JOSÉ CASAS PARDO:

ECONO[illegible] THE EUROPEAN E[illegible]

BEITRÄGE ZUR WIRTSCHAFTS- UND SOZIALGESCHICHTE

Herausgegeben von
Rainer Gömmel und Jürgen Schneider

Schriftleitung: Markus A. Denzel und Oskar Schwarzer

Band 51

In Kommission bei
Franz Steiner Verlag Stuttgart

Economic Effects of the European Expansion, 1492 - 1824

Ed. by José Casas Pardo

1992
In Kommission bei
Franz Steiner Verlag Stuttgart

Anschrift der Schriftleitung:
Otto-Friedrich-Universität
Lehrstuhl für Wirtschafts-
und Sozialgeschichte
Am Kranen 12
D - 8600 Bamberg

CIP-Titelaufnahme der Deutschen Bibliothek

Casas Pardo, José (Ed.):
Economic effects of the European expansion : 1492 - 1824 / ed. by José Casas Pardo. - Stuttgart : Steiner, 1992

(Beiträge zur Wirtschafts- und Sozialgeschichte ; Bd. 51)

ISBN 3-515-06240-8

NE: Casas Pardo, José [Hrsg.]; Casas-Pardo, José; GT

Kommissionsverlag: Franz Steiner Verlag Wiesbaden GmbH,
Sitz Stuttgart
Druck: difo druck GmbH Bamberg

Introduction

The papers included in this volume are the papers presented at the international congress on "*Consequences of the Discovery of America for Different Economies and for the Development of Economic Thought*". This congress took place in Valencia on the 16th - 19th of September 1991. The congress was jointly sponsored and financed by the *Comissio per al Cinque Centenari del Descobriment d'America* of the Generalitat Valenciana (the regional government of the Autonomous Community of Valencia) and the *Universidad Internacional Menéndez Pelayo* in its branch of Valencia. This University undertook the material organization of the congress and the congress itself took place at the seat of the University.
The purpose of the congress was to analyse in the light of the latest developments in research and knowledge the effects of the discovery of America both on economic activity in the different areas of the world and on the development of economic thought. The congress was organized to celebrate the Vth centenary of the discovery of America, and, as far as we know, it has been the only one on this topic to take place on this occasion.
The specific feature of this volume is that the papers presented at the congress and therefore included in this book cover two fields of reserach: Economic History and History of Economic Thought. The papers on Economic History are those by Michel M. Morineau, Renate Pieper, Antony Reid, Antonio Miguel Bernal Rodriguez, Ruth Vornefeld, José Maria Delgado Ribas, Pedro Pérez Herrero, Patrick Karl O'Brien, Jürgen Schneider and Joaquin da Costa Leite. The papers on the History of Economic Thought are those by Oreste Popescu, Marjorie Grice-Hutchinson, Francisco Gomez Camacho and Peter Bernholz. Finally there is a summary and conclusions written by Jürgen Schneider.
The authors are all well known specialists in these fields and come from several countries which enriches the perspective and the outlook of the analysis. Naturally the papers included in this volume do not exhaust the topics dealt with, but they make an important contribution to the knowledge we have on the impact that the discovery of America and the subsequent economic relationships that were established and developed

among the different areas of the world had on various fields of economic activity and on the ideas held on economic phenomena, particularly on the later called quantity theory of money. The papers range from covering topics concerning the XVIth century to dealing with aspects referring to the XVIIIth century. No doubt this volume represents a major contribution to our understanding of the consequences of the discovery of America.

I have to thank all the participants for their major efforts to attend the congress and to present such high quality papers. In particular I must thank Mrs Grice-Hutchinson and Professor Popescu who, in spite of their advanced age, undertook the task of attending the congress and presenting outstanding papers. I am also grateful to Professor Schneider for undertaking the job as rapporteur of the congress. For the composition of the volume I thank Dipl.-Hist. Markus A. Denzel, University of Bamberg.

The editor is greatly indebted to Professor Alfons Cuco who, as chairman of the *Comissio per al Cinque Centenari del Descobriment d'America* of the Generalitat Valenciana supported enthusiastically the idea of holding the congress and contributed generously to its financing. I am also very greateful both to Professor Ernest Lluch, Rector of the *Universidad Internacional Menédez Pelayo*, and to Professor Joan Romero, Director of the Valencian branch of this University at the time of the congress. They took my proposal to hold the congress with great interest and did everything in their hands to its succesful celebration: from organizing it and supplying all the necessary means to contributing to its financing. Finally, I must also thank Professor Joaquin Azagra, present director of the *Universidad Menendez Pelayo* at Valencia, for his encouragement to publish this volume. As secretary of the congress, Amelia Garcia-Valdecasas greatly contributed to its organization and success.

University of Valencia
Valencia, 12.10.1992 (Columbus' Day)

José Casas Pardo

Table of Contents

Five Hundred Years Ago Since That Day ...*

By MICHEL MORINEAU

We all know the 12 October 1492 was an exceptional day in the history of humanity. To celebrate it, roman trumpets will blare, chorus of the opera will sing, and the production of television shows, with fake indians and fake descubridores, will be renewed it. It'll be better than the original. It will be possible to assist, in direct to Christophe Colomb disembarkation on Guanahani's isle (or one other, let's not be chauvinist ...) from igloos, from Mandchouvian Yurts or from Bophuthastswana's huts, not to mention Bagnolet's two rooms flat in Paris suburb. In the same way as, just over twenty years ago, on our satellite, we could see the first step of Neil Armstrong on th moon. Perfect time to bring out, to dust, to regild all the old columbine panoplies as it was done in 1989 for the French revolution's second centenary. And may it be a lost opportunity, as for the same event, to fully grasp an act, the actors and the consequences!

We sill see the partisans, for or agains, shocking each other, as they have already done, during the commemoration of the frenh revolution. The onfrontation had been bloody (intellectuallly only, fortunately, the guillotine was out of order ...). The champions did brandishcd bludgeons facing each other: We did compared the siege of the Bastille bicentenary, the 14th of July 1989, to a Capetian's millenary (in 1987); people will recriminate the old regime and the bloody terror, without forgetting the *vendéen* genocide. We will talk about an economic collapse, and also the late manifestation of progress towards the

---

* Translation by Alice CLOTHIER.

modernism not knowing for sure, to heard one's say, if it could have been prepared by the evolution of the absolutism rising in the last few years, or if was due to the politics conserning the constituent Assembly and the convention, if it had taken place.

It all did take its end with an international congress at the Sorbonne, almost unanimously in spirit for the celebration and the exaltation of an apotheosis on the "Champs Elysées" from "l'Etoile" to "la Concorde" with a "haute couture" fashion show or some fun fair parade, signed by Jean Goude, and compensated by the touching Marseillaise of Jessye Norman[1].

The hypothetic repetition of such procedure in 1992 on some other topic, is not inconsistent. The multitude of publications, already out and to ome on the fifth centenary, points out the mediatic attraction and the real fascination of many readers and spectators. Hurrah and groans will be heard and exclamation such as "Vive l'Europe"[2] as well as some maledictions against an undefendable Europe[3], the cardinal's hand to bless the erection of the cross for the new world[4], the ethnocide denunciation perpetuated by the Whites, the exaltation for the "the globe's revealer"[5], the assembler of God's earth[6], the

---

1 Impressions entirely personal, that no one is obligated to adopt. The organizers, besides, had certainly their reasons.

2 Jean-Baptiste DUROSELLE in the special edition of the review *L'Histoire* concerning 1492: The discovery of America (July - August 1991), pp. 46 - 47.

3 Aimé CÉSAIRE, Discours sur le colonialisme, Paris 1973 (édition of 1989 in: *Présence africaine,* p. 7).

4 The first cross was erected in Cuba, the 14th November 1492.

5 Book title from Léon BLOY (1859).

6 Expression of Paul Claudel, who has dedicated a drama to the navigator. The German Werner Eck did an opera from it.

accusations against the enflicter of sickness, destruction of autochtonal civilisations and distruction of the environment[7].

In brief, a mêlée, within this extremity the believers in prudence, the eclectics taken by surprise, with no definite opinions, some partisans believing in a systematic balance, ideology so brilliant and so difficult to find in reality. In addition, bored people, tired precocity of popular songs too quickly let loose, the hermits of actuality and history[8].

Such a device would brush the presumptuosness, and would, coming from us, rightly indispose if we had implied to it some king of immaculate conception, and had expose an essay with a higher value exempted off all weakness and ignorance. Such pretention is far from our mind! Yes indeed, we wish to look for as unpassionately as possible but this aim passes, as much by the refusal of exaggeration from one and the other side, by the humility brought from an ambigious and distressing problem, still, as well as the respect for the remembrance, and the scares. So, this will bring us to present and to develop three simple observations:

The first one is about the discovery itself, the second is about the contacts that rise from it; and the last one on the value of America's discovery. We have no revelation to produce, only proposing a framework: we do not overestimate it, but find it rather necessary, and we wish, in the worse case, to attract enough attention towards the meaning of its content hoping it will help with the exam's preparation and for a deeper consideration.

---

7 One of the most vehement among Christophe Colomb's swaggerers is the American (from the United States) Kirkpatrick Sale in *La conquête du Paradis* (1990).

8 *Comment échapper au 92.* The Spanish work seems to echo Eugene Ionesco's *Comment s'en débarrasser*. But it would be about a Golem rather than a corpse.

I. The Discovery

First we must understand the nature of the event to the remembrance to which we are invited and the personage's importance. What ever documentary is consulted, we will never have a whole and clear vision of it, at once. This observation holds an allusion, which will be short, concerning the dark side of Christophe Colomb's birth and boyhood to the point that we have from the discovery, only a one way relationship, coming from the admiral or some of his companions (in the depositions in ulterior proceedings), in every way European and without Arrawak opposition for obvious reasons[9]. In spite of an almost comical carriage, the thought is not to be entirely put aside[10]. But we wish to insist on one other constraint of the actuel historiography. We arrive to the Genoese only through some hyperboles and some controversy which surrended him[11]. His narratives have a tinge of magnifience and of mysticism that grew as his life was unfolding and as he met, more and more resistance concerning his credits. Fernando Colomb, the son, and Bartolomeo de Las Casas, the biographer in admiration, have preserved the sort of aureole that surrounded him, and that goes with also, may be, the man and the way he was. The contestation that already rose in his days, came from various sources that we will not enumerate here[12], it reduced his importance, turned him into a tell-tale or an ignorant; chosen by luck or good fortune. Later on, his reputation varied from hight to low during the last five centuries, accordingly to one or the

9 No account, either, from Martin Pinzon, dying (providentially ...?) shortly after returning, nor, of course, from the companions of the Navidad ...

10 The Arrawaks didn't write. We can nevertheless imagine the lost in the information if we think about what we have, On the Mexican's side for the undertaking of Cortés. CF. M. Léon PORTILLA, Le Crépuscule des Aztèques. Récits indigènes de la conquête, Brussel 1965.

11 In calling Christophe Colomb a Genoese we only follow the most concrete version up to now.

12 The Pinzon, Juan de Fonseca, some of the Catholic King's surrounding, etc ...

other association of tradition, and often due to a lack of contrary informations on a long period of time. On this compound opinions started to germinate, the ones we have talked about, which are brought into opposition today. Fed beside, with the time, of other aliments: enthusiasm of proselytes, search of scholars, looks given from where we did not expect, that is, on the Indians' side[13]; it is difficult to establish the dominating wind direction. Probably, in 1992, with the coming festivity in Spain, in Italy and in America, will it be in the rhombus of the fame. Which will not stop anyone to preserve their doubts, or their scepticism or their opposition. As for us, we only retain that the critic analytic of the textes source - semantic, dialectic, or phenomenology - has not been pushed as far as in the case, for example, among others, of Herodote[14].

Christophe Colomb has presented his discovery as sensational, unheard of, unthinkable by his contemporary; espacialy in his letters and his requests to the Catholics Kings. He has revealed a "new world" (ambiguous expression) in the west, where no one had the courage to explore before him. He did offer some new possessions, somw new land, some new subjects, some new wealth (he thought fabulous). He has opened a grand perspective to the church and to the propagation of the Gospel.

We will stop on the first of those affirmations. Did the voyage and its consequence really had the extraordinary character that he gave to it and to whiht many people have enriched by adding to it the obstination against the erudite knowledge, the risk and the challenge of the unknown? The Portuguese historians are right about their anteriority in the exploration of space, on the african coast and the exploration in

---

13 The columbine biography is huge. It will certainly be up dated and filled out with the fifth centenary. What we wish to signal here is the mobility of the points of view within the litterature and the way of approach.

14 F. HARTOG, Le miroir d'Hérodote. Essai sur la représentation de l'autre, Paris 1980. Cf. however I. LUZZANO-CARACI, Colombo Vero e falso: La construzione delle Historie fernandine, Gênes 1989.

whih the future admiral of the ocean sea did participate himself. It is not insulting to compare the expedition that left from Palos the 3rd August 1492 to an operation of *rescate* which somewhat is a bit relative to the usual. Was navigating "to Cap West all" senseless to the eyes of the expert cosmographers in the end of the XVth century? On the fact and the theory the answer is no. The confirmation on the earth's rounder, Pierre d'Ailly's map often consulted by Christophe Colomb, proves it. The surrounding of the King of Portugal will dismiss the grantee on the possibility to reach Cipango and Cathay within reasonnable times, on its possibility and not the principle. How was it empirically? The advance of the Portuguese towards the Azores can't be denied nor the acquired experience by the Genoese, about the winds and the courses, during his stay in the Canaries. It ist no probable he heard nothing in Iceland concerning the existence of Greenland at sunset, as a land much further away[15]. The story of the sailor back from "over there" and confiding his secret is unverifiable. But the brother Barthelemy's shop was a meeting place in Lisbon for pilots and old seamen. The conditions of the embarkement in Palos suggest a haste or an intuition of what was to be discovered on the behalf of Pedro Vasquez de la Frontera and of Martin Alonso Pinzon, at least[16]. It would be unprobable that men had accepted to embark on

---

15 Christophe Colomb's voyage in Iceland is situed in 1477. The abandon of Greenland by the Vikings is dated differently from the end of the XIVth to the end of the XVth century. In the worse case, the memory of it will stay in mind for the Icelanders. Further more, if the Anse-aux-Meadows, in Newfounland and the short establishment of Vinland on the Cap-Breton island could have been forgotten, the cod fishing did probably attract the fishermen on the "banks". This point was studied in Rennes (France) in May 1992.
We are unfortunately very poorly informed on the frequentation of Newfound-land by the Basques, which has nevertheless, left a mark on the toponymy, and even less on the eventual relations of Portugal and Spain with Iceland to purchase of falcons. Would it be there a track to identify the mysterious "*lo que ha descubierto*" of the *capitulaciones*? We won't mention a thing about the scouring act of Luis Coin on Colomb's logbook.

16 Christophe Colomb could not pretend to attract to him the population of the small atlantic harbour, even with a comission from the Queen Isabelle. From

those caravels without knowing for certain how they would get there or would come back. Morever, the Catholic Kings, has niggerly as they were, would not have fully financed, in advance and certainly, a venture without any hope of success. This one was "in the air" as Marianne Mahn-Lot wrote[17].

This doesn't abolish the credit of the faith, of the disployed obstination to reach a project. The light only is changed. In any case the prehistory of the voyage has a lot less importance, more so, that the following point: Christopher Colomb has not discovered America. Let's us warn you straight away that here we change the register. We will not talk about such obscure point of an account anymore, we can't deny: to whom should come back the honour for having revealed, first, officiously and officially the news (the blow of the bombard came from the *Pinta*). We will not bring back to the surface the mistake of the cartographer form Saint-Dié, Waldseemüller, who deprived America of its legitimate inventor, the Genoese, to offer it - on a worldmap - to Florentine Amerigo Vespucci (and why not *Vespuccia*?). We will go further[18]. The 12 October 1492 Christopher

---

what we know concerning the embarkement's preparation, it does show the decisive role for the engagements of the personages we have mentioned earlier.

17 M. MAHN-LOT, Portrait historique de Christophe Colomb, Paris 1988, p. 42. The same author indicates the affirmation done by the Portugal's king to the Genoese, about the existence of some firm land to the west, and we know that Cabral; went decisively toward Brazil, that he had to "discover" in 1500.
On Christophe Colomb's caravels, the sailors were worried about the length of the voyage, and about the incertain return which was understandable if we try to remember the limits that *ipso facto* means, all revictualling for a race across the sea. The Admiral's acount, at this point, accentuates the polarization, on the searched discovery and doesn't seem quite equitable. Our remarks joint those from Bartholomé and Lucile BENASSAR, 1492: Un monde nouveau, 1991.

18 According to Consuelo Varela, there wasn't any indelicate or caddish attitude from Amerigo, but the treachery form one of his fellow citizen, who was worried about linning up the number of voyage on the Genoese's ones, as florentine chauvinism obliged.

Colomb discovered Guanahani or San Salvador, a confetti among the Bahamas, infinitly small by comparison to the American continent. What came out of this voyage, and from the three other periplus, was the recognition of some islands, land's littoral ends, ridiculous fragments. He had no thought concerning North America in spite of what he did suspect of it in Iceland. Some costal prolongations in the south Hemisphere, beyond the Orinoco's mouth, he only did heard an echo about it, coming from Pedro Alvarez Cabral after his success in Brazil, an outcome of a fortunate hazard, he did not acknowledge the isthmus existence that connected both sides, and he kept searching for a passage towards Asia and did not see the Pacific. The discovery of America was a breathless work, a succession of discoveries adding up to Christopher Colomb's own, and the ones accumulating to the others, no need to mention Spanish names nor the XVIth century. Is it reasonable to condemn the credit to Cabot, Magellan, Jacques Cartier, Walter Raleigh and Wilhelm Schouten for revealing some novelity, in turn and for everyone's concern? But mostly having to recognize the caps and the straits, or even to establish the beach heads, "biaise et tronque" a process spreaded over several centuries with the crossing of the Alleghanys, the prairies of the Rocky Mountains, in the North, the intrusion on the plateaus and in the Amazonie (until today) in the South[19].

Many voices will rise againsts a sophisme, a quibble, but at first a confusion of the genus, should we distinguish, the difference between the descubridores, the exploradores, the conquistadores? The quibble is reversed. To consent a dissociation and to admit a perfect impervi-

---

19 The question, if Christophe Colomb has recognized the existence of the new continent on his third voyage, in 1498, is, for us, rather otious. About him touching the Bay of Paria is certain, that he did identify it as such, is a topic to controversy. When he is taking of a "great earth" could as well been a "large island" (after all, Madagascar is well called as the Grand Island and New Caledonia the Great Land). Otherway, by searching still for a passage toward the north, in the central isthme, the Admiral, did not think, of course, about a real soure and the existence of a barrier between his dicovery and his dream.

ousness within those groups, and to reduce the first one as the only inventors of those regions tied to nothing would be a must. In this case, it would have been only one discovery, the one of Guanahani (leaving Spain, the Canaries, the Azores, the Sargasso's sea forgotten ...). On his return Christophe Colomb explored waters and islands, especially along the hispanic coast. And the taken possession in the name of the Catholics's Kings, the Indians vasselage as early as the first disembarkment, the taxation on gold, then the slavery and the deportation of the "sauvages" to Spain, constitue without a doubt, to a conquest and to an expropriation - new devolution. In fact, to explore and depart to discover, China, Eldorado, Eden or to evangelize a population, was a whole. To realize it, we ascended mountains, we came down to Orinoco or the Amazon, sailed up to Saint-Laurent or the Mississipi, and the effective or the symbolic conquest simply followed[20] - the sophism, then would be marked by denying the evidence, refusing to admit the initial worthiness of Christoph Colomb versification worthiness initium. But the reproach is with the telescoping of dishonesty or bad faith and reverses itself rapidely once we closely study it like the previous and alleged quibble.

Datelessly, the admiral of the oceann sea's sucess had awaken, or incited some vocations: Cabot, Cabral and Amerigo first. To connect to the first chronologically enumerate movement what happened after, during five hundred centuries would represent a fraud. It, this time, would be denying the autonomy and the deliberation, the conception's independence, and the will to resolve the following discovery, its character, in relation to the hazards[21]. As the conquests, the opening

20 By denominating China to be the rupture point on which he was arrived on the Saint-Laurent, Samuel Champlain witnessed the persistence of illusions at the beginning of the XVIIth century, still.

21 We must distinguish, we believe, in the heat following the discoveries after Christophe Colomb's return, two influences: The must for not coming back empty handed from a voyage in the west, and the *cupiditas*, as the publicity that was done on his wealth and on his discoveries, did awaken. This means, that eventually, the territories previously discovered were not taken into ac-

of the mines in Potisi, of the plantations, of the forced or spontaneous immigration, the landing of the Mayflower's passengers, and the Yankees rush towards the west in the XIXth century. The discovery of America has taken five hundred years and has just recently ended, at the exception of some unexploded territories in the Amazonie and Matto Grosso. The discovery didn't unroll as genealogical tree with a unic filiation, with no interruptions since the three caravels in Guanahani's horizon. Its outcome was a succession of independant acts from which everyone drew its legitimate lineage[22]. So, if Christophe Colomb did not discover Cipango nor Cathay he did not discover the United-States either[23].

---

count if they were possibly not exploitable. After 1492 and the accounts form the Admiral, it was an other story. It became urgent to proclaim to be the discoveror and to take possession of the discoveries to preserve the treasures property that they may be hid. Because, their exploitation could not be the same; the previous discovery of the oceanic islands, of the Australian and Tasmanian cost did not generate such a fever. The same goes for North America in the XVIth century.

22 We must note, in the exploitation of America, that often a reiteration was needed, like a new discovery. Mainly Portuguese, Brazil stayed exposed to all navigation tasks, to the timber cutting, etc ... undertaken by the French or others, because they were inoccupied by the propertied nation.
Until 1540, when a systematic colonization took place. Jacques Cartier's voyages in Canada did not immediately have a following and Samuel Champlain proceeded up the Saint-Laurent on new expenses. Walter Raleigh's expedition in Virginia - itself, near one century late on Cabot's expedition - did not amount to an effective implantation and twenty years had to pass for the English colonist to move in North America. CF. also the opportunity that the French, the English, the Danish catch from the abandoned spaces left by the Spanish: Guadeloupe, Jamaica, the Virgin islands, etc.

23 Guanahani's discovery was a happy surprise, fruit of a happy mistake (the faith to an exiguity of the globe). We shiver at the thought of the navigator did not find the futur America and did continued, without a stop, his never ending voyage towards Asia. But no one will follow this exagerated and contrefactual hypothesis to an end. The 10.000 maravedis reward directly went to the Admiral, initiator of the project and commander of the flotta. He gracefully promises recompence to Martin Pinzon for the blare coming from the *Pinta* (5000 maravedis that were never paid as the benefactor died). It was in the

II. The Contacts

We'll have to remember of those temporal and spatial dimensions to analyse the contacts and to emphasize its value. To say that, all was concluded, as early as the 12 October 1492, for the people belonging to civilizations divided by an enormous gap, due to their development is, in a way, true and false. After all, there is the Indians and some existing problems, still from those days, not yet resolved. In the other hand, the handfull of armed Spanish with halberds, succeded by some troops carrying muskets[24] and partially horse riding, and waves of white emigrants and the force in number was reversed, not the force in power, the cohabitation became difficult with the Indians but even more so, with the black slaves and their descendants, the Asian coolie with their offsprings.

However, let us stay faithful to the event, that we are going to comemorate, and let's ask ourself, the nature of the very first contact between the European and the Bahamas and the Antille's islanders. We can easily reconstitute the traveller's feeling when they arrived: the excitement, and the exaltation of an accomplishment for Christophe Colomb, the "ha!" of relief from his crew. On the Arawak side, a fearless curiosity dominated, according to the narration that we hold[25].

Thereby, the point is more prominent than it seems if we put together some alarming foreteeling's rumours on the arrival of some oppressors dressed like phantoms of some ancestrals's souls, or the terrified reaction from the Angolian blacks by this reappearance. It is through a mixture of divine halo, of the incredulity to conquer, and the delighted attraction that the men from beyond the sea did envolve. If

---

following order, to attribute a gratification, if he wanted to, to Rodrigo de Triana.

24 This appears in about 1525 ... after Colomb, so, and before Cortés.

25 On the other hand, Indians had a success of curiosity in Seville then in Barcelone in 1492, and this one was not denial for a long time (Cf. the entry of Henry II. in Rouen).

the surprise and the questioning rose into the discoveror's mind, those, very quickly gave, to the encounter an other meaning. Taking hold of possessions in presence of a notary was then a leonin act, which, for the natives would have been some aggressive and degrading connotations, if they had been albe to understand the meaning of it[26]. Simultaneously, the first exchanges between sailors and "sauvages" were not disinterested, nor the avidiy for the admiral's gold, of an inferieur value to the one of his subordinates. *Cupidas* for *Curiositas*, accordingly to the acceptable norms today, which was'nt the case in those days[27]. The gospel's propagation had not been forgotten. Christophe Colomb - Christ holder - as he named himself, had straight away grabbed the opportunity that it offered for people, he judged, at once, innocent and suited for baptism[28]. He gave, furthermore, and took back in his voyages to come some guarantees of kindness, in the christian proselytism. But contradiction and scorn were there.

Contradiction, because the infeodation of ruled kingdoms to catholic sovereigns hold a beginning of coercion itself. It was already considered as a prelude to an ineluctable conversion and which, should the ocasion arises, was hasten by kidnapping and deportation to Spain.

Scorn, because the Indians had their own belief, their gods and their rituals, unperceived in 1492, and they understood more or less quickly, the mortality, the cruelty, and the pitiless demand for a trib-

---

26 The act itself call for a remark. Thinking to be, more or less, arriving on the Great Khan's land, Christophe Colomb would retreat on the perspective to offend the monarch for whom he had an introduction letter. If he had arrived in China, he would have been emprisoned then thrown out as a vulgar "barbarian".

27 Owing to the scales of differente valuations for some and for others, an "inequitable exchange" is not questionable. The Indians were just as satisfied about the barter as the Europeans were.

28 This judgement involved the recognition *ipso facto* of the Indian's men quality. The pope Alexander VI thought alike. It wasn't about some animals nor some freaky beings (which the meeting would not have been inexpected for Christophe Colomb). The discussions on the Indian's soul were posterior.

ute, and for work, and the intolerance of their unexpected hosts[29]. Their reactions were not all alike: some of them spontaneously collaborated, and some jibbled and ran away; others became christian by belief, as far as martyrdom. The revolt took place, followed by repression, if not extermination[30].

To talk about a lost opportunity would be quite ridiculous. And misleading, in spite of the appareance, to create a background for a scenario to be reconstituted later, to numerous specimens, even that we can find here and there more than one component. Let's take the conquest of Mexico as an example: the expeditions preceeding the ones to Cortes, did meet some hostility from the costal population. On the other hand, the Aztec's emperor was left incapacitated by the fear of Quetzacoal's return. The conquistador takes advantages of an uncertain hegemony and the freewill of revenge in Tlaxcala and other cities. the Spanish force and native alliance brought about the fall of Tenochtitlan. The resistanes already well alive during Moctezuma's existence, and there more with his sucessors were crushed.

To a large extent, the organization of the Empire served to establish the new domination. Christianizing came later through the assault of the temples, and with blows from aspergilliums. In Peru, the internal divisions in the Inca's world were equally profitable to Pizarro. He added to it a good dose of trachery, of false christianity, with a tinge

---

29 Victim of some superficial impressions, of some interpretations, or a self-intoxication. Christophe Colomb has instantly transposed in pre-christian terms what he did hear (Cf. the old man's speach, one sunday in June 1494, in Cuba. What did he read in brother Ramon Pané's inquest, that he however encouraged?).

30 The European's "humanity" was released to the Indians since the departure of Christophe Colomb by his companion's one he left to the Navidad.
For the different observed attitudes in front off the new comers, we can refer to those of the chief Guacanagari's (favorable), the chief Caonabo's (hostile), the chief Guarionex (relapsed). One of the most strange figure is the one of Diego Colon, Guanahani's native, who was among the first contingent of "deporteed" to Spain, he learn the castillan language and faithfully became the interpreter for his won people; some kind of pre-Malincha.

of total lack of scruples, and cruelty. Boundless territories and numerous tribes changed of masters during those subsidences. The substitution from one domination to the other meant no alleviation to the burden previously endured: its reinforcement, like in the case of the *mita*, the forced labour work at the mine, with the complicity more or less given from the traditional chiefs, the *curacas*[31], the freewill was still restrained, or destroyed by the *encomiendas* and the *repartimentos*. The poor indian souls were greatly at stake. Priests and monks, brought form Europe, gave their best to the destruction of the idols, to erase the ancient practices, to the supression of anything looking more or less like paganism, including the dances[32]. All this is well known. What we wish to underline - which is not a entirely new point of view, either - is, in the concerned case, that process seems to have been or has been, irreprimable, notwithstanding the diversity of the ways that it took.

That, this would have been the consequence of a primorial lack of balance is a sure thing: poor equipment and arming, psychological inferiority of the Indians; superiority of the Europeans, the christian faith and the received education by those baptized in the XVth or the XVIth century's way - the inaccessible conciousness of being right, God's excutants and, nearly, to free themself from a duty, the fierce enlistment of the *descubridores* and *conquistadores* ... The alternatives were limited, and none were satisfying untill the end.

The resistance? By choosing it, the Incas survived a while, then failed. By an early start, the Behotuks, in Greenland and in Newfoundland, and the Mayas in Yucatan, managed better: nevertheless not untill the term of five hundred years. As well, the "Chichimeques" the "Araucans", the people from the Prairies or from the Rocky Mountains resisted to their subjection a while but finally did not escape from it.

---

31 A. MÉTRAUX, Les Incas, Paris 1962.

32 P. DUVIOLS, La lutte contre les religions autochtones dans le Pérou colonial - L'extirpation de l'idolâtrie entre 1532 et 1660, Lima 1971.

Running away? It became a repeated retreat as they were caught back either by the *bandeirantes* in Brazil or by the pioneers in the United-States. It only offered a guarantee of success by always going further into some inaccessible places to Europeans. The untouched tribes could keep their life style (and many times, their lifes); and being penalized by the absence, the frangibility to the contemporary world.

The alliance? It did not always resolve the conflicts, local and ethnical (confert: the Hurons against the Iroquois). The agreements were not respected one day nor the other, even in Pennsylvania. Those were bluntly violated as the ones concerning the Sioux, Apaches or Navajos (confert: the opening of the reservation in Oklahoma in 1906).

The quest for a refuge beside the mighty whites? Yet it had to occur the experience of the diocese in Chiapas and in Paraguay did not last. It had an artifiial howbeit, that made it vulnerable.

The cross breeding? Ambiguous solution (if we dare) which geared down the problems without resolving them, and brought more of them, reinfored by the appearance of the black race and its lineage for once by the social veolution, as well[33]. Perhaps, in a very, very "*longue durée*"...

The survival in the reductions? It is nearly always a synonym of etiolation, of an insidious change, of the lost of customs and especially, of some old virtues, of a denaturation.

---

33 The reduction of the problems came with the formation of a group of intermediate colour, pulled apart by two identities, often refected by one side or the other, sometimes with the oppressed, sometimes with the oppressors, when it didn't want to take power for itself. The introduction of blacks created a parallel structure of mulattos, quadroons, octavons, etc. Owing to the social evolution, it added to the scale a larger gap between the individuals. The most underpriviledged classes often belonged to the ethnical group, ratio which we just talked about, where as, a syndrome of "poor whites" seems to raise a barrier more and more rigid to the encounter of the individual ascensions, a fortiori collective in order of the well being, of the education, and of the politic's responsabilities.

We do not presented the previous remarks to justify a past, to exonerate some crimes or to raise the arms helplessly in the sky[34]. As it happened in the past, we have proceeded to a report, to a kind of inventory. A little comparaison is usefull. The Spanish had some experiences with "primitive" people[35]. This did result in a desaster for the Guanches in the Canaries. In the other hand, along the cost of the occidental Africa, the Europeans (Portuguese and other nationalities navigating under the same banner) were trafficking in a respectful way with an equal species, either as silent barter or in some negotiations with the black chiefs, even for the acquisition of slaves and except for some relatively isolated cases, which could have been different[36]. The first contacts on the Indian Ocean took place more so, on a level of parity. The use of force was straight away instored; to obstain a tribut from a local sultan (Sofala); to interrupt the traffic of muslims; to force a prince with whom one's was angry, often of his own doing (the Samorin from Calicut). Meanwhile, the military exploits of the Portuguese did not reach the construction of an empire deeply rooted inland. The pressure put on the autochtons was therefore very limited, sometimes annihilated by the power of a sovereign (China's Emperor) or by his official deputy (the Japanese Shogun). The situation here is very different from the Indian one in America. Too many historians, in Europe, ignore it, fooled by marine's sailing vessels, by the guns in the ports. However, the established distance did last untill the XIXth century and did succumb, before the Dutch, for example, only in the

---

34 History must not judge, indeed. No to erect itself as a guide for the future. But, this soft pillow for historians would be, also, a retro-subterfuge. What is arrived, is arrived and we cannot change it. The time mistake is as to close our eyes as well to anachronism.

35 The word "primitive" hold no pejorative connotation and doesn't need to resume with the theory form LEVY-BRUHL.

36 In the silent barter, the Portuguese had their goods on the shore, while the blacks were hiding further away. Once the whites were gone, their "mute" interlocutors approached, estimated the goods in bond according to their quotations and put the equivalent on their own products near by. Then they left. The negotiation took place as such without physical contacts.

regions where people could not afford or defend themself, same as in America[37]. Enslaving the Indians therefore, is well the fruit of their weakness, picked up by the Europeans of whom the power, itself, must not be surestimated. We can only say, that Africa and Asia have known the roughness of the European cane (before the emancipation in the XXth century); which does not bring the matters to an equivalence in 1492 but open the panorama and guide the reflection for 1992.

The alteration in time should not be the only thing to consider. America would have lost a lot more than the other continents. Every one here will think about the mortality fallen on some populations without immunity against the virus coming from beyond the Atlantic Ocean. We hesitate on the number but the biological catastrophe doesn't have its equivalent in the world, except in Polynesia after the discovery in the XVIIIth century. Even the constant drain practised in the trade of blacks in Africa could not hold the comparaison[38]. Even more pernicious, if possible, would have been the real de-civilization and the depersonnalizing generated by the conquest and by the baptism, again, with no equivalent on the others continents apart form Oceania. The events and the ruins give evidence but the question is complex. The eradication of ancient cults and their "idols" is combined with a reflection for the gods whom had not filled their part. Let us think about the revengeful fury of the Indians from Canada: "The beaver did

---

37 The most spectacular episode in the dutch expansion was the repeated massacre in the banda islands. CF. our article: Myristica Flagrans in: Mélanges d'histoire économique offerts au Professeur Anne-Marie Piuz, Genève 1990, pp. 191 - 210. The Dutch took near a century to control Indonesia.

38 On the demographic problem, we send back to Nicolas SANCHEZ ALBORNOZ, The population of colonial Spanish America, in: Cambridge History of Latin America, 1984 and from the same author, more recently: Demographic changes in America and Africa induced by the Europeans expansion, 1500 - 1800, in: The European Discovery of the world and its economic effects on the pre-industrial society 1500 - 1800, directed by Hans POHL (VSWG-Beiheft 89), Stuttgart 1990.

not protect us, let's kill the beavers and let's sell their skins"[39]. The tradition has been usely deserted by the aristocracy members, anxious to mix with the vanquihers and to share their power. The tradition has been a lot more respected by the people, to the extent that their conversion to christianity looked very epidermic to the missionary of the XVIIIth century, spoiled by a pagan reminiscences, more than that, today, we are back to it. What good points can we attribute, at the end, to these religions and civilizations, gone of baried? the ethnologists have professionally dedicated themself to rehabilitate as much the "way of thinking of the sauvages" and its myths, as possible, that the Aztec and Incas society, discribed as sophisticated, by taking out anything disappointing, including the humain sacrifies, and choosing only the artistic splendors and more, in spite of the evolution dynamic factors, clearly obsolete to the XVIth century ... and the civilization in XXth century[40], a tendency willingly archaistic and ecological of the public opinion provide them an audience[41]. Let's be serious and not spread confusion. The undeniable human dramas, past and present does not impede the recognition of the evolution taken by the economy and its means. The archaeological nostalgia must not let us forget the realistic parameters. To imagine that the progress - as

---

39 Calvin MARTIN, Keepers of the Game. Indian - animal relationship and the fur trade, Berkeley (Ca.) 1978.

40 Supported tendance in Jacques SOUSTELLE, La vie quotidienne des Aztèques, Paris 1955. More withholding from A. MÉTRAUX (op. cit.). We hold nothing against the *Pensée sauvage* from CI. Lévy STRAUSS (Paris, 1956) that we consider as a grand book. On the other hand, in his last work: Histoire de Lynx, published after redaction of this communication, he has succumbed to the anthropological propensity for the idyllic fussion ... It only is a sweet dream as we have pointed out earlier.

41 The reconstitution of a medieval floating windmill on the Lot in Cuzals-en-Quercy or of a neolthic village on the Chalain lac's shores in the Jura gives rise to any reticence other than a technical one. No need to generalize the principle for our contemporary (even that the biological agriculture ...). The reconstitution of the human sacrifices in Mexico would rise, we think, some reserves; at least if they were integral.

debatable as it may be - could have agreed with the ancient civilizations perpetuance and their facts, with a restoration (regression?) would be thoughtlessly sacrified to a counterfeiting story perfectly illusive and to divert from the real problems. We had the occasion to say something about that on an other topic just as tender and burning - the trade of the blacks[42].

III. The Valuation

When Christophe Columb had to make a forced stay in Jamaica, on his third voyage an 1503 - 1504, his crew and himself were stocked by the Indians with cassava bread and could, so, wait for help. When the Pilgrims Fathers had disembarked on the cost of New England the 21 December 1620, their provisions dried up rapidly and the famine threatened to make entirely dissappear the small troop, already decimated by the harthness of the voyage and by the winter, the survivors were saved by a troop of Indians passing by, who offered to them some of their food and did show them how to cultivate Indian corn. The two anedoctes show us that America was not eveywhere a desert and its people were not without ressources even for the Europeans. If the manioc had no success, the maize was one of those gift to Europe from America and that, we know well: beans, tomatoes, potatoes, turkeys ... It is frequent to whisk it away with ease as an epilogue for

---

42 We did show twice that the trade of the blacks wouldn't have generate a diminution in the population if the rate of birth had reach a certain level, analogue, for example, to the one of Portugual at the end of the XIXth century and at the beginning of the XXth century. Cf. our contribution to volume II of: L'histoire économique et social du monde, directed by P. LEON, Paris 1978, and one other published in the number of the VSWG mentioned on note 38: L'Afrique et l'Amérique découvertes, pp. 62 - 72). Would the african economy have known a drastic start in the absence of such puncture? We are touching here, an hypothesis of contrefactual history from which we can't have any sort of verification nor confirmation.

some highly coloured tales from the navigators, the battles and from the conquests. It's a shame because the acclimatization of those American plants on the European soil had an extremely important role in the history of the populations. Thanks to the maize, the Portugal, the Netherlands, the Northwest of Spain, mostly, have known a demographic growth, since the XVIIth century[43]. In some areas of the continent, the potato, brought in a bit late, had some identical effects, even if we can with L. M. Cullen to ask about its quality of take off or its support[44]. We don't have to exagerate an influence neither its demographic consequence, as we find synchronisticly some parellel phenomenons in Asia to which we have to attribute some other causes. It is even clearer for an "industrial revolution" and its outcomes until those agricultural progress. Otherwise, to reach the absurdity: why the culture in *Conuco* with a prolific production such as the maize, could not have engendered the steam engine, and that, before 1492[45].

We did say we were taking things out of the absurdity. But, without any good reason. The historians have been very prompt to give rise to the development of Europe from the discovery of America. A continent would have fatten itsself up by despoiling the other. Was the revolution born in the bottom of the mines, in Potosi for Karl Marx? It is true that we have diagnosed, as well, a same monopolizing at the expense of Africa (we will come back to it) and of Asia, for now let's talk about the new world. The mentioned opinion lean on an extraordinary intellectual tangle in which the amalgam. the agreed idea, and the heavy silences of final apophtegms. We end up asking ouself if

---

43 And in the Asturias, as soon as the last decades of the XVIth century. CF. The evalution from J. - M. GARCIA, El maiz en España norte atlantica en los siglos XVIII, in: Actes du Comité Scientifique de l'Ecomusée de la Lomagne, Flamarens 1988.

44 L. M. CULLEN, Irish History without the potato, in: *Past* and P*resent* 1968, pp. 72 - 83.

45 CF. the critic of the divagations from the culture in conuco in C. VERLINDEN, The pre-colombine population of America. A question of methods, in: Mélanges en l'honneur de Fernand Braudel, Paris 1973, vol. II, pp. 453 - 462.

Europe ever had any other natural quality than of a bird of prey. What is the verse meaning about his creative genius, his ability to govern the world, to turn gold into assets ... We are back to the initial dilema, to the five hundred years of polemic. Let's us to clarify it a little.

Even so, the first invested assets were appreciated more than one way. They were not very important in the firms beyond the Atlantic. 375 maravedis per unity, the two millions maravedis that Colomb's outfit did not cost in 1492, represented only about 5300 ducats. The million stingly granted by the catholic kings did cut off their incomes by a few thousand only[46]. In some certain contracts, slightly posterior, some merchants in Seville invested a few hundred of ducats in the adventure. Luque, the moneylender for Peru's conquest, provided 224.000 ducats at the time when the value's scale had already changed[47]. What matters was the men employed and the enormous profits that they could anticipate to realize in America by using a dialectic easy to understand and to establish. The gap in prices never stopped from one bank to the other, necessary to keep the traffic going[48]. The European goods were in demand as the discovery exposed its charms and that America revealed its attractions. Among those, the gold and the silver extracted from quarries and mostly from the mines - by the atrocious forced labour of the Indians - were very tempting. Those were not the only ones[49]. Talking only about the direct consequences, let's us mention the establishment of the Carrera

---

46 The only post of the *alcabalas y rentas* reached more than 295 millions of maravedis Citation from A. ARTOLA, La Hacienda del Antiguo Regimen, Madrid 1967, vol. III.

47 A few figures in R. CARANDE, Carlos quinto y sus banqueros, Madrid 1967. Cf. also M. MORINEAU, Incroyables Gazettes et Fabuleux Métaux. Les retours des trésors américains d'après les gazettes hollandaises, Paris - Cambridge 1984/85.

48 The gold and the silver were less interesting than the cochineal and the indigo on which we could make, on the way back a second profit that we did not come across with the precious metals.

49 M. MORINEAU, (op. cit.) and: Pour une histoire économique vraie, Lille 1985.

between Seville, the New Spain, Tierra Firme, the afflux of merchants and goods and the manufacturing from the chief contries in Europe for the loading of the vessels.

Upon this a few guys have erected a huge edifice. The American treasures have given an A mark to the economy. Those would be the driving force of its study: for the prices of wheat, for the prices of revolution of the XVIth century, for the economic depression of the XVIIth century, for the birth of capitalism ... We quote "pell-mell ..." it's about here that the difficulties to assent appear. As important as it has been the Atlantic "Carrera" didn't erase the other traffics pre-existing in Europe and even, out of Europe[50]. We can't tell either that proper timing (the sensibily of the recolts such as the cereals harvest) has been broken, or changed by the American arrivals. Besides one of those crucial problems, and until now, hardly touched, resides in the diffusion by its mode as well as its extension zone and by the tempo of such one[51]. It fell on one of the supported propositions: the influence, decisive, on the capitalism formation, and beyond the bourgeoisie we will see it as revolutionary, like it should be. Not without provoking some rumours, and demanding a sophistication. Spain, first favourite receiver of the treasures does not seem to have changed according to the scheme put in place. We get away with it by evoking the vanishing of gold through the border, its accumulation in the purveyor's countries and having at home, a sort of melting-pot of crucible or of magic caldron capable of transforming the treasures in assets and those into a production machine in spite of the continual dwindling endured beyond and even so, the absence of dynamic effect equivalent and among the ultimate beneficiary: Poland, Russia, India, China ... We must

---

50 M. MORINEAU, Incroyables Gazettes ... (op.cit.).

51 The silver didn't integrally stay in the United Provinces, by example, but took the way toward the Baltic, the Levant, of the West Indies. We can find some similar re-exportations, therefore less important, in England and even in France.

acknowledge, by a last effort of adjustment that something had to be missing ...[52].

The projected simplification results in a quite mysterious compilation which isn't enlightened, in any way, by its disguise in an economic transfer of European pole, from south to north explaining just as little[53]. The sort of contradiction (to which we arrive) derives from some litigious premises mentioned at the beginning of the previous paragraph[54]. To escape it we must change of conception, re-establish the real framework, and accept to follow a humble and prosaic path. Those two last ones were not kept constant during the tree centuries of colonization. We will keep a pencil while waiting for a favourable opportunity to do better. Let's start with the king during his fame, in the XVIth century and at the begining of the XVIIth presenting up to one third of arrivals that made the sovereign of Spain the first and the most important devolution's figure of the manna. The other chancelleries were dying of envy, though it wasn't the totality of each cargo[55]: What was the use of it? Partly, for the expenses of the monarchy's functioning or to some sumptuary's expenses, but any way, staying in the kingdom, and so so to the population (people and *grands* together). The rest was use to finance the politics exterior, the war, and took the road or the sea toward foreign places under some exploitation[56]. Eufemio Lorenzo Sanz has estimated that the king's treasures came to one quarter of his revenu, in the days of Phillip II. Optimistic evaluation that probably only took into account the liquid assets, once

---

52 More especially as many authors persist to make Seville then Cadix the economic pole of Europe ... Contradiction.

53 Aporia: the gold and the silver are the driving force for the development; the development supposees a previous structure; so, the gold and the silver don't command everything.

54 What we have called the noria in "Incroyables Gazettes" (CF. op. cit).

55 The confusion is frequent in the texts, it did nevertheless happen that the king of Spain confiscated a whole cargo coming back by issuing in rebursement of *juros*.

56 Money towards the soldiers enlistment, to the garnisons, ...

the deduction already engaged[57]. Some other computations give from 9 to 10%. Therefore, that it may be some three quarter or nine teenth, it is the king of Spain's subjects who have provided the biggest contribuation to his budget, in a massive manner. No sketch needed to understand that the relation between Spanish economy (and prices) and American treasures must under go a serious revision. This will be more necessary, especially as the gold ans the silver returned to the King, have served as a bait for some loans conclusion, the issuing of *juros* and at last a rise of the fiscal pressure on the *pecheros* and others. Meanwhile the metals were taken to be "buried in Genoa" according to Lope de Vega's formula, that only covers a fragment of the reality[58].

To follow the American gold and silver's labyrinth through an other door, out of Spain shows also some irregularities. The increase in value made in America, or in Seville (later in Cadix) on the sell of a *blancard* from Rouen, of a *sayette* from Hondschoote or of *bayette* from Colchester didn't come back as such in the weaver's home. All along the chain between the producer and the buyer, on the way in and the way back, the middlemen took some deductions in advance, and leaving to the artisans only some odds ans ends more or less proportionate to the needs to cover, in fact, apparently inadequate to raise their livehood[59]. The absolute or relative pauperism is not in accord with the idea of the growth of the progression of prices from the base[60]. So! concern for the middle man or the greatman? We are

57 E. LORENZO SANZ, Comercio de España con America en la epoca de Felipe II, Valladolid 1980, vol. II, p. 223, from a document of 1598.

58 It would be necessary to examin all tracks of gold, as well the commercial ones as financial ones. Genoa wasn't the only destination for the American treasures.

59 Yes, the real salaries are lower. CF. M. MORINEAU, in: Histoire économique et sociale du monde (op. cit.).

60 We don't forget that the wage-earner (the workers and the town peoples, generally) did only constitute a small minority among the residents in most European contries. However they constituated a large numbers of buyers on the

betrayed by the words and the associations of common ideas between them. In the conditions of cereal's production during the XVIth century (ans the XVIIth), the rise in prices wasn't the factor nor the result of progress, it was an illness that people had to prevent the best they could[61]. Money was spend on the occurence only if it was necessary. As for the use of the liquidity, it was varied: some people were able to assign it to develop their business, others to buy some land or an office, the third one to build or to dress for the ball. The reversion in the public was not automatic nor given to eveyone. Neither the investment. Not to mention that it did cut down the incomings of the individuals, returning, *mutatis mutandis* to the Spanish case. Not to mention either the fluctuating situations in comparison to Madrid, taking away all the regularity to the supply of precious metals. At the upmost the gold and the silver have been a support - feeble - for a movement that didn't define[62].

Let's abandon this track which would take us far from our fundamental topic. Measuring the part of the discovery of America into the development of Europe. The capitalism is the second problem. Two petitions of principal: the surplus of metals controls, the formation and the efficiency of the capital. This one act by itself, and create a spiral of development. Those are denied by the facts. Lots of firms had taken off with small money. They did prosper only after finding convenient outlets[63] appropriate outlets to its breath[64]. Those data - of experience

---

markets (the peasants lived from their own productions) but were pushed aside as soon as the prices of cereals rose too much.

61 Of course, those who still could sell during the scarcity and the high prices, profited from it.

62 Mediocre support because they did not escape to the devaluation in many contries.

63 This is what we have defended in colloquium on *Capitalisme hollandais et Capitalisme mondial*, in Paris in 1980, and which, in spite of a character touching the truism hasn't been understood from some minds tortured by the computers. Cf. *Actes* published in 1982 by the Maison des Sciences de l'Homme in Paris and for the Cambridge University Press.

- taken into consideration, we just have to become entangled now in some pseudo-laws of development which occult a whole reality side: more than half.

The Spanish and the Portuguese Americans have been one of the outlets for the Europeans producers. They were not the only ones. A quick glance to the English and French trades during the XVIIIth is enough to dissipate the equivocations. The European market count more so and we have no documentation, sadly enough, about the interior market that did prevail over it. How can we be unaware the ever-growing part of the thirteen colonies that didn't bring any money but some sugar, some coffee, some rice, some tabacco and some timber? Miracle in Callao and in Lima: the deletion of the treasures in the loading towards Europe, in the XVIIth century's second half did not lessen the value of it, on the opposite![65] It could be the chance to drive the nail further in and leaving every thing else out of account to attribute to the plantations of colonial food products ans to the work of black slaves, and to the wealth's origine of the whites and their ulterior success. But notwithstanding the irrecusable injury on the slave trade on the African costa, it would be useless to imagine an industrial area dawning on Jamaica or Saint-Domingue's shores. The history on the islands hold another lesson: the ephemeris. Their undeniable wealth during the XVIIIth century did not stand to time nor the occurences. Those went into a category that have known a sectorial economic development, as cicumscribed in the space as in the chronology[66].

A first conclusion becomes apparent after a facts's study: it would be specious and in truth it is historically and/or scientificly mistaken, to deduce only from Guanahani's discovery one evolution of five hundred years, even from the discovery of the Spanish America (in adding Brazil), of the French or English Antilles. The case of the thirteen

64 The concurrences could have also come from another producer (Cuba or the Brazil) or from a substitution's product (the sugar-beet).

65 In the war time of the French Revolution and of the Empire (napoleonic).

66 Cf. M. MORINEAU, Incroyables Gazettes ... (op. cit.).

colonies, that will be the United-States needs some supplementary investigations. Its independance towards the Spanish colonization doesn't lack of arguments even if it did profit from the mexican exchanges at certain times[67]. We will not come back on its importance - to calibrate - for the English economy. But, its development itself, in the XIXth century, untill today hasn't been the simple deduction of an initial factor (*Pilgrim Father's* disembarkement, foundation of Jameson, a fortiori exploration of Raleigh and Cabot). The ratified secession in 1783 wasn't either some king of power force that could have engendred by itself many states ans the economic rise with the wordly supremacy to the XXth century the formation of a geographic pole ans an economic strengh. The crossing of the Alleghanys, the setting up in the Prairies, the forced back Indiens, the inner continental wars (with the Mexico), the arrival of immigrants (one nationality after an other) and the culture of some huge spaces, the railway's construction, the industries's emancipation. the dissapearing of concurrents, the network set up of schools and universities, the given and allways new impulsion to the research: so many elements - and we aren't exhaustive - each have, in its own time, came in association, engendering in a perpetual creation, within itself in an steady and unsteady manner[68].

The second conclusion, then, links up with the first one: "une rente de situation" is not *ad aeternitatem*. There is no unexhaustible mine, no production without the rise of contestation, emulation, competition. The effort must be sustained, the initiatives must intervene at a given point, and deliberatly, the attention, indefectibly brought to the surrounding world, taking up a challenge or adapting to it the best we can.

---

67 The effect of fusion generally mask those "recalls" of the economy for each intervention of a new element. It has nothing to do with the cycles, in their traditional acception.

68 It doesn't exclude the responsability of some - patrons, ministers, etc. ... in varied occasions.

It is why we have to insist about the contingences that permanently ponder on the conjectures, with the inconstancy of the ancient fortune. This is visible on one sight: in the past with the degradation of Cibao and of the Potosi; in the XIXth and the XXth centuries with some examples, as varied as those of silver and gold mines in Arizona and in Alaska, the coal fields in Newcastle, of Belgium and of the North of France, the iron of Lorraine, the natural heveas (para rubber-plant) of Manaos, etc ... This threaten some entire countries when their economy is suspended to only one resource: We had, so, a rent in beef in Agentine and a rent in pyrethrum in Central Africa which were within term or dated and not perpetual: a rent is sugar in Cuba, some cocoa in Ivory Cost (attacked by the plantations of Malaisia) with mutton in New-Zealand, with oil, a bit everywhere, (Mexico, Nigeria, Algeria, etc ...). The parades caught in a decline, the diversification themself are threatened to have a similar fate, without the men's implicatio, who are on the spot[69]. If the brazilian coffee has resisted the attacks until now, it was not the case for the productions from the ancient vice royalty of Lima on which we self congratulated so much during the XVIIIth century. The Saga of Lowell (Massachussetts) two hours north of Boston is instructive. There the textile industry was created in 1814, with Francis Cabot Lowell's funds. Thanks to his inventive mind, by using the Merrimack's waterfalls and of the women enlisting in neighbouring countries, later realyed, by the immigrants. The town was a working hive, and had a leadership in its party. Its population reached 113.000 peoples by 1921. The factories rivaled by Atlanta (Georgia) or Birmingham (Alabama) closed down, one or two manukactures did substain, an industrial national park - may as well say an archaeological museum. On the other hand, in this century's seventies, a chinese immigrant, Wang, wake up the activity by public funds, and the arrival of Asian congeneres as workers. A boom happened: other firms agglomerated according to a classical phenomenon of the snow

---

69 Production from the region of Guayaquil, mainly. The lost place to the far away exploration was able to survive, sometime, on the local market or South-American.

ball. Than the wind of recession blew. Wang reduced his menpower, the engineers abandoned him, the municipality's budget sank into deficit. We could count more than 15.000 unemployed in march 1991. The fund saving, established in 1829, and becoming a bank an 1980, in euphoria, had recently declared bankrupcy, its stock auction went from 9 and even 12 Dollars to ten cents[70]. When I was boating between Honshu and Shikok, in the interior sea, my charming japonese guide, suddently did point at the coast direction with her finger to Mizushima. "Look", she tells me, "ten years ago there we could find the biggest shipyards, launching some gigantic oil tanker ... Today electronic microships are fabricated there. What a difference!" Are we getting away from the discovery off Christophe Colomb in Guanahani or Waiting's island, on the 12 October 1492? Yes: from five centuries. We did it voluntarily. To refuse the poisonous seduction of a factitious come back to the sources. As long as this one is billeted to the search and to the erudite discussions, he is authentic (historically) and doesn't do any harm. But the derivations are tight and cautious by some orchestrated infatuations. Between the romantic admiration of a navigator between stars and sea, the inventor of a new continent, the Christ's holder. For the hate toward the first one who come from Europe, and brought from across the Atlantic or announced, the iron and the fire which destroyed some millennial civilisations. We don't have to spare the cabbage, the goat, and the wolf. What is remarkable must be remarked, what is condemnable must be condemned. Anniversary calls for modesty; nostalgia for reserve[71]. The interest in an memorandum does not only reside in the

---

70 Excellent report from Roel Jansen about Lowell in the number of *NRC Handelsblad* from the 15th of june 1991. With some legendes and eloquent titles: *Welvaart in sepia ..., Lowell-monument van het Amerikaans bankroet ...* (a bit rushed, really; may be)

71 We did not study here the effects of discovery - *largo sensu* - on the environment: the Saint-Domingue's deforestation, for example: draining of the "purple lands" in Brazil: formation of the "*dust bowls*" in the United States: threats on the Amazon: exhausting of metal or oil-feld ... It would be of cour-

retrospective of an event. More fruitful and, in a certain way, more realistic is the perspective setting of the time that has passed since. The long perspective setting, not only of the discovery of a continent but of the exploitation of men. Closely connected to it are the two other fundamental analyses: What does result from the evolution? How was it accomplished? It is usual to raise the inequality between the peoples, from the Baffin sea to the Cape Horn and among themself: it isn't so to weigh the factors of progress and the down fall which have sometime favoured one, sometime the other. The recognition is essential, therefore from the process's multiplicity, and from the balance's instability. It is true, that even today the first place in the world is contested to the United-States. May be we should beg pardon to the auditory for having taken them through so many detours from San Salvador to New England and from Lowell to Seto Nakai, i.e. the Japanese Mediterranean. Gone for the setting sun, we welcome the "rose's fingers dawn" of the rising sun. Differently to Christophe Colomb, five hundred years ago after that, *sono asa kara go hyaku men go*, we have discoved, us, Cipango.

---

se, taking into account by reminding, however, that a certain destruction of the nature is co-adjacent to the humanity's development since the beginning of history, if not the prehistory. To analyse communication to the Colloquium franco-indian of may 1990 to the Maison des Sciences de l'Homme, in Paris: Le défi indien XVIth - XVIIIth century (to be published in the *Actes*).

Crédito, Financiación y Beneficio en el comercio colonial español a través de los cambios y préstamos marítimos (ss XVI - XVII)*

De ANTONIO-MIGUEL BERNAL

Como ha escrito E. Otte en fecha reciente, tenida cuenta lo que era la actividad marítima y mercantil de Sevilla y puertos bajo-andaluces durante el siglo XV, *el descubrimiento de América fue inevitable*, inserto en ese proceso de incipiente expansión colonial que Castilla y Portugal protagonizaban, mano a mano, en las rutas atlánticas. Y aunque no es hasta el siglo XVIII cuando los españoles llaman, sin eufemismo, *colonias* a sus territorios de América, a semejanza de lo que holandeses, ingleses y franceses venían haciendo con las suyas, de lo que no hay lugar a dudas es que, desde el primer momento, como *negocio colonial* fue concebido y organizado el tráfico indiano. En 1495, tres años escasos después del Descubrimiento, se pone en manos de particulares la *explotación* directa de las Indias, con renunciación implícita, por parte de la Corona, de la adaptación del modelo portugués de monopolio público de los frutos coloniales. Ya desde el primer momento, la participación del Estado - Corona de Castilla - en la expedición inicial de 1492 y en las siguientes fue, en términos monetarios, ridícula siendo el dinero empleado, en su casi totalidad, de

* Investigación financiada en su día con una ayuda del Banco de España.

procedencia privada y en buena parte extranjera (genoveses y, al parecer, los florentinos que acreditaron a Colón). Como dejara escrito un coetáneo, Fernández de Oviedo, que tan bien conociera lo que estaba sucediendo en las décadas iniciales a partir de 1492, *casi nunca sus magestades ponen su hacienda y dinero en estos nuevos descubrimientos, excepto papel y buenas palabra*. Lo que con igual rotundidad expresaría Carande, tan buen conocedor del tema hacendístico castellano, al decir que *los gastos de la hacienda real, en las Indias, en tiempos de los reyes católicos y de Carlos V, fueron insignificantes*.

La iniciativa privada al instrumentalizar y financiar tales operaciones lo hacía bajo los supuestos más evolucionados del capitalismo mercantil que por entonces se configuraba, poniendo en juego las modernas técnicas contables, las formas asociativas comerciales más complejas y los instrumentos de créditos más idóneos - cambios y letras de cambios - con el claro y único objetivo de maximalización de beneficios, al margen de cualquier pretendida limitación de naturaleza eclesiástica, lo que fue desde el primer momento entendido y apoyado por el propio Estado. Los nuevos territorios eran, ante todo, *mercados* donde la especulación y el riesgo marcaban la tasa de beneficio.

La Corona, a través de la Casa de Contratación, el Consulado - en cuanto agrupación de mercaderes que estaban facultados para negociar desde Sevilla - y los proveedores - castellanos o extranjeros - de capitales y mercancias, más que contrapuestos, tenían intereses convergentes cuando no complementarios y para todos era requisito imprescindible mantener la funcionalidad del comercio colonial en términos de privilegio y mercado reservado. Desde la economía real, el elemento que vertebra y sostiene dicho sistema era el crédito, de ahí lo necesario de un ordenamiento, aunque fuese mínimo, que estableciese las garantías necesarias ante el nivel elevado de riesgo asumido por los partícipes activos. En este contexto el control de las operaciones de cambio marítimo y préstamos a riesgos adquieren relevancia capital.

De 1492 a 1498 no parece que prestasen especial interés los medios empresariales sevillanos por negociar con las nuevas colonias, actitud que cambiaría a raiz del tercer viaje de Colón, en 1498, con el descubrimiento de las perlas en la costa venezolana. A partir de entonces la actuación privada en el comercio transatlántico iría en aumento con menoscabo de lo que fueran las capitulaciones de Santa Fe; en enero de 1503 se crea la Casa de Contratación, cuyas primeras ordenanzas instruyen sobre los cuidados a tener en la elección de los capitanes de naos y en la obligatoriedad del *registro*, o manifiestos de carga de las mercaderias depositadas a bordo, a la ida como a la vuelta, todavía en régimen comercial de monopolio por la Corona. No obstante, desde febrero de 1504 el régimen de monopolio regio queda cancelado y el comercio con América se abre a todos los súbditos de Castilla. En seis años, de 1498 a 1504, el panorama había cambiado por completo hasta el punto de que los capitanes de armada, salvo uno, se convierten en maestres de la Carrera y prefieren la negociación a los descubrimientos en las nuevas tierras y los extranjeros se muestran solícitos a invertir sus capitales por via de préstamos marítimos generándose tal actividad, como consecuencia de ello, que ha de requerir muy pronto la primera intervención y regulación del crédito en el comercio colonial.

Por la RC.de 1509 la obligatoriedad de manifestar los *cambios* que se tomaren afectaba no sólo a maestres de naos sino a cualquiera que contratase para las Indias, de manera que se establece la práctica de formalizar las escrituras de préstamos ante los escribanos de la Casa a fin de quedar incursas en la validación especial que a los documentos registrados se les concedía sobre cualquier otro aunque fuera hecho ante escribano público.

Las reiteradas crisis financieras de la Corona y la necesidad que tuviera ésta de recurrir al auxilio económico del Consulado de los cargadores a Indias determinó que dicha institución, como contrapartida, fuese ampliando su capacidad de control sobre el tráfico colonial en detrimento de la Casa de la Contratación. Varias fueron las cuestiones sobre las que el Consulado no dejara de manifestar su interés en ampliar las competencias inciales: reducir a la mínima expresión la obligatoriedad de los "registros" de carga e inspección de los mismos a efectos fiscales, asumir plena competencia en asuntos de quiebras mercantiles y financieras de quienes estuvieren ligados a la Carrera de Indias y adquirir el control del crédito tomando bajo su jurisdicción las licencias de cambios y préstamos marítimos. Por la R.C. de 1587 se traspasaba la facultad de dar licencia sobre cambios al Prior y Cónsules ante quienes, a partir de entonces, habrían de tramitarse las escrituras y contratos pertinentes. En realidad la exigencia de control vendría impuesta por las propias vicisitudes del comercio colonial, resultado de una expansión incontrolada del crédito a partir del último tercio del siglo XVI que favorecía una situación de fraudes, alzamientos ficticios de mercaderes y quiebras dolosas; situación que, por otra parte, era coincidente con lo que estaba pasando por las mismas fechas en las plazas mercantiles europeas y que habían obligado a tomar, en fechas similares, medidas parecidas de control sobre el crédito y financiación del comercio marítimo, colonial o no.

El maestre interesado en conseguir una financiación externa - en capitales contantes y mercaderias - para su expedición mercantil dirigía una solicitud, de acuerdo con la mandado en la R.C., al Prior y Cónsules indicando *tener necesidad* de tomar a cambio sobre su nao, que se apresta para viajar a Indias, una determinada cantidad de dinero por lo que pide y suplica manden dichas autoridades recibir información al respecto. Visto el escrito por el Prior y Cónsules, éstos disponian que el maestre diese la información necesaria sobre el valor de la nao para proveer en justicia; pocos dias después, vista la petición y conocida la información requerida, la autoridad consular procedía a fijar la cantidad o cuantía del crédito para la que se daba licencia al maestre peticionario. Eran tres los diferentes tipos documentales generados: a) la petición inicial, con las informaciones oportunas y licencia correspondiente, de las que hemos localizado un buen número de ellas desde abril de 1588 hasta 1603; b) la toma de razón, o asiento en un libro - registro de la cantidad global autorizada, consignándose la fecha, nombre de la persona autorizada a tomar a cambio, profesión de la misma y nombre del navio, destino final y puertos intermedios donde hiciere escala etc., del que se ha conservado un cuadernillo con 37 hojas que comprende la cuenta y razón de los 502 cambios y permisiones concedidas desde febrero de 1598 a marzo de 1612 y c) la fé de las cantidades parciales que sobre lo autorizado iba tomando el maestre, que son en realidad los traslados autentificados de las escrituras originales de cambio o préstamo formalizadas ante algún escribano público, con la mención de ser dinero prestado con licencia consular, y de cuyas cantidades parciales se va efectuando la correspondiente toma de razón hasta completar la suma total autorizada. Si el maestre necesitase alguna cantidad suplementaria habrá de volver a solicitarlo y, considerado de nuevo por el Prior y Cónsules, éstos volverán a resolver si procede conceder la autorización para ampliar el crédito o su denegación. Los expedientes de petición de cambios se llevaban mezclados con otros similares que habían de hacerse para los seguros a fin de que la cantidad asegurada no sobrepasase las 2/3 partes del valor estimado de la nao.

En resumen, en el lapso de tiempo que va desde mediados del siglo XV a principios del siglo XVII, la apertura del comercio con las Indias no supuso innovación alguna pues se limitó a adoptar el instrumento de crédito marítimo usual en el comercio europeo desde hacía varios siglos si bien hubo de adaptarlo a circunstancias nuevas impuestas por el tipo de navegación o por la novedad que supusiera el que fuese oro o plata, amonedada o sin amonedar, el medio de pago a utilizar. Lo más importante a tener en cuenta es que por las características del sistema del comercio colonial, el préstamo marítimo mantuvo la connotación de cambio monetario y es a partir de él como se introducen y ejecutan las prácticas de financiación propias de los mercados de capitales realizadas a través de la letra de cambio, razón por la cual ésta, tal como ocurriese con los cambios terrestres y de feria en Europa, se introduce con extrema lentitud y debilidad en los circuitos americanos. Por último, los sistemas de control de los cambios, bajo la supervisión de la Casa o del Consulado, fueron modelo, por la fecha temprana en que se impusieron y modo de llevarlos a cabo, de los que finalmente se adaptarian en los distintos paises europeos y por razones similares, a saber el desarrollo inusitado del crédito a raiz del auge que fuere adquiriendo el comercio con las colonias.

¿De dónde provenían y a quiénes pertenecieran, en última instancia, los capitales que hicieran posible no sólo el descubrimiento y conquista del Nuevo Mundo sino también la explotación de las riquezas que éste aportara a la economía de Europa? ¿Requirieron la explotación de las Indias y la organización del mercado colonial aportes ingentes de capitales? ¿Hasta qué punto los beneficios obtenidos fueron proporcionados a las inversiones realizadas y cómo se distribuyeran entre financieros, mercaderes e intermediarios? Estas interrogantes, y muchas más de igual naturaleza, como veremos, no fueron contestadas o carecieron de respuestas ya fuera por desconocimiento de las posibles fuentes documentales que aportasen los datos necesarios, ya porque se considerasen interrogantes retóricas que, por pretendidamente sabidas, no necesitaban respuestas demostrables. El temprano control que por el Estado se llevaba de los cambios y préstamos y el haberse conservado, aunque fragmentados, parte de los registros nos van a permitir abordar las cuestiones planteadas aunque consciente de las limitaciones que todavía subsisten en un estudio de esta naturaleza.

De 1492 a 1614, primer periodo en que dividimos nuestro estudio, hemos analizado 2.784 contratos o escrituras de cambios y préstamos marítimos por un importe total de 670.881.552 de maravedies. De ellos, el 42% proceden de los registros de cambios llevados por la Casa de Contratación y Consulado y el 58% restante provienen de los Protocolos notariales de Sevilla, resultado del muestreo en ellos efectuado. La distribución por años, el importe total anual y los valores medios es el que se recoge en el siguiente cuadro:

CUADRO I:
Distribucion anual de contratos de cambios y escrituras de prestamos
Periodo: 1492 - 1614 (A.G.I. + A.P.S.)

Años	Nº	Total ms.	Ms./Esc.	Años	Nº	Total ms.	Ms./Esc.
1492	1	12000	12000	*1519*	1	24000	24000
1493	1	6375	6375	*1520*	16	410250	25640
1495	2	24750	12375	*1522*	1	8085	8085
1496	1	5400	5400	*1523*	26	681282	26203
1497	4	10255	2563	*1524*	74	2847535	38480
1500	4	47700	11925	*1525*	126	4055001	32182
1501	9	62335	6926	*1526*	114	3305961	28999
1502	7	58670	8381	*1527*	124	4307978	34741
1503	3	18750	6250	*1528*	118	4694084	39780
1504	9	51050	5672	*1529*	54	1698719	31457
1505	7	135095	19299	*1530*	139	5705136	41044
1506	49	1164812	23771	*1531*	9	258187	28687
1507	69	3037542	44022	*1536*	3	109437	36479
1508	368	14416269	39174	*1537*	3	58125	19375
1509	107	4392391	41050	*1538*	44	1981421	45032
1510	61	3037399	49793	*1539*	4	168750	42187
1511	14	367160	26225	*1540*	4	204000	51000
1512	56	1714543	30616	*1542*	10	419067	41906
1513	97	2776053	28619	*1543*	1	8625	8625
1514	125	4445219	35561	*1544*	2	98250	49125
1515	105	3850357	36670	*1545*	1	56250	56250
1516	49	1169494	23867	*1546*	9	473550	52616
1517	84	2206554	26268	*1548*	6	579000	96500

CUADRO I:

Años	Nº	Total ms.	Ms./Esc.	Años	Nº	Total ms.	Ms./Esc.
1549	3	155750	51916	*1598*	48	26493750	551953
1550	1	18562	18562	*1599*	57	58125000	1019736
1551	4	92625	23156	*1600*	74	66232500	895033
1557	1	309000	309000	*1601*	40	41756250	1043906
1574	1	35250	35250	*1602*	58	65700000	1132758
1576	2	40526	20263	*1603*	52	66675000	1282211
1577	1	10880	10880	*1604*	53	54093750	1020636
1580	18	3648443	202691	*1605*	48	55725000	1160937
1582	1	51000	51000	*1606*	18	15011250	833958
1584	2	318750	159375	*1607*	32	38336250	1198007
1588	21	5925000	282142	*1608*	22	15162375	689198
1590	3	2062500	687500	*1609*	38	39487500	1039144
1591	13	3600000	276923	*1610*	11	9150000	831818
1593	2	---	---	*1611*	19	19800000	1042105
1594	2	97600	48800	*1612*	2	2250000	1125000
1596	1	562500	562500	*1614*	1	2250000	2250000
1597	3	2250000	750000				

Aunque en principio el cambio marítimo consistía en obtener un préstamo dinerario con la garantía de la nao, esta operación podía ofrecer modalidades múltiples según la finalidad: ya sea para fornescimiento de la nave en cuyo caso el dinero conseguido se destinaba a la adquisición de útiles, aparejos, armamento etc. necesarios para la navegación, o para abastecimiento y avituallamiento, empleándose en tal caso para la compra de víveres y demás vituallas necesaria para la tripulación durante el viaje; si se destinaba el crédito para atender ambas necesidades a la vez entonces se denominaban escrituras de "abastecimiento y despacho de naos". Si el crédito no estaba afecto a la nave sino a la carga que transportaba entonces se suscribía bajo el nombre de "préstamos" o *despacho de mercaderías* y constituía la forma regular por la que accedían al crédito los mercaderes. En tales préstamos eran las mercaderías sobre las que se corría el riesgo, quedando hipotecadas a la paga, sin obligar al maestre ni a la nao. La fórmula de afectación solía ser: "hipoteco las mercaderias que en la dicha nao llevo cargadas para que si así non feciere i compliere sean vendidas e rematadas a buen precio o a malo sin aguardar ni orden ... e de los ms. por que se vendiesen sea fecho el pago". En los años iniciales las mercaderias compradas a crédito eran en buena parte víveres y productos alimenticios - vino, harinas, aceite, bizcochos etc. - aunque muy pronto el dinero así obtenido iba destinado a la adquisición de lo que en el argot indiano se denominaría *ropa*, es decir manufacturas con predominio de las mercaderías textiles en general, confeccionadas o no. Utilizaron con profusión esta modalidad de crédito los mercaderes estantes en Sevilla pero con residencia habitual en Indias quienes se proveían de lo que les interesaba adquirir sin necesidad de desembolso previo aunque el precio del dinero así obtenido resultase muy caro - entre el 60% y el 120% de interés, según circunstancias -; también la practicaron los pasajeros que estando faltos de recursos propios aprovechaban su desplazamiento para traficar aunque fuese como mercaderes ocasionales y aunque los intereses a pagar eran muy altos siempre cabía la posibilidad de ganancia cierta dado los altos beneficios que proporcionaba el mercado colonial. Los préstamos sobre mercaderías no obligaban a la nave ni al maestre; pero si el préstamo para despacho de mercadería se hacía mancomunadamente entre mercaderes y maestres, salvo que formasen expresa compañía, lo usual era que fuese el mercader el único responsable empleandose tal argucia para ampliar la capacidad de crédito al contarse entonces con la garantía de la nave, previa escritura de sacar en paz y salvo el mercader al maestre de la deuda contraida.

Ignorados por la historia oficial, más atenta al relumbrón de los conquistadores y gobernantes, fueron hombres grises los que dieron vida a la Carrera desde la economía real. Los que se encargaron de mantener el contínuo ajetreo de las idas y venidas de los barcos, los que proveían de víveres y vituallas a los colonos asentados en las Indias, quienes dirigieron la explotación de las colonias y retornaron a Europa las riquezas del nuevo continente fueron hombres de la más variadas condiciones sociales y económicas a quienes guiaba, según circunstancias, la maximalización de un beneficio empresarial o el afán de lucro puro y simple aunque en todos persistía como meta el logro de un enriquecimiento fácil y rápido a la vez. Si, como parece, una incipiente configuración del capitalismo ya estaba latente desde mediados del siglo XV, no es de extrañar que se considere que éste llegase a su "florecimiento" a raiz del del descubrimiento americano.

La aventura económica americana sobrepasó rápidamente las posibilidades de Castilla. Nada más simple, pues, que pretender reducirla a localismos excluyentes - burgaleses, vascos, andaluces, extremeños etc. - como quiere la tradición historiográfica hispánica o darle la exclusiva prioridad a otros grupos nacionales o raciales, como por ej. genoveses o conversos, como pretende una profusa bibliografía en buena parte de historiadores no castellanos. Como veremos de inmediato, hombres, capitales y productos llegaban a la Carrera de Indias desde una geografía muy diversa y durante los tres siglos del comercio colonial se fueron sucediendo relevos que no hacen sino acentuar el *internacionalismo* que tuviera desde los momentos iniciales. Las pretensiones de monopolio, que resultaron tan frágiles en lo que respectaba al comercio, no dieron mejores frutos aplicadas a los agentes personales de la actividades naviera y mercantil. Las disposiciones inciales de restringir la participación a los que no fuesen castellanos apenas si se aplicaron; la etapa del emperador Carlos V fue de claro aperturismo internacional con las concesiones que hiciera a negociantes y banqueros extranjeros para intervenir incluso directamente en el comercio colonial y, más tarde, el déficit crónico presupuestario y la penuria de la hacienda abrieron de par en par las puertas a las naturalizaciones de extranjeros. La pretensión de excluir a los extranjeros de la negociación indiana resultó fallida en la parte principal pues, aunque a aquéllos no se les facilitase el pasar a Indias, a causa de los controles establecidos por la Casa de la Contratación, nada les impedía participar en la negociación directamente o por persona interpuesta gracias a las operaciones de cambio y préstamo marítimo.

Desde el principio, la Carrera de Indias fue en cierto modo un oligopolio donde un número reducido de armadores, maestres, mercaderes y financieros controlaban lo sustancial de la negociación e impusieron las maneras y ritmo de las operaciones. Para seleccionar a los que fueran en verdad los grandes perceptores del crédito hemos tenido en cuenta el doble criterio de número de escrituras suscritas y la cuantía del dinero adeudado. La síntesis de las operaciones efectuadas nos permitió elaborar los siguientes cuadros:

CUADRO II:
a) Grandes Deudores (con 4 escrituras, mínimo)

Años	Deudores	%Total	Escrit.	%Total	Maravedies	%Total
1492-1530	76	6.7	559	27.4	23.997.052	33.7
1588-1611	23	4.8	132	21.4	147.638.450	25.1
1492-1510	29	8.8	226	32.1	9.801.258	37.0
1511-1520	26	7.1	143	25.6	5.738.486	33.2
1521-1530	21	4.9	190	24.4	8.457.308	30.9

b) Grandes Deudores: según cuantía total

Años	Deudores	%Total	Escrit.	%Total	Maravedies	%Total
1492-1556	A 88	7.3	772	35.6	37.348.822	49.2
1492-1556	B 17	1.4	276	12.7	14.589.104	19.2
1557-1614	C 51	10.2	192	29.8	264.544.700	44.4
1557-1614	D 18	3.6	104	16.1	140.607.700	23.6

A = Mínimo 200.000 mrs.; B = 500.000; C = 3 millones mrs.; D = 5 millones mrs.

Es el reducido número de quienes entre 1492-1556 operan con más de medio millón de maravedies los que conforman la élite exportadora de la Carrera: siendo sólo el 1.4 % del total de deudores suscriben 9 veces más escrituras de cambios y 13.7 veces más del dinero contratado. Ya tendremos ocasión de identificarlos personalmente más adelante; de momento sirva señalar cómo la llamada aventura del descubrimiento y colonización no fue sino producto de una organización y decisión empresariales de un reducido grupo naviero-mercantil interesado desde décadas antes en la expansión atlántica e islas adyacentes, y en los negocios de los esclavos, del oro y especerias en las costas africanas. Sólo más tarde, en la segunda mitad del XVI, conocida la amplitud de los nuevos territorios se inició una cierta participación popular aunque todavía, según los datos expuestos, poco más de un centenar de hombres asumían el peso principal como agentes del tráfico y del comercio con las colonias.

En una aproximación, general también, a lo que pudiera ser una tipología sociológica de los deudores, según el status social, profesión o actividad realizada por los mismos, con indicación de la importancia numérica y económica, los resultados obtenidos son los que se resumen en el siguiente cuadro. A efectos de comprensión del mismo se recuerda que hay ciertos matices diferenciadores en los componentes de cada mitad de siglo: en 1466 - 1556, el cómputo de escrituras se ha elaborado con las aportadas por los registros oficiales de la Contratación más las obtenidas de la muestra efectuada en los protocolos notariales, mientras que para el periodo de 1557 - 1614 sólo se tuvo en cuenta la relación del registro oficial del Consulado. Por esa razón, en la primera mitad del siglo aparecen los mercaderes con cuantía importante - corresponden a las escrituras protocolizadas ante notarios públicos - mientras que en la segunda sólo figuran maestres y señores de naos, para quienes era preceptivo obtener la licencia consular para consequir un crédito bajo la garantía de la nao.

CUADRO III:
Escrituras de cambios y riesgos maritimos
Deudores: Distribución por actividad

		1466 - 1556			*1557 - 1614*	
Actividad	NºEsc.	Maravedies	Ms/Escr.	NºEsc	Maravedies	Ms/Escr
Maestres/capitanes, solos	639	23081183	36120	192	166000956	864588
Maestres señores de naos	344	13762864	40008	203	204226450	1006041
Señores de naos, solos	85	3289718	38702	185	178050750	962436
Maestres y señores, juntos	350	14748479	42138	39	35212500	902884
Maest.sres y mercaderes	139	5089598	36615	5	663198	122640
Maest.sres y gente de mar	33	1294970	39241			
Pilotos,escr.naos,marineros	88	991739	11269	3	42180	14060
Funcionarios etc.	40	2075619	51890	3	539490	179830
Mercaderes, varios	200	5362433	26812			
Artesanos y mercaderes	227	5234830	23060			
Prof.liberales	14	558195	39871			
Corredor de lonja	5	97575	19515			
Clero	2	213000	106500			
Apoderados de naos				5	6562500	1321500
Sin especificar				9	3912050	434672
TOTALES	2166	75800203	34995	644	595160074	924161

Es sabido que desde mediados del siglo XV en los puertos bajoandaluces se iba perfilando un importante grupo naviero involucrado en las expediciones atlánticas destacando entre ellos conspícuos miembros de la gran nobleza señorial que, aparte del control territorial de las tierras conquistadas, había tomado posiciones en las zonas de litoral y puertos pues no en balde la economía del valle del Guadalquivir, desde la conquista cristiana, estuvo abierta al doble movimiento export - import de sus puertos. Sólo por inercia histórica puede mantenerse el tópico manido de una nobleza al margen de la negociación mercantil. Apenas acababa de regresar Colón del primer viaje descubridor cuando el duque de Medinaceli, en marzo de 1493, escribe al cardenal de España manifestándole que él tuvo dos años a Colón en su casa, que le impidió que se fuese con el rey de Francia y que él mismo fue quien propuso a los Reyes que tomasen bajo su protección el viaje realizado, por todo lo cual, en vista de tan renombrados servicios prestados a la

Corona, solicitaba la merced de poder enviar el duque cada año a las tierras descubiertas varias carabelas suyas. No era éste un caso excepcional ni mucho menos. Organizado mínimamente el tráfico con las Indias, desde el primer momento destaca la presencia de naves que pertenecían a la nobleza, en particular a los Medinaceli, asentados señorialmente en la villa del Puerto de Sta.María, y a los Medinasidonía que lo estaban en las de Sanlúcar y en las villas marítimas del litorial onubense bajo el control de la rama secundaria de los Portocarrero.

A la hora de lucrarse con los pingûes negocios que los nuevos mercados coloniales prometían, todos querían participar, incluida la más alta magistratura del Reino. Precisamente el primer asiento del Registro oficial de cambios de la Contratación, de fecha 4 de diciembre de 1507, se hace por el maestre Diego Rodríguez Grajeda quien era coopropietario con la Reina, convertida en hábil comerciante, de una nao que habilitaba para ir a las Indias a negociar; el maestre compensaba a la Reina con 300.000 ms. No era la única participación pues pocas semanas despúes, el 6 de febrero de 1508, se abre nuevo registro del dinero tomado a cambio por Esteban Santaçelay, maestre de una nao mediana llamada la Magdalena que era también propiedad de la Reina, en este caso al completo; todavía en 1514 se cita la carabela Consolación, propiedad de S.A., que tenía por maestre a Andrés Niño. También, en el primer libro registro, aparecen doña Francisca Ponce de León, como propietaria de dos naos - S.Cristobal de 150 ts.y S.Telmo de 80 ts. - y don Pedro de Portocarrero como coopropietario de 1/5 de la nao Sta.María de la Rábida. En el del año de 1509 figura la duquesa de Medinaceli como propietaria de la Trinidad, que lleva como maestre a Juan Ortiz, vecino de su feudo del Puerto de Sta.María. Otros miembros distinguidos son Fco. Despíndola, del que se dice sea alcaide y vecino de Sanlúcar, propietario en 1508 de la mitad de la nao S.Cristóbal y dueño en 1509 de la nao Sta.Catalina, o el caso de los representantes de la pequeña nobleza sevillana, muy pronto encumbrada, como lo fueran el caballero veinticuatro Fco. de Alcazar y el jurado Alonso de Medina, señores ambos de naos en

1509 con el nombre de S.Salvador, o el veinticuatro J. Fdez Melgarejo dueño de la cuarta parte de la S. Miguel, en 1508. Por último, como se dirá después, hay señores de naos que son altas dignidades eclesiásticas, inquisidores etc.

De los restantes señores de naos, en los años inmediatos al descubrimiento, entre 1507 y 1514, destacan, en primer lugar, los cómitres cada vez menos vinculados a los servicios de la Real Armada y convertidos en emprendedores mercaderes, como Bartolomé Díaz propietario en 1509 de las naos Sta.María de la Luz y Sta.María de la Antigua, en 1510 de la S.Salvador y en 1513 de la S.Francisco. Inclusive, entre quienes firmaron con la Corona los primeros asientos de Armada - La Cosa, Guerra y Bastidas -, éste último renuncia y se hace mercader actuando en próspero negocio, desde 1509, como vecino de la Española, con su nao Sta.María. Aunque el ejemplo más representativo de la ambigûedad inicial entre descubridores, transportistas y mercaderes lo ofrezca Diego de Nicuesa propietario de 4 naos - Trinidad, S.Leon, Santiago y Sta.María del Cabo - con las que organiza la expedición de 1508 - 1509.

Lo más usual sería el de propiedad de naos compartida entre señores - o dueños - y maestres, que aparecen asociados no sólo por el condominio de la nave y la función de transportista que ello conlleva sino que juntos participan, además, en operaciones mercantiles, de forma mancomunada e insolidum, al responsabilizarse ambos por igual de las deudas contraidas por cambio marítimo, dejándose de ello constancia tanto en los asientos del registro como en las peticiones de licencia para tomar a cambio; pertenecen a esta clase el conjunto de escrituras que hemos agrupado como suscritas por *maestres y señores, juntos*. A veces la propiedad era compartida por mitad y no son infrecuente los ejemplos en que el maestre a lo sumo lo que poseía fuera tan sólo 1/3 o 1/5 de la misma repartiéndose el resto entre acaudalados vecinos de los puertos bajoandaluces de la más diversa jerarquía social. La presencia de esos "socios capitalistas" vendrían impuesta tanto o más que por la precariedad económica de los maestres, tal vez faltos de los recursos suficientes para afrontar la travesía atlántica y el largo tiempo de navegación que suponía, como por el afán participativo de quienes sin ser "gente de la mar" querían acceder de manera directa al tráfico mercantil con las nuevas tierras; más aún, en ocasiones eran un grupo de mercaderes y particulares los que adquirían la nave designando luego al maestre que hubiera de gobernarla cediéndole una cuota participativa en la propiedad de la misma por razones de interés mercantil y de seguridad de los capitales invertidos. Sería una fórmula mixta de propiedad y actividad económica a la que se recurriría con frecuencia hasta los años de 1534 - 1535 cuando se promulgan las ordenanzas específicas sobre la navegación indiana y se establecen con nitidez la separación de competencias y funciones de transportistas y mercaderes de la Carrera. Entre 1492 - 1530 dicho grupo suscribiría el 22.7% de las escrituras y el 25.7 del dinero contratado por la gente de la mar. Con la erección de la Universidad de mareantes, por un lado, como asociación gremial de la patronal naviera, y la del Consulado por otro, como Universidad de cargadores que agrupaba a los mercaderes, hacendados y comerciantes capacitados para intervenir en el tráfico colonial, las formas mixtas de condominio fueron cediendo en favor de la propiedad exclusiva de las naves por los propios maestres, de modo que entre 1557 - 1614 las operaciones conjuntas efectuadas por ambos apenas sobrepasaban el 6% del total de contratos y dinero prestado a la gente de mar. Desde las décadas de 1540 - 1550 los cargadores no consideran ya necesario ni rentable invertir en naves, aceptando al pago de fletes y seguros y beneficiándose de los préstamos marítimos en cuanto mercaderes bajo la garantía de las mercaderías por ellos cargadas.

En lineas generales se puede dar por válida para todo el periodo colonial la definición de Veitia de que comerciar con Indias era enviar cargazones allá para venderlas al por mayor, entendiendo por cargazón, tal como aparece en Mercado, el conjunto de mercaderias y ropa que bajo un mismo y único registro se embarca por un mercader en Sevilla consignado a otro mayorista en Indias para que proceda a su venta.

Como en otros aspectos, el descubrimiento de América no supuso ruptura con las prácticas y usos vigentes en el comercio marítimo bajoandaluz. Entraron en funcionamiento los mecanismos que regulaban la actividad mercantil en la ciudad de Sevilla, que a su vez respondían a los comúnmente aceptados en el ámbito mediterráneo. La continuidad en las modalidades de comerciar, propias del Mediterráneo traspasadas al Atlántico, pronto se verían modificadas por circunstacias y condicionamientos que dieron al negocio colonial un perfil y aire propios y que van a favorecer, en lo que a la financiación de dicho comercio respecta, la implantación del cambio marítimo como instrumento crediticio dominante. Ante todo, quiebra la principal virtud que regulaba el comercio exterior en aquella época: para los mercaderes afincados en América no hay, desde Europa, *confianza* y en consecuencia no se establece trato *directo*. De otra parte, sin embargo, el recurso masivo al crédito era insoslayable y, como tantas veces se ha reiterado, vender *al fiado* y a largos plazos era consustancial al comercio colonial. Para resolver esa contradicción - falta de confianza y necesidad imperiosa del crédito - el cambio marítimo resultó ser el instrumento más eficaz y operativo. Más aún si se tiene en cuenta que al utilizarlo se reducían de manera importante los problemas del cobro y la cuestión de las deudas, verdadero talón de aquiles del negocio indiano.

Es cierto que las modalidades de comerciar fueron cambiando con el tiempo y que a principios del siglo XVII no operaban exactamente los mismos mecanismos que a raiz del Descubrimiento. Esto reconocido, vamos a hacer abstracción de las alteraciones y subrayar, por ahora, los rasgos generales que favorecieron el desarrollo del préstamo marítimo. El comercio colonial, desde el inicio hasta su liquidación, se sustentaba en una red donde se interrelacionaban compañias, factores, consignatarios y comisionistas. Y aunque en principio pudiera parecer igual a la que venía siendo habitual en el comercio marítimo europeo desde el siglo XIV pronto se diferenciaría de aquélla a causa del distinto peso específico que cada uno de los elementos alcanzaría dentro del sistema; del mismo modo que, pareciendo semejante, el modo de comerciar con Indias diferiría del aplicado en los comercios coloniales de Holanda, Inglaterra o Francia. Precisamente, en "ese modo de hacer diferente" de los castellanos se ha querido ver la raiz de la distinta trayectoria del papel que jugaran las colonias respecto a la economía de la metrópolis.

Las diversas configuraciones de compañias servían, en primera instancia, para movilizar recursos y minimizar riesgos. La funcionalidad de las compañias no podría culminar sin los restantes elementos que configuraban la red mercantil del comercio colonial: las actividades de factoría, consignación y encomienda. Ninguna de ellas fueron de creación original del comercio colonial pero las tres conocieron, a raiz de la negociación con Indias, una evolución tal que se convirtieron en piezas determinantes de dicho comercio. Desde las primeras expediciones aparecen ya factores en Indias, responsabilizados de los asuntos encomendados por las compañias sevillanas y de fecha tan temprana como 1514 son las primeras disposiciones legislativas de la Casa respectos a ellos, en particular en lo que concierne a que vuelvan a Sevilla a rendir cuentas. En su mayoría, los factores eran criados y parientes de los socios principales de la compañia y para principios del siglo XVI eran frecuentes que figuren ente ellos algunos italianos vinculados con las principales familias asentadas en Sevilla. En la encomienda como en la consignación se mezclan tanto el apoyo mutuo de mercaderes asentados a uno y otro lado el Atlántico como el interés mercantil: por razones de amistad y también por la comisión del 7 u 8% estipulada para Indias.

Los altos costes financieros y los elevados gastos de gestión se compensaban con creces gracias a los cuantiosos beneficios generados por el comercio colonial en parte debido a los altos precios a que se realizaban las ventas de mercaderias en Indias, en parte a las ganancias derivadas del cambio monetario y agio en las remesas de oro y plata.

Aunque permanece como tema inexplorado, los datos que vamos a exponer nos parecen suficientemente reveladores sobre la cuantía de los beneficios en el comercio colonial. Parece fuera de duda que en la etapa inicial, aun antes de contar con las remesas, los beneficios fueron fabulosos. Así en los medios mercantiles sevillanos se calculó que en la primera expedición privada a Indias, autorizada en 1502 por los Reyes Católicos a Riberol y Sánchez de la Tesorería para abastecer la Española, los beneficios oscilaron entre un 300 y 400%; también en un 300% se estimaron en 1505 los obtenidos por la compañía de Bastidas en la venta de vino y aceite; en 1509 el alcalde de Espera comunica al cómitre D. Rodríguez que las mercaderías que le dio para vender en Sto.Domingo hacía nueve meses por valor de 600 ducados podrían valer 2000 ds. lo que supondría un beneficio del 233%. Muy pronto la fiebre de ganancia rápida se extendió por la ciudad del Guadalquivir y todos querían participar en una empresa que auguraba tan halagûeños resultados. La correspondencia de los factores en Indias con los socios sevillanos, dándole cuenta de la marcha de los negocios, transparentan sin reservas las ganancias obtenidas como la de F. de Herrera, desde Santiago de Cuba en 1522, a A. de Nebreda, en Sevilla, en la que le da cuenta de lo bien que se han hecho los negocios de las mercaderias enviadas y que "si me oviera enviado alguna ropa por qualquier otra quenta yo oviera hecho muy bien della ... que juro por Dios que se ovieran ganado dozientos e aun trescientos por ciento"; en 1564 el factor G. de Valladolid informa que las cargazones enviadas a Tierra firme se han vendido con un 100 y 120% de ganancia, e igual para las de Perú, para 1568 con un 70 y 90% a plazo y con un 50% en ventas al contado y, por último, en las de 1569 se alcanzaron beneficios del 80, 90 y 100%. En productos de la tierra, como el vino de Cazalla por ej., a mediados del XVI se estipulaba una ganancia del 150%. En otros casos las noticias se insertan en cartas de mercaderes asentados en Indias dando cuenta a su familia, que quedó en Andalucia, de la marcha próspera de sus asuntos: uno comunica a su sobrino en 1570 tener más de 10000 pesos empleados en pipas de vino para Zacatecas "y creo que se doblarán"; otro, desde Guatemala, escribe al cuñado animándole a irse con él que "tiene un grande trato ... y es a ciento por ciento la ganancia"; por último, los hay quienes sin ser mercader, como Celedón Falavis, de

Madrid, se lamenta de no haberse aplicado al negocio toda vez que decidiera ir a Lima en 1587: "yo fui desgraciado en no acertar a traer, aunque no fuera sino seiscientos ducados empleados en algunas cosas de las cuales sin duda ninguna hubiera hecho más de tres mil pesos, que era quedar rico para siempre". Y pese a las vicisitudes que el comercio colonial conociera en el siglo XVII no parece que las expectativas de ganancias muy remuneradoras se hubiesen interrumpido si nos atenemos a las cifras que da Osorio estimando los beneficios de un 100 a 150% hasta alcanzar en ocasiones un 300%.

Dándose por sentado, como lo hacían los coetáneos que traficaban en la Carrera, que fueran los altos precios pagados en Indias los responsables directos de tan cuantiosa ganancia quedan en el aire muchas interrogantes que responder. El diferencial de precios, aparte de la explicación monetarista clásica - menor valor del dinero en Indias que en la metrópoli -, podría estar determinado por altos precios ya en *origen* o bien como consecuencia de una continuada presión de la *demanda,* respecto a la oferta de productos europeos, en los mercados americanos. Cuando aún no se conocía el alcance de los viajes descubridores ya los proveedores de las naos expedicionarias se hacían pagar a crecidos precios los suministros proveidos hasta el punto que los Reyes Católicos, por R.C. de 23 de abril de 1497, disponen para que "los proveimientos para las Indias que ha de comprar la persona que haya los poderes de D. Cristóbal Colón se compren a los precios justos y razonables e según suelen valer en las ciudades, villas e lugares, sin que los mercaderes encarezcan los dichos proveimentos". Disposición que, como todas las dictadas a fin de tasar los precios, quedaría sin cumplimiento y efecto. A partir de entonces, y durante el primer tercio del siglo XVI, hasta 1538 al menos, se suceden reiteradas disposiciones y escritos diversos que se hacen eco de los subidos precios en las colonias, hasta tres veces superior a los que corrían por Sevilla, alza que afectaba inclusive a los derechos que los curas cobraban por entierros y velaciones. Y en términos similares se expresaban los agentes privados del comercio como el factor F. Lapi que, en 1535, comunica a sus socios florentinos Strozzi y Capponi lo fácil que era labrar en Sevilla fabulosas fortunas en muy poco tiempo negociando con el Nuevo Mundo gracias a los altos precios de venta de allá y dice no querer insistir demasiado en ello "para no ser tenido por mentiroso".

Era cierto que ya en origen las mercaderías que se adquirían para enviar a América se compraban a subidos precios. En primer lugar, como diría Mercado, porque los que compran en Sevilla lo hacen al fiado y a largos plazos, y por consiguiente, caro: de ahí que los altos precios de Indias vengan impuestos, en primer término, por los altos precios de Castilla. La "ropa fiada" solía cargarse con un 33% de su "justo valor"; en ocasiones la ambición desmedida de un "necio comprador" en fecha inmediata a la salida de la flota podía hacer subir en Gradas los precios en un 25% tan sólo en cuestión de dias por un excesivo afán acaparador de determinado producto del que la ciudad no estuviese muy bien abastecida. Sin embargo sería el elevado coste financiero, a causa de los mecanismos e instrumentos empleados para acceder al crédito o fiado, los que determinarían, a mi modo de ver, los elevados precios en origen de las mercaderias contratadas para exportar. Esos mecanismos e instrumentos serían la *barata* y el *préstamo marítimo*. La primera, como se sabe, consiste en un mecanismo por el que se compra al fiado y se vende de inmediato al contado a más bajo precio como medio de conseguir liquidez inmediata a corto plazo, operaciones que fuese habitual se hiciesen en el siglo XVI en las Gradas sevillanas con un quebranto del 20 al 25% por término medio. Y a la barata recurría el mercader falto de liquidez porque las remesas de la anterior expedición no le hubiesen llegado a tiempo con lo que repercuten, a la hora de vender en Indias, el coste adicional que han debido sufrir por la falta de liquidez a corto plazo. La segunda opción podría ser adquirir las mercaderias a embarcar por operación de cambio marítimo, y en tal caso, dado que el vendedor corre el riesgo del viaje, pues el pago no se ha de hacer efectivo sino hasta la llegada a salvo de la nave a Indias, recrece el precio de venta amén del tipo de interés del dinero. De cualquier forma, la necesidad de recurrirse al crédito por los exportadores propicia, para quienes venden a los cargadores en Sevilla, el poder participar en las previsibles ganancias via alza de precio en origen.

De cualquier modo, los precios de partida tendrían una incidencia limitada por cuanto el precio final de venta en el mercado colonial - que era el que en última instancia hacía subir o bajar el % de los beneficios - dependía de la coyuntura de la llegada de las naos y flotas, en último término de la *demanda*. En parte por las dificultades organizativas del tráfico pero sobre todo por los intereses monopolistas de los cargadores sevillanos el resultado fue "que las colonias estuvieron irregular e insuficientemente abastecidas de bienes de consumo europeos ... lo cual les posibilitaba una venta a precios más altos y hacía que atrayentes ganancias compensaran todos los riesgos". Pocos años después del descubrimiento quedaba claro que para la monarquía española las medidas que fomentasen el desarrollo económico de las colonias quedarían pospuestas al interés financiero de la metrópoli. Del pretendido monopolio estatal de los primeros viajes se pasó a un sistema de monopolio compartido entre la Corona y los grandes comerciantes sevillanos, en particular a partir de la creación del Consulado. Dicha institución facilitaba la *armonia* entre los grandes cargadores - a mitad del siglo XVI aquellos que hubiesen embarcado por cuenta propia mercaderias por valor de 300.000 ms. de plata -, y era el órgano a partir del cual se determinaba la naturaleza y magnitud de las exportaciones que permitían el ajuste conveniente entre oferta y demanda para dictar los precios e imponer, en su caso, el precio máximo.

A medida que la demanda - los mercaderes en Indias - fue contrarrestando el monopolio imperativo de la oferta lo más destacado sería la presencia en la Carrera de los encomenderos de los mercaderes de Indias como agentes activos que vienen a Castilla a efectuar las compras que fueren menester reduciendo la dependencia e intermediación de los cargadores a Indias. Son los llamados *peruleros*, que aparecen a principios del siglo XVII mezclados con los cargadores de las flotas, y en quienes el Consulado muy pronto vería a un poderoso competidor. En realidad, el perulero, tal como lo describe F. de Mandojana en

1622, era un encomendero que venía de las Indias a emplear dinero ajeno, comprando parte al fiado y a pagar en Indias; parece que los que primero se situan en la Carrera son aquellos que estaban favorecidos por personas poderosas de Lima, a cuenta de quienes hacían cargazones para el virreinato. Desde el primer momento se intentaría excluirlos achacándoseles que desde que venían a España a emplear los capitales encomendados "se habían reconocido atrasamientos <en las salidas de las flotas> y fraudes en los derechos", y en algún momento determinado, como en la flota de 1617, se les llegó a prohibir expresamente que se embarcasen. Sin embargo, parece que terminan imponiendo su presencia - la flota de 1622 se decia que no podía cargarse por no haber peruleros - gracias al apoyo adicional que recibían de los mercaderes extranjeros para quienes resultaba beneficioso venderles a crédito y poder recibir de Indias su procedido registrado a su nombre.

El problema de los *peruleros*, y según parece la causa también de la mayoría de los conflictos surgidos entre los cargadores sevillanos y los mercaderes en Indias, se debía a la incidencia que su actuación hubiera de tener en la formación de los precios en el mercado americano. Como se reconocía en uno de los informes arriba mencionados - el de Mandojana, de 1622 - la presencia de los encomenderos que vienen de los virreinatos a comprar a Sevilla significaba encarecer los precios en origen más de un 20% por las formas y usos en que dichas compras se realizan y, después, como han de pagar en Indias lo principal de su importe, los compradores se abstienen de comprar hasta que los encomenderos se vean obligados a vender a los precios más bajo posible. Con tal proceder los cargadores sevillanos se resienten por cuanto, satisfechas las primeras necesidades, quedan a merced de la demanda. Mantener una situación de esa naturaleza mucho tiempo hubiese significado el fin inmediato del monopolio a lo que, de otra parte, no estaban dispuestos a renunciar las oligarquias mercantiles beneficiarias, ni las de Sevilla ni las criollas. No quedaba pues más camino que el entendimiento y éste pudo conseguirse a través del ajuste de los precios de feria.

Durante el siglo XVII las dos principales ferias, como se ha dicho, habrían de ser las de Portobelo que se inicia en 1598, y era continuadora de la feria de Nombre de Dios, donde se realizaban las transacciones de las cargazones destinadas al Perú, y la feria de Veracruz con idéntico cometido respecto a México; más tarde adquiriría renombre la de Jalapa. Una norma básica mantenida por los cargadores sevillanos había sido mantener en secreto la cuantía y diversidad de las cargazones para que de ese modo los precios obtenidos fuesen lo más remuneradores posibles, proceder que habría de encontrar sistemáticamente la oposición de los mercaderes criollos y que, una vez creado el Consulado, llevó a los de México incluso a pedir el libre comercio en fecha tan temprana como la de 1613. Como medio para tener acceso a la información sobre las cargazones, el Consulado de México consiguió de la Corona el arrendamiento de las alcabalas lo que habría de convertirse en fuente contínua de conflictos como el surgido a raiz del aplazamiento de la flota de Nueva España de 1674. La petición de aplzamiento la hizo el Consulado de Sevilla por entender que el mercado estaba tan saturado que hacía inviable la obtención de beneficios compensadores, decisión que fue recurrida por el Consulado mexicano por sentirse perjudicado en cuanto arrendador de las alcabalas, al suspenderse la feria que hubiera de celebrarse. Como consecuencia del pleito se llevó a cabo un interrogatorio por el que se puso en claro la no conveniencia, para los exportadores, de que se conociese en detalle las mercaderias llevadas por cuanto los mercaderes del Consulado de México "reconociendo por menor las calidades y géneros se ajustan a comprar los precios que ellos quieren y confieren deteniéndose en la compra y esperando a que la abundancia de un género obligue a venderlo al precio que ellos entre sí disponen y en otros géneros proponiendo la tasa que quieren". Para subsanar las diferencias se reguló con minuciosidad las diligencias que habrían de llevarse a cabo hasta conseguir el ajuste de precios de una feria, tal como se refleja en el siguiente expediente correspondiente a la celebrada en Veracruz en 1683.

Llegada la flota se dicta auto de inmediato (10-VII-1683) por D. de Zaldívar, capitán general de la Armada, ordenando se reunan los 4 diputados nombrados por el Comercio de México con los nombrados por él entre los comerciantes que venían en la flota, a fin de que "no se pierda minuto de tiempo". El mismo dia se celebra Junta de los diputados nombrados al efecto y se acuerda que los comerciantes que representan a la flota entreguen a los de México una Memoria con relación de los géneros que traen y primeros precios "para abrir y celebrar feria y compra hasta en cantidad de 100.000 pesos y que lo referido sirva de ejemplar a todo el reino". El 11 de julio se entrega la Memoria solicitada que es devuelta por los mexicanos a los diputados de España el dia 13 con la contraoferta de precios que ellos, a su vez, hacían. Ante la disparidad de precios, se realizan nuevas ofertas y contraofertas, con respectivas modificaciones, hasta conseguir el 23 de julio los primeros acuerdos, ya en firme, sobre algunos de los 174 diferentes tipos de mercaderias en negociación. Dos dias después se elabora una última Memoria sobre los productos en que aun había desacuerdo y superado éste, el dia 26 de julio se celebra la última junta donde se ajustan al completo las propuestas de los 7º y 8º precios propuestos respectivamente por los diputados de España y México. Los precios últimos aprobados, a efectos de la contratación de los cien mil primeros pesos son los correspondientes a la 8º propuesta, es decir los últimos méxicanos ofertados si bien en algunos productos, muy pocos, el precio queda libre al arbitrio de la propia contratación. Como síntesis y ejemplo del proceso indicamos la fluctuación producida en el ajuste de precios de 32 de las 174 tipos de mercaderias negociadas:

CUADRO IV:
Ajustes de primeros y ultimos precios: Feria de Veracruz, 1683

Mercaderia	*Primeros* España	*Precios* México	*M/E* %	*Ultimos* España	*Precios* México	*M/E* %	*Dif.Total* %
Olanes	22p.	12p.	54.5	20p.	13p.	65.0	10.5
id. de parís	8p.	4p.	50.0	7p.	4p. 6rs.	67.8	17.8
Bramantes florete	9rs.	4.5rs.	50.0	7rs.	5rs.	71.4	21.4
id. redondos	7rs.	3.5rs.	50.0	5.5rs.	4rs.	72.7	22.7
Ropillla de Olan	6p. 4rs	3p.	46.1	5p.	3p. 4rs.	70.0	23.9
Cera	28p./a	15p./a	53.5	22p./a	17p./a	77.2	23.7
Papel	3p. 4rs.	2p.	57.1	3p. 2rs.	17rs.	65.3	8.2
Sempiternillas	26p.	8p.	30.7	19p.	9p.	47.3	16.6
Bayetas Inglaterra	28rs.	10rs.	35.7	23rs.	10rs.	43.4	7.7
Palmetas anchas	14rs.	5rs.	35.7	11.5rs.	5.5rs.	45.6	9.9
Fernandinas	15rs.	6rs.	40.0	12rs.	7rs.	58.3	18.3
Sargas grana holanda	17rs.	7rs.	41.1	13.5rs.	7.5rs.	55.5	14.4
Olandilla ancha Ingl.	6rs.	3rs.	50.0	5rs.	3.7rs.	65.0	15.0
Paños de Holanda	4p.	20rs.	62.5	28rs.	21rs.	75.0	12.5
Damasco de Toledo	30rs.	2p.	53.3	28rs.	18rs.	64.2	10.9
Seda torcida Granada	10p.	3p.4rs.	35.0	9p.	4p.	44.4	9.4
Chistoneria Napoles	18p.	8p.	44.4	16p.	8p. 4rs	62.9	18.5
Acero	22p.	8p.	36.3	19p.	9p.	47.3	11.0
Vaso labrado Sevilla	3p.	12rs.	50.0	20rs.	13rs.	65.0	15.0
Medias Venecia,par	6p.	3p.	50.0	5p.	3p. 2rs.	65.0	15.0
Cintas reata,docena	7p.	2p.	28.5	6p.	18rs.	37.5	9.0
Manteleria ordinaria	24rs.	11rs.	45.8	22rs.	14rs.	63.6	17.8
Colchones Hamburgo	24rs.	14rs.	58.3	23rs.	2p.	66.6	8.3
Ruanes floretes	9rs.	4.7rs.	52.7	7rs.	5.5rs.	78.5	25.8
Blancartes	8rs.	4rs.	50.0	6rs.	4.5rs.	75.0	25.0
Creas anchas Lyon	8rs.	4.2rs.	53.1	6.2rs.	4.2rs.	68.0	14.9
Chamelotes, Genova	15rs.	8rs.	53.3	?	9rs.	?	?
Media seda Napoles	3p.	14rs.	58.3	3p.	15rs.	62.5	4.2
Tafetanes de pisa	7rs.	3.5rs.	50.0	6.5rs.	?	?	?
Hierrro	9p.	6p.	66.6	8p. 4rs.	6p. 6rs.	79.4	12.8
Platillas	4p. 4rs.	2p. 4rs.	55.5	4p.	3p.	75.0	19.5
Lienzos listados	5rs.	2.2rs.	45.0	4rs.	2.2rs.	56.2	11.2

Mucho había cambiado la situación respecto a como sucedían las negociaciones durante el siglo XVI. Los primeros precios ofertados por los diputados mexicanos, en término medio, suponían tan sólo el 48% de los precios propuestos por los cargadores de la flota; luego, tras ardua negociación, en la que tenían que intervenir las autoridades tanto virreinales como de la Armada, se alcanzaban unos últimos precios mexicanos que, de media, venían a representar el 63% de los últimos precios solicitados por los españoles, de manera que el incremento medio final entre primeros y últimos precios habría sido del orden del 15%. Margen pequeño que revela, a nuestro entender, lo ajustado de la negociación y un claro posicionamiento selectivo y no dependiente de la demanda respecto a la oferta - se estima, por quienes se han ocupado de las cuestiones del tráfico, que "hacia 1686 las flotas surtían sólo una tercera parte a los mercados indianos"-. El modo de negociar empezaba a cambiar durante el siglo XVII y ello habría de tener sus consecuencias tanto en el sistema de financiación como en las expectativas de beneficios.

Las nuevas circunstancias y las innovaciones introducidas en el comercio colonial en los últimos años del siglo XVI y primera década del XVII produjeron notables modificaciones en la financiación de la Carrera: un control oficial menos riguroso sobre las operaciones de crédito, una ampliación de los partícipes españoles pero al mismo tiempo una participación creciente de los capitales extranjeros y, por último, la configuración de modalidades nuevas en los instrumentos crediticios y una mayor flexibilidad en el manejo de los mismos.

A lo largo del Seiscientos quedarían en manos de los extranjeros, casi en exclusiva, la provisión de las manufacturas para el comercio colonial; a ello vendría a añadírsele, como veremos, la negociación de los seguros y, en último término, la propia financiación de la Carrera. Con su presencia, se daba la paradoja de que mientras se acentúa la decadencia de España en el siglo XVII más se afianza su importancia como centro comercial europeo aunque, como escribieran Brunel y

Van Aerssen en 1655, de las riquezas de dicho comercio sólo permanecieran en España el regusto de las migajas que quedan entre los dientes.

No obstante, para los extranjeros, el modo de operar en el comercio colonial español debía resultar lento - casi dos años para cada operación - y caro a causa de los costes de intermediación; pero sobre todo, si se atenían a la estricta legalidad no resultaba todo lo beneficioso que pudiera ser al dificultársele las ganancias elevadas y complementarias derivadas de la especulación con el oro y plata recibido al tener fiscalizados sus registros. La necesidad por acceder lo más directamente posible a los recursos metálicos indianos se iría acrecentando durante el siglo XVII a consecuencia de los desajustes monetarios que afectaron a las economías europeas a causa de la disparidad creciente entre el numerario circulante y el crecimiento de la economía real. La presencia de los peruleros como agentes muy activos de la Carrera favoreció, en el tránsito del siglo XVI al XVII, el cambio en el modo de negociar de los extranjeros con otro más acorde a sus intereses. Como hemos señalado, los peruleros operaban sin apenas recursos propios manejando capitales y créditos ajenos y una de las causas principales por la que los extranjeros les querían fiar sus mercaderías, al decir de J. Gallardo de Céspedes en su Memoria, sería porque en su caso habrían de ser pagadas en Indias, facilitándose de ese modo un acceso más directo a las remesas metálicas bajo menor control. O bien, como recordaban Mandojana y Neve en su Informe de 1622, vendían al fiado, con un recargo del hasta el 20% en los precios habituales, y a continuación descontaban en Sevilla las escrituras de riesgos y cambio recibidas con un daño del 8 o 9 %; de ese modo obtenían liquidez inmediata, no tenían necesidad de comprar frutos de la tierra ni tampoco coloniales, salvo los que tuviesen a la venta en sus paises de origen beneficio asegurado, y sobre todo podían con impunidad sacar el procedido por cuanto no había constancia oficial ni registro del oro y plata percibido por los extranjeros en dichas transacciones. Por tales razones, aunque sin efecto, no cesarían de publicarse desde 1592 a 1616, y con menor intensidad hasta 1645, disposiciones y órdenes prohibiendo a los extranjeros contratar para cobrar en Indias al tiempo que se solicitaba la prohibición de descontar las escrituras de riesgos a favor de extranjeros como si fuesen letras de cambio.

La fase de transición parece que pudiera darse entre los años de 1635 y 1648. Aunque con dificultades, hasta 1635 el doble comercio europeo-americano se efectuaría en Sevilla de manera conjunta y en la confluencia de esa interrelación se considera que radicó desde finales del siglo XV la prosperidad de la ciudad convertida a la vez en centro de aprovisionamiento interior, en foco de exportación nacional y de reedistribución internacional y centro financiero y monetario de primera magnitud. Pero a partir de 1635 con la guerra con Francia todo varió al cerrársele las puertas al comercio de ese país e igualmente al de Holanda. Una mención aparte merecería el caso de los portugueses, aunque por desgracia está por estudiar lo que fuera su participación activa en el comercio colonial. Se sabe que, desde 1629 están sólidamente implantados en Sevilla desde donde comercian directamente en compañía de sevillanos, como ellos, judaizantes; también parece que lo hacen con profusión desde Portugal empleando la intermediación canaria, a cuyas islas se dirigen simulando allí la venta del barco y mercaderias cargadas a un isleño y luego continúa a las Indias permaneciendo al frente de la expedición el mismo maestre aunque so color de "asalariado" del fingido nuevo dueño.

Excluidas oficialmente sus mercaderias de la Carrera, los comerciantes franceses y holandeses hubieron de recurrir a ciertas fórmulas de intermediación dando con ello principio a "extraviar" las mercaderias "y embarcarlas por alto en flotas y galeones" gracias a la ayuda de agentes, comisionados y hombres de paja asentados en los pueblos de la bahía y disponibles a tal servicio. En este sentido, como dejara escrito Van Aersen por aquellos mismos años, destacaría el papel favora-ble de Sanlúcar de Barrameda, villa señorial perteneciente al duque de Medinasidonia quien se lucraba de la *protección* que daba a dicho comercio clandestino, percibiendo a través de sus administradores unos emolumentos ya tarifados según la cuantía del embarque;

proceder que llegó a adquirir tales proporciones que fuera un elemento coadyuvante, cuando no decisivo, - más que la pretendida traición del duque con motivo de la independencia portuguesa -, de la pérdida del señorio de Sanlúcar por el duque y su reintegro en la jurisdicción realenga. Lo de Sanlúcar, sin embargo, no era un fenómeno aislado sino que circunstancias similares se dieron en los distintos núcleos que enmarcan la Bahía, principiando por la propia ciudad de Cádiz.

Dentro de la relativa similitud en los modos de negociar pueden percibirse diferencias significativas según nacionalidades. Para los flamencos la segunda mitad del siglo XVII viene marcada como una etapa de esplendor debido al aumento considerable de sus exportaciones textiles hacia el mundo hispano-colonial fabricadas en Flandes y Hainaut. Las casas flamencas no autorizadas a participar en el tráfico colonial lo consiguen haciendo uso de dos técnicas comerciales refinadas que, según Everaert, sirve a la vez como medio para eludir las prohibiciones del comercio directo y como solución a la falta de liquidez de los adquirientes y la necesidad de venta al fiado: a) el primer procedimiento consiste en una venta a crédito mediante prima a los cargadores y b) un segundo por el que las mercaderias a exportar se consignan al fiado a un cargador el cual procede con ellas como si operase por su cuenta y riesgo. En la primera modalidad los productos eran llevados de Amberes a Cádiz y el cargador que los importaba pagaba 1/3 a la recepción de las mercaderias y para los 2/3 restantes extendía una *obligación descontable* para pagar en Indias, por procuración, o bien al retorno de la flota; la obligación descontable podía revestir el carácter de una escritura de préstamo *llana*, a interés normal de tierra y fijo (a mitad del siglo XVII estaba en un 12%), que eran los menos casos, o bien por escritura a riesgo o a la *grosse aventure* cuyo interés dependía según que cubriese sólo el viaje de ida o ida y vuelta. En la segunda modalidad, el cargador que embarca y registra las mercaderias como si fuesen de su cuenta y riesgo es un simple hombre de paja, que figura como propietario ficticio de las mercaderias a los efectos de conocimientos de embarques, liquidación impositiva, facturas etc. En este caso el compromiso de cargador con el exportador extranjero y dueño efectivo de la carga se instrumentaliza por medio de un documento que es resultante del conocimiento de carga, de la factura de la misma y de un contrato específico realizado entre el intermediario español y el consignatario de modo que quedaban en manos de éste todos los instrumentos necesarios para hacer efectivo el cobro de lo exportado quedando el cargador u hombre de paja como un mero vínculo para legalizar la exportación de la que era usual no tuviese siquiera conocimiento de la carga.

Bajo esta última modalidad operarían los franceses hacia 1670 según escribía M. Lemonnet a Colbert: las mercaderias serían cargadas a nombre de españoles quienes, para mejor tener guardado el secreto del tráfico pues de ello dependía en buena parte la expectativa de beneficio, no sabrían siquiera lo que se cargaba en su nombre; la información pertinente y los instrumentos acreditativos necesarios permanecen en poder del *comisionista*, con funciones similares a los encomenderos de antaño que viajan con las manufacturas y son ellos quienes al regreso de las naos con el procedido de la venta entran en contacto directo con los verdaderos dueños de las mercaderias para hacerle entrega de la plata que les corresponda, que casi siempre traen sin registrar. La fórmula no puede considerarse, sin embargo, como universal por cuanto los modos de negociar fueron cambiando según las circunstancias del comercio y también de la capacidad competitiva de los productos franceses en el comercio colonial. Por suerte, disponemos para el comercio francés durante la segunda mitad del siglo XVII de informaciones diversas y muy detalladas: la principal y más completa es la contenida en la instrucción general para el comercio de Francia de J. Savary conocida como Le parfait negociant cuya primera edición fuera de 1675 y que practicamente fuera utilizada en casi todos los informes y memorias redactadas con posterioridad y utilizada con profusión por A. Girard en su libro al abordar esta cuestión; la llamada Memoria de Patoulet, intendente de marina en Dunquerque, que viaja a Cádiz en 1688 y donde recoge y anota las informaciones obtenidas de los comerciantes franceses allí asentados, utilizada en sus respectivos estudios por Morineau y Kamen, entre otros; por último, la Mémoire touchant le commerce des Indes occidentales par Cadix, con fecha de 1691, que fuera publicada y estudiada en 1927 por H. Sée.

En Cádiz los franceses ejercitan el doble comercio de aprovisionamiento interior de España, pues allá iban a proveerse los negociantes de las principales ciudades, y de reexportación a las Indias. No es nuestra intención analizar el contenido de dicho comercio en este escrito - sí lo hacemos en el estudio mas detallado que hemos dedicado al comercio colonial español y su financiación en los siglos XV al XIX - sino limitarnos a considerar las modalidades en cómo se realiza. Hasta los años de 1660 aproximadamente, según dice Savary, el sistema ordinario que seguían era el de venta directa a los cargadores, lo que suponía una operación mercantil corta en el tiempo y con riesgos mínimos aunque también de beneficios limitados. Muy conservadores en la forma de negociar, los franceses procuraban eludir los "grandes tiempos" usuales en el tráfico indiano así como las cuestiones de liquidez, de ahí su preferencia por el contado eludiendo el préstamo, a ser posible tanto a la hora de comprar como de vender; respecto a los comisionados o corresponsales, personas que representan a la firma en la plaza gaditana y quienes han de efectuar por cuenta de aquélla la venta a los negociantes españoles y remitirles el pago en reales, oro, plata o productos coloniales, siguen lo practicado por holandeses e ingleses, a saber, enviar como tales a sus hijos, hermanos u otros parientes próximos procurando no designar nunca, a ser posible, a nadie que no sea sino de la propia familia para dirigir el comercio filial de la casa matriz persuadidos de que, de no ser así, el comercio a comisión no era un medio adecuado para tener éxito en el negocio. A partir de la década de 1660, por la fuerte competencia que deben soportar las manufacturas francesas, la realidad les fuerza a cambiar y adoptan la modalidad de parte de venta al contado y el resto a pagar al retorno de los galeones devengando un interés del 12%. Por último optan por cargar ellos mismos en las flotas utilizando como testaferro a un español, quien a su vez se encargaba de vender las mercaderias en Indias, dando "leurs cédules ou promesses" de rendir cuenta a su vuelta de las ventas o cambios que hayan efectuado en las ferias de Portobelo; perciben por ello un 7 u 8% de comisión más un 5 o 6 % del importe de las remesas.

El excesivo conservadurismo francés les hace perder, sin embargo, cotas de mercados con rapidez inusitada, en particular frente a los ingleses - en menor medida, respecto a los holandeses también - por cuanto éstos el sistema que adoptan es el de consignación directa a un cargador, al que pagaban un 9 o 10% de comisión, al tiempo que camuflaban la operación como una "venta a crédito simulada" de manera que la persona interpuesta, u hombre de paja, resultaba innecesaria. El sistema anglosajón sería más fluido y la aparente menor participación en los beneficios del comercio la compesaban con una mayor agresividad en las condiciones de oferta - calidad y precios - de manera que hacia 1686, como reconoce Patoulet en su Memoria, era notoria la caida de las manufacturas francesas en el comercio indiano. Y no por la mala voluntad de los comerciantes gaditanos, cuya fidelidad llegaría a ser proverbial signada no más que por un gentleman's agreement, sino por buscar a mejor precio las manufacturas que necesitaban para sus registros sin mirar la nación de procedencia.

Después de 1680 se perciben ciertos cambios cualitativos importantes: mientras que franceses, genoveses, alemanes o flamencos, con ciertas variantes de menor entidad, persisten en comerciar de manera indirecta enviando sus mercaderías a Cádiz y utilizando la intermediación española, los ingleses y holandeses se orientan más al comercio directo con las colonias, o modalidad que los franceses denominan "commerce à la longueur de la pique". Así, en 1681 - 1682 se hace notorio por el Consulado de los perjuicios que originan los holandeses por su intervención dirtecta en el comercio de cacao; en 1683, desde la isla de S. Gabriel se detallan al por menor los daños que ocasiona al comercio la intervención directa de portugueses e ingleses; también desde 1682 - 1685 se empieza a percibir la importancia de la intervención directa de los extranjeros sobre el tráfico de barras de plata en Lima, indicándose la necesidad de crear una nueva Casa de Moneda en dicha ciudad a fin de evitar tal intromisión. Incluso los flamencos pretenden en 1688, a título de pobladores, un comercio directo con Sto. Domingo y Puerto Rico. Los franceses, en cambio, apegados al sistema tradicional gracias a la preeminencia que sus comerciantes habían adquiridos en Cádiz y Sanlúcar asisten a una decadencia continuada de su comercio que sería notoria hacia 1691; las causas serían diversas: según el autor de la Memoire de dicho año en parte se debería a la envidia de los españoles contra los franceses intentando hundir su comercio como represalias a las conquistas territoriales que Luis XIV hiciera a España si bien, como insiste Patoulet, fueron más por razones técnicas y mercantiles debido a la disminución de calidad de las manufacturas de Rouen, Morlaix, Laval, Quintin y Coutances y por el establecimiento de talleres manufactureros similares en Holanda (en Leyden, particularmente, con sus anascotes), Hamburgo y Flandes por fugitivos franceses cuya oferta a más bajo precio las hacen preferibles para el comercio colonial. Los datos no podían ser más elocuentes: en 1682 los galeones llegados a Cádiz trajeron 22.809.000 de pesos de los que pasaron a Génova el 19.7%, a Holanda el 15.3%, y a Inglaterra y Francia el 10.9 respectivamente; en conjunto, el 57% del procedido de las remesas. Tales avatares no supondran, sin embargo, la retirada de las firmas francesas: a fines del siglo XVII se hacía perceptible que la contracción del comercio iba siendo sustituida por la negociación y especulación financiera pues cada vez eran más voluminosos los capitales franceses enviados a Cádiz para su empleo en préstamos a cambio marítimo.

Sobre el beneficio obtenido por los extranjeros en el comercio colonial los valores que se insertan en sus informes y memorias no se adecuan con la realidad por cuanto éstos centraban todo su interés, como dijera Alvarez Ossorio, en mostrar sólo la cuantía de los costes en su afán de conseguir unos gastos de intemediación y una fiscalidad lo más baja posible. Por ello, sin duda, especifican con todo lujo de detalles la relación de gastos y derechos fiscales que habrían de pagarse por quienes aceptasen comerciar dentro de los límites de juego establecidos por el monopolio indiano; un ejemplo paradigmático es sin duda el libro de Savary, por el carácter de manual o prontuario con que fue concebido al servicio de los mercaderes interesados en dicho comercio. El coste de intermediación, que es lo que percibían los comisionados y hombres de paja se estipula en un 8%; los costes fiscales - almojarifazgos, indultos etc. - se valoraban para la segunda mitad del siglo XVII en un 23% y por último los gastos generales de fletes, seguros y almacenamiento que, por término medio podría oscilar alrededor del 10%. Savary, que analiza en detalle la relación de gastos, los estima alrededor del 45 al 50% en su conjunto. Se comprende el magnífico negocio que para los extranjeros ya suponía poder "meter por alto" sus mercaderias en la Bahía, traspasándolas directamente de los barcos en que las traían a los galeones que habrían de llevarlas a América: en tal caso se ahorraban un 23% en derechos y gabelas fiscales si bien habían de pagar un 1% a los *metedores*, que la tradición literaria francesa quiere ver en ellos a jeunes gentilshommes ... cadets des meilleures maisons du pays, qui n'ont pas de bien, en una visión tópica más que sobre España, y de Andalucia particular, circulara en el pais vecino. El fraude fiscal así cometido no suponía sólo un beneficio adicional sino que colocaba de manera ventajosa en las ferias de Portobelo, Cartagena y Veracruz a las mercaderias negociadas por cuenta y riesgo de los extranjeros quienes, según se denunciaba por la R.C. de 17 de julio de 1677, llegaban a ofertarlas "hasta un 30% menos que los vasallos de estos reinos", quedando aún así con ganancias considerables mientras que los naturales, si adecuaban sus precios a los de los extranjeros, liquidarían con pérdidas sus operaciones. El control de la Carrera a través de los modos de financiación era tal que llegaba incluso a eliminar la posible competencia que pudieran ejercer los cargadores españoles que se decidiesen operar por cuenta propia.

Del estudio de Everaert sobre la firma flamenca Boussemart aparece que en la negociación de mercaderias reexportadas a Indias según el sistema de venta a prima proporcionaría un beneficio bruto entre el 45 y 65%, con un aumento probable de un 12 a un 18%, de lo que habría que disminuir de un 22 a un 38% como gastos generales, quedando un beneficio neto del 30 al 55% en condiciones óptimas. En las ventas por medios de comisionados, es decir asumiendo los flamencos los riesgos de la operación, el beneficio bruto oscilaría entre un 60 y 100% respecto al valor de las mercaderias declarado en Cádiz, no en origen; si se le añade el beneficio de compra, estimada en un 25% y se deducen los gastos generales el neto obtenido sería de alrededor de un 40 a un 75%. Entre los franceses, los diferentes escritos e informes (Savary, Memoria de 1691 etc.) estiman que el "profit" de las mercaderias que envían a las Indias a su cuenta y riesgo se sitúa entre el 40 y 50%., e incluso valores inferiores (Patoulet cifra en un 25 o 30% el beneficio de las que se enviaban a Indias), cifras que consideramos mínimas por subvaloradas. Más viso de realidad, como veremos al estudiar los tipos de interés del dinero destinado a la financiación de la Carrera, tienen las cifras que en 1686 aportara Alvarez Osorio a fin de cuantificar las ganancias que los extranjeros tuviesen en sus tratos con las Indias. Como base de partida en el cálculo establece los diferenciales de precios en origen, en España y en las Indias:

CUADRO V:
Precios - Beneficio bruto

a) Productos coloniales, a Europa

Productos	*Precio* en Indias	*Incrementos en %* España / Indias	Europa / Indias	Europa / España
1. Cacao Caracas, fga.	10ps.	300	---	---
2. Tabaco varinas, arr.	5ps.	300	800	266
3. Manojos de tabaco	1.5rs.	333	800	240
4. Grana de Campeche,arr.	20ps.	250	500	200
5. Grana silvestre	8ps.	250	700	280
6. Grana fina	80ps.	175	250	142

b) Manufacturas extranjeras, a Indias

Mercaderias	*Precio* en origen	*Incrementos en %* España / Origen	Indias / Origen	Indias / España
1. Lienzos de Cambrai, Holanda	3.5ps.	100.0	243	71.5
2. Rouanes, bretañas, morlaix	2rs.	100.0	300	100.0
3. Creas,crudos, brabantes	1 rs.	100.0	300	100.0
4. Hilos de Bayona, Cambrai	4ps. 16rs.	100.0	300	100.0
5. Estameñas fr. e inglesas	3	100.0	300	100.0
6. Sedas, brocados	7	71.5	185	66.0
7. Sargas, varios tipos	4	75.0	200	71.5
8. Tafetanes dobles	3	66.0	233	100.0
9. Muaré	4.5	100.0	122	11.0
10. Felpa	10	100.0	220	60.0
11. Tafetanes simples	1.5	100.0	300	100.0
12. Cintas de sedas	4.5ps.	55.0	77	14.0
13. Encajes finos seda	1.5	100.0	300	100.0
14. Encajes finos de hilo	6	100.0	300	100.0
15. Tisús de oro y plata	2.5ps.	100.0	220	60.0
16. Lienzos ricos	6ps.	66.0	166	60.0
17. Camelots plata	2.5ps.	20.0	140	100.0
18. Encajes oro y plata	1.5ps.	100.0	233	66.0
19. Galones oro	2ps.	100.0	200	50.0

En las manufacturas extranjeras, los precios de España respecto a los que tuvieran en los centros de producción en sus paises de origen tenían, de media, un incremento del 87%; en Indias, los precios en origen se incrementaban un 228% por término medio y un 75% los que hubieran alcanzado en España. Si se deducen los gastos ocasionados, entre un 20 a 25% en el comercio con España, y entre el 40 y 50% para Indias, obtendríamos un beneficio neto del 55 al 65%, aproximadamente en el comercio de mercaderias extranjeras para ser vendidas en Cádiz y entre un 160 a 180% si se enviaban a Indias por cuenta y riesgo de los propios extranjeros; si por el contrario, la reexportación la hacían cargadores españoles a su propia cuenta ese beneficio hubiese quedado limitado a un 40 o 45%. Bien es cierto que tales cifras han de der continuamente matizadas. En primer lugar, por la relación beneficio-tiempo: la duración media del ciclo de los negocios coloniales se aproximababa a los tres años, tiempo de duración entre dos convoys sucesivos en el viaje de ida y vuelta, con los tiempos adicionales de carga y liquidación correspondientes. En segundo lugar, la oscilación de los precios de primera venta en feria podía ser considerable de una flota a otra; la extrema inestabilidad a que estaban sometidos dependían, como advertía Savary, del encaje entre volumen de mercancias europeas ofertadas en feria y las disponibilidades de lingotes de oro, barras de plata y productos coloniales y también del capricho de la demanda, demasiado ostensible cuando de un mercado de productos de lujo se trata. Del cuadro anterior se desprende que el mayor beneficio, o a veces incluso pérdida, depende " du plus ou du moins des marchandises qui ont été portées à cette Foire de Puerto-Bello, tant de la part des espagnols que des indiens". En los productos coloniales el beneficio bruto en España sería del 268%. Vendidos en Europa, el beneficio bruto medio, respecto al precio de origen en Indias, sería de del 610%, según los datos de Alvarez Osorio aunque hemos de hacer constar que la muestra era muy selectiva y compuesta por los productos donde era notorio el incremento desmesurado; en relación a los precios que tuviesen los coloniales en España, el beneficio medio sería del 225% - los extranjeros reconocían para los precios coloniales en sus paises de origen respecto a los que tuviesen en Cádiz una plusvalía bruta del 150% como máximo y un margen de beneficio neto entre el 60 y el 100%. Hay que tener en cuenta, por descontado, que los riesgos eran múltiples - quiebras, demoras por impagos etc.- y que podían darse vicisitudes inesperadas que hacían subir de forma alarmante los gastos - por ej. indultos extraordinarios etc.- o alteraciones anormales en precios lo que convertía al comercio colonial en una empresa especulativa por excelencia.

American Silver Production and West European Money Supply in the Sixteenth and Seventeenth Century

By RENATE PIEPER

Gold and silver influenced to a great extent the process of conquest and colonization in the New World. Up to the eighteenth century their export provided one of the most important links between the economies on both sides of the Atlantic. The effects of the American treasure on European economies troubled economists and historians alike since the reign of Philipp II. Research on this topic received a revived interest over the last years, as new methods and theories developed. Nevertheless,in the discussion of the reasons for the European Price Revolution of the sixteenth century and the "crisis of the seventeenth century" old arguments are still being debated[1]. Taking into consideration those new approaches, an analysis of American silver produc-

---

1 Douglas FISHER, The Price Revolution: A Monetary Interpretation, in: *The Journal of Economic History* XLIX (1989), pp. 883 - 902; Jack A. GOLDSTONE, Monetary Versus Velocity Interpretations of the 'Price Revolution': A Comment, in: *The Journal of Economic History* LI (1991), pp. 176 - 181; Immanuel WALLERSTEIN, Y a-t-il une crise du XVIIe siècle? in: *Annales E.S.C.* XXXIV/1 (1979), pp. 126 - 144; enforcing the American point of view: Ruggiero ROMANO, Algunas consideraciones sobre los problemas del comercio en Hispanomérica durante la época colonial, in: *Boletín del Instituto de Historia Argentina y Americana "Dr. E. Ravignani"* Tercera Serie I/1 (1989), pp. 23 - 49.

tion, bullion exports and European coinage may give some clues to the evolution of European money supply and thus of one crucial factor of economic development during the sixteenth and seventeenth century.

The voyages of discovery and the first settlements in the New World were financed by the merchant community, and to a lesser extent by the Spanish crown. Due to the heavy financial burden the conquistadores had incured, the search for valuable trade goods for the European market was of major concern to them. The profitability of the exploration process was so crucial that the lack of easily available riches in the very first years put the whole enterprise into danger, and led to a revision of the colonization concept. Following the portuguese example, interest at first concentrated on gold, spices and slaves. As mining operations appeared to be profitable, European capital was invested in the gold and copper mines and refineries on the Antilles. Export of European mining technology and the emigration of miners from central Europe followed[2]. Despite these efforts, neither the Antillian gold nor even the copper excited so much interest in Europe and America alike, as did the silver from the mines of Mexico and Peru. Very soon after the conquest of the Aztec and Inca empires Mexican and Peruvian silver was exported to Europe. Not until the mid-sixteenth century did silver mining and silver exports become dominant compared to gold. This process was paralleled by the decline of Central European silver mining from the 1550's on. American silver production reached its peak in the first decades of the seventeenth century, when European silver mining had almost come to a halt and monetary devaluation and disorder spread. In the following years overseas output dropped and the levels of 1590 - 1630 were never regained during the Habsburg reign in Spain. But even under these worsening conditions, America still remained Europes' most

---

2 Hermann KELLENBENZ, Der mexikanische Silberbergbau (16. und 1. Hälfte des 17. Jahrhunderts). Zum Stand der Forschung, in: Hanns-Albert STEGER / Jürgen SCHNEIDER (ed.), Wirtschaft und gesellschaftliches Bewußtsein in Mexiko seit der Kolonialzeit, München 1980, pp. 227 - 240.

important supplier of silver and even of gold, following the Brazilian discoveries[3].

The traces of American silver might be perceived most clearly in the regions that had an almost direct contact with overseas economies. Even if the thesis of E. J. Hamilton on the spread of the Price Revolution from Spain to the rest of Europe has been contested[4], the question of the diffusion of Mexican and Peruvian bullion is still open to discussion[5]. During the sixteenth century and to a lesser degree even during the seventeenth century the majority of American silver reached Europe within the Spanish trade monopoly. Therefore, its spread throughout Europe must have followed the network that linked the Peninsula, and especially Seville, with the rest of the continent. Until 1630 almost three quarters of the officially declared silver imports to

---

3 Artur ATTMAN, The Bullion Flow from Europe to the East: 1500 - 1800, in: Eddy H. G. VAN CAUWENBERGHE (ed.), Precious Metals, Coinage and the Changes of Monetary Structures in Latin-America, Europe and Asia (Late Middle Ages - Early Modern Times), Leuven 1989, pp. 65 - 68; Renate PIEPER, The Volume of African and American Exports of Precious Metals and its effects in Europe, 1500 - 1800, in: Hans Pohl (ed.), The European Discovery of the World and its Economic Effects on Pre-Industrial Society, 1500 - 1800, Stuttgart 1990, pp. 100 - 112.

4 Earl J. HAMILTON, El tesoro americano y el florecimiento del capitalismo, in: idem, El florecimiento del capitalismo y otros ensayos de historia económica, Madrid 1948, pp. 3 - 26; Carlo M. CIPOLLA, La prétendue révolution des prix, in: *Annales E.S.C.* X (1955), pp. 513 - 516; Kerry W. DOHERTY, Dennis O. FLYNN, A Microeconomic Quantity Theory of Money and the Price Revolution, in: E. CAUWENBERGHE, Precious Metals, pp. 185 - 208.

5 Antonio Domínguez ORTIZ, Los caminos de la plata americana, in: *Boletín de la Academia Nacional de la Historia* LXII (Caracas 1979), nr. 248, pp. 811 - 825; Adon A. GORDUS, Jeanne P. GORDUS, Identification of Potosí Silver Usage in Sixteenth-Century European Coinage through Gold-Impurity Content of Coins, in: Coinage of the Americas, New York 1989, pp. 22 - 41; Emmanuel LE ROY LADURIE, Jean-Noël BARRANDON, Bruno COLLIN, Maria GUERRA, Cécile MORRISON, Sur les traces de l'argent du Potosí, in: *Annales E.S.C.* XLV/2 (1990), pp. 483 - 505.

Seville belonged to private persons[6]. For this reason, most of the silver must have reached other European countries by trade, as payment for the Castilian commercial deficit. Spains major trading partners were France and Italy. Relations with the Netherlands, upper Germany, the Hanseatic towns and England were intense. Because of obvious political connections crown silver was mainly exported to the Netherlands and Italy. But it served as well to finance envolvement in Austria, Germany and France.

According to this framework, the considerations that follow will deal mainly with the influence of American silver on the Western parts of Europe. The beginning of the American mining boom in the second half of the sixteenth century was more remarkable than the attenuate recession of mining activities from 1620 on. For this reason, it might be easier to determine the effects of the former than those of the latter. Changing internal and external conditions in different European regions represent serious obstacles to the application of a simple monocausal model, even if European gold and silver markets formed a very well connected network. European silver production and export, deliberate monetary policies in order to attract gold or silver, the spread of billon coins, and the improvement of credit mechanisms must be taken into consideration. Moreover, even in modern economies quantitative models of changes in monetary supply and demand and their links with other economic variables are still being debated. Nonetheless, to follow the traces of American silver in Europe might provide a limited but nevertheless important insight in early modern economic structures.

In order to distinguish the effects of American bullion on European monetary systems from other factors, it is necessary to consider first the evolution of overseas mining in some detail. The first remittances

---

6 E. J. HAMILTON, American Treasure and the Price Revolution in Spain, 1501 - 1650, Cambridge (Mass.) 1934. For the present article the Spanish translation is used: El tesoro americano y la revolución de los precios en España, 1501 - 1650, Barcelona 1975, pp. 45 - 47.

of the conquistadores to Spain consisted mainly of gold and to a lesser extent of silver. They came from booties of gold and silver objects which were melted down.

In Mexico, silver mining and refining continued only a few years in the hands of the indigenous population, as autochtonous silver mining techniques were not as highly developped as in Peru. As early as 1524, in the mines of Zumpango, Spanish colonists entered the production process. But as they were not experienced miners, output dwindled very soon, as the rich ores were exhausted[7]. In 1537 the Fugger Factors in Seville bought a mine in Súltepec and sent German miners, who introduced and adapted Central European mining technology to the condition of New Spain[8]. Especially the use of lead as an agent in the smelting process, the improvement of furnaces which were now fired with charcoal and the installation of hydraulic machinery were due to their activities. The discovery of new mines like those of Zacatecas in 1546 and Guanajuato in 1548 led to an increase in silver production. In the middle of the sixteenth century rich ores were exhausted, and Central European refining methods which depended on extensive use of wood and water, proved to be too expensive for the processing of low grade ores. Moreover, up to the 1550's Mexican lead or galena production was insufficient, and English lead was imported to New Spain via Seville as ballast on the fleets. But, as English lead exports to the European continent were severely restricted in 1552 and fell to one-half until 1554, until new Mexican deposits were explored, lead supply to Mexico became increasingly difficult[9].

---

7 Relaciones geográficas of Tasco and Zumpango, in: René ACUÑA (ed.), Relaciones geográficas del siglo XVI: México, Mexico 1986, vol. 2, p. 114 n. 5, p. 117 n. 7, vol. 3, p. 197; Demetrio RAMOS PÉREZ, Minería y comercio interprovincial en Hispanoamérica (siglos XVI, XVII y XVIII), Valladolid 1970, pp. 39s; Modesto BARGALLÓ, La minería y la metalurgia en la América Española durante la época colonial, Mexico-Buenos Aires 1955.

8 H. KELLENBENZ, Der mexikanische Silberbergbau, note 14.

9 Ian BLANCHARD, England and the International Bullion Crisis of the 1550s, in: Hermann KELLENBENZ (ed.), Precious Metals in the Age of Expansion, Stutt-

That is why the European bullion crisis of the 1550's favoured the development of the amalgamation method. The invention of this process in 1554 - 1557 is attributed to Pedro de Medina. Instead of adding lead, *galena* or *cendrada*[10], mercury was now used as an agent. Furthermore, the new technique required less wood or charcoal and less water. It spread rapidly throughout New Spain. Nonetheless, New Spain's mining industry continued to depend on imported raw materials, as European lead exports were supplanted by mercury supplies from Almadén and Idria. For this reason, the smelting process was used until the end of the colonial period for those silver ores best suited to it. During the seventeenth century mining and refining techniques were improved but no substantial innovation occured.

In Mexico no central mining district developed, instead production was scattered over a great number of mining camps from Central to Northern New Spain. In the middle of the Chichimecas territory, where the northern mining districts were situated, the crown administration needed some time to establish themselves. For these reasons, official control of silver production was limited during the first decades of mining. Nevertheless, tax records remain the best source of information on silver output, even if they were subjected to the problem of evasion, facilitated by the great distances between the mining camps and the respective royal treasuries (*caxas*). Tax records start in the second half of the century, so that for the first decades even recent

---

gart 1981, pp. 90ss. The *alcalde mayor* from Nombre de Dios on the border of New Galicia and New Biscay related, that in 1554 Spaniards had set out from Zacatecas, where they exploited not only the silver deposits but also those of lead, Peter S. BAKEWELL, Silver Mining and Society in Colonial Mexico. Zacatecas 1546 - 1700, Cambridge 1971, p. 23. E. HAMILTON, El tesoro, p. 337, reports lead prices only for Andalusia during the first half of the sixteenth century.

10 *Galena* is a silver ore with a high content of lead. *Cendrada* is the residual of the copellation process with a high lead percentage.

studies rely on the figures published by C. H. Haring[11]. Records for Zacatecas, which in its years of splendour (1615 - 1635) represented almost 50% of the recorded Mexican silver production, are available from 1559 on[12]. Accounts for other *reales de minas* are not at our disposal until the 1580's. For the seventeenth century the data basis seems to have improved although the problem of undeclared and untaxed silver remained or even worsened. To cross check tax records with accounts from the royal mercury monopoly is also limited in the results it yields. Appart from the fraud problem, mercury was only needed in the amalgamation process. Silver obtained by smelting, especially important in times of mercury shortage, needed no mercury and cannot be estimated by looking at the mercury consumption of New Spain. But even these records are only available from the 1570's on[13].

These circumstances allow at best very approximative data on Mexican silver production during the sixteenth century[14]. Nonetheless, the available information seems to confirm, that due to the search for new

---

11 Peter S. BAKEWELL, Mining in Colonial Spanish America, in: Leslie BETHELL (ed.), The Cambridge History of Latin America, vol. 2, pp. 141.

12 P. BAKEWELL, Silver Mining and Society, table IV, p. 241.

13 David A. BRADING / Harry E. CROSS, Colonial Silver Mining: Mexico and Peru, in: *Hispanic American Historical Review* LII (1972), pp. 545 - 579; cf. P. BAKEWELL, Silver Mining and Society, p. 256.

14 Production numbers are indicated in *pesos de 272 maravedis* and estimated on the basis of: Adam SZÁSZDI, Preliminary Estimate of Gold and Silver Production in America 1501 - 1610, in: H. KELLENBENZ, Precious Metals, pp. 162, 163, 166; P. BAKEWELL, Registered Silver Production in the Potosí District 1555 - 1735, in: *Jahrbuch für Geschichte von Staat, Wirtschaft und Gesellschaft Lateinamerikas* XII (1975), pp. 92 - 96, 101 - 103; idem, Mining in Colonial Spanish America, pp. 139-140; Herbert S. KLEIN / John J. TEPASKE, The Seventeenth Century Crisis in New Spain, Myth or Reality, in: *Past and Present* 90 (1981), pp. 124 - 127. The data offered by A. SZÁSZDI probably are somewhat to high. For Mexican silver production during the seventeenth century amounts given by P. BAKEWELL and H. KLEIN / J. TEPASKE are more or less in accordance.

deposits, the introduction of new technologies and the improvement of old ones, silver production constantly expanded from the times of Cortés until the 1560's. At that time, 2.5 - 3 millions of silver *pesos* were refined yearly. Until the first decade of the seventeenth century this level was maintained. Afterwards output increased once again, attaining between 1615 - 1635 approximatly 3.5 - 4.5 million *pesos* of silver per year. From the 1630's on, there were signs of reduced output falling back to the levels registered at the beginning of the century. A new production increase could only be perceived thirty years later, from 1665 on. This time, even the levels of the 1620's were surpassed. The second boom lasted until 1695.

In relative terms, compared with American mining activities as a whole, the evolution of Mexican production was different. Until 1545 Mexican mining activities were more important than those of South America. An exception was the five-year period 1531-1535 when, due to the conquest of the Inca empire relatively great amounts of silverware (0.75 million *pesos* per year) were melted down. With the discovery of Potosí (1545) and other lesser mines, the situation changed. During the 1550's the Potosí mines accounted for 2 - 2.5 million *pesos* yearly. But whereas Mexican mining activities increased steadily, in Peru up to 1574 mining and refining were largely left to the indigenous population. Consequently, as no technological innovations occured, once the rich ores were exhausted, production diminished. In contrast to Mexico and in spite of the discovery of the Huancavelica mercury mines, the amalgamation method was not introduced, even in a modified version until 1574. For this reason, Peruvian silver production fell during the 1560's below the Mexican level. In the five-year period of 1571 - 1575 a nadir was reached with an average output of 1.4 million *pesos* per year, less than half of the Mexican production.

Due to the reforms of the Peruvian viceroy Francisco de Toledo in 1574, silver production recovered to an unforeseen degree. For the indian population these measures meant a lot of suffering. They lost their control of mining activities and were subjected to forced labor (*mita'*) in the silver mines of Potosí and Oruro and, even worse, in the mercury mines of Huancavelica. The supply of cheap labor helped to increase output in Potosí alone until 1591 - 1595 to a maximum of 7.4 million *pesos* per year. Total Peruvian production must have been even higher. This level was almost maintained until 1605. From then on, a steady decline in Potosí output began. Thanks to the discovery of the deposits of Oruro total Peruvian output reached its climax in 1611 - 1615 with an average of nearly 9.2 million *pesos* of silver per year. The Oruro mines stabilized the Peruvian dominance until 1635 - 1640. Nevertheless, Potosí contributed more than 50% of the Hispanoamerican silver production during 90 years, and at its best, in 1580 - 1610, more than two thirds. Due to the steady decline of Peruvian silver production from 1620 on and the recovery of Mexican mining activities after 1665, the relative position of northern and southern silver production changed. When Mexican mining industry had its first boom in the 1620's, Peruvian output was almost twice as large. However, at the time of its second peak, Mexico contributed up to 60% of the whole.

Total American silver production (Graph 1) fluctuated on a relatively low level until 1545. Due to the discovery of the Peruvian and Mexican mining centers output increased nearly fivefold during the next years (1545 - 1550), then stabilized until 1575. From then on it more than doubled until 1620. The later reduction by almost 50 % to nearly "pre-Toledo" levels ended in 1665. At the end of the seventeenth century American silver production accounted for only two thirds of the maximum reached at the first mining boom 80 years before. Nonetheless, the high level of output once reached in the 1580's had been maintained.

Graph 1:
American Silver Production, 1530 - 1695[15]
(Average Annual Production per five-year periods)

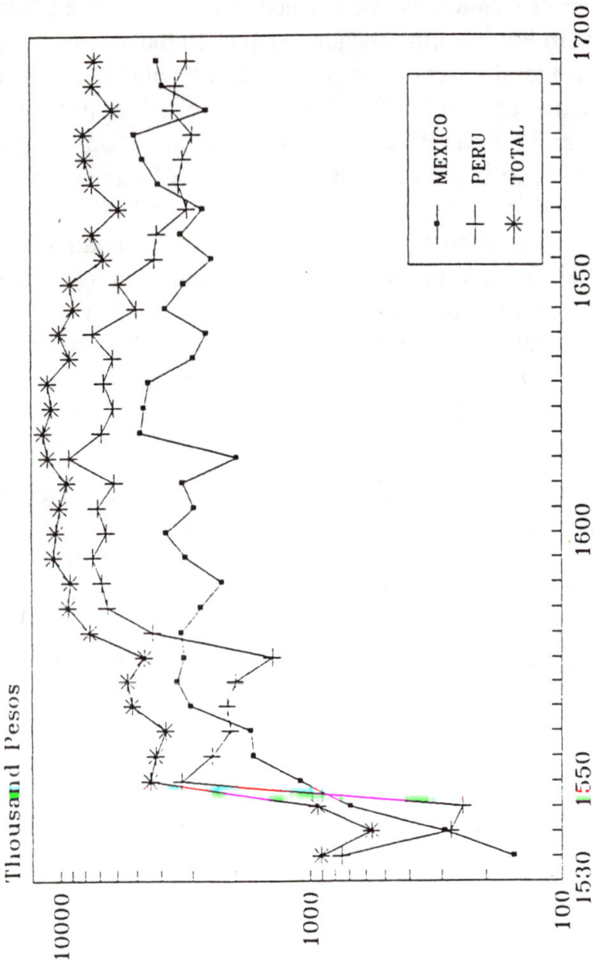

15 Source: Note 14.

Silver left the colonial mining centers in exchange for services and goods and as remittances for the gains of the great mine owners, who lived in Lima or Mexico, and for tax payments. Thus, part of the metal entered the colonial economies, but to a greater extent bullion was exported. Silver was needed to settle the American trade balance deficit with Europe and with Asia via Manila. Furtheron, the colonial administration sent considerable sums from its tax income to the motherland. The percentage of precious metals retained in the New World increased during the sixteenth and seventeenth centuries. The development of the colonial economies, growing intercolonial trade, manufactures and agricultural exploitation, all required substantial amounts of specie. Demographic recovery of the indian population and an increase in the number of the mestizo population from the mid-seventeenth century on, accelerated this process. Frequent complaints of officials and merchants about a lack of silver coins indicate a growing monetary demand overseas[16]. Comparing the development of mining activities with changes in European monetary variables, a certain time lag must be taken into account. But as nearly all indications on production, bullion imports and even on coinage are calculated on five or ten years averages, direct effects are hidden by this time span. Secondary repercussions may have required more than ten years.

European money demand was met by its own mining activities, and by bullion imports from Africa and America. Furthermore, coin debasement usually connected with recoinage and melting of church and secular treasures, incremented the monetary stock. Money supply may have augmented also because the coins continued to be in use longer than before, and by a higher rate of circulation. A broader diffusion in the use of credit and the improvement of credit instruments up to the

---

16 Horst PIETSCHMANN, Anmerkungen zum Problem einer Geld- und Finanzgeschichte des kolonialen Hispanoamerika, in: Jürgen SCHNEIDER (ed.), Wirtschaftskräfte und Wirtschaftswege. Festschrift für Hermann Kellenbenz, vol. 4, Stuttgart 1978, pp. 103 - 115.

spread of fiat money, offer clear hints of a growing monetary demand in Europe during the sixteenth and seventeenth centuries. But one has to keep in mind that up to the nineteenth century all forms of payment were based on the stock of precious metals. Credit could multiply the monetary stock represented by coins and bars. On the other hand, due to the same multiplier, relatively small changes, i.e. increases and reductions of the amount of precious metals, could seriously affect overall money supply. For this reason, changes in American silver production, even if they contributed only in part to the monetary supply of Europe, were an important economic factor.

One may assume that only the proportion of Peruvian and Mexican precious metals actually exported, directly affected European monetary systems. There is ample evidence that up to the 1620s' most of the silver exported reached the Old World within the framework of the Spanish trade monopoly. Even the famous booty of Piet Heyn, who in 1628 captured up to 4.8 million *pesos*, represented less than one year of Potosí production in the year of 1627 or 1626, and accounted for only 12% of the precious metals that officially reached Spain in the five-year period 1626 - 1630[17]. The figures on the Spanish imports of precious metals from 1503 to 1630, published by E. J. Hamilton in 1934, still remain the best approximation. They are based mainly on official accounts of the house of trade in Seville[18]. During the seventeenth century smuggling of silver coins and ingots became more intense. For this reason the numbers given by E. J. Hamilton do not reflect all the silver that reached Europe. Besides, production must have been higher than official records reveal. From the 1630s' on, the estimate of European silver imports is much more difficult since no reliable and exact sources are available until the end of the century[19].

---

17 E. HAMILTON, El tesoro, p. 47.

18 E. HAMILTON, El tesoro, pp. 23ss; R. PIEPER, The Volume, pp. 106 - 110.

19 Michel MORINEAU, Incroyables gazettes et fabuleux métaux. Les retours des trésors américaines d'après les gazettes hollandaises (XVIe-XVIIIe siècles), Paris - Cambridge 1985, tries to include the smuggled silver in his accounts.

For this reason, to measure the effects of American silver on European money supply one can rely on production numbers and not on official import figures only. This way at least part of the smuggled silver may be included.

Considering the impact of silver from overseas it is first of all necessary to refer briefly to the amount of European production and exports of precious metals to the East. European silver mining reached its peak in the 1520's and 1530's, when an equivalent of 2 million *pesos* (50 tons of silver) were refined per year. In the following decades output decreased slightly, with European mining in the fifties accounting for 1.6 million *pesos* of silver. From then on, central European mining operations declined rapidly[20]. Nonetheless, European silver production did not extinguish completely but survived on a low scale. As the example of the Spanish mines of Guadalcanal shows, there were even some years of splendour. During the five-year period of 1555 - 1560 output in Guadalcanal reached the equivalent of 0.5 million *pesos* per year. But production dwindled very soon afterwards[21]. European exports of specie developed in the opposite direction than mining activities. Rough estimates are given by A. Attman[22]. Exports to the Levante, the Baltic and the East in the mid-sixteenth century accounted for 2 - 3 million *pesos*. By 1600 remittances reached 4.4 million *pesos*, increasing further during the seventeenth century. 5.8 million *pesos* were transfered in 1650 and 8.5 million *pesos* in 1700.

Cf. Fernando SERRANO MANGAS, Armadas y flotas de la plata (1620 - 1648), Madrid 1989, pp. 315 ss.

20 Valentín VÁZQUEZ DE PRADA, La coyuntura de la minería y de la metalurgia europeas (siglos XII - XVIII), in: *Revista de Historia Económica* VI (1988), p. 264; Ekkehard WESTERMANN, Zur Silber- und Kupferproduktion Mitteleuropas vom 15. bis zum frühen 17. Jahrhundert. Über Bedeutung und Rangfolge der Reviere von Schwaz, Mansfeld und Neusohl, in: Der Anschnitt V - VI (Bochum 1986), pp. 187 - 211.

21 Julio SÁNCHEZ GÓMEZ, De minería, metalurgica y comercio de metales. La minería no férrica en el Reino de Castilla. 1450 - 1610, vol. II, Salamanca 1989, p. 523.

22 Artur ATTMAN, The Bullion Flow.

Even if these sums include gold exports, silver formed the bulk of the remittances. These data reveal that already in 1550 exports largely surpassed European production. They could only be paid thanks to the great increase of American mining at the end of the 1540's. As American silver production decreased from 1620 on, in the mid-seventeenth century European exports accounted for two thirds of Mexican and Peruvian silver output. At the end of the seventeenth century, when Brazilian gold led to a revival of imports of American precious metals, the exports of the Old World nearly equaled the silver production overseas. Therefore, it might be expected that the most visible impact of American specie on European money supply will be perceived especially after 1546 - 1550 and after 1576 - 1580. Its influence may have been reduced after 1640. The traces of Potosí silver probably diminished from the second decade of the seventeenth century on.

Direct proofs and reports on the influence of American silver in Europe are very scarce. Nevertheless, developments came about which ought to be explained by the influx from overseas. First of all, one has to mention the change in the official gold-silver ratios throughout Europe. Although in the short run these might not accurately reflect market trends, over longer periods they responded to the relative scarcity or abundance of gold or silver. Due to the availability of gold at the end of the fifteenth and the beginning of the sixteenth century, gold-silver parities dropped slightly until 1520 - 1530. Afterwards, until 1560 some fluctuations of the European average can be observed. After the 1560's, gold-silver ratios experienced a steady and continous increase of about 50% until 1730, when Brazilian gold stopped the process. The constant devaluation of silver in terms of gold in Europe and even in Asia must be mainly attributed to the output of the American silver mines[23].

---

23 R. PIEPER, Die Preisrevolution in Spanien (1500 - 1640). Neuere Forschungsergebnisse, Stuttgart 1985, p. 21; Om PRAKASH, Precious Metals Flows in Asia and the World Economic Integration in the Seventeenth Century, in: Wolfram FISCHER / R. Marvin MCINNIS / Jürgen SCHNEIDER (eds.), The Emergence of a World Economy 1500 - 1914, Stuttgart 1986, pp. 83 - 96;

The evolution of gold-silver ratios was accompanied by the spread of heavy silver coins as a supraregional means of payment, displacing gold coins to a great extent even in long distance trade. The coinage of great silver nominals began at the end of the 15th century but gained general acceptance only in the second half of the sixteenth century. The first *Talers* were minted in Tirol in 1486 and the famous *Joachimstaler* was struck in great quantities between 1500 and 1518. In southern Germany minting represented some peculiarities. The coinage of *Talers* did not start until 1537 gradually displacing the *guilder*. In the second half of the sixteenth century gold coinage recovered its importance, whereas at the same time the number of foreign gold coins increased[24]. In Northern Germany, in the first half of the sixteenth century gold coins represented up to 90% of the value of greater coins in coin hoards. On the other hand, account books reveal that the importance of gold coins gradually vanished in favour of heavy silver coins[25]. Due to the close contacts of Italy with the Iberian Peninsula and via Venice with Hungary, gold supply in this area might have been better than in Northern Europe[26]. Therefore, the coinage of silver *ducatoons* as an equivalent to the gold *scudo* did not begin until the middle of the sixteenth century. The mint of Milan issued big sil-

---

K. N. CHAUDHURI, World Silver Flows and Monetary Factors as a Force of International Economic Integration 1658 - 1758 (America, Europe and Asia), in: The Emergence of a World Economy, pp. 61 - 81.

24 Joachim SCHÜTTENHELM, Zur Münzprägung und Silberversorgung süddeutscher Münzstätten im frühen 16. Jahrhundert, in: Werner KROKER, Ekkehard WESTERMANN (eds.), Montanwirtschaft Mitteleuropas vom 12. bis zum 17. Jahrhundert. Stand, Wege und Aufgaben der Forschung, Bochum 1984, pp. 159ss; idem, Problems of Quantifying the Volume of Money in Early Modern Times. A Preliminary Survey, in: E. CAUWENBERGHE, Precious Metals, pp. 89 - 95.

25 Michael NORTH, Geldumlauf und Wirtschaftskonjunktur im südlichen Ostseeraum an der Wende zur Neuzeit (1440 - 1570), Sigmaringen 1990, pp. 72 - 76, 80ss.

26 Up to the seventeenth century *Hungarian ducats* were exported to Poland; idem, Bullion Transer from Western Europe to the Baltic and the Problem of Trade Balances: 1550 - 1750, in: E. CAUWENBERGHE, Precious Metals, p. 59.

ver coins for the first time in 1551. Venice, Genua and Florence adopted the same measure in the 1560's due to the scarcity of gold on the Italian market[27]. In Hispanoamerica big silver coins were struck since 1536. But only thirty years later, in 1566, did the *peso corriente*, a coin that already circulated in the colonies, receive an official value in the motherland. It was the famous *peso de a ocho reales*, with a weight of 27.92g and a fineness of 93.1%. In America at the same time, other forms of *pesos* were used: The *peso ensayado*, another big silver coin, that contained 42.29g of pure silver, but never received the status of an official means of payment. Officially no gold coins were minted overseas until 1627. Nonetheless, the *peso de oro de minas*, with a gold content of 4.2g, and the *peso de oro común*, with a gold content of 2.61g, were officially valued a silver *peso* with *450 maravedís* and *272 maravedís* respectively[28]. The fact that the *peso de a ocho* gradually displaced the *peso of 450 maravedís* as an accounting unit overseas at the beginning of the seventeenth century was a sign of its importance.

To prove the influence of overseas silver on European coinage in a more direct and detailed form represents serious difficulties. Mint account books only register the origin of metals coined from time to time. In the case of Spain there are references that during the reign of Philip II most of the crown silver and even that of private persons was coined by the mints of Sevilla and the water powered mint of Segovia. There are also notices of direct remittances to the mint of Barcelona. But in none of these cases do we have yet any studies to what extent other metals, for example those from recoinage, contributed to mint

---

27 Carlo M. CIPOLLA, American Treasure and the Florentine Coinage in the Sixteenth Century, in: E. CAUWENBERGHE, Precious Metals, p. 75.

28 Cf. Günter VOLLMER, Goldwährung in Neu-Spanien im 16. Jahrhundert, in: *Jahrbuch für Geschichte von Staat, Wirtschaft und Gesellschaft Lateinamerikas* V (1968), pp. 103 ss.

output[29]. Investigations of English mint accounts reveal that in 1562 two thirds of the melted silver consisted of Spanish coins, that is mainly of American metals[30].

Another possibility to determine the origin of the bullion used for European coinage and the role American silver played is provided by neutron activation analysis. Recent studies point to the fact that Potosí silver differed substantially in its indium and gold impurities from that of Mexico or Europe. Whereas the European and Mexican coins had an average gold contents of 1.0 - 0.05mgAu/100mgAg, those from Potosí contained only 0.007 - 0.002mgAu/100mgAg. Due to the influx of Peruvian bullion, gold impurity dropped more than 30% in Aragonese coins and over 80% in Castilian ones. Until 1590, French money had a content of 1.2mgAu / 100mgAg, whereas the average of the coins issued in 1590 - 1652 amounts to 0.6mgAu / 100mgAg. Data for England and Italy show a similar developement[31]. A drop in the average gold content could also be perceived in the coinage of the southern and northern Netherlands. Moreover, in coins minted in Castile, France and the Netherlands, extremely low gold impurities could be detected. So they must have been struck almost exclusively

---

29 Modesto ULLOA, Castilian Seignorage and Coinage in the Reign of Philipp II, in: *The Journal of European Economic History* IV (1975), pp. 459 - 479. Recently Glenn MURRAY tries to fill the gap.

30 Christopher E. CHALLIS, Spanish Bullion and Monetary Inflation in England in the later Sixteenth Century, in: *The Journal of European Economic History* IV (1975), pp. 385 - 386; idem, The Tudor Coinage, Manchester 1978, p.197.

31 E. LE ROY LADURIE et al., Sur les traces, pp. 502 - 505; Adon A. GORDUS, Jeanne P. GORDUS, Potosí Silver and Coinage of Early Modern Europe, in: H. KELLENBENZ, Precious Metals, pp. 230 - 236; idem, Identification of Potosí Silver, pp. 29, 32. Indications on gold contents in silver coins are not totally in accordance considering the data of the French group and A. and J. GORDUS. Nevertheless, their tendency is the same. On the other hand, the interpretation of their own data offered by A. and J. GORDUS is wrong. They only tried to detect coins with a pure Potosí silver contents, but did not take into account, the relatively small drop of gold impurity caused by a high percentage of Potosí silver.

from Potosí silver. The previous data suggest that at least 50% of the metals coined in Europe after the reforms at Potosí until the mid-seventeenth century, proceeded from Upper Peru. A rate that roughly equals the share of total American silver production of this *real de minas*.

Furtheron these data are corroborated by the analysis of indium impurities. Contrary to gold, indium was nearly absent in European and Mexican silver. The indium contents of French coins struck in the western mints augmented from 1575 on. An increase of nearly 700% of its indium impurities must be attributed to the coinage of ca. 40% of Potosí silver. In the Spanish mints Potosí bullion contributed up to 60% of the metals entering the mints. In Spain the decline of indium impurities started during the reign of Philipp IV, paralleling the drop of silver production in Peru. In the French mines on the atlantic shore, silver coinage was reduced rapidly after 1610. Nevertheless, the relatively few coins struck afterwards contained a high percentage of Peruvian bullion[32]. So it may be assumed, that Spanish coinage responded more directly to silver production overseas, whereas in France effects were more attenuated. But these results might be due to the small number of coins analyzed from this period.

Whereas chemical analysis corroborates the importance of American silver for European coinage and therefore for its money supply from 1575 on, data on mint outputs present somewhat different information. In Florence until 1557 the value of gold coins struck was higher than those of silver. This tendency was reversed severely in 1558 but monetary policies did not accept the fact until 1568. In England and the Netherlands the importance of gold was reduced steadily from the mid-sixteenth century on. In France a similar development could be observed. On the other hand, considering the development of silver output only, the picture changes somewhat. Whereas in Florence and Milan the highest quantities of silver were struck between 1580 and 1590, in the southern Netherlands the peak had been passed in 1555 -

32 E. LE ROY LADURIE et al., Sur les traces, pp. 502 - 505.

1574, when silver production overseas had not yet reached its absolute maximum. In England the highest point was attained even earlier, between 1545 and 1564. In France and in Spain silver mint output was a little more in accordance with absolute changes in production, or at least with registered silver imports.

Considering the silver coinage of the seventeenth century in France and the southern Netherlands it has to be stated that mint outputs in France, measured in kgs. of pure silver, were at their highest point in the 1640's and 1650's. In the Southern Netherlands silver coinage reached its peak in the third and fourth decade of the seventeenth century, when output was many times that of 60 years before. In Milan the levels of silver coinage during the seventeenth century were lower than they had been during the last decades of the sixteenth century, and reached their minimum in 1630 - 1655[33].

In order to offer a valid interpretation of these data, it has to be taken into consideration that the volume of mint output depended largely on regional monetary policies. Coin debasement connected with recoinage provided an additional source of income to the always exhausted treasuries. Moreover, gold-silver ratios were fixed above or below market conditions in order to attract a given sort of specie. Nevertheless during the sixteenth century the examples mentioned above show a clear connection either with the relative or with absolute changes in American silver production. Whereas in Spain and France, Spain's major trading partner, the absolute maximum of silver coinage paral-

33 C. CIPOLLA, American Treasure, pp. 71 - 73; John H. MUNRO, The Central European Silver Mining Boom, Mint Outputs, and Prices in the Low Countries and England, 1450 - 1550, in: Eddy H. G. VAN CAUWENBERGHE (ed.), Precious Metals, Coinage and the Changes of Monetary Structures in Late-Medieval and Early-Modern Europe and Asia, vol. II, forthcoming; Eddy VAN CAUWENBERGHE / Rainer METZ, Coinage and the Coin(Money) Stock: Problems, Possibilities and First Results (The Southern Low Countries 1334 - 1789), in: E. VAN CAUWENBERGHE, Precious Metals, vol. I, pp. 7 - 24; Frank C. SPOONER, L'économie mondiale et les frappes monétaires en France (1493 - 1680), Paris 1956; M. ULLOA, Castilian Seignorage. Carlo M. CIPOLLA, Mouvements Monétaires dans l'État de Milan (1580 - 1700), Paris 1952.

leled the evolution of overseas mining, in the other cases mentioned, silver minting reached its highest point when European production was still important and the relative increase in American mining reached a maximum. During the seventeenth century, compared with the situtation of the previous period, no dramatic changes in overseas output occured. For this reason fluctuations of mintages were dependent on monetary policies.

To estimate monetary circulation, a mathematical model has been developed on the bases of local mint outputs for the Southern Netherlands[34]. On the assumption of an average of 30 years of circulation for a given coin, monetary volume in terms of domestic silver coins reached its peak in the 1640's and a first maximum in the last quarter of the sixteenth century. Due to the excellent data on mint output, this method may be preferred to the estimate of money volume derived from coin hoards. Nonetheless, at least in some regions, the importance of foreign coins must be taken into consideration as the example of the *Schwäbische Kreis* in southwestern Germany reveals. The analysis of coin hoards shows that domestic large silver and gold coins reached their highest percentage between 1540 and 1560, representing nevertheless only one fourth of total coin volume. Afterwards foreign gold and large silver coins contributed more than 90% of the total circulation of coins of high value. The share of silver coins in circulation reached its peak before great quantities of American silver could have arrived, which might be explained by the relatively good connections of this region with Central European mining centers. Nonetheless, in northeastern Germany, silver continued to be the dominant metal for coins of high value during the second half of the sixteenth

34 Articles published in Eddy VAN CAUWENBERGHE / Franz IRSIGLER, Münzprägung, Geldumlauf und Wechselkurse, Trier 1984, by E. VAN CAUWENBERGHE / Didier HAENCAERT, Mintage and Coin Circulation in the Southern Low Countries (14th - 18th Centuries). Some theoretical reflections, pp. 151 - 179, and E. VAN CAUWENBERGHE / Rainer METZ, Geld und Währung in den südlichen Niederlanden während der frühen Neuzeit, pp. 123 - 149; idem, Coinage, pp. 12 - 15.

century[35]. Moreover, one has to keep in mind that really large sums of silver were floating through the European economies as bullion or circulated in *pesos fuertes*, the coin struck overseas.

Considering the previous data, two different effects and two periods of influence of American silver on European money supply can be distinguished: From the mid-sixteenth century until the discovery of Brazilian gold, overseas bullion determined European monetary structures, i.e. the composition of coins and coinage. This was due to the fact that during the whole period, Peruvian and Mexican silver supplied the raw material for European silver coins. This way it enforced the rise of heavy silver coins as the dominant means of payment for interregional trade, a process that had already started with the Central European mining boom. As could be proven by the traces of Potosí silver in European coins, changes in American production almost inmediately led to similar changes in the composition of metals coined in Europe. These effects could be perceived during the end of the sixteenth century as well as during the Thirty Years War. In addition, the *peso fuerte* or *real de a ocho*, struck overseas, was a very well known means of payment all over Europe.

It is more difficult to determine the influence of American silver on monetary volume, even if most of the silver coined from the 1580's on originated from overseas. The development of monetary circulation based on mint accounts suggests that the high increase of silver production in the New World during the 1540's and 1550's was more important for the increase of the money volume than the influx of foreign specie during the first American mining boom thirty years later. This result was due to the opposite development of European mining industry which had reached its peak shortly before. As American metals were added to a high European silver output, the relative annual increase of "fresh" silver (European and American combined) was higher during the mid-sixteenth century than between 1560 and

35 J. SCHÜTTENHELM, Problems of Quantifying, pp. 92 - 94; M. NORTH, Geldumlauf, pp. 72ss.

1600. Growing silver exports further diminished the relative increase of the stock of precious metals in Europe at the turn of the sixteenth century. During the seventeenth century, changes in American silver production had almost no direct influence on the monetary volume as it can be deduced from mint accounts. As the examples of silver coinage in France and the Southern Netherlands show, the quantity of specie struck was at its maximum when American silver production had already started to decline. On the other hand, the sum of the silver yearly minted in the Southern Netherlands and in France during this period did not even account for one third of annual American silver production at the same time. As money supply and demand did not depended exclusively on the influx and production of precious metals, the influence of American riches during the second half of the sixteenth century strongly differed from that of the seventeenth century. This latter period was characterized by great monetary demand that overseas bullion could not satisfy alone, mainly due to European warfare, as constant coin devaluations, massive copper and bullion coinage as well as the improvement of credit mechanisms suggest. Furthermore, changes in the structure and volume of money supply had serious repercussions on other economic variables, i.e. interest rates and prices.

The influence of Mexican and Peruvian silver on European money supply in quantitative terms was more decissive during the period when overseas mining was only starting than afterwards. On the other hand, American production was almost the only supplier of raw materials for European coinage and other uses of silver from 1550 - 1560 on. The importance attributed to that silver stream by European merchants and administrations alike can be perceived in nearly any document related with the New World.

Latin American Contributions to the Development of the Quantity Theory of Money*

By ORESTE POPESCU**

1. Introduction

The Columbus enterprise of the discovery began the 12th October of 1492, but the foundation stage of Spanish colonization in America, which serves as a reference frame to these considerations, extends with the attempt in the Antilles and in the Continent and afterwards

* I thank Prof. Lucy Gómez de Mainer and Mrs. Mónica Mainer de Ohde their generous and efficient technical support in the translation and transcription of this work, respectively. I also thank my assistant, Lic. María Angélica Tietjen who carried out the final supervision of the transcription of the Notes and Bibliographic References.

** The author is Professor emeritus of the Argentine Catholic University, where he is also Profesor Ordinario in the Economic Faculty of UCA, and Director of the Latin American Institute of Economic Thought; Superior Researcher of the National Counsel of Scientific Research and Member of the National Academy of Economic Sciences of the Argentine Republic in Buenos Aires. For scientific contact with his colleagues the address of his permanent domicile is given: Calle 8, N° 491, City Bell (1896), Argentina. Telephone: 021-800265.

with the prowesses of Hernán Cortés in Mexico and Francisco Pizarro in Peru until well after the middle of the XVIth Century[1].

From the beginning of the conquest the most important Indian industry was the extraction of gold and silver and its drainage to Seville. The impact produced by the overflow of the Indian precious metals on the level of Spanish prices and later, due to expansive waves on the other European countries, was so great, that already in the past century the expression: "the revolution of prices" was borne to design this event[2]. And furthermore, towards the middle of the present century Earl J. Hamilton engaged himself in establishing a strict correlation between the American treasure flux and the price revolution which took place in Spain between 1501 and 1650, and with these data to verify the quantity theory of money for this period. As it should be expected the subject stimulated the renewal of studies in the area of the history of the facts as well as in that of economic doctrines. It was Hamilton who posed the question: Why did the prices raise? What answer did the Spaniards of the XVIth Century give to this question?[3]

If we give a passing view on the answer given up to now we shall see that in most cases it is rare to find a reference to an Indian author, that is a Spanish American one[4]. Phillip IInd liked the title "Hispaniarum et Indiarum Rex". Today they are different worlds though they are united in the common faith, the language and the history. Therefore there remains the ineluctable task for the Latin American scholars of

---

1 CÉSPEDES DEL CASTILLO (1961, II and III).

2 THORP / TAYLOR (1957), 12, pp. 375ss; BONN (1896).

3 HAMILTON (1934), p. 299.

4 SAYOUS (1928), 20, pp. 289ss; DEMPSEY (1936), 50, pp. 174ss; HOEFFNER (1941; 1955); GRICE-HUTCHINSON (1952; 1978; 1989; 1990); SCHUMPETER (1954); WEBER (1959; 1962); VILAR (1964; 1969) and BAECK (1988), 20, pp. 381ss among the foreign hispanists; LARAZ (1943), ULLASTRE CALVO (1941, I), pp. 375ss; (1942, II) pp. 51ss; (1965, LV) pp. 11ss; IPARRAGUIRRE (1954, 2 - II), 79ss; (1957); SIERRA BRAVO (1973), 64, pp. 273ss; SÁNCHEZ ALBORNOZ (1959), 47, pp. 95ss; (1979), pp. VIIss); and GÓMEZ CAMACHO (1981), pp. 7ss; (1985), 172, pp. 55ss) among the Spanish researchers.

our time to look far backwards to the horizon of the foundation times and be responsible of all the specific works. Among them, one of the first that stands out is the answer to the most precise question: Which has been the understanding of the Spanish American thinkers on the revolution of prices?

I believe that the response to the Quantity Theory was evident since the first day of the discovery: has gone on being studied and verified on the light of events, and it has had a permanent echo in Europe; and that it has attained it highest point in works, which, though unknown in our century because they were written in Latin, are of lasting value in the history of economic doctrines. In colonial America we have also lived under the influence of mercantilists and late scholastics, brought up in the thirty three Spanish American universities for a population that did not reach fifteen million inhabitants[5]. The papers of American mercantilists swarm in the form of report- letters, briefs, reform projects, and the works of the chroniclers, and their authors are conquerors or royal officers, governors and viceroys. I have grouped them in second Section, which is dedicated to the quantitativism of the Discoverer exhibited in the journal of the first voyage which covers his stay in the Bahama islands and the Big Antilles between the 12th October 1492 and the 16th January 1493; in the third Section, dedicated to Quantity Theory already well outlined after the "ransom of Cajamarca" in 1533; and in the fourth Section on the mature quantitativism which came forth with the discovery and exploitation of the Potosí mines, in 1545. In the fifth Section I summarize the life and work of the most conspicuous authors of treatises of the second half of the XVIth Century belonging to the West Indies Scholastics, whose great works, real treasures of the West Indie remained covered by dust of forgetfulness in the American Libraries of the Colleges and Universities of the religious orders, created and given life by more than eleven thousand missionaries with which those orders counted at the

5 POPESCU (1965, 1988).

end of the XVIIth Century[6]. In the sixth Section I present a retrospective view together with a general conclusion of the foundational period.

2. The Navigation Journal of the first voyage of the discovery (1492 - 1493)

The same day of the discovery the first fair took place between the Admiral's people and the crowd of natives of the Guanahaní islet of the Bahama who witnessed the landing[7].

> "Because I desired that they were friendly towards us (Columbus said), because I understood that they were people who would free themselves and convert to our Sainted Faith by means of love, and not by force, I gave some of them a few red bonnets and some glass beads which they hang to their necks and many other things of little value, which brought them great pleasure and it was marvelous how they were ours ... Afterwards they came swimming to the boats of our ships where we were, and brought us parrots, balls of cotton thread and spears and many other things, which they bartered for other things we gave them, such as little glass beads and hawk's bells (brass timbrels)[8], finally, they took all and gave of the things they had"[9].

This was a good start to establish the free trade market between the Spaniards and the Antilian Indians of the Taino nation of Guanahaní[10], christened with the name San Salvador. Columbus never stops

---

6 FURLONG (1969), POPESCU (1966 y 1986 a).

7 BALLESTEROS BERETTA (1945), FERNÁNDEZ DE NAVARRETE (1825), SANZ (1962).

8 THACHER (1903, I), pp. 533ss, 548, 626s, and (1974), p. 67.

9 COLÓN (1492 - 1506), p. 30.

10 KRICKEBERG (1946), pp. 246ss.

stressing the increasing demand, or as he states with his own words "the want of our things" that the Indians showed.

At next days' market the Admiral ponders:

> "I was alert and trying to know if there was gold and I saw that some of them brought a little piece (of gold) hanging through a hole in their nose, and communicating by gestures he could know that going South or coming back to the Island by the South way, there was a king that had big vases of it, and that he had a lot".

That was very important news, a real event which would be taken into account in the rest of the exploring trips. From San Salvador the chosen route follows to the Santa Maria de la Concepcion Islet and after to Fernandina Island, which they reached on the Tuesday 16th of October. The news of the discoverers "who came from heaven" had already reached Fernandina's population with the natural wonder among the pacific Tainos.It was so that the first night

> "there was no lack of canoes aboard the ships - Columbus states - that brought us water and what they had. I ordered that everyone should be given something, that is to say some little beads, ten or twelve of them of glass on a thread, and some brass timbrels that in Castile are worth a maravedi each, and some laces, all of which they had in very great esteem".

The marketing also went on the morrow.

> "The people were all of the same condition, and they gave of what they had in change of any thing given to them; and here I saw that the crew changed little pieces of broken bowls and glass for spears".

And two other sailors

> "found an Indian who had in his nose a piece of gold that was about half a castellano, in which they saw letters engraved and I scolded them because they did not bargain for it and gave whatever they demanded in order to see what it was,

> and whose money it was; and they answered that they did not dare to bargain for it".

The news was not very encouraging for the Admiral, but a few days later another event would change his mood.

In the navigation Journal of the 22nd October we read actually that even if most commerce with the Indians took place through the already mentioned spears and balls of cotton thread, this time a novelty occurred: "some of the Indians brought pieces of gold hanging from their noses which they readily changed for a hawk's bell suitable for the foot of a sparrow-hawk, and for little glass beads". This established a great novelty in the bartering market of the Fernandina Tainos. Gold that was only to serve as an ornament and indirectly to be treasured, lowered in its condition and became a means of change as the rest of Indian goods. This change shows us clearly, in economic terms, of a change in the level of gold value in the market of Fernandina. However, the change in the value of gold was not only not general but it was neither very accentuated, as gold only accepted being changed for one of the most treasured Spanish products, the hawk's bells, and only secondarily for the glass beads. Anyway, the event of the gold from Fernandina kept the Admiral pondering for several days, until the 1st November when he took a dangerous decision. At that time he was near cape Las Palmas in the Island of Cuba. The Indians of the place neared the ships with more than sixteeen canoes full of spun cotton and others and great was their surprise when they were told the news that "the Admiral ordered nothing should be taken because they had to know that the only thing that the Admiral looked for was gold". The decision of limiting the interchange with the natives only to gold, stopped suddenly the flux of commerce. For a month and a half the exploring of the discoverers pursued successfully in Cuba and in La Española, but there is a complete silence about the gold exchange.

They were already in Haitian land in front of La Tortuga Island in Paradise Valley and after two timid attempts, the expeditionaries unexpectedly charged again with their demands for gold from Monday 17th December.There were good news everywhere. The attempt of a bartering in the nearest village where he sent several Spaniards, was satisfactory: "They change glass beads for some thin pieces of carved gold". Due to the avalanche of the sailors onto the village after this attempt, the chief of that village devised to have the natives carve the first small gold tiles ("tejuelos de oro") of the Indias, breaking a sheet of gold as large as a hand: "and he made little pieces of it, and bringing one small tile he bartered it (in the plaza)". The same day Columbus received the visit of a chief of La Tortuga Island in whose canoe fourty men came with him, in which opportunity he was told by Haitian natives that in La Tortuga there was more gold than in La Española Island "because it was nearer Babeque". The Babeque Island (the Great Inagua? or Jamaica?), was known by the Discoverer since the 12th November when he had tried unsuccessfully to discover it, as he had heard "that its inhabitants picked up the gold by candlelight at night and they said that they made bows with it with hammers". Facing these first considerations of space economics in the West Indies, the Admiral remarked that more than the distance or at least at its level, it was fundamental to take into account what we, nowadays, call the volume of transactions, which was very low in La Española and in La Tortuga. In fact, the Admiral said

> "I do not believe there were gold mines in La Española Island or in La Tortuga, but that they brought it from Babeque, and they bring little because they have nothing to give for it, and the land is so rich that they do not have to work much to feed themselves or to dress as they go naked".

The Discoverer did not know that introducing in the discussion the volume of transactions he contributed with a first brick to Irving Fisher's "change equation", but he records that he affirmed it in La Española Island the 17th December 1492.

The riches in gold of Babeque Island were confirmed by the young king of La Española Island who lived in the Haitian area today called Gros Marne and who visited for the first time the expeditionary ships the 16th December in the gulf between La Tortuga and La Española. In this first visit, the young king, accompanied by more than five hundred men watched the bartering market in the morning, in which "some brought some grains of very pure gold in their ears and nose, which they gave readily", and ordering (the king) to all of them afterwards, to honor the Admiral. The second visit of the king of Gros Marne took place the 18th December and followed a more pompous pattern. More than two hundred men accompanied the king and four men brought him in a litter. Of course in the ceremony there was no lack of the food and drinks offered by the Spaniards. But the most interesting item was the interchange of gifts.

> "I - wrote Columbus - saw that he liked a drapery that I had over my bed and I gave him it and (added) some very good amber beads that I had on my neck and red shoes and a flask of orange flower water, of which he was so happy that it was a wonder".

As the Indian king already knew that the discoverers' expedition was in the search of gold and wanted to go to Babeque Island, we can guess his option. The remarks of Columbus in the Journal were:

> "the king gave me also two pieces of carved gold which were very thin; and I think they obtain very little of it here as I believe that they are very near from where the gold is born, and there is a lot" ("el rey me dio dos pedazos de oro labrado que eran muy delgados, que creo que aquí alcanzan poco de él, puesto que tengo que están muy vecinos de donde nace y hay mucho").

In spite of the ironic tone of the comment there is no doubt that we are facing remarks of great interest for our subject. It is a clear thesis of Columbus that the value of gold decreases ("they obtain very little of it here" - "aquí alcanzan poco de él") with the nearness of its place of extraction ("if they are very near from where gold is born" - "si están muy vecinos de donde nace") and of its abundance in the market ("and there is a lot" - "y hay mucho"). This happened at Puerto de Paz in La Española the 18th December 1492.

In the ceremony given in homage to the king of Gros Marne, the Admiral learned from a principal of the souverain, a person of long age and experience, "that there are many islands near at a hundred leagues in which there is a lot of gold, and even one of them is all gold, and in the others there is so much that they pick it up and sift it with some sort of sieves and they melt it and make bows and thousand other things". Immediately Columbus decided "to go there". In the night of the 19th December they left La Tortuga Gulf and the 20th December the expeditionary ships entered Acul Bay were they discovered a big settlement whose inhabitants seeing the ships ran towards them. "So many came that they covered the land" to bring them bread, water "and all that they had and knew that the Admiral wanted; and it must not be said that because they gave liberally, what they gave had little value - said the Admiral - because the same did those who gave pieces of gold and those who gave the gourd of water". More than a hundred and twenty canoes also visited the vessels on the 22nd December; and the great chief Guacanagarí, who was in his village of El Recreo, sent the Admiral the most valuable present they had seen up to then: "a belt that, instead of a bag had a mask with two big ears of hammered gold, and the tongue, and the nose". The 23rd December the ships were visited by about fifteen hundred persons; then the Admiral received the very important news that among the sources where gold was found, was the region of Cibao, that is located in La Española Island itself", and that to it they came to buy gold from other parts "and that there is as much gold as one would want" could be found; "and that in finding the place from which it is obtained he would get it very cheaply and as he imagined, even for nothing" ("y que hallando el lugar donde se saca habrá gran barato de ello, y según imaginaba, que no por nada").

In the meeting with Guacanagarí, in the Niña Caravel on Wednesday 26th December Columbus could ratify again his thesis that his gold trade was more prosperous because of the major quantity of gold in La Española. When the king from Recreo had just arrived, a canoe that carried a chief from other province appeared, and they "brought pieces of gold which they wanted to change only for a hawk's bell, because nothing they wanted more than hawk's bells". The canoe had not yet reached the vessel where they called and showed the pieces of gold, saying "chuq chuq" meaning hawk's bells, so they were about to go crazy for them. So that we would not be mistaken if we stated that from then on, gold got to be a type of money-merchandise of the American Tainos, while the hawk's bells played the role of merchandise-money among the discoverers of the Indias together with the Spanish monetary system. The chief Guacanagarí did not lose the opportunity to link his name to the new parity of the two pre-money standards. A hawk's bell was equal to four pieces of gold as big as a hand. Actually, once that the change operation of the chief was closed, the king Guacanagarí approached the Admiral to suggest that "he ordered a hawk's bell to be kept for him until the next day, because he would bring (in payment) four pieces of gold as big as the hand". Competition was also working wonders in the market economy established by Columbus in Indies.

But the meeting between king Guacanagarí and Admiral Columbus has an special interest also for the history of economic doctrines. While the interchange of pieces of gold as big as a hand for a Spanish hawk's bell happened, it was evident that an increase of the value of the hawk's bell in relation to the purchasing power of "the piece of gold as big as a hand" was taking place. Undoubtedly this was satisfactory for the Spaniards: "The Admiral was glad to know about this". To which the response on the Indian side was quick:

> "The king was glad to see the Admiral happy and understood that he (the Admiral) wished to get a great amount of gold, and he told him by gestures that he knew where they could find a lot of it near where they were; and to be optimistic because he would give him all the gold he would wish, and that he informed him that there was a lot specially in Cipango, which the indians called 'Civao', where there was so much that the Indians there consider it nothing, and that he would bring it from there, but that in this island, Española, called 'Boh'o' and in that Caribata province there was much more".

And as if to insist in the formulation of the quantitativist doctrine of the Indian king of the island Española, in the navigation journal of the 1st January 1493 we find the following remark:

> "The Admiral believed that king Guacanagarí might have forbidden everybody to sell gold to the Christians, so that all of it should pass through his hands. But as I told the day before yesterday, he knew the places where there was gold in such a quantity that it may not be considered to have a price for them".

Today Christopher Columbus would tell us that the abundance of gold in Cibao was such that its value was null and so that it entered into the cathegory of free goods. In not more than three months of the "honeymoon" between the Spaniards and the American Indians he could verify empirically an observation that he transcribed daily in his navigation journal and that sometimes rendered the opportunity to ponder upon economic doctrines: that the value of gold could oscillate among an almost prohibitive level of purchase power, as it happened in the experiments of the Guanahaní islet, and with very rare exceptions also in Fernandina and the island of Cuba; and a moderate level of esteem as he verified in the region of the chief of the Valle del Paraiso when the necessity of "creating" a sort of small tile to make the transactions easy, up to reaching the third stage to the region of the chief Guacanagarí who will accompany Columbus in the history of American quantitativism, which took place in the Acul Bay the last days of December of 1492 and the beginning of January, 1493, remarking that the acquisitive power of gold "is enough for little" if it is abundant, that is "if there is a lot", and, of course, "nearer it is from its source" its abundance will be greater and with this "lower will be its price", and an extreme case may happen as he thought it happened in Cibao, that "there was a great quantity of gold" making it "extremely cheap", and because of this decreasing its worth "to nothing", meaning that it could be bought with almost nothing or "that it may not be considered to have a price". Here, we are essencially in front of an advanced quantitativist idea.

It is important to add that the optimism about the success of the enterprise of the discovery would incorporate in Columbus's doctrine of quantity the equally optimistic expectations that in a very short term as they gave pieces of gold that equaled two "castellanos" for a needle that would be nothing as compared with what would happen in a month from then (the 26th December); or, as Guacanagarí had told the Admiral that he had sent for gold and that he (Guacanagarí) would cover him (the Admiral) all in gold before he left; as in a mediate or long term the Admiral said: "I hope in God that on my return from Castile, I will find a barrel of gold that those who stayed will have bargained and they will have found the gold mine and the spicery, and this in such quantity that before three years have passed the King and the Queen can start and prepare the conquest of the Sainted House (of Jerusalem)".

The inclusion of the expectations in his theory is also useful as a bridge between his quantity theory and his chrisohedonist theory - in their essence evidently antagonistic - whose evocation of gold as the higher symbol of wealth reaches notes of bullonistic lirism in the Admiral's letter of the fourth trip, which reads:

> "Genoveses, Venetians and all people who have pearls, gems and other valuable things, all of them take them to the end of the world to change them into gold. Gold is most excellent, with gold treasures are made and with it he who has it can do whatever he wants in the world and even send souls to Paradise"[11].

3. The Ransom of Cajamarca (1533)

The conquest of Perú shows the other side of the contact between the Spaniards and the natives. The violence and the fierceness of the struggles were widely exploited by the enemies of Spain; the triumph

---

11 COLÓN (1492-1506), pp. 200s.

of the Spanish expeditionaries, sometimes almost miraculous, filled the conquerors with a well deserved vanity; while in the mother country the astounding news refering to the Indian treasure, instead of vanishing, as happened in the Columbus enterprise, were absolutely confirmed, because the magnitud of "the ransom of Cajamarca" (el rescate de Cajamarca) surpassed all estimates.

If in the prowess of the discovery made in the first trip the names of Guacanagarí and Columbus are outstanding, in "the ransom of Cajamarca" the major characters are Francisco Pizarro and the Inca Atahualpa. And in spite of the course of fourty years time that separate them, there is a strong bond between them in respect to their monetary remarks. The Inca Atahualpa plays in the development of American Quantity Theory the same role played by king Guacanagarí fourty years before. In one of the first accounts about the ransom of Cajamarca sent to the king by "the Governor of Panamá and other trustworthy persons" in 1533, we are surprised with the clear quantitativist approach. The same account reports that:

> "after Governor Pizarro had advanced, on foot and on horseback, with 200 Spaniards, they reached the place where a chief, great lord, called Atabalique, brother and General Captain of the Souverain of those lands; that after peace was oferred to him, as he resisted, they fought him and he was imprisoned and they took from him more than fifty thousand castellanos of gold and more than twenty thousand silver marks ..., that said chief promised to give Pizarro and the Spaniards a piece of land as extensive as the courtyard of a castle, or more, and from it they had already taken more than four hundred thousand very large pieces (of gold), and of strange shapes; ... and that after said battle, native people brought fifty thousand Castellanos of gold, so they had already received from the chief more than two million twenty carat gold; and the duty of ten percent, corresponding to what would be brought, would be of more than four hundred thousand castellanos ..., and those who write this believe that the ships are detained for a long time to load and bring the aforesaid gold that they expect it will be a marvelous quantity".

This is the principal idea of this casual report that would reach the king's courts and the markets of Europe with the same velocity and spread of Columbus's first letter about the voyage of the Indias discovery. Its authors are unknown, but there is no doubt that the source is only one; some of Pizarro's people who participated in the conquest of Perú and who, already satisfied, returned on the first ship that carried part of the Inca's treasure, on the 5th December 1533, or on the second, on the 9th January 1534. Today we know that this news was spread almost simultaneously in French, German and Italian, so that we can say that at the beginning of 1534 it had rounded the world[12].

But what has this news, which data are common to almost all latter accounts and cronicles, related to the conquest of Perú, to do with our subject? It is precisely due to its clear quantitativist approach that it calls our attention. Actually when therein it is stated that the Inca had already delivered more than four hundred thousand pieces of gold, he was surprised to see that the Spaniards immediately broke them up to store and load them.

> "Seeing this, said Indian chief asked them why they did so[13], as he would give them as much as they wanted. And he also had his subjects bring more than sixty thousand marks of pure silver and he told them that, in his country, there was also cinnamon, of which they could order ten thousand loads to be fetched. He also told them that to have the silver they wanted it sufficed to put fire to a rock he showed them and from which they could extract as much melted silver as they wanted, ready to be hammered; so that there is as much gold and silver in this reign as there is iron in Vizcaya, and that is why they do not think it is important".

This of putting a rock on the fire is not untruthful, as the Inca referred to the melting method, which takes place melting the metal veins on the fire in small furnaces which they called "guairas" and of which

---

12 Anónimo (1533).

13 Carande (1977, II), pp. 82ss.

there were a great number in the slopes of the mines and which were seen at night as if they were festival lights.

The fundamental thing for us is the general awareness among the conquerors of Perú of the enormous abundance of gold and specially of silver mines, due to which these "precious" metals had among the Incas so little value that "they give them no importance".

The conquerors, who used gold and silver as means of payment, became immediately aware of the deterioration of the value of those metals. This is proved in the "Relación" made by Francisco López de Jerez, who, after the victory over Atahualpa in Cajamarca, in which he participated as secretary of Captain Francisco Pizarro, and when he returned to Spain on the 3rd June of 1534 he had said "Relación" printed the same year. After reviewing the most important aspects of the "ransom of Cajamarca", Francisco de Jerez tells us that on the 13th May, 1533 the melting of all the gold and silver was started and it was alloted. In fact, after taking His Majesty's fifth and the foundry rights, all the treasure of the Incas was distributed among the conquerors, who earned it,

> "eight thousand eight hundred and eighty gold pesos and three hundred and sixty two silver marks corresponded to the cavalry men, and four thousand four hundred and forty gold pesos and a hundred and eighty one silver marks to the infantry men, and to some more than to others in the measure the governor thought they deserved it, the quality of the persons or their work. A quantity of gold that the governor separated before the allotment, he gave to the neighbours who had remained in the town of San Miguel and to all the people who came with the Captain Don Diego de Almagro and all the merchants and sailors who came after the war had finished, so that all (the Spaniards) who were in that land obtained a part".

We regard the sudden appearance of a society of newly rich whose members could not yet believe that this were true. Francisco Jerez himself was beneficiary of a boot of "a hundred and ten good silver 'arrobas' (twenty five pounds each)", earned in only one of the twenty years spent there: "nineteen in poverty and in only one the riches I brought here". We can foresee the price revolution that this historic allotment would produce, in the first place in the region of Cajamarca and San Miguel. Jerez himself described the madness of prices and stated that suddenly they have become "so high, and I can say it truthfully, as I saw it and bought some things". More still, after having registered a list of the most high prices that in this land had been payed those days, he expressed a consideration that, now that we know that they were acquainted with it in Panamá and from there spread by the Conqueror to all Europe, we can understand it correctly. In effect, writes Jerez, many things should be said "about the increased prices at which everything has been sold, and the little value given to gold and silver". We already know that among the Incas those "precious" metals had an unimportant value. And now that the Indian treasure had changed hands and it was in possesion of the Cajamarca conquerors the depreciating effect accompanied its new owners. Jerez himself says: "if someone owed something to somebody else, he gave him a piece of gold without weighing it; and even if he gave him twice what he owed he gave nothing; and from house to house went the debtors, with an Indian loaded with gold looking for the creditors to pay what they owed". Formerly, in the 1533 "Relación" we only knew of Indians who rejected "precious metals", but in this 1534 account of Francisco Jerez we learn that gold"was held in contempt both by the Spaniards as by the natives"[14].

The exconqueror and ex "encomendero" (commissionaire) Licentiate Bartolomé de Las Casas, later converted to the Order of the Dominicans, presented in 1542 by order of the "Emperor king ... in the City Halls of Valladolid", a work which he entitled "Remedios para Reformación de las Indias", afterwards printed in Sevilla in 1552. In it he pleaded for the abolition of the system of "encomiendas". The argument he uses to justify this measure is devolped thus:

---

14 LÓPEZ DE JEREZ (1534).

"As the priviledge granted to the Spaniards to give them the Indians in 'encomienda' has been so iniquitous and so damaging ... and has borne such very enormous and irretrievable evils to God and to royal crown of Spain, and has destroyed those kingdoms and lands and killed so many people and devastated so many settlements. And even these reigns of Castilla are flagellated by God every day; and there is great fear that He should plunder them because of the great sins that the Spanish people have comitted in the Indies, of which we see an evident punishment, that everybody sees it and says everywhere, that with it God afflicts us and shows that he is very offended with us in those parts due to the destruction of those nations: and it is that of so infinite treasures have been brought from them, that never king Solomon nor other King of the world owned, nor saw, nor heard about so much gold and silver, nothing has remained in those reigns, and even from what there was in Spain, little before the Indies were discovered, there is nothing at all. Because of this everything costs thrice the price they were worth before, and poor people suffer great poverty and need, and to Your Majesty, who so well employs his life in the increase of the Catholic faith, it becomes necessary and impossible of carrying out great heroic feats in the service of our Almighty God, as you really could acheive if so great disorders, due to said damaged 'encomienda' and to what precedes it, which are the unjust wars, would not have happened in the Indies; therefore it follows that that privilege is so iniquitous and evil and that so great damages and mischiefs it has caused, though at the beginning it did not seem bad but good ... Therefore it is true and just that the Indians take it away from the Spaniards ... because it is iniquitous and tyrannical and against our sainted Catholic faith ..., against all natural law and of enormous damages and grievances and the finishing of all those reigns, and matter of provocation of the terrible wrath of God, Who He will spill over us in vengeance for our sins we committed on them (the Indians)"[15].

---

15 LAS CASAS (1974, II), pp. 763 - 765.

In a work of mine in 1984, examining the "Remedios" of Las Casas I observed the deep metaphysical frame in which the economical subject was established. Las Casas feared that God would punish his homeland, due to the slavery of the Indians, and one of the signs of this punishments, that was already taking place, he saw in the escape of the American treasure towards other kingdoms and the accelerated increase of prices in Spain. In his more still famous work: "Brevísima relación de la destruición de las Indias", wrote in Valencia the same year 1542, edited in Sevilla in 1552, he repeated that he acted so to "drive away hell from the Indies ... and from pity towards his country whish is Castilla, and God would not destroy it because of so great sins commited against His faith and honour ..."[16].

With the analysis limited to the quantitativist subject imbued in Las Casas's mysticism, neither the course of reasoning of the correlation among the different variables was very clear. Inclusively it was possible to construe that Las Casas related the revolution of prices in Spain more with the flight of money from the treasures brought from the Indies than with its abundance. But, in spite of the inaccurate terminology, it could be supposed that Las Casas could have thought in a causal relation flux of metals, price revolution.

What lacked in the elucidation of this matter was to know that Las Casas was well acquainted with the first quantitativist experiences that took place in the Antillas in Columbus's first voyage. It was Las Casas who knew the Navigation Journal drafted by Columbus, which he transcribed in the first Book of his History of the Indies and which constitutes - as we have above seen - the basic source of the primitive quantitativist American theory from October 1492 to January 1493[17/18].

---

16 Popescu (1984, 1986 b.), Las Casas (1542), p. 13.

17 Las Casas (1951, I), pp. 200ss, Hanke and Sanz (1962, Preliminary Study).

18 Piqué (1974) has the merit of arousing our attention in page 25, on Las Casas remarks stated in the Treaty on "Remedios" which I was not acquaintedwith, affirming that with this "Fray Bartolom' perceives the relation between the in-

4. The discovery of Potosí (1545)

The discovery of the silver mines of Potosí at the beginning of 1545 is another event which would have immediate repercussion in the debate about the theory of money value in the Indies. The first American position we know about is that of a conqueror soldier, very obscure and totally ignored in the history of the conquest. The only reference I find and which rescue him from forgetfulness is owed to Garcilaso de la Vega (1539 - 1616). It is Gonzalo Bernal, who towards the last days of April of 1545, when the fabulous silver mines of Mount Potosí had just been discovered as he contemplated them and saw the start and the legal registration of the first vein, he exclaimed: "The mines (of Potosí) promise such riches, that after a few years of working them iron will be more valuable than silver". This event is higly significative. The discovery of the Potosí silver mine has not only a meaning in the history of quantitative theory - and as such is a powerful tool - surely not the only one, nor the first - to produce chain reflections on the field of the value of money theory. It is in this sense that this remark of Gonzalo Bernal must be considered, from whom the only thing I know is what Garcilaso de la Vega said, that is: that he had been a steward of General Pedro Alonso de Hinojosa. Someone links his remark with an event that happened much later between December 1553 and 1554, that is the raising from "El Cuzco" of Francisco Fernández Girón, who ended by being executed in Lima. But this is a misunderstanding. Gonzalo Bernal made his remark before Diego Centeno, a few days later of the registration of the first vein in the name of Diego de Villarroel. "Villarroel ... registered it the

---

crease of gold and silver and that of prices". In my former work (Popescu, 1984) I expressed my doubt if I should or not accept this interpretation, though this doubt did not imply an skeptical vision. But today, after studying the Journal of Columbus's first voyage, that Las Casas knew and transcribed in Book I of his "General History of the Indies", I have no doubt that he was familiar with Columbus's Quantitative ideas, and that he supported them, more still that Las Casas anticipated Hamilton's thesis, understanding that the price revolution in Spain was caused by the late treasures of the Indies.

21st April 1545, staking the vein ..., which is the same of taking posession of the yards that the law concedes, to those who find it so that they mine it as owners". This is categorically affirmed by Antonio Vázquez de Espinosa[19]. Though it was uttered as a prediction, there is no doubt that here we find an important mile stone in the history of money quantitativism. And so Garcilaso de la Vega also understood it in 1605.

In September 1545 from the city of Santiago, Pedro de Valdivia (1510 - 1554) in operation of the conquest of Chile decided to send a messenger to Spain with news about his conquesting and colonizing "journey". To finance this embassy he resorted to "the gold that some Indians of mine had extracted and what the neighbours had, that all of them loaned it to me readily ... making a total of almost sixty thousand pesos". It was in the opportunity that the vessel and those who sailed in it set sail from the port of Valparaiso, "That the conqueror of Chile tried to grasp how much those sixty thousand pesos were worth. Valdivia himself tried to evaluate them making a difference between what it would be if the embassy went to Peru or to another different place. If the ship went "to a place other than Peru" it was evident that sixty thousand pesos was very much", it was a sum of very great value. And what would happen if this embassy were to Peru? Valdivia was well acquainted with the monetary effects of the discovery and the start of the exploitation of the silver mines of Potosí, and his answer was readily given: "At that land has been and is so prosperous or rich in (silver) money, they would little esteem that amount". That as Valdivia gives the quantitative doctrine of money a citizenship card for Peru, as if he would have wanted to say that everybody knew this. And he states this remark when the messengers to His Majesty "set sail from the port of Valparaiso about September of said year of 1546". What does this sum represent now for the conquerors of Chile? again Valdivia asks himself. And his answer accompanied with the

19 Garcilaso de la Vega (1968), pp. 672ss, Vázquez de Espinosa, A. (1629, Punto 1649).

reason of same was: "Here (this 60.000 gold pesos) were very much for us because every peso costs us a hundred drops of blood and two hundred drops of sweat". In other words, in Chile the value of money was founded in the costs of its exploitation[20].

By May 1549 another young soldier, but who this time was a chronicler, Pedro Cieza de León (1518? - 1554), "the prince of the Indian chroniclers" had already departed from the City of the Kings towards Charcas, and he was visiting the mining settlings of the Potosí high land, the fabulous market of the "Villa Ymperial del Potosí" in accelerating growth, and the noble and loyal "Villa del Plata", a Spanish population in "Los Charcas", established in Chuquisaca[21]... The impact produced on him by the contact with the dynamic pole of potosinian development - as we would call it nowadays and with the vast area of influence that is already appearing in Cuzco in the North and in Tucuman in the South, is moving and his considerations greatly confirm the cuantitativist approaches of his predecessors Jerez, Las Casas, Bernal and Valdivia. Cieza gathers information and writes about it to enlarge the manuscript of his already bulky "Cronica del Perú". Started in 1541 in Cartago, in the Valley of Cauca, it was at the point of receiving the last touch to be printed, once that the last stretch of Cieza's itinerary had concluded. Actually this last part fills about twenty chapters of the "Crónica del Perú", that go from Chapter 95 to Chapter 115. And it is in these chapters that Cieza's quantitativist considerations appear. This occurs in two opportunities, one in which Villa de Plata is described, and other in which the metal mines are described; and the corresponding chapters according to Cieza's numbering are: "Chapter 107" and "Chapter 115"[22].

Chapter 107 begins with the already mentioned paragraph in which a praising presentation is made of the "noble and loyal Villa de Plata",

---

20 VALDIVIA (1550), CUNNINGHAME GRAHAM (1943).

21 CIEZA DE LEÓN (1972). Good biobibliographical note in CIEZA DE LEÓN (1967).

22 Starting from CIEZA DE LEÓN the works of sections 4 and 5 are a revised and enlarged edition of my publications. POPESCU (1984; 1986 b).

famous in all the world "due to the great treasures that have parted from it to Spain". Its localization was optimum. This town is located in the best place that was found, and as it is readily proved, "it has a good temperature to grow fruit trees and to sow wheat and barley, grow vines and other things". This "of good temperature" must be understood in the sense that being located in the torrid zone and at a height of 2,700 m its climate is really very agreable and also as compared with the mining Mount Potosí, 4,800 m high, very rugged and, being very cold and windy, was uninhabitable even for the natives. As Cieza was in the place he unfortunately does not bear in mind that his readers do not follow him in his comings and goings, and what is more, where he writes about Potosí, the young soldier, even if he admits the weather is cold (Chapter 109), he nevertheless judges that "it is healthy, specially for the Indians as very few or none of them are sick there" (Chapter 110). But the problem of interest for us is understood in its totality only when we find out, through other sources that because of the intense cold and the strong winds "for six leagues (measure of distance) roundabout Potosí from May to the end of August no fruit is borne, nor there are trees, nor is there grass in the mountain of the ground which is dark, red, and partially the colour of burnt ashes". Only with this information we can guess that for the Spaniards of Los Charcas the mountain and the Villa Imperial of Potosí were places of sweat and hard work while Villa de Plata was used as an oasis of rest and family enjoyment, besides being the headquarters of all the political, administrative and religious institutions of the province of Los Charcas and also the seat of certain activities that could not take place in Potosí.

Let us now examine the second paragraph of Chapter 107 of Cieza's Chronicle. This is its first proposition with which the second paragraph begins: "The farms and country estates have nowadays a very high price, caused by the riches that have been discovered in the mines of Potosí".

As the wealth discovered in the mines of Potosí is silver, not only the relation between the level of prices and the quantity of silver is established here, but, at the same time a causality order is established: the increase of the volume of silver in the Potosí mines brought about the increase of the level of prices in the Villa de Plata. But, thinking it better, such an interpretation comprises much more than what Cieza was thinking, as the relation he establishes does not include the level of all prices, but only the level of the prices of land or, still more precisely of the farms and country estates; and only in Villa de Plata. Other classes of properties and located in other places would not necessarily have "high prices" because of the growth of the quantity of silver in Potosí. This remark belongs, of course to us, not to Cieza, but we do it precisely to make clear and not equivocal Cieza's considerations in the above mentioned sentence with which this second paragraph begins. It is probable, that Cieza had bore in mind a real interpretation and not a monetary interpretation, when he related the price of the country estates with the volume of mining production. Actually, it is probable that he might have had in mind the idea that, as the volume of the mining production increased, a larger amount of labour hands, larger amounts of consumption goods are needed, and consequently a greater valuation of the neighbouring farm-lands, precisely due to the increase of the requirements of consumption goods. In such case it would be an effect of space economics or of localization or positional rent due to the vicinity of the mining developing pole, of the same category of the one seen two thousand years before by Xenophon (a.D 430 - 355 b.C). When the plan of mining exploitation, was being carried out, the localisation of the worker families in the mining settlement increased, the demand for consumption goods also increased and, consequently, the lands near the mining centre were incorporated to the production process according to the space economic order, increasing their rent and thus their prices too. It is evident that also in this case, it can be asserted that the price of the land raised due to the increase of the wealth of the newly exploited mines. Therefore, to the first quantitative interpretation of Cieza's ideas, with this a second interpretation is added of the space economic type. In which of these two interpretations should we place the first sentence, second paragraph of Chapter 107 of Cieza's chronicle? - he answer is not easy; but in the way it is stated in the context of Chapter 107 I am inclined towards accepting the real and space interpretation and not the monetary quantitative one. This questions merits to be furtherly studied by more expert minds.

Chapter 115 is titled "Cómo en esta parte deste reino hay grandes minereos de metales" (How in this part of this reign there is much metal mining). It is, actually an attempt to synthesize all that Cieza had seen from Cartagena to Potosí, to arrive to the conclusion that in the Indies "the greatest riches and treasures ever seen in the world and in many ages have been found". He follows numbering the different kinds of metal found. First it was the gold from the Cauca Valley region, from Popayan as far as Mompox village, as rich, if not richer, than Cuzco. Afterwards he states that in several areas such as Antioquia and Cartago in Nueva Granada, and also in all the reign of Perú there was gold and silver to extract "for ever after"; also determining that "there is a great quantity of copper and more still of iron in the sand banks and the collars of the ridges that lower to the plains", as also "there is lead, and this reign is well stocked with all metals that god created".

Based upon this data he states his conclusion: "And I believe that as long as there are men, there will be great wealth there; and so much has been extracted, that it has raised the prices in Spain in such a way, as never men could have thought". This conclusion brings to mind similar ideas - we have above seen - in Las Casas; and we will also find them later in 1567, reproduced almost verbatim, but recognizing his debt with Cieza, in the "Gobierno del Perú" of Juan de Matienzo. Moreover, we must bear in mind that he had made that kind of remarks including before Potosí was famous and even before it was discovered. But to localize them we have to regard with greater attention the part of the Crónica related to his actuation in the Valley of Cauca, in Nueva Granada. We can read his considerations when he knew the "renowned and rich Mount Buriticá, from which great quantity of gold has been taken" which he describes in Chapter 14 of the Crónica. Cieza participated in its discovery when he was part of the army of Captain Juan de Vadillo en 1539, that is ten years before knowing the other famous mountain, but of silver, of Potosí, and he again traversed it towards the end of the same year 1539, this time being enlisted in the army of Captain Jorge Robledo. It was in this opportunity that he could contrast the "great quantity of gold" that the Indians took from this mountain (that even nowadays occupies an outstanding place in the works of monetary History), with "the very great need of supply of provisions" caused by the setting on fire of the village and of all the harvests produced by the Indians when the Spaniards entered.

> "I remember - tells Cieza in his Crónica, in the part that corresponds, as I believe, about the year 1542, that is, in the same year when Las Casas was constructing his ideas - that, going to look for food, a soldier called Toribio, found in a river (of the town of Buriticá) a stone as big as a man's head, full of gold veins that penetrated the stone from one side to the other, and when he saw it he put it on his shoulders to bring it to the camp. And climbing a hill he met a little dog that belonged to the Indians; and when he saw it he rushed to kill it for eating it, letting go of the gold stone; which rolled back into the river, and Toribio killed the dog having it of greater price than gold because of the hunger he had which was the cause of the stone staying in the river, where it at first was. And it it should change into something that could be eaten, surely someone would go back to search for it, because we really have great need of food".

Cieza's account is a double of the "theory of the mouse" - as I called somewhere else - sketched in the Natural History of Plinius the Aged (23 - 79); but there is no doubt that here, under the same view of the subjective approach to value, at the same time a subjective approach to the law of demand and supply is established, in a market in which one of the parts is represented by the precious metal: to the abundance and scarcity of any product,that abundance and scarcity of gold mining is opposed. In this case the abundance of gold was such that the man who let it go did not take the trouble to "go to fetch it back". Once broken the objective taboo of precious metals, in Chapter 26 of the "Crónica" Cieza had the intuition of placing one after the other the three parts of the quantitative problem as he saw it, which reminds us of Jerez's point of view: In the first place he stressed "the very excessive prices of goods in the Cauca Valley", then he observes that "for the glory of Spaniards", the conquerors of the Indias "so low considered the monies that, even if they had needs they despised it". And few lines after we find the confirmation of the remark that the Indian lands and rivers "are very rich and there is abundance of this metal (gold)". That is, in a same page he placed, one after the other three ideas: (i) abundance of gold, (ii) excessive prices, (iii) low value of money. But the author does not deem necessary to correlate them explicitely. And this occurs when Cieza de León writes the chapter dedicated to the description of the Valley of Cauca, valley which he travelled so many times between the years 1539 and 1547 as when he enlisted with the royalists who followed the summon of La Gasca in July 1547, Cieza was in Cartago. It is probable that this chapter 26 had been written towards the end of 1546.

From Chapter 30 on, Cieza describes the road from the city of Cali to that of Popayan, with which he confirms that he is actually and speedily marching towards the place of encounter with La Gasca's troups in Túmbez. In chapter 31 we read that Cieza already has "reached the city of Popayán", and he finds that he has to give a last backward look, as he is practically in the Sierra of the Coconucos where the two great branches of the river Magdalena are born. The great hastiness in the drafting of the Crónica is notorious and also the tight and very synthetized style, which makes the reading difficult. In this panoramica vision of chapter 31 again is posed the subject of our interest. Here is the part of major importance for us:

> "There are so many Indian provinces and towns from the birth of this river up to where it enters in the Ocean sea, and so much riches, rich gold mines and riches that the Indians had, and some still have, and so big is the trade of it that it

> cannot become dearer, as it is much, it makes it become cheaper that the natives of those regions have not much reasoning, and they speak such different languages, that it was necessary to take many interpreters to travel through them".

In spite of the difficulty of the reading and of the quantity of subjects this long phrase contains, it is evident that Cieza again establishes the problem and he is determined to give it a final solution. In the first place he underlines the great abundance of gold in Nueva Granada. In the second place he marks the importance of the great trade of gold with which it seems he wants to emphasize that there is a great demand of gold in the market. In the third place, he establishes that, in spite of the great supply of gold or as it is expressed in the text "as it is much", in face of the great demand or, as it is also said in the text before "so big is the trade" in gold, the price in gold cannot increase, that is "it cannot become dearer". There is a fourth consideration, related to the possibility that the price of gold might tend to decrease, "and it makes it be come cheaper" because of particular reasons of the Indians, or rather, because of the knavery of the conquerors, but this question was, later, in chapter 46 annulled by Cieza himself, when he says: "It is another time and they know well how to sell what they have and trade for what they need" and also it has no interest for our purpose. If the interpretation the long paragraph of chapter 31 transcribed above is correct, we can admit that Pedro Cieza de León, following the way open in chapter 14, which we have examined before, insists, in chapter 31 with greater emphasize in the subjective view of the value of gold in function of its abundance or its scarcity. Concluding, we can therefore affirm that Cieza de León's contribution to the theory of money has as a basis the thesis that with the abundance or scarcity of gold its value raises or decreases respectively. And as in the place and time in which he wrote, gold was used as money, it is possible that ultimately his thesis contains the germs of the quantitative theory, and as such it has surely influenced in preparing the way to the quantitative ideas in the Hispanic American world as including in the other countries in XVIth and XVIIth centuries. To these ideas borne in the opportunity of his sojourn in the Valle de Cauca, we must add those who surged during his stay in the province of Los Charcas in 1549, when he visited the city of La Plata, the Villa Imperial and Mount Potosí the grade of irradiation of these last ideas could have been greater, even if the establishing on a basis and the coherence of said suffer certain formal deficiencies. In other respects it is sure that the "Crónica del Perú" has been known, appreciated and very frequently quoted by the Licentiate Juan de Matienzo, in his "Gobierno del Perú" who will be object of our research in the following sections of this work. It would not be very audacious to hint that Cieza's conclusions together with those of his predecessors and contemporaries are an important start for the quantitativism of the "Second Scholastic Economics" both in Europe as in the West Indies.

A contemporary of Cieza's is the Licenciate Pedro de La Gasca. Cieza was in Cartago when he enlisted with the royalists who followed La Gasca's call in July of 1547. The Licenciate de La Gasca only remained a pair of years in the West Indies, between 1546 and 1550, and they were years dedicated to pacifying Perú, enterprise which ended with the defeat and trial of Gonzalo Pizarro in the valley of Xaquixaguana the 9th of April of 1548[23]. But this short time sufficed to grasp with no difficulty the effects of the flood of Potosinian silver on the general level of prices and its space grading both American and European. In fact, immediately after contacting the American lands, in a letter of 12th July 1546 forwarded to the Counsel of Indies he was aware of the regional discrepancy of the system of prices within the same American space, passing from the coast to the hinterland, when he stated that the road was long and painful (from Cartagena) to the New Reign (Santa Fé de Bogotá), and what there was spent, he believed that (the Licenciate Armendáriz) not only would have a lot of work, but he would spend more than what his salary could afford; even if it is not said explicitely that by "hinterlands" they meant spaces rich in gold and silver or emerald mines. In a letter of the 2nd May of

23 LA GASCA (1549).

1549 he not only repeated the principle of the devaluation of gold and silver with the exploitation of new sources, as was the case of the recently discovered mines in the limits of Guamanga and El Cuzco: "Such abundance is expected in these lands, that silver may be worth almost nothing, that it may be considered as unbelievable, because even now it is so for those who do not see it". But in this last letter it is evident that La Gasca wanted to demonstrate - mentioning concrete cases of prices of the most different products, goods and services - that in the mining areas, specially in the silver focus of Potosí high land, prices were very high as compared to those of the same products in Lima, precisely due to the major abundance of silver in those areas. But we find considerations of major interest for us in his letter to the Counsel of Indies of the 28th January of 1549, in which he establishes his awareness of the great difference of the purchasing power of gold in the West Indies as compared to Spain: "What in Spain may be bought with a 'real' is not bought in the Indies with a gold peso". With this, all the problem that is behind what we today formulate with the abbreviation PPP (Purchasing Power Parity), is forestalled, as it makes us see that the parity of the purchasing power of a gold peso in the Indies is given by a "real" in Spain. The Licenciate de La Gasca establishes with this the foundation of the monument that will be built in 1556 to the glory of Dr. Martín de Azpilcueta Navarro and of the following European and American constructors of the PPP.

But the record of velocity of intuition of the violent inflation that was lived in Perú in the middle of the XVIth Century is due to Don Andrés Hurtado de Mendoza, Marquis of Cañete, the third Peruvian viceroy, that in that time was the same as to say South American viceroy of the Spanish province in the Americas[24]. He entered the waters of Nombre de Dios in Terra Firma together with the fleet of Sevilla and a few days after landing and crossing the isthmus he wrote concisely to the king in a long letter dated in Panamá the 16th March of 1556: "Only here I have understood what happens here and there". The first thing

---

24 HURTADO DE MENDOZA (1566).

that called his attention, or better still, he experimented personally having to pay the expenses "of having to go from his house in Nombre de Dios to Chuquisaca" with money of his own; he immediately underlined the phenomenon of the Indian high prices remarking with worry that he was sorry for the Spaniards in the West Indies when he saw that land was so expensive, and associating right away the American high prices with the growing abundance of gold and silver of the Peruvian mines our newly arrived viceroy offered his quantitativist explanation: "Because as the land is rich, money is worth very little". In the very short time of thirty American days, Don Andrés Hurtado de Mendoza diagnosticated accurately that the revolution of prices which was suffered, first in the Indies and later in Spain, was due to the opulence of its gold and silver mines and above all to the powerful mining centre of Potosí. And if this could be understood in only a month and placed in a site like Panamá it can be presumed - in addition that he had at least copies of the letters of his predecessors, and of course correspondence of the Licenciate La Gasca, the Pacifier of Perú - that the idea for long floated in the air, specially in the poles of mining exploitation, and it was common knowledge to the persons who were acquainted with business in the West Indies.

A more detailed examination of the writings produced by the Court (Audiencia) of Charcasallows to verify, actually, that this doctrine cropped out from the beginning of its activities in Chuquisaca the 7th September of 1561. The President and two judges of the Court of the Charcas - as if they would have wanted to mark the birth of a real economic school - stated the essence of their quantitative doctrine by means of a formal "Letter to His Catholic Royal Majesty" dated in the city of La Plata the 1st February 1562. In this letter is made evident what any connoisseur of the province of Los Charcas could not but know, that is the great difference in the level of prices between Lima and Potosí: "In Potosí things ordinarily are four times dearer than in Lima", is established in the Letter to the King of 1562, and presently the magistrates of Chuquisaca review two fundamental explanations of this anomalous gap of 400 % in the level of the prices between

Lima and Potosí. In the first place they insist on the influence of spatial economy factors: distance, the means of transportation of the goods who came from Spain via Porto-Bello - Panamá - Lima - Arequipa and their respective transportation costs. But at the same time they emphasize the decisive influence of the quantitative factor, precisely in an environment toward which gravitate the irradiating forces of a real focus of development gravitates, the Mountain of Potosí, the symbol of the fabulous riches and also of the price revolution as far as the ultimate boundaries of the recently born Capitalism.

It is that - as the President and judges of Charcas argued - "Where there is more money always things are more expensive". It is a brief and clear reply similar to the one given by Matienzo years later in his "Gobierno del Perú", and much more precise than the classical thesis of Juan Bodin (1530 - 1596), who "will discover" in 1569 the half loose nexus between the level of prices and the volume of precious metals instead of the volume of the money[25] as the magistrates of La Plata had confirmed so exactly (1562) the thesis of La Gasca (1544) and Marquis de Cañete (1566).

If the members of the Court of Charcas could deem evident their quantitativist thesis in an environment like Chuquisaca and Potosí, they did not have great expectations as to the receptivity of their doctrine in the metropolitan world. They knew that there their thesis could find oppositions and produce reticences. To counteract such possibility they decided "on demand of some officials of this Court", to gather testimonies of people learned in the affairs of Indian businesses and send this "Information" to the king together with the letter of February

25 "I believe that the high prices we suffer come from three causes: the principal and almost the only one is the abundance of gold and silver; the second cause is due to the monopolies, the third to the penury originated by the exportations as by the ravage; the last is the entertainment of the kings and great lords, that raises the price of the things they like" in Jean BODIN, Responses aux paradoxes du Sire de Malestroit ..., Paris 1568. The Spanish Version of the text in Oreste POPESCU, Introducción a la Ciencia Económica Contemporánea, Barcelona ^{3}1968, p. 240.

1562. We ignore the contents and the destiny of those "Information" but its mere mentioning them is a clear sign of the popularity and ample attachment of the people from Chuquisaca and Potosí to the quantitativist thesis of the value of money.

Here we totally transcribe this important text, which doctrine will unite in the economic approach, since their first steps, the magistrates of the Court of Los Charcas:

> "... they order (by command of the Viceroy of Perú) that in Potosí must be kept the fees of Lima; the zeal could be good but they have been misinformed because in Potosí things are four times more expensive than in Lima ordinarily and when they are cheaper they are the double than in Lima, and this is easy to understand as the goods are brought from Lima, which is three hundred leagues far, half by land and half by sea ... and furthermore, where there is more money things are dearer as everything will be explained to Your Majesty by the information that goes together with this on demand of some of the officials of this Court".

To all this another consideration should be added, which rises from a "letter to the king" from the city of La Plata the 22nd October 1561. This is too an adjoined letter signed by the President Licenciate Pedro Ramírez, and the Judges Licenciate Matienzo and Licenciate López de Haro, and in which we find that the Souverains of Castilla had already been informed by the *door keepers* of the Court of the spectacular expensiveness of this land "because in this city everything costs very high prices", and they (the souverains) demanded the newly arrived magistrates of the Court, by the Royal Decree of Valladolid of the 15th July 1559, to send report on the situation of this province so as to decide on salary policies. It is highly expressive that the magistrates of La Plata answered the king that "in fulfilment of Your Majesty's orders by means of (the decree), the information that adjoins this was gathered, and Your Majesty will see by means of it the *great expensiveness* of everything that is suffered in this Province"[26].

Neither this "Information" of October 1561 got to us, but we must be aware of the likeness of this information of October 1561 to the one mentioned in the letter to the king of February 1562. May it not be that they are the same documents, but whichever were the answer there are no doubts that the purpose of the documents if not identical is very similar; to verify and explain the reason of the *great expensiveness* in the city of La Plata and the Villa Ymperial de Potosí.

5. The Indian Scholastics (1567 - 1791)

The West Indies scholastics extends - as well as Indian mercantilism - from the beginning to the end of the colonial period. Its born representatives are the doctors, generally theologians, whose working places are the universities or convents of the religious orders. As the West Indies scholastics was a transplant of Spanish scholastics, the former has equally deep Aristotelian roots, and as such, the world of business is localized in moral philosophy and its three branches: ethics, politics and economics. But also, according to the doctors in both laws, with their seats in the universities; or according to the entries of the royal audiencies, said business has an origin in the world of contracts, among which an important place is occupied by the contract of bargain and sale, commonly called, since Raymundo de Peñafort, of the "Tratos y contratos", that is "trade and contracts of merchants". The treaties on moral philosophy, including the treaties with rules for confessing, on justice and law and of deals and contracts are the three basic sources for the world of business of the scholastical economics in the West Indies as well as in Europe.

---

26 RAMÍREZ, MATIENZO and LÓPEZ DE HARO, "Carta a su Majestad", La Plata, 22nd. October 1561, in: LEVILLIER (Ed.), (1921), pp. 21s.

The identification of the writings that interest the world of business is more difficult in the scholastic works because they have rarely been published in Spanish. It is convenient to recall, concerning this, the brilliant considerations of Guillermo Furlong when he published his History of Rioplatense philosophy in colonial epoch:

> "Almost all documents with which we have worked are written in Latin. The ignorance of this language on the part of those who have wanted to write about the philosophical doctrines of the (colonial) past has prevented them to reach the sources. That explains so many and so deplorable extravagancies, even in writing, that carry the signature of studious and well meaning men"[27].

To explore the process of the spread of late scholastics in Hispanic America we have made a sampling of the principal works drafted among us, in order to guarantee, on one side its temporal distribution along the three centuries of the Hispanic period (Spanish and Portuguese); and, on the other hand, its regional expansion in all the West Indies area. As a result we have been able to prove the weight of these authors concerning the period 1550 to 1700, but with a dispersion circle from the beginning of the XVIth Century until the ending of the XVIIIth Century, as demonstrated in the writings of the Dominicans on the first half of the XVIth Century and those of the Jesuits on the XVIIth and XVIIIth Centuries. Its regional distribution is polarized in the surroundings of Mexico in the North and Chuquisaca (Sucre, at present) and Córdoba in the South. At the starting point, about 1567 / 1569 is the Licenciate Juan de Matienzo[28] and the Master in Theology Tomás de Mercado from de University of Mexico[29], and at the end of colonial dominion in America, in 1791 Professor Domingo Muriel

---

27 FURLONG (1952).

28 MATIENZO (1558, 1567, 1580), LOHMAN VILLENA (1966), POPESCU (1982).

29 MERCADO (1571), SAYOUS (1928), LARAZ (1943), GRICE-HUTCHINSON (1952, 1978, 1990), SÁNCHEZ ALBORNOZ (1959, 1977), WEBER (1962), POPESCU (1967, 1968, 1986, 1987, 1988, 1990), VILLAR (1969), CRAVERO (1983), BAECK (1988).

from the Universitiy of Córdoba. Moreover, as we have just seen we must advance the starting point of West Indies scholastics beginning, in 1542, with the Licenciate Bartolomé de Las Casas, who was, without doubt, one of the most learned West Indies scholastics, as it can be seen from the study of his treatises, even if his field was more that of social philosophy. But we must acknowledge that the field of economic analysis was not his strong point even though as he was interested in social development programs, and as we have read, we have found him participating actively in the controversy about the quantitativist theory of money, and especially anticipating, in 1542, the thesis that the revolution of prices in Spain was the consequence of the flux of the American treasure. His solid knowledge was the field of social philosophy, the tools of which he used as firearms to near his goal, the liberation of the Indians, even if it only were a centimeter more. Also from this section we have from him some remembrances for the history of Indian economic thought, such as, for example, the correct use of the sentence "*ceteris paribus*" which he mentions expressely or the repeated use of the expression "natural liberty" so dear to the author of the "Wealth of Nations".

When the writings of the West Indies scholastics appeared it was evident that they found all the basic pieces of their "New Economics" already elaborated, with sweat and blood, by their predecessors, "the West Indies mercantilists" with the help of their science and their West Indies "*ispiriencia*". But far from us to impair their intrinsical merits, the principal of which is to have known how to weld in a consistent theory the flux of Aristotelian-Thomistic contributions and of the Spanish and foreign scholastics together with the contributions of the West Indies mercantilists and to strengthen and to polish them.

Juan de Matienzo published the following works which are of interest to us "Dialogus Relatoris et Advocati Pintiani Senatus" (Valladolid 1558), "Gobierno del Perú" (Chuquisaca 1567 m.s), and "Commentaria in librum quintum recolectiones legum Hispaniae"

(Madrid 1580, 3rd edition Madrid 1613)[30]. If Mercado founded the School of Mexico, Matienzo has the merit of founding the School of Chuquisaca in Hispanic America, integrated by all the magistrates of Charcas[31].

Tomás de Mercado's fundamental work is, to our purpose the "Summa de tratos y contratos", published in Salamanca in 1569 and newly edited in Sevilla in 1571 and 1587. With the manuscripts of his Summa in his knapsack, Mercado travelled to Spain to publish his works, whose doctrine was elaborated on the facts of Indian economic life that was partaken by his order in the Mexican Province (Dávila Padilla). His work is one of the most important, not only in America but also in the world of his time[32].

Bartolomé de Albornoz published his "Arte de los contractos" in Valencia, in 1573[33]. Because of his agressive polemical spirit his works

---

30 He was born in Valladolid the 22nd February 1520, city where he coursed universitary studies, reaching the degree of Licentiatein Law. After seventeen years in the Valladolid Court of Justice he was sent to America as Judge in the Charcas Court of Justice that was just created. He remained there from the 7th September 1561 until his death, on the 15th August 1579.

31 RAMÍREZ DE QUIÑONES (President), MATIENZO, LÓPEZ DE HARO Y PÉREZ DE RECALDE.

32 According to the Spanish editors contemporary of the Summa (Madrid, 1975 and 1977) Mercado would have been born in Sevilla, but those who have researched his life and work, Nicolás Antonio in 1648 and in our time the Professor Wilhelm Weber in 1962, repeatedly certified that Tomás de Mercado was born in Mexico. There is no doubt that he entered in the Convent of Santo Domingo of Mexico, where he obtained the degree of Master in Theology granted by the University of Mexico and he was lecturer in the Dominican Convent of that city. In 1575, loaded with the glory of having withnessed the tremendous success of the two editions of his work in Spain, Mercado decided to return to Mexico. But he fell ill during the sea voyage and he died on sight of the Mexican coasts. His mortal remains rest in Mexican waters in front of San Juan de Ulloa in Veracruz.

33 In the works of the last two Centuries his name appears as Díaz Albornoz (Canga Arguelles 1808), Bartolomé Fr'as de Albornoz (Iparraguirre 1954), Doctor Frías (Picón Salas 1944) and Frias Bartolomé de Albornoz (Rahola

have been censured. Notwithstanding, we must stress that Nicolás Antonio, as Oñate and Solórzano dared to quote him, the latter greatly praising him. The importance of his work is that he poses questions and gives answers in the line of economic scholastics and that his doctrine was built based on his American experiences and surely also on his teaching experiences acquired during his long stay in the University of Mexico.

Luis López (Ludovicus Lopez), in many aspects a follower of Bartolomé de Las Casas published his writings "Instructorium conscientiae, duabus contentum partibus" (Salamanca 1585, 2nd ed. Lyon 1588, 3rd ed. Salamanca 1592) and the "Tractatus de contractibus et negotiationibus" (Salamanca 1589, Lyon 1594, Brescia 1596, translated to Italian, Venice 1590)[34]. We know that during his long sojourn in the Indias he was closely acquainted both with the policies practiced by the Indian "encomenderos" and with the merchants.

The theologian Luis López is contemporary of Molina and probably that is the reason why his writings and also his life are seldom mentioned by the Spanish spoken critics. Among the Hispanic American

1885). The same happens with the title of his work that almost always appears mentioned in scientific writings as "Arte de los contratos". He was born in Talavera, probably around 1510 and 1515, and he was a disciple of Diego de Covarrubias. He obtained his degree of Licentiate in Law at the University of Osuna. He arrived to the Indias in 1550. He was the first professor of Civil Law of the recently created University of Mexico.

34 His biographic data are very poor. Luis López was born in Madrid about 1520, where he studied Theology. Afterwards we find him as missionary in the province of Chiapa and in Guatemala, where "plures annos Indorum saluti vigilanter incubuit" (Nicolás Antonio). The comments gathered in his two works arose, greatly from the overwhelming quantity of problems he had to endure in the American lands. We ignore the date of his return to Spain. But we have information that he returned with the purpose of interesting King Phillip IInd to remedy the condition of the American Indians. Hoeffner affirms that he was professor in Salamanca. He was also Provincial of the Dominicans of Spain. There (in Spain) he took care of the edition of his two works that have had an important echo in the scientific world because of its numerous editions and translations. He died in 1595.

scholastics mostly Oñate and Avendaño quote him frequently. Yet, his theory of just price is well developed in Chapter 63 of the "Instructorium Conscentiae" (Part II, 1585) and in Chapters 14 and 42 of the "Tractatus de contractibus et negotiationibus" (Book I, 1589). His bibliographic quotings, are very frequent. The high polemical content of his critic considerations have been very fruitful for the continuing development of late scholastic economy, and the grade of influence that it undoubtedly had, including in the ideas of Molina and Lesio (Lessius) has not been sufficiently studied yet.

The name of Pedro de Oñate was forgotten on the shelves of the libraries of the Hispanic American cultural past. His works "De Contractibus", whose three volumes with 3.586 pages in two columns and published in Rome, 1645 - 1654[35], was rescued by Father Guillermo Furlong, who roused the attention of the Argentine jurist Vicente Osvaldo Cutolo, author of a work titled "La Primera Obra de Derecho Escrita en la Argentina del Siglo XVII" ("The First Work of Law written in the Argentine of the Seventeenth Century") published in 1954. The work of Cutolo - lately also endorsed by the Argentinian historian Vicente D. Sierra ("Historia de la Argentina", Buenos Aires 1957, 2nd ed. 1967 V.2. p.590) - compels us to infer that also with this was located "The First Work of Economic Theory, in the Argentine of the Seventeenth Century", because the two parts of the third volume of "De Contractibus" are a complete and oustanding work on economics, probably the greatest work on Indian scholastic economics. The fact that the bibliographical material used, is concentrated in its last stage, in the first twenty years of the XVIIth Century strengthens the hypothesis that the manuscript referred to economic subjects could have been started during his sojourn in Córdoba, as Provincial of the Jesuitic Province of Paraguay (including the regions of Rio de la Plata, Tucumán, Paraguay, Uruguay and Chile; it is the area that today is named "el Cono Sur") between 1615 and 1624, though it is possible that the gathering of material and the examination of cases

35 OÑATE (1646 - 1654), POPESCU (1980 a, 1986 c, 1987 and 1988).

had taken place previously, between 1592 and 1614, when he was Master of Novices in the city of Lima and Rector of the Colleges of Potosí, La Paz and Chuquisaca, which was seat of the Court of Charcas with jurisdiction over all the provinces of the Rio de la Plata.

We must stress the great effort of systematization carried about by Oñate and his purpose of synthesizing the multiple aspects that were being evident in the scientific production of the XVIIth Century. In this respect I believe that it is correct to place Oñate in the same line with the great systematic works of Juan de Lugo in Spain and of Giambattista de Luca in Italy[36].

A little after the publication of the last volumes of Oñate's "De Contractibus", there appeared in the Virreinato of Peru, another work, the

---

36 A serious biographical research on this author is needed. Apparently he was born in Valladolid the 7th January 1567, and died in Lima the 31st December 1646. He entered the Compañia de Jesús the 12th March 1586. After getting his degree of Bachellor of Arts in Salamanca and of Licentiate in Law in the University of Alcalá, where he also started his Theology studies We know "that being still a student he was sent to Perú" under the direction of Father Diego de Zuñiga, who obtained the authorization by a royal decree of the 11th July 1590 - that is, when Oñate was twenty three years old - and he arrived at Lima the 20th December 1592. His professional and missionary training continued in Perú; there he was Master of Novices (destined to the Indians) for three years in the School of El Cercado. After, he was Rector of the Colleges of the Compañia de Jesús, in Potosí, La Paz and Chuquisaca for nearly ten years. We know for certain that he was granted the profession of four vows in the Compañia de Jesús, the 18th October 1604, in the Jesuitic mission of Juli, by the Titicaca lake, experimentation plant of missional training of the Compañia. His first important position in Lima was that of associate (coadjutor) of the Provincial and finally he was nominated Provincial of the Jesuitic Province of the Rio de la Plata, Paraguay, Tucumán, Chile and Uruguay, which see was Córdoba, since 1615 until 1624. As Provincial he founded several Jesuitic Colleges and showed great interest in securing the high academic level of the University of Córdoba that was recognized as University by the Pope and the King under his administration, and Oñate himself drafted its academic Constitution. After this he retired to the Colegio Máximo de Lima, where he was in charge of very high positions in the Jesuitic Province of Perú. He died a week before his eightieth birthday.

"Thesaurus Indicus", in six volumes with about 2.500 pages in Latin, published in Amberes (1660 - 1678), by the Professor of the University of Lima and of Chuquisaca, Diego de Avendaño (1594 - 1668). It is really difficult to ascertain which of the two works soars higher. But if we limit ourselves only to the field of economic science, I believe that Diego de Avendaño could rival Oñate, but his proficiency is not the analytical field in which Oñate excells, but is more in the area of economic policy in the broad sense of the statement, including consequently, in the social policy also the specific aspects of the economic wellfare policy.

In 1791 there appeared, in Venice, the work of Cyriaco Morelli "Rudimenta juris naturae et Gentium", in a 388 pages volume. For more than a century Hispanic American criticism was unconcerned with the author who had an Italian surname and whose work was written in Latin. When, at the beginning of this century - because of some testimonies from the end of the XVIIIth century - the critics started to investigate the matter, they could "discover" that the Italianized "Morelli" and the Hellenized "Cyriaco" (Kyrios, Greek; Dominicus, Latin; Domingo, Spanish) were the pen-names of Domingo Muriel[37]. His work is in the line of the late scholastics, but to be able to duly appraise it, it is necessary to take into consideration that it was drafted in a time agitated by the appearance of the Encyclopaedia, the Declaration of the Independence of the United States of America and the outburst ot the French Revolution. A work entitled "Elements of natural law and law of nations" could not but reflect these events. The roots of the doctrine supported in the work start from the Aristo-

---

37 He was born in Tamames, Salamanca, in 1718, and entered the Compañia de Jesús in 1734. He was one of the most conspicuous Hispanic-American Historiographers and glory of the University of Córdoba del Tucumán where he had been professor of Philosophy (1751) and of Moral Theology (1753) and he had been appointed University Rector (1767) but he could not take possession of the latter position due to the expulsion of the Compañia de Jesús from the Indias. Still more adverse was the fortune of his work, that was not only object of a very deficient translation but the translator also ingored Muriel's real surname.

telian-Thomist doctrine and furtherly continues through the works of the great Spanish and Hispanic American Scholastics, to end opposing the philosophers of Illuminism. Thus, Muriel establishes a strong connection between Late Scholastics and Neoscholastics. Muriel's theory is one of the scientific productions that follows the line of Spanish Scholastics, but simultaneously it is one of the first with which the scholastical restoration in Europe was started, via Italy, and also in Hispanic-America.

We have now to try to take inventory of the theorical contributions of Indian economic scholastis. The starting point of the quantitativism of Hispanic-American scholastics is monetary theory and this, in its turn is a chapter of the general theory of value and of prices. Respecting the theory of value, its considerations revolve about two subjects: The labour theory of value and the subjective theory of value. The attitude of the Hispanic-American scholastics is that of a total and unanimous rejection of the first. "One of the greater errors of the merchants - reflects Mercado - lays on the obstinacy in taking as a basis of their estimates the costs of their wares" (Vol. II, Chap. XV). Albornoz states identical terms. Matienzo, López and Oñate reprove John Duns Scotus (1266 - 1308) for claiming that the production cost was the source or the cause of value. They reply in unison: "It is a most fallacious rule". López affirms:

> "... haec est alea sortis & fortunae mercatorum, quoad duritia negotiantur debent victrix; sorti sicut lucrandi,ita & perdendi se exponere, iuxta temporum & circunstantiarum praedictarum varietatem; unde fallacissima regula est si semper quanto emit pretio; & quantum periculi & laboris subivit, tantum velit vendere" (Instr. Consc., Pars II, cap. 63).

To determine the logical source of value, the Hispanic- American scholastics resort to the subjective Theory of Value. Following the line of Aristotle, Aurelius Agustinus and St. Thomas Aquinas, Mercado emphasizes that "in no nation is anything appraised according to its natural value, but according to our necessity and usage, which give them esteem and value" (Book II, Chapter 6). Albornoz, who follows

Mercado closely was on the brink of reaching the analysis of marginal utility, without finally succeeding (Book II, Tit. 16). López binds closely the "raritas" to the concept of the subjective theory of value; Matienzo accomplishes to pose the question and find the solution of the paradox that Adam Smith will expound two centuries later in his Theory of Value. And Oñate systematizing all the contributions in the defense of the theory of subjective value, synthesizes his thoughts thus: "Value is not something intrinsical and real in things"; its basis takes root in "the estimation of men ... which is unimportant to be truthful or to be false, ... as also, that which is false has true effect of causing a real and just price". That is, following Oñate, that the subjective Theory of Value, leads to the theory of prices: "Price is the just measure of the saleable value expressed in terms of money" (Treat. 21, disp. 63). It is as if we read Alfred Marshall who, in 1890 stated: "Price is the value of everything expressed in terms of money". Domingo Muriel, who wrote in a time in which the objective theory was outstanding in Political Economy, does not even mention it. For him, the preferred authors of treatises are always Vitoria, Azpilcueta, Covarrubias and Leiva, Matienzo, Mercado, Molina, López, Lugo, Oñate and, of course the "Very Eminent" Suárez, giving full evidence of his having known the great scholastics and not forgetting to mention St. Thomas Aquina: the basis of value is inaltered, just as it was characterized by the scholastic orthodoxy, "according to the common estimation of the goods".

Also in the theory of prices the contributions of the Hispanic-American scholastics have been really fruitful. In the first place, they had a clear concept about the determining forces of the formation and variations of prices. They clearly differentiated between the forms of open market and closed market. In open markets they worked with theory of "natural just price" (also called: current, vulgar or accidental) while in closed markets they did it with the theory of "legal just price" (also called: "la tasa"). On the other hand they differentiated very well between the free competition and the monopolic markets. Tomás de Mercado had already talked about the "trader agreements (that we call the monipodio)", and this happens on the side of the buyers, as on the side of the sellers (Book II, Chapter 8, G. 2 and 3).

Albornoz suggests maintaining the name of "monipodio" only for the buyers, since the sellers go by the name of monopoly, which is more correct, since etymologically, and in this Oñate also agrees, in Greek, "monos" means single, and "poleo" means sell, anticipating by several centuries the typology of Joan Robinson. Tomás de Mercado, Matienzo and López even identify the market in which a monopolic seller comes face to face with a monopolic buyer. While Mercado continues to condemn this type of market, López thinks that the buyers' monopoly may be an effective way of confronting the sellers' monopoly, and as such justifies its existence, Oñate on the other hand, not only christens it "pandopolium" but better justifies its advantages. Actually, observes Oñate, the "pandopolium" is almost a normal market in Panamá. If, to the cunning of the Peruvian buyers, who agree not to buy if it is not at a price lower than the just price, the Spanish traders reply with identical agreement and cunning establishing prices above the natural price:

> "They would compensate reciprocally for the two identical delicts and as one nail knocks another out, one monopoly would prevent another one or better, from the mutual agreement, there would result a just price ... In this joint determination of the price, there is nothing unjust ... one could consider it a very just and fair global agreement".

It is evident from here, that we are dealing with a double monopoly and in fact he labels it "monopolia bina" which is nothing more than the "Bilateral Monopoly" by Bowley (1928) - foreseen by Marshall (1890)-, by Zeuthen (1933) and others.

Oñate also points out its nature detected with almost the same foresight as Galbraith expresses in his theory of countervailing power (1952). Even more, Oñate following closely, the conclusions of López in the discussion of the well-known case of the merchant of Venice becomes sharply aware of the duopolistic market, which he condemns as severely as he does the monopolists. This will later be thoroughly investigated in economics following the publications of Cournot (1838), Bertrand (1880) and Edgeworth (1897). On the other hand, Oñate, following up the linings of Tomás de Mercado and the warnings of Albornoz, will find various elements for the identification of the partial oligopolic market, which later economics will develop thanks to the concentrated efforts of Chamberlin (1929 - 1933), Schneider (1930 - 1932), Frisch (1933), Stackelberg (1933 - 1934), etc. With regard to the public monopolies the attitude of the Hispanic American Scholastics was benign. The justification was based in fiscal considerations; in reasons relevant to social welfare - as Mercado understood the "estancos", and Albornoz understood the "cotos", which were formed to import goods and to protect the produce of the farmers hoarded by the oligopolists and put it up for sale at moderate prices; or for the promotion of certain trades, such as editorial firmes and restaurants, suggested by López; or finally the promotion of silver mining, like the well known "estanque del azogue" in Juancaválica, in Perú, which Oñate considered a "just monopoly".

The theory of the natural just price had its roots in the idea of competition and the Hispanic-American scholastics made their contributions having in view not only the writings of their Spanish teachers but also the empirical knowledge gathered as observers of the economic process in the fairs and markets of our regions. Their remarks are important. Actually, in spite of the fact that in the formulation of the theory of value they insisted in the concept of subjective value, in the formulation of their price theory, they took into consideration, in a Marshallian way, the subjective elements on the side of the demand together with the objective aspects on the side of the supply. Of course they did not use the terms demand and supply, but incidentally, as in the case of Mercado, who stressed several times the role of the "demand" (Book II, Chapter 18 and 20), which is significative for the History of Economic Thought. Neither did they give the word "concurrence" the sense it has in the specialised literature in German and French languages of our time and whose usage goes as far back as the Roman jurist Paulo. Our scholastics have been more inclined to use the terms competition (competencia), outbidding (puja), bidding at auction (licitación), including contest (contienda), words which frequently appear, not only in the Spanish writings but in those written in Latin, from Mercado (Book II, Chapter 8, G.4), Albornoz (Book II, Tit. 16, f. 66 E) and Oñate (Tract. 21, disput. 63, No. 61, 63, 164 and 167) up to Muriel (Book I, disp. XI, p. 164). True it is that our writers have had the intention of something related to the game of supply and demand, but, excepting Oñate who most neared the goal (Tract. 21, disput. 63, No. 60) referring to St. Agustine, have they never formulated it in such terms. The focal point of their considerations always revolve about the factors that cause the raise and fall of prices in the free market. Mercado offers a good example: "We see in the market that if there are many garments, they are cheap; if there are few buyers, cheaper still; if there is little money they are given away for almost nothing. On the contrary if there are few garments, this makes them to be esteemed; if there are many who buy, the price increases and more so they do if there is an abundance of money" (Book II, Chapter 7, F.1).

Still more illustrative is Matienzo, who from the beginning observes that for the formation of the just price a great many elements have to be taken into account. The two pairs of fundamental factors - and I would add common to all Hispanic- American scholastics - are "abundance and scarcity of merchandise and the affluence of buyers and sellers in the market". But to this he adds considerations related to the "necessity of the thing; the merchant's work and his cares, its industry and its risks; if the goods were changed into something better or suffered any damage; and the abundance or scarcity of money". Matienzo adds still more to the theory of prices: the variations produced by temporal or spatial factors, factors related to the personality of the participating parties in the market, the prevalence of monopolic or competitive structures of the market, the more or less explicit expectations on the future behaviour of the different variables and its weight at the time on the general level of prices, etc. (Tit. 11, Act. 1, gl. 2; Tit. 14, Act. 1, gl. 9; Tit. 12, Act. 1, gl. 1; Tit. 14, Act. 1, gl. 9).

And after producing this inventory of the most important factors to be incorporated in the theory of prices, he considers his duty to add that the vicissitudes in the level of prices caused by the total of these permanently changing factors is a process that he, himself could verify: "All this happens every day in the occasional fairs and markets, as occurs daily in the Reign of Perú" (Tit. 11, Act. 1, gl. 2).

Still more impressing is the inventory carried out by Oñate, who added for every situation a great deal of cases, equally compiled, in the most part, by his own observation carried out "frequently in the Paraguayan region" (Treat. 21, disput. 61, No. 47).

When the Hispanic-American scholastics effected this detailed inventory of almost all the elements which influence or conform at their turn the analytical tools of those who participate in the market confrontment, they have carried out a pioneering effort towards the building of a theory of prices in a time in which the world just started to prepare itself to profit fruitfully from such amount of knowledge.

As to the policy of prices, Oñate participates in the opinions of his predecessors, that both the legal price and the price of the free market are two real forms consistent with the ideal type of natural price, but he observes that both are not equally just, and as such they require permanent adjustments concerning the natural price of the scholastic theory. "The natural price does not always coincide with the current market price", severely states Oñate, who immediately explains: "These two prices are very different, and according to our judgement they must be well distinguished one from the other. Actually, the current price, even that of all the country may sometimes be unjust on account of frauds, monopolies and the power of the rich. Instead, the natural price, the price dictated by honest reasoning after all the circumstances of the case have been considered and pondered, can never be unjust but it corrects and rectifies the legal price and the current price when they distort" (Tract. 21, disp. 64, No. 36).

Let us now try to examine more closely some considerations about the area of monetary theory, and particularly the quantitativist theory of the value of money. The aspect which draws more our attention is the attempt of integrating monetary theory to the general theory of prices, an imperative issue which lasted until the present time. The linking bridge of both subjects was the idea of *estimatio*, "esteem", that is the purchasing power of money, which depends in its turn on *ceteris paribus*, of its *abundantia vel penuria*, abundance or scarcity. From this fundamental vision, product of the Indian experience and of the study of their teachers of classical and late scholastics, came forth two other contributions of great importance for the development of economics: one related to the internal value of money, the quantitative theory of money; the other a logical consequence of the former, related to the external value of money, the theory of the purchasing power parity.

The most brilliant representative of the monetary theory and the most celebrated by the specialised criticism is Tomás de Mercado (cf. A. E. Sayous, 1927 and 1928; J. Larraz, 1943 and Wilhelm Weber, 1962 who, besides, and like Marjorie Grice Hutchinson knows he is talking about a Mexican Scholastic).

The most interesting fact is that in his statements Mercado develops simultaneously both theories. This is the key text:

> "... It must be taken into account that the value and price of money and its esteem are not the same thing. A very clear example of this is that in the Indies the value of money is the same as it is here; one real, thirty four marvedis, one mine peso, thirteen reales, and the same is its value in Spain. But, notwithstanding the value and price are the same, the esteem is very different in both places: that much less is it esteemed in Indies than in Spain ... After the Indies where it is less esteemed, is in Sevilla, as it is a city that recieves all that is good that comes from the Indies, then the other parts of Spain follow. It is very much esteemed in Flanders, in Rome, in Germany, in England. Such esteem and appreciation is caused in the first place because there is a great abundance and scarcity of these metals and as in those parts of the Indies they are found and gathered, they are lowly considered ... A

very clear example of this is that even within the boundaries of Spain (having the ducados and the maravedis the same value) we see that they have a much greater esteem for them in Castilla than in Andalucía. And even in the same city, because of the diversity of the times we find the same discrimination: that thirty years ago 200,000 maravedis was a handsome sum, at present they are estimated in nothing, yet being the maravedis of the same price of money. Because, the different estimation that the times have made in a same nation on account of several events, cause the reasons I expounded at the same time in different reigns" (Book IV, Chapter 5, cc. 3 y ss).

Once that the essence of the purchasing power of money which he calls "esteem" (estima) is made clear, we should try to find a trace of the concept of the velocity of circulation of money. I believe he was bordering the subject, as it follows from this text:

"Money is better present than absent, many learned teachers say ... Finally, as they say, it is better to have a bird in the hand than two in the bush ... speaking plainly it is better to have money in cash than to wait for it. Though for many men it is better not to have it. For the merchants present money is not better than the absent one, on the contrary, the absent money has more value than the one in the hand".

Hitherto the quantitative theory has been expounded. It remains to find the theory of the purchase power parity in Mercado. Now then, this different esteem of money confirmed from one country to another and from one time to another in the same country is the dynamic resource of international changes; their cause and, at the same time their justificarion. Referring to justice he states the following:

"The justice of the exchanges now in use, lies upon and is originated in the different esteem of money that occurs in different places, and this suffices to justify them".

Referring to the cause, he states his reality in the following way:

"Modern changes are based in the different esteem of money, of the totality of a republic or reign: as we see that, in all

Flanders, in all Rome, money is more esteemed than it is in all Sevilla, and in Sevilla more than in the Indies; and in the Indies more in Santo Domingo than in Nueva España; and in Nueva España more than in Peru ... And the money changers and the exchange have an eye to appraise this different esteem".

Mercado enunciates the principle of purchase power parity in the following paragraph, meaning that the unequal esteem of money in different places equals itself by means of the unequal quantity of interchanged money.

"In this way it happens in money, that because they are more esteemed in some places than in others, they come to be equal, even if the quantity is diverse: ninety three in Flanders against a hundred in Sevilla, not because the ducado is another legal standard or it has another value, but because that land itself pays more attention to money ... Therefore as it is great the advantage the Indias made in the abundance of gold and silver in these kingdoms, there are of equally esteem and reputation seventy "ducados" in the Court (of Castilla) as hundred in Lima and ninety in La Veracruz ... The same is from these lands (of Spain) to Rome, that hundred in Burgos will be as well ninety four in Rome: so that changing the hundred for the ninety four is the same change ... Three things are of the essence of exchange, namely: if the esteem of money be unequal, the unequal quantity makes it equal, this necessarily demands a diversity of places, as a hundred ducados in Sevilla and ninety five in Antwerp are equal in esteem because they are unequal in quantity. The unequal quantity equals the different reputation of money there is in these places".

Mercado's doctrine found an ample accord among the other Hispanic-American scholars, but with different hues; in Albornoz (Book II, Tit. XVI, f. 64 C and Book III, Tit. IV, f. 131 and 132), Matienzo, who did not know neither the author nor his work (Tit. 11, Act. 1, gl. 2 No. 2 and 7), López (Tract. de Contr., Book 11, Chapter 7 and 9; Instr.

Consc., Part II, Chapter 63), to reach, in Oñate, the dimension and grandeur of a complete treaty (Trat. XXIV, pp. 521 - 603).

The monetary problem has not, from the formal point of view a separate treatment in Matienzo's *Commentaria*. This must be undoubtedly due to the fact that its systematic consideration together with the theory of usury would be incorporated in another work which was planned or was probably being prepared and whose destiny we ignore. Consequently, his theory is expressed in fragments that are dispersed in the corpus of his writings, making difficult the work of inventory and analysis of his considerations in this field.

In spite of this formal difficulty the effort of the search and integration of materials in the economic area is compensated by his contributions being so substancial. Effectively as we have aforeseen, and it is convenient to repeat, the factor money is one of many others that have to be taken into account in the formation of prices. Prices rise or fall, he said "with the abundance or scarcity of money: - *Pecunia abundantia vel penuria*. Saying it in other words, Matienzo's monetary theory is another chapter, and as such is an integrant of the general theory of prices. The desire of contemporary economists of integrating the theory of money in the general economic theory is, for our author a solved problem. If we should ask Matienzo about the basic ingredients of the so called law of supply and demand, he would undoubtedly answer that at least in this area, we should incorporate the theory of demand, the theory of supply, the theory of prices and the theory of money.

The incorporation of the theory of money in the theory of price should take place also on account of another reason. Actually Matienzo states, money also, like any other merchandise oscillates in its value, price or esteem. Of course it is necessary to distinguish the intrinsical and the extrinsical variations of money. In the intrinsical variation money is modified in its weight and material, while in the extrinsical variation of money: "with the same weight and the same material, it increases or decreases extrinsically in regard to price or esteem". *Vel quoties pecunia eodem pondere et materia manentibus, vel augetur, vel minuitur extrinsecus quoad eius pretium, vel aestimationem*. But Matienzo does not consider that this very important subject could be furtherly analyzed in the chapter about "Weights and measures to buy and sell goods and maintenance and iron-works" which is the object of the aforementioned chapter 13. And surely thinking in Book 8 of the "Recopilación", he interrumpts the development of the subject, excusing himself thus: "This due to lack of space here we shall expound in another place": *cuius examinatio, quia non vacat modo alibi fiet*. And yet, from the scanty considerations about the intrinsical and extrinsical factors of the variations of the value of money, we can extract the conclusion that effectively for Matienzo, also in the consideration of the monetary problem they should have recoursed to the tools of supply and demand, of abundance and scarcity.This is a quite familiar idea among the Hispanic scholastics of the XVIth Centuries, as Wilhelm Weber demonstrates.

The other monetary aspect we can find in the *Commentaria* is related to the delicate question of money interest. The discussion of this issue is also delayed by this author, as we have already mentioned in the comments about Book eighth of the "Recopilación". But Matienzo's brief statement respecting the possibility of the loan of money being licit, to the concept "just interest" - *interesse justum* - and the compatibility of just interest with an anual rate of ten percent is astonishing. Surprise is increased due to the spontaneous association of ideas produced in the reader's mind when he reminds that Matienzo knows and frequently quotes Carolo Molineus's treaty, nowadays known by historians of economic thought. But, if we bear in mind that formerly, on one side the Church in the Vth Letran Assembly of Bishops in 1515 and on the other the Spanish Monarch himself in 1534, had laid the positive foundations of the doctrine sustained by Matienzo, the question changes its aspect. Actually, we know today that there were very few authors who followed in the XVIth Century the doctrine of "just interest", and this sole fact is enough to emphasize Matienzo's presence among the very few inventoried up to now for said Century.

The third monetary subject and which undoubtedly will interest most of the contemporary studious men, is Matienzo's contribution in the field of the money value theory. The afore mentioned thesis that the prices rise or fall "with the abundance or scarcity of money" is, in itself a consideration which contains the germ of the quantitative theory of money. We should avoid, of course, the dangerous statement that this happened for the first time as the critics did when they dealt with the treaty "Sobre la Justicia y el Derecho" (On Justice and Law) by Luis de Molina. Today we know that at least four authors who were not American and whose works were written before Matienzo's, sustained an identical idea or a more or less similar one. Around 1557 the Spanish chronicler, Francisco López de Gomara (1511 - ca. 1565) wrote in the "Anales del Emperador Carlos V" that the level of prices had raised "because the great quantity of silver and gold that has arrived here from the Indias". In December 1556 and January 1557 Doctor Martín de Azpilcueta Navarro (1492 - 1586) published in Salamanca the first edition of his work "Comentario Resolutorio de Cambios", that the criticism of our time considers as a pioneer in Spain in the development of the quantitivist theory of money value; about thirty years before, Nicholas Copernicus (1473 - 1543) had stated in his work *Monetae cudendae ratio* written in 1526 by suggestion of king Segismund of Poland, that "money is normally despised when it becomes too abundant ..."; and almost a century before, St. Antonino de Florencia (1389 - 1459), affirmed still more vigorously, that "one of the causes of things being more or less valuable is the scarcity or abundance of money among the citizens". Of the four works only the *Summa Theologica* of St. Antonino de Florencia was known by Matienzo, but not the other three, of which two remained unpublished, Gomara's until 1912 and Copernicus's until 1861. It is incredible that Matienzo ignored precisely this writing of Dr. Azpilcueta, whose other works he knew since he was at the University of Valladolid and who he quotes quite frequently; but it is so. Neither Tomas de Mercado quotes him (Azpilcueta) in his Summa. It is also incredible but true. And also respecting the Summa of St. Antonino it must be made clear that though he was acquainted with it, Matienzo ignored completely his thesis related to the influence of money on the general level of prices, as if he would have known it he would have gladly resorted to the authority of the Archbishop of Florence whom he quotes in several opportunities, and not to the authority - in this case we could say "with no just title" - of Domingo de Soto.

There is a second text in the *Commentaria*, of great interest for the history of the quantitativist money theory. In it Matienzo ratifies and enlarges the thesis formulated in the former paragraph. The approach is genuinely inductive and it contemplates, together with the quantitative theory, aspects related to the purchase power parity. The starting point of his consideration is the problem of bread price: "Bread - Matienzo states - is of the same nature in Spain and in the Indies. But here, it is sold dearer than in Spain, because this product is scarcer, but also because there is an abundance of gold and silver, which are the causes of the increased price. *Panis eiusdem naturae est in Hispania et apud Indos, ed maiori hic pretio venditur quam in Hispania, propter indigentiam et argenti aurique abundantiam, quae causae augendi pretium.* This approach is much more advanced in comparison with the three aforementioned predecessors. It also totally covers the approach of Dr. Martín de Azpilcueta Navarro expounded almost a quarter of a century before, and inclusively it seems he surpassed it. Actually while Azpilcueta only takes into consideration the effect of abundance of money immobilizing the other effects with the hypothesis *ceteris paribus*, Matienzo adds to the abundance of money effect, the effect of the demand, in this case the scarcity of demand, as if he would have wanted to insinuate, in modern language that, for him, the level of prices is a direct function of the quantity of money and an inverse function of the volume of transactions: What seems true, however is that also in the case of Azpilcueta, Matienzo passed by his points of view on the theory of money value and so, he lost another opportunity to remit himself to an authority of first level of Spanish scholastics, with the addition that Dr. Azpilcueta's work was published twelve years before Bodin published, in 1568 his reknowned doctrine on quantitative theory which made him famous to our times, but which is in all aspects inferior in its approach to Dr. Azpilcueta Navarro and to Dr. Matienzo.

A more careful exploration of Matienzo's scientific production allows us to conclude that his quantitivist considerations are not only superior to those of Juan Bodin (1530 - 1586) but also to those of former authors. Actually, if we read attentively his "Gobierno del Perú", the writing of which was finished in Chuquisaca, the 24th August 1567, consequently a year before the "Respuesta al Señor de Malestroit" by Juan de Bodin - we find that among other considerations of interest for the scientific researcher, Matienzo specially underlined the close relation, induced in his direct experiences, between the volume of currency and the general price level. Thus is how the subject is narrated by the judge from Charcas: "There are opinions among those who are curious to understand the things of this land, about if it were convenient that gold and silver coins were made here - Some say that land will decrease in value and that everything will be cheaper, because: Who would want to give in 'reales' a hundred 'castellanos' for the making of a garment as they now give? Who would give for a head-dress, that is worth ten 'reales' in Castilla, a thousand or twelve hundred? It will be necessary, therefore, that everything decreases in value. But, none of this inconveniences, in my opinion is enough... to say that land will decrease in value, and that things will lower their price is to guess; rather the contrary is seen everywhere by experience: where there is more money everything is more expensive".

And what would happen if instead of being more abundant, money were less abundant? Matienzo's answer is drastic: "and there being less money, it is clear that everything would be cheaper". Therefore we can conclude that also in the "Gobierno del Perú" the variation of the quantity of money - if the other things remain constant - causes proportional changes in the level of prices. This would be tantamount to say, that within Hegeland's typology - who differentiates three principal variants of the quantitative theory - Matienzo's quantitative theory would be localized in the second variant, because it adds the causality element.

Also, it is worth to point out that the chapter of the "Gobierno del Perú" that has as a rather long title "If it is convenient that there were farms (de pancoger) and that sugar- mills, and cloth mills, and vegetable gardens and vineyards were made and that there were cattle ...", etc.), the Licentiate Matienzo gives an answer of great importance for the history of Hispanic-American economic thought, for that reason we transcribe it almost completely:

> "All this is necessary for the conservation of this land (of Perú); and even though some believe that it is better that there were not of these things, but that they were brought from Castilla, so with them to extract the silver and take it to Spain, I do not know how those who assert this is better, could found their arguments, nor than this should be coveted because the more silver is taken to Castilla and more goods are brought to this land, more expensive will everything be in Spain ...; and if we confess that due to this Spain gets richer, not because of it we should stop trying to make richer and greater this land and its natives because they are the cause of ours being rich ... I would like that those who come to govern it had this consideration in mind perpetually and not to profit from it while they live in it, and returning rich to Spain, do not care if it is lost and finished. This is to tell the truth, whether some like it or not, as all the riches and gifts in the world, in exchange for not telling the truth, I do not give a feather or a fig".

In the paragraph we have just transcribed, in addition to the seeds of the most diverse economic and social conditions we find again the ample image that Matienzo reproduced in his *Commentaria* and accepted the authority of Didacus Pérez de Salamanca, and in which we see together with the effect of the abundance of money also that of the scarcity and demand of goods, and at the same time aspects related to the international changes. But we find all this in a larger or smaller scale in the *Commentaria.* What is new is the consideration on the nature of the Hispanic inflationary tendency of his time, establishing that the historic cause of the increase of the general level of prices in Spain and through it also in the other European countries of its time was due, in the first place to the flux of the American gold and silver. With this Matienzo anticipated two other foreign authors, John Hale or Thomas Smith or William Stafford, to whom is ascribed a writing which is more or less similar and whose date is not very precise, it may probably be 1581, and Noel du Fail, in a work titled "Balivernes et contes d'Eutrapel" published in 1548 of which it is affirmed that it would have anticipated the thesis of the price revolution caused by the American treasure, which is only true for the second edition published in 1584. And he also anticipates in the quantitative theory of money, his American countryman, Master Tomás de Mercado, who, in the same year that Bodin but gathering experiences accumulated in Nueva España, and as Matienzo, with total independence of thought, formulated his quantitativist theory in identical terms.

As in the case of Tomás de Mercado, our author reached his goal because he had the knack of joining to the reading of the classics the sagacious observation and analysis of American economic life. In addition to Matienzo's scholastic doctrinary sources, Matienzo's considerations surge from his observations as a judge in Chuquisaca. This hypothesis is furtherly confirmed by the fact that there is proof - as aforementioned - that in a brief signed by the president and two Chuquisaca magistrates the 1st February 1562, it is collectively formulated - as if he would have wanted to leave a constancy of the birth of the School of Chuquisaca - the germ of the new monetary theory of Hispanic-American scholastics.

Finally, we must remember that Juan de Matienzo also left in his "Gobierno del Perú" a clear constancy that he well knew all the writings of the Hispanic-American chroniclers of the time since the discovery on, and among them he also quotes Cieza de León, who in his

"Crónica del Perú" (1553) stated the considerations about the American quantitativism[38].

6. Retrospective View and Conclusions

It is now the time to look backwards over the road travelled along the foundational period of the Hispanic colonization in America with the aim of making an inventory of the principal contributions to the development of the quantitativist theory of money.

If we want to evaluate the first commercial contact between the Tainos and the Spaniards which is the object of the Navigation Journal of Columbus's first voyage to the Indies, it seems unavoidable to reach the conclusion that during the first trip the free market was the prevailing note with the Taino natives of San Salvador (name given to Guanahaní), the Santa María de la Concepción islet, the Fernandine

---

38 It is not easy to determine precisely the references gathered by Matienzo of Cieza's Chronicle of Peru. This is due to the fact that the original of the manuscript of Matienzo "The Government of Peru" up to now has not been found. Effectively, as he reported in his "letter to the King" of La Plata, 28th. Nov. 1567, with which he sent the original manuscript for its approval and publishing in Spain, this had "marginal notes about philosophers, theologians and many other serious authors". (Cf. Roberto LEVILLIER [ed.], The Charcas Audience, I. p. 238). Unfortunately Matienzo's original manuscript sent to the Counsel of Indies has "disappeared into thin air" and none of the copies found up to now carry the original marginal notes made by Matienzo himself. The editor contemporary of the Government of Peru, Dr. Guillermo Lohmann Villena, has found four or five of Matienzo's extracts of "The Chronicle of Cieza", without specific mention in the corpus of the text. This is a sure indication that the scrupulous and very learned magistrate of Chuquisaca, has gloried his bibliographic learning in the marginal notes of the original manuscript. To clucidate this matter it is necessary to consult in addition to the work of Guillermo Lohmann Villena, in Juan de Matienzo, Gobierno del Perú (1567), Edition et Etude préliminaire par Guillermo Lohman Villena, Col. Travaux de l'Institut Français d'Etudes Andines, Tome XI, Paris - Lima, 1967, specially all the references made in pp. LXIX, 7, 89, 162, 275 and 332.

Island, the island of Cuba and the Española Island. Once that the existence of gold was confirmed among the natives, a second prevailing note is made evident: the establishing of a sort of premoney gold standard in the transactions with the natives. A third aspect is related to the shiftings in the price of gold, according to Columbus's direct remarks that he transcribed daily in his log-book, remarks made during almost three months of stay in the West Indies in the first voyage.

Actually, the value of gold had oscillated most of the time, from an almost prohibitive level of purchasing as it happened in the experiments with the premoney of treasuring in Guanahaní, La Fernandina and Cuba; to a moderate level of appraisal, as it was proved in the region of the Indian Chief of the Paradise Valley in Haiti in front of the island of La Tortuga, when among the Taino natives rose the need of creating a sort of small gold tiles, the first "tejuelos de oro" in the Indies, to facilitate the transactions with the Spaniards; and reaching a third stage in the land of Indian Chief Guacanagarí, in Acul Bay, in which a great decrease in the esteem of gold by the natives is apparent. So that we would not be mistaken if we stated that from then on, gold got to be a type of money- merchandise of the American Tainos, while the hawk's bells played the role of merchandise-money among the discoverers of the Indias together with the Spanish monetary system. The chief Guacanagarí did not lose the opportunity to link his name to the new parity of the two pre-money standards. A hawk's bell was equal to four pieces of gold as big as a hand.

There are many questions related to the reason of this oscillations, and simultaneously the first discussions take place in the West Indies about the theory of the value of money. So happened the 17th December when an Indian chief of the Tortuga island tried to approach the discoverers, in which opportunity Columbus was noticed that in La Tortuga there was more gold than in the Española Island "because it was nearer Babeque". The Babeque island (the Great Inagua or Jamaica?), was news for the Discoverer since the 12th November as he had understood that its inhabitants picked up the gold at night by candle light and they said that they made bows with them with hammers. Facing these first considerations of space economics in the West Indies,the Admiral remarked that more than the distance or at least at its level it was fundamental to take into account what we, nowadays, since Irving Fisher's equation call the volume of transactions, which was very low and that was why "they bring very little gold, as they have nothing to give for it". A firmer step towards quantitativism is given the 18th December, when Columbus received the visit of the king of Gran Marne from Haiti. The young Haitian king interchanged presents with the Discoverer and offered him among other things two pieces of gold. The remarks of Columbus in the Journal were that "the king gave me also two pieces of carved gold which were very thin; and I think they obtain very little of it here, as I believe that they were very near from where the gold is born; and there is a lot" ("el rey me dio también dos pedazos de oro labrado que eran muy delgados, que creo que aquí alcanzan poco de él, puesto que tengo que están muy vecinos de donde nace y hay mucho"). In spite of the ironic tone of the comment, there is no doubt that we are facing remarks of great interest for our subject. It is a clear thesis of Columbus that the value of gold decreases ("they obtain very little of it here" - "alcanzan poco de él aquí") with the nearness of its place of extraction ("as I believe that they were very near from where the gold is born " - "puesto que tengo que están muy vecinos de donde nace") and of its abundance in the market ("and there is a lot" - "y hay mucho"). This same thesis would be repeated and enlarged in the interviews with king Guacanagarí, who will accompany Columbus in the history of American quantitativism, which took place in the Acul Bay the last days of December of 1492 and the beginning of January, 1493, remarking that the acquisitive power of gold "is enough for little" ("alcanza poco") if it is abundant, that is "if there is a lot" ("si hay mucho") and, of course, "nearer it is from its source" ("cuanto més cerca de la fuente de donde nace") its abundance will be greaterand with this "lower will be its price" ("menor será su precio") and an extreme case may happen as he thought it happened in Cibao, that "there was a great quantity of gold" ("habúa una gran cantidad de oro") making it "very cheap" ("muy barato"), and because of this decreasing its worth "to nothing" ("no por nada"), meaning that it could be bought with almost nothing or "that it may not be considered to have a price" ("que no la tenga en precio"). Here, we are essencially before a presentation almost as advanced as the quantitativist formula of our last European competitor after the discovery, Nicholas Copernicus[39], who in the Prussian Assembly of 1522 sustained that "money normally depreciates itself when it is too abundant", then, it is not necessary to pursue asking oneself about the source of inspiration of this theory. It is important to add that the optimism about the success of the enterprise of the discovery would incorporate in Columbus's doctrine of quantity the equally optimistic expectations that in a very short term as they gave pieces of gold that equaled two "castellanos" for a needle that would be nothing as compared with what would happen in a month from then (the 26th December); or, as Guacanagarí had told the Admiral that he had sent for gold and that he (Guacanagarí) would cover him (the Admiral) all in gold before he left; as in a mediate or long term the Admiral said: "I hope in God that on my return from Castile, I will find a barrel of gold that those who stayed will have bargained and they will have found the gold mine and the spicery, and this in such quantity that before three years have passed the King and the Queen can start and prepare the conquest of the Sainted House (of Jerusalem)".

In the "Ransom of Cajamarca" of 1533, the principal characters are Pizarro and Atahualpa. The conquerors understood, from the explanations given by Atahualpa himself, that there gold and silver existed in such abundance as iron in Vizcaya, and that was why Peruvians did not consider it had any value. The conquerors themselves were who spread to every wind that blew the immensity of the richness in precious metals in the New World. But it was also they who felt in their own flesh the burn of the quantitativist effect expressed in the general raise of the prices in the same neighbouring of Cajamarca and they

39 COPERNICUS (1864).

who witnessed the spread of the inflationary fire throughout the area of Castilla del Oro, Terra Firma and Española Island. And that is the reason why the conquerors, as formerly the Incas, easily understood the process of decay of the value of gold and silver when they used them as means of payment. Pizarro ordered his secretary Francisco Lopez de Jerez to complement the Inca quantitativism with that of the Christians; in his well known "Relación" printed in Seville in 1534. Jerez describes minutely the price revolution which took place mainly in the region of Cajamarca and San Miguel due to the depreciating effect of gold and silver which accompanied the newly "rich". Jerez himself says that if someone owed something to somebody else, he gave him a piece of gold without weighing it; and that even if he gave him twice what he owed he gave nothing; and that from house to house went the debtors, with an Indian loaded with gold looking for the creditors to pay what they owed. Formerly, in the 1533 "Relación" we only knew of Indians who rejected precious metals, but in this 1534 relation of Francisco Jerez we learn that gold was held in contempt both by the Spaniards as by the natives.

If the conquerors were those who witnessed the spreading of the inflationary fire at an American regional level, a pair of years later, but this time from Valladolid, through the voice imbued with mysticism of the Apostle of the Indies, and passing over the lack of precision of vocabulary, there is the testimony of the historical fact that the terrible conflagration started in Cajamarca had already crossed the ocean together with the treasures of the Inca Atahualpa plunging Spain into consumption, destroying industries and sowing misery and discourage among the Castilian, while the American treasure was already filtering to Flanders, Italy, France, and in successive waves to the other regions of the European continent. The exconqueror and ex commissionaire of Indians in Cuba, Licenciate Bartolomé de las Casas already converted to the order of the Dominicans, was who gave this historical testimony in 1542 in the Valladolid Assembly, describing in a very complete way both, the internal physiognomy of monetary quantitativism and its outward projection provoking enormous unleveling in foreign exchange rates, or in Earl Hamilton's words, making well clear the relation between the American treasure and the revolution of prices in Spain. Or, as Las Casas stated, "of so infinite treasures that had been brought from the Indies to European nations, that neither Solomon nor other king of the world so much gold ever had or saw, or heard of, nothing remained in that kingdom, not even what they had before the discovery. Due to which every thing had three times the price that they had before, and for that reason poor people were in great misery and need".

It must be remembered that Las Casas was very aware of the first quantitative experiences that took place in the Antilles in Columbus's first voyage to America. It was Las Casas who was familiar with Columbus journal of his first voyage, which he transcribed - saving with this the disappearance of this document whose original copy has been lost - in the first book of his "History of the West Indies", which is, as we have seen, the basic source of the primitive American Quantity Theory from October 1492 to January 1493. Furthermore, Las Casas was acquainted with some of the predecessors of Columbus's quantitativism. Only if these antecedents are taken into account, it is possible to duly understand the remarks of Las Casas included in his "Remedios para Reformación de las Indias", of 1542, printed in Seville in 1552, in which Las Casas feels the quantitativist causal relation: flux of metals, revolution of prices. With this all doubts disappear and the place of Las Casas in the American and Spanish quantitativism is definitively established.

The "magnificent Potosí" once discovered, marks the most important stage in the development of the history of modern quantity theory. Truly, nothing knew the Inca of this maximum source of the Indian treasure. Pizarro's conquerors were who stumbled on it, in the middle of April in 1545. As it happens many times in the events of great world resonance, destiny chose a humble soldier, Gonzalo Bernal, who also by mere chance was present, being he who predicted "the Potosí mines promise so much wealth, that few years after it is carved, iron will be worthier than silver". The only information I found about this very obscure and totally ignored soldier in the history of the conquest, and the only mention made about his prediction is due to the Inca Garcilaso de la Vega[40].

Very long before, in September 1546, from the city of Santiago (Chile), the Captain Pedro de Valdivia in full operation of the conquest of the Araucanian lands already wrote to the king of Spain that it was known that the value of precious metals in Perú, because of its extreme abundance, had decreased very much. He had collected sixty thousand gold pesos to finance his embassy to the king. If the vessel went to Perú, it is evident, he says, that "as that land has been and is so prosperous or rich in silver, they would appraise this quantity as very poor". And he remarks thus when "the messengers to his Majesty set sail from the port of Valparaiso". What did this sum of sixty thousand gold pesos mean for the conquerors of Chile? Valdivia asks himself again. And his answer, accompained with the reason of it was: "Here (these sixty thousand gold pesos) we value a lot because every peso costs us a hundred drops of blood and two hundred of sweat". May this message be, at the same time a first seed in the American history of the theory of the value of money founded in the costs of its exploitation?

By May 1549 another young soldier, but who this time was a chronicler, Pedro Cieza de León, "the prince of the Indian chroniclers" had already departed from the City of the Kings (Lima) towards Charcas, and he was visiting the mining settlings of the Potosí high land, the fabulous market of the "Villa Ymperial del Potosí" in accelerating growth, and the noble and loyal "Villa del Plata", a Spanish population in "Los Charcas", established in Chuquisaca, ... The impact that the contact with the dynamic pole of potosinian development - as we would call it nowadays - which is already evident in Cuzco in the North and in Tucumán in the South is moving, and his remarks greatly prove the quantitivist approaches of his predecessors: Christopher Columbus, the followers of Pizarro in Panamá of 1533 (whose relati-

---

40 Inca GARCILASO DE LA VEGA (1968), pp. 672ss.

on was already divulged, almost simultaneously in French, in German, and in Italian, so we can say that in the begining of 1534 it had travelled round the world), the relation of Francisco López de Jerez in 1534, the memorandum of Las Casas in the Valladolid Assembly of 1542, Bernal's testimony in 1545 and Valdivia's remarks in 1546, most of those texts he surely knew. His chronicle of Perú, started in 1541, in Cartago, in the Valley of Cauca and finished in Potosí in 1549, and printed in Seville in 1553, shocked the Castilians, and breaking the language barriers would be eagerly read in the rest of the world, that would devour its translations. As I have shown in another place, it was Cieza de León who, besides repeating the relation between the level of the prices and the Indian treasure, established that the abundance of silver was the cause of the increase in prices and that this effect "would spread in successive waves all over the Indies and all the kingdoms of Spain so that it had raised its prices in such a way, as never men ever thought", as if they had been pronounced by Las Casas in Valladolid, and those that we will find later in 1567, reproduced almost verbatim, but recognizing his debt with Cieza, in the "Gobierno del Perú" of Juan de Matienzo. It would not be very audacious to hint that Cieza's conclusions together with those of his predecessors and contemporaries are an important start for the awakening of the "Second Scholastic Economics" both in the European as in the West Indies.

The Licenciate de La Gasca only remained a pair of years in the West Indies, between 1546 and 1550, and they were years dedicated to pacifying Perú, enterprise which ended with the defeat and trial of Gonzalo Pizarro in the valley of Xaquixaguana the 9th of April of 1548. But this short time sufficed to grasp with no difficulty the effects of the flood of Potosinian silver on the general level of prices and its space grading both American and European. Nevertheless we find considerations of major interest for us in his letter to the Counsel of Indies of the 28th January of 1549, in which he establishes his awareness of the great difference of the purchasing power of gold in the West Indies as compared to Spain: "What in Spain may be bought with a 'real' is not bought in the Indies with a gold peso". With this, all the problem that is behind what we today formulate with the abbreviation PPP (Purchasing Power Parity), is forestalled, as it makes us see that the parity of the purchasing power of a gold peso in the Indies is given by a "real" in Spain. The Licenciate de La Gasca establishes with this the foundation of the monument that will be built in 1556 to the glory of Dr. Martín de Azpilcueta Navarro and of the following European and American constructors of the PPP.

Don Andrés Hurtado de Mendoza, Marquis of Cañete, the third Peruvian viceroy, a few days after landing and crossing the Isthmus, wrote concisely to the king in a long letter dated in Panamá the 16th March 1956: "Only here I have understood what happens here and there", anticipating the basic ideas sustained by the Court of Charcas. In the very short time of thirty American days, don Andrés Hurtado de Mendoza diagnosticated accurately that the revolution of prices which was suffered, first in the Indies and later in Spain, was due to the opulence of its gold and silver mines and above all to the powerful mining centre of Potosí.

Although the members of the Charcas Court of Justice could believe in the evidence of their quantitativist thesis in an environs like Chuquisaca and Potosí, they had no great expectations with regard to the receptivity of their doctrine in the metropolitan world. They knew that their thesis could be resisted there; to counter-work such probability they decided: "at request of some officers of this Court", to gather testimonies of people learned in Indian businesses and to forward this "information" to the king together with the letter of February 1562. We ignore the contents and destiny of those "informations" and we deeply regret their disappearance, but nevertheless its being mentioned is a clear sign of the popularity and ample support given by the people of Chuquisaca and Potosí to the quantitativist thesis of money value. Here we totally transcribe this important text, which doctrine will unite in the economic approach, since their first steps, the magistrates of the Court of Los Charcas "... they order (by command of the Viceroy of Perú) that in Potosí must be kept the fees of Lima; the zeal could be good but they have been misinformed because in Potosí things are four times more expensive than in Lima ordinarily and when they are cheaper they are the double than in Lima, and this is easy to understand as the goods are brought from Lima, which is three hundred leagues far, half by land and half by sea ... and furthermore, where there is more money things are dearer as everything will be explained to Your Majesty by the information that goes together with this on demand of some of the officials of this Court".

When the writings of the West Indies scholastics appeared it was evident that they found all the basic pieces of their "New Economics" already elaborated, with sweat and blood, by their predecessors "the West Indies mercantilists" with the help of their science and their West Indies "*ispiriencia*". But far from us to impair their intrinsical merits,the principal of which is to have known how to weld in a consistent theory the flux of Aristotelian Thomistic contributions and of the Spanish and foreign scholastics together with the contributions of the West Indies mercantilists and to strengthen and polish them.

In several works I have studied carefully the contributions of the principal West Indian scholastics. In that opportunity, I have attentively examined the writings of six authors: two theologians, Tomás de Mercado (México 1569) and Luis López (Chiapas and Guatemala 1585 and 1589); two jurists, Juan de Matienzo (Chuquisaca 1567 and 1580) and Bartolomé de Albornoz (México 1573); and two theologian-jurists, Pedro de Oñate (Córdoba and Lima 1645 - 1654) and Domingo Muriel (Córdoba 1791). From the examination of their works it results that the principal contribution of Spanish American scholastics is rooted in the development of the subjective theory of value, the prices theory system, the market morphology, the integration of the monetary theory with the general prices theory and with this, the ample development of the quantity theory of money and the theory of the parity of the purchasing power of money. We must stress that in the development of monetary theory, due to the powerful influence of the effects produced by the "ransom of Cajamarca" (1533) and the dicovery of the silver mines of Potosí (1545), the nucleus formed by the school of Chuquisaca grasped beforehand its essencial elements.

A general view both of the Spanish scholastics as of the West Indian ones, allows us to see that the common denominator of their contributions is the approach to the prices system and the monetary problems as an integrating part of the New Economics. In the second place it calls powerfully our attention that the three great forerunners of the Spanish New Economics: Azpilcueta, Matienzo and Mercado elaborated their system with complete independence one from the other. Neither the Spanish American Matienzo and Mercado knew each other, nor the two of them knew the Azpilcueta of "Comentario Resolutorio de Cambios" published more than a decade before the finishing of the manuscripts of the two Americans. Who is dedicated to the study of the History of Economic Doctrines knows very well that this does not happen for the first time. This is a very important aspect to bear in mind. If at present and in spite of the thousand refinements received by the electronic revolution, many of the scholars are obliged to live in watertight compartments, how can we reject that possibility in a world in which people lived at not only geographic and cultural or scientific distances which sometimes were impossible to surmount; as was evidently the martyrdom of Matienzo's solitude in Chuquisaca until the moment of his death? Tomás de Mercado had been in Seville and some contemporary critics also affirm he had reached doctoral titles and proffesorships in Salamanca University, subject with which I do not agree and which I will not discuss at this moment. Notwithstanding, Mercado leaves no evidence in his work about the "Comentario Resolutorio de Cambios". Instead he knows and quotes extensively Domingo de Soto, whose work was object of a special course at Mexico University. Whatever could be said about Mercado as a person, his work is an American product and that is attested by his brother in religion, Father Agustín Dávila Padilla, who advises everybody that the theory sustained by Mercado in his "*Summa*" and his principal resolutions "were taken from the resolutions and arguments of Santo Domingo of Mexico"[41] ("Historia de la Fundación y Discurso de la Provincia Santiago de México por las vidas de sus varones insignes y cosas notables de Nueva España").

But Azpilcueta is chronologically former to the two great forerunners West Indian scholars even if sometimes the influence of American mercantilists is evident, as, for example when he affirms: "even in Spain, in the time when there was less money, for much less, salable things were given... that after the Indies were discovered, they covered it with gold and silver" (XII, 51). Notwithstanding, his "Comentario Resolutorio de Cambios" is a glory of Hispanic Economics and the only thing to regret is that it has not been translated to the *lingua franca* of our times - English - taking as reference the exellent edition published in 1965 in the collection "Corpus Hispanorum de Pace" of the Superior Counsel of Scientific Investigations of Spain. And after, when the circumstances allow it, to do the same with the works of his peers Matienzo and Mercado.

Finally, and even if it might seem a redundant question, I believe that it is imperious to stress the precision and constancy that have been evident for all the foundational period, thanks to which a series of writings have been drafted in America, writings that are placed in the first lines of monetary quantitativism history. We know that the enemies of Imperial Spain have lifted the banner of the "black legend". But today, at a long enough distance from those difficult days with a clear mind and supported by serious research works we may add in full justice that it was in that time of the "contemptible" mercantilism and of the "decadent" scholastics that Spanish America has borne fruits of unsuspectable value for the progress of learning in the pith of the New Economics from the XVIth Century.

We know very well indeed that we are scarcely nearing the lands contiguous to the "mar oceana" of documents, ready for exploration, but we are sure that the researchers of the History of Spanish Ameri-

---

41 DÁVILA PADILLA (1596), p. 587.

can economical thinking of the generations to come will accomplish in successive waves, with enthusiasm and responsibility, the full schedule of works that await them.

Today, my humble effort has been aknowledged by the international community and also my proposal found a good response among a line of Latin American scholars; some of which are performing exellent researches[42]. The cultivation of the colonial past of the Hispanic American economic doctrines is apparently assured.

Bibliographic References

1. Introduction

CÉSPEDES DEL CASTILLO, 1961: Las Indias en el Reinado de los Reyes Católicos, in: J. VICENS-VIVES, Historia de España y América, Barcelona, II, pp. 492ss.

------ 1961: La Sociedad Colonial Americana en los Siglos XVI y XVII, in: J. VICENS-VIVES, Historia de España y América, Barcelona, III, pp. 387ss.

FURLONG, 1969: Historia cultural y social del Río de la Plata. 1536 - 1810, Buenos Aires, 3 vols.

HAMILTON, E. A., 1934: American Treasure and the Price Revolution in Spain, 1501 - 1650, Cambridge (Mass.); Spanish transl.: Barcelona 1975.

POPESCU, O., 1952: El sistema económico en las misiones jesuíticas. Un vasto experimento de desarrollo indoamericano, Bahía Blanca; 2a. ed. Barcelona 1967.

------ 1965: L'histoire de la pensée économique et sa division en periodes, in: *Revue Int. Sc. Sociales* XVII/4, pp. 655ss.

------ 1966: Lehrgeschichtliche Anfänge der sozialökonomischen Entwicklungsbestrebungen Lateinamerikas, in: *Weltwirtschaftliches Archiv*, Sondernummer für Latein-Amerika (Kiel); Spanish version entitled "Estructura económica de las Misiones", in: *Cuadernos del Milenio* 2, 1991.

------ 1986a: Estudios en la historia del pensamiento económico latinoamericano, Bogotá.

------ 1988: Económica Indiana, Academia Nacional de Ciencias Económicas, Buenos Aires.

THORP, W. L. / G. R. TAYLOR, 1933: Price History. Encyclopaedia of the Social Sciences; E. R. A. SELIGMAN (Ed.), repr. 1957, vol. 12, pp. 375ss.

---

42 PIQUÉ (Argentina, 1976); CRAVERO (Argentina, 1983); CHAFUEN (USA, 1986 y 1991); ARENAS RODRÍGUEZ (Perú, 1986); BRAND (El Salvador, 1987); CONSUEGRA HIGGINS (Colombia, 1987); RUBLI KAISER (México, 1987); GUMUCIA (Bolivia, 1988); and others.

2. The Navigation Journal of the First Vogage of the Discovery (1492 - 1493)

BALLESTEROS BERETTA, A., 1945: Cristóbal Colón y el descubrimiento de América, Barcelona - Buenos Aires, 2 vols.

COLÓN, C., 1492 - 1506: Los cuatro viajes del Almirante y su Testamento, Edition and prologue Ignacio B. Anzoátegui, Espasa Calpe, Colección Austral. No. 463, Madrid 1946, 5a. ed. 1971.

FERNÁNDEZ DE NAVARRETE, M., 1825: Colección de los viajes y descubrimientos que hicieron por mar los españoles desde fines del siglo XV, T. I. Viages de Colón: Almirantazgo de Castilla, Madrid.

KRICKEBERG, W., 1922: Etnología de América, German translat., Fondo de Cultura Económica, México 1946.

MORISON, S. E., 1974: The European Discovery of America. The Southern Voyages A.D.1492 - 1616, New York.

SANZ, C. (Ed.), 1962: Diario de Colón. Libro de la Primera Navegación y Descubrimiento de las Indias, with a preliminary study by the editor, Madrid, Biblioteca Americana Vetustísima. English translation in: MORISON, S. E., 1963: Journals and Other Documents on the Life and Voyages of Christopher Columbus, New York, pp. 41 - 179.

THACHER, J. B., 1903: Christopher Columbus. His life, his work, his remains as revelated by original printed and manuscript records, New York - London, vol. I.

3. The Ransom of Cajamarca (1533)

ANÓNIMO, 1533: Conquista del Perú, por Francisco Pizarro. French translation by Ramón Carande, in: R. CARANDE, Carlos V y sus banqueros, Abridged Edition II, 1977, pp. 82ss.

BRANDI, K., 1933: Berichte und Studien, Berlin.

------ 1941: Kaiser Karl V. Werden und Schiksal einer Persönlichkeit und eines Weltreiches, 3 ed. München.

CARANDE, R., 1977: Carlos V y sus banqueros. Abridged edition, II, pp. 82ss.

CIEZA DE LEÓN, P. de, 1553: La crónica del Perú, Sevilla; reprinted in: Historiadores de Indias: América del Sur, Barcelona 1972.

------ 1967: El señorío de los Incas, Instituto de Estudios Peruanos.

COPERNICUS, N., 1526: Monetae cudendae ratio; ms. edited by L. WOLOWSKI, together with the treaty of Oresme 1355, Paris 1864.

HANKE, L. y M. GIMÉNEZ FERNÁNDEZ, 1954: Bartolomé de las Casas 1474 - 1566. Bibliografía crítica, Santiago de Chile.

LANZ, K., 1844: Correspondenz des Kaiser Karl V, Leipzig.

LAS CASAS, B. de, 1952: Brevísima relación de la destrucción de las Indias, Valencia ms., Sevilla 1552; reedición Ed. Louis MICHAUD, Paris - Buenos Aires S.F.

------ 1951: Historia de las Indias; edition from Agustín Millares Carlo and preliminar study from Lewis HANKE, México and Buenos Aires.

------ 1974: Tratados, México 1965; reprint.

LÓPEZ DE JEREZ, F., 1534: Verdadera relación de la conquista del Perú ..., Sevilla.

PIQUÉ, A., 1976: Las ideas económicas de Fray Bartolomé de las Casas, en: *Cuadernos de Historia del Pensamiento Económico Hispanoamericano* (1976), pp. 1ss (mimeo).

POPESCU, O., 1984: Orígenes hispanoamericanos de la teoría cuantitativa, Buenos Aires; reed. Madrid and Bogotá 1986.

------ and others, 1986b: Aportaciones del pensamiento económico iberoamericano siglos XVI - XX, Madrid.

4. The Discovery of Potosí (1545)

CUNNINGHAME GRAHAM, R. B., 1926: Pedro de Valdivia Conqueror of Chile; Spanish transl.: Pedro de Valdivia conquistador de Chile. Su biografía y epistolario, Buenos Aires, 1943.

GARCILASO DE LA VEGA, El Inca, 1609: Primera parte de los comentarios reales que tratan del origen de los incas, Lisboa; various reeditions: 1723, 1941 - 44, 1945, 1959, last edition: Barcelona 1968.

HURTADO DE MENDOZA, A. Marqués de Cañete, 1566: Carta a su Majestad, Panamá 16 de marzo, in: LEVILLIER, R. (1921).

LA GASCA, P. de, 1549: Cartas al Consejo de Indias, in: LEVILLIER (1921).

LEVILLIER, R., 1921: Gobernantes del Perú, Cartas y Papeles, Siglo XVI, Documentos del Archivo de Indias, T.I, Madrid.

LÓPEZ DE GOMARA, F., 1912: Anales del emperador Carlos V, Madrid.

POPESCU, O., 1984: Orígenes hispanoamericanos de la teoría cuantitativa, Buenos Aires; reed. Madrid and Bogotá 1986.

------ and others, 1986b: Aportaciones del pensamiento económico iberoamericano siglos XVI - XX, Madrid.

(VALDIVIA, P.,) 1550: Relación hecha por Pedro de Valdivia al Emperador, dándole cuenta de lo sucedido en el descubrimiento, conquista y población de Chile y en su viaje al Perú, in: Colección de Documentos Inéditos relativos al Descubrimiento, Conquista y Organización de las antiguas Posesiones Españolas en América y Oceanía sacados de los Archivos del Reino y muy especialmente del de Indias, Madrid 1865, Volume IV, pp. 5ss.

VÁZQUEZ DE ESPINOSA, A., 1628: Compendio y descripción de las Indias Occidentales, English version Smithsonian Miscellaneous Collections, vol. 102 (Whole Volume), 1942; Spanish version, unabridged transcription from the original document by Charles Upson CLARK, Washington 1948.

5. The Indian Scholastics (1567 - 1791)

ALBORNOZ, B., 1573: Arte de los contractos, Valencia.

AVENDAÑO, D. de, 1660 - 1678: Thesaurus Indicus, 6 vols., Amberes

AZPILCUETA NAVARRO, M. de, 1556: Comentario resolutorio de cambios, Salamanca; modern ed., Madrid 1965.

BAECK, L., 1988: Spanish economic thought: the school of Salamanca and the 'arbitristas', in: *History of Political Economy* 20/3, pp. 381ss.; 2nd ed. entitled "Imperial Spain: The School of Salamanca and the Arbitristas", linotype 1991.

CRAVERO, J. M. J., 1983: La ley natural en la filosofía económica de Fray Tomás de Mercado (1575), Buenos Aires.

DÁVILA PADILLA, A., 1596: Historia de la fundación y discurso de la Provincia Santiago de México por las vidas de sus varones insignes y cosas notables de Nueva España, Madrid.

DEMPSEY, S.J., B., 1936: The Historical Emergence of Quantity Theory, in: *The Quarterly Journal of Economics* L, pp. 174 ss.

DORNBUSCH, R., 1987: Purchasing Power Parity, in: The New Palgrave: A Dictionary of Economics, London - New York - Tokio 1987, vol. 3, pp. 1075ss.

FURLONG, G., 1952: Nacimiento y desarrollo de la filosofía en el Río de la Plata, 1536 - 1810, Buenos Aires.

GÓMEZ CAMACHO, F., 1981: Introducción, in: Luis de Molina, La teoría del justo precio. Edition by F. Gómez Camacho, Madrid, pp. 7ss.

------ 1985: La teoría monetaria de los doctores españoles del siglo XVI, in: *Moneda y Crédito* 172, pp. 55ss.

GRICE-HUTCHINSON, M., 1952: The School of Salamanca: Readings in Spanish Monetary Theory, 1544 - 1605.

------ 1978: Early Economic Thought in Spain (1177 - 1740), London; Spanish transl.: El pensamiento económico en España (1177 - 1740), Barcelona 1982.

------ 1989: El concepto de la Escuela de Salamanca: sus orígenes y su desarrollo, in: *Revista de Historia Económica* VII/2, pp. 21ss.

------ 1990: Aproximación al pensamiento económico en Andalucía: de Séneca a finales del siglo XVIII, Málaga.

HOEFFNER, J., 1941: Wirtschaftsethik und Monopole im fünfzehnten und sechzehnten Jahrhundert, Jena.

------ 1955: Statik und Dynamik in der scholastischen Wirtschaftsethik, Köln - Opladen; Spanish transl.: Estática y dinámica en la ética económica de la Filosofía Escolástica, in: *Investigación Económica* XVIII 72 (1958), pp. 629ss.

IPARRAGUIRRE, D., 1954: Las fuentes del pensamiento económico en España en los siglos XIII al XVI, in: *Estudios de Deusto*, 2a. II, pp. 79ss.

------ 1957: Francisco de Vitoria. Una teoría social del valor económico, Bilbao.

LARAZ, J., 1943: La época del mercantilismo en Castilla, 1500 - 1700, Madrid, 3a. ed. 1963.

LOHMAN VILLENA, G., 1966: Juan de Matienzo autor del "Gobierno del Perú". Su personalidad y su obra, Sevilla.

LÓPEZ, L. (Ludovicus Lopez), 1585: Instructorium conscientiae, duabus contentum partibus, Salamanca; 2nd. ed. Lyon 1588, 3rd. ed. Salamanca 1592.

------ 1589: Tractatus de contractibus et negotiationibus, Salamanca; Lyon 1594, Brescia 1596, Italian transl. Venice 1590.

MATIENZO, J., 1558: Dialogus relatoris et advocati pintiani Senatus, Valladolid.

------ Gobierno del Perú, Edition et étude préliminaire par G. Lohmann Villena, Travaux de l'Institut Français d'Études Andines, Paris - Lima 1967.

------ 1580. Commentaria in librum quintum recollectionis legum Hispaniae, Madrid 3a. ed. 1613.

MERCADO, T. de, 1569: Tratos y contratos de mercaderes y tratantes discididos y determinados, Salamanca; second edition, considerably enlarged under the title: Summa de tratos y contratos, Sevilla, 1571; third edition Sevilla 1587; Italian transl.: De negotii, et contratti de mercanti, et de negotianti, Brescia 1591; new reprint by G. SÁNCHEZ ALBORNOZ, 2 volumes, Madrid 1985.

MURIEL, D. (Cyriaco Morelli), 1791: Rudimenta juris naturae et gentium libri duo, Venecia.

OÑATE, P. de, 1646 - 1654: De Contractibus. Tomi tres ... Romae, Ex Typographia Francisci Caballi, 3 vols. fol. 20 h. 688 p., 28 h. 1024 p., 12 h. 946 p.(third volume): Romae Apud Angelum Bernabà haeredem Nanelphi (1646 - 1654), pars secundae 790 p.

POPESCU, O., 1967: Historia de las doctrinas económicas:antiguedad mercantilismo, Bogotá. 1964; 2nd. ed. enlarged with a chapter about the economic thought in Hispanic America, Bogotá 1967.

------ 1968: Dinero y Crédito, Bogotá.

------ 1982: Aspectos analíticos en la doctrina del justo precio de Juan de Matienzo (1520 - 1579), Buenos Aires; reed. 1984.

------ 1986c: El pensamiento económico en la escolástica hispanoamericana, Buenos Aires; reed. Bogotá 1986, Buenos Aires 1990.

------ 1987: Price theory in the hispanic american scholastics (Festschrift in Honour of Anghel N. regina, Part I), in: *International Journal of Social Economics* XIV/3-5, pp. 61ss.

------ 1991: Latin American Economica during the Hispanic Domination, in: Festschrift in Honour of Lazaros Th. Houmanidis, Piraeus.

SAN ANTONINO DE FLORENCIA, 1740: Summa Theologica, Verona.

SÁNCHEZ ALBORNOZ, C., 1959: Un testigo del comercio indiano: Tomás de Mercado y Nueva España, in: *Revista de Historia de América* 47, pp. 95ss.

------ 1977: Tomás de Mercado, entre la tradición escolástica y la práctica económica del siglo de oro, in: Tomás de Mercado, Summa de tratos y contratos, Madrid, I, pp. VIIss.

SAYOUS, A. E., 1928: Observations d'écrivains du XVIe siècle sur les changes et notamment sur l'influence de la disparité du pouvoir d'achat des monnaies, in: *Revue Economique Internationale* 20, pp. 289ss.

SCHUMPETER, J. A., 1954: History of Economic Analysis, New York; Spanish version: Historia del Análisis Económico, Barcelona, 1971.

SIERRA BRAVO, R., 1973: La 'Suma' de Tratos y Contratos de Tomás de Mercado, in: *Revista de Economía Política* 64, pp. 273ss.

ULLASTRES CALVO, A., 1941 - 1942: Martín de Azpilcueta y su comentario resolutorio de cambios, in: *Anales de Economía* I, pp. 375ss; II, pp. 50ss.

------ 1965: Las ideas económicas de Martín de Azpilcueta, in: Martín de Azpilcueta, Comentario resolutorio de cambios, Madrid, pp. LVIIss.

VILAR, P., 1964: Crecimiento y desarrollo, Barcelona.

------ 1969: Oro y moneda en la historia, 1450 - 1920, Barcelona.

WEBER, W., 1959: Wirtschaftsethik am Vorabend des Liberalismus, Münster.

------ 1962: Geld und Zins in der spanischen Spätscholastik, Münster.

6. Retrospective View and Conclusions

ARENAS RODRÍGUEZ, M., 1986: Controversias históricas, in: *Desarrollo Indoamericano* XX 85, pp. 51ss.

BRAND, S., 1987: El origen latinoamericano de las teorías de la moneda y la inflación, Bogotá.

CHAFUEN, A. A., 1991: Christians for Freedom. Late-Scholastic Economics, San Francisco 1986; Spanish edition: Economía y Etica - Raíces cristianas de la economía del libre mercado, Madrid.

CONSUEGRA HIGGINS, J., 1987: El pensamiento económico latinoamericano contemporáneo, Caracas.

GUMUCIA, F. B., 1988: La Escuela de Chuquisaca o los Orígenes del Pensamiento Económico Latino Americano, La Paz.

RUBLI KAISER, F., 1987: Qué sabemos de las teorías cuantitativas de la inflación que no se conociera cuando menos desde 400 años?, in: *El Trimestre Económico* (Mexico) LIV 213, pp. 179ss.

Contributions of the School of Salamanca to Monetary Theory

By Marjorie Grice-Hutchinson

"The discovery of America and that of a passage to the East Indies by the Cape of Good Hope", said Adam Smith, "are the two greatest and most important events recorded in the history of mankind". And, if we look back on all that has happened since Smith wrote, we may well decide that he was not greatly exaggerating. Even if we limit our viewpoint to events in Spain in the sixteenth century, we must recognise that the Discoveries inaugurated a notable phase of commercial expansion and brought about profound modifications in our view of the world and our place in it. I have been invited to talk to you today about the way in which monetary theory in Spain was affected by the Discoveries.

Most people would agree, I think, that the Spanish doctors of the sixteenth century who occupied themselves with economic theory devoted a great part of their efforts to trying to bring the traditional canonical and theological doctrine of usury into line with business practices which had existed since medieval times but which, largely as a result of the Discoveries, had become more general and more sophisticated than before.

This attempt may be looked at in two ways. It can be held that the Spanish Doctors of the School of Salamanca had come to realise the impossibility of rigidly controlling the unruly commercial spirit of the age, and to see that a certain liberalisation was necessary if business life and the teaching of the Church were not to go their separate ways. On the other hand, we can take a rather different view, and say that by turning traditional doctrine into paths that I shall try to indicate, they succeeded in bringing whole areas of dubious practice back into the fold of the Church, and to some extent, and for some time longer, in keeping them under her guidance.

The Pursuit of Profit in the Middle Ages

Some historians write as though medieval people were in general content with the sort of life they were born into, and had no ambition to rise in the world. In the Middle Ages, it is said, there were few opportunities of acquiring wealth, and the whole idea of money-making was foreign to feudal society.

This may be true of many parts of Europe but can hardly be said of Spain. To begin at the top with the nobility and gentry, enormous possibilities were open to them in the course of the Reconquest.

Take the story of the Cid, for example. We know that he lived in the beginning of the eleventh century, but the epic poem that bears his name was probably composed between 1201 and 1207, and reflects the popular mentality of the early thirteenth century.

The profit motive is taken for granted throughout the poem. Many of us will remember the scene in which the exiled hero tricks the Jews, Rachel and Vidal, into lending him 600 marks on false security to enable him and his followers to invade and sack the lands of the Emir of Toledo[1] Three years later we find him encamped before Valencia and sending out messengers to every part of the Peninsula to invite prospective recruits to join his new enterprise.

> Andidieron los pregones, sabet, a todas partes, al sabor de la ganançia non lo quieren detardar, grandes yentes se le acoien

1 Poema del Mio Cid, p. 80 - 120.

> de la buena christiandad, creciendo va en riqueza Mio Cid el de Bivar[2].
> (Know that the heralds went to every part, for the sake of the gain they want no delay. Great crowds of good Christians join him, and my Cid of Bivar is getting richer and richer).

The Cid was true to his word. At Valencia "the men who went on foot became knights. The gold and silver, who shall count them? Everyone there was rich"[3].

The Cid took as his share of the booty some thirty thousand marks in gold and silver, apart from other things. He sends for his wife and daughters, and, after cavorting before them on his newly-acquired horse, Babieca, escorts them up to the top of the alcazar, not a stone's throw from where we are meeting today. They contemplate on the one hand the sea and on the other the lush countryside, and thank God for this "ganancia, como es buena y grand". A further victory against the Moorish forces brings in another three thousand marks in gold and silver, and of "las otras ganancias non avia recado".

The poet does not suggest that there is anything reprehensible in what to us seems a somewhat excessive desire for profit. His sympathies are all with his hero. As he says, "mala cueta es, señores, aver mingua de pan".

The Cid of the poem is, of course, the creation of the poet. But this wonderful work of art was based on real life. The initial borrowing of the necessary funds is confirrned by the *Fuero viejo de Castilla,* a collection of laws, probably made in the year 1212, about the same time as the composition of the *Poema,* by Alfonso VIII of Castile to regulate the rights and privileges of his nobles. It includes a section on the pledges that could be given by noblemen to Christian as well as Jewish moneylenders. Anything seems to have served as a pledge. Houses, orchards, vineyards, clothing, bedclothes, stuffs, silver, arms,

---

2 Poema del Mio Cid, 1195 - 1200.

3 Poema del Mio Cid, 1215.

animals - all are mentioned in that connection[4]. After reading the *Poema del Mio Cid* we shall not be surprised by the readiness of the Castilian nobleman to pawn even his bedclothes. The Reconquest was approaching its final phase, when only the kingdom of Granada would remain under Moslem rule. The hidalgo would naturally wish to take part in whatever military expedition seemed likely to yield the enormous profits we have just been considering.

What could the Cid have done with the vast sums that were now at his command? He could not have spent the whole amount on his daughters' weddings or on repairing his house at Bivar. Fortunately, opportunities for investment were not lacking.

If the hidalgo was able to profit from the peculiar circumstances of the Reconquest, the mercantile classes did not fail to share in the general economic expansion which, from the tenth century onwards, benefited the Mediterranean peoples.

Italy was ahead of other nations, and Italian business men are often regarded as having been the leaders of the nascent commercial economy. But progress was helped in the Spanish peninsula by the presence of Jewish and Moslem merchants whose age-long business experience surpassed even that of the Italians. The last two centuries of the Middle Ages, from the end of the thirteenth century to that of the fifteenth, were marked in the Peninsula by considerable cultural and economic vitality, at first in Aragon and later in Castile.

The Church and the Business World

In the eyes of the Church there would have been nothing sinful in the material success of the Cid or in the financial activities of Rachel and Vidal. The Cid's campaigns were waged against the enemies of the Christian faith. As for Jewish money-lending, speaking generally it

---

4 Fuero Viejo de Castilla, vol. 1, lib. 3, at. 5 & 7.

was permitted by the civil law, the maximum rate of interest being fixed.

But, with the quickened rhythm of economic growth and an increase in the numbers of the mercantile community, there was concern among canon lawyers and theologians about the ever-widening gap that was opening between the way of life of the early Christians and that of the contemporary business world. Merchants, after all, are out to make a profit, and the profit motive was viewed with suspicion. A moderate profit on sales was approved, but profit on loans was virtually forbidden by the canon law. This prohibition was perhaps framed in order to protect the poor debtor from the depredations of the moneylender. Had it been observed, it is difficult to see how any further economic expansion would have been possible. But it was often not observed. Many documents have come down to us in which interest-bearing loans are disguised as some other form of transaction.

In the course of the Middle Ages there grew up in various parts of Europe, and more especially in Italy, a, substantial body of doctrine by which philosophers, theologians and jurists sought to explain and direct the activities we now call "economic". Up to quite recent years medieval economic thought was frequently treated as though it were almost uniform in character, and historians discussed, sometimes with a good deal of heat, such questions as (for example) did the scholastic Doctors hold a labour or a utility theory of value? Fortunately those days are past. Professor Langholm, to mention only one of the numerous specialists who have contributed in recent years to a better knowledge of the history of economics, has traced and disentangled the widely divergent threads that ran through the earlier scholastic analysis of wealth and money, price and value, and usury, chiefly in the Aristotelian tradition.

The rediscovery of Aristotle in the West dates from the middle of the thirteenth century, and a considerable part of the basis of economic science is to be found in the writings of the Philosopher. Among the more important Aristotelian texts are some brief passages on justice in exchange included in the *Nichomachean Ethics* and some fairly elaborate monetary theory in the *Politics*. In the course of the next four centuries several hundred commentaries were written on these texts, coming to form what may be regarded as the main body of scholastic teaching on economic subjects, including money.

In their discussions of commutative justice the schoolmen were not concerned with the fair division of the whole product of a community but with the justice of the individual transactions that made up economic life. It was not a question of whether everyone was getting a fair share of the collective cake, but of fair dealing between man and man. Were buyers paying the proper price for their neighbours' goods? And were some people taking advantage of their neighbour's need by making them a loan and charging them for it? These two problems did not occupy the whole field of medieval monetary theory. But they were central to it, and as the contributions of the School of Salamanca were chiefly concerned with them I shall limit the rest of this paper to discussing some aspects of the doctrines of Just Price and Usury.

The Medieval Doctrine of the Just Price

The medieval Doctors accepted the teaching of Roman law that the just price was the price currently obtainable from buyers, supposing them to be well informed, and in the absence of all fraud and constraint.

But this did not really get them much further forward. They needed a theory of value to explain what determined the prospective buyers' choice and what regulated the demand for a thing. Aristotle had provided the makings of one. In the first Latin translation of the *Ethics* to reach the West he had said that the measure of all things was *indigentia,* indigence, a highly suggestive word that signified both the lack of a thing and the need that was felt for it.

It came to be generally agreed among the Doctors that the relative scarcity of a useful or otherwise desirable thing was what in the long run determined its value and hence its price. The scarcer a thing became, it was thought, the greater the rise in its value. Abundance of goods tended to lower their price and abundance of buyers to raise it. We need not insist further on this simple supply-and-demand theory of value. It was also recognised that labour and costs played a part in the determination of value, but the role of these factors was less well defined.

Some Medieval Views on Money

During the greater part of the long Middle Ages this predominantly subjective theory of value was not applied to money. The functions of money, as Aristotle had said, were to serve as a medium of exchange, a measure of the value of goods, and a store of value or "guarantor against future need". Clearly, money could not fulfil these functions unless its own value were stable.

We cannot always tell just what a scholastic writer means by the "value" or "estimation" of money. He might mean the tale of the coin which determined its ratio to other coins and was stamped with the mark of the prince whose servants had minted it. Or it might mean the market value of the metal of which it was made. Some writers stressed the first of these sources of value, and some the second. The matter was neatly summed up by John Buridan (1300 - 1358), rector of the University of Paris, who says that the material cause of money is some rare metal, its efficient cause the State, its final cause the need of men to exchange goods, and its formal cause the sign set upon it[5].

In the later Middle Ages it came to be glimpsed that the value of money might vary under the influence of supply and demand, just as

---

5 BURIDAN, op. Bk. I., Q. II, art. 2. See NOONAN, pp. 67 - 68.

that of goods varied. This tendency appears most clearly in the discussion of foreign exchange. It was taken up and developed by the School of Salamanca, as we shall see.

Medieval Views on Interest

The condemnation of usury, defined as the act or intention of charging a profit on a loan, is not exclusively Christian. I doubt whether any one of the sources that are often listed as having originated the prohibition of interest-bearing loans, - that is to say, the Bible, Aristotle, the Church Fathers, the medieval Doctors, natural law, and the modified view of time that foreshadowed the age of Newton - played a decisive part in its development. Jewish sources are important for our subject but tend to be overlooked. Less seminal for western monetary theory is the Islamic legal tradition, although in Spain the frequent bracketing together of "Jewish and Moorish" usurers in the medieval legal texts suggests that some part of the sophisticated Islamic teaching, as well as the Jewish, may have survived to reinforce the sources mentioned above.

It seems reasonable to suppose that the condemnation of usury common to the three Semitic religions (with the exception of the eastern Church, which permitted interest) did not spring from learned sources alone but from the daily experience of the common man. In any poverty-stricken community the chief object of economic life is to keep starvation at bay, and the cost of doing so has always been heavy. The struggling farmer, beset by problems of every kind, has had to seek credit that has often sent him into the ranks of the day-labourers; while in the towns the small shopkeepers, obliged to grant credit or go out of business, have willynilly become moneylenders and been hated for their pains.

The search for a theory that would protect the poor man from ruin and yet permit the sort of loans without which the Commercial Revolution, and perhaps even the Reconquest itself, would have been impossible, was the chief task that confronted the pre-Salamancan monetary theorists.

The juridical principles on which the usury doctrine depended were the following.

All loans must be gratuitous. There are two classes of loans. In the first, which is called in Latin the *commodatum*. the ownership of the thing lent does not pass to the borrower, and the actual thing borrowed must be returned - for instance, a house or a mule. In the second class of loans the ownership passes to the borrower. Such a loan is called a *mutuum* which is the free loan of a good that is consumed in use and may be weighed, counted or measured, for example, money, oil, gold, silver, or corn. Since the borrower needs the thing in order to consume it, he obviously will not be able to return it and must instead return another good of the same kind, quantity and quality. Usury is only to be found in a *mutuum*. Since in this kind of loan ownership naturally carried the right of use, it was universally regarded as unjust for the lender to charge separately for the use of the thing lent, and he was entitled only to the return of the principal.

There were other standard arguments that were used by the Church to discourage moneylending. Time, it was held, was the essence of a loan, and a lender had no right to sell time, which belonged to all God's creatures. Again, money was barren by its very nature and so could not bear fruit. Finally, Christ had enjoined his followers to "lend, hoping for nothing in return". These and other arguments against usury were incorporated into Gratian's *Decretum* compiled between 1139 and 1141, and into the *Decretals* of Gregory IX, compiled in 1234. In these compilations of canon law we may follow the growth of the Catholic doctrine of usury, which tended, on the whole, towards an ever-increasing severity.

A key-figure of the history of usury in Spain is that of Saint Raymond of Peñafort (1180 - 1278), the compiler of the *Decretals* and the patron saint of canon lawyers. Raymond spent most of his life in Barcelona, at that time a busy seaport. The problem of usury engaged his anxious attention. Among other "manifold shifts and stratagems" used to conceal interest-bearing loans were the following: profiting from the fruits of a pledge; taking horses in pledge and over-charging for their fodder; forestalling; usury cloaked as a partnership, "as when a man lends money to a merchant on condition that he shares in the profits but not in the losses"; usury disguised as a penalty for failing to return the loan by a certain date; and usury charged through a third party. In an attempt to reconcile the severity of the Church's doctrine with the legitimate needs of commerce, Raymond makes use of the Roman law concept of *interesse* "that which is between" the amount due under a contract and the amount actually paid, or damages arising from the default of one of the parties. Among the titles to *interesse* approved by Raymond are the following: expense incurred in caring for pledged property; loss suffered by the lender owing to the borrower's failure to return the loan on the agreed date; and loss of the profit the lender might have expected to make if, instead of allowing himself to be persuaded into lending his money, he had used it for the purpose of his business[6].

We may well ask what was the net result of the long duel between mercantile practice and ecclesiastical control. That the prohibition of interest-bearing loans was taken very seriously is evidenced by the considerable number of testators who made restitution in their wills for the usury they had committed. As to daily business life, a Genoese document of 1369 alleges that debtors unwilling to pay their creditors often introduce "many obstacles and hindrances" by alleging that the contract under which they are being sued was illegal and usurious, and by resorting to the canonical courts in order to delay payment[7].

Once usury was condemned by the canon law, the ban came general. Henceforth usury was a mortal sin, and the usurer open to the charge of heresy. In Spain, the civil law followed the canon law, though in a

---

6 GRICE-HUTCHINSON (!978), pp. 3 - 36.

7 LOPEZ, R. S. / RAYMOND, I. W., pp. 276 - 277.

vacillating manner. In Castile usury was made a punishable offence in 1348, and in Aragon a little later. Usury at a maximum rate was generally allowed for Jewish moneylenders, though there were times when even that was banned[8].

We may perhaps conclude that despite the development of alternative contracts the prohibition of usury did to some extent hamper economic progress, and that it sometimes troubled the conscience of merchants who were otherwise blameless in their business dealings.

The Age of the Discoveries

The Reconquest, as J. H. Elliott says, "was not one but many things. It was at once a crusade against the infidel, a succession of military expeditions in search of plunder, and a popular migration"[9]. We are here concerned only with the second of these motives, the desire for wealth, which for the hidalgo had traditionally been won by force of arms and which consisted of land and booty.

The end of the Reconquest came in 1492 with the fall of Granada to the Catholic Kings. In August of that same year Columbus set sail for the unknown regions of the west. He himself was not a hidalgo but a representative of tlie Mediterranean commercial tradition who saw his task as primarily an economic enterprise. Nevertheless, by the *conquistadores* who followed him the discovery of America was envisaged as a continuation of the Reconquest: that is to say, as a military advance that would lead to the sharing-out of freshly-won land and booty, as well as to the conversion of the heathen.

The opening of the American market brought a new prosperity to the motherland. With the arrival and settlement of the Spaniards in the New World there arose a growing demand for the products of the

---

8 CLAVERO, pp. 38 - 59; GRICE-HUTCHINSON (1978), pp. 33 - 36.

9 ELLIOTT, p. 20.

metropolis. In compensation for the Spanish exports to the colonies, American gold and silver began to reach Spain from the beginning of the sixteenth century onwards. Seville, the home-port of the treasure-fleet, attracted businessmen from every part of Europe. A trade-boom, set in. Prices rose, first in Seville, then throughout New Castile, and later in Old Castile, Valencia, and the rest of Spain, doubling in the first half of the sixteenth century, and again in the second.

Of the American treasure that arrived at Seville between 1503 and 1660, it appears that rather more than a quarter passed to the crown. Yet it was insufficient to meet the needs of the Spanish treasury. In the reign of the emperor Charles V it became necessary to borrow in every part of the imperial domains. In Spain these loans took various forms: fixed-interest bonds or "juros", forced loans on the arrival of the treasure-fleet, loans "suggested" to the great nobles and prelates, and short-term debt contracted by the local authorities in the form of bills-of-exchange payable at the next settling-day or "fair" to be held at Medina del Campo, Medina del Rioseco, Lyons or Besançon.

For a little time fortunes could still be made in the New World by the old traditional method of conquest, the acquirement of land and booty, and the virtual enslavement of the conquered peoples. But in Spain itself things had changed. Accounting skills, quickness of intellect, and knowledge of commercial practice were now the keys to prosperity. And of such training the hidalgo had but little, contenting himself with consolidating the territorial gains he had achieved in the Reconquest. The dynamic role in the economic leadership of society was assumed by the merchant families, many of Jewish or foreign origin, who knew how to exploit the changed economic situation created by the discovery of America. There were openings in the Church, too, for some of the newly converted, who carried into their Christian life the high standards of scholarship that had been attained by their forefathers, the rabbis, and whose zeal and administrative ability soon brought them into prominence. They contributed to the formation of a well-trained professional group whose members were able to explain the economic events of their time and to attempt to guide their course, though not always with success.

The School of Salamanca

It is clear that a phenomenon such as the rise in prices that took place in Spain in the sixteenth century could not pass unnoticed in the Spanish universities. The sin of avarice which according to the medieval doctors had accompanied the growth of commerce in their day now reappeared with redoubled virulence. As the evangelisation of the New World proceeded, even the activities of the *conquistadores* were looked at askance, because, unlike the Cid, they were plundering fellow-Christians. A few of the more compassionate Doctors (including Vitoria) went so far as to maintain that heathens, too, had rights under natural law. As for the merchants and bankers who were profiting from the American trade, the Doctors held them to be in dire moral peril. Often, however, they were sinning out of ignorance, which the Doctors saw it as their duty to dispel. In their bulky treatises, generally written in Latin, they examined many aspects of economic life: the institution of private property, poor relief, taxation, price, interest, foreign exchange and banking.

Many of the Doctors taught at the university of Salamanca, hence the name by which the group is known. Its prestige as a source of economic doctrine was established by Francisco de Vitoria in 1526 and lasted through several generations, spreading far beyond Salamanca. Among the earlier members of the School there were several Dominicans; among the later, some of the more celebrated were Jesuits. I have chosen to devote the rest of this paper to considering three of the pioneer members of the School of Salamanca, rather than their successors, because it seems to me that their "contributions to monetary theory", the prescribed subject of this paper, can be more readily distinguished from the work of the medieval Doctors. Their views were discussed, accepted by some of the later writers and refuted by others; and some of their ideas, at least, were carried forward into modern times. The relative success of their monetary theory must to a great extent be attributed to their custom of vigorous controversy, by which illogical, unrealistic, or otherwise untenable opinions were weeded out as soon as they appeared. The subtlety and complexity of their teaching was not as excessive as is sometimes thought, but was, on the contrary, necessary if monetary theory was to advance on sure ground.

Francisco de Vitoria and his Theory of Value

In the earlier decades of the sixteenth century the centre of European culture was the University of Paris, where the Spanish Dominican friar, Francisco de Vitoria, took his degree in theology in 1522. After teaching for three years in Valladolid, Vitoria was appointed, in September 1526, to a chair of theology at the University of Salamanca.

Vitoria took no part in public life and published little. He was absorbed in his academic work, and here his influence was great, his lectures coming to form the cornerstone of theology in Spain. The principal reform that he brought with him from Paris was the replacement as text-book of Peter Lombard's *Sentences* by the *Suma Theologica* of Saint Thomas Aquinas, an innovation that was generally adopted by the Spanish theologians of the sixteenth and seventeenth centuries. When Vitoria came to hear that in the New World, despite the efforts of the Catholic Kings to protect their "barbarian" subjects, fortunes were being made illegally by the time-honoured methods of the Cid - that is, by slaughter, enslavement and rapine - he was filled with horror. In his lectures on the Indies, delivered in 1538 and 1539, he stresses the need for peaceful and fair trading between the Spaniards and the native peoples, thus bringing the newly-created

American society into the orbit of international law and of the Law Merchant that was in process of development.

Vitoria's monetary theory follows the path that had been marked out by three celebrated Thomist theologians of a somewhat earlier period: the Austrian, Conrad of Summenhart, and two Italians, Cardinal Cajetan and Silvester of Priero. These authors accepted and enriched the medieval doctrine of the just price whose main lines I have already roughly sketched. We now have to consider in what way Vitoria may he said to have improved on the generally-accepted supply-and demand theory of value, and whether his teaching on the matter was in any way influenced by the discovery of America. An answer to the first part of this question was put forward by the late professor Demetrio Iparraguirre[10]. Vitoria, he tells us, differed from earlier authors by distinguishing between necessary and superfluous things.

Vitoria's ideas about value may be summarised as follows. He holds that when the price of a thing is fixed by law, then the legal price is also the just price. As regards other things, he adheres to the doctrine that utility is the principal source of value and that the just price is determined by common estimation: that is, by the play of supply and demand. The common estimation of the market is, for Vitoria, the only factor that enables us to compare things that are diverse in their nature, such as gold and silver, or horses and pearls.

But Vitoria's insistence on the utility factor is by no means indiscriminate. He makes a careful distinction between the price of necessities and that of luxury goods. The just price of necessities, when it is not legally fixed, is the common market price, which, once established, must be respected. But if no common market price exists for a necessary good, then the just price must be settled between the contracting parties, and in this case such factors as cost, labour, risk, and scarcity may be taken into account.

---

10 IPARRAGUIRRE, passim.

Coming to the price of superfluous goods, or luxuries, Vitoria explains that here there need be no extraneous limitation to the play of the contracting parties' personal tastes. He insists firmly on this doctrine, which he claims to be novel. In fact, it appears that the distinction between necessities and luxuries was not altogether unknown before Vitoria's time, but he seems to have given it a new emphasis[11]. His vision of several markets, perfect and, imperfect, in which social conditions vary, has led Iparraguirre to speak, with much reason, of his "social theory of value".

Vitoria's thesis was accepted by some of his successors and rejected by others. Why did he make an exception to his general teaching by' permitting the vendor of a luxury article to sell it for any price he could get? I would suggest that he was trying to reconcile his basic concern for justice, the common welfare, and tradition, with a certain acceptance of the inflationary conditions of his day - conditions that followed upon the Discoveries- and that he was unwilling to condemn as sinful any profit that might be made by traders in luxury goods, for which the demand was greater than it had been before.

Vitoria applies his theory of value to services as well as goods. He especially mentions those of singers and other musicians. "If a man refuses to sing unless he is paid a thousand ducats, and he gets them, who is to say that he ought to return the money?"[12]

Another example of a certain liberalisation in Vitoria's economic thought is his treatment of the resale or *mohatra* contract. This was an ancient Jewish device, described in the Talmud and often debated among the rabbis, by which a loan could be passed off as a sale. There were several forms of *mohatra*. I need only mention the commonest, which was when the moneylender pretended to sell some good to the borrower at an agreed price payable at a future date, and immediately bought it back at a lower price, the difference between the

---

11 IPARRAGUIRRE, par. 24 and 25, pp. 78 - 81. See LANGHOLM, (1982), pp. 276 - 277.

12 IPARRAGUIRRE, par. 41, pp. 84 - 85.

two prices being the usury on what was really a loan. A third party could be brought into the transaction to make it more plausible, and it had been held that the contract was licit if the sale and resale were not made by the same person. Vitoria now says that even this is allowed so long as no previous agreement had been reached between the parties[13].

Little did Vitoria foresee that a hundred years later, in 1656, the *mohatra* was to be used by Pascal as a weapon against the Jesuits, since, although officially condemned by the Church, it was half approved in some manuals of moral theology, including that of the Spanish Jesuit, Antonio de Escobar, which was mainly based on the teaching of the Spanish Doctors[14].

Vitoria, in my opinion, did take some tentative steps towards a certain flexibility in business morality, and he may well have been prompted to do so by the increased volume and complexity of commerce that resulted from thc Discoveries. But he made no decisive break with earlier teaching, nor does his monetary theory constitute a milestone in the history of economic thought in the way that his doctrine of empire does in the history of international law. His most cherished aim, perhaps, was to speak with the voice of Saint Thomas Aquinas to the people of his own day.

Quantity Theory and Theory of Money

After Vitoria's death in 1544 his economic thought was perpetuated and developed by his colleagues and disciples. Bearing in mind the main purpose of this talk, which is to distinguish the original contributions made by the School of Salamanca to monetary theory from amongst the vast mass of doctrine they had inherited from earlier

13 IPARRAGUIRRE, par. 21, p. 79.

14 PASCAL, Lettres Provinciales, Letter 8.

authors, we may say that in their general outlook and in their overall treatment of economic subjects we find a new realism and a new readiness to take the facts of contemporary business practice into account. Some of the most complete and lucid descriptions of the commercial customs of those times are included in their writings. This marriage of descriptive and prescriptive economics seems to add a new instrumentality to the work of the School of Salamanca.

A hint that pointed the way towards the quantity theory of money had already been dropped by Vitoria. In accordance with his predominantly subjective theory of value he observes that if the Duke of Alba, for example, wishing to transfer money from Spain to Germany, were to deliver 1000 ducats to a banker in Medina, he would receive a lesser sum in Germany owing to the higher value of money in Germany. Some such doctrine had been current in the later Middle Ages, though never very clearly stated, since the pre-Salamancan writers do not elucidate the meaning of the words "valor" and "aestimatione" in reference to money or tell us what they mean by money's being "worth more" and "worth less" in this context. We may conjecture that they had the purchasing-power of money in mind, but we cannot be sure of it.

Mention of exchange-business brings us to the subject of the fairs. A celebrated piece of descriptive economics is the account of them given by Domingo de Soto in 1553. He tells us that there were four fairs. Two were held at Medina del Campo and the others at Medina del Rioseco and Villalón, corresponding to similar fairs held in Flanders[15].

The fairs dated back to medieval times and had not ceased to serve the community by supplying it with goods, but they were tending to engage more and more in purely financial business. They had become great international clearing centres, "the beginning and end of all payments", as Tomás de Mercado said in 1569, and "mainly places for

---

15 Domingo de Soto, De Justitia et Jure, Lib. VI, Q. 12, a. 2.

settling accounts, not for true buying and selling", though of such there was still "a good share"[16].

Following Vitoria's lead, Soto explains how the system of payment in force at the fairs gave rise to a rate of exchange for moneys remitted from fair to fair by means of bills. This rate, according to Soto, varied according to the supply and demand for bills in the different financial centres. Money, he continues, was sometimes so scarce in Flanders that small coins were there worth as much as coins of large denominations in Spain, just as a measure of wheat in a place where wheat is scarce is worth two measures in a place where it is plentiful. For this reason, a merchant who pays 410 *maravedis* to another merchant or fair-banker in Spain is justly repaid only 360 *maravedis* in Flanders, thus suffering an apparent loss of 50 *maravedis*.

> Similarly (adds Soto), if a merchant pays out 300 *maravedis* in Flanders he is repaid 375 in Spain,so that he gains more by sending money to Spain than he loses by sending it to Flanders. The same thing is happening now between Spain and Rome, because money is generally scarcer in Rome.

Like other apologists of exchange transactions, Soto is careful to minimise the importance of the time element in the deal, since interest paid simply for the use of money during a certain period of time was universally condemned as usurious. His general conclusion is that

> it is lawful to exchange money in one place for money in another, having regard to its scarcity in one and abundance in the other and to receive a smaller sum in a place where money is scarce in exchange for a larger where it is abundant.

When the two sums are exchanged by reason of a divergence of place, not of time, the transaction is not a loan but "the true exchange of two things present that are of equal value"[17].

---

16 Tomás de Mercado (1569), pp. 88 - 89.

17 Soto, lib.VII, Q. VII, Q. V., art. 2.

The celebrated Augustinian doctor, Martín de Azpilcueta, called Navarrus, in his commentary on the exchanges, written in Spanish, makes the definitive advance in the formulation of the quantity theory of money by equating the "value" of money to its purchasing-power. By doing so he at once explains the events of his time and justifies the business of the exchange-dealer. The following passage is well known but may perhaps bear repeating here:

> Other things being equal, in countries where there is a great scarcity of money, all other saleable goods, and even the hands and labour of men, are given for less money than where it is abundant. Thus we see by experience that in France, where money is scarcer than in Spain, bread, wine, cloth and labour are worth much less. And even in Spain, in times when money was scarcer, saleable goods and labour were given for very much less than after the discovery of the Indies, which flooded the country with gold and silver. The reason for this is that money is worth more where and when it is scarce than where and when it is abundant[18].

In this text Azpilcueta clarifies a point that had not been well defined by earlier authors: that the "value" or "estimation" of money is determined, in certain circumstances, by its purchasing-power. Earlier in the same text he had remarked on the contemporary practice of merchants to "increase their fortunes" by smuggling ducats out of Spain to Flanders and France, "some in barrels like olives and others hidden in wine, on each of which they make a large profit, buying merchandise that is cheap abroad and dear at home". He thus considers the purchasing-power of money in the shape of coins as well as bills of exchange, and suggests one of the channels by which the inflation of prices in Spain was spread to other countries by increasing the demand for goods that were cheaper in countries where money was scarcer.

---

18 AZPILCUETA, Comentario de cambios, Ch. XII, par. 51.

Azpilcueta on Usury

In another commentary, also written in Spanish, in which he treats the subject of usury in general, Azpilcueta devotes his opening chapters to defining the Spanish word "usura" and recapitulates the principles of Roman law on which the prohibition of usury still largely depended.

> Usury (he reminds us) is only to be found in a *mutuum:* that is, the loan of things that are spent when used and that are sold by weight, measure or number.
> Concealed usury (he goes on) is committed in the trading of all these things, and even in credit transactions in which more than the maximum just price in charged because the vendor agrees to wait for his money, or less than the minimum just price is paid because the purchaser advances payment before he receives the thing sold.

This text suggests that the concept of usury had come to engulf a wide range of business practices. Azpilcueta calls for repentance and restitution not only from bankers and merchants but from landlords who charge more than the normal rent because they postpone payment, tax-farmers who take over the revenues at an unfairly low rent because they pay in advance, clerics and rich laymen who let their land to their labourers at an unduly high rent in return for allowing them longer credit, or lend them wheat to consume or sow, or money for other necessities, on similar unjust terms, "thereby compelling them to work unduly hard and live worse than if they were slaves ...". Such things, he adds sadly, were unknown in Spain before our present age[19].

Azpilcueta's rigorous treatment of usury in contracts of sale contrasts with his relative permissiveness in the matter of foreign exchange. On the whole, I think, we may say that he was determined to remain within the bounds of orthodoxy in cases where liberalisation would result in hardship and injustice for one of the parties concerned in the deal, but that he took care not to condemn too harshly the normal

19 AZPILCUETA, Comentario de usuras, Ch. 12, pp. 15 - 20.

business practice of bankers and merchants. That this was his basic aim is suggested in the concluding paragraph of his *Commentary on the Exchanges*:

> "To this extent, and no further, may we allow the merchants their profit. We have stretched every possible point in just defence of the souls, reputations and fortunes of so many honorable and important people".

Later Developments

The path laid by Vitoria, Soto and Azpilcueta was followed by many of the Spanish schoolmen, including Diego de Covarrubias (1512 - 1577), Tomás de Mercado (died 1575), Luís de Molina (1535 - 1600), Leonard Lessius (1554 - 1623), and Juan de Lugo (1583 - 1660), whose death marks the close of the scholastic renaissance in Spain, so far as monetary theory is concerned. By the later decades of the sixteenth century the wave of prosperity evoked by the Discoveries was already spent. It was succeeded by a depression that deepened as time went on and was not to lift for another century. The moral problems born of excessive profits gave way to those evoked by material disaster. Pressing economic questions of the day came to occupy the minds of churchmen as well as laymen. In monetary theory, currency problems replaced usury as a matter for primary and universal concern.

We may usefully compare the development of the usury doctrine in Spain with the course taken by the same doctrine in England during the period when the School of Salamanca was at its zenith. The Anglican Church was hostile to loans at interest. When in 1571 the government of the Tudors recognised the legality of interest provided it did not exceed the rate of 10%, there were protests among the Anglican divines.

A leading opponent of the bill was Dr. Thomas Wilson, whose *Discourse on Usury* was published in the following year. His attitude is less tolerant than that of the Spanish Doctors, and the fact that he christens the merchant of his dialogue by the name of "Gromelgaynor" is enough to show what he thinks of the business world.

A later opponent of interest was the Reverend Miles Mosse or Moses, rector of Combes in Suffolk, whose sermons against usury were published in 1595. His little book offers a knowledgeable summary of the evasionary devices as they existed in his day, and he condemns them all as "fair cloaks to shroud the ragged garments" of usury. His vivid description of the *mohatra* recalls the account given by Tomás de Mercado in 1569. Mosse shows, indeed, a certain familiarity with Catholic teaching on usury but adopts the more rigorous attitude of an earlier age. It would seem that the moral doctrine of the Anglican clergy was, in the matter of usury, less flexible than that of the School of Salamanca, and that as far as concerns economic analysis, the Spanish Doctors were considerably more advanced.

In England it was left to Bacon to solve the dilemma that lay at the heart of the usury prohibition and had troubled moralists ever since the early middle ages. Confessing himself unable to reconcile the positive and negative aspects of usury, in his essay of 1625 he suggests that two maximum rates should be introduced: one for the "common borrower", and a higher rate for business loans But this idea, besides being unworkable, was too simple to appeal to theologians and lawyers.

The history of usury remains something of an enigma. According to a leading authority, the last word on the subject has not yet been said. Credit has grown up surreptiously, in the shadow of guilt and cynicism. If we try to follow the usury debate, "we come up against a certain opacity that is difficult to overcome"[20]. This last judgement, at least, I can heartily endorse.

---

20 GAZIER, pp. 120 - 121.

Conclusion

The doctors of Salamanca accomplished a good deal, so far as monetary theory is concerned. They conserved tradition in a rapidly changing world and adapted theory to fit contemporary events. They developed medieval value-theory on subjective lines, and brought money and merchandise under the same doctrine of value. They connected the rise in the Spanish price-level to the influx of American gold and silver, and to the increased volume of credit that resulted from the American trade, thus laying the foundations of the quantity theory of money. They formulated a theory of foreign exchange based on the diversity in the purchasing-power of money in the different countries concerned. And they retained the formal ban on usury while moderating some of its more irksome effects, and directed the metamorphosis that changed the reprehensible "evasive devices" into the approved "extrinsic titles" to interest.

But what was the fundamental object of all this intellectual labour? And can we say that it had any permanent success? Let us return for a moment to the Salamancan theory of value. The doctors accepted that, as Domingo de Soto said, "prices are a primary concern of the republic and its governors, who ought really to fix the price of every article. But since they cannot possibly do so in all cases, the task is left to the discretion of buyers and sellers"[21]. Their subjective or utility theory of value was not designed to promote business interests. On the contrary, their tendency to underplay the influence of cost and labour on price, which they sometimes carried to extremes[22], was intended to prevent merchants from overcharging on the plea of recuperating their original outlay. Price should correspond to the "estimation" or demand for a good that was "common" to the market as a whole, and not to the claims made by sellers about their costs.

---

21 Soto, lib. VI, Q. 2, Art. III.

22 As in Saravia de la Calle, Ch. III.

When the School of Salamanca had long since passed away and scholasticism no longer dominated men's way of thinking, this subjective or utility view of value was preserved and handed down through successive generations until it came to form one of the bases of modern economic science. The Salamancans, of course, could not know that the seeds of economic liberalism were latent in their work, nor can we say what their reaction would have been if they had known it. The relevance of Salamancan monetary theory to our own day has been important. But, by one of the paradoxes that enliven the history of economic thought, it was fortuitous and incidental to the doctors' two overriding aims: to uphold the authority of the canon law while relieving the burden of moral condemnation that weighed on the conscience of merchants.

Bibliography:

AZPILCUETA, Martín de, Comentario resolutorio de cambios, Salamanca 1556; modern edition, Madrid 1965.

AZPILCUETA, Martín de, Comentario resolutorio de usuras, Salamanca 1556.

BURIDAN, J., Quaestiones super VIII libros politicorum Aristoteles, Paris 1513.

BAECK, L., Spanish economic thought: the School of Salamanca and the arbitristas, in: *History of Political Economy* 20/3 (1988).

BARRIENTOS GARCIA, J., Un siglo de moral económica en Salamanca (1526 - 1629), Salamanca 1985.

CLAVERO, B., Usura: del uso económico de la religión en la historia, Madrid 1984.

DEMPSEY, B. W., Interest and Usury, London 1943.

ELLIOTT, J. H., Imperial Spain. 1469 - 1716, London 1963.

Fuero viejo de Castilla, in: Los códigos españoles, Vol. 1, Madrid 1847.

GAZIER, Michèle and Bernard, Or et Monnaie chez Martín de Azpilcueta, Paris 1978.

GOMEZ CAMACHO, F., Introduction to Luís de Molina *La teoria del justo precio*, Madrid 1981.

GOMEZ CAMACHO, F., Introduction to Luís de Molina *Tratado sobre los préstamos y la usura.*

GOMEZ CAMACHO, F., Introduction to Luís de Molina *Tratado sobre los cambios,* Madrid 1990.

GOMEZ CAMACHO, F., La teoría monetaria de los doctores españoles del siglo XVI, in: *Moneda y Credito* 172 (1985).

IPARRAGUIRRE, D., Francisco de Vitoria: una teorla social del valor económico, Bilbao 1957.

LANGHOLM, O., Price and Value in the Aristotelian Tradition, Bergen 1979.

LANGHOLM, O., Wealth and Money in the Aristotelian Tradition, Bergen 1983.

LANGHOLM,O., The Aristotelian Analysis of Usury, Bergen 1984.

LANGHOLM, O., Economic Freedom in Scholastic Thought, in: *History of Political Economy* 14/2 (1982).

LOPEZ, R. S. / RAYMOND, I. W., Medieval Trade in theMediterranean World, New York 1955.

MERCADO, Tomás de, Tratos y contratos de mercaderes, Salamanca 1569; enlarged edition, Suma de tratos y contratos, Seville 1571;. modern editions Madrid 1975 (ed. R. SIERRA BRAVO) and Madrid 1977 (ed. N. SANCHEZ-ALBORNOZ).

MOSSE, M., The Arrangement and Conviction of Usurie, in: TAWNEY, R. H. / POWER, E., Tudor Economic Documents, London 1934.

NOONAN, J. T, The Scholastic Analysis of Usury, Cambridge (Mass.) 1957.

Poema de Mio Cid, ed. Ian MICHAEL, 2ª edición renovada, Madrid 1984.

RAYMOND OF PENAFORT, St., Summa pastoralis, ed. J. G. RAVAISSON, Catalogue géneral des Mss. des Bibliothèques publiques des Départements, Vol. 1, Paris 1849, pp. 621 - 623.

RAYMOND OF PEFIAFORT, St., Summa de Poenitentia, 1st edition 1840; reprinted under the title of "Summa ad manuscriptorum fidem recognita", Verona 1744.

ROBERTSON, K. M., Aspects of the Rise of Economic Individualism, Cambridge 1933.

ROOVER, R. de, La pensée éonomique des Scolastiques, Paris 1971.

ROOVER, R. de, Business, Banking and Economic Thought in Late Medieval and Early Modern Europe, Chicago 1974.

SARAVIA DE LA CALLE, L., Instrucción de Mercaderes muy provechosa, Medina del Campo 1544; edición moderna Madrid 1949.

SCHUMPETER, J. A., History of Economic Analysis, New York 1954.

SIERRA BRAVO, R., El pensamiento social y económico de la escolástica, Madrid 1967.

SOTO, Domingo de, De Justitia et Iure, Salamanca 1553.

TAWNEY, R. H., Religion and the Rise of Capitalism, London 1926.

TORTAJADA, R., Justes Prix, Usures et Monnaie, in: *Economies et Sociétés,* serié Oeconomia, P.E. 15 (1991), pp. 61 - 91.

VINER, J., Religion and Economic Society. Four chapters of an unpublished work, in: *History of Political Economy* 10/1 (1978).

WEBER, W., Geld und Zins in der spanischen Spätscholastik, Münster 1962.

WILSON, T. A., Discourse upon Usury, London 1925.

Spanish Economic Thought of the Seventeenth Century

By FRANCISCO GÓMEZ CAMACHO

Introduction

For guides to the economic thought of the seventeenth century we can turn to either Adam Smith or John Maynard Keynes. If we choose Smith we will obtain a basically negative view, as exposed in the fourth Book of *The Wealth of Nations*; if we prefer Keynes our vision will be essentially positive, and its general lines are to be found in Chapter 23 of *General Theory*. In order to truly understand the economic thought of the seventeenth century, perhaps we should leave aside the go-betweens, and examine it face to face, bearing in mind that it was in this century that the so-called "Newtonian Revolution", or the "Scientific Revolution" took place. The seventeenth century, when Galileo and Newton both lived (Galileo died in 1642, the year that Newton was born),

> "... underwent, and accomplished, a very radical spiritual revolution of which modern science is at the same time the root and the fruit"[1].

---

1 A. KOYRÉ, From the Closed World to the Infinite Universe, London 1970, p. 1.

Smith wanted to be part of this scientific revolution when he wrote his economic work; he envisioned a dynamic and stable society that, propelled by the interests of the individual, could live in the absence of authority without falling into chaos and irrationality. Smith wrote *The Wealth of Nations* in 1776; Newton had published his *Principia Mathematica* in 1687. Why did the Newtonian Revolution have to wait almost a century before it was applied to economics?

I. Scholasticism and the Scientific Revolution of the Seventeenth Century

A. Koyré tells us that the question of the origins of modern science and its relationship to the Middle Ages "is still a greatly debated *quaestio disputata*"[2]. In contrast, there seems to be no dispute about the origins of the economic sciences. No one would be so imprudent or bold as to cast doubt on Smith's paternity. And I am not about to do so; however, there is one point that surprises me, and I feel that economists have not awarded it the attention it merits. In the area of modern sciences, those developed by Galileo and Newton, historians accept that

> "The late medieval scholars, the Scholastics in particular, not only provided the rational atmosphere in which modern mathematics and science were born, but they infused the great thinkers of the Renaissance with the belief that nature was the creation of God and that God's ways could be understood. It was this fundamental article of faith that dominated and inspired the Renaissance mathematicians and scientists"[3].

---

2 A. KOYRÉ, Estudios del pensamiento científico, Madrid 1977, p. 51.

3 M. KLINE, Mathematics in Western Culture, Penguin Books, 1987, pp. 119 - 120.

If this is true in the area of natural or empirical sciences, how can we explain that these same Scholastic philosophers, who so influenced modern mathematics and science, made no scientific contribution to economic thought? Had J. A. Schumpeter exaggerated when he said in his *History of Economic Analysis* that if a group deserved the qualification of "founders of scientific economics", these were the Spanish Scholastic Scholars[4]. This question, sparked by my own curiosity, is what lead me to study the economic thought of the Spanish Scholastics of the sixteenth and seventeenth centuries.

Naturally, the economic thought of seventeenth century Spain was not reduced to the work of the Scholastics; however I should clarify here that I will not discuss the works of the "Arbitrist", or those from the same time which dealt with "Mercantilism", but will concentrate instead on the writings of the doctors who taught in the universities. Were Spanish seventeenth century economic thought reduced exclusively to the Arbitrists' propositions, this body of study would have contributed very little to the economic sciences. Fortunately, however, such is not the case. As Marjorie Grice-Hutchinson writes:

> "For most historians this period constitutes the 'age of mercantilism'. And certainly, in Spain as elsewhere, mercantilist doctrine was preached by many writers. But for the historian of economic thought it does not, perhaps, represent the most interesting work of the period. The high level of Spanish sixteenth-century economics noted by Schumpeter was largely the achievement of the late Scholastics - the School of Salamanca, as they have sometimes been called"[5].

Obstacles of varying importance must be overcome to explore in depth the economic thought of this School. The first, and perhaps the least important of these arises from the language the doctors used to write the bulk of their work. As we know, Latin was the academic tongue of

---

4 J. A. SCHUMPETER, History of Economic Analysis, Oxford 1967, p. 97.

5 M. GRICE-HUTCHINSON, Early Economic Thought in Spain 1177 - 1740, Oxford 1978, p. 81.

the seventeenth century, and we cannot forget that at the end of this period, when Newton wrote his *Principia Mathematica*, Latin was still used for scientific writings[6]. This problem has been solved at least in part, as today several of the treatises on economic topics by the Scholastic philosophers have been translated into Spanish. The second obstacle is more important since its origins reside in the character of the Scholastic works themselves. These were not written for theological or moral purposes[7], but were conceived from what today could legitimately be called an "interdisciplinary" perspective. We are so accustomed to the one-dimensional approach to science, to its compartmentalization into airtight specializations, that it is difficult to comprehend the interdisciplinary concept of reality. The Scholastics, nonetheless, produced a body of interdisciplinary thought where

> "Science, philosophy, even theology, are, all of them, legitimately interested in questions about the nature of space, structure of matter, patterns of action and, last but not least, about the nature, structure, and value of human thinking and of human science"[8].

---

6 I think it is also important to note that the Scholastic doctors were concerned with making reading and understanding their ideas available to those who did not read Latin. T. de Mercado, for example, expressly says that he wrote in the common language so that he would be understood (Prologue to the *Suma*); Dr. Navarro wrote his Confessors' *Manual* in Castillian Spanish; the *Treatise*, by Melchor de Soria, was written in Castillian Spanish, etc. One thing were academic writings, which were in Latin, the language of the universities at that time, and another were works published to propagate the school of thought.

7 This moral purpose has always been present in the great economists, who considered themselves "moral philosophers". Why does Keynes call Chapter 24 of the General Theory "Final notes on social philosophy to which the general theory may lead" if not because he considered his work a book on social philosophy or, as would have been said in the seventeenth century, on moral philosophy?

8 A. KOYRÉ, From the Closed ..., p. ix.

Without doubt Pierre Vilar has best expressed the Spanish Scholastics's "interdisciplinary" outlook when describing economic phenomena when he observed, perhaps in reference to Doctor Navarro's *Confessors's Manual* that, in the hands of this thinker "The Confessors's Manual became a book of economic analysis!"[9]

Within this "interdisciplinary" perspective, we must place the Scholastic philosophers' use of mathematics; and this constitutes the third obstacle to understanding their economic thought. So little is known of this aspect of the Scholastics's work that it merits careful exposition. Furthermore, this is a topic I consider essential to properly comprehend what the Scholastics wrote about money and usury, as I hope to show below.

In the Faculties of Arts, the doctors taught Euclides's geometry, explained Pythagorean thought and discoursed on Aristotle's physics in the tradition of the "calculators" from Oxford. In other words, they *separating themselves* from what Aristotle had to say with respect to certain points, for example, in their explanation of the dynamics of bodies. In this manner, they developed a clear awareness of the role mathematics played in the analysis of specific problems, *including theological matters*. They preached an infinite character of God, and a mathematical infinity that could not be applied in arbitrary fashion to substantives, so the *actu* existence of an infinite reality constituted one of the problems they dealt with in their treatises. This concern prompted the Scot John Mair, Smith's predecessor as the chair of Moral Philosophy at the University of Glasgow, to write at the beginning of the sixteenth century one of the first works "On the Infinitive". It also bears mention that it was one of his Spanish disciples, Antonio Coronel from Segovia, who, apart from criticizing some of the treatise's points, worked with Mair on the moral reply that the Sorbonne gave after the consultation by a certain group of merchants about their economic practices. From the beginning, the doctors made an epistemological distinction between mathematical infinity and real infinity,

9 P. VILAR, Oro y moneda en la historia, 1450 - 1920, Barcelona 1969, p. 179.

and developed a body of thought in which they clearly distinguished the magnitudes or nominal values from the reality which these values were to be applied. This divergence, which Domingo de Soto clearly exposed in his *Comments on Aristotle's Physics* is the fruit of the neo-Platonic thought that at the time opposed Aristotelianism. The Scholastic doctors projected the controversy to the analysis of the concepts of space and time, in which the idea of continuity and divisibility *ad infinitum* played an essential role. In mid seventeenth century Juan de Lugo followed the same mathematical tradition, and wrote a brief treatise on *The composition of continuity and its divisibility in finite parts*[10]. This study clearly shows the extent to which the doctors practised an interdisciplinary endeavour. It also highlights the role they attributed to mathematics. Juan de Lugo resorts to the mathematical analysis of continuity, as he himself says,

> "... to deal with the current theological problem of whether or not merit, because of the duration of the act, is raised to the infinite. (Later he adds that) the theologian studies this question in order to show clearly how the duration of a good deed or a bad deed does not result in an infinite merit or infinite demerit ...; the topic - warns Cardinal Lugo - is totally philosophical, and the Councils and the Pontiffs can define nothing about it, as Valencia, among others teaches"[11].

According to the doctors, the problem embodied in the duration of human acts had a direct and immediate bearing on the economic behaviour of the subjects. This applies specifically to the period of time a loan is granted a person, and underlines the problem, analogous to the theological merit of good deeds, of defining the relationship between the duration of the loan and the amount of interest paid, which was derived from the length of the operation. For this reason I consider of particular importance the analytical meaning granted the ex-

---

10 Juan DE LUGO, Quo modo possit explicari compositio continui ex solis indivisibilibus finits juxta sententiam recentiorum philosophorum, reproduced in: *Arch. Teolog. Granadino* 47 (1984), pp. 165 - 191.

11 Juan DE LUGO, ibid.

pressed reference to the "mere passing of time" that frequently appeared in the doctors's treatises on loans, transactions and usury. Without studying the doctors's analysis of time (and space) in relation to causality, it does not seem possible to correctly understand their monetary thinking in reference not only to usury, but to the shifts in the value of money that the public Authorities perpetrated as well. The doctors's thinking cannot be removed from the Nominalist philosophy in which it was developed and, as we know, Nominalist thought was particularly rigorous in the logical analysis of the concepts it used. It is for this reason that I believe that when at the end of the seventeenth century Newton was forced to define what he understood by *absolute* or scientific space and time in contrast to "vulgar" or relative space and time, he proceeded in a manner that prolonged a tradition developed previously by the Scholastics. The same occurs with his analysis of infinity, from which infinitesimal calculus eventually grew[12].

To conclude this introduction to the economic thought of the Spanish Scholastic philosophers of the sixteenth and seventeenth centuries, I should say something about the view that they held of natural law, and of the decision-making process when faced with uncertainty. In other words, I should say something about Probabilism and the fact that this philosophy was forsaken for Scientific Determination in the eighteenth century.

II. Natural Law, Probabilism and Scientific Determination

It would be difficult to find an author who has done more than J. A. Schumpeter to bring to light the meaning of Spanish Scholastic

---

12 Independently of the order of priority between Leibniz and Newton, it seems that both drew from the same philosophical sources.

thought and its place in the history of the economic sciences[13]. As is well known, one of his theses affirms the continuity of the method of natural law in eighteenth sociology and economics[14].

It seems to me that what Schumpeter wrote in his *History of Economic Analysis* is still one of the most complete and valid works that can be read on the methodology of natural law and its importance in the origin of the social sciences. In one aspect, nonetheless, his presentation of the Spanish Scholastics seems inadequate: in reference to *probabilism* and its importance in the moral decision-making process[15]. It surprises me, for example, that Schumpeter says nothing about probabilism and the importance it had for the Scholastics when deciding among more or less probable alternative economic courses; it also surprises me that he says nothing of the Nominalist philosophy and its importance in the origins not only of the Scholastics reflections on economics, but also in the origins of the modern sciences[16]. But if Schumpeter said nothing about the probabilistic element in Scholasticism or about the influence on it of Nominalism, his contemporary, Keynes called attention to this point. Precisely in his *Treatise on Probability* he expressly recognizes that

> "The first contact of theories of probability with modern ethics appears in the Jesuit doctrine of probabilism. According to this doctrine one is justified in doing an action for which there is *any* probability, however small, of its results being the best possible ... The correct application of probability to conduct naturally escaped the authors of a judicial ethics, which was more interested in the fixing of

---

13 See M. Grice-Hutchinson, Los economistas españoles y la Historia del Análisis Económico de Schumpeter, in: *Papeles de Economía Española* 17 (1983), pp. 72 - 184.

14 J. A. Schumpeter, History of Economic Analysis, Oxford 1967, p. 141.

15 For example, on how the juridical structure relates to non-juridical material. Cfr. op. cit., p. 141.

16 With reference to this point see my introduction to Tratado sobre los cambios (Treatise on change), by Luis de Molina, Madrid 1990, pp. XXXVII - XLVI.

responsibility for definite acts, and in the various specified means by which responsibility might be disposed of, than in the greatest possible sum-total of resultant good"[17].

Leaving aside the question as to the accuracy of Keynes's judgement and interpretation of the Scholastics's probabilism, I believe there is no denying that he was able to perceive an aspect of the economic thought of Spanish Scholasticism that the doctors considered essential, and that has generally been ignored by economists. Along these lines, perhaps now is a good time to recall something that the anthropologist Julio Caro Baroja said. This author has chosen to interpreted Scholastic probabilism and its casuistry as the expression of a specific view of the human person, and of Spanish society of the sixteenth and seventeenth centuries. In contrast to the widely held notion of a highly inquisitorial and monolithic society and mentality, Caro Baroja has stressed that sixteenth and seventeenth Spain lived through enormously complex times ideologically and socially. The title of one of his works: "*The complex forms of religious life: Religion, society and character in the Spain of the sixteenth and seventeenth centuries*"[18] states this thesis perfectly. In reference to the method of Scholastic moral thought, to which economic thought belongs, Julio Caro Baroja writes:

> "That the casuistics sought "causes in cases" of conscience, without resorting *either to chance or to a rigid application of certain principles of evangelical moral*, can be interpreted in various ways today. Some continue to believe that in this search they threw themselves into a simple dialectic, almost

---

17 J. M. KEYNES, Treatise on Probability, the Collected Writings, vol. VII, New York - London 1973, p. 340.

18 J. CARO BAROJA, Las formas complejas de la vida religiosa; Religión, sociedad y carácter en la España de los siglos XVI y XVII, Madrid 1978, p. 525. Those who still repeat mechanically M. WEBER's thesis on the protestant ethic and the origin of capitalism would learn much from reading this book.

> rhetorical game[19]. Others have sought deeper explanations in their research into the root of moral diversity ... It was not a question (says Caro Baroja) of a conflict between "moral theory" and "practical theory" ... It was a question of delving into the world of doubtful or little understood probabilities and finding causes that were not easy to detect to explain the facts of moral life"[20].

If the anthropological explanation of Scholastic probabilism goes back to what Keynes was to call "animal spirits"[21] centuries later, its philosophical and rational roots were in Nominalism. The origins of the Nominalist movement were connected to Oxford University, where in the fourteenth century Ockham studied and later taught philosophy and theology in the Faculty of Arts. Called the *modern way* in the sixteenth century in as compared with classical Thomism and Scotist Realism, Nominalist philosophy was propagated by the European universities and, most particularly, by those that were founded throughout the fifteenth century[22]. It was taught with special force in the Spanish universities of Alcalá and Salamanca, thus creating a community of thought with the university of Paris where many of its defenders has studied under the Scottish master John Mair, to whom I have already referred[23]. In the sixteenth century Mair founded

---

19 This seems to be the interpretation that KEYNES received in his education, as he writes in Chap. 23 of General Theory.

20 J. CARO BAROJA, op. cit., p. 523.

21 All of Chapter 12 of the General Theory is important in this respect. Particularly illuminating is, in my opinion, what Athol FITZGIBBONS writes in his book Keynes's Vision: A New Political Economy, Oxford 1988, pp. 84 ss. on "rationality under uncertainty" ... Later on we will have the opportunity and the need to return to the end of Chapter 12 of the General Theory.

22 On the influence of Nominalism on the universities of Alcalá and Salamanca, see, for example, R. VILLOSLADA, op.cit. in note 25, p. 308. Cfr. my introduction to Tratado sobre los cambios (Treatise on changes), by Luis DE MOLINA, Madrid 1990.

23 Cfr. J. DURKAN, J. KIRK, The University of Glasgow, 1451 - 1577, Glasgow 1977, p. 161.

Europe's most advanced school of Nominalist philosophy, and his fame reached throughout the continent to such an extent that European merchants frequently came to consult him concerning moral doubts on economic matters[24]. A disciple of the Spaniard Jerómino Pardo, Mair counted many Spaniards among his students, and enjoyed great friendships with them[25]. Among these were the Coronel brothers and the mathematician Juan Martínez Silíceo.

Nominalist philosophy stresses aspects of knowledge that are of great significance and reach far into the subsequent development of scientific thought. It defended, for example, "that a general term or 'class name' represents in the proposition individual things, and only individual things". Claims like these placed the defenders of this notion in conflict with the Essentialist philosophical current, particularly with respect to the problem of the universals[26]. Furthermore, the Nominalists claimed that only those propositions which could be reduced to the principle of contradiction would be considered absolutely real, turning the causal propositions of science into merely probable affirmations, and therefore, not necessary ones[27].

For Nominalist philosophy, the correlation between general concepts and individual reality, therefore, constituted a required point of reference. From here arose its particular insistence on the empirical dimension of knowledge about the natural sciences. The logical coher-

---

24 Cfr. D. DE SOTO, De Iustitia et Iure (1553 - 1554), Salamanca 1573, lib. VI, q. XII, a.v.; fol. 173, col. B.; A RENAUDED, Pré-Reforme et Humanism à Paris pendant les Premières Guerres d'Italie (1497 - 1517), Paris 1953, p. 697.

25 R. GARCÍA VILLOSLADA, La universidad de París durante los estudios de Francisco de Vitoria, O. P., Rome 1938; H. ELIE, Quelques maitres de l'université de Paris vers l'an 1500, in: *Archives d'histoire doctrinal et littéraire du Moyen Age* 1950/51, pp. 193 - 243; J. DURKAN, J. Major: After 400 years, in: *The Inees Review* 1 (1950), pp. 131 - 157; F. GÓMEZ CAMACHO, El Triángulo Glasgow, París, Salamanca y los orígenes de la ciencia económica, in: *Miscelánea Comillas* 48 (1990), pp. 231 - 255.

26 F. COPLESTON, History of Philosophy, vol. III, chapt. 29, 1971.

27 Ibid.

ence of reasoning needed to be completed by withstanding the test of specific circumstances that defined the "case" under study. While at the same time, the empirical knowledge of the circumstances of the "case" could not stand without a general theory which was logically coherent. This is why we can affirm that the epistemological differences existing between Nominalism and Realism in the sixteenth and seventeenth centuries were manifest logically in different attitudes concerning probabilism and its role in decision-making. To the Scholastics the decision-making process did not obey empirical knowledge that uncovered *empirical legal necessities*. Rather it was born of a fallible subject who took a chance on a specific *reasonable probability*, that was neither truly necessary nor mathematical.

In my opinion this concept cannot be forgotten if we want to correctly interpret the economic thought of the Spanish Scholastic doctors with respect to the "paradigm" of natural law. Hence it is surprising that when he deals with Spanish Scholastic thought in his interpretation of natural law, Schumpeter, as I have already pointed out, makes no mention of either Probabilism or Nominalist philosophy. If the origin of modern science is linked to the triumph of Rational Determinism, the economic writings of the Scholastics must be considered as pre-modern reflections; compared to the *Mechanistic necessity* that came to dominate the modern vision of economic laws, the economic writings of the Scholastics were governed by *Probability*. For this reason, and from the epistemological point of view, when the seventeenth century leaps into the eighteenth, with the a jump from de Scholastic doctors to the classical school founded by Smith, I believe this can be interpreted as the triumph of absolute *necessity* over a greater or lesser *probability*[28]. As opposed to the imperfect and limited know-

---

28 On the origins of science and its link with medieval thought, I. Prigogine has written the following: "In this respect, perhaps reading The Name of the Rose by Umberto Eco has taught us more than many epistemological treatise about the origin of the science that was born in Europe four centuries ago. It submerges us, in fact, into the heart of the "cultural turbulence" of the end of the Middle Ages ... Eco shows us the long term implications of the problems that

ledge of human beings, Laplace's "omniscient understanding"[29] took hold. This called for the hypothesis of a necessary natural order, which beginning in the eighteenth century became an "article of faith of the orthodox creed of classical science"[30], interpreted as a guarantee of rational behaviour that made all concern for the moral unnecessary. One of the most significant texts on this subject can be found in the work of Mercier de la Rivière, written in 1767 with the significant title of *The natural and essential order of political societies*:

> "Do not feel any concern now for our morals or our customs. It is socially impossible for these not to conform by their principles; it is socially impossible for men who live under such simple laws (property and the freedom of the market), that *men* who, once they have achieved knowledge of absolute justice, have submitted to an order whose base is by essence justice, and whose limitless advantages are evident, not to be, humanly speaking, the most virtuous men"[31].

The interpretation of natural law that rests on Laplace's hypothesis of the omniscient devil, and therefore, on legal necessity, was not shared by the Scholastics, whose interpretation was based on probability. The God that the natural law of the Scholastics referred to was not a God of necessity, but quite the opposite. It was a God that respected free-

---

agitated Medieval thought. What can we know of the world? What does a name teach us? Can the truth of an individual give us generic knowledge? Is the investigation of signs enough to guide us in the labyrinth of phenomena? Similar questions, he reminds us, resonated throughout the most diverse fields, from politics to ethics, aesthetics or religion and reciprocally (I. PRIGONINE and I. STENGERS, Entre el tiempo y la eternidad, Madrid 1991, p. 39).

29 LAPLACE, Ensayo filosófico sobre las probabilidades, Paris, 1814. Edición preparada por el INTEMAC, Madrid, p. 18. On the shift from probability to necessity, see F. GÓMEZ CAMACHO, Filosofía moral y ciencia económica: Una reflexión histórica, in: *Revista ICADE* 19 (1990), pp. 167 - 185.

30 M. CAPEK, El impacto filosófico de la física contemporánea, Madrid 1965, p. 134.

31 Quote taken from A. MARZAL, Ciencia y anticiencia en el dominio de las ciencias sociales, in: Ciencia y Anticiencia, ed. A. DOU, Bilbao 1979, p. 169.

dom, error and even the reality of sin. The suppression of freedom in the vision that the Scholastics held of social and human reality would mean the suppression during the sixteenth and seventeenth centuries of what Caro Baroja has called "the greatest theme of a time", the theme of pre-destination[32]. Perhaps it is a inexact, as Caro Baroja says, to relate theological providencialism to scientific determinism[33]. Nonetheless, it does not appear that the origins of the modern sciences, including the economic sciences, can be understood without understanding the theological climate from which they evolved[34]. When studying the famous controversy between Leibniz and Newton (Clarke) it is hard to reject the idea that the ambiguity pointed out by Caro Baroja, if indeed it exists, was very much present in the origins of the modern sciences[35]. In the area of economic behaviour, it seems impossible to separate the economic "laissez-faire" from the theological "laissez-faire" that Newton and Leibniz debated. Perhaps on another occasion I will be able to write about this relationship.

---

32 J. CARO BAROJA, Las formas complejas ..., Chap. 10, "El mayor tema de un tiempo".

33 J. CARO BAROJA, op. cit., p. 241.

34 On the importance of theological thought in the origins of the Newtonian sciences, see I. PRIGOGINE, ¿Tan sólo una ilusión?, Barcelona 1982; La nueva alianza: Metamorfosis de la ciencia, Madrid 1990. A. FUNKENSTEIN, Theology and Scientific Imagination from the Middle Ages to the Seventeenth Century, Princeton 1986.

35 On this controversy, see A. PÉREZ DE LABORDA, Leibniz y Newton: Física, Filosofia y Teodicea, Salamanca 1981; Voltaire referred to this controversy as "perhaps the most beautiful monument that exists among literary battles". Cfr. I. PRIOGOGINE, Del Tiempo ..., p. 42.

III. Prices and the Market in Seventeenth Century Thought

The problem of setting the right price and the laws governing legal prices give us a specific example of how probability, and not necessity, was the dominant principle in the economic reasoning of the Spanish Scholastics. By the same token, one of the best explanations of how the Spanish sixteenth- and seventeenth-century doctors understood the market's mechanisms, and the government's role in setting prices is revealed in this problem. I will begin by referring to the distinction made between natural price and legal price, and the government's role in these matters.

a) Legal Price and Natural Prices

No one who has read the sixteenth- and seventeenth-century Scholastic works will question the knowledge that these authors enjoyed of the mechanisms of a free market, and the rejection they manifest toward monopolies. Hence, to give an example, Molina writes the following on the market and prices:

> "It should be observed that there are many circumstances that cause the price of things to rise and fall. Thus, for example, a shortage of goods, due to a bad harvest or similar causes makes prices go up. Abundance, nonetheless, makes them go down. The number of buyers that go to the market, at times there are more and at times less, and their greater desire to buy also makes prices rise. Equally, the greater need that many have for a specific item at a particular time, assuming a constant supply of the good, will force its price up, as occurs with horses which are worth more when war is near than in times of peace. The same happens when money is in short supply in a specific place, the price of the other goods drops, and an abundance of money makes them rise. The less money there is in a place, the greater its value, and therefore

> 'caeteris paribus', with the same amount of money more goods can be bought"[36].

I will return to this clear and expressed reference to quantitavism later, but will concentrate now on how prices were determined and the forces of the market. Knowledgeable as they were of the forces that acted on the market, as we have just seen, did the Spanish doctors defend fixing prices legally or, on the contrary, did they advocate the natural price? The answer must distinguish between the general principle and its application in specific circumstances. As a general principle, Domingo de Soto would say in mid sixteenth century,

> "judging the motives and the causes for establishing the price of things is the role of society and its governors, who after considering the circumstances should indicate the price for all goods; ... since it would be much safer and more prudent ... for the general good for the law to set the price of all things, if this were possible"[37].

However, as this is not possible, it is necessary to resort to the natural price which people fix in the market. This general principle, defended by Soto in 1556, was defended by most of the Spanish doctors. For example, one author who criticized the law governing legal prices was the Jesuit Luis de Molina who had no qualms about saying,

> "Everyone recognizes that it is the role of the public Authorities to establish and define the price of things in the way that, respecting the limits of equality, they consider appropriate for the common good ... The power to fix legal prices - he adds - resides principally in the prince of chief of the republic; the governors and other public authorities receive from him the authority customarily granted them,or conferred expressly by law, or privately"[38].

---

36 L. DE MOLINA, De Iustitia el Iure, t. II, Cuenca 1597, Edition prepared by F. GÓMEZ CAMACHO of Luis DE MOLINA, La Teoría del justo precio, Madrid 1981, Disp. 348, no. 4, p. 169.

37 D. DE SOTO, De Iustitia et Iure, Salamanca 1556, lib. VI, q. 11, a. 3.

38 L. DE MOLINA, op. cit., Disp. 344, no. 1.

Melchor de Soria defended the same general principle in 1633 and Juan de Lugo did so in the middle of the seventeenth century. But the general principles were one thing and their application to specific circumstances were quite another. The principle is abstract, and does not descend to the analysis of specific socio-economic circumstances. For this reason it cannot be applied immediately and directly to reality. In other words this cannot happen without the mediation of the analysis of the circumstances. *Mediation* in the application of the general principles became the task that the Spanish doctors would commend to *ratio recta* in its analytical dimension, and not in its normative dimension. Melchor de Soria, for example, writes very clearly in this respect in an exposition that leaves no room for doubt. At the beginning of Chapter IV of his *Treatise*, after devoting the first three chapters of the book to an exposition of the general principles of natural law, he comments that,

> "Until now we have given some general principles of moral theology, and will give others later; and from them alone a valid conclusion cannot be drawn about whether it is right for there to be a legal price, or whether the price is fair, if the farmer and the people of the Republic are not consulted with particular attention ... and many detailed circumstances considered, that are necessary for such a domestic and vulgar matter, before condemning (or approving) a law imposed by the Kings"[39].

Luis de Molina expressed himself with the same clarity when he wrote,

> "In moral problems, the change of one or several circumstances is usually the cause that changes the case, and what would be one way on the basis of the principle alone, would be another due to the circumstances"[40].

---

39 M. DE SORIA, Tratado de la justificación y conveniencia de la tassa de el pan ..., Toledo 1627.

40 L. DE MOLINA, De Iustitia et Iure, Cuenca 1597, t. I, col. 649, D and 650, A.

Correct solutions to problems cannot be found on the basis of general principles alone; rather it is necessary to analyze and study the circumstances that define a specific "case". To the normative dimension of moral reflection, we must add the analytical dimension. And it is when we add this other dimension precisely when the Spanish doctors offer the best of their economic analysis and thought. Hence, for example, if the price of wool is being discussed, Molina would not limit himself to saying that this price must be fair. He would proceed to analyze the futures markets between the Genovese merchants and the Castillian shepherds to find out the circumstances under which these prices have been set. When fixing the price of wheat, Melchor de Soria would not limit himself to recommending that it be a fair price either; he would take on the task of analyzing the productivity of the various lands, the costs of producing wheat, and even the periodicity of the agrarian cycles before emitting a moral judgement. In order to find out all of these specific facts, the Bishop of Toledo had the best documents available: the tithe registers that the parish priests had to show during his pastoral visits. With these documents it was possible to get to "the truth of the fact", to use an expression of Melchor de Soria's, since it was to that truth that the general principle was to be applied in more or less probable form. Let us examine a specific example: the fixing of the price of wheat. This is a problem, as Melchor de Soria informs us, around which, in Spain in 1627,

> "There were two opinions concerning this matter; some think it would be better to eliminate the legal price, and let the price of bread rise and fall with the times, according to its abundance or scarcity, as occurs in the other markets. Others hold constantly that is necessary to fix the price, and this - adds Melchor de Soria - is the most valid and and true opinion"[41].

---

41 M. DE SORIA, Tratado de la justificación y conveniencia de la tassa de el pan y de la dispensación que en ella haze su Magestad con todos los que siembran, Toledo 1633, p. 39.

"Voting" in the wheat market

Doubtlessly many of you are familiar with, or have heard of the manner of setting prices in the free market that bears a lot in common with voting in democratic systems. A classical text which refers to this similarity is the Introduction to Milton Friedman's *Price Theory* where he specifically says the following:

> "... the controlling force is pecuniary demand; voting is in proportion to the number of dollars a person has. This is not obviously 'just'. The basic inequality, it should be noted, is an inequality in the ownership of resources ..."[42].

Although it is not necessary to enter here into an analysis of how Friedman understands freedom in voting in the free market, and what he means when he affirms that it is not "just" for the weight of the votes to be proportional to the amount of money a person possesses, I do feel that attention should be drawn to the two following facts: 1) the idea of these voting in the market is not new, and can be found in the seventeenth century in the works of Melchor de Soria; but 2) when recognizing that the weight of the vote is proportional to the wealth of a man, Melchor de Soria finds it necessary to take into consideration the distribution of wealth and its influence on the fixing of prices. He concludes that a price cannot be considered to have been "calculated commonly", and therefore to be fair when it is reached through voting carried out from such unequal economic standpoints as those that were created in Spain by bad harvests, and unequal distribution of wheat and land. In such unequal circumstances, Melchor de Soria writes,

> "if on the basis of their needs poor farmers are disqualified from casting valid and legitimate votes in setting the fair price of the bread they sell, those who buy the bread should also be disqualified because of the need with which they buy it in a very sterile year, and for this reasons the lords of the bread, rich and powerful, should be all the more disqualified

---

42 M. FRIEDMAN, Price Theory, Chicago 1967, p. 11.

> from voting because of the little or lack of need with which they sell it to those who are forced to buy it"[43].

Melchor de Soria recognized in the seventeenth century that there exists a perfect analogy between the setting of a price in the market and the democratic process in a free election; but, apart from recognizing this analogy, Soria insisted on the existence of specific circumstances that disqualified the election in years when the harvest had been poor. It was disqualified, for example, by the pressing needs of the poor farmers, and the few needs, or none at all, that the lords of the bread, rich and powerful, had in selling their bread. Voting in these circumstances, just like "haggling", was not the proper method of reaching the "commonly calculated" price, whether it was called the "fair" price or the "balanced" price, since the voting weight of one of the parties overruled the other. Let us examine the Scholastic analysis of the "haggling" process.

"Haggling" and the "Common Calculation" of Prices

Think back to Walras's *tâtonnement* or "auctioning process", Edgeworth's "recontracting process" and Hicks' "false transaction". These are iterative processes, based on trial and error, that do not try to reproduce the markets of the real world, but that are used analytically as a step toward reaching balance. Against this analytical background, let us listen to the following words that Melchor de Soria wrote in 1633 about fixing the price of bread, and the differences between this product and other goods.

> "with goods that are not so necessary for human life ..., the seller, in order to better use his goods, to earn more money for himself gives in to selling them at the agreed upon price, and the buyer, as he is not buying out of need, is grudging with his money and gives the lowest price he can, and between them they haggle and adjust the price, in such a way

---

43 M. DE SORIA, Tratado ..., p. 33. Another author who used the voting process to explain the thought of the doctors was Bernard W. DEMPSEY, The functional economy, Englewood Cliffs 1958.

> that it is commonly fair. But at midday, how can the poor official or labourer, who are exhausted from working and ravenous, begin to haggle over the price of bread in a sterile year, when it is bought by the rich, who sell it without need. From here we can evidently infer, that then the price is not natural, but violent, because of the violence wrought by the sellers and that which the buyers receive"[44].

The haggling that Melchor de Soria mentions is a real process; it is this process that can still be observed in some popular markets where the agreed price between supply and demand is reached after adjusting the various offers. Perhaps it is easier to understand the place in the history of economic thought the Spanish doctors of the sixteenth and seventeenth centuries occupy if their explanation of setting the "natural" price is compared with the explanation that Smith defended in *The Wealth of Nations*. Below are some points that I consider significant in this comparison.

From the fair "natural" price to the balanced "natural" price

If I have stressed Melchor de Soria's expressed reference to "voting" in the market and the "haggling" process between the parties that

---

44 M. DE SORIA, Tratado ..., p. 32. Adición ..., p. 48; "of the great difference there is between bread and other goods, it follows that these are priced not only by the seller, but also by the buyer, because as they are not necessary to live, like bread, they are bought freely, and for them a price is discussed with the seller, in such a way that the man who buys shoes, or a hat, if asked for fifty reales by the seller, he will reply that he will wear his old one another thirty days, and then the hat seller will ask him how much he would give, and thus they haggle over the price, and agree upon it between them; and as all hat makers eat from selling their wares, and other people will sell theirs, he gives in and sells for a moderate price. But in a very sterile year ..., only the seller sets the price, because the buyer, famished with hunger, cannot say that he will go another thirty days without eating it, and the seller will not ask how much he will give for it either, nor will he allow him to have a vote in setting the price, but will ask what he wants, and the poor buyer will have to pay it, because in a sterile year, bread is in the hands of a few sellers, and these are powerful men who sell without need".

gather there, it has been to satisfy two ends: 1) because of the importance these processes have in themselves in order to understand the thought of the Spanish doctors on the market and prices, and, furthermore, 2) because I believe that the explanation of these processes will help us to correctly situate the doctors's thought within the history of the economic sciences, particularly with respect to Smith and his successors.

In Chapter VII of *The Wealth of Nations* Smith writes about "the natural price and the price of the market of goods", and says

> "The natural price, therefore, is, as it were, the central price, to which the prices of all commodities are continually gravitating. Different accidents may sometimes keep them suspended a good deal above it, and sometimes force them down even somewhat below them. But whatever may be the obstacles which hinder them from settling in this centre of repose and continuance, they are constantly tending towards it"[45].

Later on, Smith observes again that, although the market price continually fluctuates around the natural prices,

> "... sometimes particular accidents, sometimes natural causes and sometimes particular regulations of policy, may, in many commodities, keep up the market price, for a long time together, a good deal above the natural price"[46].

The concept of the natural price belongs to the Aristotelian tradition (5 *Eth.*, Chapt. 7) and is found in the writings of the Scholastics in contraposition to the legal price. The latter is fixed by the public Authorities, and on the contrary, the natural price is called "natural",

> "not because it does not depend in large measure on the higher opinion that men usually have of some things over others ...; nor because it does not fluctuate or change, since it is evident it changes, but it is called natural because it comes

---

45 A. SMITH, An Inquiry into the Nature and Causes of the Wealth of Nations, edit. E. CANNAN, New York 1965, p. 58.

46 A. SMITH, op cit., p. 59.

> from the things themselves independently of any human law or public decree, but depending on many circumstances with which it changes, and of the opinion men have of the goods"[47].

The Scholastics set the natural price against the legal one in a well-known contraposition. Also worth asking is what they thought of the market price, which as Smith tells us "fluctuates continually around the natural price". Did the Spanish doctors recognize the existence of a market price that was different from the natural price? If they recognized its existence, what was the relationship between this market price and the fair natural price? I believe the answers to these two questions will allow us to uncover one of the essential differences between what could be called the Scholastic paradigm for the setting of prices, and the Smithian or classical paradigm.

First, it is important to note that for Smith the natural price is the ideal price, a goal towards which we move thanks to the fluctuations of the price in the market. Differences exist between the market price and the natural price that will be eliminated by the fluctuations of the price in the market. Using the Newtonian image of gravity as did Smith, we could say that the fluctuations in the market price are similar to the swing of a pendulum that rotates around its centre of gravity. The natural price is its position of repose which will be reached with time.

Now, Smith himself warned that "various contingencies", "particular accidents" and "particular natural causes", apart from legal decrees, can come between the market price and the natural price, and separate the former from the latter for a shorter or longer period of time. In other words, there are "particular accidents" or circumstances that can affect the gravitational dynamics of the market price, and thus delay its reaching the position of repose which is the natural price. Transactions carried out in this period will be realized at the market price, but

---

47 L. DE MOLINA, op. cit., t. II, Disp. 347, no. 3.

not at the natural price[48]. If we now focus our attention of those "different accidents" and "various contingencies" that Smith mentioned we can easily understand the thought of the Spanish doctors.

For them, the first question that has to be posed was whether in the case under study these "various contingencies" are present and; second, though related to the first point, it needs to be explained whether the adjustment of the marked price as it converges towards the natural prices is interpreted as a mechanistic necessity and "necessary", or on the contrary, as a moral necessity that can be frustrated by the freedom of the subjects. For the Spanish doctors, the necessity for the market price to adjust until it coincided with the natural prices is a *moral necessity*, not mechanistic and incapable of failure. The dynamics of the adjustment, just as the dynamics of the haggling and the voting, do not *necessarily* lead to the natural price, but could lead to what the doctors called a "violent price", as distinct and opposed to the natural one. Furthermore, the recognition of the possible existence of "certain accidents" that made the converging process, or the adjustment to the natural position of equilibrium difficult, lead them to defend the need to investigate in each specific case for the existence "accidents" or "various contingencies", since, as M. de Soria writes, there are arguments

> "that seem to only have force when contemplating very general principles, but are satisfied with duly observing particular circumstances and events that occur commonly"[49].

This is the idea we saw earlier in Luis de Molina, "the change of one or various circumstances is often the cause of a change in the case." For this reason, the general theories and principles need the mediation of *ratio recta* in its analytical function to explore the circumstances.

---

48 In the terminology used by HICKS, the "false transactions" would correspond to those carried out at market prices, and transactions carried out at balanced prices would be the equivalent of those realized at the natural price.

49 M. DE SORIA, Tratado ..., p. 74.

From the relative price to the general level of prices

Both "haggling" and "voting" are processes that play a role in setting the relative price of goods, since it is the transaction of selling and purchasing that is being analyzed. The problem is different in reference to the general level of prices. When Molina told us earlier that "the lower the amount of money in a place, the higher its value and, therefore, *caeteris paribus*, with the same amount of money, more things can be bought", he is referring to the general level of prices and, therefore, was formulating what we know today as the quantitative theory.

There are fewer and fewer historians of the economic sciences who can allow themselves to ignore that, in the words of Pierre Vilar,

> "the Spanish "quantitavists" ... have understood the relationship between the price of goods and the amount of money in circulation, on one hand, on having recorded a well-founded Scholastic tradition around this point, and on the other hand, on having observed empirically in the Indies and in Spain, the double simultaneous and brutal phenomenon of the influx of metals and the rise in prices"[50].

Pierre Vilar takes pains to stress that this affirmation is not more or less valid in the works of the Spanish doctors, but part of the "well-founded Scholastic tradition". However, of Bodin, he says

> "A less good theorist than the Spaniards, Bodin describes the phenomena accurately and tries to see beyond the possible causes; he is fairly subtle and sometimes analyzes the problems well, but an error has been made in believing him when he said (in 1568) that we was the first to search for the cause in the silver from America ("a cause which until now no one has touched"), since in Spain it was a common opinion and

50 P. VILAR, Crecimiento y Desarrollo, Barcelona 1976, p. 140. On the Scholastic tradition in the Indies, see the works of Professor Oreste POPESCU, particularly: Orígenes Hispanoamericanos de la Teoría cuantitativa, in: Aportaciones del Pensamiento Económico Iberoamericano. Siglos XVI - XX, Madrid 1986, pp. 4 - 33.

> almost a theory formulated by Mercado (1569) and Azpilcueta (1556)"[51].

Earl J. Hamilton's studies have underlined again in the twentieth century the extraordinarily strong correlation between the increase in the volume of the imports of precious metals and the rise in the price of goods throughout the sixteenth and seventeenth centuries; and although the conclusions of these studies have been criticized, I believe we can affirm, as does Marjorie Grice-Hutchinson, that

> "It is probable that the influx of American Treasure was the principal but not the sole cause of the price-revolution in Spain. "Real" factors must also have played their part"[52].

This allusion to the "real" factors seems important to me when interpreting the thought of the Spanish Scholastic scholars, since the presence of these elements introduces a dimension that is not strictly monetarist into the doctors's analysis. The connection between the amount of money and price levels was not independent of "real" factors, such as the decisions of the subjects to set prices relative goods. For this reason, their monetary thought can be interpreted, as I have already indicated, in accordance with Hicks's "suggestion" to fuse the monetary theory with the value theory[53]. Below I will deal with the monetary theory of the sixteenth and seventeenth doctors.

---

51 P. VILAR, Oro y moneda en la historia, 1450 - 1920, Barcelona 1969, p. 213. The world of T. de Mercado, Suma de tratos y contratos ..., came into the public light in 1569, but "The manuscript must have been concluded in 1567 or, at the latest, at the beginning of 1568". Cfr. "Preliminary Study" by N. SANCHEZ ALBORNOZ to the edition of Mercado's work. Suma de tratos y contratos, published by the Inst. de Est. Fiscales, Madrid 1977, p. XI.

52 M. GRICE-HUTCHINSON, Early ..., p. 107.

53 Cfr. "Introducción" to the works of Luis DE MOLINA, Tratado sobre los préstamos y la usura, Ed. Inst. de Est. Fiscales, Madrid 1989, pp. XX, ss.

b) Money in the Scholastic Thought of the Sixteenth and Seventeenth Centuries

The monetary theory of the Scholastic doctors was explained in some depth in the review *Moneda y Crédito*, and I would like to add a few considerations to what has already been published.

Several years ago Pierre Vilar, in an article on "The Spanish primitives of economic thought", tore down some of the errors that the famous manuals on the History of the doctrines had founded among economists. Specifically, he pointed out how the accusation of "bullionism" that used to be levelled against the Scholastic doctors was unfounded. In truth, when we understand the importance that the Nominalist philosophy had for the Spanish Scholastics of the sixteenth and seventeenth centuries, and the controversies that the Nominalists and Realists maintained during that time, it is difficult to explain how they could have been accused of "bullionists".

Alberto Ullastres knew of the importance of the Nominalists among the Scholastic doctors, and for this reason when he presents "The economic ideas of Martín Azpilcueta" he expressly referred to the problem posed by the relationship between Nominalism and Realism:

> "One can be Nominalist or Metalist - wrote Ullastres - as long as, if the former, the unit of account materializes into something physical with no intrinsic value. But a system that uses an economic good such as money cannot be sustained if a legal, arbitrary value is assigned its monetary function that is different from the real value of the goods. This is the basic fault of the ancient nominalisms which without exception, were built on the noble metals"[54].

It is true that this poses a difficult epistemological question that has yet to be solved: the problem of the relationship between our abstract concepts and the reality we want to design with them. Today, and as

---

54 A. ULLASTRES, Las ideas económicas de Martín Azpilcueta, in: Martín AZPILCUETA, Comentario resolutorio de cambios, ed. from the C.S.I.C., Madrid 1965, p. LXXXV.

part of the monetary theory, J. R. Hicks has formulated the question in terms of an "anchoring" the abstract Walrasian numéraire to a real and specific economic good. The numéraire is only an abstract value, a nominal "unit of account" that belongs to the Platonic ideas, and for this reason it must be "anchored" in economic reality, to a real "economic unit". Until this empirical "anchoring" of the numéraire occurs, and we explain the relationship between the "nominal unit of account" and the "real unit of account", our monetary and economic reasoning are still nothing but purely mathematical or arithmetical calculations, and in no way can they be considered empirical knowledge or a scientific explanation of economic reality[55]. It is in this philosophical context of the relationship between Nominalism and Realism that Luis de Molina's words, which were upheld by most of the doctors, take on their true importance:

> "A coin can be considered in two ways; one, as a coin; another, as metal, or as gold of greater or lesser purity, of greater or lesser weight"[56].

Taken as just a coin, our appreciation of money and of the coin will be purely Nominal and mathematical; this would correspond to what today we economists understand as "numéraire" or an "unit of account". When considered as a specific amount of gold, with a series of characteristics, the money, which is the coin, becomes something real. The problem was posed in the sixteenth and seventeenth, and holds true today, when trying to explain how one passes from the concept of nominal unit to this real object which we call unit standard. Not only must the monetary theory answer this question, but the problem is posed in all the sciences that wish to apply a specific measuring system to the analysis of reality[57].

---

55 J. R. Hicks, Critical Essays in Monetary Theory, Oxford 1967.

56 L. de Molina, De Iustitia et Iure, Disp. 406, col. 986, C; Disp. 410, col. 1036, B, C, D.

57 Cfr. H. Reichenbach, The Philosophy of Space and Time, New York 1958.

The Role of the Authorities in the Scholastic Monetary Theory

A simple and evident way to answer our question could be as follows: The coin shifts from a nominal unit to a real unit by means of a decree or a law imposed by the Authorities, just as the abstract units of length and weight become the real standards which are the meter and the kilogramme. However, it is not the political fact which interests us here, but the scientific and economic meaning that this political fact carries. I think a text by Keynes can help understand the meaning of this shift, when he wrote in 1923 about the re-establishment of the gold standard:

> "If, indeed, a providence watched over gold, or if Nature had provided us with a stable standard ready-made, I would not, in an attempt after some slight improvement, hand over the management to the possible weakness or ignorance of boards and governments. But this is not the situation. We have no ready-made standard. Experience has shown that in emergencies ministers of finance cannot be strapped down. And - most important of all - in the modern world of paper currency and bank credit there is no escape from a "managed" currency, whether we wish it or not; convertibility into gold will not alter the fact that the value of gold itself depends on the policy of the central banks"[58].

Translate the world of paper money into the world of metal money, and it would not be very difficult to apply Keynes's works to seventeenth century Spain. As P. Vilar wrote, in the sixteenth and seventeenth centuries, "the die used to mint coins was at times as wasteful and unwise as is the modern plate used to print bills"[59].

The fact that the "anchoring" of the nominal monetary unit to the real world is a step that is juridically delegated in the Authorities is something that is hard to deny; it is the political power or the legal authority the entity which is in charge of fixing the convertibility

---

58 J. M. KEYNES, Essays in Persuasion, vol. IX, p. 178.

59 P. VILAR, Oro y moneda ..., p. 14.

relationship and thus "anchor" the nominal concept to a real object. A decree or a law passed by the legitimate Authorities constitutes in this way the legal bridge that makes it possible to join the realm of concepts and nominal values to the realm of real objects or economic goods. The Scholastics did not overlook this matter, but considered it insufficient. The *recognition of the fact* brought about through a specific decree or law was not enough for them. Above this was the judgement of the natural law. It did not suffice them that the public powers could exercise their functions *de facto*, they wanted to know if they exercised them correctly, or in other words, in accordance with the *ratio recta* which is the foundation of the law. For example, once the convertibility relationship was established, could the Authorities change the relationship between the nominal and the real value of the unit of account? This brings us to the topic of the constancy and invariability of the standard measurement of the value and the manipulation of money by the public powers.

Constancy in the standard used to measure value

The fact that the standard of measurement of any magnitude had to be constant was all too evident in the sixteenth and seventeenth centuries for the standard used to measure economic value to be an exception. The Scholastic doctors recognized this, and Tomás de Mercado wrote specifically that

> "it is a universal rule and necessary for (money) to be any fixed measurement, that is sure and permanent. Everything else can, and even must, change, but the measurement must be permanent, because as a fixed sign we can measure the changes of the other things. We all complain that things have changed a lot in our times, and we know this because things that cost thirty now twenty years ago cost, as it were, three. So through money we can measure the difference and the cost, and if the *real* were not worth thirty four as then, we

> would not be able to appreciate and understand this change"[60].

It shouldn't vary, but wasn't it evident that it varied? The experience of the seventeenth century, with repeated new mintings of coins, had demonstrated that in emergency situations, like those that the Crown frequently experienced, it was not possible for royalty to keep its word; repeated manipulations of the currency meant an equal number of changes in the convertibility relationship between the nominal unit of account and the real unit of account. In view of this manipulation, the doctors reacted in the only way that a moral philosopher could: they condemned the Authorities' failure to keep their word. Altering the value of the currency, just like altering the length of the meter or the weight of the kilogramme, constituted a fraud that could not be tolerated morally. Manipulating in this way the unit used to measure the value of money amounted to robbing society, and theft was a practice that could not be tolerated morally. Juan de Mariana was extremely explicit on this point.

In Chapter III of his *Tratado de la moneda de vellón* (*Treatise on "Vellón" Coins*) (Colonia, 1609), when he asks if the king can lower the weight of a coin against the will of the populace, in other words, if he could go back on his word without society's consent, he writes:

> "Two things are certain here: the first, that the king can change the form or the mint of money, as long as he does not make it worse ... the second, due to some difficulty like war or a seige, he can lower its value on two conditions: one, that it be for a short period of time, or as long as the circumstances require; two, once the difficulty has abated, (he must) restore the losses occasioned the interested parties ...; because if the prince is not a lord, but the administrator of the goods of the citizens, he cannot take part of their patrimony by

60 T. DE MERCADO, Suma ..., vol. 1, p. 220. D. Ricardo posed the same question in his Principles.

> these means or by others, as occurs each time money is devalued, since more is charged for what is worth less"[61].

The expressed reference to the need that arises from "war or siege" allows us to enquire about a third need: can this be applied to re-activating the economy? Would Mariana be in favour of "lowering" the currency in order to re-activate the economy? Mariana's answer is conceived in terms that may be surprising, formulated as they were at the end of the sixteenth century and beginning of the seventeenth.

Mariana clearly distinguished two time frames in which the manipulation of money by the Authorities would produce its effects: in the short and the long run. This manipulation, he writes, "is like the drink given the sick person unduly, which first refreshes him, but later causes more serious accidents and makes the illness worse"[62]. Mariana devotes Chapters VII and VIII to an exposition of the "disadvantages" and "advantages", respectively, of minting "vellón" coins, and although he recognizes that the short term advantages are undeniable, this does not justify, he says, forgetting the disadvantages that will arise in the long run. For example, it is true that "vellón" coins will not be taken out of the kingdom, and there will, therefore, be many in circulation and thus the economy will be stimulated in two ways: by increasing domestic production, "which will lead to an abundance of fruits and goods, which will all be cheaper", and, furthermore, debtors would find money cheaply "where time passed, if it were not at high interests, nobody, or very few would look to loaned money for help"[63]. In relation to foreign nations, imports would decreased for two reasons: greater domestic production would make them unnecessary and, what is more, they would be reduced to being paid for with a currency of lower value. (*Ibidem*) Finally, the foreigners who still bring their goods to Spain would prefer to be paid in kind rather than in cash,

---

61 Juan DE MARIANA, Tratado de la moneda de vellón, Biblioteca de Autores Españoles, t. XXXI, p. 579.

62 Ibid.

63 J. DE MARIANA, op. cit., p. 582.

which would stimulate domestic production once again. Mariana recognizes all of these short term advantages, and does not hesitate to affirm, furthermore, that

> "the king would benefit greatly from this, since he would fulfill his needs, pay his debts, remove the annuities consuming him, without hurting anybody. There is no doubt that the immediate interest is great"[64].

But these immediate benefits will turn into future impediments. In fact, observes Mariana, farming would be abandoned; commerce with foreign countries would cease, and due to these shortages, the people and the kingdom would become impoverished and change (*Ibidem*). Before this general increase in prices and the decrease in business activity, Mariana observes,

> "The King will want to fix a legal price on everything, and that would make the wound fester, because the people will not want to sell at higher prices"[65].

The conflict between short term and long term interests is thus outlined, and as with all conflicts of interest, the doctors will solve this one by offering the probable solution, not the necessary one. In summary, as a general principle, the Scholastic doctors rejected the notion of the Authorities' being able to legitimately manipulate the value of the standard unit for their convenience. A rapid and superficial reading of Juan de Mariana's *Treatise on the "Vellón" Coin* suffices to prove this. But, at the same time, the doctors also recognized that socio-economic circumstances could evolve over time in such a way that the empirical definition of the standard unit no longer corresponds to the first "anchoring" of the nominal or abstract definition, thus making it necessary to change. The role of the public Authorities with respect to the standard unit was twofold: on one hand was *respect for the definition given*, and avoiding any practice that would involve cheating or robbing society; on the other hand, they had to be aware of

---

64 Ibid.

65 Ibid.

how circumstances had developed in order to, when these circumstances called for it, modify the previous definition which had become out-dated; this is the function of *adjusting to reality*. If we were to ask them now what they thought of the success or failure of the practical judgement exercised by the Authorities, we would have to answer that they did not always opine that the actions taken by the public powers were correct.

We have slipped almost imperceptibly from discussing the convertibility between nominal unit of account and the real unit of account to the general price index, and this is a step that should be explained.

The Convertibility Relationship and the General Price Level

There are two relationships in all monetary theories that are not easy to bring into harmony: first, the relationship we have just seen between the nominal unit of account and the standard that serves as the real unit, and second, the relationship that exists between the total amount of money and the real goods in an economy, and which we normally refer to as the general price level. In both cases, nominal magnitudes are related to real ones, and what we must explain are the connections between these relationships. The Spanish doctors raised this question, although they did it indirectly, by analyzing the "caeteris paribus" clause.

An initial difference between both relationships is that the first, as we have just seen, consists of one that the Authorities establish by juridical means at the time of minting; the second is a relationship that can be called "autonomous", or, if you prefer, "natural". Now, we are interested in analyzing whether the second relationship, which is the general price index, is expressed in terms of the nominal unit of account, or, on the contrary, of the real unit of account. The answer was not easy at all, since if one defends, as did the Scholastics, that it is a measurement of value, money had to possess a fixed value that was true and permanent. The general price index could not come into conflict with, or contradict this "universal and necessary rule"[66]. The doctor's reply was based on the natural value of the metal used in coins. Molina, for example, writes that,

> "if circumstances vary over time...and the value of the metal of these coins increased considerably it cannot be thought that the legislators want to uphold the laws that fixed the old rate; and even if they wanted to, it would not be just and equitable. (Since the natural value of money) is not so rigid that it cannot rise and fall just as the other goods do whose price is not fixed by law, or in other words, according to their abundance or shortage, or the number of people who require them"[67].

As I have already expressed[68], from the epistemological point of view, the discrepancy or difference between the legal value of money and its natural value means that the legal (or nominal) value has been "falsified" by the "natural" economic reality. This, as you will recall, is the problem that Ullastres called the "fundamental failure of the old Nominalisms", but that is raised in all scientific theories that aspire to empirical relevance. As the natural value becomes independent of the standard unit for its nominal value, we find ourselves before *two numerary systems*, before two different measurement systems supported by measurement standards that possess two equally different dynamics: one is constant and the other, variable. For this reason, it may be of interest to know how the Spanish doctors reacted to the fact of the duality of the standards used to measure the value (of money). And it must be said, that faced with the necessity to choose between both standards, the legal-nominal one, or the real-natural one, the doctors, in general, opted for the natural standard and measurement system, and subordinated the legal system of measurement to the former. Changes in economic circumstances involved a change in the natural

---

66 Cfr. note 62.

67 L. DE MOLINA, op. cit., Disp. 401, col. 988, B; 983, C, D.

68 Cfr. Introduction to Tratado sobre los cambios, of Luis DE MOLINA, Inst. Est. Fiscales, Madrid 1990, p. L.

appreciation of the value of goods, including monetary metal. As I have stressed throughout my exposition, a change in circumstances warranted a change in the application of the general principle.

I have deliberately left out of my exposition the problem of interests and usury, as well as the distinction between monetary and financial operations. There is not sufficient time to delve into these two issues which I otherwise consider fundamental in the economic thought of the Spanish doctors. Those who are interested in these topics can consult the Introductions to the two works of Luis de Molina that I have mentioned earlier: his *Tratado sobre los préstamos y la usura* (*Treatise on loans and usury*) and *Tratado sobre los cambios* (*Treatise on changes*).

The Discovery of the New World and the Development of the Purchasing Power Parity Theory

By PETER BERNHOLZ

1. The Discovery of the Purchasing Power Parity Theorem

M. Grice-Hutchinson published her book on "The School of Salamanca: Readings in Spanish Monetary Theory, 1544 - 1605" in 1952 (see also Grice-Hutchinson [1978]). At least since then it is well-known that the Theologians of the School of Salamanca were the first to find the purchasing power parity theory long before D. Ricardo (1811), not to speak of Gustav Cassel (1923). And even earlier in 1935, Bernard W. Dempsey, in a comment on Hamilton (1934), already showed that Molina (1615) had presented the Quantity and the Purchasing Power Theory in 1593, and that he referred approvingly to the earlier work of M. Azpilcucta dc Navarro and of Domingo dc Soto (1583). As L. Baeck (1987) put it: "L'analyse de Tomás de Mercado concernant la parité internationale du pouvoir d'achat anticipe de trois siècles sur la formulation d'Irving Fischer et de Gustav Cassel. Tomás de Mercado est fort bien conscient de son originalité (Suma, Lib. IV, cap. 3): "Cierto nunca la he visto enteramente explicada en ninguna obra".

To recall the facts, let me just give two quotations. The first comes from Martín de Azpilcueta Navarro (1556, pp. 80):

> "Now we maintain that the value of the two monies may diverge for one of eight reasons: ... Seventh, because of scarcity and need ... As to the seventh respect which causes money to rise or fall in value (namely, whether it is scarce and greatly needed, or abundant), money is worth more when and where it is scarce than where it is abundant.
> Second, and of great importance, that all merchandise becomes dearer when it is in great demand and short supply, and that money insofar as it may be sold, bartered, or exchanged by some other form of contract, is merchandise and therefore also becomes dearer when it is in great demand and short supply.
> Third, that (other things being equal) in countries where there is a great scarcity of money all other saleable goods, and even the hands and labor of men, are given for less money than where it is abundant. Thus we see by experience that in France, where money is scarcer than in Spain, bread, wine, cloth and labor are worth much less. And even in Spain, in times when money was scarcer, saleable goods and labor were given for very much less than after the discovery of the Indies, which flooded the country with gold and silver" (translated by Grice-Hutchinson [1982], pp. 91 - 95).

The second quotation is from Thomás de Mercado (1589):

> "After the Indies, the place where money is least esteemed is Seville, the city that gathers unto herself all good things from the New World, and, after Seville, the other parts of Spain. Money is highly esteemed in Flanders, Rome, Germany, and England. This estimation and appreciation are brought about, in the first place, by the abundance or scarcity of these metals; since they are found and mined in America, thus they are there held in little esteem" (p. 92, translated by Grice-Hutchinson [1982], pp. 98 - 99).

> "Thus, corresponding to the advantage which the Indies enjoy over Spain in their abundance of gold and silver, so are

> 70 ducats in Madrid esteemed as highly as 100 in Lima and 90 in Vera Cruz; and if I were to state that the excess were larger I do not think that I should be deceived, It is the same between Spain and Rome, for 100 in Burgos are certainly worth 94 in Rome" (p. 95, Grice-Hutchinson, p. 102).

Even earlier Domingo de Soto (1553) had stated:

> "The more plentiful money is in Medina the more unfavourable are the terms of exchange, and the higher the price that must be paid by whoever wishes to send money from Spain to Flanders, since the demand for money is smaller in Spain than in Flanders. And the scarcer the money is in Medina the less he need pay there, because more people want money in Medina than are sending it to Flanders".
>
> "It is lawful to exchange money in one place for money in another, having regard to its scarcity in the one and abundance in the other and to receive a smaller sum in a place where money is scarce for a larger where it is abundant" (quoted from Grice-Hutchinson [1978], pp. 103 - 104).

The above quotations show already that the Doctors of Theology of the School of Salamanca were also well aware of the Quantity Theory of Money (see, e.g., Baeck [1987], pp. 18 - 22; Grice-Hutchinson [1952], pp. 51 - 52; Popescu [1986]) and thus predated the work of Jean Bodin (1568). Popescu (1986) showed that the development of the theory can be even followed back to earlier statements in Latin America, where the "price revolution" preceded that in Spain since the additional silver and gold originated there. For instance, the Viceroy of Peru, Pedro de la Gasca (1485 - 1560) on July 20, 1549, wrote a letter to the Consejo de Indias, in which he asked for an adjustment of the salaries of the members of the Audiencia de Lima. In this letter he wrote:

> "Y ansi me parece lo que antes, que aun cada dia crece la carestia de esta tierra como va creciendo la riquesc dclla"[1]

1 "And so it even seems to me that the dearness of this country grows each day as its richness increases".

(Levillier [1921], vol. 1, p. 214; quoted from Popescu [1986], p. 19).

Still, though the Quantity Theory of Money was certainly developed in Spain and earlier in Latin America, it seems that Copernicus was the first to invent it (Jastrow [1923]; Popescu [1986], p. 23). He first stated it in a memorandum to the Prussian diet meeting in Graudenz in 1522, which was expressed in German[2]. From this he worked out a more careful Latin version presented to the Polish king. Copernicus stated in this *Monete cudende ratio* (1526):

> "Vilescit hec ut plurimum multitudinem, utpote si tanta argenti copia in monetam transierit quoadusque argenti massa ab hominibus magis quam moneta desideretur: perit nempe hoc modo dignitas monete, quando per ipsam tantum argenti non licet emere quantum ipsa pecunia continet"[3] (Wolowski [1864], p. 53).

---

2 "Es kann auch die Münze in Verachtung kommen aus derselben unmässigen Vielheit, wo zu viel Silber vermünzt wird, (so) dass das Rohsilber von den Leuten mehr als gewöhnlich begehrt wird; denn dadurch nimmt die Achtung der Münze ab, wenn ich mit derselbigen nicht so viel Silber kaufen kann als sie in sich selbst hat und alsdann einen grösseren Nutzen befinde, dass ich die Münze schmelze und tilge" (COPERNICUS [1522], p. 23; I have put the old German into modern spelling).

3 In making use of the earlier German version I translate this as: "The coin can also fall into contempt by too great an amount of it, as it is possible if too much silver is minted, until the silver is more desired by the people than the money; for in this way the money certainly loses reputation, if it cannot buy so much silver as it contains itself".

2. Problems of the Development of the Purchasing Power Parity Theorem: The Formulation of the Theory and its Relevance for the Metallic Standard

Already in an earlier article I have pointed out that the formulation of the Purchasing Power Parity Theorem under a monetary regime based on gold or silver convertibility poses a problem (Bernholz [1982], pp. 5 - 6). The same is true for the Quantity Theory of Money if formulated, as by e.g. Copernicus, for a single country. In this section we will first formulate the simple macroeconomic mathematics and then describe the problem. As a consequence, it will become obvious that the problem is related to the facts on which the members of the School of Salamanca based the development of the Purchasing Power Parity Theorem. We will thus try to get a picture of the facts in Section 3 and discuss how far they are in accord with those the Doctors perceived. The paper will be concluded by stating some problems which remain for future research.

Let us assume that nominal money demand increases proportionally with the price level, P, and with real national income, Y, and that it is equal to money supply

(1) $M = k\,P\,Y\,.$

This formulation is consistent with the above quotations concerning the Quantity Theory, since P rises monotonically with M. Note, however, that the texts quoted do not speak of a *proportional* increase. The same relationship may be postulated for a foreign country:

(2) $M^{*} = k^{*} P^{*} Y^{*}\,.$

Finally, purchasing power parity is assumed

(3) $P = a r P^{*}$.

Here r denotes the exchange rate and a allows some deviation from absolute purchasing power parity, e.g. because of transportation costs and of untraded goods.

(1) to (3) imply

$$r = \frac{1}{a}\frac{P}{P^{*}}$$

$$P = \frac{1}{k}\frac{M}{Y}$$

$$P^{*} = \frac{1}{k^{*}}\frac{M^{*}}{Y^{*}}$$

(4) $$r = \frac{k^{*}}{ak}\frac{Y^{*}}{Y}\frac{M}{M^{*}}$$

Equation (4) shows that the value of "two monies may diverge [from $r = 1$ if they have the same metal content] ... because of scarcity and need. ... money is worth more when and where it is scarce than where it is abundant" (Martín de Azpilcueta Navarro). For an increase (decrease) of M (M^*) raises r and thus makes domestic money less valuable in terms of foreign money. The figures, given by Mercado in the last of our quotations, favors this interpretation. Also if we take logarithms of (1) and (4), we get by rearranging terms

$$\ln P = \ln M - \ln k - \ln Y$$

$$\ln r = \ln k^{*} - \ln a k + \ln Y^{*} - \ln Y + \ln M - \ln M^{*}$$

Taking a, k, k^*, Y and Y^* as constants, we derive by differentiating these equations with respect to time t:

(5) $$\frac{\dot{P}}{P} = \frac{\dot{M}}{M}$$

(6) $$\frac{\dot{r}}{r} = \frac{\dot{M}}{M} - \frac{\dot{M}^*}{M^*},$$

where $\dot{x} = \frac{dx}{dt}$.

The rate of inflation or relative price increase is caused by the growth rate of the money stock according to (5). Also (6) shows that the rate of depreciation of the domestic currency equals the difference between the growth rates of the domestic and the foreign stocks of money.

Now let us turn to the difficulties such an approach faces under monetary regimes in both (all) countries based on the same metallic standard, with full convertibility at fixed silver (gold) parities. In such a system the amount of money circulating in individual countries is endogenously determined and the exchange rate kept between specie points. Sir Thomas Gresham (1519 - 1579) already described the latter mechanism (1588) and the two relationships have been nicely connected by David Hume (1742; 1955):

> "Again, suppose, that all the money of Great Britain were multiplied five in a night, must not the contrary effect follow? Must not all labour and commodities rise to such an exorbitant height, that no neighbourlng nations could afford to buy from us; while their commodities, on the other hand, became comparatively so cheap, that, in spite of all the laws which could be formed, they would be run in upon us, and our money flow out; till we fall to a level with foreigners, and lose that great superiority of riches, which had laid us under such disadvantages?

> Now it is evident, that the same cause, which would correct these exorbitant inequalities, were they to happen miraculously, must prevent their happening in the common course of nature, and must for ever, in all neighbouring nations, preserve money nearly proportionable to the art and industry of each nation.
> What other reason, indeed, is there, why all nations, at present, gain in their trade with Spain and Portugal; but because it is impossible to heap up money, more than any fluid, beyond its proper level? The sovereigns of these countries have shown, that they wanted not inclination to keep their gold and silver to themselves, had it been in any degree practicable" (pp. 63 - 64).

Martín de Azpilcueta Navarro (1556) had an inkling of these relationships but apparently did not see their consequences for his theory:

> "Thus, in our own day many people have greatly increased their fortunes by carrying to Flanders and France ducats of two, four, and ten, some in kegs as though they were olives, others in barrels hidden in the wine, on each of which they made a big profit; and they bring merchandise from abroad which is worth little there and here much ..." (p. 88, Grice-Hutchinson [1982], p. 90).

Let us formalize the ideas expressed above and in doing so, abstract from minting, transportation and insurance costs as well as from any expected value of possible penalties and fines for exporting coins. We call the silver (gold) stock circulating as currency at home or abroad G and G^*. No other money (paper money or token money) is used. Assume next that the total world stock, S, is constant:

(7) $G + G^* = S$.

Parities are given by p and p^*, so that

(8) $M = pG$

(9) $M^* = p^* G^*$.

With no transportation costs of specie the law of one price requires that

$$(10) \quad r = \frac{p}{p^*}$$

This means that r is fixed with the parities. By inserting (10) into (4) it follows that

$$(11) \quad \frac{M^*}{M} = \frac{p^*}{p} \frac{k^*}{ak} \frac{Y^*}{Y},$$

also by using (8) and (9)

$$(12) \quad \frac{G^*}{G} = \frac{k^*}{ak} \frac{Y^*}{Y}.$$

Equations (11) and (12) tell us that the distribution of the world gold stock between countries is determined endogenously by the ratio of their money demand functions. Given the parities, this ratio also determines the ratio of domestic to foreign money stock.

Similarly, by inserting (10) into (3) one obtains

$$(13) \quad \frac{P}{P^*} = \frac{a p}{p^*}.$$

The ratio of domestic and foreign price levels is determined by the ratio of the silver (gold) parities, given a.

Finally, it follows from (7) and (12)

$$S - G = \frac{k^* Y^*}{ak\, Y} G$$

$$\frac{akY + k^*Y^*}{akY} G = S$$

(14) $$G = \frac{akY}{akY + k^*Y^*} S,$$

and because of (8)

(15) $$M = \frac{pakY}{akY + k^*Y^*} S.$$

The domestic amount of monetary silver (gold) and the money supply are both determined endogenously as soon as the world stock of silver (gold), S, and the parity are given. The same is true for G^* and M^*.

Combining (15) with (1) we derive

(16) $$P = \frac{paS}{akY + k^*Y^*},$$

which implies that the Quantity Theory cannot be applied to an individual country, if it has no control of S. It can only increase P and r (see [10]) if it changes p, i.e. if it debases its currency.

On the other hand, if S, the world stock of silver, increases we get from (16)

(17) $$\frac{dP}{dS} = \frac{pa}{akY + k^*Y^*} > 0.$$

The price level changes proportionately with the world specie stock. But according to (10) the exchange rate remains unchanged.

Confronting these results with the theories put forward in Section 1, several puzzles arise. How could Copernicus find the Quantity Theory by looking at the Prussian experience? For this theory is not applicable to an individual country on a metallic standard. The School of Salamanca, Bodin (1565) and the Latin American observers are better off in this respect. For (16) or (17) tell us that the price level increases everywhere with the stock of silver (or gold). But Doctors of the School of Salamanca are in a bad position concerning the Purchasing Power Parity Theory, since the exchange rate is according to (10) not influenced by an increase of *S*.

Thus, if the above theories were completely correct, Copernicus should not have found the Quantity Theory and the School of Salamanca the Purchasing Power Parity Theorem. But, paradoxically, the above theories just summarized their findings. Thus, if their findings were completely valid, they would never have found them. How can this puzzle be solved?

3. Possible Solutions to the Puzzle

The puzzle stated above can only be solved if the theory formulated for an international monetary regime with metallic standard and free convertibility is a valid approach to reality but is in some respects inadequate to explain it. If this were the case there might be room for empirical observations diverging from the conclusions of the theory which would allow to invent the Quantity Theory of Money and the Purchasing Power Parity Theorem.

In this Section we propose possible solutions. First, the theory stated above neglects transaction costs like those incurred for minting or melting coins, for separating the silver from the copper alloy contained in them, for transport and insurance costs to bring them abroad. Secondly, there may be time lags which are absent in the static model presented above. E.g., it obviously takes time to transport silver from Potosí to Spain, or even from Spain to France or Flanders. Especially under the conditions of the 16th century the transaction costs mentioned and the time lags for transportation cannot be neglected.

Let us first turn to the Quantity Theory of Money. There is, as we already pointed out, no problem for the Doctors of the School of Salamanca or the Latin American proponents of the theory if and as far as they base their ideas on the worldwide increase of gold and silver stocks and the rise of the price level in the same countries or places over time. Things looked different for Copernicus. In the Prussia of the 15th and early 16th centuries, to which he referred, the local inflation certainly was not caused by a worldwide increase of the silver stock, but by debasement of the currency. Copernicus himself points out that whereas in 1410 2 1/3 Prussian marcs were minted out of a half pound of pure silver, at his time (1522) the figure rose to 15 Prussian marks (1564, pp. 85 and 61). How then could he make his famous statement quoted above "The fact that the coin is valued less is most often caused by its being available in too great amounts ..." (pp. 52 - 83, my translation).

The explanation is probably given if we take into account the costs for melting the coins and for separating the different metals contained in it. An overissue of coins could then decrease their value below the market value of its metal content up to the amount given by these costs. Note that these costs are relatively higher for coins with a lower market value of the metals contained in the coins. And since the Prussian marcs in 1522 had a much higher copper than silver content, these costs were relatively high for them. Thus it is possible that an overissue of marcs led to a fall of their value until this lower boundary was reached. Copernicus may have perceived this phenomenon, for he continues after the statement just quoted:

> "In this case the value which has been added by minting is lost and it is not possible to buy with the coin as much silver as it contains; one could even find an advantage in melting

the coin. The remedy is not to mint any more money until it has reached its equilibrium and has become more expensive than the silver" (pp. 52 - 83).

We turn next to the Purchasing Power Parity Theorem. Here the costs incurred by transporting silver (or gold) from one country to another leave some room for the exchange rate to fluctuate between upper and lower silver (or gold) points, so that (10) does not hold between these points. Note that these costs may not only comprise transportation and insurance costs but also the expected costs of fines and penalties if governments forbid the export of silver (gold) and sanction detected transgressions of such decrees.

A simple model may help to clarify the relationships. Let c be the costs for bringing one unit of domestic silver (gold) money abroad or vice versa. Then, neglecting the costs of minting or melting coins, an arbitrageur of silver (gold) could make a profit by exporting one unit of silver (gold) if

$$(18) \quad (1+c)p < r p^* .$$

Note that p and p^* are the values of a unit of silver (gold) at home and abroad expressed in the respective monetary units and as determined by the parities. cp are the transportation costs etc. in domestic currency for bringing one unit of silver (gold) abroad. rp^* is the price of it abroad also in domestic currency. From (18) we get

$$(19) \quad r > (1+c)\frac{p}{p^*}.$$

Similarly, it is profitable to import silver (gold) if

$$p > r p^* + c r p^*,$$

$$(20) \quad r < \frac{p}{p^*} / (1+c).$$

Assuming perfect competition, profits from arbitrage are reduced to zero, so that (19) and (20) do not hold. It follows that

$$(21)\quad (1+c)\frac{p}{p^*} \geq r \geq \frac{1}{1+c}\frac{p}{p^*}.$$

The upper and lower silver (gold) points are thus given by the left and right hand sides of these inequalities. Within this band r is determined according to (3) or (4). Note that the band is wider if no perfect competition dominates the arbitrage market and if minting and melting costs are included.

If we assume now that only at home (say in Spain) the silver stock is increased by mining, then it follows from (8) and (9) that

$$\dot{M} = p\dot{G},$$

$$\dot{M}^* = 0$$

so that because of (5), (6) and (8)

$$(22)\quad \frac{\dot{r}}{r} = \frac{\dot{M}}{M} - \frac{\dot{M}^*}{M^*} = \frac{\dot{G}}{G},$$

$$(23)\quad \frac{\dot{P}}{P} = \frac{\dot{M}}{M} = \frac{\dot{G}}{G},$$

$$(24)\quad \frac{\dot{P}^*}{P^*} = 0.$$

This means that the exchange rate would (according to [22]) be driven up until it reached the upper silver point of (21). Until then only the domestic (Spanish) price level would increase. Afterwards silver would be exported, G^* and M^* would begin to rise and drive P^* upward. It follows that the price increase in Spain should precede that abroad (in France and Flanders) and the exchange rate should remain above its parity

$$(25) \quad r = (1+c)\frac{p}{p^*} > \frac{p}{p^*}$$

as long as silver is mined at home (in the Spanish dominions). We will have to look, in the next section, whether the facts correspond to this picture. If it should be the case, the puzzle, as to how the Purchasing Power Parity Theorem could be found under a metallic standard, would be solved.

A final reason to be mentioned for a divergence of r from p/p^* could be time lags. Here I do not speak about time lags in the adaptation of the price levels which were certainly present in reality. No, such time lags could not invalidate (3) inside the silver (gold) points, nor the validity of (22) if r would fully and immediately react and if no lags in silver (gold) arbitrage were present. If, however, such a lag is taken into account (and it has to be for the 16th Century), then the boundaries set by (21) may be surpassed by r, so that the deviation of the exchange rate from p/p^* may be even greater than expressed by (28).

4. Looking at Historical Developments

Let us first look at the development of prices (Fig. 1, 1a and Fig. 2, 2a). Here price indices have been taken which have been calculated by Hamilton (1934) for Andalucia and Old Castile/Leon, for Brabant by Van der Wee (1975) and for Utrecht and Leyden by Postumus (1964). We observe first that the price indices show a rising trend over the whole century, as required for the finding of the quantity theory. Until about 1550, they increase from 100 to 231% for Andalucia, to 138%

for Old Castile/Leon, to 176% for Brabant, to 128% for Utrecht and to 144% for Leyden. In the second half of the century, the price levels rise again from 100 around 1550 to 205% for Andalucia, 190% for Old Castile/Leon, 310% for Brabant, 303% for Utrecht and 326% for Leyden at the turn of the century.

As far as the statements of the Doctors of Salamanca are concerned, one should expect that the price level in Andalucia rose earlier and remained above that in the other places. This is certainly true until 1550 and remains true for Old Castile/Leon and Utrecht even until about 1600. The respective price indices (1500 = 100) reach 474, 262 and 388% in these cases. It is not true or more dubious for Brabant and Leyden with price indices of 526% and 469% for 1600 - 1608. On the other hand, there is no evidence that the price indices of the Dutch places increased later and remained below that of Old Castile/Leon. In the second half of the century the price index of the latter was even strongly surpassed by those of Utrecht and Leyden. I do not know whether this can be interpreted as evidence against the Doctors or the above theory. For it may well be that maritime transportation was cheaper to the Netherlands than transport costs to Old Castile. Also, much Spanish silver flowed directly (or via Genoa) to Flanders and probably from there to the Netherlands because of the war expenditures of the Spanish crown against the rebellious provinces.

Let us now look at the exchange rates (Fig. 3). Unfortunately, only figures for the second half of the 16th century were available (they have been taken from Vazquez de Prada). Since the rates are quoted in Flemish Groots per Spanish Ducats, Flanders must be considered to be the home and Spain the foreign country. We should thus expect from the theory exposed above that the Spanish ducats were quoted permanently below parity. This is, in fact, the case for the (spring) quotations on Medina del Campo. Things are, however, not as clear concerning the exchange rates quoted for Sevilla, where the discount from the parity should be even more pronounced than for Medina according to Purchasing Power Parity Theory and to the writings of the Doctors of Salamanca. This is certainly not the case. As far as the empirical observations of the Doctors are concerned, we have to admit that M. Azpilcueta de Navarro's refer to the earlier half of the century, since his book appeared in 1556. Thomás de Mercado's treaty was published in 1569, so that his experiences can only have reached up to, say, 1567 - 1568. And for the years from 1563 - 1568, the exchange rate on Sevilla is certainly below parity, but not below that on Medina del Campo.

5. Summary and Conclusions

In this paper we have recalled that the School of Salamanca was probably the first to develop the Purchasing Power Parity Theorem. These ideas came about by referring to observations which could be made during its time about the rise of prices in several countries and the behavior of exchange rates as a consequence of the inflow of gold and especially silver (Figure 4) from Mexico and Peru first to Spain (mosty by way of Seville) and from there to France, Flanders etc.

We demonstrated, however, that paradoxically, the facts which they asserted to have observed could not have happened according to a strict simple formulation of their model. Only an extension of their model including minting, melting, transportation and insurance costs and/or a time lag for silver (gold) arbitrage to other places allows for such observations.

After developing these relationships we finally looked at the facts concerning price levels and exchange rates, to find out whether they matched the empirical evidence brought forward by the Doctors of Salamanca in support of their arguments. Whereas the price levels in several places rose, and whereas they lagged behind the rise of the price level for Andalucia, no such difference could be found between the development of the price levels in Utrecht und Leyden compared to Old Castile/Leon. On the contrary, they moved ahead of the price level of the latter in the second half of the 16th century. This happened, however, only after Azpilcueta de Navarro and Thomas de Mercado had published their works.

The exchange rates in Antwerp on Medina del Campo and Seville show the discount from parity expected by the Doctors until 1568. But the rate on Seville is not lower than on Medina as should have been expected from Purchasing Power Parity Theory. One possible reason could be that it had reached the limit given by the lower silver point and/or time lags of silver arbitrage. It seems that more detailed empirical work on transport and insurance costs is necessary to determine the location of the lower silver points for different places. The same is true for the length of time lags in silver arbitrage. Without such knowledge not much progress in elucidating the remaining problems can be expected.

References

AZPILCUETA NAVARRO, Martín de (1586, 1968): Commentario resolutorio de cambios. Introduced by A. ULLASTRES / J. PEREZ PRENDES / L. PERENA, Madrid.

BAECK, Louis (1987): La Pensée Economique en Espagne aux 16e et 17e Siècles, in: H. VAN DER WEE (ed.), L'Or et l'Argent des Indes dans l'Economie Européenne, Louvain, pp. 3 - 39.

BERNHOLZ, Peter (1982): Flexible Exchange Rates in Historical Perspective (= Princeton Studies in International Finance No. 49), Princeton University.

BODIN, Jean (1565): Résponse aux paradoxes de M. de Malestroict touch. l'enchérissement de toutes les choses et des monnayes, Paris.

CASSEL, Gustav (1923): Money and Foreign Exchange after 1914, New York.

COPERNIC, Nicolas (1526, 1864): Monete Cudende Ratio (Traité de la Monnaie), edited and translated into French by M. L. WOLOWSKI, Paris, pp. 48 - 83.

COPPERNICUS, Nicolaus (1522, 1884): Das Gutachten über die Verbesserung der preussischen Münze, dem preussischen Landtage auf der Tagfahrt zu Graudenz im März 1522 überreicht, in: Leopold PROWE (ed.), Nicolaus Coppernicus, Vol. 2: Urkunden, Berlin, pp. 21 - 29.

DEMPSEY, Bernard W. (1935): The Historical Emergence of Quantity Theory, in: *Quarterly Journal of Economics* 80/1, pp. 174 - 184.

GRESHAM, Thomas (1588, 1839): Information of Sir Thomas Gresham, Mercer, touching the fall of the exchainge, MDLVIII. To the Quenes most excellent maiestye, in: J. W. BURGON, The Life and the Times of Sir Thomas Gresham I, London.

GRICE-HUTCHINSON, Marjorie (1952): The School of Salamanca. Readings in Spanish Monetary Theory, 1544 - 1605, Oxford.

GRICE-HUTCHINSON, Marjorie (1978): Early Economic Thought in Spain 1177 - 1740, London.

HAMILTON, Earl (1934): American Treasure and the Price Revolution in Spain, 1501 - 1650, Cambridge (Mass.).

HUME, David (1742, 1955): Of the Balance of Trade. In Writings on Economics, edited and introduced by Eugene ROTWEIN, London, pp. 60 - 77.

JASTROW, J. (1923): Textbuch 4, "Geld und Kredit", 5th edition Berlin.

MERCADO, Tomás (1869, 1975): Suma de Tratos y Contratos, introduced by R. BRAVO, Madrid.

LEVILLIER, Roberto (1921): Gobernantes del Perú - Cartas y Papeles - Siglo XVI - Documentos del Archivo de Indias, Tomo I, Madrid.

MOLINA, Luís (1893, 1615): De Jure et Iustitia, vol. II, Antwerp.

POPESCU, Oreste (1986): Origenes Hispanoamericanos de la Teoría Cuantitativa de la Moneda, in: *Desarrollo (Indoamericano)* XX No. 84 (Barranquilla), pp. 18 - 25.

POSTHUMUS (1964): Inquiry into the History of Prices in Holland, vol. II, Leiden.

RICARDO, David (1811, 1969): The High Price of Bullion. A Proof of the Depreciation of Bank Notes, in: E. C. K. GONNER (ed.): Economic Essays by David Ricardo, 4th edition London, pp. 1 - 60.

SOTO, Domingo de (1553): Libri decem de justitia et jure, Salamanca.

SPOONER, Frank C. (1972): The International Economy and Monetary Movements in France, 1493 - 1728, Cambridge (Mass.).

VAZQUEZ DE PRADA, V.: Lettres Marchandes d'Anvers, 2 vols., Paris.

VAN DER WEE, Herman (1978): Prijzen en lonen als ontwikkelingsvariabelen. Een vergelijkend onderzoek tussen Engeland en de Zuidelijke Nederlanden, 1400 - 1700, in: Album, Aangeboden aan Charles Verlinden, Gent, pp. 413 - 447.

WOLOWSKI, M. L. (1864) (ed.): Traictie de la Première Invention des Monnaies de Nicole Oresme et Traité de la Monnaie de Copernic, Paris.

Figure 1:

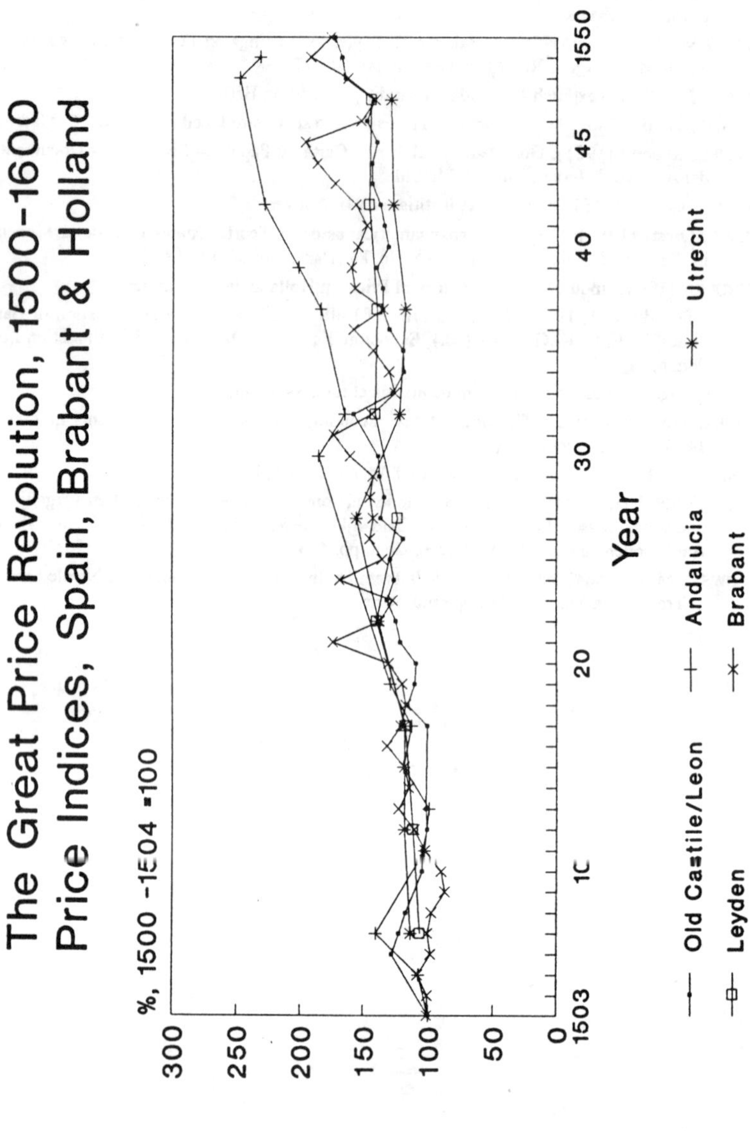
The Great Price Revolution, 1500-1600
Price Indices, Spain, Brabant & Holland
%, 1500 -1504 =100
300
250
200
150
100
50
0
1503
10
20
30
40
45
1550
Year
Old Castile/Leon
Andalucia
Utrecht
Leyden
Brabant

Figure 1a:

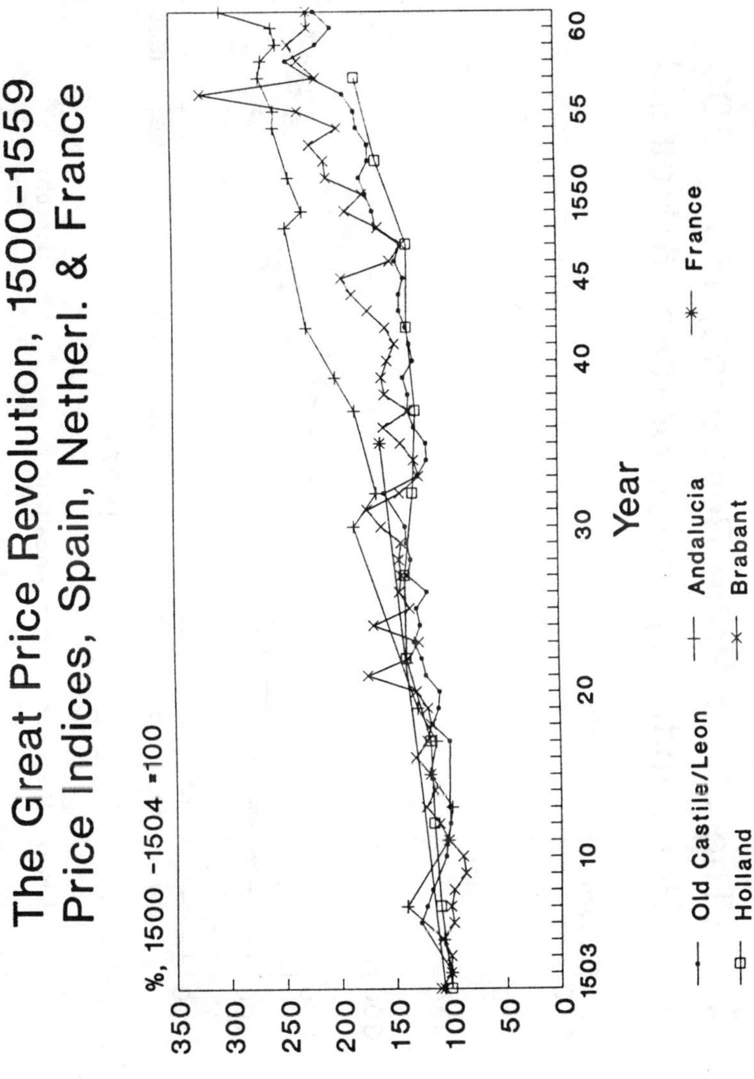
The Great Price Revolution, 1500-1559
Price Indices, Spain, Netherl. & France
%, 1500 -1504 =100
350
300
250
200
150
100
50
0
1503
10
20
30
40
45
1550
55
60
Year
Old Castile/Leon
Andalucia
France
Holland
Brabant

Figure 2:

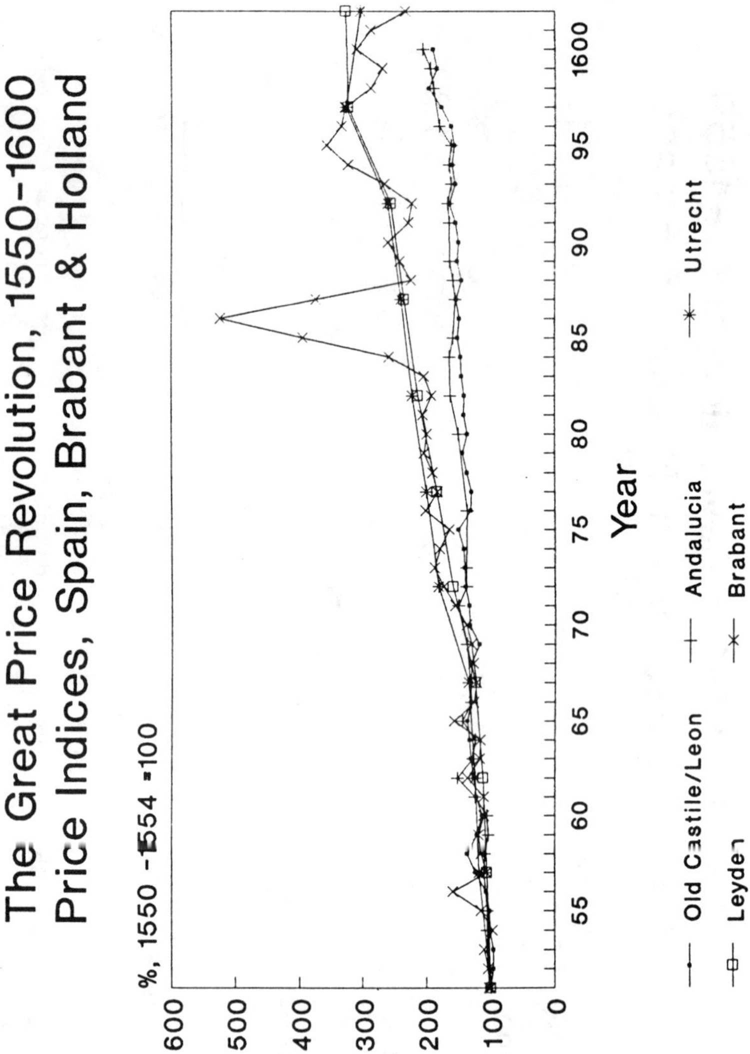
The Great Price Revolution, 1550-1600
Price Indices, Spain, Brabant & Holland
%, 1550 -1554 =100
600
500
400
300
200
100
0
55
60
65
70
75
80
85
90
95
1600
Year
Old Castile/Leon
Andalucia
Utrecht
Leyden
Brabant

Figure 2a:

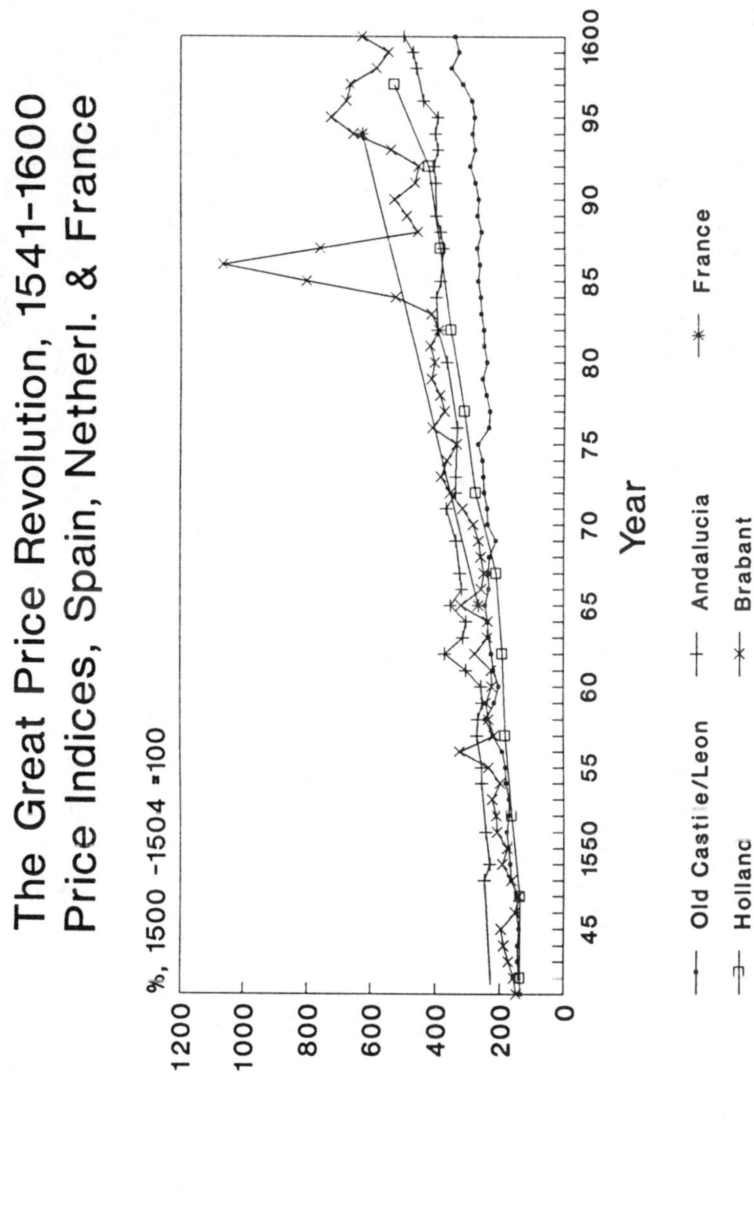
The Great Price Revolution, 1541-1600
Price Indices, Spain, Netherl. & France
%, 1500 -1504 =100
1200
1000
800
600
400
200
0
45
1550
55
60
65
70
75
80
85
90
95
1600
Year
Old Castile/Leon
Andalucia
France
Holland
Brabant

Figure 3:

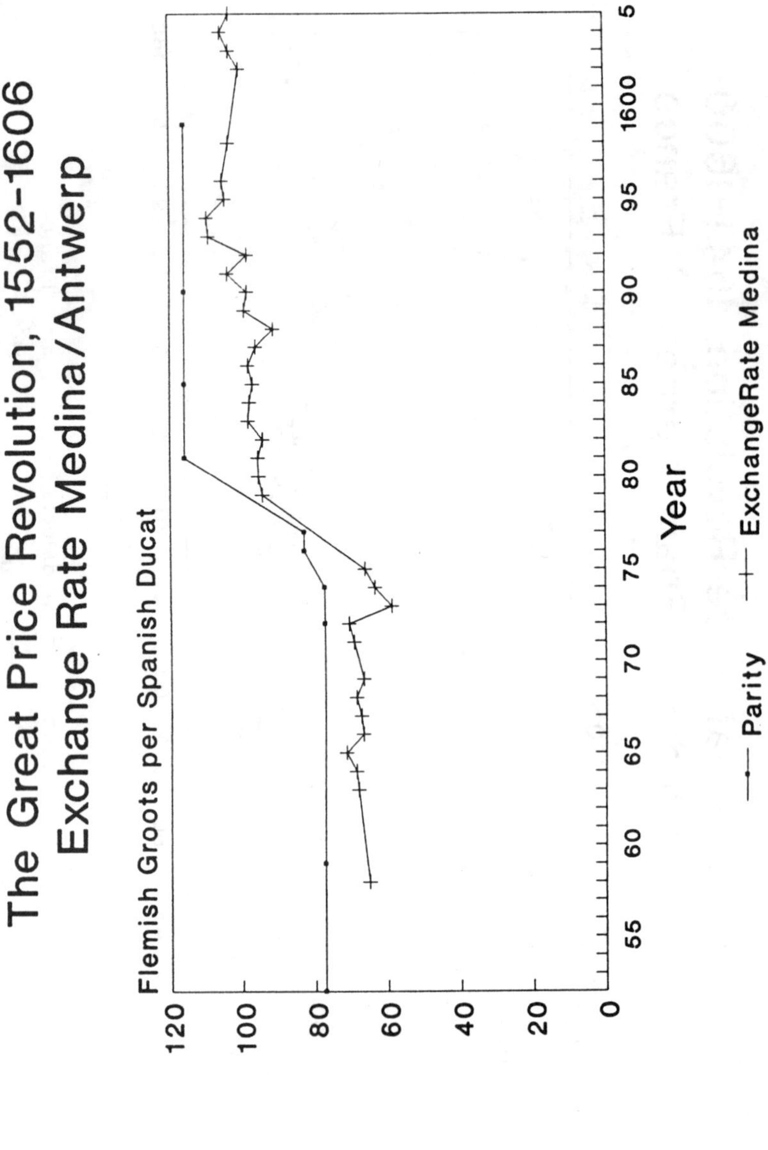
The Great Price Revolution, 1552-1606
Exchange Rate Medina/Antwerp
Flemish Groots per Spanish Ducat
0
20
40
60
80
100
120
55
60
65
70
75
80
85
90
95
1600
5
Year
Parity
ExchangeRate Medina

Figure 3a:

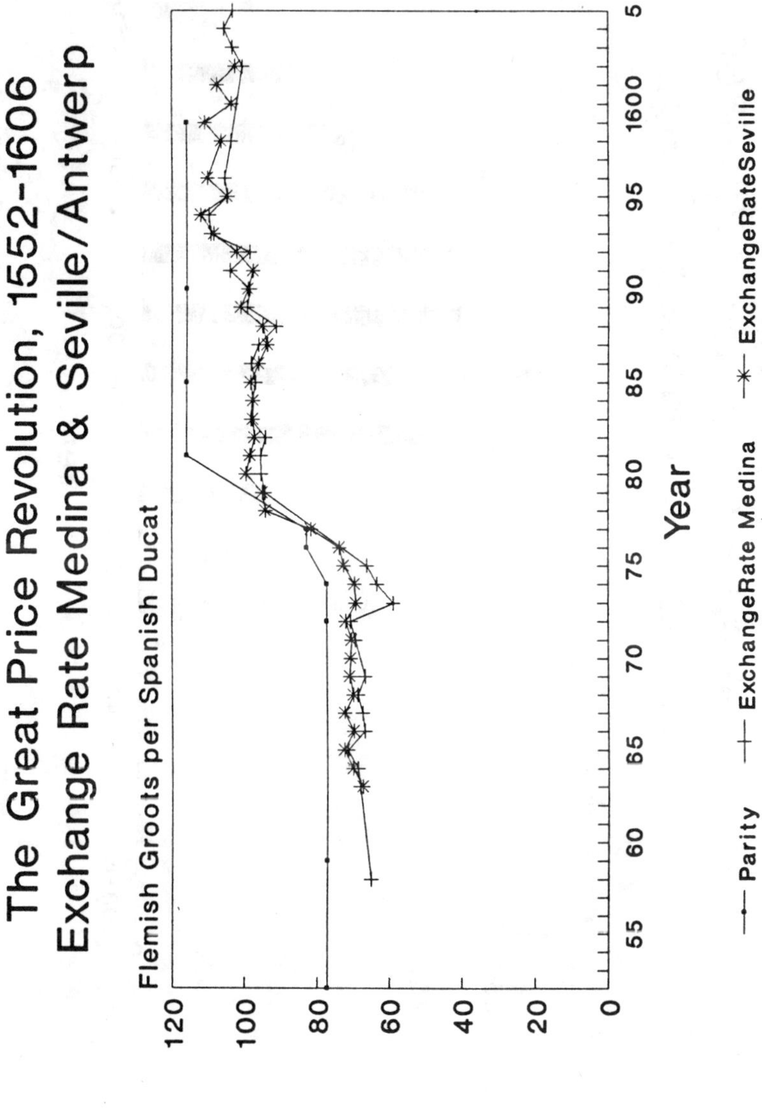
The Great Price Revolution, 1552-1606
Exchange Rate Medina & Seville/Antwerp
Flemish Groots per Spanish Ducat
120
100
80
60
40
20
0
55
60
65
70
75
80
85
90
95
1600
5
Year
Parity
ExchangeRate Medina
ExchangeRateSeville

Figure 4:

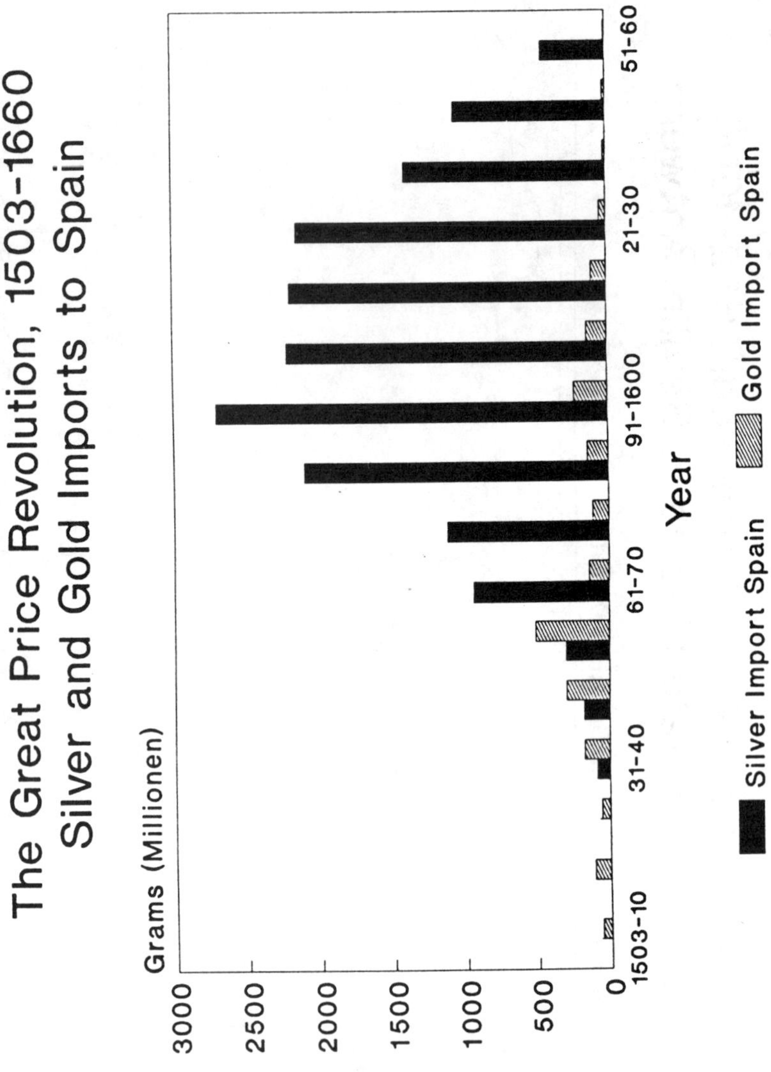
The Great Price Revolution, 1503-1660
Silver and Gold Imports to Spain
Grams (Millionen)
3000
2500
2000
1500
1000
500
0
1503-10
31-40
61-70
91-1600
21-30
51-60
Year
Silver Import Spain
Gold Import Spain

Figure 5:

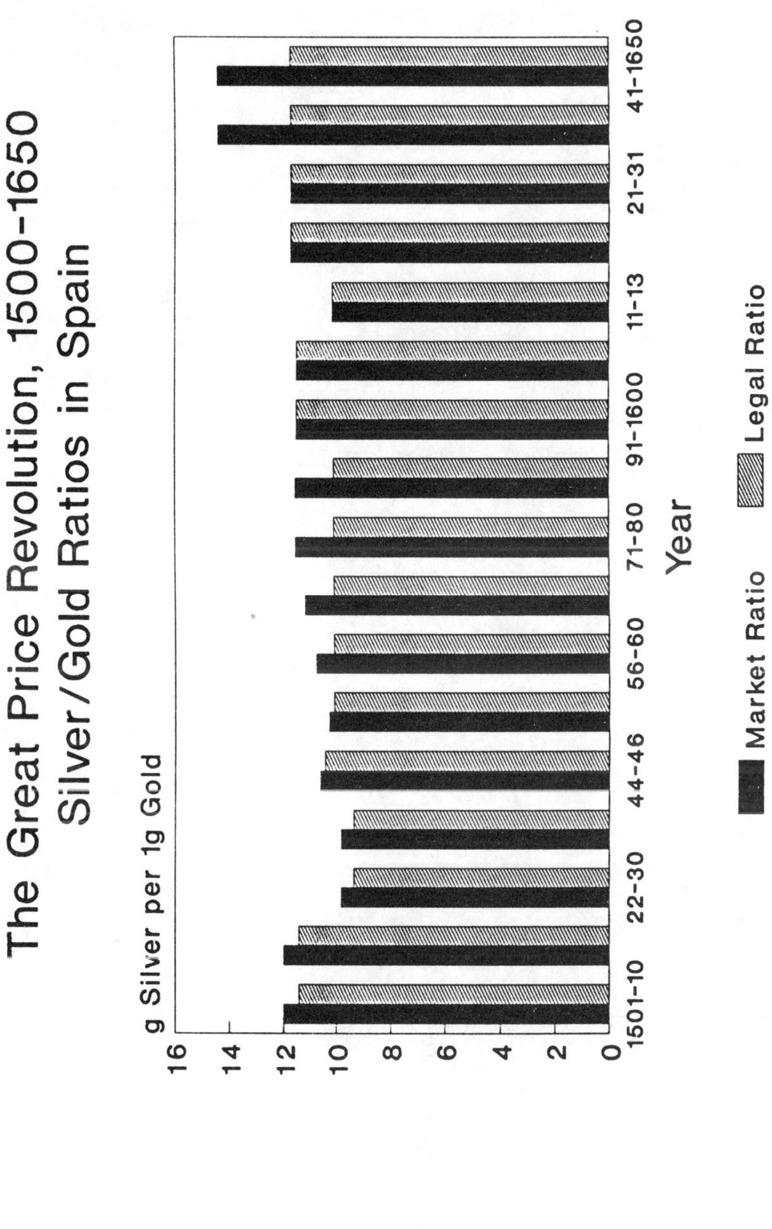

The Great Price Revolution, 1500-1650
Silver/Gold Ratios in Spain
g Silver per 1g Gold
16
14
12
10
8
6
4
2
0
1501-10
22-30
44-46
56-60
71-80
91-1600
11-13
21-31
41-1650
Year
Market Ratio
Legal Ratio

The American Factor in Portuguese Economic and Demographic Growth

By JOAQUIM DA COSTA LEITE

From a Portuguese perspective, the discovery of the Americas and the transatlantic exchange of the following centuries had diverse and complex consequences. A brief evaluation of those consequences necessarily involves a selection of relevant problems in the context of a proposed debate. In order to deal with the American factor in Portuguese economic and demographic growth, I begin with a few examples to suggest the diversity and complexity of the theme; I will then proceed to analyze the characteristics of local and regional markets which contradict traditional assumptions based on commercial treaties and political alliances; finally, I will take issue with the increased relative weight of the Northwest during the seventeenth and eighteenth centuries, discussing its economic transformation under the stimulus of maize cultivation, emigration and Brazilian trade.

In the Portuguese Northwest sedentary agriculture has been practiced by peasant communities organized within a relatively stable administrative framework for about a millenium. Yet, some of the elements of the agrarian system are fairly modern: maize was introduced from America via Spain, to become the major bread grain in the area sometime during the seventeenth century; another American crop, the potato, gained importance in the late eighteenth through to the nineteenth century; resistant American vines replaced the old ones ravaged by the phylloxera in the second half of the nineteenth century. Completely integrated, these foreign elements can now be described as essential elements of the traditional landscape of the Northwest, with maize fields bordered by vineyards, and the hills covered by pine trees. In parish churches and chapels, many of them constructed or rebuilt in the eighteenth century, Brazilian gold still shines in baroque altars[1].

The discovery of America had evident repercussions in the region. Some resulted directly from Portuguese colonial involvement; others were like maize, becoming available through a process of cultural diffusion which cut across imperial boundaries. As in the case of the introduction of new crops the effects were concentrated in specific regions, but in other aspects they concerned the whole country.

When Columbus touched Portuguese soil - first in the Island of Santa Maria, then in Lisbon - on his return from Hispaniola, he was in fact anticipating a change in the strategic position of the country. The mainland territory had been the *finisterra* of Antiquity, the end of inhabited land; oceanic navigation and the colonization of America changed a marginal into a strategic position, strengthened with Portuguese settlement of the Atlantic Islands. This new position stimulated participation in transatlantic trade and migratory flows, and became essential to the definition of political alliances down to the present time[2].

---

1 See, for example, Vitorino MAGALHÃES GODINHO, Os Descobrimentos e a Economia Mundial, vol. 2, Lisbon 1965, pp. 343 - 380; Orlando RIBEIRO, Portugal, o Mediterrâneo e o Atlântico, 4th ed., Lisbon 1986, pp. 8, 111 - 122; id., "Milho", in: Joel Serrão (Ed.), Dicionário de História de Portugal, Lisbon 1971; J. COSTA LEITE, A Portuguese Contrast: Agrarian System and Common Lands in Two *Freguesias*, in: *Economia* 7/1 (1983), pp. 1 - 50; David JUSTINO, A Formação do Espaço Económico Nacional, Portugal 1810 - 1913, vol. 1, Lisbon n. d., pp. 34 - 44.

2 In a classical evocation, *Finisterra* is the name of the most important Portuguese geographical journal; for concrete aspects of the new economic and geopolitical situation see, for example, T. Bentley DUNCAN, Atlantic Islands: Madeira, the Azores and the Cape Verdes in Seventeenth-Century Commerce and Navigation, Chicago 1972; Jorge BORGES DE MACEDO, O Bloqueio Continental: Economia e Guerra Peninsular, Lisbon 1962.

Of course, discovery carried no automatic consequences. Access to a whole new continent, complete with its different plants and animals, constituted a potent new factor but the precise historical outcome depended on the interplay with preexisting factors and their mutual evolution. The present reality of Brazil as a Portuguese-speaking nation is in a broad sense a consequence of discovery, but this predominantly cultural element is itself the product of many other factors: for example, the integration of the future territory of Brazil in the Portuguese sphere of influence by the Treaty of Tordesillas; the very low density of the native population; and the attraction of Portuguese immigrants during the gold rush of the eighteenth century, have all contributed to shape the linguistic reality of Brazil.

To give another example, the adoption of new crops was not a simple consequence of more productive plants being made available to hungry peasants. The degree of compatibility with existing practices of cultivation, the landed structure, even prevailing tastes seem to have affected a process of diffusion still barely studied[3]. A comparison of the different chronology and regional distribution of maize and potatoes in Portugal is enough to show that it was not an easy process.

Having made clear that the consequences of regular contacts with the Americas were many, complex, and diversified, I will now proceed to do the opposite: choose only a few, simplify, and adress the consequences from a particular standpoint. I will give precedence to the more enduring demographic and economic aspects, observed from

3 Seigneurial dues prescribing payments in kind also interfered in the process, discouraging experimentation with new crops in the fields customarily reserved for the required products; see João NUNES DE OLIVEIRA, A Produção Agricola de Viseu entre 1550 e 1700, Coimbra 1987 (mimeo.), quoted by Guilhermina MOTA, Estruturas Familiares no Mundo Rural: Grupos Domésticos no Bispado de Coimbra em 1801, in: *Revista Portuguesa de Historia* 24 (1988), pp. 13 - 14; Aurélio DE OLIVEIRA, A Abadia de Tibães, 1630/80 1813: Propriedade, Exploração e Produção Agricolas no Vale do Cávado Durante o Antigo Regime, vol. 1, Oporto 1979 (mimeo.), p. 202; Albert SILBERT, Le Problème Agraire Portugais au Temps des Premières Cortes Libérales, Paris 1968, pp. 183 - 184, 301 - 302.

within the present frontiers of Portugal; colonial relations will not be ignored, but from this long-term perspective the political element is not of primary concern[4].

Considering a growing European economic activity, with a consequent increase in the need for silver as a means of payment, Adam Smith made the following observation:

> Since the discovery of America, the greater part of Europe has been much improved. England, Holland, France, and Germany; even Sweden, Denmark, and Russia, have all advanced considerably both in agriculture and in manufactures. Italy seems not to have gone backwards. The fall of Italy preceded the conquest of Peru. Since that time it seems rather to have recovered a little. Spain and Portugal, indeed, are supposed to have gone backwards. Portugal, however, is but a very small part of Europe, and the declension of Spain is not, perhaps, so great as is commonly imagined[5].

Without establishing a causal relationship the author of *The Wealth of Nations* expressed the conviction, common to many or his predecessors and contemporaries, that the Iberian Peninsula stood out as a declining area in a prosperous Continent. Measured in terms of their relative maritime and military power, or in their capacity to develop an active manufacturing sector to retain precious metals received from the Americas, the Iberian countries were undoubtedly declining. To statesmen and political economists foreign trade was a crucial element in the bid for power on the international scene; the flow of goods and precious metals across national boundaries received considerable attention, but in a predominantly agrarian era, with high transport costs and regional economies, foreign trade was not an entirely reliable indicator of general economic conditions.

---

4 This is not intended to dismiss politics from the scene; political choices matter, but within the same institutional framework different regions develop their own fundamental characteristics resistant to policy changes and revolutions; in this qualified sense political events may be regarded as secondary.

5 Adam SMITH, The Wealth of Nations, vol. 2, London 1964, pp. 184 - 185.

In an imperial era it seemed natural to consider imperial relations as a major factor in the explanation of whatever occurred: prosperity in Great Britain, decline in the Iberian Peninsula. Colonial profits and the monetary stimulus of the inflow of Brazilian gold were seen as direct causes of British industrialization; in Portugal the same elements were thought to relax the pressure for protection of domestic manufactures - the state enjoyed large revenues, commercial deficits were easily covered, - and deindustrialization followed[6]. The empire was even regarded as an element of Iberian dependence, and many authors extended their arguments into the cultural sphere, believing that easy colonial incomes confirmed the Portuguese and the Spaniards in their contempt for manual work, further compromising any prospects for economic redemption[7].

Such interpretations were sometimes eloquently argued in the context of each country, but a comparative analysis reveals that they did not go to the heart of the problem: when the same elements produce different results in different countries, they have to be either irrelevant or mere contributing elements whose impact depends on the manner of their appropriation by other factors which are themselves crucial to the final outcome. (As a third possibility, the whole analysis may be wrong.) In comparative perspective, a failed experiment is just as illuminating as a success story.

---

6 See, for example, Sandro SIDERI, Comércio e Poder: Colonialismo Informal nas Relações Anglo-Portuguesas, Lisbon 1978; and in a critical perspective Jorge BORGES DE MACEDO, Problemas de História da Indústria Portuguesa no Século XVIII, 2d ed., Lisbon 1982; Patrick K. O'BRIEN, European Economic Development: the Contribution of the Periphery, in: *Economic History Review* 35 (1982), pp. 1 - 18.

7 Carl A. HANSON, Economy and Society in Baroque Portugal 1668 - 1703, London 1981, chapter 11: section on "Portugal, England, and the Roots of Modern Dependency", pp. 270 - 276; J. H. PARRY, The Spanish Seaborne Empire, New York 1979, chapter 12: "Economic Dependence", pp. 229 - 250; J. H. ELLIOTT, The Decline of Spain, in: Trevor ASTON (ed.), Crisis in Europe, 1560 - 1660, London 1980, pp. 167 - 193.

Using the terminology in a loose sense, the first attempt to industrialize Portugal is commonly dated back to the early 1670s. This coincided with a fall in the price of sugar and other colonial products, reducing export earnings; the War of Restoration further aggravated the situation, widening the trade deficit and draining the country of precious metals for coinage. The government responded with sumptuary laws restricting the use of imported goods, and promoted the establishment of manufactures. The first industrial spurt is supposed to have reached an end around 1690 when colonial exports recovered, followed by the discovery of gold mines in Brazil.

In subsequent periods the same basic connections were identified: a commercial crisis, usually due to a fall in colonial exports, led to protectionist measures and the promotion of manufactures; with the return of commercial prosperity the policy of industrial protection was abandoned. The whole period from the late seventeenth century to the middle of the nineteenth century has been interpreted in that light, as a series of industrial spurts interrupted by cycles of commercial prosperity[8]. It should be noted, however, that this interpretation is based on policy directives and the fate of manufacturing establishments closely associated with the state; it is by no means certain that the whole manufacturing sector followed the same ups and downs, a reasonable doubt which is also instilled by difficulties of a theoretical nature[9].

---

8 Vitorino MAGALHÃES GODINHO, Le Portugal, les Flottes du Sucre et les Flottes de l'Or, 1670 - 1770, in: *Annales: Economies, Sociétés, Civilizations* 1 and 2 (1950), translated and reprinted in: Ensaios II: Sobre História de Portugal, 2d ed., Lisbon 1978, pp. 423 - 448; id., Prix et Monnaies au Portugal, 1750 - 1850, Paris 1955. For a summary and anthology, see Joel SERRÃO / Gabriela MARTINS (eds.), Da Indústria Portuguesa: Do Antigo Regime ao Capitalismo, Lisbon 1978.

9 Jorge BORGES DE MACEDO, Problemas de História da Indústria Portuguesa no Século XVIII; Jorge Miguel PEDREIRA, Industrialização e Flutuações Económicas, Preços, Mercados e Inovação Tecnológica: Apontamentos e Reflexões Sobre o Caso Português (1670 - 1890), in: Estudos e Ensaios em Homenagem a Vitorino Magalhães Godinho, Lisbon 1988, pp. 276 - 292.

The connection between commercial prosperity and industrial decline has in the Methuen Treaty a privileged example. In 1703, with gold flowing in from Brazil, there was no concern with the trade deficit and the Portuguese could readily agree to favor imports of British textiles in return for a privileged position in the export of wine. The treaty was discussed by Adam Smith - who was sceptical of the proclaimed benefits for England, - and David Ricardo, among lesser known authors. It became probably the most famous treaty in the history of international economics, and has generally been regarded as an important, if not decisive element, in the specialization of the two countries: Britain prepared the first industrial revolution, while Portugal followed an agrarian path[10]. The abstract reasoning is clear, but the concrete implications deserve a close examination, at least on the Portuguese side[11].

In fact it has been shown that, contrary to prevailing assumptions, the treaty did not signify the ruin of Portuguese manufacturing activity. It is true that British woollens penetrated the Portuguese market, but when account is taken of technological conditions and transportation costs, their impact was confined to the coastal area; moreover, the persistence of many artisans even in the Lisbon area decades after the treaty, revealed that the commercial supremacy of British textiles had been greatly exaggerated[12].

---

10 Nuno VALÉRIO, Portugal nos Séculos XVIII e XIX segundo Adam Smith e Friedrich List, in: *Revista de História Económica e Social* 6 (1980), pp. 105 - 115; Bo SÖDERSTEN, Internationell Ekonomi, Stockholm 1969, pp. 27 - 34.

11 It deserves to be stressed that the Methuen Treaty dealt exclusively with woollen textiles; cotton products of future industrialization were not included, and were indeed prohibited in Portugal; see A. O. FRANCIS, The Methuens and Portugal, 1691 - 1708, Cambridge 1966, pp. 197 - 198; Jorge BORGES DE MACEDO, Methuen, Tratado de, in: Joel SERRÃO (ed.), Dicionario de História de Portugal; Valentim ALEXANDRE, Os Sentidos do Império: Questão Nacional e Questão Colonial na Crise do Antigo Regime Português, Lisbon 1989 (mimeo.), pp. 121 - 122, 127 - 129.

12 Jorge BORGES DE MACEDO, Problemas de História da Indústria Portuguesa no Século XVIII; id., Methuen.

Once the notion of large industrial enterprises is discarded as uncharacteristic of the pre-steam age, there is perhaps nothing surprising in the resistance of small artisan shops, and small manufacturing units, holding their own in local markets: their products were adjusted to local consumption patterns and traditional tastes, marketed through local networks of exchange and credit[13]. Foreign products of good quality could reach potential customers among the "middle classes" of the areas close to the ports, but in order to dislodge local production a whole range of goods would have to be produced much cheaper, and to be transported at very low rates; this would have to wait for a mechanized industrial system, serviced by a transportation network based on steamships and railways[14].

Similar questions arise concerning agriculture. Many authors, observing a continued dependence on grain imports, have concluded for the inability of Portuguese agriculture to change[15]. It cannot be denied that there was a persistent agrarian problem in Portugal, but the verdict of unqualified immobilism is not warranted. It should be noted that the chronic grain deficiency was in essence a shortage of wheat for the supply of Lisbon; to take that as the verification of an absence of agrarian change implied the existence of a unified national market, an assumption which was manifestly not met. The grain market was geographically divided, and segmented in socio-economic terms.

---

13 For a concrete example, see David JUSTINO / Mafalda SOARES DA CUNHA, As Feiras de Estremoz: Uma Primeira Contribuição para o Estudo dos Mercados Regionais no Antigo Regime, in: *Revista de História Económica e Social* 11 (1983), pp. 102 - 123.

14 Even in Western Europe, economic activity was still predominantly regional down to the middle of the nineteenth century; see Sidney POLLARD, Peaceful Conquest: The Industrialization of Europe, Oxford 1981.

15 António Sérgio, Antologia dos Economistas Portugueses (Século XVII), Lisbon 1974; Carl A. HANSON, Economy and Society in Baroque Portugal, 1668 - 1703, London 1981, chapter 8: "Economic Expansion and Foodstuff Shortages", pp. 185 - 206.

Different grains, mixtures, quality of grindind and baking, resulted in many sorts of bread, and in normal years the shortage was not so pressing as to make everybody willing to eat whatever was available. The ordinary people of Lisbon could not afford the best white bread made with imported wheat, having to content themselves with a cheaper kind made with local wheat; but they looked down on an inferior kind of bread, apparently made of millet, which was left to the most miserable elements of the population[16].

In times of famine the common people could not be choosy, but their social superiors insisted even then on satisfying their particular tastes. A measure of the extraordinary hunger of 1680 is given by the story of the friars of S. Marcos near Coimbra, who were prepared to eat maize bread for lack of wheat, a trial from which they were reportedly spared by the grace of God[17].

Socio-economic differentiation was cut across by regional divisions. Different bread grains predominated in different parts of the country, resulting in regional patterns of consumption; but even the existence of true regional markets cannot be taken for granted in the early eighteenth century. Table 1 shows the example of the prices of wheat, rye and maize, in two urban centers of the Portuguese Northwest from 1725 to 1729.

---

16 António DE OLIVEIRA, A Vida Económica e Social de Coimbra de 1537 a 1640, vol. 2, Coimbra 1972, pp. 132 - 146, Lisbon reference on pages 140, 142.

17 Ibid., p. 144.

TABLE 1:
Grain Prices in Viana do Castelo and Ponte de Lima, 1725 - 1729

	Viana do Castelo			*Ponte de Lima*		
	Wheat	Rye	Maize	Wheat	Rye	Maize
1725	400	260	240	400	190	190
1726	410	290	280	400	300	300
1727	480	240	190	700	300	180
1728	570	240	200	580	240	200
1729	425	240	200	400	180	180

Prices in *réis* per *alqueire*.

Sources: For Viana, see Vitorino MAGALHÃES GODINHO, Introdução à História Económica, Lisbon n.d., pp. 168 - 169; for Ponte de Lima, António DOS REIS, O preço dos cereais em Ponte de Lima (1625 - 1925), in: Almanaque de Ponte de Lima 1980 (Câmara Municipal de Ponte de Lima, 1979), p. 156.

Viana was a seaport, Ponte de Lima a small town just over twenty kilometers inland. Located in the same region, connected by the Lima River, they enjoyed favourable circumstances for the integration of their local grain markets, but this had clearly not been achieved in the first quarter of the eighteenth century. Wheat, for example, cost the same in the two places in 1725, but two years later the price had increased only 20 percent in Viana, and 75 percent in Ponte de Lima; perhaps more significantly, the maximum price for the quinquenium was reached in 1727 in Ponte de Lima, and the following year in Viana.

In the case of maize discrepancies are less pronounced, but it is possible to verify that it was cheaper to buy maize in Ponte de Lima in alternate years (1725, 1727, 1729), and in Viana in 1726; only in 1728 did it cost the same in the two markets. The popular bread of the Northwest, *boroa*, was made with a mixture of maize and rye, and the two grains were closely associated in Ponte de Lima, where in three out of five years they cost the same; but in neighbouring Viana rye was consistently more expensive than maize. Even in Ponte de Lima the apparent rule of parity was suddenly broken in 1727, when rye cost 67 percent more than maize.

In spite of the cultural and geographical proximity of the two urban centers, their prices were differentiated by a relative autonomy in the variation of purchasing power and preferences of different groups of consumers; this varying demand was exerted against the quantity of grain brought to the market, which was itself distinct - namely because of peasant domestic consumption and transportation difficulties, - from total production. Even small variations in supply or demand could produce large price fluctuations which could not easily be corrected by a quick inflow of grain from outside. (Notice that wheat prices in Ponte de Lima were more unstable than in Viana, a larger town with access to the sea.) In such circumstances it was impossible to transpose conclusions or to make simple assumptions from one product to the other, from one market place to the next.

Taking insufficient account of the nature of small fragmented pre-industrial markets, authors who tried to infer general economic conditions from policy directives or foreign trade were often wrong. They were wrong when they expected the Methuen Treaty to lead directly to the ruin of Portuguese manufacturing activity. And they were wrong when they interpreted continued grain imports as evidence of agrarian inertia, precisely when a remarkable transformation was taking place in the Northwest. But in order to perceive the change it is necessary to take a different approach.

In the pre-industrial era population and production moved in close step. Increased production allowed the population to grow, leading to a further increase in the labour force and more production, until diminishing returns led to a significant reduction of average productivity, forcing a demographic adjustment. Apart from this interaction of a general nature, in the case of Europe west of the Elbe the marriage pattern - with its emphasys on the nuclear family and its minimum economic requirements for marriage, - established a closer association between general employment conditions and the formation of new households. It therefore seems justified to take population as a rough long-term guide to aggregate economic activity[18].

Table 2 shows the number of households counted in Portugal in 1527 and 1801, suggesting a population increase of approximately 2.7 between those two fairly complete censuses. To put this into perspective, it can be pointed out that from 1500 to 1800 the population of the whole European Continent may have increased about 2.2 times, while in Spain there were difficulties denounced by a modest increase (only 1.4) from 1541 to 1797[19]. From this point of view there are no signs of decline; on the contrary, it would be tempting to propose Portugal as a dynamic economy if this formulation were not misleading: production may have grown in a subsistence context, without a significant change in a capitalist direction.

---

18 Although the precise connections between population and the economy are admittedly not simple, in the long run they are closely associated. See Robert I. ROTBERG / Theodore K. RABB (eds.), Population and Economy: From the Traditional to the Modern World, Cambridge 1986; Jan DE VRIES, The Economy of Europe in an Age of Crisis, 1600 - 1750, Cambridge 1976, pp. 4 - 16; J. HAJNAL, European Marriage Patterns in Perspective, reprinted in: D. V. GLASS / D. E. C. EVERSLEY, Population in History: Essays in Historical Demography, London 1974, pp. 101 - 143. Concerning Portuguese demographic characteristics, see Robert ROWLAND, Sistemas Familiares e Padrões Demográficos em Portugal: Questões Para Uma Investigação Comparada, in: *Ler Historia* 3 (1984), pp. 13 - 32; Maria Norberta SIMAS BETTENCOURT AMORIM, Guimarães, 1580 - 1819: Estudo Demográfico, Lisbon 1987, especially chapter 1: "Nupcialidade", pp. 63 - 143.

19 Colin MCEVEDY and Richard JONES, Atlas of World Population History, Harmondsworth 1978; Jordi NADAL, La Población Española (Siglos XVI a XX), 4th ed., Barcelona 1976), p. 16. In approximately the same period of time population growth was about 1.9 in France, 2.2 in the Netherlands, and 3.5 in England and Wales; see Robert I. ROTBERG / Theodore K. RABB (eds.), Population and Economy: From the Traditional to the Modern World, pp. 64, 102, 160.

TABLE 2:
Portuguese Population (Households) in 1527 and 1801

	1527	1801	Increase
Northern Coast	82,158	285,134	3.5
Alentejo	25,637	57,936	2.3
Portuguese Mainland	280,415	758,501	2.7

The Northern Coastal Area comprises approximately the present-day *distritos* of Viana, Braga, Porto, Aveiro, and Coimbra. Alentejo comprises Portalegre, Beja, and Evora.

Sources: The population count of 1527 - 1532 has been published in separate sections; a useful list of administrative units and respective households has been assembled by Júlia GALEGO / Suzanne DAVEAU, O Numeramento de 1527 - 1532: Tratamento Cartográfico, Lisbon 1986, appendix 1, pp. 91 - 106. The 1801 census was compiled, and later published, as Taboas Topograficas e Estatisticas, ed. by Instituto Nacional de Estatística, Lisbon 1948; for a summary, see Joel SERRÃO, Fontes de Demografia Portuguesa, 1800 - 1862, Lisbon 1973, pp. 77 - 78.

Where should we look for the economic foundations of demographic growth? Little attention has been given to agriculture and internal trade, but the regional figures in table 2 provide a valuable indication. Alentejo registered a moderate growth while the Northern Coast surged ahead: considering that Alentejo had a low population density to start with, and the North included the most densely settled areas since at least the late medieval period, the contrary was to be expected[20]. An essential element in the explanation is that the wet, irrigated lands of the north, were excellent for the cultivation of maize which was not readily suited to the dry plains of Alentejo[21].

---

20 A. H. OLIVEIRA MARQUES, A População Portuguesa nos Fins do Século XIII, in: Ensaios de História Medieval, 2d ed., Lisbon 1980, pp. 51 - 92.

21 This observation applies to maize as a major crop for human consumption; it can also be used as fodder, introduced as a secondary crop in a rotation system, justifying the assertion made in the 1970s that the full potential of the maize revolution had not yet been exhausted; see Eugénio DE CASTRO CALDAS,

The new plant was adopted by Portuguese peasants who learned to cultivate maize in association with beans, as Columbus had seen in the West Indies[22]. Suited to intensive cultivation in the small fields of the Northwest, the new crops were quickly adopted because they required only minor adjustments in the usual crop rotations. Already tried in the late sixteenth century, maize seems to have spread vigorously during the first half of the seventeenth, increasing productivity per hectare and sustaining a remarkable demographic growth[23]. When gold was found in Brazil towards the end of the century, the Northwest could send thousands of emigrants there every year for decades, and still keep growing faster than the rest of the country[24].

The evidence of a remarkable demographic growth in the Northwest is unmistakable. Doubts arise when decisive questions for the prospects of economic development are put forward: Did population increase entirely absorb the increased production of foodstuffs, merely enlarging a subsistence peasant sector? Were productivity gains claimed by well-connected *foreiros*, the middlemen of the landholding system, to increase their income and reinforce their social status? Or was there a

---

A Agricultura Portuguesa no Limiar da Reforma Agrária, Oeiras 1978, pp. 42, 109 - 110.

22 Carl Ortwin SAUER, The Early Spanish Main, Berkeley 1969, pp. 54 - 55; Orlando RIBEIRO, Milho; Aurelio de Oliveira, A Abadia de Tibães e o Seu Domínio (1630 - 1680): Estudo Social e Económico, Oporto 1974, p. 264.

23 The gains have not been quantified, but if later figures are any indication, productivity per hectare probably doubled relative to other grains; in the Northwest, however, the revolutionized agrarian system registered much larger gains in overall productivity; see Margarida MATEUS / Abel MATEUS, Technological Change, Trade Regimes and the Response of Agriculture in Portugal During the 19th Century, Lisbon (Universidade Nova, Faculdade de Economia, Working Paper no. 52), pp. 13A (table 3), 20 - 24; Pedro LAINS, A Evolução da Agricultura e da Indústria em Portugal (1850 - 1913): Uma Interpretação Quantitativa, Lisbon 1990, table 2, p. 11.

24 Vitorino MAGALHÃES GODINHO, L'Emigration Portugaise (XVe - XXe Siècles): Une Constante Structurale et les Réponses aux Changements du Monde, in: *Revista de História Económica e Social* 1 (1978), pp. 9, 20.

surplus for the market, favouring economic specialization and strengthening the urban component in the region?

There was certainly a bit of everything. Irrigated fields with less than one hectare could sustain a whole family, and this helped peasants keep the market at arm's lenght. It is also true that *foreiros* were particularly prominent in maize regions, both in Portugal and in Spain. There is also clear evidence of small-scale manufacturing production in town and countryside[25].

In view of these contradictory elements, it would seem possible to classify the Portuguese Northwest as an economically blocked region where the bulk of agricultural production was consumed without ever going through the market; any surplus was appropriated by middle and upper strata with aristocratic pretensions, and spent on manors and churches; some artisans were required to build the manors or carve saints for the altars, while the surplus population emigrated. In outline, this is an interpretation which has been coherently argued for Galicia, so close to the Portuguese Northwest in geographical, economic and socio-demographic terms[26].

In the Northwest the scenario of stagnation does not seem adequate. Important questions remain to be answered concerning the precise chronology of change, or the characteristics and relative weight of various elements, but it is nevertheless clear that commercialization and specialization gained ground. Although in the early eighteenth century market development still left much to be desired, the multiplication of population in a small area enlarged the potential market and lowered transaction costs. The increasing role of merchants in the

---

25 Orlando RIBEIRO, Milho; Aurelio DE OLIVEIRA, A Abadia de Tibães, 1630/80 - 1813, pp. 296 - 298; Raymond CARR, Spain 1808 - 1939, Oxford 1966, pp. 8 - 10; for manufacturing see references below.

26 Jaime GARCIA-LOMBARDERO, La Agricultura y el Estancamiento Economico de Galicia en la España del Antiguo Regimen, Madrid 1973; see also Ramón VILLARES, Foros, Frades e Fidalgos: Estudios de Historia Social de Galicia, Vigo 1982.

rural areas shows that larger quantities of grain were being bought and sold, escaping both the subsistence economy of the peasants and the traditional consumption networks controlled by aristocratic and religious institutions. This progress in the commercialization of agriculture (extensive to wine, olive oil, livestock and timber), points to an increase in the share of the non-agricultural population, which is confirmed by a diversification of occupational skills, and growing urban centers[27].

The dynamic nature of the region was evident in its capital, Oporto, which doubled its population in the half-century from 1732 to 1787[28]. In spite of this remarkable growth the city was well-supplied with fooodstuffs; indeed, it could dispense with large quantities of maize, beans, smoked ham and wine, which were regularly shipped to Lisbon. An annual movement of some five hundred sea-going vessels, mostly Portuguese and British in approximately equal proportions, ensured connections with Brazilian, British and other ports. There was a significant reexport trade, but Oporto merchants also handled agricultural and manufactured products of the Northwest. Importation of British manufactures (especially woollen textiles) was not incompatible with the existence in the city and its hinterland of a dynamic sector, producing and exporting a variety of linen and woollen cloth, silk,

---

27 See, for example, Aurélio DE OLIVEIRA, A Abadia de Tibães e o Seu Dominio (1630 - 1680); id., A Abadia do Tibães, 1630/80 - 1813; id., A Renda Agricola em Portugal Durante o Antigo Regime (Séculos XVII e XVIII): Alguns Aspectos e Problemas, in: *Revista de História Económica e Social* 6 (1980), pp. 1 - 56; José AMADO MENDES (ed.), Memória Sobre a Provincia do Minho pelo 2° Visconde de Balsemão, in: *Revista Portuguesa de História* 18 (1980), pp. 31 - 109; Cândido DOS SANTOS, Subsidios para a História da Demografia da Região de Santo Tirso, in: Actas do Colóquio de História Local e Regional: Santo Tirso, 17 e 18 de Março de 1979, Santo Tirso 1982, pp. 181 - 208.

28 Cândido DOS SANTOS, A População do Porto de 1700 a 1820: Contribuição Para o Estudo da Demografia Urbana, in: *Revista de História* 1 (1978), p. 288.

lace, buttons, hats, nails, etc. Perhaps close to a half of this export trade was carried in ships built and fitted in the city or its environs[29].

The productive agriculture and dense population of the Northwest provided the foundation for the manufacturing and commercial prosperity of Oporto[30]. Once this was assured, Brazilian gold could indeed bring an extra stimulus; this was exerted in a complex way which may be schematically presented: exploration of gold and diamonds produced an economic boom in Brazil, paying for imports and attracting immigrants, mostly from the Portuguese Northwest; these immigrants retained connections with their native region, and contributed to extend the commercial network of merchants in Viana do Castelo, Figueira da Foz, and above all in Oporto; immigrants and goods stimulated shipping, and this in turn kept busy the naval construction sector[31].

It should be stressed that the multiple interaction (maize - high population density - manufacturing and emigration - trade - shipping and shipbuilding), which was probably established in the early eighteenth century under the stimulus of gold in a colonial context, has been

---

29 Agostinho REBELO DA COSTA, Descrição Topográfica e Histórica da Cidade do Porto, 2d ed., Oporto 1945, esp. pp. 242 - 283.

30 This raises an issue concerning the role of domestic versus foreign - especially colonial - trade. See Valentim ALEXANDRE, Os Sentidos do Império: Questão Nacional e Questão Colonial na Crise do Antigo Regime Português; id., Um Momento Crucial no Subdesenvolvimento Português: Efeitos Económicos da Perda do Império Brasileiro, in: *Ler História* 7 (1986), arguing for the crucial role of the Brazilian market, and the ensuing debate in *Penélope* 3 (1989) and 5 (1991), with Pedro Lains stressing the importance of the domestic market.

31 It seems justified to look at the Northwest in the late eighteenth century as a proto-industrial region, but a study of manufacturing activity is required; some complementary agricultural, demographic, and foreign trade data are already available, for example, in Aurélio DE OLIVEIRA, A Abadia de Tibães, 1630/80 - 1813; Maria Norberta SIMAS BETTENCOURT AMORIM, Guimarães, 1580 - 1819: Estudo Demográfico; and Valentim ALEXANDRE, Os Sentidos do Império: Questão Nacional e Questão Colonial na Crise do Antigo Regime Português.

more clearly documented for the closing decades of the century when gold was no longer prominent; it could still be found in the mid-nineteenth century without gold or colonial ties. During such a long period, trade and migration fluctuated according to the relative prosperity of both countries, but they were never interrupted long enough to break the human and commercial nexus. From this perspective, the first radical alteration in the transatlantic exchange occurred in the 1870s, when packet steamships (predominantly British) replaced sailing ships (almost exclusively Portuguese) in the transportation of Portuguese emigrants to Brazil[32]. The irresistible force of technological superiority was then clearly demonstrated.

In conclusion, it may be said that before the technology of the industrial revolution enabled modern entrepreneurs to outsell their competitors in distant unprotected markets, the decisions of the Portuguese government or its agreements with the British Ambassador in Lisbon could be very important, but their concrete repercussions in the rest of the country would depend on the characteristics and vitality of the regional economies. An excessive attention to foreign trade and tariff policies resulted in wrong assumptions concerning both industry and agriculture. Commercial situations which affected consumers with incomes above the average, predominantly in the Lisbon area, were wrongly interpreted as characteristic of the country as a whole.

The importance of a regional analysis is confirmed by demographic data, and it is in a regional context that the consequences of the discovery of America are clearly revealed in their most persisting elements. The American factor (defined in a broad sense) was particularly strong in the Northwest, in a mutual interaction of agricultural, demographic and economic elements.

The transatlantic flow established under the stimulus of Brazilian gold constituted the most complex manifestation of the American nexus. Important in itself, because of the regions and populations involved,

---

32 J. Costa Leite, O Transporte de Emigrantes: Da Vela ao Vapor na Rota do Brasil (1851 - 1914), in: *Análise Social* 112 - 113 (1991), pp. 741 - 752.

the Oporto-Bahia-Rio connection is also relevant in its suggestions. For example, the sugestion that something important may be missed in a simple analysis of trade flows between Portugal and Brazil, when the human and commercial elements were so closely related. (Lacking this human complement, Lisbon was more heavily dependent on state support, and in this sense more vulnerable to political contingencies.) From the perspective of the Northwest the colonial factor, essential to the creation of an administrative framework and the orientation of early transatlantic flows, does not seem to have carried a decisive weight in the alteration of the pace and composition of later demographic and trade flows. The competitive edge conferred by industrial technology was instead of primary importance.

Finally, I would like to conclude that productive new crops had the potential to become more important than trade. In the case of the Portuguese Northwest maize was more important than gold; but one did not exclude the other, and after allowing for a few decades of initial demographic growth, the combination of maize and gold produced visible changes. Maize provided subsistence to a larger population, creating opportunities for economic specialization; gold provided the extra stimulus to attract an increasing number of people away from subsistence agriculture, further activating manufacture and trade.

In the Northwest as in other proto-industrial regions the promise of early industrialization did not materialize, but the failure does not erase the importance of the changes which took place during the seventeenth and eighteenth centuries. Their imprint is still recognizable today in a region characterized by its demographic vitality, fragmented landholdings and scattered industries, integrated in a conservative yet flexible socio-economic structure.

The Effects on European Markets of Imports of Overseas Agriculture: The Production, Trade and Consumption of Coffee (15th to late 18th Century)

By JÜRGEN SCHNEIDER*

Introduction

The most important products of overseas agriculture and forestry on European markets (1500 - 1800) were spices, sugar, dyestuffs, cocoa, coffee, tea, and tobacco. Other overseas products, such as potatoes, did indeed come to be cultivated in Europe, but did not figure in international trade. For this reason they do not belong in the group of goods under discussion.

According to Fernand Braudel

> "(...) braucht jede Zivilisation ihre Luxusartikel und ihre ganz bestimmten Simulantien. Im 12. und 13. Jahrhundert waren es der Pfeffer und die Gewürze, im 16. Jahrhundert der Alkohol, dann der Tee und der Kaffee, ganz zu schweigen vom Tabak, der (...) zwischen dem 16. und 17.

---

* Translation by Peter ORAM.

> Jahrhundert die ganze Welt erobert, und zwar nachhaltiger noch als Kaffee und Tee, was einiges heißen will"[1].

Spices such as pepper had been reaching Europe since ancient times[2]. Sugar cane was originally native to the Bengal coast between the Ganges Delta and Assam. It crossed the Atlantic by way of Egypt (10th century), Cyprus, Sicily, Valencia, Madeira, the Azores and the Canaries, reaching Brazil and from there, in the second half of the 17th century, the Caribbean[3]. Among the dyestuffs indigo was already known in antiquity; there is evidence of it from the 12th and 13th centuries on, first of all in Italy and then in France and England[4]. The discovery of America made further dyes available for the European textile industry: logwood (campeachy-wood), Brazil wood, quercitron, orlean and cochineal.

Around 1600 Europe discovered three new stimulating and envigorating beverages: cacao, coffee and tea. "Die Schokolade gelangte in Brot- und Tafelform von Mexiko und den spanischen Kolonien um 1520 nach Spanien"[5]. By the end of the 16th century coffee had become a familiar commodity throughout the Islamic world. During the 17th and 18th centuries coffee-drinking spread over the whole of Europe. Tea was introduced into Holland around 1610. There is first mention of its use in 1637.

> "Comme le thé commence à entrer en usage chez certaines personnes, écrivent les directeurs de l'Oost-Indische-Com-

---

1 Fernand BRAUDEL, Die Geschichte der Zivilisation. 15. bis 18. Jahrhundert. München 1971, p. 279s.

2 Eberhard SCHMITT, Pfeffer, Vom Reichtum an Gewürzen in: *Kultur und Technik. Zeitschrift des deutschen Museums* 4/1988, pp. 214ss.

3 Thomas SCHLEICH, Das weiße Gold der neuen Welt. Zuckerherstellung und Zuckerhandel 1415 bis 1815, in: Ibid., pp. 238ss.

4 Thomas BECK, Indigo. Cochenille und Brasilholz. Farbstoffhandel und Technologietransfer im ersten Kolonialzeitalter, in: Ibid., pp. 222ss.

5 BRAUDEL, op.cit., p. 265.

> pagnie, nous en attendons quelques jarres de Chine ou du Japon sur chaque vaisseau"[6].

The Spaniards had already come into contact with tobacco during their first voyages of discovery. Both forms of consumption -smoking and snuff-taking - were already employed by Indians of North and Central America and spread from Spain across the whole of Europe during the 17th and 18th centuries.

Hans Chr. Johansen's schematic representation of interregional trade routes to and from Western Europe around 1750 conveys a picture of worldwide pre-industrial currents of trade[7]. The most important colonial goods in the 18th century may well have been sugar and coffee. Colonial goods appeared on price lists already at an early date. Thus in the "*Prys-Courant*" of Hamburg, 1672, we find indigo, cochineal, orlean, (an orange-yellow dye), the woods Pernambuco and Campeche, tobacco, pepper and sugar.

Adam Smith considers the discovery of America and the sea routes to East India round the Cape of Good Hope to be the two greatest and most significant events in human history:

> "... in consequence of those discoveries, the commercial towns of Europe, instead of being the manufacturers and carriers for but a very small part of the world (that part of Europe which is washed by the Atlantic Ocean, and the countries which lie round the Baltic and Mediterranean seas), have now become the manufacturers for the numerous and thriving cultivators of America, and the carriers, and in some

---

6 Lettre du 2ième Janvier 1637 au gouverneur de Batavia, zitiert nach: Louis DERMIGNY, La Chine et l'Occident. Le commerce à Canton au XVIIIe siècle. 1719 - 1833, t. I, Paris 1964, pp. 379s.; extensive bibliographic references in Vol. III, p. 1502s.; W. H. UKERS, The Romance of Tea. An Outline History of Tea and Teadrinking through Sixteen Hundred Years, New York 1936.

7 Hans Chr. JOHANSEN, How to pay for Baltic Products? in: The Emergence of a World Economie 1500 - 1914. Papers of the IX. International Congress of Economic History, ed. by Wolfram FISCHER / R. Marvin MCINNIS / Jürgen SCHNEIDER, Stuttgart 1986, Vol. I, pp. 123ss.

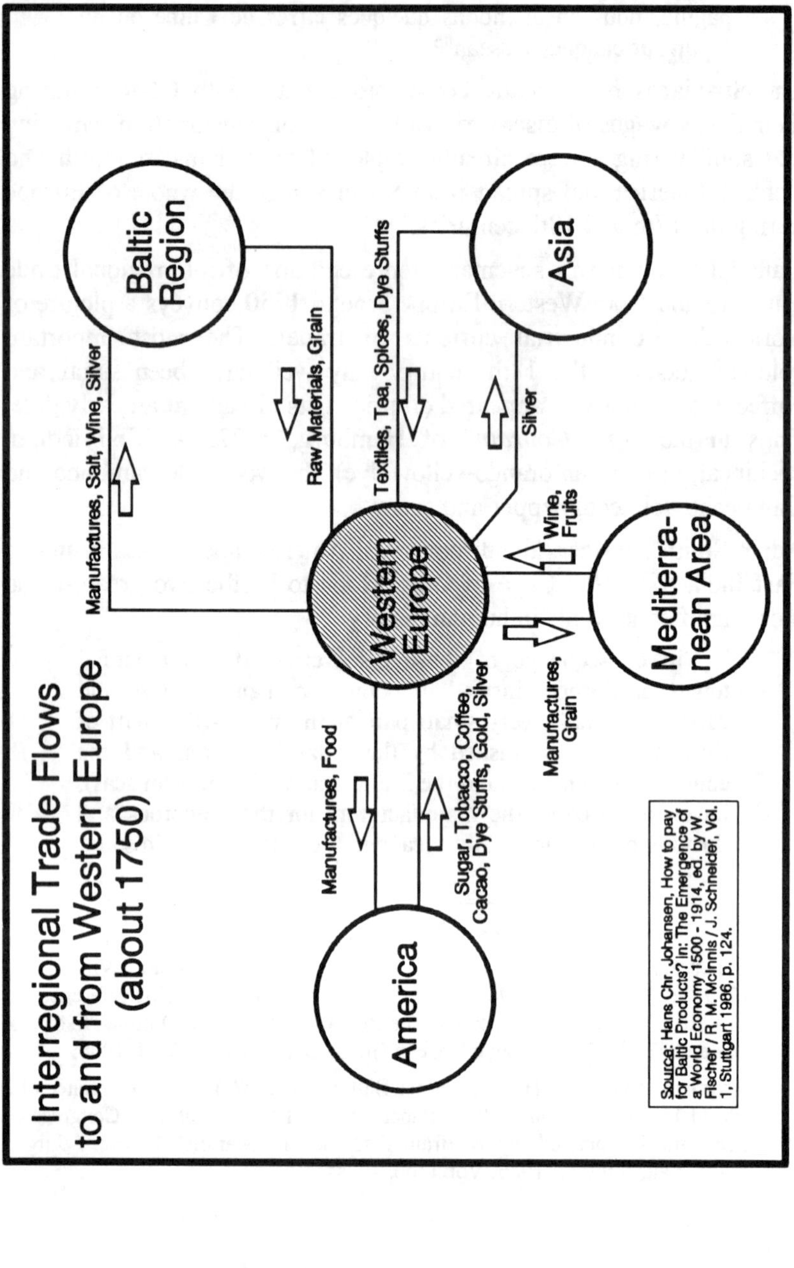

Source: Hans Chr. Johansen, How to pay for Baltic Products? In: The Emergence of a World Economy 1500 - 1914, ed. by W. Fischer / R. M. McInnis / J. Schneider, Vol. 1, Stuttgart 1986, p. 124.

respects the manufacturers too, for almost all the different nations of Asia, Africa and America. Two new worlds have been opened to their industry, each of them much greater and more extensive than the old one, and the market of one of them growing still greater and greater every day"[8].

The expansion of the trade and the associated international division of labour between 1550 and 1750 is also highlighted by K. N. Chaudhuri:

> "The final sequence of international division of labour between 1550 and 1750 may be drawn up in the following scheme. American treasure helped to finance Spain's balance of indebtedness. The cost advantage enjoyed by the Genoese bankers, an later by the Dutch ans English in entrepôt trade accumulated capital in the Hands of Europe's most efficient entrepreneurs. This capital helped to finance the imports of Indians cotton textiles, Asian spicesand Chinese silks and tea. Indian textiles and cowries were in turn exchanged for African slaves who produced new agricultural commodities in the New World for consumption in the Old. The circuit seems to have ended as Barbados sugar sweetened Cinese in porcelain cups copied from the products of Ching-te-chen kin in imperial China"[9].

We shall discuss here the production, marketing and consumption of coffee. We know but little of the penetration into Europe of this product. The economic and social historian must attempt to go beyond previous treatments of the topic. Perhaps the advance of such products may be integrated into the civilization process that is described by

---

8 Adam SMITH, The Wealth of Nations. In two volumes: volume two. Introduction by E. R. A. SELIGMAN, London - New York 1962, p. 122.

9 K. N. CHAUDHURI, World Silver Flows and Monetary Factors as a Force of International Economic Integration 1658 - 1758 (America, Europe and Asia), in: The Emergence of a World Economy, p. 76.

Norbert Elias[10]. Ethno-historical nutritional research can also contribute a wider understanding of the subject[11].

1. Coffee[12]: The Early Period (15th - 17th Century)

Kahwa, an Arabic word of uncertain origin, forms the basis of the word "coffee" as it appears in numerous languages. The contributions of C. Van Arendonk and K. N. Chaudhuri in the *Encyclopédie de l'Islam*[13] provide us with much information concerning coffee's early years. Coffee grew in the wild in great profusion in the highlands of Ethiopia, from where it was brought to the middle altitudes of the Yemeni highlands in S.W. Arabia, probably in the late 14th century. The custom of coffeedrinking probably originated in the Yemen with the religious order of the Sufis. There were already a few coffee-houses in Mecca at the very end of the 15th century. Islam and the Osman Empire formed the vehicle for the spread of coffee. Coffee was introduced to Cairo by the Yemeni Sufis in the first decade of the 16th century. As a result of lively contact with the holy cities and with Egypt coffee was brought as a trading commodity to Syria, Persia, Turkey and North Africa. Pilgrims also played an important part in its

---

10 Norbert ELIAS, Über den Prozeß der Zivilisation, 2 Vols., München 1969.

11 Hans J. TEUTEBERG / Günther WIEGELMANN, Unsere tägliche Kost. Geschichte und regionale Prägung, Münster ²1986.

12 The library of the Jacob Suchard Museum, CH-8034 Zuerich, Seefeldquai 17, includes sources and pertinent literature on the subject of coffee, together with manuscripts and early prints in most languages. With some 3000 titles from the 16th century to the present it may be considered the largest specialist library on this subject in the world. - Cf. also Wolf MÜLLER, Bibliographie des Kaffees, des Kakao, der Schokolade, des Tee und deren Surrogate bis zum Jahr 1900, Bad Bocklet 1960.

13 C. Van ARENDONK, Art. Kahwe, in: Encyclopédie de l'Islam, Tome IV, Leiden - Paris 1978, pp. 469 - 473; K. N. CHAUDHURI, Art. Kahwe, in: Ibid., pp. 473 - 475.

spreading popularity. In 1554 two merchants, Hakim of Aleppo and Djens of Damascus, opened Constantinople's first coffee-house.

Coffee was first mentioned in Europe by Leonhard Rauwolf, a Swabian merchant's son, botanist and Augsburg doctor. In the guise of an Armenian merchant and with a large supply of goods, Rauwolf travelled the Middle East during the years 1573 - 1576 and by way of Tripoli and Aleppo reached Baghdad. There he stayed for some time. It was his particular intent to explore the ways which according to secret reports would lead from there to the riches of India. Rauwolf had however to return to Aleppo earlier than intended, and in 1576 he made his way via Tripoli and Venice back to Augsburg. In 1582 he published "*Raisz in die Morgenländer*"[14]. In Chapter VII, headed "*Von großen Gewerben und Handlungen der Stadt Halepo, item der Türcken mancherlay Speysen, Getränken, Ceremonien und auch ihrer sonder weiß zum Essen und Trinken zusitzen*", he states:

> "Unter anderem haben sie ein gutes Getränk, das sie hoch halten. Chaube von ihnen genannt. Das ist beinahe wie Tinte so schwarz und bei Gebrechen, besonders des Magens, sehr dienlich. Diese pflegen sie frühmorgens zu trinken, auch an öffentlichen Orten, vor jedermann ohne Scheu, aus tiefen Schalen von Ton oder Porzellan, so warm, wie sie es ertragen können. Sie setzen oft an, machen aber kleine Schlücklein und lassen es gleich weitergehen, so wie sie nebeneinander im Kreise sitzen. Zu dem Wasser nehmen sie Früchte, die von Einwohnern Bunnu gennant werden, die außen in ihrer Größe und Farbe wie Lorbeer aussehen: sie sind mit zwei dünnen Häutchen umgeben und sollen den alten Bräuchen nach aus Indien eingeführt werden...".

The coffee tree was first described by Prospero Alpino (1553 - 1617). Alpino travelled to Cairo with the Venetian Consul as a doctor in 1580, a trip which furnished him with rich material for his exceptional powers of observation. In his celebrated work "De plantis Aegypti"[15]

---

14 Leonhard RAUWOLF, Raisz in die Morgenländer, Lauingen 1583.

15 Prospero ALPINO, De plantis Aegypti, Venetiis 1592.

over 50 hitherto unknown plants are described in detail, including the coffee tree.

Merchants from the Levant and European travellers to the East brought news of coffee-drinking and coffee-houses in those parts. The Roman Patrician Pietro della Valle, after ceremoniously donning pilgrim's robes in Naples, boarded a ship in Venice in 1614 to make a pilgrimage to the East. His journey took him to Turkey and Egypt, from there to Jerusalem, then on through Syria and Persia to India, and lasted over eleven years. Only in 1626 did he arrive with a sizeable oriental retinue in Rome, where Pope Urban VIII bestowed on him the honorary title of Chamberlain. In 1615 Valle made a stop in Constantinople. Of the enjoyment of coffee during the fasting-month of Ramadan he reports:

> "...ils <les Turcs> dorment presque toute la journée, et la nuit ils vont a la Mosquée, d'où après avoir achevé leurs prières, ils s'en retournent chez eux, pour veiller joieusement, en se traitant le mieux qu'ils peuvent, & s'exicitant les uns les autres à bien manger et à boire souvent; de sorte qu'ils passent tout le reste de la niut dans les divertissements et les jeux, particulierement en certains lieux publics, destinenz et entretenus express pour cet office, ou meme en d'autres tems s'assemblée beaucoup gens pour y passer quelques heures a se regaler, en buvant souvent tour-a-tour et a diverses reprises et gorgees, a cause qu'ils boivent tout chaud, et plus d'une tasse, d'un certain breuvage d'eau noire qui enivre, et qu'ils nomment Cahué, en quoi ils mélent le divertissement de leur conversations, comme nous ferion à peu près au jeu des dames et des échets. Et meme en se moiis de leur grand jeune, dans ce Cabarets de Cahué, qu'ils apellent. il y a des bateleurs et des boufons qui entretiennent la compagne de mille bagatelles: entr'autres. ils font voir, comme je vis aussi le soir précédent, derrière une toile ou une carte peinte, par la lumiére de quelques flambeaux, diverses representations d'ombres et de figures de fantomes, qui se movent, qui marchent et font mille postures, de meme qu'on en fait paroitre aussi parmi nous en quelques spectacles. Néanmoins

> ces figures, ou ces marionettes, en sont pas muétes comme les notres, mais ils les font parler, ainsi que les Charlatans étalent à Naples le long du Chateau, et en la Place Navonne"[16].

He also describes the effects of drinking coffee:

> "... elle contribue notablement à la santé, ardant la digestion, fortifant la estomach, et arrétant le cours des fluxions et des caterres: ce sont de bonnes proprietez, si elles sont éfectives. Il s'en debite ici une telle quantité, que l'on dit que l'impot sur le Cahué monte à und somme très - considerable au profit du Grand Seigneur. Quand je ferai sur le point de m'en retourner, j'en porterai avec moi, et ferai connoitre a l'Italie ce simple, qui lui est peut-etre inconnu jusqu'à present"[17].

The arrival of European traders in Mocha and at the Red Sea was important for the history of coffee. Up to that point South Yemen and certain regions of Ethiopia had been the exclusive suppliers of coffee beans to the entire Islamic world. The Yemeni rulers had taken strict measures to block every attempt by foreigners to export coffee seed or plants. The descriptions by European traders and the archives of the Dutch and English East India Companies not only provide general observations concerning the coffee markets in Mocha and Bayt-al-Fakih, the most important centres of the coffee trade, but also give detailed information on the exports of individual countries, on buying methods, production sites, and the marketing of coffee.

The European merchants trading in Mocha at first imagined that price structures with regard to coffee would be similar to those on West European trade exchanges. Yet this was not the case. The local producers often had only extremely small plots of land on which to grow coffee and could grant no discount for bulk trade. Smaller guantities could be traded without difficulty. In the event that the price

---

16 Pietro DELLA VALLE, Viaggi di Pietro della Valle, 4 Vols., Roma 1650 - 1663 (Voyages de Pietro della Valle, t. I., Rouen 1745, pp. 90ss.).

17 Ibid., p. 134.

on the coast was too low for the small-scale producers, they simply did not bother to come to the coffee market in Bayt-al-Fakih.

Coffee was transported from the inland regions to the coast on the backs of camels, and from there it reached the Osman Empire by one of two ways. The most important route was the one that ran via Jeddah and Suez to Cairo. From the international trading centre of Cairo coffee was conveyed not only further into the interior of the Osman Empire, but also to Europe, in particular to Marseille. Considerable quantities of coffee travelled up the Euphrates via Basra. Philippe Sylvestre Dufour reports on trade in 1686 in his "Traitez Nouveaux & Curieux du Café, du Thé et du Chocolate":

> Je vous écris puis que vous le voulez tout ce que j'ai apris du Café sur les lieux meme d'où l'ons nous l'aporte où j'ai fait quelque sejour. Il n'en vient que dans un seul petitcanton du monde, à cavoir dans l'Yemen, ou Arabie Heureuse. On l'aporte des Montagnes du Paris à Moka, à Louhaia et autres ports de mer qui sont le long de la mer Rouge, d'où on le charge sur de petits barques pour Gidda ou Zyeden, qui est un port de mer de l'Arabie Petrée dans l'etat du Cherif de la Meque, qui n'en est éloignée que de sept ou huit lieues. Les Arabie en transportant beaucoup sur leurs Chameaux à la Meque pour cette espace de soire qui s'y tient tous les ans à la Plaque des Mahometans: et c'est là que toutes ces grandes differentes Caravanes qui s'y trouvent alors, s'en chargent à leut retour chacune pour leur pais; mais la plus grande partie est transportée de Gidda à Suez, Port de mer à la Tete de la mer Rouge, éloigné du Caire d'environ vingt-deux lieues, tant sur deux Galeres, que sur sept ou huit grosses Barques, qui vienent là exprez d'Egypte tous les ans. Les Caravans le transportent ensuite de Suez au Caire, d'où il se repand par toute le Turquie et ailleurs jusqu'en à Marseille.
> Presentant les Anglois et les Hollandois, qui tous les ans viennent des Indes Orientales à Mokka dans la mer Rouge, à deux lieures du détroit de Babel-Mandel, en chargent beaucoup sur leurs Vaisseaux depuis que cette boisson s'est introduite en Europe.

> L'on n'en use que tres-peu dans les Indes et dans la Perse, il ne passe presque pas le Ports de mer, et n'entre que peu point dans les terres; mais il se repans, comme je viens de dire, par tout la Turquie"[18].

In 1609/10 the English East Asia Company was already dispatching ships to Mocha to explore the commercial possibilities. Since the mid-17th century coffee was regularly exported around the Cape of Good Hope to Europe. Exports by the English East India Company were significant between 1664 and 1700, but only in 1716 did the Company establish a permanent depot. Chaudhuri gives two reasons for this late establishment of a trading post: (1) opposition by the merchants of Surat and (2) non-Muslim ships were not allowed to come too near Jeddah and the holy city of Mecca. The export of coffee was responsible for a growing supply of precious metals, above all silver. This allowed Arab traders to import luxury goods from India which in turn had to be paid for with the precious metal. The export of coffee brought about considerable increases in rural and urban incomes in the production regions.

2. The Expansion of Production

As the habitual enjoyment of coffee spread swiftly across Europe and the rest of the world in the 17th and 18th centuries, and as demand increased, the monopoly hitherto held by the cof fee-producing regions around the Red Sea came to an end. Arabia, with its relatively low production levels, could no longer satisfy the rapidly growing demand. Cultivation spread increasingly, finally extending to all suitable regions across the whole world. In 1658 the Dutch began to cultivate coffee in Ceylon and in 1711 the first coffee from Java was auctioned in Amsterdam. In the year 1713 the coffee-tree came to Haiti and

---

18 Philippe Sylvestre DUFOUR, Traitez Nouveaux & Curieux du Café, du Thé et du Chocolate, Lyon 1685, pp. 207 - 209.

Santo Domingo, in 1715/17 to Réunion, in 1718 to Surinam, in 1723 to Parà on the Amazon and to Martinigue in the Caribbean. In 1760 the Portuguese brought the coffee-tree from Goa in India to Rio de Janeiro.

In 1789, with 400,000 slaves and 30,000 white planters, Haiti produced 60 million pounds of coffee. Fifty years earlier total European consumption lay at a mere 4 million pounds. In 1787 France imported some 38,000 tons of coffee; of this however 36,000 tons were re-exported, in particular from Bordeaux, Nantes and Le Havre to the Netherlands and above all to Hamburg. Paul Butel (1974) points out the growing significance of the Hanseatic ports and of Prussia for the re-export of colonial goods from Bordeaux, in particular coffee and sugar, from ca. 1740. Le Havre and Rouen also took part in the growing re-export of colonial goods (Pierre Dardel, 1963). From 1730 Marseille re-exported coffee from Martinique to the Eastern Mediterranean. From 1815 on Brazil was able to increase steadily its share of the world market: in 1841 Brazil was producing 38.8% of the world's coffee, and in 1848 50.0%.

Whilst studying archives in Nantes I came across the letter-book of a trading company still unknown at that time. The letter-book, containing duplicates of all dispatched correspondence, comprises 565 letters in Dutch, French and above all German. The correspondence concerns 217 merchants in 61 Middle European towns. From these letters it can be seen how coffee from the French Antilles was traded on to the whole of central Europe. This firm in Nantes delivered among other things coffee to Frankfurt, Kitzingen, Marktbreit, Fuerth, Nuremberg, Regensburg, Kaufbeuren and Munich. The trading company Johann Valentin Schmidt in Kitzingen, for example, received in 1763 seven barrels of St. Domingo coffee, two barrels of finest Martinigue coffee, 59 bales of Bourbon coffee together with several barrels of indigo[19].

---

19 Cf. Peter HÖFER, Deutsch-französische Handelsbeziehungen im 18. Jahrhundert. Die Firma Breton frères in Nantes (1763 - 1766), Stuttgart 1982.

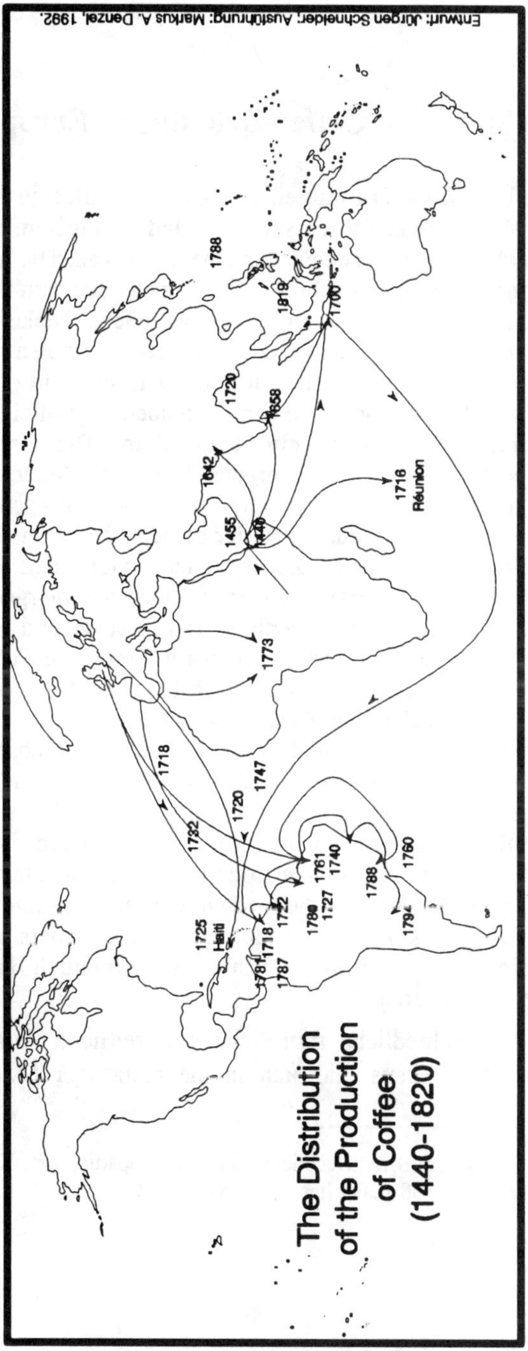
The Distribution of the Production of Coffee (1440-1820)
Entwurf: Jürgen Schneider; Ausführung: Markus A. Denzel, 1992.
1440
1455
1642
1658
1720
1700
1819
1788
1716
Réunion
1773
1718
1747
1720
1732
1725
Haiti
1718
1781
1787
1722
1727
1761
1740
1788
1760
1794

3. The Spread of Coffee-Drinking in Europe

> "Jede Nation hat fast ihre eigene Art, den Kaffee zu trinken. Die Türken trinken ihren stärkeren und geistigeren, aus der Pulpe der Frucht, jederzeit nur eine Tasse voll. Die anderen Nationen trinken ihn gebrannt in Bohnen. Bey dem Trinken pflegen die Morgenländer etwas gestoßene Nelken, oder Zimmet, Cardomomen. oder etliche Tropfen graue Ambraessenz, oder ein wenig Zucker mit Ambra angefeuchtet, oder einen halben Löffel voll Pomeranzenblüthwasser hinein zu thun. Die Engländer trinken ihn fast nur des Morgens, bey einer Butterschnitte, und überhaupt sparsam. Die Holländer morgens und nachmittags, wenig und stark, der gemeine Mann meist ohne Zucker, oder er beißt Zucker dazu, oder, statt dessen, Lakritzensaft. Die Franzosen essen meist des morgens eine große Tasse voll Kaffee, denn sie thun Zucker und Semmel hinein, und machen sich einen Kaffeebrey. Die Schweden trinken ihn vorzüglich nach der Mittagsmahlzeit, an drey Tassen, mit Milch und Zucker. Bey den deutschen sind alle diese Gewohnheiten, und noch mehrere, vereinbaret; sie trinken morgens und abends, alt und jung, von vornehmsten Manne bis zum ärmsten; sie essen und trinken ihn, wie man es verlangt; sie sieden ihn auf, und filtrieren ihn; der gemeine Mann labet sich sogar am Kaffespühlicht, mit Syrupp versußt, um nur die mode mit zu machen, und Kaffee zu lutschen; kurz, alle Unarten der Ausländersind hier einheimisch, und werden sich auch vermutlich hier am spätesten verlieren"[20].

"Über die unterschiedliche räumliche wie zeitliche Ausbreitung der Sitte des Kaffeetrinkens, die sich in die bisheriger Mahlzeitsysteme

---

20 Johann Georg KRÜNITZ, Oeconomische Encyclopädie, Art. Kaffee, Vol. 32, Brünn 1789, pp. 100 - 264, here: pp. 183s.

einfügen mußte, d.h. über die vorwärtstreibenden und behindernden Faktoren wissen wir wenig"[21]. The establishment of coffee-houses may however be seen as a certain indication of the spread of coffee-drinking. First reports come from the countries which had had the longest and most intensive commercial connections with the Levant: Italy, France, England and Holland.

The oldest coffee-house in Europe, the Café Florian, was opened in 1647 beneath the arcades on St. Mark's Sguare in Venice. The most famous cafes in Rome was founded by a Greek entrepreneur in the Via Condotti in 1760: the "Café del Greco", to which was later added the epithet "antico". The "Greco" became such a notable meetingpoint for German artists and writers that it became known as the "Café Tedesco". Here could be found, among others, Johann Wolfgang von Goethe, Heinrich Tischbein, Karl Moritz, Friedrich Rückert, Richard Wagner, Schopenhauer, Lenbach and Böcklin.

Jacob, a Syrian Jew, opened the first coffee-house in England in Oxford in 1650. Only two years later the Greek Pasqa Rosee, who had formerly been a servant to Daniel Edwards, a London merchant trading in the Levant, opened a cafe' in London. The Strasbourg merchant Zetzner, who was staying in London in 1702, found over a thousand coffee-taverns there.

In 1696 Edward Lloyd, owner of "Lloyd's Coffee House" in Lombard Street, founded for his guests the mercantile weekly "Lloyd's News", which however due to its lack of political discretion was soon suppressed and only reappeared from 1726 as "Lloyd's List". "Lloyd's List" mainly served maritime interests, above all the insurance business, whose representatives conducted their negotiations in "Lloyd's Coffee House". This was the origin of the company which opened up as "New Lloyd's" on the east side of the stock exchange in 1771. "Lloyd's Coffee House" was thus the seed for the insurance company that is still today the largest in the world.

---

21 Hans J. TEUTEBERG, Kaffeetrinken sozialgeschichtlich betrachtet, in: *Scripta mercaturae* 14/1 (1980), pp. 27 - 54, here: p. 28.

Around 1650 the wealthy Marseille merchant Jean de la Rogue[22], on his return from a journey as envoy to Constantinople, imported a small amount of coffee to his home town. In 1671 merchants trading in the Levant opened the first coffee-house in Marseille.

In 1669 Louis XIV received the Turkish ambassador Soliman Aga as representative of Sultan Mohammend IV in Versailles. During the political discussions Soliman Aga performed his country's traditional coffee ritual. In this way the French court adopted the custom of coffee-drinking. While gluttony and inebriation at table were nothing out of the ordinary even in respectable circles in the late Middle Ages and early modern times, the 17th century, with France in the lead, brought the art of eating to new levels which are by and large still valid today. The "kitchen revolution" took place initially only in very small courtly circles, and from there gradually spread throughout the population. The exclusive eating habits of a small upper class gave rise to a striving to imitate such habits in other social strata. The devaluation of eating-etiquette that automatically ensued sparked off in turn further developments in such customs at the top levels of society. Norbert Elias believes that through French cuisine and the associated refinement of eating-habits a new type of social mechanism was set into motion which had not previously existed in such a form. To the subject of the refinement of the culinary arts in France also belongs the adoption of coffee-drinking via the French court and the associated ceremonies, which became a role model for the rest of Europe. In Germany the imitated French customs, first practised in the courtly circles of particularist rulers, became in turn a model for the upper and middle classes.

The letters of the Duchess Elisabeth Charlotte of Orléans (1652 - 1722), daughter of the Elector Karl Ludwig of the Palatinate, offer

---

22 Jean DE LA ROQUE, Voyage de l'Arabie Heureuse par l'ocean oriental et le Détroit de la Mer Rouge. Et un traité historique de l'origine et du progrès du café, tant dans l'Asie que dans l'Europe; de son introduction en France et de l'etablissement de son usage à Paris, Paris 1715.

very rich material relating to the spread of coffee-drinking in the French courtly society of the Ancien Régime. Ranke refers to the Prince's daughter as a woman of "pure Germanness". Liselotte had no taste for the court life of Versailles. In her correspondence with her aunt, the Electress Sophie of Hannover, and with her halfsister Luise of the Palatinate she allows us some deep insights into the courtly life of her time. According to her, everything is better in Germany, not only the people but also, especially in the Palatinate, the air, clothing and above all good German cooking. Even in her ripe old age she preferred to eat broccoli with fried sausage or cabbage salad with ham.

> "Viele Leutte hir drincken thé und caffé und chocolat, aber ich nehme nichts von dießen zeug, bilde mir ein, es saye nicht gesund".

On the advice of her doctor she took coffee for medicinal purposes, but she found no pleasure in its taste:

> "Ich trincke alle tag einen becher mit caffé, daß jagt mir die windt weg und verhindert mich, dicker zu werden, drum continuire ich es, aber ich muss gestehen, dass mir der Geschmack gar nicht gefällt, dass es wie stinkender Atem schmeckt".

In 1672 an Armenian by the name of Pascal had opened a coffee-house in Paris:

> "Da es aber nicht recht damit fort wollte, ging er nach London. Ihm folgten verschiedene andere Armenianer und Persianer, doch aber, weil es ihnen an der gehörigen Geschicklichkeit mangelte und sie keinen guten Plätze hatten, auch Personen vom Stande und einer guten Lebensart an solche schlechte Oerter nicht gehen wollten, mit gleich schlechtem Gefolge. Endlich schmückten einige Franzosen besonders große Zimmer dazu sehr gut aus, und versahen sie mit Tapeten, großen Spiegeln, Gemälden und prächtigen Kronleuchtern, und verkauften daselbst nicht nur Kaffee, sondern auch Thee, Chocolate und andere Erfrischungen. Dieses veranlaßte, daß auch bald Leute von guter Lebensart

> und Gelehrte sich in diesen Häusern versammelten, und daß deren Anzahl in kurzer Zeit auf 300 anwuchs"[23].

The Florentine Procopo Cultelli, who invented ice cream in Italy in 1660, is considered the founder of the French type of coffee-house. In 1689 he established, opposite the old Comédie Francaise, the "Café Procope", which assumed an eminent position among the literary cafés of the 18th century, and was patronised by, among others, Voltaire and Rousseau.

In no other place in the world did the coffee-house make such a mark on its time nor reach such a degree of sophistication, nor exert such a movingly human influence as in Vienna. It became the ultimate symbol both for the genius loci of the city and for the mentality of her inhabitants. It has long been claimed that coffee was introduced to Vienna by Georg Franz Koltschitzky. (It was he who in 1683 established the link between the besieged city of Vienna and Duke Karl V. of Lorraine who was camped beyond the tents of the Osman army). However, more recent research shows that he had no involvement in the brewing of coffee. The first Imperial licence to set up a coffee-house was granted on the 17th January 1685 to the Armenian Johannes Diodato, son of a Levantine merchant. He had been granted freedom by the court and had already been trading small quantities of coffee. Diodato soon found "bourgeois" competition in Isaac de Lucca, born in Eriwan, who in 1697 is mentioned as a coffee brewer. By this time however the Armenians Andreas Pain and Philipp Kamberg, together with Leopold Riess and the baptised Turk Stephan Devich had also been granted concessions[24].

Tacitus, in his treatise of 98 A.D. "De origine, situ, moribus ac populis Germanorum" - commonly known as "Germania" - had already claimed of the German peoples: "Least of all can they put up with being thirsty" (*Germania 4*). The permanent battle of the Germans against thirst had already in the 16th and 17th century

---

23 KRÜNITZ, op.cit., pp 119s.

24 Karl TEPLY, Die Einführung des Kaffees in Wien, Wien 1980.

assumed the worst of forms. Alcoholism, and degenerate and uninhibited drinking orgies had permeated all layers of society. Contemporary reports, including those of foreigners touring Germany, paint a hair-raising picture.

Coffee found powerful rivals in Germany in the form of wine, beer and brandy. The first coffee-house in Germany was established in 1677 in Hamburg by an English merchant. Other towns that followed included Frankfurt am Main, Dresden and Regensburg. A certain Stoer opened the first coffee-house in Nuremberg in 1684 behind the town hall, while David Ulrich Aulber opened a similar establishment in Stuttgart in 1712 under the name of "König von England". The first coffee-house in Berlin was opened by a negro named Oliver. He had fled to Germany with the stream of French Huguenots after the repeal of the Edict of Nantes. In 1711 Oliver obtained a licence to open the "Café Royal".

The Dutch doctor and philosopher Cornelius Bontekoe, personal physician to the Grand Elector Friedrich Wilhelm, introduced the drinking of coffee and tea as early as 1675 to the Brandenburg court, where they became household drinks. Bontekoe's so-called 'Cartesian Cure' consisted mainly in the prescribing of unbelievable guantities of coffee and tea, which was purported to stimulate blood circulation and thus heal all sorts of disease. His miracle cures at least helped to moderate the inordinate consumption of alcohol.

The first coffee-tavern in Wuerzburg was opened by a Turkish prisoner of war, who after the appropriate preparation was christened Johann Ernst Nicolauss Strauss in the church of the Julius Hospital. Work as a craftsman or in administration, or a career in the Church were forbidden him, but he received 50 Taler from the Hospital, in order to "damit seine gelernte Kunst Cavé, Schokolade und andere Zuckerbäckereien anzufangen". The Turkish convert must have turned to Bishop Johann Gottfried von Guttenberg, for on the 23rd of March 1697 "Supplicanten gnädigst verwilligt, daß er mittels Aushengung einer Tafel oder Schildes eine Profession mit Caffeesieden und anderen männiglich dahier treiben und ecerviren möge".

> "Der Fürstbischof wollte dem getauften Türken ein Unterkommen verschaffen, ohne zu bedenken, daß das Getränke, mit welchem dieser die Würzburger bekannt machte, dereinst in acht Kaffee-Schenken öffentlich und in allen Wohnungen der Armen und Reichen privatiim in großen Quantitäten werde verzehrt werden, während Tausende von Gulden dafür ausser Landes gehen"

as Denzinger notes in 1847 [25].

The first coffee-house customers came principally from the landed nobility and from merchant circles, who were in a position to afford such a luxury drink. In the first decades of the 18th century the enjoyment of coffee spread to all larger towns, particularly in North Germany. From 1740 on larger and larger amounts of coffee arrived in the Atlantic ports of Bordeaux and Nantes from the French Antilles. The bulk of these imports were re-exported to the Netherlands and to Hamburg.

> "... In Schweden (...) ist der Kaffee nicht vor 1700 im Gebrauche gewesen, welches noch viele dasige alte Leute bezeugen können; diese sagen aus, die schwedische Nation sey damit von einigen aus Frankreich zurück gekommenen Reisenden angestecket worden. Dieses ist eine Klage, die auch wohl andere nordische Länder und Deutschland führen möchten. In Polen und Preußen ist der Kaffee gleichfalls erst seit dem Anfange des 18ten Jahrhunderts in Aufnahme gekommen. Die alten Leute in Sachsen wissen noch, das er erst um das J. 1720 in diesen Ländern in rechten Gebrauch gekommen sey. Man ging damit sehr sparsam um; man trank ihn nur bey Feyerlichkeiten. Man hatte damals nur

---

25 J. DENZINGER, Erste Kaffee-Schenke in Würzburg, in: *Archiv des historischen Vereins für Unterfranken und Aschaffenburg* 9/2 (1847), pp. 161 - 162.

> levantinischen, wovon das Pfund mit 1 Rthlr. 16 Gr. bezahlt wurde"[26].

In the second half of the 18th century coffee also reached the villages.

> "Doch blieben große räumliche, wie soziale Unterschiede weiterhin bestehen. Entscheidend war, ob der Kaffee bereits vorhandene Getränke erstetzen konnte oder nicht. Recht einfach war die Ablösung der wenig geschmacksanreizenden Biersuppen und des teuren Branntweins.
> Sehr viel schwieriger war der Ersatz des Hafer-, Buchweizen- oder Roggenbreis durch Kaffee mit Brot und Aufstrich, weil dies einen starken Eingriff in die bäuerliche Wirtschaft bedeutete (z. B. in die Häufigkeit des Brotbackens), was nicht schnell und reibungslos vor sich gehen konnte. Insgesammt gelang der Einbruch in das herkömmliche Mahlzeitensystem zunächst sehr viel eher in Nord- und Mittel- als in Süddeutschland. Die süddeutsche Küche mit ihren vielen Mehlspeisen behinderte nicht nur die Eingliederung des Kaffees, sondern auch der Kartoffel"[27].

In 1789 Johann Georg Kruenitz contrasts in his Economic Encyclopedia the advantages and disadvantages of drinking coffee:

> "Der Kaffee macht munter und vertreibt den Schlaf; in dieser Absicht würde er also in manchen Fällen als ein nützliches Mittel, besonders bey fetten, trägen, schläfrigen und phlegmatischen Personen, zu gebrauchen seyn. Wenn aber Gelehrte, um die Nacht durch studieren, oder auch Andere, um sich des Schlafes zu erwehren, des Abends spät Kaffee trinken, so ist ein solches gar nicht zu billigen"[28].

But coffee drinking has its disadvantages too:

---

26 KRÜNITZ, op.cit, pp. 125s.

27 TEUTEBERG, op.cit., p. 4.

28 KRÜNITZ, op.cit., p. 186.

> "Es ist also auch so sehr unwahrscheinlich nicht, daß ein übermäßiger Gebrauch des Kaffees die männliche Kraft benehme ..."[29].
> "Westindische Kaffeeinseln hat Deutschland auch nicht; also ist alles Geld, was der Kaffee kostet, für Deutschland völlig verloren".[30]

A doctor claimed that he could tell from the first glance at the people of a village whether or not coffee drinking had been habitual there for a few years:

> "Die Leute hätten durchgängig das frische robuste Aussehen nicht mehr, sondern eine bleiche Farbe, und etwas schwächliches in der Mine. Die Bauernweiber bekämen Nervenkrankheiten, wie Damen aus der Stadt, würden empfindsam hysterisch etc ..."[31].

At the assembly of the Royal and Electoral Agricultural Society at Celle in 1777, five gueries concerning coffee were raised; these were answered by the Archdeacon Ress of Wolfenbuettel. To the question,

> "was der jetzige häufige Gebrauch des Kaffees für merklich und sichtbare Veränderungen im ökonomischen Zustande der Menschen bisher gewirkt habe",

he replied:

> "Manchen neuen Aufwand veranlaßt, nämlich:
> 1. Den Ankauf des Porzellans. Man muß, die Methode befiehlt es, nicht allein zum eigenen täglichen Gebrauch, sondern auch für Fremde besondere Tassen haben.
> 2. Die auch ganz neue Verwahrung des Hausrathes durch das übrige Kaffeegeschirr. Man hat jetzt Brenner, Mühlen, Töpfe, Kannen und mehrere Kleinigkeiten nöthig, die unsere Vorfahren nicht brauchten.
> 3. Die Anlegung der Besuchszimmer, die unstreitig in den meisten Häusern ihren Ursprung dem Kaffee zu danken

29 Ibid.

30 Ibid., p.193.

31 Ibid., p. 194.

> haben, da alle alten Leute wissen, daß sie zu Anfange dieses Jahrhunderts noch in den wenigsten Häusern vorhanden waren, weil man sie durchaus nicht eher brauchte, als bis es anfing zu guten Lebensart zu gehören, daß wenigsten die Hausfrau Kaffeebesuch annahm.
> 4. Die Ausgabe für den Kaffee und dessen Zubehör selbst. Die Nahrung des Bierbrauens fiel an den meisten Orten so, wie der Gebrauch des Kaffees gestiegen ist."

Coffee led to the custom of the afternoon visit - the so-called coffee-visit. In earlier times people would meet in the summer in gardens or in the winter in public houses,

> "und versparte die kostbaren Versammlungen auf Hochzeiten, Kindtaufen, Begräbnissen und andere Familienfeste. Und dies waren fast, außer der kirchlichen Zusammenkunft, die einzigen Gelegenheiten, wobey sich Frauenzimmer, das nicht nahe verwandt oder vernachbart war, einander sah".

The housewife would remain with the children and servants, and discuss family matters with her cousin or household topics with a neighbour or schoolfriend; on Sunday she would spend time in her garden or go for a walk. The indisputable increase in the rapidity and extensiveness of change in clothing trends and other fashions is the very visible result of such freguent gatherings. To mitigate the tedium of coffee-visits people turned to playing games,

> "nicht das scherzhafte, unschädliche unserer Vorfahren, sondern das neuere, vornehmere, das Spiel um Geld".

Man has shown such a keen instinct in the search for a new stimulant drinks that no suitable plant, no matter how modest, has pass ed unnoticed. The hot drinks coffee, tea and cocoa brought about a revolution in thousands-of-years-old drinking habits and mealtime routines. Hans Juergen Teuteberg believes the main reason to be the following:

> "Der Kaffee (auch in seinen Suggeratformen!) befriedigt die wichtigen psychosozialen Bedürfnisse des Menschen: Er regt

nicht nur alle Sinnesorgane an, sondern trägt zugleich zum Vergnügen, zur Entspannung und vor allem zur mitmenschlichen Kommunikation bei. Der gesellschaftsverbindende Charakter des Kaffeehauses, das jahrhundertealte ständische Barrieren durchbrechend, Literatur, Kunst, Musik, Wirtschaft und Politik mannigfach inspirierte, kann für den Fortgang der Zivilisation und damit auch für den sozio-kulturellen Wandel nicht hoch genug verschlagen werden. Das Kaffeetrinken darf daher ohne Übertreibung als eine spezifische Ausdrucksform der entstehenden bürgerlich-industriellen Gesellschaft begriffen werden, da es neue Formen der sozialen Gesellung beförderte. Durch den Abbau der sozialen Schranken in den Kaffeehäusern wurden der bürgerlichen Freiheit wie Freizeit neue Wege eröffnet. Nicht zufällig sind viele Zeitungen sowie politische Clubs und damit Ideen zu den bürgerlichen Revolutionen in Kaffeehäusern entstanden. Der ernährungsphysiologische Wert der Kaffeebohne war sicherlich stets gering, desto wichtiger wurde aber der Symbolgehalt der entstehenden Kaffeepause. Sie ist als wichtiges Gegenstück der Erholung und Entspannung zu der sich rationalisierenden Arbeitszeit nicht immer fortzudenken"[32].

---

32 TEUTEBERG, op.cit., p. 52.

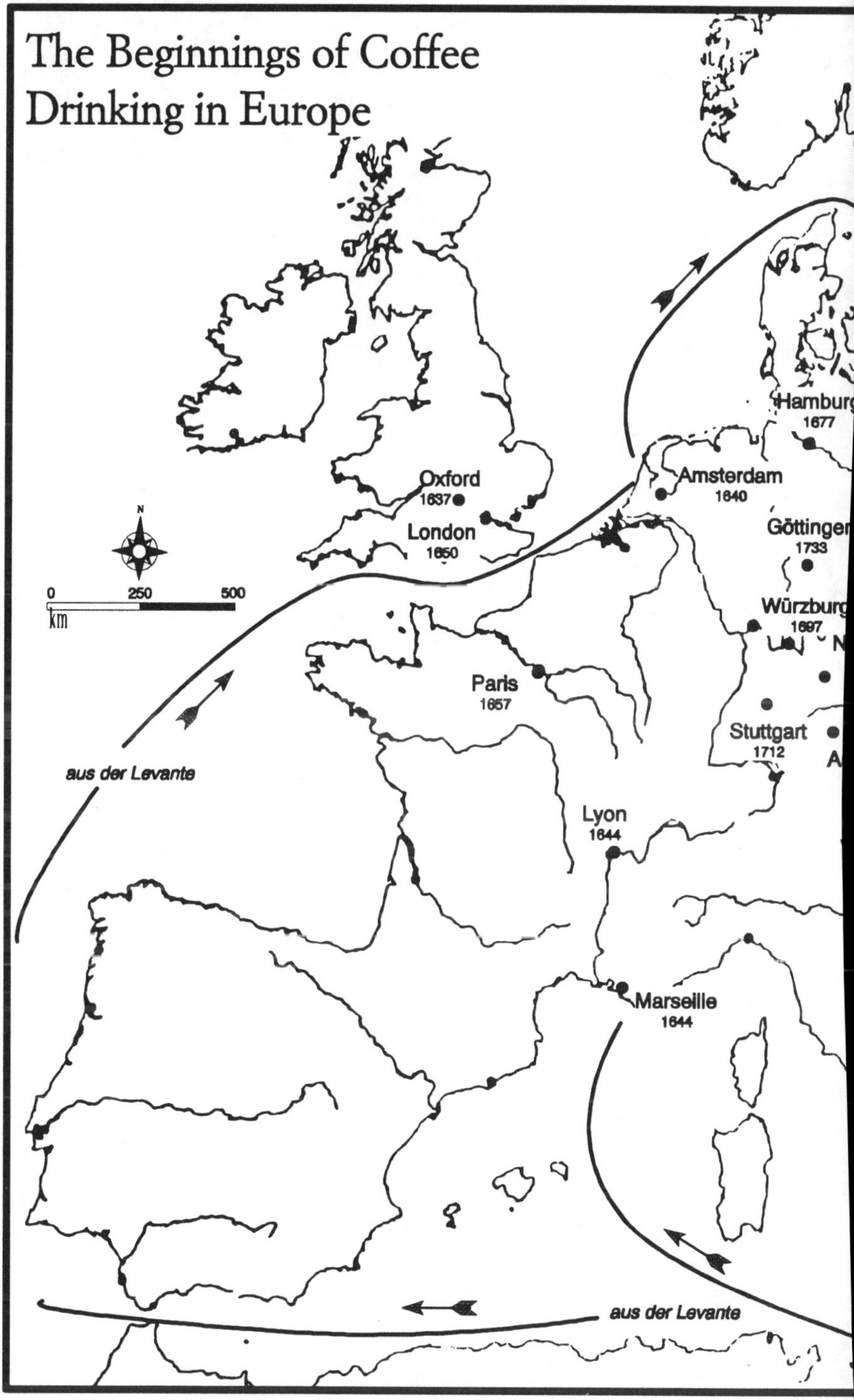

The Beginnings of Coffee Drinking in Europe
Oxford
1637
London
1650
Amsterdam
1640
1677
1733
1697
Paris
1657
Stuttgart
1712
Lyon
1644
Marseille
1644
aus der Levante
aus der Levante
0
250
500
km
N

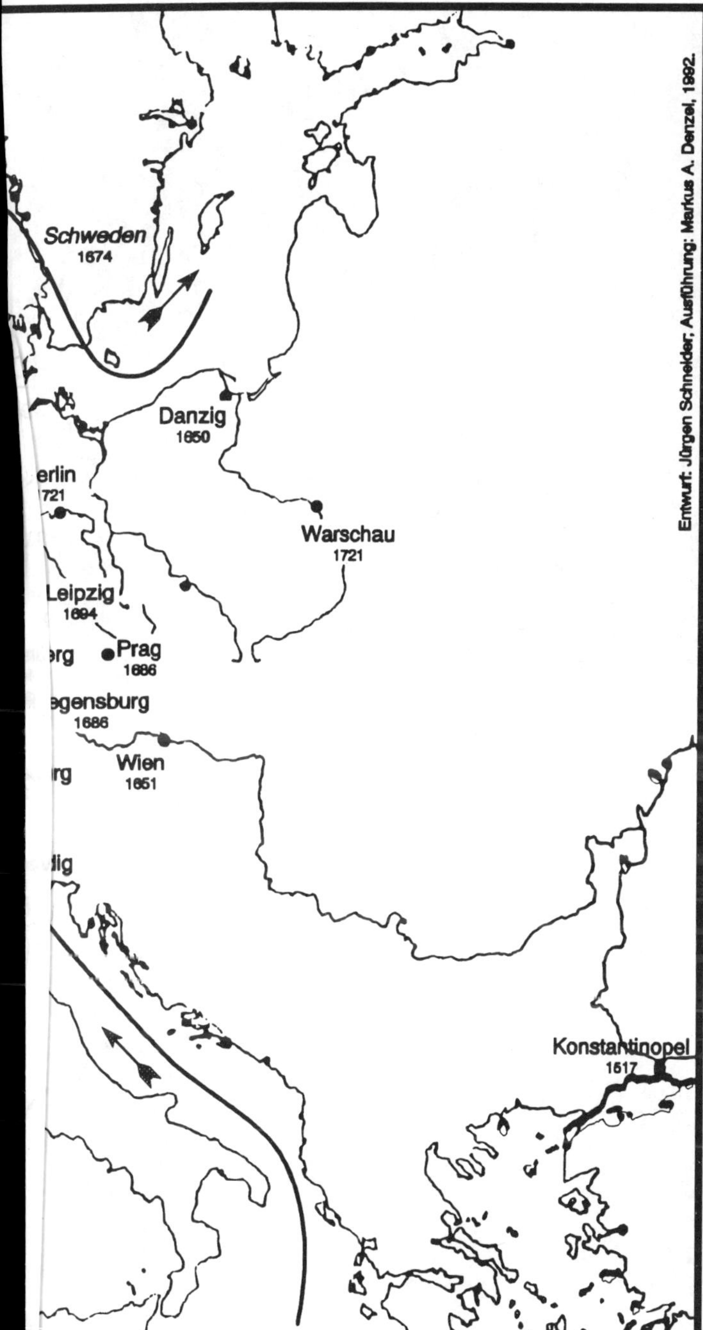
Schweden
1674
Danzig
1650
erlin
1721
Warschau
1721
Leipzig
1694
Prag
1686
egensburg
1686
Wien
1651
Konstantinopel
1617
aus der Levante
Entwurf: Jürgen Schneider; Ausführung: Markus A. Denzel, 1992.

The Transfer of European Know-how and its Effects on Economic Development in Colonial Hispanic America

By RUTH M. VORNEFELD

I. Introduction

European discovery, conquest and settlement not only influenced autochthon societies and economies in America, but had also shaped an entirely new economic and social order in their colonies. Nearly every part of material life, such as economy, science, techniques, and even the so called social sphere[1], i.e. language, religion and law, had been deeply changed by the invaders. The Spaniards brought with them new products, followed by new modes of production. The most impressive example may be the changes in agriculture by the introduction of European animals: cows, pigs, horses, sheep and chicken and European plants: wheat, rye, vegetables and fruits which provoked a revolution in ecological equilibrium and nutrition habits[2].

---

1 Cf. Gustav SIEBENMANN, Zur Problematik des Kulturtransfers zwischen Europa und Lateinamerika, in: Wirtschaftskräfte und Wirtschaftswege, Festschrift für Hermann Kellenbenz, hrsg. v. Jürgen SCHNEIDER et al., Bd. 5, Stuttgart 1981, p. 599.

2 A survey offers Pieter EMMER, European Expansion and non-western agriculture before 1800, in: The European Discovery of the World and its Economic

Spanish political and economic aims occasioned a shift of economic activities towards mining and far distance trade, neglecting traditional subsistence economies. Spanish laws and not at least language and religion had considerable influence on the economic framework. The coerced labour systems, encomienda, repartimiento and mita, finally the catastrophic decline of the population affected traditional Indian subsistence economy, too, and even the sheer lifes of those who did not come into direct contact with the invaders.

We could subsume such global consequences of the discovery of America as initiated by a transfer of European know-how and knowledge, but it cannot be my aim to deal with so vast a subject. Neither the main question should be if exports of European know-how (or their refusal) let to a peripherical status of the colonies, a "modern world system" (Wallerstein) or the disequilibrium of the 19th century world economy, preceding actual problems of Latin America as underdevelopment and debt crisis[3].

As space is limited here, this paper will focus on the period of the so called Bourbon reforms, the second half of the 18th and the first two decades of the 19th centuries. The subject will be mainly the transfer of know-how in the fields of technology, labour organisation, monetary and administrative improvements from Europe to Hispanic America.

Why this temporal restriction? There are three reasons in favour of such a decision:

1. In Europe, there were many new inventions, older ones were improved or applied in industry; the leading European states (above

Effects on Pre-industrial Society, 1500 - 1800, ed. by Hans POHL, Stuttgart 1990, p. 207 - 222.

3 Cf. Ruth VORNEFELD, The "Export" of European Knowledge and European Products and its Significance for the Economic Development and the Structure of Mining and Business in Overseas Territories, in: POHL (Ed), European Discovery, p. 223 - 236.

all the United Kingdom) started the so called "Industrial Revolution".

2. Spain aimed at reinforcing her relations to the colonies, their intensified economic exploitation and her own economic modernization by the means of new economic and technical science and invention. Though conservative in the field of religion and politics, Spain eagerly received new developments in foreign "useful sciences".
3. A sort of Spanish American identity arose among the Creole population of colonial Hispanic America which augmented tensions between Americans and the Spanish mother-country. At the same time Indian revolt reached a new peak (Tupac Amaru revolt in Peru e.g.). There may be economic reasons for this new pattern of conflict.

The effects of the European transfer of know-how will be studied with reference to the "old" economic system of colonial Hispanic America. Main questions will be the origin of innovation (only a small part was of Spanish origin), the medium of transfer, the velocity of their spread and the general diffusion.

Following Kuznets, we can discern five different types of augmenting scientific and technological knowledge:

1. a scientific discovery, an addition to knowledge;
2. an invention, the application of knowledge to a useful end;
3. an innovation, the first industrial use of an invention;
4. an improvement, a minor application;
5. the spread of an innovation (accompanied by improvements)[4].

The transfer of knowledge does not always refer to the spread of an innovation. The transfer of ideas or scientific discoveries was made possible quite early by the art of printing. Printing itself was an innovation which was brought very early to Hispanic America. As early as

---

4 Simon KUZNETS, Economic Growth of Nations. Total Output and Production Structure, London 1971, p. 328 - 333.

1539 the first printing press was installed in Mexico[5]. But the pure knowledge of discoveries or inventions did not mean that they were applied as innovations in the New World, even not if they had been successful in Europe (see II). The innovation is of central economic interest because it can increase economic productivity. As conditions for successful introduction of an innovation Musson names three factors: [a.] capital investment, [b.] entrepreneurial talents, [c.] the market[6].

We also may enquire who encouraged the transfer of knowledge and technology, where resistance can be found and what role especially the Bourbon state played. So it may be of special interest to look at industries under direct management of the crown (estancos), private industries which were subjected to royal control (e.g. the mining industry) and private ones the state was little concerned with.

The following procedure seems appropriate:
After a few considerations on general problems in dealing with the transfer of know-how and a glance at primary sources and recent research we will discuss the importance of this transfer for contemporal Spanish economic thought. The main part will treat a few examples of sucessful and unsucessful transfers of European technology and knowledge to Hispanic America in private and public economic activities. Finally, we will try to evaluate the importance of imported improvements for the economic development in late colonial Hispanic America.

---

5 Hermann KELLENBENZ, Technik und Wirtschaft, in: CIPOLLA / BORCHARDT (Ed.), Europäische Wirtschaftsgeschichte II, Stuttgart 1983, p. 115.

6 A. MUSSON, Editor's Introduction, in: Idem (Ed.), Science, Technology and Economic Growth in the Eighteenth Century, London 1972, p. 15.

II. Methodological problems, references and recent research

The transfer or, more generally, the spread of knowledge can be effected by a rather large variety of channels, e.g. by skilled personnel, import of goods, licences and patents, capital transfer, books or exhibitions. With the exception of exhibitions all other media were already employed in early modern times. The channels may be combined and often were as shows e.g. the introduction of European dyestuffs in Mexico during the 16th century which nevertheless proved unsucessful in the long run[7].

Besides the import of new products, the transfer of knowledge by books is the most common and widely used way of "exporting" know-how. For the economic and social historian, however, the export of scientific or technical books poses special problems. So the presence of certain books in Latin American libraries or their being named on export lists in Seville indicates that certain techniques must have been known in Hispanic America, but it does not tell us anything about their application. This can also be illustrated the other way round: the common American technique of extracting silver from silver ore, the amalgamation method, was known in Europe since Roman times, but never applied in the thickly-wooded middle European mining areas. Abundance of fire-wood and scarcity of mercury compelled the miners of Saxonia, Bohemia and Moravia to smelt their ore instead of employing the amalgamation technique. On the other hand, only in rare cases we have the possibility to learn something about numerous, not isolated use of certain production modes or forms of organisation. So, nearly all statements made on the introduction of new techniques have

7 Cf. Jacques HEERS, La busqueda de colorantes, in: *Historia Mexicana* 11 (1961/62), pp. 1 - 27; an authorised German tried to introduce woad and madder. A general framework of technology transfer is provided by Hans POHL, Aufbruch der Weltwirtschaft, Stuttgart 1989, p. 141 - 142.

a character of hypothesis and cannot be proved as large quantity phenomena[8].

At the same time, many forms of know-howtransfer have no measurable results. How can we describe the effects of a new educational system, university reform, or the introduction of a technical school? In many cases we have to confine ourselves to purely qualitative statements, inferring more than analyzing the economic effects of improvements and reforms. Moreover, instead of working with methodically sound quantitative data we have to give evidence to our hypotheses by examples, a doubtful method for economic historians.

Bearing these limitations of perception in mind, we can take a look at the possible sources for our subject. As primary sources may serve the relations of European experts who travelled through Hispanic America and proved economic and technical interest beside their biological, botanical or geological main interests[9]. Particulary useful are some analyses of Bourbon reform politicians, e.g. the pamphlets of Fausto de Elhuyar or the "Instrucciones reservadas" of some enlightened viceroys which offer a very broad picture of set up reforms[10]. Unfortunately, pictures of new machines etc. are quite rare in edited source collections; the excellent collection of Elias Trabulse focuses on the 17th century and offers few technical drawings of the 18th century[11]. The inventories of Hispanic American libraries also give us additional reference material - with the restrictions just mentioned above. Some

---

8 Thomas GOMEZ, Ciencias y tecnicas en la formación de las Elites ilustradas en Nueva Granada, in: *Asclepio* 39/2 (1987), p. 245 - 246, points out that e.g. 25 % of the scientific library of the enlightened viceroy Caballero y Góngora consisted of French books, but that there is no evidence how many of the readers were able to understand French.

9 Two very important references are the "Noticias Secretas"and the "Essai politique" by Alexander von Humboldt.

10 Instrucciones reservadas of the Viceroy Marqués de la Croix and the Viceroy Conde de Revillagigedo (II).

11 Elias TRABULSE, Historia de las ciencia en México, vol. II, México 1984.

inventories were analyzed by Ildefonso Leal with reference to libraries in colonial Venezuela[12].

Until very recently, the history of the transfer of knowledge and of sciences and technology in Spanish America in general did not attract the attention it deserves. In Germany, there is a certain tradition to explore the German attempts to introduce modern techniques - especially in the mining sector - in colonial Latin America. This was not always done in a purely scientific way: the studies are of very differing qualities[13]. No doubt because of language problems these writings were hardly recognized in international research.

In Spain and Latin America these items were neglected for a long time, but during the last ten years history of science and of knowledge transfer became quite fashionable. A research survey on the scientific relationships between Spain and Latin America which refers mainly to the 19th century names mainly titles published after 1982[14]. In 1987 the review "Asclepio" published the contributions of a colloquium on science and technology in Spanish America during the 18th century

---

12 Ildefonso LEAL, Libros y bibliotecas en Venezuela colonial (1633 - 1767), Caracas 1979; see also note 9.

13 A summary of older German research with a lot of her own research work is presented by Renée GICKLHORN, Die Bergexpedition des Freiherrn von Nordenflycht und die deutschen Bergleute in Peru (= Freiberger Forschungshefte D 40), Leipzig 1963; she also published biographical essays on German miners in Latin America and a study on chemists in the Jesuit missions of South America (Missionsapotheker. Deutsche Pharmazeuten im Lateinamerika des 17. und 18. Jahrhunderts (= Veröffentlichungen der Internationalen Gesellschaft für Geschichte der Pharmazie, N.F. Bd. 39, Stuttgart 1973). A very fine study, though ignoring completely older German research, presented by Rose Marie BUECHLER, Technical Aid to Upper Peru: The Nordenflicht Expedition, in: *Journal of Latin American Studies* 5 (1973), p. 37 - 77.

14 Leoncio LOPEZ-OCON CABRERA, Las relaciones cientificas entre España y la América Latina en la segunda mitad del siglo XIX: Un balance historiográfico, in: *RI* 50 (1990), p. 305 - 333.

which had taken place in Madrid a year ago[15]. In Mexico one must mention the research work of Elias Trabulse, but he, like his Spanish counterparts, paid less attention to applied improvements and their economic effects than to the development of "pure" sciences in Spanish America[16].

A lot of information on innovations from Europe can be taken from general publications on economic history of late colonial Spanish America. Especially some recently published research on industrial development (primarily the textile sector) makes us see new patterns of business administration and labour organization[17].Despite these promising beginnings a history of the progress of productivity in Spanish America and it's European contribution is yet to be written. This paper, however, does not claim to fill the gap. In the following examples we will only try to outline some developments which perhaps are representative for general difficulties in the "export" of knowledge from Europe to Latin America.

III. Know-how transfer - conditions and examples

During the 18th century, Spanish attitudes towards the introduction and the employment of new sciences and technologies changed remarkably. It may have been the humiliating experience of economic decline in the 17th century that provoked a growing interest of Span-

15 Coloquio "Ciencias y tecnicas en la America Españiola del siglo XVIII", ed. by José Luis PESET, in: *Asclepio* 39/2 (1987).

16 Elias TRABULSE, Ciencia y religión en el siglo XVIII, México 1974, deals mainly with astronomy and physics; an exception: "Aspectos de la tecnologia minera en Nueva España a finales del siglo XVIII", in: *HM* 30 (1981), p. 311 - 357.

17 Cf .the monographs of TYRER, SALVUCCI, THOMPSON, et al. who published regional studies on the textile sector in New Spain and in Spanish South America (see below).

ish economists and administrators in foreign doctrines and ideas. The transfer of foreign economic ideas to Spain, mainly from France and England, may illustrate this development. Early in the 18th century Gerónimo de Uztáriz and Bernardo de Ulloa promulgated English and French mercantile thought in order to revive Spain's trade with her colonies. During the second half of the 18th century, the Spanish education and university system was increasingly critizised. A part of Charles III's later secretaries, e.g. Campomanes and Floridablanca, belonged to the group of so-called *manteistas* who revolted against scholastic tradition and aristocratic privileges at Spanish universities. The protests provoked certain reforms: In the last third of the 18th century some private universities for technical and natural sciences were founded[18]. During the second half of the 18th century members of the government, first of all the "enlightened" group around Campomanes, and the semi-official *Sociedades económicas de los amigos del país* encouraged and financed the translation of foreign studies in economics. From 1700 until 1750 only two essays in economics were translated into the Castilian language, from 1750 until 1794 an additional forty. John Reeder, however, indicates in his analysis of these translations that they not only aimed at promulgating foreign economic thought, but also at censuring those texts. For the potential readers of economic literature were mostly able to read at least Italian and French, if not English, originals[19].

So, we may conclude that Spanish intellectuals and the Spanish government had been prepared to promote a know-how transfer from European countries other than Spain to Latin America - an important

---

18 Mario HERNANDEZ SANCHEZ-BARBA, La administración de los reinos americanos, in: Historia de España 31/2, 2nd ed., Madrid 1988, p. 31 - 37; Pedro VOLTES, La politica económica, loc.cit., p. 215 - 219.

19 John REEDER, Economia y ilustración en España: Traducciones y traductores 1717 - 1800, in: *Moneda y Crédito* 147 (1978), p. 63 - 68, 43. A complete bibliography of translations offers REEDER, Bibliografía de traducciones al castellano y catalán, durante el siglo XVIII, de obras de pensamiento económico, in: *Moneda y Crédito* 126 (1973), p. 57 - 66.

condition for economic progress for two reasons: [1.] Spain was backward compared to the technical and economic knowledge of central and especially western European states and [2.] despite the liberalization of trade and traffic to and from Hispanic America since 1778 most scientific or commercial contact between Europe and America needed Spanish intermediation and support. Nevertheless, the Spanish attitude towards the colonies remained ambiguous: The national character of Spanish enlightenment which focused mainly on Spain herself and excluded the colonies from major infrastructural improvements proved to be slightly unfavourable to the knowledge-transfer to Latin America. On the other side, Spanish reform policy in the colonies created a more favourable climate at least in special sectors of the Spanish American economy[20].

In the colonies, intellectuals often showed an anti-Spanish bias in favour of French and also German thought and research. Enlightenment encouraged both Spanish American government representatives and the creole élite to take a growing interest in European scientific progress. While travelling around in 1803, Alexander von Humboldt remarked with astonishment the Creole youth's interest in natural sciences[21]. However, Humboldt's observations may have been less representative, though he ennumerates an impressive list of Creole self-made scientists.

---

20 For a characterization of the Spanish enlightenment see Ricardo KREBS, La renovación de España en el pensamiento de los economistas espanoles del siglo XVIII, in: *Historia* 2 (1962/63), p. 168 - 177; for the aims of Bourbon reform policy: Manfred KOSSOCK, Der aufgeklärte Absolutismus in Spanien, in: *Zeitschrift für Geschichtswissenschaft* 30 (1982), p. 118; John LYNCH, The Spanish American Revolutions, London 1973, p. 5, but also Ricardo LEVENE, Las Indias no eran colonias, Madrid 1951, p. 99; Richard KONETZKE, Staat und Gesellschaft in Hispanoamerika am Vorabend der Unabhängigkeit, in: *Saeculum* 12 (1969), p. 164 - 165.

21 Alexander von HUMBOLDT, Essai politique sur le Royaume de la Nouvelle Espagne, Paris 1811, t. I, l.II, c. VII, p. 118.

As this study's concern is mainly the economic implications of know-how transfer, some examples will tell us more about the ambiguous attitude of private and public, Spanish and Creole representatives towards various forms of knowledge distribution in late colonial Spanish America.

The transfer of mining technology is one of the best-known cases of the spread of knowledge from Europe to America in an economically important sector. Almost exclusively concerning the processing of silver ore, the early Spanish American mining industry could not be called technologically backward. The greater part of refining mill owners (*azogueros*) had employed the amalgamation system since its introduction by Bartolomé de Medina in 1556. The traditional method of smelting ore in wind furnaces, however, was never completely abandoned. The amalgamation method had been known in Europe probably since Roman times[22], but it had scarcely been employed. The temperate zones of central European mining areas offered abundant ressources for fuel, completely lacking in the highlands of Mexico and Peru. The amalgamation method employed in Spanish America had been developped by an empirical try-and-error process and showed considerable deficiencies because of its waste of mercury and the long processing time (2 - 5 months)[23]. But already during the 17th century some improvements led to a diminishing danger to the workers' health who came into direct skin contact with mercury or had to inhale its poisonous fumes. A procedure developped in America faciliated the mixing of mercury and crusted silver ore: The *azoguero* surrounded the *patio*, where the amalgam should be spread, with a small circular wall, put a stake in the middle of the circle and tied a

---

22 Helmut WILSDORF, Trapiche und arrastra - Die Mechanisierung des Amalgamationsverfahrens in Mexico und Peru seit 1556, in: Sympózium "200 Vyrocie zavedenia nepriamej almagamäcie a zalozenia I. Medzinárodnej vedeckej spolocnesti na svete", Zbornik 1986, p. 117.

23 A fine technical description of the amalgamation method gives Peter BAKEWELL, Silver Mining and Society in Colonial Mexico. Zacatecas 1546 - 1700, Cambridge 1971.

trail-rake (*arrastre*). A mule or oxen then could move the arrastre like a whim, running around on an elevated path. A heavy stone, moved by the same principle, had a similar effect. In analogy to the sugar refining mill this stone technique was called "trapiche". Of course, these procedures were not very sophisticated and technically trailed the belt-driven puddle-machine suggested by Agricola already in 1530 (in his "Bergmannus"). Nevertheless, they had the advantage of being stout and suitable[24].

Exploitation technology itself remained on a rather low level (the so-called rat-hole-system, an incorrect but illustrative translation of the Spanish term "sistema de rato"). Unthoughtful and unsystematic construction of galleries, pits and air-shafts led to frequent accidents and major problems with mine drainage.

Not until Charles III's reform policy did a certain interest arise in a systematic promoting of mining techniques. At the same time, good opportunities for international technology-transfer in the mining sector presented themselves. In central Europe, a systematic professional training of miners had taken place by starting the 17th century and also had been supported by several princes, because the importance of mining production for government income had been obvious[25]. The growing employment of scientific methods went along with an internationalization of natural, especially mining sciences during the Enlightenment, though this field had been kept secret in former times in

---

24 WILSDORF, Trapiche und arrastra, p. 122; TRABULSE, Aspectos, p. 339 (figure 5).

25 The high prestige of mining in econmic policy becomes evident while looking at the "scientific excursion" of the Austrian Prince Leopold and his brother, the Roman King and later Emperor Joseph II. On their mother's order (Maria Theresia), in 1764 they travelled to several Moravian mining centres, e.g. Schemnitz, Kremnitz and Neusohl. The visit encouraged the composition of a detailed description of the mining towns, the mines, their technical outfit, the processing techniques and the annual production of silver and copper. This manuscript is now published (in German and Slovakian language) and forms an excellent reference for mid-18th century mining technology in central Europe; "Das goldene Bergbuch", ed. by Joseph VOZAR, Bratislava 1983.

order to guarantee national advantages. So, the Mining Academy of Freiberg/Saxony, founded in 1765, opened its doors for foreign scientists, engineers and students who could participate in the courses for a fee. Many of the Saxonian students obtained fellowships. In Freiberg, regular teaching contained mathematics, mechanics, metallurgy, assaying of metals, mineralogy, subterranean geometry (surveying) and later also physics, geology, law, iron-metallurgy, chemistry, engine-building and construction[26].

One of the first foreign graduates of the Freiberg Mining Academy were Fausto de Elhuyar, later the reformer of New Spain's mining industry, and his brother Juan who later went to the Viceroyalty of New Granada. Both started their studies in 1778. Another celebrate Spanish graduate was Andrés Manuel del Rio who started studying in Freiberg in 1789 and became the first professor of mineralogy at Mexico City's *Colegio de Mineria* in 1795[27].

Two other events underline Freiberg's importance for Spanish American mining: Firstly, the academy served as model for the foundation of the *Colegio de Mineria* in Mexico City in 1792 which had already been planned in 1774 (like for the *Ecole des Mines* in Paris founded in 1783)[28]. Secondly, Fausto de Elhuyar's contacts to the Academy fomented a big project of know-how transfer from Saxony to Spanish America. In 1786 Elhuyar was named director general of New Spain's mining industry. Before he took up his new post he went on a journey to Central Europe, visiting Schemnitz where a Mining Academy had

---

26 Jan-Pieter BARBIAN, Deutsch-französische Beziehungen in der Wissenschaft und Technologie des 18. und frühen 19. Jahrhunderts. Das Beispiel der montanwissenschaftlichen Ausbildung, in: *Technikgeschichte* 56 (1989), p. 307 - 308.

27 Carl SCHIFFNER, Aus dem Leben alter Freiberger Bergstudenten, t.3, Freiberg/Sachsen 1940, S. 2 - 5.

28 Cuauthémoc VELASCO AVILA / Eduardo FLORES CLAIR / Alma Laura PARRA CAMPOS / Edgar Omar GUTIERREZ LOPEZ, Estado y minería en México (1767 - 1910), México 1988, S. 180; BARBIAN, Deutsch-französische Beziehungen, S. 305.

been founded already in 1762, Glashütten, where the famous Austro-Hungarian metallurgist Ignaz Edler von Born presented his new amalgamation method (the so-called "warm" method), and several other mining centres. In Glashütten, he joined the recently founded "Society of mining sciences" (Sozietät der Bergbaukunde), the first international technical society, which unfortunately was to dissolve in 1791[29].

Finally Elhuyar came to Freiberg where he succeeded in recruiting several graduates of the Academy and some miners, in total 33 men, who obtained the permission of the Saxonian government to go with him to the American overseas territories. Contracts were made up for 10 years (1788 - 1798). A part of the group went with Elhuyar to New Spain, another part accompanied his former co-student and friend, Fürchtegott Leberecht Freiherr von Nordenflicht to the Viceroyalties Rio de la Plata and Perú[30].

The project to introduce modern mining technology in Spanish America by "importing" skilled personnel and engineers failed completely. There were several reasons for this failure:

- The miners from Saxony were not or only insufficiently able to speak Spanish and could not defend and carry their ideas; fur-

---

29 László MOLNAR, Die erste internationale Bergbauwissenschaftliche Konferenz und der erste Bergbauverein, in: László MOLNAR / Alfred WEISS, Ignaz Edler von Born und die Sozietät der Bergbaukunde 1786, Wien 1986, p. 28 - 29; R. SENNEWALD, Die "Sozietät der Bergbaukunde" - erste internationale montanwissenschaftliche Gesellschaft (1786 bis 1790), in: Studien zur Geschichte der Montanindustrie vom 16. bis zum 20. Jahrhundert. Beiträge zur Geschichte der Produktivkräfte XXI, Leipzig 1987, p. 75 - 102; in Spain, the Conde de Floridablanca and the Marqués de Senora (sic!) were enlisted as honourary members of the society; cf. list of members in MOLNAR / WEISS, Ignaz Edler von Born, p. 122.

30 Concerning this mining expedition there is a lot of German literature which remained hardly noticed by international research - probably because of language problems. A summary of this older German research offers the Viennese historian Renée GICKLHORN, Eine deutsche Bergexpedition in Latein-Amerika (1788 - 1798), in: *Technikgeschichte* 37 (1970), p. 268 - 275.

thermore, they obviously lacked personal qualities, such as patience, diplomacy and a sense of humour and understanding[31].

- Established groups of miners, in Peru supported by the viceregal adminstration, were reluctant to accept any improvement and even boycotted new measures.
- Finally, some processing methods and techniques could not be adapted to Spanish American conditions, though they had been sucessfully employed in Central Europe.

Nordenflicht e.g. who tried to introduce Born's modified amalgamation method in Peru met unknown difficulties even in dealing with simple problems. So, a blacksmith as well as some iron tools that Nordenflicht needed in order to construct the necessary engine had to be brought from Buenos Aires up to the Andean highlands. The local miners lost patience and finally denounced the Germans as impostors who had forced them to spend a fortune for nothing. The unsatisfactory results of some experiments, extremely high cost and not at least a different mentality guaranteed the failure of the Nordenflicht mining mission[32].

The group under Elhuyar's leadership in New Spain behaved more carefully and prudently. Nevertheless, its success was very limited, too. Federico Sonneschmidt first tried to introduce Born's amalgamation technique, but then turned to be a passionate defender of the traditional patio-method which he described in his "Tratado de Amalgamación". He improved it slightly by the suggestion that coppery soda or coppery sal-ammoniac should be mixed with silver ore and mercury in order to speed up the chemical reactions[33].

---

31 Cf. BUECHLER, Technical Aid, p. 73.

32 John FISHER, Silver mines and silver mining in Colonial Peru, 1776 - 1824, Liverpool 1977, p. 54 - 73; GICKLHORN, Bergexpedition, p. 270 - 272; BUECHLER, Technical Aid, p. 37 - 77.

33 Renée GICKLHORN, Friedrich Traugott Sonneschmidt, in: *Der Anschnitt* 20 (1968), p. 8 - 10.

Maybe the introduction of Born's warm amalgamation method failed because of its technical shortcomings: The method saved time and mercury, but it was not well developped, complicated and could not be adapted to Spanish American conditions. Suprisingly, there was hardly progress in the planning of mines, the construction of galleries and shafts and in hauling-techniques. Still on his voyage in 1803, Humboldt observed that many mines including the celebrate "Veta Vizacaina" in Real del Monte were drained not by whims or pumps, but that the water was carried out in leather bags[34].

These primitive methods persisted while better techniques were theoretically well-known in New Spain. Already in 1727, the creole author Juan Antonio de Mendoza y González had published a study of modern drainage methods for silver mines[35]. But inventions and their spread did not necessarily lead to their application: The miners lacked capital and were not willing to take additional risks. Even innovations which had been well established in Europe meant risks to American enterpreneurs. For example, a group of miners which wanted to introduce British steam-engines for drainage in the Peruvian mining industry at the beginning of the 19th century proved to be unsuccessful and went bankrupt[36].

The same results may be observed in the development of mine-surveying. The systematic construction of galleries and air-shafts had been described and technically explained by Francisco Xavier Gamboa in his famous "Comentarios de las Ordenanzas de Minas" (1763)[37]. Fausto de Elhuyar himself was a qualified specialist in the field of

---

34 "On doit être surpris que l'on n'ait pas songé à substituer à ce misérable moyen de retirer l'eau par des sacs, des équipages des pompes, mus par des baritels à chevaux, par des roues hydrauliques, ou par des machines à colonne d'eau". HUMBOLDT, Essai politique, t. II, l.IV, c. XI, p. 541.

35 Published in TRABULSE, Historia, T. II, p. 221 - 231.

36 FISHER, Silver mines, p. 114 - 115.

37 The corresponding chapter is published in TRABULSE, Historia, t. II, p. 231 - 247.

"geometría subterránea". He taught this subject from 1781 until 1786 at the Real Escuela Metalúrgica in the city of Vergara in Spain[38]. Nevertheless, only small parts of knowledge from this science could be successfully applied in Spanish America. One of the specialists Elhuyar had recruited in Freiberg, Gottlob Friedrich Mothes who went with Nordenflicht to Peru, told of strong resistance that Peruvian officials and miners showed against the innovations he was aiming at. But there is also some evidence that a small group of miners was interested in correct methods of digging of galleries and the results of subterranean geometry: When his official contract ended in 1798, Mothes got private employment in Peru at least until 1818 as geometer and surveyor[39].

Altogether, such single activities had little effect on the state of silver mines in general. In 1803, Humboldt critized the whole condition and design of silver mines: drilled holes for blasting rocks were always made too big and too deep, in consequence a lot of powder was wasted. Generally, shafts and galleries would be built too big and broad. This would offer no airing-advantages but create a lot of unneccessary costs. Instead of small side-galleries towards the ceiling and the walls, miners used to build big exploration-galleries. But the worst mistake was the complete lack of side-connections between the different galleries. Humboldt compared these mines to a building where the visitor had to go through every room in order to get around[40]. As a result, a lot of labour-saving methods like chain-conveyors or trams could not be used in Mexican and Peruvian mines.

The Spanish and Creole resistance to European innovations in mining techniques cannot be explained only by language problems or national and religious antipathies, though older German research tradition tries

38 GICKELHORN, Sonneschmidt, p. 14.

39 Renée GICKELHORN, Gottlob Friedrich Mothes, in: *Der Anschnitt* 17 (1965), p. 30 - 33.

40 HUMBOLDT, Essai politique II, 1. IV, c. XI, p. 549 - 550.

to do so and there is some evidence of what Aguila calls "patriotismo tecnológico"[41]. But native Creole scientists met the same difficulties. Velázquez de León, e.g., an assistant of general visitor José de Gálvez on his journey to Baja California and later president of the *Tribunal de Minería*, did not succeed in introducing his set of innovations though he was of Creole origin[42]. Finally, Humboldt's argument seems to be most conclusive: He underlines that the purely private organization of the Spanish American mining industry offered no opportunity to enforce reforms ordered by the government.

Maybe a little more successful was the transfer of institutions for the formation of mining engineers, though it should not be overestimated. In 1774, a plan was already developped in New Spain to found a mining school where gifted young people could be trained technically and even politically. But only with Fausto de Elhuyar's arrival those plans ripened. In 1790, he presented to the *Tribunal de minería* his plans for a "Colegio de minería" which started working in the beginning of 1792. Following the example of German mining academies, fellowships were granted to apt persons who had to be sons of miners, aged between 14 and 20 years and who had already received elementary instruction in geometry, arithmetics and Castilian grammar. They were mainly trained by European teachers[43].

The Colegio claimed to teach practical professional skills at the highest scientific and technological standard to the largest possible group

---

41 Cf. the above mentionned studies of QUELLE, HELMER and GICKLHORN; Yves AGUILA, Innovación técnica y estado en la Nueva España ilustrada, in: *Asclepio* 39/2 (1987), p. 301.

42 Cf. Salvador BERNABEU ALBERT, Ciencia y Minería in Baja California: El informe de Joaquín Velázquez de León (1771), in: *Asclepio* 39/2 (1987), p. 103 - 122.

43 Besides Elhuyar, the German Louis Lindner tought chemistry and metallurgy since 1794; with Andrés del Rio and the Creole Joaquín de Velázquez the Colegio contracted two well-known scientists; VELASCO AVILA et al., Estado y minería, p. 180, 192 - 193; GICKLHORN, Sonneschmidt, p. 5.

of young mining specialists. This purpose could be only partially realized. Between 1792 and 1811, the colegio had only 92 students, only about 30 of them passed the exam[44]. The Colegio's proximity to the practice also may be questionned. Alexander von Humboldt, a rather good friend of the Colegio and its aims[45], critized that lectures and even the mineralogical collections of the Colegio showed little regional reference and did not regard the specific necessities of the Mexican mining industry[46]. So, we can conclude that the practical effects of the Colegio on the mining sector were limited despite its good scientific reputation. Probably, the boom of the Mexican mining industry in the last quarter of the 18th century was due more to government measures such as tax exemption, a bigger and cheaper availability of mercury and a greater influx of merchant capital than to the timid introductions of modern European mining techniques.

An economic sector which is characterized by less state intervention may serve as a second example for our quest if and when know-how transfer from Europe had a certain influence on late colonial economic development in Spanish America. the manufacturing sector, more precisely the textile industry. Since the 16th century we can discern two different modes of textile manufacturing: the traditional artisan production and the centralized production in the so-called obrajes. Both artisanal and plant production were imitations of European production modes with slight modifications[47], but technically backward and so with purpose, because Spanish American textile production was only tolerated by the Spanish government if it was restricted to

---

44 José Joaquín IZQUIERDO, La primera casa de las ciencias en México; el Real Seminario de Minería, 1792 - 1811, México 1958, p. 48 - 49.

45 To his relations to the colegio cf. Otto QUELLE, Das Colegio de Minería in Mexiko unter deutschem wissenschaftlichen Einfluß, in: *Ibero-amerikanisches Archiv* 11 (1937/38), p. 376 - 381.

46 HUMBOLDT, Essai politique, t. I., l. II, c. VII, p. 121; t. II, l. IV, c. XI, p. 506.

47 Richard E. GREENLEAF, The Obraje in the Late Mexican Colony, in: *The Americas* 23 (1966/67), p. 229.

poor qualities and did not impede the import of Spanish and European luxury textiles. Generally, we cannot observe a supersession of old production forms by modern ones, but emphasis shifted from artisanal organization to obraje-production and finally to the putting out system (*Verlagsystem*)[48].

It has been discussed if the obraje may be interpreted as a factor of protoindustrialization in Mexican or Andine economy. Because of the complete lack of technical progress recent research tends to answer this question in the negative. Obrajes had no cost advantages, there were no economies of scale to be realised. Profits remained on a low level and investment in better equipment or machines was a rare exception even in the 18th century[49].

Nevertheless, European know-how certainly influenced the introduction of the cottage industry (Verlag), mainly in Southern New Spain's cotton production. The highly capitalist structure of business crowded out native Indian craft tradition. *Aviadores* bought cotton from the cotton farmers, supplying them with credit and goods, then sold the raw cotton to merchants, the so-called "algodoneros" or "regalones de algodón". They in turn organized and financed the distribution and further manufacturing among the spinners and weavers[50].

In New Spain as in the Audiencia de Quito, this typical protoindustrial European production mode proved to be very successful. The number of looms expanded rapidly and only diminished when British and

---

48 Manuel CARRERA STAMPA, Los gremios mexicanos. La organización gremial en Nueva España, 1521 - 1861, México 1954, p. 283; Manuel MIÑO GRIJALVA, Capital comercial y trabajo textil: Tendencias generales de la protoindustria colonial latinoamericana, in: *HISLA* 9 (1987), p. 62.

49 MIÑO GRIJALVA, Capital, p. 65; GREENLEAF, Obraje, p. 240; John C. SUPER, Querétaro Obrajes: Industry and Society in Provincial Mexico, 1600 - 1810, in: *HAHR* 56 (1976), p. 200.

50 Guy THOMPSON, The Cotton Textile Industry in Puebla during the Eighteenth and Early Nineteenth Centuries, in: N. JACOBSEN / H. - J. PUHLE (Ed.), The Economies of Mexico and Peru during the Late Colonial Period, 1760 - 1810, Berlin 1986, p. 169, 180 - 181.

East-Indian textiles were allowed to compete in the Spanish American market[51].

The successful introduction of an approved European capitalist organisation scheme was, however, well prepared by the economic and demographic circumstances: the growing population, the decline of the obrajes since the mid-18th century and not at least additional mercantile capital that had been activated with the introduction of "free trade" in 1778. In contrast to the government-directed mining missions, the introduction of the putting out system had been a half-conscious imitation of European examples mixed up with well-known elements of Spanish American economic life (like the avío-system). So, we cannot really speak of a 'transfer' of European knowledge, but only of a certain European influence which is difficult to separate from other elements. Nevertheless, this way of introducing economic innovations proved to be more successful than the mining mission and certainly had discernable though not quantifiable effects.

In the public sector, reform politicians tried to transfer European knowledge both to economic activities of the crown (like the monopolies for tobacco, gunpowder or playing cards) and to sovereign rights (like minting). Bourbon reform politics generally followed the example of other European countries. When introducing the intendant system, Spain followed the French example and so she did in restructuring the system of public finance and tax-farming. (Somewhat ironically one could add that the Spanish Empire was also abolished by imitating France, for the independence was strongly influenced by and in more than one way a consequence of the French Revolution[52].)

---

51 THOMPSON, Industry, p. 170; Brooke LARSON, The Cotton Textile Industry of Cochabamba, 1770 - 1810: The Opportunities and Limits of Growth, in: PUHLE / JACOBSEN (Ed.), Economies, p. 156 - 161.

52 Cf. e.g. Manfred KOSSOK, "Mögen die Kolonien verderben!" 1789 und die koloniale Frage, in: *Zeitschrift für Geschichtswissenschaft* 32 (1990), p. 494 - 497.

In smaller details, we see too how crown officials set to work a lot of minor improvements. The gun-powder-monopoly in New Spain may serve as an example: The monopoly was administered by a private contractor up to 1765. As he was not willing to improve the quality of the gunpowder by technical innovations and investments, the Crown decided to take the plant into direct administration. As a first step to amelioration, Ordenanzas prescribed the working modalities. In 1779, the minister of the Indies, José de Gálvez, succeeded in gaining Salvador Dampierre, a French chemist, as Director de Salitres of New Spain. He visited the Mexican niter mines, wrote new instructions and introduced some improvements in order to obtain pure and better gunpowder. But like the German miners a few years later, Dampierre was not well received in New Spain. He had to suffer ironical remarks as well as open hostility[53]. Despite Humboldt's statement that Creole intellectuals were always very fond of talking with Europeans[54], the direct transfer of knowledge by non-Spanish European experts seems to have caused serious problems and xenophobic reactions.

Even the introduction of new techniques and production methods from Spain sometimes proved to be difficult. So did Charles III's attempt to modernize the colonial minting system. Between 1733 and 1770 all offices in the royal mints of Spanish America had been incorporated into the Crown. In 1771, Charles made an effort to withdraw the current coins, the *macuquina*, and to introduce a circular and uniform new coin to Spanish America. The *macuquina* showed considerable deficiencies: its irregular shape encouraged clipping and counterfeiting, a great number of the coins left the mint too light. Its substitution by the so-called *moneda de cordoncillo*, ordered by Ferdinand VI, had failed 20 years ago. Charles' new type of money, the *moneda del busto*, had a regular form, was difficult to counterfeit and stamped by machines instead of hammers. Accompanied by a secret reduction of

53 AGUILA, Innovación, p. 299 - 301.

54 HUMBOLDT, Essai politique, t. 1., p. 118.

the coin's silver content, the new money should be introduced at the same time in all parts of Spain's American empire[55]. For this purpose, in march 1771 Madrid sent ordinances, technical equipment, improved matrixes and coin-stamps to all the royal mints[56] and advised the superintendants of the mints to start coining in 1772. Although well prepared the operation was only partially successful: some of the dispatches arrived with delay or were damaged. Initially, the local administrations did not succeed in withdrawing the *macuquina* in an adequate period of time. As the mints had insufficient capacities to substitute the old coins by new ones and in particular to provide enough small denominations, the different sorts of coin all circulated during the late colonial period. Besides the benefits for the Crown from the secret debasement, the *moneda del busto* added little positive effects to the Spanish American money-system[57].

IV. Conclusion

Although often depicted as self-restrained and xenophobic the Bourbon government as well as viceregal administrations in Hispanic America were often vividly interested in technological progress and the transfer of so-called "useful sciences" whenever measures seemed apt to increase government income. Transfer of know-how was carried out by various means: The Crown encouraged the founding of technical schools, the teaching of natural sciences at the traditional universities, invited and payed generously foreign specialists and even "ordered" technical progress by ordinances. Yves Aguila thinks it

---

55 Earl J. HAMILTON, Monetary Problems in Spain and Spanish America, 1751 - 1800, in: *Journal of Economic History* 4 (1944), p. 21 - 48.

56 México, Guatemala, Santa Fé de Bogotá, Popayán, Lima, Potosí, Santiago de Chile.

57 Cf. Ruth VORNEFELD, Spanische Geldpolitik in Hispanoamerika, 1750 - 1808, (= VSWG-Beiheft 102), Stuttgart 1992.

quite paradoxical and it really is astonishing that the state employed its compulsory forces to serve the technical progress[58].

Nevertheless, the transfer of know-how seems not to have been very successful. Concerning one of the most prestigious projects, the Nordenflicht mining mission to Upper Peru, Fisher judges: "The failure of the Nordenflicht mission to introduce modern European methods of mining and refining silver ores to Peru meant that the industry as a whole saw no technical improvement in any aspect of silver production in the period underconsideration (...)"[59].

Various other projects with foreign specialists, like the mining missions to New Spain and New Granada, showed similar results: nearly none!

The attitude of the creole élite towards a know-how transfer remained ambiguous. On the one hand, there is a lot of evidence that Creoles admired French culture and sciences and - certainly to a lesser degree - German skill. On the other hand, the creole élite remained conservative in the field of economics, observed critically and even boycotted every attempt to further economic exploitation of the colonies. This may be one reason for the lack of cooperation and the "patriotismo tecnológico" foreign specialist experienced. Furthermore, Creole entrepreneurs, especially miners, were chronically short of capital and even government improvements mostly lacked solid financing, a crucial condition for successful innovation.

Given a solid financial basis, knowledge transfer could be remarkable and followed by splendid economic results. The influx of foreign know-how and capital to Cuba, e.g., during the British occupation in 1762 and even more after the flight of the "grands blancs" as a consequence of the mulatto and slave revolution in Haiti in 1790/91 made

---

58 AGUILA, Innovación, p. 299.

59 FISHER, Silver mines, p. 67.

Cuba the "phenix of the late Bourbon period" and produced the "most solid and brilliant bourgeois class" in all of Latin America[60].

Slow economic transformations that are surely influenced by European technical and organisational know-how are very difficult to trace like the gradual take-over of the cottage industry in the Spanish American textile industry. Without doubt, until the 1790s most areas of the Spanish empire received a long continuing economic impetus, but there is no evident link of a transfer of European knowhow.

Single projects which are well documented in general refer to government activities. Dirigist measures to improve productivity or quality in the export-oriented sectors of the Spanish American economy mostly showed rather poor results as the examples demonstrate. So, we have to conclude that at least the documented part of the European contribution to economic development of Spanish America during the late Bourbon period was not very impressive. Although several attempts were made, the Spanish colonies on the eve of independence made up their technological backwardness only marginally. In encouraging the transfer of European know-how to Spanish America, Bourbon reformers mainly achieved an increase in cost rather than in government income.

---

60 Quotations from A. L. ALLAHAR, The Cuban Sugar Planters: The Most Solid and Brilliant Bourgeois Class in All of Latin America, in: *The Americas* 41 (1984) and John FISHER, Commercial Relations between Spain and Spanish America in the Era of Free Trade, 1778 - 1796, Liverpool 1985, p. 75.

The Beneficiaries of the Bourbon Reforms: Spain versus the New Spanish Elite[1]

By PEDRO PÉREZ HERRERO

Introduccion

Traditionally, the 18th century in Latin America has been interpreted as follows:

a) Economic growth accelerated during the second half of the century and more specifically starting with the reign of Charles III. At the same time, it is usually emphasized that this economic upturn was the direct consequence of the modernizing policies of the Bourbons and thus posterior to them (Brading [1987]).

b) The new Bourbon dynasty, by improving the colonial administrative operations, was able to considerably increase the shipments of wealth to Spain and thereby strengthen the imperial structure. This revitalization undertaken by the Bourbons, alternately called the "reconquest of America", "governmental revolution", or "expansion of the royal authority", signified for

1 Translated by David Markowitz. The basic ideas of the present article were discussed in the course titled "Consequences of the Discovery of America"' which took place at the Universidad Internacional Menéndez Pelayo, Valencia (Spain) September 16 - 19, 1991. The original spanish version was published in: *Historia Mexicana* XLII/2 (1991), pp. 207 - 264.

the New Spanish elite a parallel decrease in the level of political autonomy they had gained during the previous epoch of the Habsburgs. From this point of view, fiscal income has been used as a gauge to measure the success of the Bourbon reforms (Lynch [1973]; Lynch [1989], pp. 341 - 374; Brading [1987], pp. 120 - 132; Burkholder-Johnson [1990], pp. 234 - 289; Fisher [1990], pp. 573 - 594).

c) The wars of independence occurred in a climate of economic growth and coincided with the highest level of fiscal income, which signified, following the above interpretation, a strengthening of the capacity of the monarchy to impose its authority. To explain the birth of the social unrest preceding the revolution and the destruction of the imperial structure, theses have been proposed focused basically on the unequal distribution of wealth (Florescano-Gil [1977]), on anti-Spanish sentiments raised by the strengthening of the centralization process through the Bourbon policies, and on the famous abdication at Bayonne: economic growth exaggerated existing social differences, reforms excited anti-Spanish sentiments, and the power vacuum generated by the abdication of Charles IV and Ferdinand VII to José Bonaparte triggered the push towards political independence in the overseas territories (Lynch [1973]).

In general, these interpretations are for the most part inherited from the historiographies of 18th century enlightenment Europe and liberal 19th century Latin America. During the 18th century, the Bourbons were interested in demonstrating that their "modernization" policies had caused an economic take-off in both Spain and the colonies, to justify the process of political centralization. As a consequence, they made an effort to contrast the differences between the 18th century and the preceding period of the Hapsburgs, creating a black-and-white image composed of the "crises" of the 17th century and the "growth" of the 18th. This interpretation was "'sanctified"' and endowed with a scientific facade by A. de Humboldt, who with official documentation and without any criticism of the figures, spread the thesis that as a result of the Reglamento de Comercio Libre of 1778, the public earnings of New Spain doubled and the entire vice-regal economy shot up in similar proportions (Humboldt [1966], p. 499 - 502).

The 19th century Latin American historians, conservatives as well as liberals, praised with different intentions the government and administration of the final colonial period. The conservatives of the first half of the 19th century wanted to demonstrate that the loss of the authoritarian and centralist colonial political apparatus had given rise to a period of social revolts, division of territory, and a general economic crisis. Those of the second half of the century emphasized that the introduction of liberal theses had provoked a general economic awakening, for which they contrasted the "order and progress" that reigned during the second half of the 19th century with the "anarchy and crisis" (terms coined by this historiography) of the first half of the century and the "growth" of the Bourbon period. Evidently, in this case they tried to place emphasis on the "political failures" of the first half of the 19th century and not on the colonial victories.

Next, we will examine some of the aforementioned supposedly interpretative historiographies. For this, we will begin by examining the veracity of the numbers used traditionally, so that from the concrete case of New Spain we can begin to analyze the relations between fiscal success and the strengthening of the imperial structure.

Documented Evidence of Bourbon "Economic Growth"[2]

If we put ourselves in Spain and utilize the official documentation, the results of the Bourbon reform plan were indeed spectacular: mineral, agricultural, and cattle production increased, commercial traffic im-

---

2 This section synthesizes the ideas that appeared in PÉREZ HERRERO (1989).

proved, reaching by 1776 volumes unimaginable for the era, and royal income soared, breaking mythical barriers.

In accordance with the official coinage totals, considered indicators of the extraction of precious metals, the production of silver and gold increased notably, reaching in 1804 a record 27 million pesos of silver coined in the mint (see diagram no. 1).

If we utilize the number of ships or the income from alcabalas, almojarifazgos, and averias (taxes levied on mercantile transactions), it may be concluded that throughout most of the 18th century there was a both general and continuous increase of commercial activity in Latin America. The number of ships (see diagram no. 2) that did business across the Atlantic rose clearly during the third quarter of the 18th century: from an average of 20 ships annually arriving in Veracruz between 1728 and 1739, it reached 103 between 1784 and 1795, following the numbers of M. Lerdo de Tejada (Lerdo de Tejada [1853]) and J. Ortiz de la Tabla (Ortiz de la Tabla [1978]). Income from alcabalas (tax on internal commerce) increased again in the case of New Spain from a gross, for example, of 191.136 pesos in 1730, to 527.299 pesos in 1740,1.129.285 pesos in 1750, to 2.172.882 pesos In 1781, and 2.440.767 pesos in 1784 (TePaske et al. [1976]).

Ir we use the information proceeding from the income from diezmos (tax of 10% on agricultural and cattle production that every cultivator, with the general exception of the indigenous peopies, had to pay to the Church), it could be assumed that the agricultural production rose spectacularly as well. In New Spain, the official income from the diezmo rose from a total (in current values) of 302.055 pesos in 1771, to 612.022 pesos in 1780, and 724.014 pesos in 1790 (Pérez Herrero [1989]).

Utilizing the official numbers for fiscal income it has been concluded that the new Bourbon administration sensibly multiplied its profits, so that it is not surprising to see why the Bourbon reforms have been considered an authentic success. Specifically, for example, it can be proved that in New Spain fiscal income multiplied by more than 11 from beginning to end of the 18th century. The gross profits of the Peruvian viceroyalty did not rise as spectacularly (they multiplied only by four from beginning to end of the century), perhaps due to the fact that the area of Peru was divided both territorially and fiscally, to create the new viceroyalties of Rio de la Plata (1776) and of Nueva Granada (1739), and that mineral recovery was not as intense in this area as in the case of the northern viceroyalty. It is not surprising, therefore, that the tendency for the fiscal revenues to rise is seen to have halted in 1776, the year of the creation of the southern viceroyalty of Rio de la Plata (Humboldt [1966]; Tepaske et al. [1976]; TePaske-Kleine [1982]; TePaske-Kleine [1986]) (see diagram no. 3).

We could continue adding more examples of different quantitative series, proceeding from official fiscal sources, in which are shown a steady and growing increase in official income. However, it is necessary to underline that the problem inherent to these numbers is that fundamentally they have been used by historians as economic indicators, without making the necessary preliminary adjustments; interpreting, for example, that an increase in the volume of collections in the section of alcabalas signified an increase of an equal proportion in mercantile transactions; that a rise in the quintos (tax on mineral production) represented a rise of equal calibre in the production of silver; that a larger intake from diezmos (tax on agricultural and cattle production) corresponded with a like increase in agricultural production, etc., or that the oscillations in the number of ships utilized by the merchant marine was a reliable indicator of the variations in the number of transactions realized and therefore of the evolution of economic activity as a whole.

In the first place, it is necessary to remember that the rise in fiscal income at the end of the colonial era does not reflect solely and exclusively an economic upswing both in production and in trade, but as well (although again not exclusively) certain administrative improvements. It is evident that the cancellation of the practice of renting the administration of certain divisions, the creation of a true royal administration, the introduction of the double-entry-system, careful watch over the accounts, the cancellation of the sale of public offices, or simply the existence of a new juridical and fiscal framework, all helped to combat, for one, the administrative corruption characteristic of the previous years and created, secondly, a new scenario in which it began to be more profitable and safe to use official trade channels rather than the old illegal ones, in which the profit margins had been reduced in some cases. One of the consequences of all of these changes was that the official fiscal income rose. The fiscal pressure grew not only vertically with the increased fiscal obligations of the contributors, but horizontally as well, by the incorporation of new sectors of the population (Garavaglia-Grosso [1985]). Some examples can be quite revealing.

We know, for example, that the amonedación (the total of silver converted into coin in the mints expressed in nominal values) and the silver quintada (that which had been paid as fiscal obligations to the Crown at the moment ofits extraction, such as the quinto, the diezmo, the cobos, according to the situation and region, and that therefore bore the royal stamp, silver acuñada) were not synonymous to production. During the 17th century it was quite common for an ample percentage of the silver to circulate in bars (called "en pasta" at that time) without being taxed the quinto and without being converted into coin, their value fixed by their weight and intrinsic standard, to which normally they deducted the unpaid duties and the costs of coinage (senoreaje). The transaction with this silver consisted of buying the bars with a reduction in their price due to the unpaid taxes and immediately selling them abroad, where what was important was the standard and not if they had been marked with the royal stamp of if they were made into coin. In other words, the totals for silver coined do not coincide with that taxed, that exported, and with that actually produced.

Following this train of thought it could follow that the variations in the amount coined, numbers used by the majority of historians as a synonym for production, may reflect at the same time as a shift in production level an increase or decrease in the circulation of silver "en pasta"' and un-taxed, which is precisely what happened in the case of New Spain. The new conditions conceded to the mining sector, which consisted of fiscal exemptions (alcabalas) or special privileges in regard to the prices of certain essentials for mineral production whose distribution was monopolized by the Crown (gunpowder, mercury, salt), along with a new financial structure (Banco de Minería) which freed the miners from their relations with the capital of the merchants (bancos de plata, aviadores), made it so that it began to be more advantageous to employ the official means of marketing the silver rather than the illegal ones. In short, during the third quarter of the 18th century the totals for silver extracted, taxed and coined began to coincide, so that only from these dates and not before can we utilize the statistics of coinage as indicators of production (Pérez Herrero [1988]). In essence, we do not doubt the fact that the level of coinage rose in the final analysis, which is beyond all doubt, but we question what this rise truly represented.

Secondly, it must be understood that during the second half of the 18th century there was a general and indisputable inflationary process, which has been described in the works of E. Florescano (Florescano [1969]), R. Garner (Garner [1985]), J.M. Larraín Melo, R. Romano, L. L. Johnson, K. W. Brown, E. Tandeter, N. Wachtel, B. Larson, R. J. Ferry, D. Alden and J. Cuenca Estaben, for distinct regions (see a synthesis in Johnson-Tandeter [1990; eds.]).

In addition to this inflationary process the true value of the silver in international markets decreased in the first half of the 18th century. Thus the silver, due to enlargement of the monetary supply, lost value in said periods in respect to gold, which can be checked in the following table (*on the next page*).

Finally, it is important to remember that if the total number of pesos nominally coined did grow, the intrinsic value of the coin decreased due to the different devaluations made throughout the 18th century. Between 1535 and 1768, the standard for silver coins in Mexico was

TABLE 1:

Decades	silver/gold
1691 - 1700	14.96:1
1701 - 1710	15.27:1
1711 - 1720	15.15:1
1721 - 1730	15.09:1
1731 - 1740	15.07:1
1741 - 1750	14.93:1
1751 - 1760	14.56:1
1761 - 1770	14.81:1
1771 - 1780	14.64:1
1781 - 1790	14.76:1
1791 - 1800	15.42:1
1801 - 1810	15.61:1

Sources: Shaw [1896], pp. 157 - 159; Lafky [1964], p. 32.

11 dineros, 4 granos (939.551 milésimos). In 1728 it was fixed at 11 dineros (916.666 milésimos), which was equivalent to 64 reales and 2 maravedies; in 1772, at 10 dineros, 20 granos, and gold coins at 21 quilates instead of 22; and in 1786, at 10 dineros, 18 granos (895.8 milésimos).

In light of these considerations, it is evident that if we want to value with precision the increase in the production of precious metals, it is necessary to adjust the annual totals by the index of prices, in order to measure the actual buying power of the produced silver, as well as bear in mind the problems which exist between silver "en pasta", coined, taxed, etc. Until recently it has been very common for historians to present the nominally official coinage totals as equal to those of production, without introducing the obligatory adjustments, the result being that the interpretative conclusions extracted from these totals were, from our point of view, hasty.

In regard to the increase in agricultural production, A. Ouweneel and C. J. H. Bijleveld (Ouweneel-Bijleveld [1989]) have indicated that the growth in income from diezmos in New Spain also reflected the elevation of prices and the improvements in administration and accounting introduced in the second half of the 18th century. If agricultural production increased, it was probably more due to an extension of the production means (colonization of new territories and incorporation of more man-power in the production process) than to an intensification of the same, which would have caused an increase in productivity, which in fact was not produced except in a few special cases, as was emphasized some time ago by R. and L. Salvucci (Salvucci-Salvucci [1987]).

Regarding the totals for transactions, it is necessary to remember that not surprisingly gross income from alcabalas doubled in 1754, the final year in which that division was rented, traditionally to the Merchant Guild of Mexico City, or to the council (Cabildo) of that same city. Aside from the improvements in administration, it must be kept in mind that the amount that the American contributors had to pay in alcabalas did not stay constant, but instead, in the event of wars or the construction of new roads, was increased continually. Specifically, in the case of Mexico, this tax rose from 2% added to the value of goods at the beginning of the 18th century, to 8% at the end. Remember that totals collected from the alcabalas, the avería (tax of 2% added to the value of goods for import-export, used to finance the Merchant Guild), the almojarifazgos (taxes on maritime commerce) and the rest of the commerce taxes, charged as a percentage of the value of the goods, grew throughout the 18th century also as a consequence of the inflationary process, so that they do not exclusively reflect an increase in transactions. In this respect, it is surprising that they even continue to manipulate figures for import-export taxes added to the value of goods without making the necessary deflations.

On the other hand, it would not hurt to remember that it is not very exact to measure the fluctuations in mercantile maritime transactions by means of the number of ships, since their tonnage varies. By general rule, the hull capacity of commercial vessels decreased during the 18th century, to attain greater agility of movement while reducing overhead.

To all of this we would have to add that as a rule the trade figures have been used to measure the fluctuations of the entire economy, arguing that the collection of alcabalas reflected the variations of supply and demand. However, this train of thought does not match reality, having been proven that they were not necessarily directly related phenomenons. It must be remembered that a reduction in transactions (alcabala) might express a contraction in the volume of monetary trade, but at the same time a growth in non-mercantile production (barter) and/or in autoconsumption (as was the case in the "crisis" of the 17th century), and, vice-versa (as was the case in the "growth" of the 18th century), that an amplification of mercantile channels might represent a decrease in non-mercantile production and/or autoconsumption. Definitively, an increase in collections of alcabalas might signify on certain occasions an increase in official monetary, mercantile channels, at the same time as a decrease in the non-mercantile production of the same proportion, so that we cannot talk about an across-the-board economic growth, but instead, of a change in internal structure.

Finally, everything seems to indicate that the intensity of the growth should be reconsidered through a revision of the indicators used. We have started this analysis, introducing some of the rectifications commented upon, allowing us to prove that behind the official figures is hidden a reality quite different from the traditionally accepted one which underlines the fact that the 18th century was one of constant growth. J. Coatsworth (Coatsworth [1986]), regarding the mineral production of New Spain, and A. Ouweneel and C. J. K. Bijleveld (Ouweneel-Bijleveld [1989]), regarding the agricultural production of Central Mexico, have employed adjusted tables of the official values of coinage and the diezmo, discovering that at the end of the 18th century, what appeared to be an increase can be interpreted in real terms as a decrease in productivity. However, there are still some problems to resolve such as: a) correcting the values to avoid differences, for example, between silver coined, taxed, and produced; or changes in the fiscal taxes between one year and the next, as for example in the alcabalas or the diezmos; b) the construction of a correct and adjusted price index that would reproduce the regional variances and which would not be based solely on the wholesale price of a few goods normally regulated by the municipal authorities (as in the case of the price of corn in the public granary of Mexico City); and c) the correlation between mercantile economies and economies of autoconsumption in an analytical diagram more complicated than that proposed by the dualist theses.

Nevertheless, it can still be maintained that the triumphal image of the age of the Bourbon reforms is not completely in line with reality. The thesis of a continuous economic growth during the 18th century will have to be revised with caution in the next few years to test the regional differences and their specific rhythms. It is evident that no generalization is valid if we take into account the diversity of the Latin American economies of this period.

The Relation Fiscal Income = Strengthening of Imperial Power

The second great presupposition of traditional historiography concerning the 18th century in Latin America has been to consider that the success of the policies of reform lay in the improvement of the fiscal machinery. The usual conclusion is that the creation of new monopolies, such as of tobacco, the modernization of the administration in order to avoid fraud, putting the accounts in order and abolishing the policy of renting out the different branches of the Real Hacienda, in addition to economic growth, resulted in a spectacular increase in royal income. This interpretation assumes that greater levels of income translate into a strengthening of the imperial machinery and finally a solidification of royal authority on the American continent and a reduction of the political and economic autonomy of the elite Latin Americans.

Next we are going to revise these general suppositions in light of the concrete case of the Real Hacienda of New Spain, considered by Spain to be one of the most "profitable"[3]. The information base that

---

3 Specifically, HUMBOLDT (1966) proposed the idea that the Treasury of Madrid received from the viceroyalty of New Spain between 5 and 6 million pesos annually in cash; one million from Peru; 600,000 from Buenos Aires; between 400,000 and 500,000 from New Granada. The rest of the colonies did not produce net profits which could have been sent to Spain.

we are going to use is that outlined by the important contribution of J. TePaske in collaboration with J. and M. L. Hernandez Palomo (TePaske et al. [1976]), which unites both the year by year and itemized income of the Real Caja de Mexico from 1576 until 1816. It deals with, therefore, known information, used and interpreted on numerous occasions by the same J. TePaske (TePaske [1983]; TePaske [1986]), by H. Klein (Klein [1985]), by J. Coatsworth (Coatsworth [1982]), or recently by B. H. Slicher van Bath (Slicher van Bath [1989]). The change that we have introduced has been to incorporate important accounting modifications as well as in the itemized presentation of the figures themselves.

It must be made clear that the aforementioned amounts for income of the Real Hacienda came to be used fundamentally as economic indicators, that is to say, read and interpreted as figures for production or trade. It is not necessary to remind ourselves that this usage in that time caused a fiery historiographical polemic. Later they began to be thought of as income of the Crown, analyzing their social and political consequences (Coatsworth [1982]). It is evident that from this perspective the difficulties that had been raised concerning their utilization as economic indicators disappear, which does not mean that we should not be cautious of new and not less important problems.

In the first place, one should remember that the aforementioned official amounts for the income of the Real Hacienda, made public by the important contributions of J. TePaske, H. Klein and J. and M. L. Hernandez Palomo (TePaske et al. [1976]; TePaske-Klein [1982] and TePaske-Klein [1986]), hide certain accounting problems, so that they cannot be used as total amounts of cargo (income) without previously making certain adjustments. D. A. Brading (Brading [1985]) and the same J. H. TePaske and H. S. Klein (TePaske-Klein [1986]; TePaske [1983]) indicated that one must keep in mind that:

a) Included in the cargo column were temporary entries of money deposited in the Caja Real and available to the royal officials during a certain period, such as, for example, surplus from the previous year (existencias, alcances de cuenta); unpaid debts (débitos por cobrar); capital deposited as a guarantee that normally was returned once the obligations contracted with the administration were fulfilled (depositos); and temporary loans from individuals to the Crown, which could be withdrawn at a desired or contracted moment by the lender (préstamos).

b) Monies are included that clearly should not be considered net profit, as is the case of those denominated cambio de platas, consisting of the re-minting beginning in 1794 of all pesos de ocho, as well as reales, because what was computed as income ended up, as time passed, used in the task of recasting, becoming an expenditure, so that with few differences (having to pay salaries and the costs of the operation), one can prove that the cargo and the data of this division cancel each other out. Assuredly, some of the deposits cannot be considered as such, as they were not strictly net income, but instead accounting adjustments or in other cases could be removed or transferred at any moment.

It is evident, therefore, that it is not possible to use the total figures for income without previously calculating the net or liquid profits. This job has already been done in part by the same J. TePaske (TePaske [1983]). To find the total net annual profit before 1786 he subtracted from the figures in the cargo column the amounts for existencias, alcances de cuentas, depósitos, préstamos and cambio de platas. After 1786, he subtracted as well the new amount for the Real Hacienda en Común. These figures of "net income" were utilized by J. H. Coatsworth in his detailed revision of the financial foundation of the absolutist colonial state (Coatsworth [1982]). For his part, D. Brading (Brading [1985]) emphasized later the need to adjust the gross totals for income of the Real Hacienda of New Spain, subtracting the depósitos, cambio de placas, real hacienda en común, préstamos and imposiciones de capitales.

J. J. TePaske's resulting figures present in our judgement some problems. In the first place, he does not establish a relation between the columns for cargo and for data to find the so-called "net" by division. For example, he computes the income from alcabalas but without subtracting the administrative expenses of this division or the expenses related to it, that is to say, that which appears in the data of the alcabala division. If what we are looking for is to compute the final net profit (the liquid money left to the Crown), it is obvious that we ought to make these corrections. Secondly, he does not reproduce the structure of the Real Hacienda of the time, so that there is no difference between the income pertaining to the masa común of the extraordinarios, the ajenos, the especiales, the suplementos, the préstamos, etc. The first problem (that of not calculating the net per entry) is not at all important if what we want to do is reconstruct the entries by item, let us suppose, of the mineral or commercial sector, to calibrate the changes in silver production or of the mercantile transactions. However, the second problem (the faulty reproduction of the structure of the Real Hacienda) is fundamental if what we want to do is reconstruct the imperial and vice-regal financial system as it is necessary to remember that the structure of the Real Hacienda of the Old Regime was different from the one that followed, so that it can not be analyzed under the same criteria. Basically, the most important fiscal concept differentiating the Old Regime from the then present one is that during the first period the majority of the different incomes are tied to certain specific expenses, so that it is absolutely necessary to understand their internal structure. In other words, it did not have the same political consequences that the growth or the decrease of the income as a whole would have made in the masa común, or in the extraordinarios, nor as well as if the income was gross or net.

To avoid these problems, we have opted to reconstruct in detail, with the help of the important contribution of A. Lira (Lira [1968]) and information from F. de Fonseca, C. de Urrutia (Fonseca-Urrutia [1845 - 1853]), and J. de Maniau (Maniau [1914]), the structure of the Real Hacienda of New Spain from the year 1750 until the end of the colonial period, at the same time that we have succeeded in calculating the net income for each of the different entries. First, we have grouped together each of the entries in each one of the groups (see table no. 2) in order to reproduce the fiscal structure of the epoch. From the point of view of the financial system of the State, it was not the same if a surplus were produced in one of the divisions of the Masa Común (from which were taken general as well as incidental expenses, salaries, war expenses, pensions, obligations to the King), or if it were produced in Particulares (called this because of having the particular destiny of paying ecclesiastical expenses, as well as for devout works, maintenance of the missions, ecclesiastical salaries, spreading the faith), los Ajenos (given this name for not belonging in theory to the royal patrimony, although they were protected and administrated as public funds by the king "to be disposed of by special attention of His Majesty", and whose product was assigned in advance to a specific end), or the Especiales (composed of special state monopolies such as tobacco, playing cards, and mercury, and whose product was sent directly to Spain). Uniquely, the division of the Real Hacienda en común, created in 1786, did not have assigned monetary egresses. This division was utilized in different ways:

> "for some accountants (...) it served the same function that the extraordinario division had in the past (taking over income or expenses for which there was no existing division). In the other provincial treasuries, the inclusion of the title Real Hacienda en Común, on the credit side, represented the sums available from the various divisions of the Real Hacienda, once expenses were paid, and on the debit side, expenses for which there was no existing division on the credit side, or expenditures from one division greater than what was produced that year in that same division" (TePaske-Klein [1986]).

This division logically increased the fiscal autonomy of the viceroy by reducing the number of expenses assigned in advance to each division.

Subsequently, we proceeded to calculate the net income of each division in particular, in doing so subtracting from the credit column (cargo) the amounts that with the same name appear in the debits (data), composed of the administrative expenses of the same division and of the specific expenses assigned in advance. In theory, we would only be able to call product "net" (from an accounting point of view) that belonging to the divisions of Masa Común and Especiales, as only in these do the administrative expenses of the same division appear in the Data column, the expenses which were assigned for guerra, situados, and sueldos having already been separated. One must remember that the doubleentry system in the royal accounts was set up in Mexico in 1786, but was abandoned in 1789, for causing "serious conflicts", according to the accountants, although we do not know if said problems were real or if the new system brought certain disorders in the accounting out into the open which they wanted to cover up.

The totals for "net income" calculated by J. TePaske do not coincide with ours for different reasons (see appendix for statistics). J. TePaske calculates "net income" up until the year 1786 adding the "gross" income (that is to say, the income before deducting administrative expenses and related expenses) from the divisions of ordinarios, extraordinarios, imposición de capitales and otras tesorerias (TePaske [1983]). After this date, the time in which the accounting problems become complicated due to the introduction of new administrations, the opening of new treasuries and the application of the double-entry system, J. TePaske does not explain in detail how he calculates his "net", so that it is difficult to reproduce his calculations. Up until 1786 our results and those of TePaske are practically in line with each other, although our net totals are logically somewhat less due to the subtraction of datas from cargos under the same heading (see appendix for statistics). After 1786 the differences increase, proven by the fact that from 1795 onwards our "net" totals are larger than those calculated by J. TePaske (see table no. 17). As we will demonstrate later, this is due to the variations in the costs of the colonial administration.

Unlike TePaske, we first calculated the "net" of each division, subtracting from the "credits" the "debits" with the same name and then made the corresponding accounting adjustments. To the total of the joint net product of the divisions of ordinarios, extraordinarios and "plus"[4], we added the net products of the divisions of ajuste de cuentas, buenas cuentas, cambio de placas and depósitos. In this way we have solved the problems of double accounting and the temporary condition of some divisions (cambio de placas, depósitos, préstamos). Finally, we corrected these "nets" with the totals of compensatory payments made between the Caja de México and the provincial branches (otras tesorerías), as well as with the amounts of existencias.

We have divided expenditure into two large blocks. On one hand are the particulares (administrative expenses and permanently assigned to each division) and temporales (temporary expenses assigned to each division by royal authority), which the colonial accounting presents as a unit, so that it is not possible to differentiate one from the other. The division total for this type of expense we subtracted from the income of the same name in order to calculate the net by division. On the other hand are the general expenditures, or perpetuos (general expenses for administration and defense, which appear specified in the entries for General y sueldos, guerra and situados) which although assigned in principle and theoretically only to the income of the Masa Común, appear in the colonial accounting separately because in practice they were an expense shared to a great extent by the ajenos and especiales divisions when they were greater than the income of the masa común, an event which occurred constantly from 1795 onwards, when these expenditures increased and ordinary income fell. Later, to these aforementioned "perpetuos"", and in order to calculate the total general expenditure, we have added the débitos atrasados and from 1786 onwards, the new division Real Hacienda en Común, which, it may he remembered, acted in certain circumstances as a division which combined all those payments or income which did not have a specific entry.

---

4 We have called income "Plus" if it was generated through préstamos, imposiciones de capitales and donativos, as we are unable to call this group "extraordinarios" or "especiales" because these titles already exist for other divisions. For more details, see the attached table showing the fiscal structure of New Spain during the 18th century.

In order to accurately reproduce the financial structure of New Spain, we have made all statistical calculations and computations of the material by computer, using the programs Lotus and Harvard-Graphics. The utilization of a double-entry data system has allowed us to verify the exactitude of the completed calculations and to eliminate problems of "double-accounting", compensatory payments between different treasuries, adverse balances of the accounts, overdue debts, stocks, deposits, etc. (see attached appendix). We have not considered it opportune to deflated the amounts, converting them into constant values instead of current prices, due to the fact that our objective is to find a relation between the behavior of the different types of income and the different kinds of expenses, rather than the utilization of these numbers as economic indicators.

From the quantitative information calculated in this way one can arrive at many conclusions. Due to the lack of space, we will only point out the most important ones.

In general terms we can establish three large epochs: a) the first, which goes from 1750 - 1780, in which net income and total expenditure grow smoothly in a parallel and nearly constant manner; b) a second epoch taking place between 1781 and 1795 in which the net income and perpetual expenses (general administration of the viceroyalty, war and situados) have a clear tendency to decrease, while the expenditure for temporales and particulares (administration profits and assigned expenses) grow in a comparatively clear way; and c) a final period understood as between 1796 and 1816 (when as a consequence of the wars of independence information ceases) in which the net income grows almost vertically, at the same time as does total expenditure. Let us analyze in greater detail each one of these periods.

A) Period 1750 - 1780

During this period the following characteristics may be observed:

1) Net income runs parallel to gross income, which signifies that a constant relation existed between income and administrative expenses

(see diagram no. 4). In other words, the increase in gross income was accompanied by an increase of the same proportion in expenditure. Since there was no alteration of the structure of income and expenditure, it would seem as if the mild increase of both reflected, apart from the evident administrative improvements as a consequence of the creation of the Tribunal de Cuentas in 1776, the slow, consistent inflationary process of the century (remember that the numbers that we have been using are in current values and not in constant ones), as well as an increase in general economic activity.

2) The principle source of net total income is ordinary income, with only small amounts corresponding to extraordinary income in comparative terms (see diagram nos. 5 and 7). If we now take a closer look at the composition of the ordinary income during this period, we see that it is for the most part made up of income from the masa común (see diagram no. 6). All of this means that the income from particulares, ajenos and especiales do not play an important role in the financing of the structure of the viceroyalty. They only took on a special function during the wars of the 1760's (Seven Years War [1754 - 1762]), when military expenditure increased beyond the normal level. In other words, there was an equilibrium between income and expenditure that was maintained even in periods of crisis. Ordinary income financed the costs of the colonial enterprise, so that it is not surprising that income bearing the title "plus" does not even appear during this period. The minimum of accounting adjustments made show the fiscal order that was reached during this period.

The perpetual expenditures make up the largest percentage of the total expenditure, and within these the military expenses are the most important (see diagrams nos. 13 and 15). This means that, administrative expenses staying more or less stable, both temporal and particular, adjustments of the deficit were made through the control of military expenses.

B) Period 1781 - 1795

During the second period, the financial behavior of the previous three decades changes completely. In broad terms, net total income and general perpetuos (general administration of the viceroyalty, war expenses, situados) decrease, while administrative and related expenses from temporales and particulares increase. Let us look at this in more detail:

1) Ordinary income, which continued to be the most important source of income, fell throughout this period, experiencing sudden drops which became more and more serious, as in the years 1782, 1784, 1786, 1787, and culminating in the worrisome descent of 1795 - 1796, when ordinary net income was reduced to a little over one million pesos (see diagram no. 5). This was not due to a decrease in gross income as much as fundamentally an increase in administrative expenses (gasto temporal y particular), showing that after a certain point the net profits obtained were decreasing (see diagrams nos. 12, 13, 14 and 15). Every new weight thrown into the fiscal basket meant a greater expenditure that reduced net income. Unfortunately for the reformers, the problems did not end here, as from 1786 until the year 1795, the Real Caja de México had to finance with important amounts of money the creation of the new Cajas Reales (Chihuahua in 1785; Michoacan in 1788; Puebla in 1789; Oaxaca in 1790 and Saltillo in 1794) and the institution from 1786 onwards of what turned out to be the extremely costly new management system. During these years, the provincial treasuries, instead of sending resources to the chief Caja in Mexico City, which was the function for which they had in theory been created, absorbed important sums of hard cash originating in Mexico City (see diagram no. 10). This means that the capital of the viceroyalty financed the costs of the administrative reorganization in the provinces instead of acting as the recipient of net profits.

2) The colonial government, led by José de Galvez from the Secretaría de Indias in Spain until 1787, and in order to finance the costly political and administrative reforms of the Bourbons [remember that this is

the epoch which saw the introduction of a new management system, the creation of the Comandancia General de las Provincias Internas (created in 1776 and modified successively in 1785, 1787, 1792, 1804, and 1812) and when the most important administrative changes were put into ef fect] and faced with the fall of net ordinary income and the growing increase in administrative costs (expenditure temporal y particular), tried desperately to increase net income: a) creating new divisions, such as the especiales (tobacco, cards, and mercury); b) strengthening extraordinary income (extraordinarios, suplementos, préstamos, imposición de capitales, donativos and especiales); and c) cutting perpetuos.

The net income from the especiales division began to occupy an important position, reaching in some years (1781 - 1785) almost 50 percent of all ordinary income (see diagram no. 6). However, this bonanza was not very long lasting, as from 1785 onward this income began to decrease in an accelerating manner.

On one hand, net extraordinary income and in particular: the division of this same name (extraordinario) grew notably from 1779 on, but, as was true in the previous case, decreased once again starting in 1785 (see diagrams nos. 7 and 8). The exceptional recourse of obliging the elite Americans to contribute directly to the colonial costs proved to have a poor reception, because only in 1782 was there a significant net income (3.656.116 pesos) gained through préstamo, so that later this division even produced negative profits. On the other hand, income under donativos and imposiciones de capitales were minimal (see diagram no. 9). The Spanish reformist government was not able to extract extra resources from the American elite, who resisted financing the new Bourbon colonialist policies.

The perpetuo expenditure and especially the military portion, which had undergone a worrisome ascent between 1779 and 1785, was restricted almost 100 percent, defense spending falling in a vertical manner (they fell to less than one-half million pesos in 1794) (see diagram nos. 13 and 15). As one may remember, given the structure of expenditure in the previous period, the reduction in military spending was the only way to adjust the deficit.

However, all of these recourses were not sufficient nor did they maintain the constancy necessary to combat the growing deficit resulting from administrative costs that had multiplied by seven between 1774 and 1790 (see diagram no. 14).

3) From the general fiscal point of view of Spain, this era can be seen as a failure, but from the perspective of the entirety of the economy of New Spain, it can be interpreted as an era in which administrative costs fell inside the borders of the viceroyalty, so that consumption increased. The decrease in the official exportations of silver from the Real Hacienda to Spain between 1780 and 1795 (Pérez Herrero [1988], p. 187) demonstrated the growth of surplus in the viceroyalty (see table no. 18). From this view, one would have to begin to rethink if the change of direction of the Bourbon policies did not end up precisely helping the elite Americans instead of Spain, the reforms being converted into a potent mechanism for redistribution of wealth. The profits suctioned off by the Real Hacienda, instead of being sent to the peninsula, were redistributed in a high percentage within the viceroyalty itself, favoring very specific social groups, such as those on salary from the new administrative posts, parties to the new troop supply contracts (food and clothing), public works contracts (paving, lighting, highways, bridges, ports, etc.) or those chosen to benefit in the monopoly of now productions such as tobacco, or of the transport of mercury, to cite only some classic examples. It is not surprising, therefore, that the American elite, if they were benefitting from the increase in colonial expenditure, did not see it opportune to utilize the mechanisms of loans or "'donations" (in order to get interest on their capital, fiscal exemptions, and priority political treatment), nor did they protest against the increase- in fiscal pressure, the Real Hacienda having been converted into a potent means of redistributing profits which they were even able control to some degree.

This important aspect of the political and financial telationship between Spain and the American elite remained totally hidden by manipulation of gross income instead of net (see diagram no. 4). For this reason also the totals of the "net" income calculated by J. TePaske do not show a fall between 1785 and 1795 but instead a slow recuperation (see diagram no. 17).

C) Period 1796 - 1816

Finally, during the third period, the relationship between the different variables in the composition of income, expenditure and of both together changed again.

1) One can observe that the net ordinary income started to decrease in 1799, after having experienced an important although transient growth during the years 1797 - 1798, perhaps due to the introduction of some new accounting methods, while the extraordinary income ("plus") grew spectacularly starting in 1798 (see diagrams nos. 5 and 8). As a consequence to the beginning of the war, the special taxes (suplementos) designed to finance the military costs increased notably and in a continuous manner starting in 1808.

By analyzing the behavior of the net ordinary income in more detail, one can detect that the income pertaining to the masa común, after a profound crisis in 1795 - 1796 and a rapid rise in 1797 - 1798 (both processes perhaps reflect variations in accounting practices), had a clear tendency to decrease. On the other hand, the income from particulares (destined for ecclesiastical expenses), after an inexplicable rise in 1797 - 1798 (they go up from an average of two million to ten million pesos annually), stayed practically stable with a slight inclination to rise, very possibly a reflection of an inflationary process. The income from especiales (mercury, tobacco, and playing cards), after the net losses of the years 1795 and 1796, caused by an increase in administrative costs in this division, grew from 1798 - 1802 to later decrease almost to the point of disappearing, due this time to the reduction in gross income more than an elevation in administrative costs. The income from ajenos (which although did not pertain to the royal patrimony, was protected and administered as public assets by the King, its product pre-assigned) was the only that clearly had an ascending tendency until 1808, when it began to decrease due to the political upheaval (see table no. 6).

From the above it can be concluded that the capacity to extract net fiscal benefits on the Crown's part fell across the board during this third period. Gross income rose as a result of economic activity, the increase in fiscal pressure, and the inflationary process, but at the same time, administrative costs (temporales and particulares) grew at a faster pace, devouring these profits (see table no. 14). Only in the case of ajenos was net income rising due to the fact that administrative costs did not grow with the same velocity. It is ironic to find that the net ordinary income descended while the economy of New Spain was experiencing, according to the traditional interpretation, its highest hour.

2) It can be observed that the Crown, faced with the decrease in this income and an important fiscal deficit, chose to: a) ask for help from the Latin American elite in the form of loans, forced and voluntary, to finance the deficit; b) juggle with the public debt promising interests to whomever wanted to invest his savings; c) impose supplementary taxes once military problems started; d) invert the relationship between the Caja de México and the provincial branches in order to transform the negative balance into a positive one; and e) try to reduce expenditure as much as possible. Let us look at each point in more detail.

By analyzing the total evolution of this income, one can prove easily that, as was said previously, it was the extraordinary income, and more specifically préstamos and the imposición de capitales, that was responsible for the growth in the net total income (see table nos. 5, 7, 8 and 9). Here is precisely where resides one of the important differences between our calculations and those offered by J. TePaske (see table no. 17). Upon incorporating this income (préstamos and imposición de capitales) that, as we have just seen, was of capital importance during this period, our totals are higher in general than those offered by Tepaske. The Crown opted to finance the deficit with easy, fast money, although it is true that to do this it had to pay a high political price such as was the concession of exemptions and priority treatment. The elite of New Spain took advantage of the opportunity to take these favors from Spain, at the same time investing their capital, benefitting from the public debt, and regaining the political autonomy which the Gálvez administration had tried to take away in the previous period. It remains to be resolved why the elite of New Spain decided to collaborate in the financing of the deficit precisely from 1798 on, but everything seems to indicate that it was due to, on one hand, the variations in their interests, and on the other, the change in the conditions offered by the administration in Spain. When, as has been shown by Coatsworth (Coatsworth [1986]), the profitability of mineral production began to decrease due to increases in production costs and the fall in the value of silver in international markets, the elite investors of New Spain began to discover that playing this market could be an alternative recourse, favored additionally by the traditional conception of "security of the State" (Pérez Herrero [1988], p. 206).

At the same time, if during the time of Charles III's government they had tried to manage American affairs from a position of force without granting many concessions, the situation changed radically during the reign of Charles IV. Remember, for example, that once José de Gálvez, minister of the Secretaria de Indias, was dead (1787), politics as relating to the colonies changed direction. American af fairs began to be dealt with by each of the corresponding departments (Estado, Gracia y Justicia, Guerra, Marina and Hacienda). Very possibly, the situation created by the closure of Atlantic commerce between 1797 and 1804 due to the war against England served, for the elite Latin American locals, as a way to win a high margin of economic autonomy by utilizing the "neutrales"' system of commerce. To this we can add that in 1796 American merchants were conceded the freedom to send out ships on their own to the peninsula. This was in practice a veiled legalization of a regimen of true free commerce, much more benign and fabricated for American interests than had been the previous Reglamento de Comercio Libre of October 12, 1778, officially applied to New Spain in 1789.

Whatever the explanation may be, the unquestionable fact is that the elite Americans decided to collaborate in the financing of the colonial deficit, an affair that they had avoided before. It is evident that the existing relationship as defined by the colonial contract varied during this period, as opposed to that which is traditionally stated, in favor of American interests. Once the New Spanish elite found that they had gained an important degree of economic and political autonomy, the distance to the transition to independence had been substantially shortened.

As a parallel recourse in order to reduce the deficit, the Crown tried to invert the existing relationship between the Caja de Mexico and the provincial branches, so that the branches would send profits to the capital and not the other way around, as had been the practice up to that time (see diagram no. 10). Notwithstanding, if we discount the brief experience of 1797, they were not able to see the fruits of this until 1803, when the Caja de México finally began to receive monetary benefits from its branches. Without a doubt, they succeeded in making the provinces finance the fiscal imbalances of México City. From this point of view, it would not be by chance that an anti-centralist resentment was created that would explode violently into the wars of independence and that would be utilized with different ends during the first half of the 19th century.

As a final means of increasing extraordinary recourses, once the independence movements had begun, fiscal pressure was increased, raising old taxes or creating new ones (suplementos, see diagram no. 8).

With respect to the policy of controlling expenditure, another of the measures taken to reduce the deficit, it can be shown that it was a battle lost in good measure from the start. Inside the general structure of expenditure, it can be clearly observed that while the perpetuo and the temporal-particular could be controlled to a certain point and except for in certain years, the new expense of the Real Hacienda en común shot up in an apparently uncontrolled manner from 1797 on (see diagram no. 13). Before moving to the detailed analysis of each of these respective behaviors, it is necessary to underline that it is extremely complicated to establish with precision any interpretation of the variations in expenditure in this period, due precisely to the appearance of the new division: Real Hacienda en Común. By serving in part, as was explained earlier, the same function as the old division extraordinario, that is to say, incorporating income or expenses for which there was no existing division, it is practically impossible to know which of these was the destination of this expenditure using the summaries of the Real Hacienda's accounts. Very possibly the Crown, in order to gain greater autonomy in the management of the Real Hacienda, preferred to create this division in which the expenditures and income would not be interdependent, that is to say, each income would not have a specific expenditure assigned to it. The fact that the largest percentage of the income was of extraordinary character (that they did not have pre-assigned expenditures) aided in this process. The result is that one must ask if the lack of growth in the expenditures perpetuo and temporal-particular was derived from the growth of the expenditure in the Real Hacienda en Común, or said in another way, if the growth of the latter was not connected with the decrease of the former. At present it is impossible, with existing information, to respond to these questions.

The total perpetuo expenditure was able to be controlled until 1805, when it grew markedly without shrinking again until 1810 (see diagram no. 15). Unlike what might be thought at first, the total war expenditure was maintained at a low level until 1807, in which it doubled. Expenditures for situados (remittances of cash to other administrations with a deficit, such as the Comandancia General de las Provincias Internas de la Nueva España, the Antillian and Caribbean area, and the Philippines) grew appreciably between 1796 and 1808, precisely the times when ordinary income had a tendency to drop. As a consequence, we could deduce that the obligations that the Hacienda of New Spain had regarding the other imperial regions helped to enlarge the deficit of the viceroyalty, which would be taken advantage of by the elite for their own profit, as we saw. For their part, the general administrative costs were held under control until the period 1802 - 1809, in which they multiplied by an average of five.

The total temporal y particular expenditure (remember that we always use figures in today's values) showed a clear tendency to rise, albeit with strong annual oscillations, such as the increases of 1796 - 1799, 1802, 1804 and 1808 - 1809 (see diagram no. 14). The date of 1808 can be explained easily, as the new political conditions increased total expenditure and therefore administrative costs. That of 1804 can be understood by the costs of the Consolidación de Vales Reales. However, those of 1796 - 1799 and 1802 are more difficult to explain.

The expenditure of the Real Hacienda en Común appeared suddenly in 1797, doubling or tripling, according to the year, the rest of the expenditures (see diagram no. 13). Aside from the difficulty in analyzing this expenditure and its connection with the rest, one can observe a parallelism between the evolution of expenditure in the Real Hacienda en Común and the curve of extraordinary income (see diagram no. 7). Certainly there seems to be no doubt that the new expenditures at the end of the colonial period were financed with extraordinary resources.

3) Evidently, and following even the most conservative and concealing calculations of the decapitalization that New Spain began to experience starting in the decade of 1790[5], the official extractions of currency realized by the Real Hacienda grew markedly from 1795 on (see diagram no. 18). In this case the exceptionally strong differences

---

5 We have used the lowest figures for the exports of cash made by the Real Hacienda, which are those found in the document entitled Icaza (AHH [Mexico], 395 - 397 and AHH [Mexico] 397 - 399). A detailed analysis of this source and a quantitative reproduction ofits calculations can be seen in PÉREZ HERRERO 1988, pp. 165 - 194.

between one and the other can be explained by the state of maritime commerce, for when the state of war required it , the commercial flow was held up to await more favorable conditions, as can be precisely proven by the figures of existencias, whose maximums coincide exactly with those years in which the extractions were delayed (see diagram no. 10).

This relation between net income and exportation of cash on behalf of the Real Hacienda show clear differences from the previous period, when, as one may remember, we emphasized that an important percentage of expenditure was realized in New Spain. The consequences of this change were important, as on one hand it helped to speed the decapitalization process, and on the other hand it showed the elite locals of New Spain that: a) a good part of the total amount of their loans were exported in order to be invested in other American regions (situados) or in Spain, but not in the vice-royalty, as it had in the past; and b) that in exchange for the loans, the Crown mortgaged as a guarantee certain divisions such as especiales (mercury, tobacco and playing cards) which clearly had income on the low side. Ef we add to this, as Coatsworth (1982) demonstrated, that the most intense total economic growth in the viceroyalty was produced in the first half of the 18th century and not at the end of the century, we will be in a position to value the consequences of the transformations in the described income-expenditure-exportation relationship. The consequence followed soon after. From 1804 on, the monies obtained through voluntary loans clearly began to decrease. The Crown, faced with the urgency of the deficit, did not hesitate, although conscious of the consequences that came along with it, to utilize ecclesiastical capital, introducing the Consolidación de Vales Reales, and in imposing obligatory loans (Stein [1983]). Thus, from 1805 on, and evidently before 1808, when there was a power vacuum caused by the famous abdication at Bayonne, both the elite investors of New Spain and the highest ecclesiastical representatives put themselves clearly against the policies of the government in Spain. The occupation of Spain by Napoleon and the absence of the monarch in 1808 was, in a way, the straw that broke the camel's back, instead of the origin of a process, as it has been interpreted traditionally. When Gabriel de Yermo, in the night of the 16th of September of 1808, struck against the viceroy Iturrigaray, it was evident that the traditional colonial contract between Crown, Church, and elite locals had been broken some time before. When the Church and the elite discovered that both were in disagreement with the Spanish government policies and, more importantly, no longer needed them as a means of redistributing wealth, independence seemed inevitable.

Conclusions

It appears that the thesis of continuous and accelerating growth under the Bourbons should be reconsidered in light of this criticism of the existing official numbers. Once the technical problems have been solved, it remains to continue digging deeply into the causes of the growth and of the links with administrative and political reforms. At present, in the case of New Spain, some have begun to reinterpret (Coatsworth [1978]; Coatsworth [1982]; Coatsworth [1986]; Pérez Herrero [1990]) the existing official tallies, with unquestionable results, although evidently it will be necessary to continue working to overcome some technical details and to continue gathering information, but these will not substantially change the most important conclusions. Through this work we now know that if we adjust the official coinage totals using the price of silver in the international market, we prove that silver production in the viceroyalty of New Spain during the second half of the 18th century, measured in constant values (and not in nominal values, current values or in kilograms) did not have the spectacular rise which the official numbers emphasize, and that it even decreased at the end of the colonial era before the independence movements began and not as a result of them.

We also know that the highest rate of economic growth, in the case of New Spain, was produced in the first half of the 18th century and not in the second (Pérez Herrero [1991]), so that we must now modify the thesis that reforms caused it, at least in this region. To summarize, one can not continue arguing that the economic growth was constant, of a growing nature, and true throughout the 18th century for the entire Latin American area, and was caused by the introduction of reformist measures. Additional regional studies will have to clarify local differences.

Regarding the links between fiscal income and strengthening of the imperial establishment, it can be proven, at least again in the case given of New Spain, that the triumphal interpretations of the 18th century and the liberal ones of the 19th century have systematically concealed socio-political behaviors of a rather more complex nature. Upon analyzing in detail the structure and evolution in the relationship between income and public expenditure in the viceroyalty of New Spain, we discover that, in contrary to what has been maintained until this date, during the period of 1780 - 1795 the greater percentage of the net profits or the complicated administrative and fiscal reforms ended up with the elite colonials instead of the Spanish government. Gross income increased, but at the same time and with a greater intensity so did public spending, which enables it to be proven that the Real Hacienda was used by the elite colonials to their advantage as potent means of redistributing income. In the following period of 1796 - 1816, the fiscal deficit created by the increase in expenditure and the reduction of net income was covered basically with the help of loans conceded by the elite subjects of the viceroyalty. When the expenditure began to be realized outside of the borders of the viceroyalty and the divisions mortgaged to guarantee the loans were losing value due to the inflationary process and the growth in administrative costs, they began to see the disadvantages in their relationship with Spain which offered little in return.

In essence, it would seem that the famous Bourbon success did not reach the "mythic" intensity given it by traditional historiography and therefore that the "force" of the metropolitan government depended in this period not so much on its capacity to extract fiscal profits, but rather on the willingness of the local elite to "donate" resources in exchange for economic protection and for political and ideological justification of their colonial structure. The interpretative consequences which can be derived are important, since one may then suggest that if there was a strengthening of the imperial structure, it was not so much due to the capacity of Spain to control as much as to the agreement of the powerful Latin American elite to maintain the status quo. The interests of the Elite, Government, and Church had been intertwined throughout the colonial period. The Bourbons recklessly broke this equilibrium.

Bibliography

BAKEWELL, Peter J. (1975): Registered silver production in the Potosi district, 1550 - 1735, in: *Jahrbuch für Geschichte von Staat, Wirtschaft und Gesellschaft Lateinamerikas* 12, pp. 67 - 103.

BRADING, David A. (1985): Facts and figments in Bourbon Mexico, in: *Bulletin of Latin American Research* 4/1, pp. 61 - 64.

------ (1987): Bourbon Spain and its American Empire, in: L. BETHELL (ed)., Colonial Spanish America, Cambridge, pp. 112 - 162.

BURKHOLDER, Mark A. and Lyman L. JOHNSON (1990): Colonial Latin America, Oxford.

COATSWORTH, John H. (1978): Obstacles to Economic Growth in Nineteenth-Century Mexico, in: *American Historical Review* 83/1 (Traducido al castellano en J. H. Coatsworth [1990]).

------ (1982): The limits of Colonial Absolutism. The State in EighteenthCentury Mexico, in: Karen SPALDING (ed.), Essays in the Political Economic and Social History of Colonial America, Newark, pp. 25 - 51 (Traducido al castellano en J. H. Coatsworth [1990]).

------ (1986): The mexican mining industry in the Eighteenth-Century, in: JACOBSEN-PÜHLE (1986), pp. 26 - 45 (Traducido al castellano en J. H. Coatsworth [1990]).

------ (1990): Los orígenes del atraso. Nueve ensayos de historia económica de México en los siglos XVIII y XIX, México.

CHAUNU, Pierre and Huguette CHAUNU (1959 - 1969): Seville et l'Atlantique, 12 vols., Paris.

FISHER, John (1977): Silver mines and silver miners in colonial Peru, 1776 - 1824, Liverpool.

------ (1985): Commercial relations between Spain and Spanish America in the Era of Free Trade 1778 - 1796, Liverpool.

------ (1990): Iberoamérica colonial (1700 - 1808), in: M. LUCENA SALMORAI (Coord.), Historia de Iberoamérica, vol. II, Madrid, pp. 549 - 662.

FLORESCANO, Enrique (1969): Precios del maíz y crisis agrícolas en México (1798 - 1810), México.

FLORESCANO, Enrique and Isabel GIL (1977): La época de las reformas borbónicas y el crecimiento económico, 1750 - 1808, in: D. COSÍO VILLEGAS (Coord.), Historia General de México, 4 vols., México, vol. II, pp. 183 - 301.

FONSECA, Fabian de and Carlos DE URRUTIA (1845 - 1853): Historia General de Real Hacienda, 6 vols., México.

GARAVAGLIA, Juan Carlos and Juan Carlos GROSSO (1985): Estado borbónico y presión fiscal en la Nueva España 1750 - 1821, México.

GARCÍA-BAQUERO, Antonio (1976): Cádiz y el Atlántico. El comercio colonial español bajo el monopolio gaditano, 2 vols., Sevilla.

GARCÍA FUENTES, Lutgargo (1980): El comercio español con América, 1650 - 1700, Sevilla.

GARNER, Richard L. (1985): Price Trends in Eighteenth-Century México, in: *Hispanic American Historical Review* 65/2, pp. 279 - 325.

HUMBOLDT, Alejandro de (1966): Ensayo político sobre el Reino de la Nueva España, México.

JACOBSEN, N. and H. J. PÜHLE (eds.) (1986): The economies of México and Peru during the late colonial Period, 1760 - 1810, Berlin.

JOHNSON, Lyman L. and Enrique TANDETER (eds.) (1990): Essays on the price history of eighteenth-century Latin America, Albuquerque.

KLEIN, Herbert (1985): La economía de la Nueva España, 1680 - 1809: un análisis a partir de las Cajas Reaies", in: *Historia Mexicana* 34/4, pp. 561 - 609.

LAFKY, J. D. (1964): Silver: National and International Problems, Ph.D. University of Texas.

LERDO DE TEJADA, Miguel (1853): Comercio exterior de México, México.

LIRA, Andrés (1968): Aspecto fiscal de la Nueva España en la segunda mitad del siglo XVIII, in: *Historia Mexicana* XVII/3, pp. 361 - 394.

LYNCH, John (1973): The Spanish American revolutions 1808 - 1826, New York.

------ (1989): Bourbon Spain, 1700 - 1808, Oxford.

MANIAU, Joaquín (1914): Compendio de la Historia de la Real Hacienda de Nueva España, México.

ORTIZ DE LA TADLA, Javier (1978): Comercio exterior de Veracruz 1778 - 1821. Crisis de dependencia, Sevilla.

OUWENEEL, A. and C. J. H. BIJLEVELD (1989): The economic cycle in Bourbon Central México. A critique of the recaudacion del diezmo liquido en pesos, in: *Hispanic American Historical Review* 69/3, pp. 479 - 530.

PÉREZ HERRERO, Pedro (1988): Plata y libranzas, México.

------ (1989): El crecimiento económico novohispano durante el siglo XVIII. Una revisión, in: *Revista de Historia Económica* VII/1, pp. 69 - 110.

------ (1990): *Crecimiento* colonial versus *crisis* nacional (México 1765 - 1854). Consideraciones acerca de un modelo explicativo (Ponencia presentada a la VIII Conference of Mexican and North American Historians), San Diego, CA. (en prensa).

SALVUCCI, Richard and Linda SALVUCCI (1987): Crecimiento económico y cambio de la productividad en México, 1750 - 1895, in: *HISLA* X, pp.67 - 89.

SHAW, W. A. (1896): The history of the currency 1252 to 1894, New York.

SLICHER VAN BACH, B. J. (1989): Real Hacienda y economia en Hispanoamérica, 1541-1820, Amsterdam.

STEIN, Stanley J. (1983): Prelude to upheaval in Spain and New Spain, 1800 -1808: Trust funds, Spanish finance and colonial silver, in: *Bibliotheca Americana* 1/3, pp. 273 - 298.

TEPASKE, John J. (1983): Economic Cycles in New Spain in the Eighteenth Century: The view from the Public Sector, in: *Bibliotheca Americana* I/3, pp. 171 - 204 (Reimpreso con el mismo título en R. GARNER y W. TAYLOR (comps.) (1985), Iberian colonies, New world societies: Essays in Memory of Charles Gibson, publicación privada.

------ (1986): General tendencies and secular trends in the economies of México and Peru, 1750 - 1810: The view from the Cajas of México and Lima, in: JACOBSEN-PÜHLE (1986), pp. 316 - 339.

TEPASKE, John J. et al. (1976): La Real Hacienda de Nueva España: la Real Caja de México (1576 - 1816), México 1976.

TEPASKE, John and Herbert S. KLEIN (1982): Royal Treasuries of the Spanish Empire in America, 3 vols., Durham N.C.

------ (1986): Ingresos y Egresos de la Real Hacienda de Nueva España, 2 vols., México.

WALKER, Geoffrey J. (1979): Política española y comercio colonial 1700 - 1789, Barcelona.

NEW SPAIN FISCAL INCOME STRUCTURE

A) ORDINARIOS

1) Masa Común:
Directos: Tributos, lanzas, Media Anata secular, Novenos, Bienes, Comunidades.
Indirectos: Casa de Moneda, Apartado, Diezmo, Derechos Oro, Ensaye, Cobre, Vajilla, Perlas, Pólvora, Afinación, Alumbres; Alcabalas, Aguardiente, Almojarifazgo, Armada Barlovento, Averia, Buques, Caldos Pulperías, Vino, Grana, Añil, Vainilla, Seda, Aguardiente, Pulques.
Penas-Confiscaciones: Comisos, Confiscaciones, Multas, Embargos, Espolios.
Bienes de la Corona:Tierras: Salinas, Minerales.
Bienes Mostrencos: Mostrencos.
Empresas del Estado: Papel Sellado Fábrica Palacio, Oficios vendibles y renunciables, Chancillerla, Cordobanes, Censos, Composiciones Tierras, Sal, Lastre, Correo Nieve, Gallos, Aprovechamientos, Factoría.
Sin Clasificación: Otros.

2) Particulares:
Directos: Diezmos Eclesiásticos, Mesadas, Media Anata eclesiástica.
Penas-Confiscaciones: Penas de Cámara.
Sin Clasificación: Subsidio eclesiástico Vacantes, Bulas Cruzada Sínodo Misiones, Fábrica Iglesia.

3) Ajenos:
Directos: Inválidos, Monte Pío, Medio Real de Ministros.
Indirectos: Muralla, Sisa, Bebidas Prohibidas, Desagüe Huehuetoca.
Mixtos: Fábrica polvora, Señoreaje.
Penas-Confiscaciones: Remisible a España, Espolios.
Bienes Difuntos: Intestados.
Empresas del Estado: Depósitos, Asignaciones, Productos, Redención de cautivos Particulares.
Sin Clasificación: California, Temporalidades, Hospital, Mezcales, Sisa.

4) Especiales: Tabaco, Naipes, Azogue.

5) Juros/Vales: Banco Nacional de San Carlos, Juros, Amortización, Consolidación.

B) EXTRAORDINARIOS

1) Extra:
Extraordinario: Extraordinario.
Suplementos: Arbitrio extraordinario, Subvención, Suplementos.

2) Plus:
Prestamos: Prestamos.
Imposición de Capitales: Imposición capitales.
Donativos: Donativos
Especial: Real Hacienda en Común

C) OTRAS TESORERIAS: Otras tesorerías.

D) TRANSITORIOS:
Cambio de platas
Depósitos

E) AJUSTE CUENTAS:
Alcance de cuentas
Buenas Cuentas
Débitos atrasados
Existencia

NEW SPAIN FISCAL EXPENDITURE STRUCTURE

A) PERPETUO [gastos generales]
General y sueldos
Guerra
Situados

B) TEMPORAL [transitorios adscritos a cada ramo por disposición soberana]

C) PARTICULAR [de administración y permanentes adscritos a cada ramo]

D) REAL HACIENDA EN COMUN

E) DEBITOS ATRASADOS

G) OTRAS TESORERIAS

Diagram 1:
Total de amonedaciones en Nueva España y Potosí
(cifras oficiales, valores corrientes)

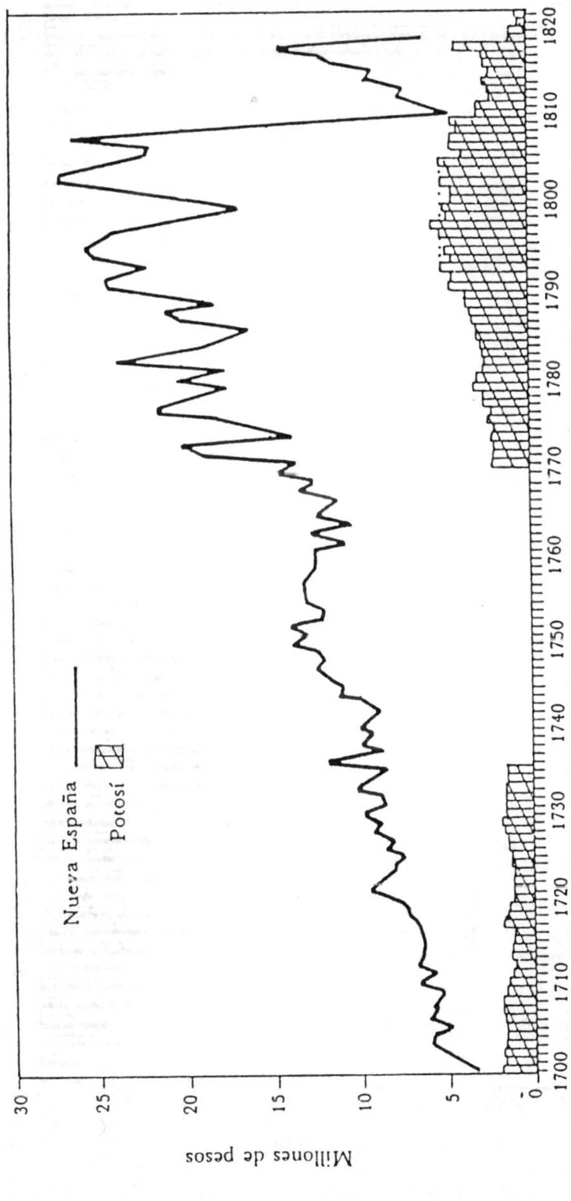

FUENTES: NE-PÉREZ HERRERO, 1988; POTOSÍ-FISHER, 1977; BAKEWELL, 1975.

Diagram 2:
Comercio atlántico entre España-América Latina
(número de barcos)

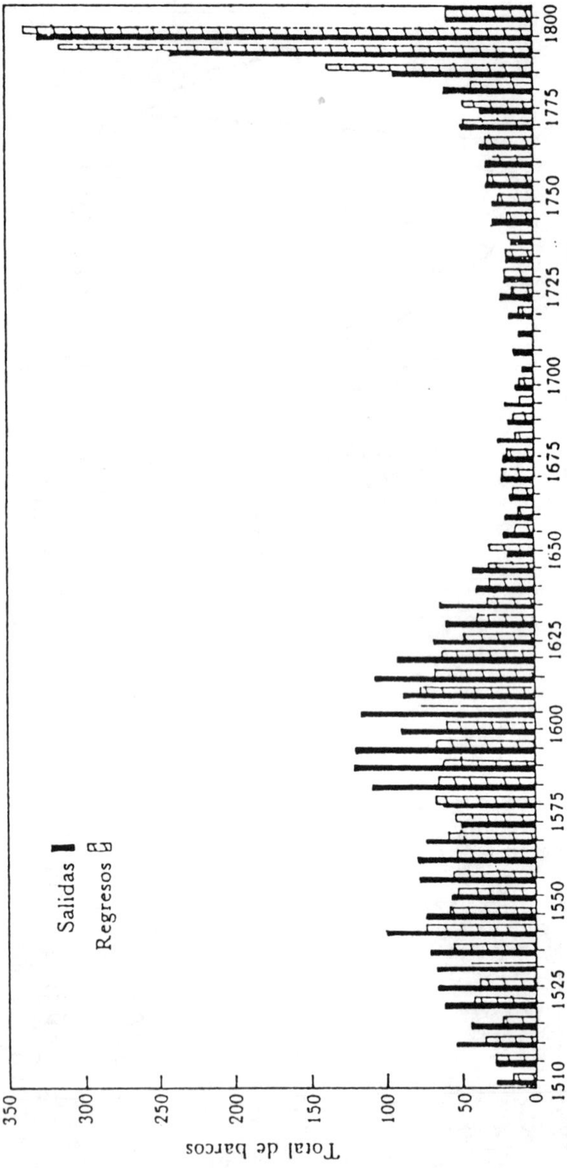

FUENTES: CHAUNU, 1959-1969; GARCÍA FUENTES, 1980; WALKER, 1979; GARCÍA-BAQUERO, 1976; FISHER, 1985.

Diagram 3:
Ingresos brutos en Nueva España y Perú
(precios corrientes)

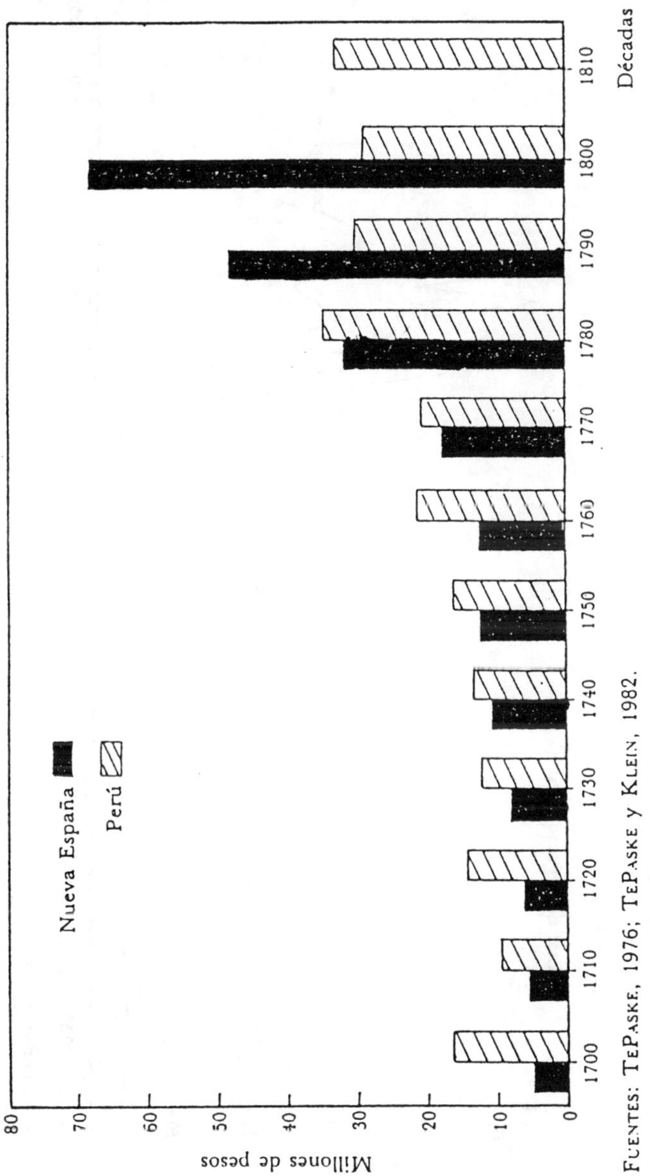

FUENTES: TEPASKE, 1976; TEPASKE y KLEIN, 1982.

Diagram 4:
Ingresos brutos / ingresos netos en Nueva España
(valores corrientes)

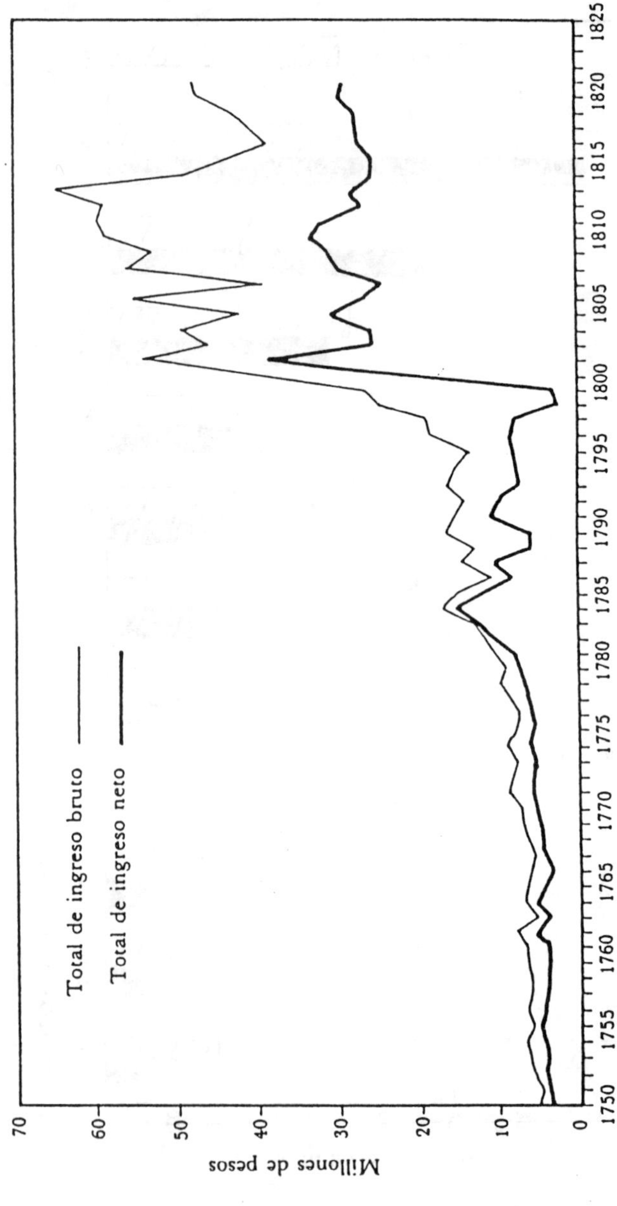

FUENTE: TEPASKE, 1976.

Diagram 5:
Ingresos netos en Nueva España
(valores corrientes)

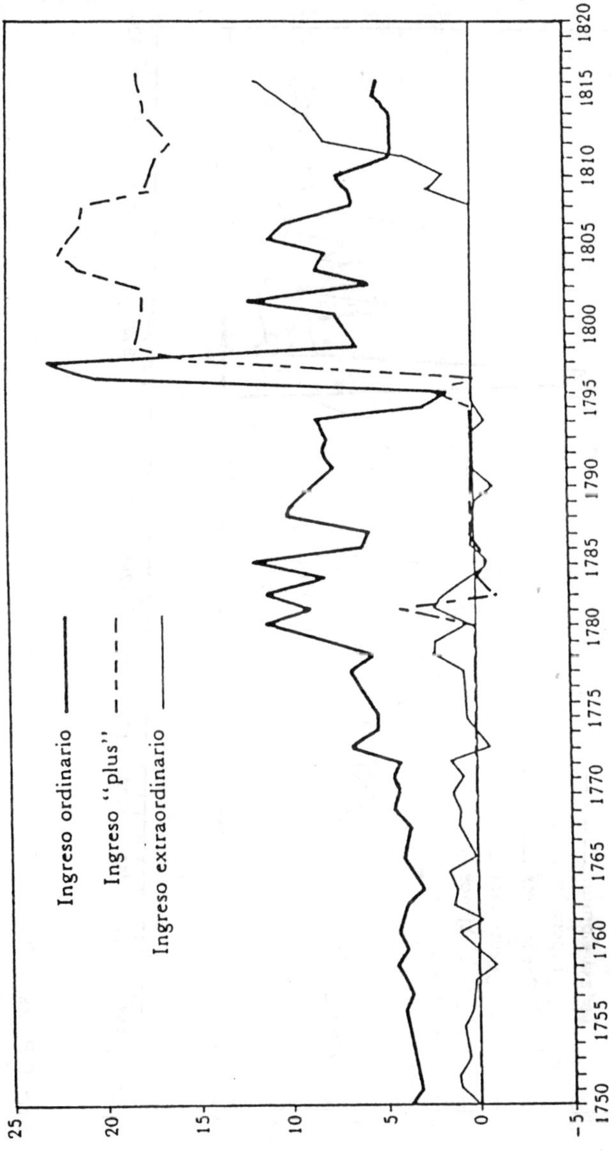

FUENTE: TEPASKE, 1976.

Diagram 6:
Ingresos ordinarios netos
(valores corrientes)

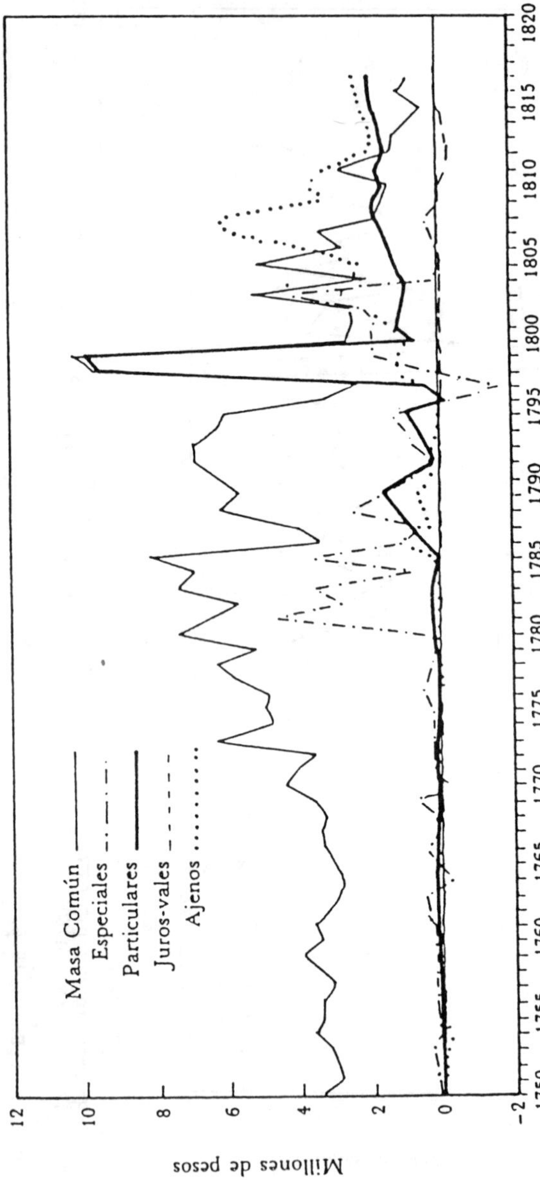

FUENTE: TEPASKE, 1976.

Diagram 7:
Ingresos ordinario y extraordinario, netos
(valores corrientes)

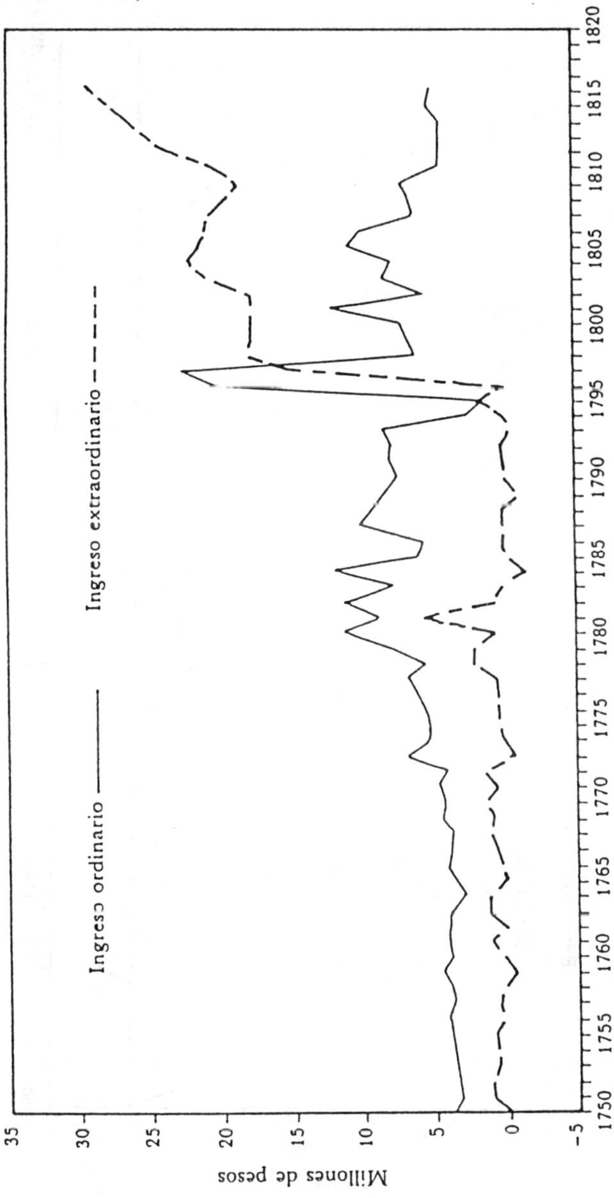

FUENTE: TEPASKE, 1976.

Diagram 8:
Ingresos extraordinarios netos
(valores corrientes)

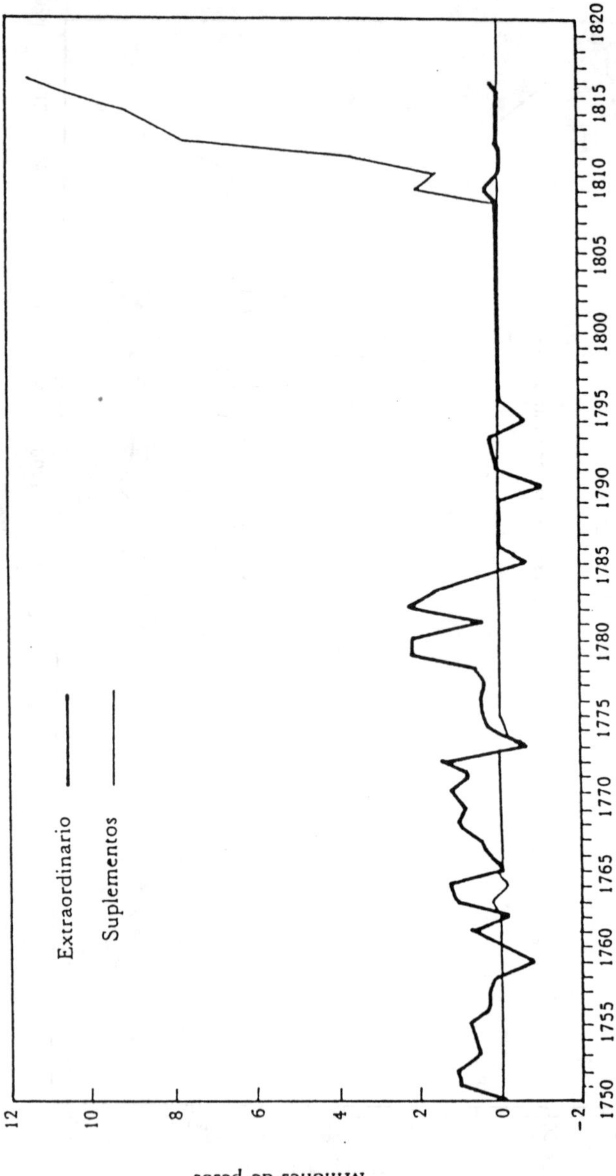

FUENTE: TEPASKE, 1976.

Diagram 9:
Ingresos "plus" netos
(valores corrientes)

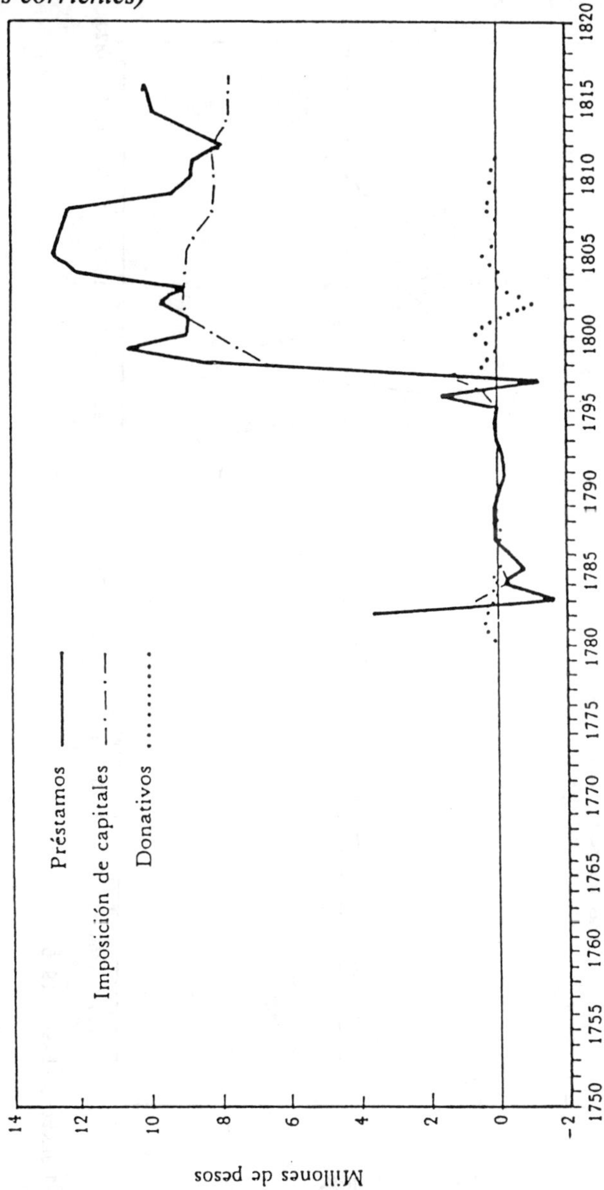

FUENTE: TEPASKE, 1976.

Diagram 10:
Ingreso neto depósitos / cambios-platas / O. Tesorerías
(valores corrientes)

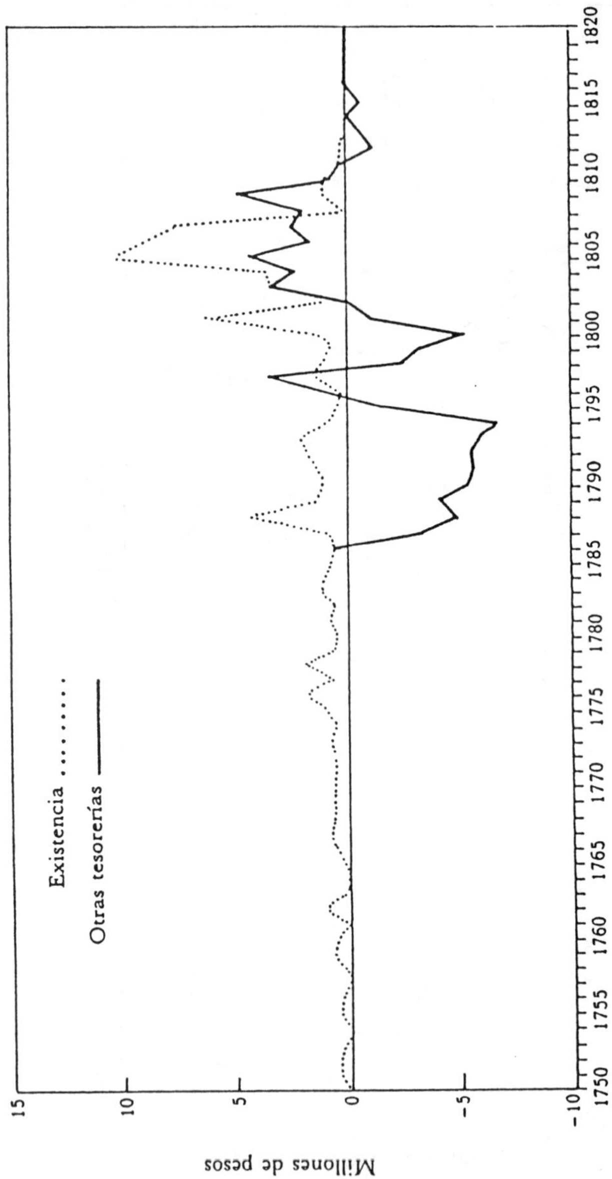

FUENTE: TEPASKE, 1976.

Diagram 11:
Tendencias de los ingresos netos en Nueva España
(valores corrientes)

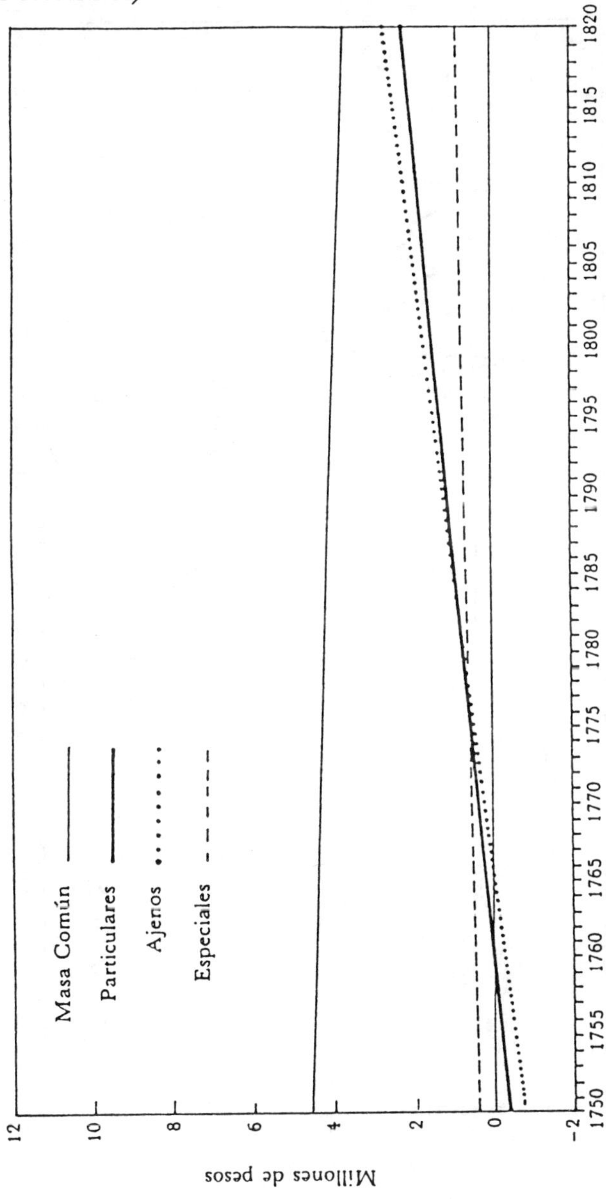

FUENTE: TEPASKE, 1976.

Diagram 12:
Ingreso ordinario/gasto total en Nueva España
(valores corrientes)

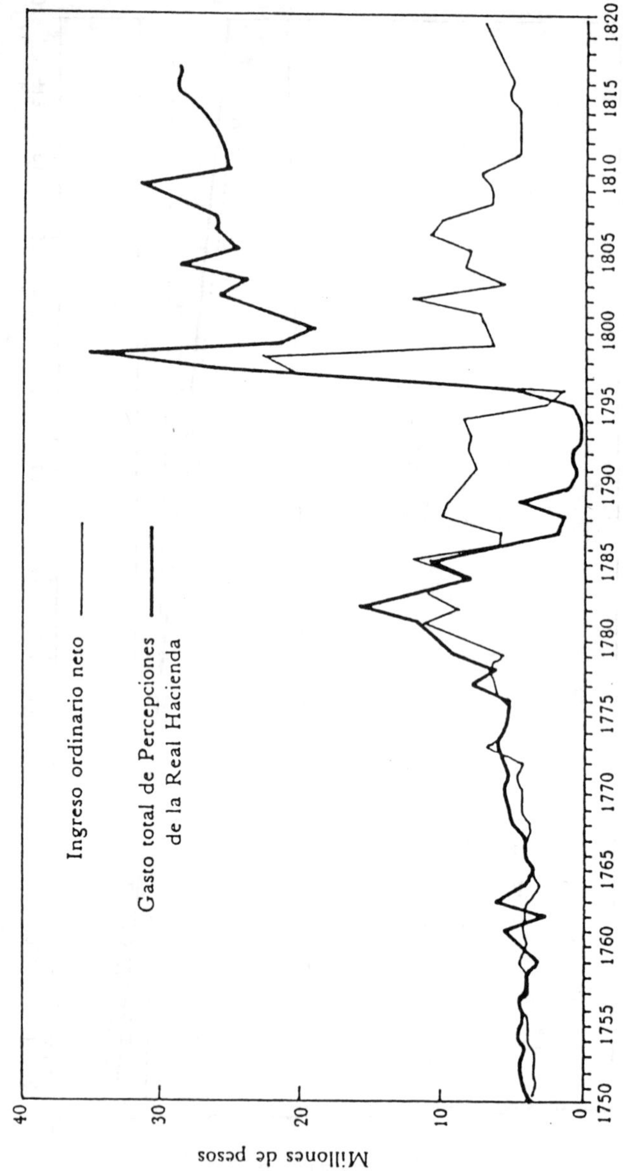

Fuente: TePaske, 1976.

Diagram 13:
Estructura del gasto general en Nueva España
(valores corrientes)

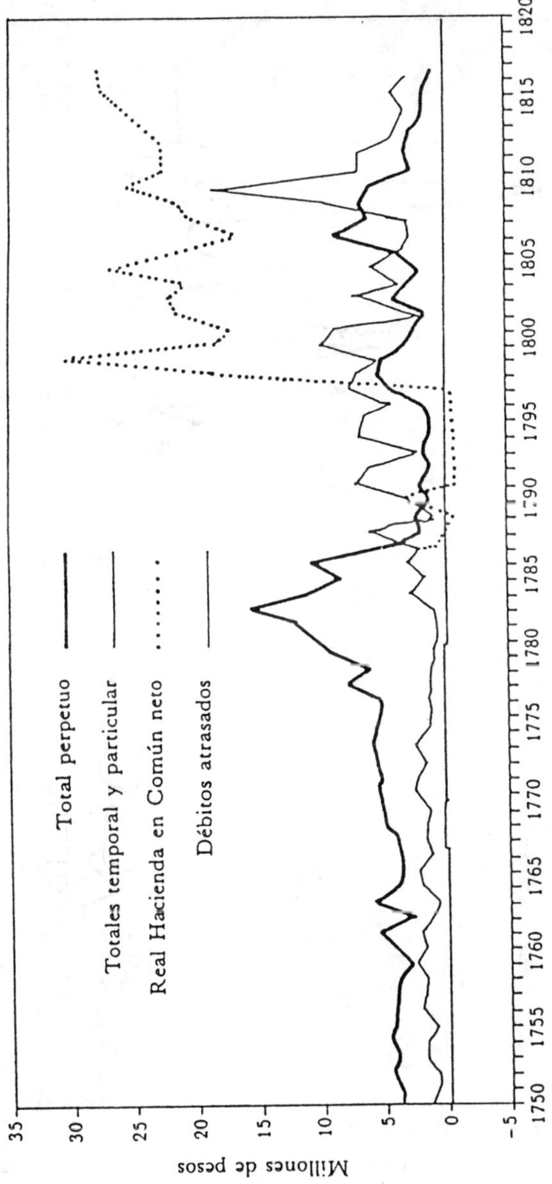

FUENTE: TEPASKE, 1976.

Diagram 14:
Estructura de los gastos temporal y particular
(valores corrientes)

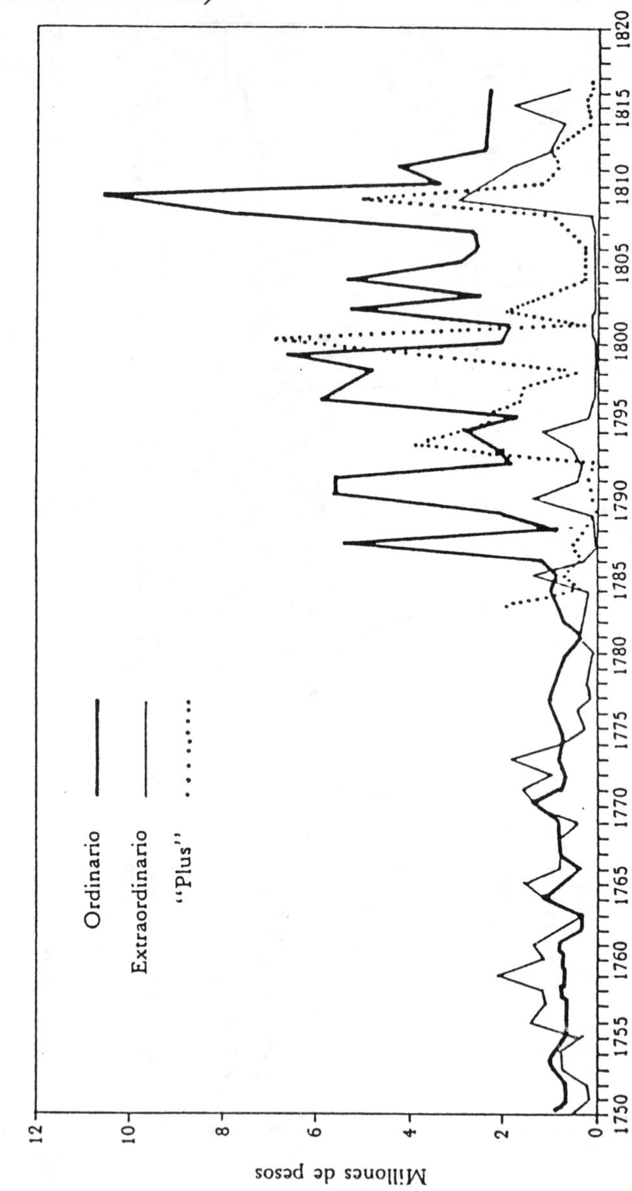

Fuente: TePaske, 1976.

Diagram 15:
Estructura del gasto perpetuo en Nueva España
(valores corrientes)

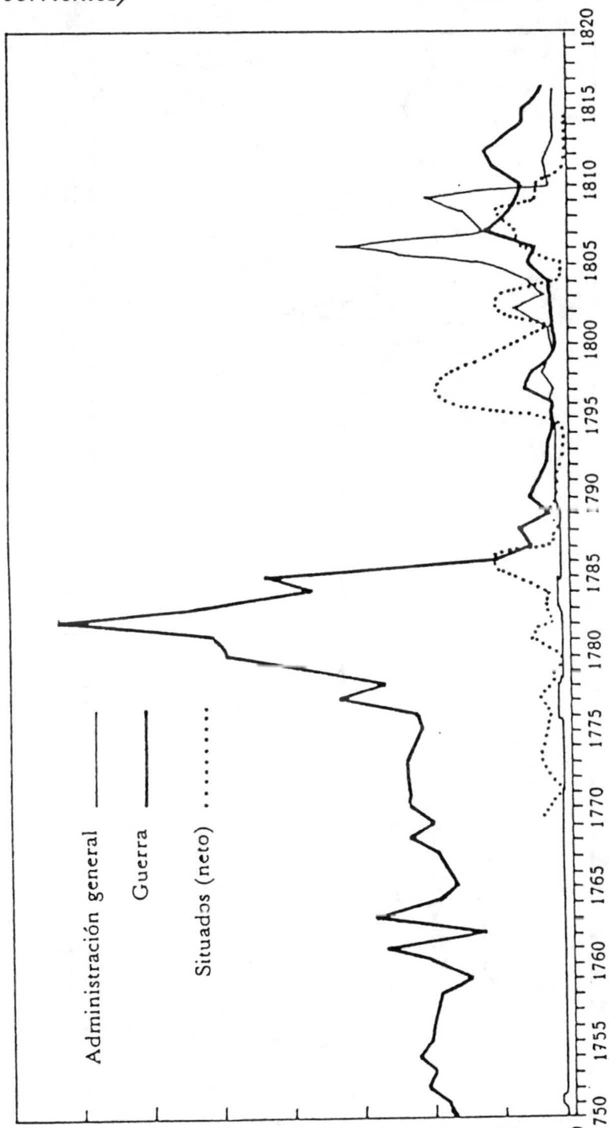

FUENTE: TEPASKE, 1976.

Diagram 16:
Ajustes de contabilidad
(valores corrientes)

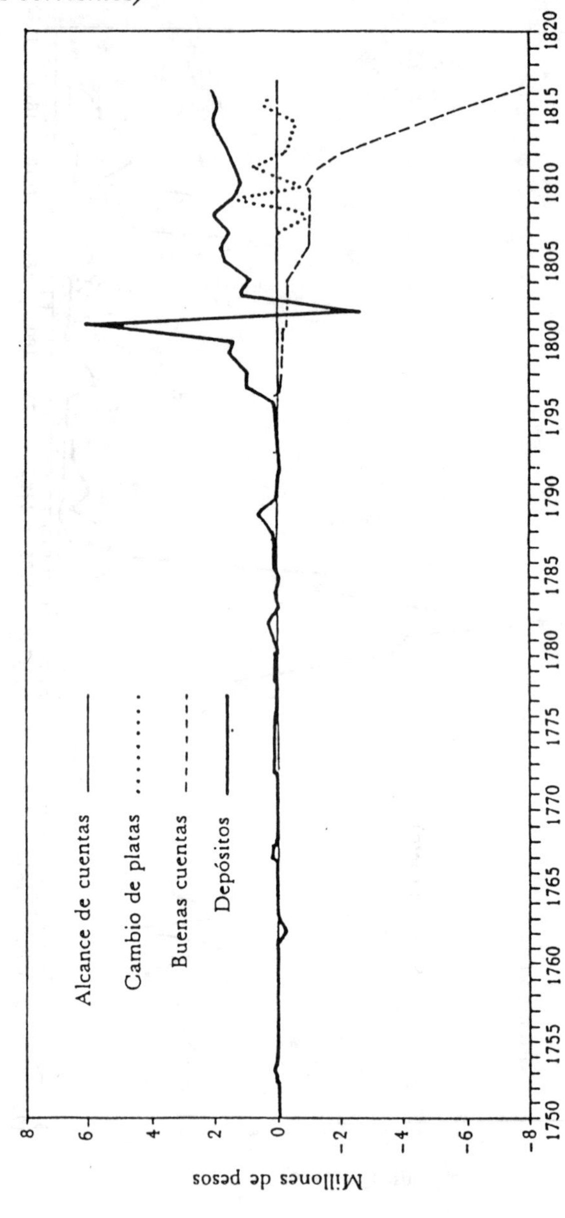

FUENTE: TEPASKE, 1976.

Diagram 17:
Ingreso neto (Pérez Herrero) - Ingreso neto (TePaske)
(valores corrientes)

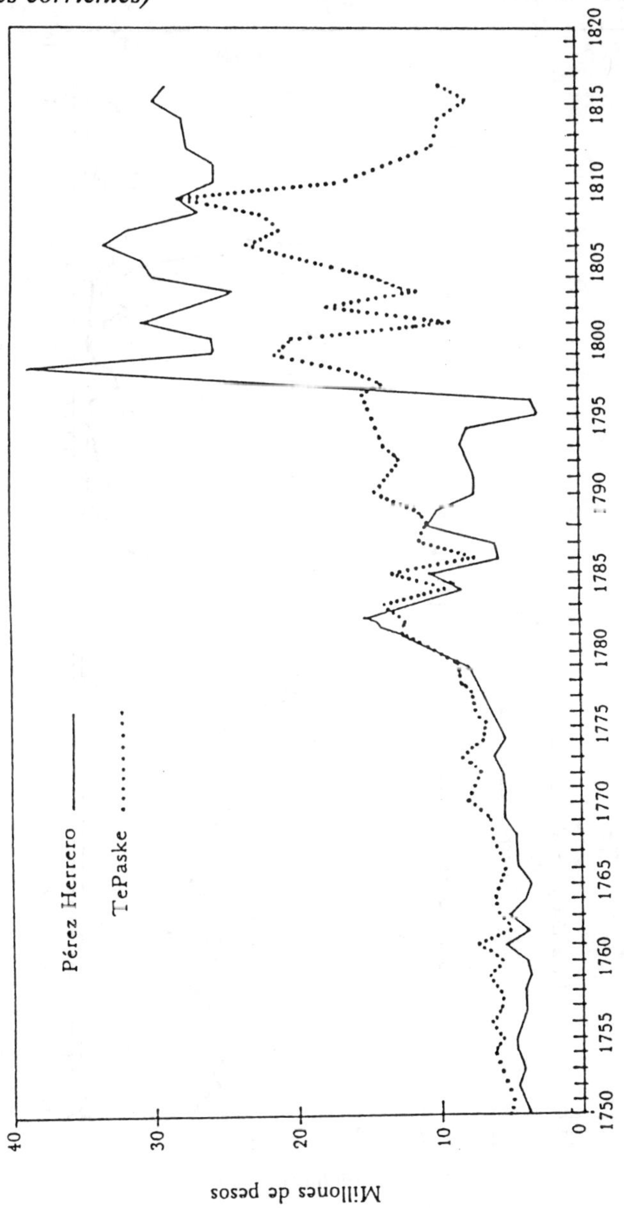

Fuente: TePaske, 1976.

Diagram 18:
Exportaciones de circulante de la Real Hacienda
(valores corrientes)

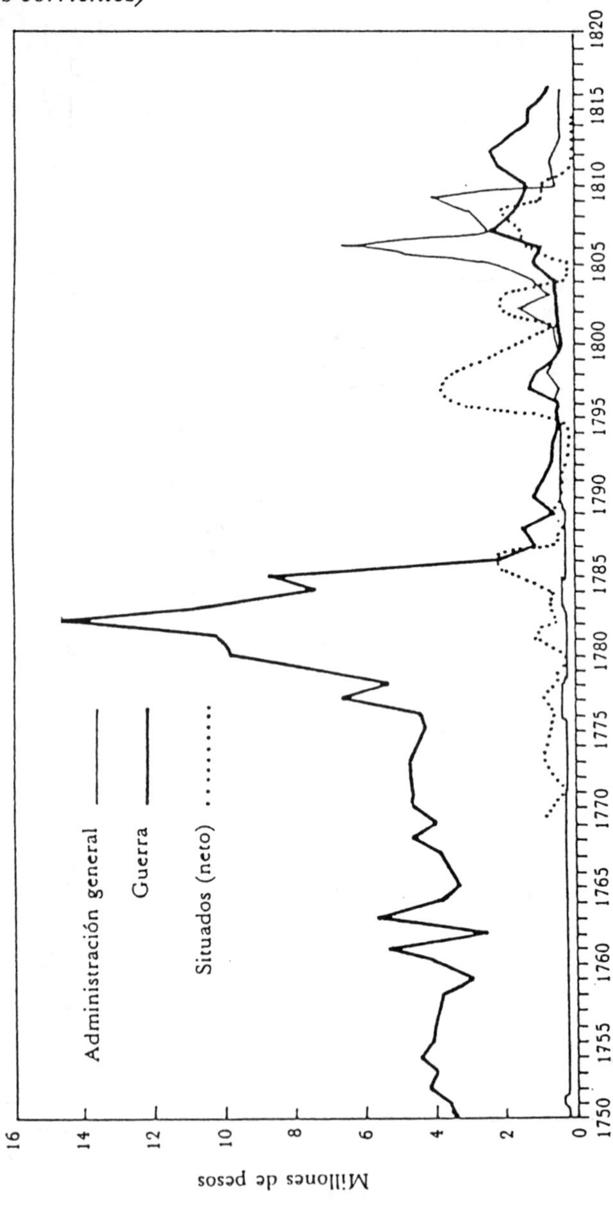

FUENTE: TEPASKE, 1976.

El Impacto de la Reforma del "Comercio Libre"

Sobre el Comercio Colonial Español[1]

De JOSEP M. DELGADO RIBAS

Introduccion

La bibliografía se ha mostrado bastante unánime a la hora de considerar el *Reglamento y Aranceles para el comercio libre* de 12 de octubre de 1778 como un cambio positivo en la organización del comercio entre España y América que abrió una nueva etapa de crecimiento y prosperidad y eliminó los obstáculos institucionales que impedían la intensificación del tráfico y la participación en la negociación de Indias a las regiones de la periferia española. Se trataría, en suma, de una de las medidas "modernizadoras" más importantes adoptadas por el gobierno "ilustrado" de Carlos III[2].

---

1 El texto de esta ponencia fué preparado durante una estancia en el Departamento de Historia de la Universidad de California en San Diego, financiada por el Comité Conjunto Hispano-Norteamericano. La versión final se ha visto enriquecida por las sugerencias recibidas por los restantes participantes en el Seminario, muy en especial, de las procedentes del comentarista crítico de mi aportación, el profesor Michel MORINEAU. En cualquier caso las opiniones aquí sostenidas sólo pueden imputarse al autor.

2 La gran mayoría de los especialistas del siglo XVIII español han ofrecido una valoración sobre el Reglamento de 1778 que responde a estos tópicos. Así,

para Rodríguez Labandeira "el sistema arancelario de libre comercio está en función de la política industrial de la Corona consagrando un proteccionismo que establece de forma generalizada la reserva del mercado americano a la producción nacional" (RODRÍGUEZ LABANDEIRA, La política económica de los Borbones, p. 174). Para GARCÍA BAQUERO, El Reglamento de 1778, acentuó el trato diferencial en beneficio de los productos españoles, "volviéndose a moderar los derechos sobre las exportaciones". En su opinión, "las cifras confirman.. el acierto de las medidas liberalizadoras capaces de impulsar en una proporción tan fuerte la actividad comercial" (Independencia colonial americana y pérdida de de la primacía andaluza, en: Historia de Andalucía VI, pp. 120 y 124; también, Cádiz y el Atlántico I, p. 254). Para COMELLAS, "las facilidades fiscales permitieron una expansión realmente extraordinaria". Dinámica y mentalidad de la burguesía gaditana en el siglo XVIII, en: La burguesía gaditana, pp. 18 - 19. Reducción de la carga fiscal y estímulo al comercio y a la producción industrial son ideas también compartidas en los trabajos de J. MUÑOZ PÉREZ, La publicación del Reglamento del comercio libre a Indias, en: *Anuario de Estudios Americanos* 4 (1947), p. 615 passim; M. NUNES DÍAS, El Real Consulado de Caracas, Caracas 1971, p. 124 - 125, 147; P. VOLTES BOU, La España de Carlos III, Barcelona 1964, p. 148; J. LANG, Conquest and Commerce. Spain and England in the Americas, Nueva York 1975; D. BRADING, Bourbon Spain and its American Empire, en: L. BETHELL (edit.), Colonial Latin America, pp. 413, 418; J. FISHER, Commercial Relations between Spain and Spanish América, p. 14 y Relaciones Económicas entre España y América hasta la Independencia, Madrid 1992, p. 170; R. FERNÁNDEZ DÍAZ, España en el Siglo XVIII, p. 44; C. MALAMUD, La economía colonial americana en el siglo XVIII, en: Historia de España, Menéndez Pidal, La época de la Ilustración, II p. 177; J. LYNCH, Bourbon Spain, p 352; G. CÉSPEDES DEL CASTILLO, América en la monarquía, en: Actas del Congreso Internacional, I p. 155; P. TEDDE, Política financiera y política comercial, en: Actas del Congreso Internacional, II p. 200, nota 95; I. WALLERSTEIN, The Modern World-System III, Nueva York 1989, p. 239.

Existen algunas diferencias, sin embargo, a la hora de atribuir la paternidad de la reforma. Para unos, el *Reglamento* es presentado como el triunfo de la periferia dinámica y mercantil sobre el inmovilismo del poder central (NUNES DÍAS, O comercio livre entre Havana e os portos de Espanha, Sao Paulo 1965, p. 124; GARCÍA BAQUERO, Cádiz y el Atlántico, I p. 91; I. DIAS AVELINO, Instituçao do comercio livre na mudança estructural do sistema colonial espanhol, p. 251; para otros, es el triunfo de una línea de pensamiento intelectual renovador, cuyos jalones más importantes son Campillo y Campomanes, que acaba imponiéndose gracias al apoyo de un monarca "ilustrado", (por citar sólo tres ejemplos bien recientes: Ch. C. NOEL, Charles

El buscar una respuesta menos trillada obliga al investigador a rechazar cualquier profesión de fe hacia la buena voluntad de los gobernantes "ilustrados". Desde una atalaya crítica, los efectos del *Reglamento* pueden analizarse de dos modos, según se tenga presente o no la evolución posterior del comercio colonial. Nuestra intención es ofrecer en primer lugar una aproximación desde una perspectiva institucional en la cual se considera el texto de 1778 como un cambio introducido en las tradicionales reglas de juego del monopolio comercial español con la pretensión de conseguir unos objetivos económicos y políticos muy concretos, y entrar luego en la consideración de su repercusión sobre el tráfico entre España y América.

III of Spain, en: H. M. SCOTT, Enlightened Absolutism. Reform and Reformers in Later Eighteenth-Century Europe, Ann Arbor 1990, pp. 119 - 143, - quien tiene la feliz idea de incluir entre los impulsores de las reformas al P. Eleta, confesor de Carlos III (p. 127), con lo que resulta difícil encontrar en su reinado un solo inmovilista -, C. MACLAHLAN, Spain's Empire in the New World. The Role of Ideas in Institutional and Social Change, Berkeley (C.A.) 1988, pp. 91 - 93, donde casi se nos convence del efecto "milagroso" del *Reglamento*, y F. VENTURI, The End of the Old Regime in Europe, 1776 - 1789, I pp. 236 - 258.

Por otro lado, también es frecuente la insistencia en que la periferia peninsular resultó especialmente beneficiada "por el incremento que produjo en el volumen de las exportaciones a América y aún de las propias remesas nacionales que aumentaron sin cesar porcentualmente respecto a las extranjeras". Pero, a fin de cuentas, esta periferia parece que se ha reducido a Cataluña donde "no hay duda de que el comercio americano fué el sector más dinámico de la actividad mercantil del Principado en el siglo XVIII y aún más allá" (C. MARTÍNEZ SHAW, Cataluña bajo el signo de la expansión, en: España en el siglo XVIII, p. 91). Desde el *Reglamento*, Cataluña tendió a solucionar sus problemas de déficit exterior gracias al superavit de su balanza comercial con América; por otro lado, como puso de relieve GARCÍA BAQUERO, Comercio colonial y producción industrial, p. 294, "el desarrollo industrial catalán de fines del siglo XVIII resulta prácticamente inconcebible de no haber contado con el mercado americano". Recientemente, GARCÍA BAQUERO se ha reafirmado en sus ideas en La industria algodonera catalana y el libre comercio. Otra reconsideración, en: *Manuscrits* n. 9 (enero de 1991), pp. 13 - 40.

El contenido de la reforma

En el cuadro I he recogido una serie de estimaciones que corroboran desde diferentes puntos de vista la rentabilidad fiscal del "comercio libre", tal como éste se configura a partir de 1778. En Ia y Ib comparo la demostración efectuada por Landázuri en 1765 sobre el beneficio que se obtenía de sustituir los derechos de Palmeo y Toneladas por su arancel "ad valorem" con idéntico cálculo pero efectuado sobre la fiscalidad aprobada en el *Reglamento*. Si la propuesta de Landázuri representaba un aumento de la base imponible sobre un cargo destinado a Veracruz del 31,7%, gracias a la aplicación de un 6% sobre los géneros "nacionales" y un 7% sobre los extranjeros, el nuevo arancel permitía a la Real Hacienda triplicar prácticamente sus ingresos pese a rebajar los derechos de salida de España sobre los géneros "nacionales" a un 3%. La explicación a esta aparente contradicción debe buscarse en el hecho de que la principal novedad del arancel de 1778 no era tanto la rebaja de los tipos de gravamen sinó la recuperación del almojarifazgo de Indias suprimido por las reformas de comienzos de siglo que ahora volvía a cobrarse de nuevo en todos los puertos americanos sobre las mercancías transportadas desde España. El mismo José de Gálvez, en carta aclaratoria dirigida al intendente de La Habana en mayo de 1779[3], le notificaba que el nuevo sistema recuperaba el almojarifazgo de Indias, abolido por el Proyecto de 1720, que no se había introducido en 1765 por "ciertas circunstancias que en el día ya no subsisten". Este impuesto no se calculaba sobre la misma base imponible que los derechos de salida de España, sinó que ésta era aumentada por el art. 21 del R.L.C. entre un 12 y un 20%, según el puerto habilitado de entrada.

---

3 Gálvez al Intendente de La Habana, Aranjuez, 20-V-1779, AGI, Indiferente General, leg. 2416.

CUADRO I:
Algunos cálculos sobre los cambios en la fiscalidad introducidos por las reformas de 1776 - 1782

a) La propuesta Landázuri sobre un cargamento representativo a Veracruz (1765)[4]

géneros	palmos	valor rs. pta.	derechos Rl. Proyecto	6%	100=Proyecto de 1720
lencería	44.000,0	10.692.000,0	270.875,00	641.520,00	236,0
lanas	11.000,0	1.443.750,0	67.718,75	86.625,00	127,9
sedas	11.000,0	5.761.250,0	67.718,75	345.675,00	510,5
telas finas	533,3	764.263,3	3.283,25	45.855,75	1.396,7
	66.533,3	18.661.263,3	409.595,75	1.967.675,75	273,4
+ Toneladas[256.000 rs.]			665.595,75	1.119.5,75	168,2
frutos	33.260	1.706.769	185.615,00	85.338,50	46,0
+ Toneladas [64.000 rs]			249.615,00	85.338,50	34,2
TOTAL			915.210,75	1.205.014,25	131,7

4 AHN, Estado leg. 2314.

b) Sobre el mismo lote de mercancías según el Reglamento de 1778
(Sin contablizar el aumento de las valoraciones arancelarias ni posibles cambios en la composición de las exportaciones).

géneros	palmos	valor rs. pta.	derechos Rl. Proyecto	14%* 6%**	100=Proyecto de 1720
lencería	44.000,0	10.692.000,0	270.875,00	1.496.880	552,6
lanas	11.000,0	1.443.750,0	67.718,75	202.125	298,5
sedas	11.000,0	5.761.250,0	67.718,75	806.575	1.191,1
telas finas	533,3	764.263,3	3.283,25	106.997	3.258,9
	66.533,3	18.661.263,3	409.595,75	2.612.577	637,8
+ Toneladas[256.000 rs.]			665.595,75	2.612.577	392,5
frutos	33.260	1.706.769	185.615,00	102.406	55,2
+ Toneladas [64.000 rs]			249.615,00	102.406	41,0
TOTAL			915.210,75	2.714.983	296,7

* salida de España y entrada en Indias, mercancías extranjeras
** Id. mercancías "nacionales"

En Ic se resume el impacto recaudatorio que el almojarifazgo tuvo en los ingresos de los dos puertos novohispanos que controlaban el comercio exterior de México. En Acapulco, el almojarifazgo comenzó a cobrarse sobre el comercio con Perú y Tierra Firme a partir de su habilitación en 1774, a razón de un 2,5% de salida y un 5% de entrada sin que llegara a ser un ingreso importante para la Caja Real hasta que, en 1782, el comercio con Filipinas pasó también a contribuir bajo este concepto según diversas tarifas que oscilaban entre un 3,5% y un 6% de salida, y un 18 - 33% de entrada, sobre los géneros manufacturados de Asia. En 1787, año que cierra el primer ciclo reformista, los almojarifazgos representaban el 90,2% de los ingresos generados

c) El "nuevo" almojarifazgo en Acapulco y Veracruz (1774 - 1785) (rs. vn)

	Acapulco	*Veracruz*
1774	0	2.558.980
1775	14.360	2.416.420
1776	22.280	2.067.360
1777	116.760	1.505.140
1778	59.860	1.155.320
1779	57.660	1.939.140
1780	322.900	1.234.480
1781	494.760	1.608.860
1782	1.594.840	8.274.760
1783	1.886.640	1.257.260
1784	2.847.260	8.888.260
1785	2.342.920	9.069.400
1786	456.540	11.203.780
1787	5.185.340	12.698.780

por la tesorería de Acapulco[5]. El caso de Veracruz es distinto porque los almojarizagos ya se cobraban antes de 1778 sobre el comercio interamericano y las expediciones en registros sueltos. Aún así, la extensión del impuesto a todas las importaciones procedentes de España convirtió a esta partida en el ingreso más importante de la Caja Real tras el ramo de alcabalas[6].

La comparación entre el arancel Landázuri y el aprobado en 1778 supone que el *Reglamento* mantuvo reglas para la determinación de la base imponible utilizadas anterioremente o que, como mínimo, recogió precios corrientes de 1778 para su estimación. Sin embargo, no fué así. Según el cálculo n. 6 de Landázuri[7] los 1091 barriles quintaleños de aguardiente que se incluían en el registro de Veracruz eran valorados a razón de 37,5 reales la arroba, mientras que la dirección de rentas estableció en 1778 un valor arancelario por arroba de 60 rs. Podría pensarse que el cambio en la valoración obedeció a un aumento del precio del aguardiente entre 1765 y 1778, como resultado de la presión de la demanda americana sobre una oferta inelástica a corto plazo. Pero las informaciones de que disponemos sobre precios del

5 J. J. TEPASKE / H. S. KLEIN, Ingresos y egresos de la Real Hacienda de Nueva España, I pp. 45 - 51. En el cálculo de 1787 hemos deducido del cargo las partidas procedentes de otras tesorerias.

6 J. J. TEPASKE / H. S. Klein, Ingresos y egresos de la Real Hacienda de Nueva Espana, II pp. 76 - 77.

7 AHN, Estado, leg. 2314, "Cálculo de una navío de 600 toneladas para Veracruz". Realizado sobre precios corrientes de 1765.

aguardiente parecen indicar lo contrario. Los precios de las variedades exportadas a América, el aguardiente "prueba de Holanda" y el "prueba de aceite", registraron en el mercado mayorista de Reus una tendencia a la baja que culminaría hacia 1785 - 1786 con las cotizaciones mínimas de todo el siglo. Entre 1781 y 1785, los precios medios computados en octubre de cada año, cuando entraban en el mercado los destilados de la nueva cosecha, se encontraban muy por debajo, no sólo del arancel de 1778, sino de los cálculos menos interesados de Landázuri: el prueba de aceite se vendía a 18,5 rs. la arroba, mientras que el de Holanda cotizaba a 13,7 rs.[8]. Si la valoración arancelaria del aguardiente se triplicaba o cuadruplicaba respecto al precio de mercado resulta indefendible la postura de los que hablan de una rebaja de derechos para la producción agrícola española, máxime si consideramos que el peso de esta partida en las exportaciones agrarias - el 47,8% según los cálculos de Landázuri - tendió a aumentar después de 1778 como resultado de las estrategias arbitradas por los comerciantes para tratar de reducir la incidencia de la fiscalidad sobre sus beneficios[9].

---

8 Información sobre precios del aguardiente en estos años en J. M. DELGADO, El impacto de las crisis coloniales en la economía catalana, 1778 - 1808, en: J. FONTANA (edit.), La Economía Española al final del Antiguo Regimen. III, Comercio y colonias, pp. 99 - 169. Mas información sobre el mercado del aguardiente, en: Fç. OLIVÉ I OLLÉ, El Valls del segle XVIII i el comerciant d' aiguardents Anton Baldrich i Janer, Valladolid 1981; S. ROVIRA I GÓMEZ, Els aiguardents del Camp de Tarragona a la segona meitat del segle XVIII, en: Primer Congres d' História Moderna de Catalunya, Barcelona 1984, pp. 305 - 320; A. SEGARRA I BLASCO; L' economía de Reus al segle XVIII: el comerç del aiguardent, Reus 1988; J. TORRAS ELÍAS, Aguardiente y crisis rural. Sobre la coyuntura vitícola, 1793 - 1832, en: *Investigaciones Económicas* 1 (1976), pp. 45 - 67.

9 Los exportadores españoles de caldos contrarestaban el impacto conjunto de fletes elevados y presión tributaria con el incremento de las exportaciones de productos refinados y de mayor valor añadido. En el caso del aguardiente, la prohibición de embarcar mistelas para Nueva España efectuada en 1763 trató de corregir con poco éxito esta tendencia al ser éstas sustituidas por orujos comunes de mayor graduación alcohólica que el aguardiente prueba de aceite

El Ministerio de Indias neutralizó parte de estas estrategias a través de la normativa paralela al *Reglamento*. En 1777, y con la excusa de un accidente fortuito sucedido en el puerto de Veracruz durante la descarga de uno de los buques de la flota de Antonio de Ulloa, José de Gálvez solicitó y obtuvo del ministerio de Hacienda que se prohibiese la exportación a América de los aguardientes catalanes refinados, con la excusa de que su alto contenido alcohólico podía provocar accidentes de graves consecuencias durante su manipulación en los puertos. En realidad, la justificación de la medida era "el notorio perjuicio que este refino ocasiona al Público y a los Derechos Reales porque son iguales los que contribuye cada barril de cada una de las insinuadas clases desde su salida de la fábrica hasta que entran en poder del mercader mexicano"[10]. El cuadro II pretende ofrecer desde la per-

---

y Holanda, que luego eran rebajados en México y otros mercados consumidores (Discurso formado con fecha de 24 de julio de 1788 sobre la decadencia de la agricultura de la Nueva España y medios de restablecerla, Biblioteca de Catalunya, Manuscrits 904, fols. 1 - 31).

10 El proceso administrativo que siguió este expediente es interesante porque ilustra cómo funcionaron los mecanismos de innovación legislativa en el reformismo borbónico. En febrero de 1777 (Manjón a Gálvez, Cádiz, 4-II-1777, AGI, Indiferente General, leg. 2412), el Presidente de la Casa de la Contratación, recién nombrado por Gálvez y con ganas de ser útil a su valedor, remitió un informe completo del accidente sucedido en la descarga de la flota de Ulloa donde se aclaraba que no había sido provocado por los aguardientes refinados sinó por la ruptura de algunas vasijas de ácido sulfúrico. Manjón quitaba importancia al incidente y señalaba que esta mercancía y otras similares no eran inflamables y su peligrosidad se limitaba a "solo el daño de corroer, tostar y manchar cuanto encuentra por donde fluye hasta que se consume el espíritu". Por tanto debían tomarse precauciones en su embalaje pero "sin restingir el envío de estos licores cuya provisión se necesita en el Reino". Pero el accidente podía ser aprovechado para prohibir "el embarco de ... aguardiente refino que. han inventado los fabricantes de Cataluña, mandándoseles no continúen en la fábrica de esta especie por los medios que aseguren su extinción en aquella provincia y pueblos de estas costas".

Manjón barajaba varios argumentos para justificar esta política. Algunos no podían ser mas "ilustrados": la medida beneficiaría en primer lugar al Principado pues reduciría el consumo de leña y se incrementaría la oferta de spectiva del cargador individual el conjunto de costes de transacción - cargas tributarias, pagos por intermediación, servicios y costes financieros - soportados por el "comercio libre" tanto a la exportación como a la importación de Indias.

---

vino catalán "escasa"? y "cara"?; también la obligación de exportar variedades que no se pueden "rebajar con el agua" sería un estímulo para la imaginaria marina mercante española pues doblaría la demanda de buque para el transporte de pipas de aguardiente. Pero la razón que hacía mas recomendable la prohibición era el interés de la Real Hacienda. El aguardiente refinado pagaba a su salida para América los mismos derechos que el prueba de aceite y Holanda cuando su concentración era del doble; seis barriles de vino destilado producían sólo un barril de orujo refinado y dos de "prueba de aceite".

Gálvez traspasó sólo catorce días después la sugerencia de Manjón a Múzquiz con ideas de su propia cosecha. No sólo era conveniente prohibir el aguardiente refino sino que debía limitarse la producción del prueba de aceite. Afortunadamente para los cosecheros catalanes, el ministro de Hacienda, no era tan "ilustrado" como Gálvez y sólo aceptó la primera de las sugerencias (Gálvez a Miguel de Muzquiz, El Pardo, 16-II-1777, AGS, Secretaría de Hacienda, leg. 2349).

Ad cuadro II b: Para los fletes y averías, ver la respuesta del el cargador gaditano Francisco Guerra de la Vega a la consulta de 1787 sobre las causas de la decadencia del "comercio libre", fechada en Cádiz el 2 de enero de 1788. (AGI, Consulados, leg. 73). Corretajes y comisiones en ANC (Arxiu Nacional de Catalunya), Borsa de Barcelona, corredor Magí Justi i Anglada, B-1 (1776 - 1779). La prima del seguro a Veracruz en tiempo de paz, en *Diario de Barcelona*, 16 de diciembre de 1792.

El capítulo de averías comprende aquellas que se consideraban completamente normales en el curso de un viaje de larga duración y que por tanto no daban lugar a indemnización por parte del asegurador. Nosotros le damos aquí una repercusión muy baja, sensiblemente inferior a la que las mismas companías aseguradoras entendían como "normal" en el comercio de manufacturas": un 3%, o en este caso 135 rs. vn. (AHPB, not. R. Font Alier, Manual de escrituras de 1772, fol. 94r - estatutos de la Cia. de Seguros Marítimos Inmaculada Concepción.

Ad cuadro II c: Fuente, libro citado del corredor Just i Anglada para las compras a crédito. Para las escrituras de riesgo a Veracruz, Archivo Histórico de Protocolos de Cádiz (AHPC), Notaría 24, Antonio de la Torre, manuales de 1780 a 1784.

CUADRO II:
Costes de transacción sobre un fardo con 125 piezas de bretañas contrahechas, valorado en 4500 rs. de vn. puesto en Veracruz
(en rs. de vn.).

a) Carga fiscal (en rs. de vn.)

	arancel entrada	exportación a Indias	almojarifazgo de Indias	alcabala +armada	total
(1) Flotas	180	45,6	---,-	270	495,6
(2) extranjero	900	315,0	352,8	504	2.071,8
(3) "nacional"	675	135,0	151,2	504	1.465,2

b) Costes de transacción privados - fletes, seguros, comisiones, intereses, etc

	flete	comisión 2%	corret. ½%	seguro 4%	averías	total
(1) Flotas	178,3	90	22,5	180	67,5	538,3
(2) extranjero	133,2	90	22,5	180	45,0	470,7
(3) "nacional"	133,2	90	22,5	180	45,0	470,7

c) Costes financieros (compra a crédito y cambio marítimo)

	int. crédit. com.20%	cambio marítimo 30%	total
(1) Flotas	900	1350	2250
(2) extranjero	900	1350	2250
(3) "nacional"	900	1350	2250

d) Total costes de transacción, en porcentaje sobre el precio de una mercancía de exportación

	impuestos	transacción	financieros	total
(1) Flotas	11,0	12,0	50	73,0
(2) extranjero	46,0	10,5	50	106,5
(3) "nacional"	32,5	10,5	50	93,0

El primer ejemplo - IIa - calcula en términos absolutos y relativos los pagos realizados por un exportador de una partida representativa de lencería[11] con destino al mercado mexicano, en los supuestos de que la operación se realizara en el marco del Proyecto de 1720 (1), del Reglamento de 1778 como mercancía extranjera (2) o como mercancía extranjera "rebautizada" (3). Nuestro ejemplo trata simplemente de mostrar el cambio inmediato que para el cargador español representó verse obligado a trabajar en el nuevo marco institucional.

Dentro del apartado de la fiscalidad, la principal novedad que incorpora el cuadro II es la inclusión de los derechos de entrada a España modificados por los Aranceles Recopilados de 1782, cuya reforma es inseparable del desarrollo del nuevo sistema de "comercio libre". La diferencia de tributación respecto al sistema de 1720 es fruto de la eliminación de los privilegios que los lienzos y otras manufacturas francesas disfrutaban desde el Convenio de Eminente en la aduana de Cadiz y su equiparación en las tarifas generales del arancel a las restantes manufacturas europeas. En conjunto, la fiscalidad sobre los lienzos de rexportación se cuadruplicaba en el caso de los que se introducían a España ya acabados y casi se triplicaba en el caso de los semielaborados o crudos destinados a sufrir una última manipulación en España. Pese a ser abrumadora, la carga tributaria era sólo uno de las que debía soportar el usuario del "comercio libre". En IIb se recogen parte de los costes de transacción privados que limitaban el beneficio mercantil de los comerciantes[12]. Salvo en la partida de los fletes, donde la desaparición del derecho de Toneladas permitió un inmediato descenso de los costes, las demás no se modificaron a corto plazo. También en este caso, nuestra estimación es forzosamente optimista.

---

11 El ejemplo que utilizamos fué propuesto por el cargador gaditano Francisco Guerra de la Vega en su respuesta particular a la consulta de 1787 sobre las causas de la decadencia del "comercio libre", fechada en Cádiz el 2 de enero de 1788 (AGI, Consulados, leg. 73).

12 D. C. NORTH, Transaction Costs in History, en: *The Journal of European Economic History* 14/3 (1985), p.558.

En primer lugar, no incluye el coste del transporte de Veracruz a México al suponer que éste era soportado por el importador mexicano que se encargaba de distribuir las mercancías en el mercado interior; pero, en la medida en que este comerciante criollo tendió a ser sustituido por "negociantes- aventureros" peninsulares, los costes de distribución en el mercado novohispano comenzaron a gravitar sobre las espectativas de beneficio del comercio español. Por otro lado, tampoco incorpora el pago de servicios y costes de protección no reconocidos por la ley, ni la pérdida de rentas de información - con el consiguiente aumento del riesgo y la incertidumbre - que debieron padecer los comerciantes obligados a adaptarse a otras reglas de juego para realizar sus cálculos de coste / beneficio, algo especialmente costoso en aquellos casos donde además comportó un cambio en los sistemas contables y de medicion.

La legislación de 1778 había prohibido el cobro por parte de la burocracia de todos los derechos, tasas y contribuciones no reconocidos explícitamente por la administración. Pero la tarea de conseguir la aplicación efectiva de estas normas dependió más de las denuncias concretas de los cargadores y navieros que de la práctica fiscalizadora de la administración. Es presumible que cuando esta protesta faltó porque la corrupción beneficiaba a los administrados, la existencia de estas prácticas permaneció oculta en beneficio de todos[13]. Afortunadamente para el historiador, este acuerdo parece que no existió entre el gobernador de Puerto Rico, José Dufresne, y los "vasallos de V.M." en Barcelona que lo denunciaron ante la dirección general de rentas por cobrar a cada capitán del comercio libre 10 ps. fs. antes de autori-

13 En el volúmen II de mi tesis doctoral, Cataluña y el sistema de comercio libre, pp. 108 - 151, describo numerosos casos de colaboración interesada entre burócratas y comerciantes en el marco del comercio libre. Véase también, ejemplos publicados en: Comercio colonial y fraude fiscal en Cataluña. Algunas consideraciones en torno a los registros del libre comercio a Indias (1778 - 1796), en: *Estudios Históricos y Documentos de los Archivos de Protocolos* VI (1978), pp. 311 - 326; y en: Fiscalidad y comercio con América: los resguardos de rentas de Cataluña (1778 - 1799), en: *Boletía Americanista* XXII n. 30 (1980), pp. 69 - 88.

zar la distribución en la isla de las mercancías traidas de Europa. El motivo de la protesta no era tanto la importancia intrínseca de la cantidad exigida sino el principio de incertidumbre que introducía en la práctica del comercio libre que privaba de sentido a la reforma:

> "no se debe llamar libre comercio, sino un negocio expuesto a arbitrios que a cualesquiera se le antoje imponer"[14].

Más frecuente aún que estos comportamientos reprobables fué la inercia del aparato administrativo a asumir a nivel regional o local los compromisos del *Reglamento* de comercio libre, en especial, aquél que declaraba la libertad de derechos "anteriores y consiguientes al Proyecto de 1720"[15]. Salvo las cargas directamente relacionadas con la tramitación de los oportunos permisos para participar desde Cádiz en el apresto de una expedición de Flotas o Galeones - visitas, reconocimiento de carenas, habilitaciones, licencias para navegar - ningún otro derecho o arbitrio municipal sobre las mercancías de la Carrera fué en realidad abolido. Mas bién al contrario, la habilitación de puertos como Málaga, Barcelona o La Coruña sirvió para que el "comercio libre" rentabilizara arbitrios y contribuciones locales de la mas diversa procedencia - almirantazgos, ancorajes, periajes, derechos de limpia, cuartillos y octavo de aguardiente, montepíos de cosecheros, derechos de puertas y lezdas, medios y unos por ciento para la construcción de aduanas etc. Paradójicamente, las diferencias en los niveles de tributación local antes y después de 1778 parece que no hicieron sino reforzar el liderazgo de Cádiz como cabecera del tráfico dado que en su caso si hubo rebaja de derechos. También en este caso fueron los comerciantes catalanes los primeros en poner de manifiesto

---

14 Unos "vasallos de S. M". en Barcelona a "los señores Directores Generales o a quien corresponda este escrito", 20, septiembre de 1778. AGI, Indiferente General leg. 2415. La protesta hacía referencia a las normas introducidas en la Real Instrucción de febrero.

15 Art. 6 del R.L.C. Se mencionaban esplícitamente, además del Palmeo y las Toneladas los de "San Telmo, extranjería, visitas, reconocimientgo de carenas, habilitaciones, licencias para navegar y demás gastos anteriores y consiguientes al Proyecto del año de 1720".

esta situación al contrastar las buenas intenciones de Carlos III con las novedades de la realidad cotidiana en la aduana de Barcelona:

> "El Administrador general de Rentas Generales de Cataluña por unos principios mal entendidos ha manifestado ya desviarse en la práctica de estas saludables máximas, pretendiendo exigir ciertos derechos que deben entenderse extinguidos en virtud de dicho reglamento, y queriendo sujetarlas la contribución de otros algunos géneros que allí se declaran absolutamente libres"[16].

Las protestas catalanas, reiteradas en años sucesivos[17], hacían especial hincapié en la "indebida" exacción del derecho de Almirantazgo[18] y en los aranceles que pagaba a su entrada en Barcelona un producto declarado libre por el Reglamento como era el azúcar - 4% por derecho de ciudad y 7 rs. por quintal en concepto de equivalente de bolla - que suponían en conjunto un gravamen "ad valorem" del 9%, superior al exigido a los generos extrangeros embarcados para América. Esta situación afectaba además al cacao y a la manufactura sedera barcelonesa, también obligados al pago de equivalente y derechos de puer-

---

16 "habiéndose esmerado el paternal amor de V.M. en prescribir las mas sabias, prudentes y oportunas providencias para el logro de los altos fines que en beneficio universal de la Nación se ha propuesto en la Real Cédula de 12 de octubre último comprensiva del Reglamento y Aranceles Reales para eel Comercio Libre de España a Indias, debían persuadirse los recurrentes que los ministros empleados en el recaudo de las rentas reales conformándose con las piadosas intenciones y declarada voluntad de V. Rl. P. sobre que antes se amplien que se limiten sus gracias, conspirarían a que pudiese el comercio disfrutar libremente todas las que V. Md. se ha dignado dispensarle, interpretando benignamente cualquier artículo que acaso pudiese considerarse equívoco, o susceptible de alguna duda. Pero el suceso no ha correspondido a esta fundada esperanza". La Junta de Comercio de Barcelona - firman J. Fç de Duran, J. Gloria, P. Puiguriquer, G. Timmermans, M. Civil, F. Prat y F. Gener (AGI, Indiferente General, leg. 1830-A).

17 Vid., asimismo, eun nuevbo memorial del comercio catalán remitido en enero de 1784 (AGS, Superintendencia de Hacienda, leg. 1110).

18 El comercio de Cataluña al conde de Floridablanca, 21 de noviembre de 1778 (AGI, Indiferente General, leg. 2415).

tas. Es interesante señalar que el dictamen final de la dirección general de rentas que desestimaba la petición catalana mas que argumentar razones de legalidad respondía a criterios puramente recaudatorios:

> "No deja de ser de consideración la suma de cuatrocientos veinte y un mil quinientos cuarenta reales de vellón a que ascienden todas las expresadas partidas del producto del año de 1779. Y no hallando motivo para que el Rey deje de percibirlos; nos parece que S. M. se sirva desestimar la solicitud de estos comerciantes como infundada"[19].

La alteración de los sistemas de peso, medida y valoracion es uno de los factores que mas inciden sobre los costes de transacción al aumentar el nivel de riesgo e incertidumbre entre los agentes económicos, sobre todo cuando su sustitución no obedece a criterios de racionalidad económica[20]. El incremento de los costes de transacción como resultado de la modificación en las valoraciones arancelarias es pefectamente descrito en uno de los memoriales ya citados del comercio catalan:

> "la tarifa de esta aduana de Barcelona corría impresa y la tenían muy presente todos los comerciantes para gobernar por ella sus especulaciones calculando sobre el importe de los derechos correspondientes a los valores senalados en la tarifa, habían acopoado varios géneros y tomado sus medidas para expedir algún registro, o cargar parte de algún buque mercantil con destino a América, y en la ocasión de verificarse esta expedición han visto desconcertados sus cálculos"[21].

---

19 El dictamen, elaborado por Sáenz de Parayuelo, y fechado en Madrid a 3 de julio de 1784, en AGS, Sup. de Hacienda, leg. 1110.

20 Sobre la importancia de estas cuestiones en la determinación de los costes de transacción, véanse las precisiones teóricas de J. NIEHANS, Money in a static theory of optimal payment arrangements, en: *Journal of Money, Credit and Banking* 1/4 (1969), pp. 706 - 726, y E. KARNI, Transaction costs and the demand for media of exchange, en: *Western Economic Journal* 11/1 (1973), pp. 71 - 80.

21 Representación del comercio de Barcelona a Carlos III, 21 de noviembre de 1778, (AGI, Indiferente General, leg. 2415. Otros factores que aumentaban

En el Principado, el *Reglamento* además transformó la práctica mercantil catalana al imponer el uso de la moneda y el sistema métrico castellano:

> "pues así como antes se arreglaban por canas y palmos que es la medida común del país, y por moneda catalana, se ha querido también variar esta práctica poniendo varas en lugar de canas, y anotando sus precios por moneda de vellón".

El aumento del riesgo y la incertidumbre no sólo perjudicó al comercio catalán. En diciembre de 1778 un colectivo de 38 cargadores gaditanos solicitaron al Rey que se definiera el marco en el cual debían organizarse las expediciones a los puertos del Perú y Chile prestas para partir a fines de mes; este marco sólo quedó finalmente perfilado cuando una R.O. de 25 de diciembre despejó las últimas dudas[22].

Los costes financieros que soportaba el reexportador de las bretañas se incluyen en IIc. La primera columna refleja el interés anual pagado por el importador español de textiles elaborados o semielaborados a su proveedor extranjero, calculado a partir de la diferencia entre el precio de la mercancía al contado, algo muy inusual en las compras al por mayor de textiles extranjeros y la venta a pago aplazado de un año, procedimiento utilizado en la mayoría de las compras. La segunda, el "premio" del cambio marítimo suscrito por el comerciante español, con la garantía de sus mercancías, para financiar los restantes costes

---

los niveles de incertidumbre en opinión de los cargadores catalanes eran el caracter incompleto de los aranceles que dejaban sin aforamiento oficial manufacturas poco frecuentes en el comercio de América y concedían a los funcionarios del resguardo la potestad de valorarlas en cada caso (El comercio de Barcelona a Carlos III, 21-XII-1778, AGI, Indiferente General, leg. 1830-A), y la obligación de depositar antes del adeudo las mercancías registradas en los almacenes de la aduana "cuya práctica sobre de ser contraria a la que se observa en Cádiz y en los demás puertos habilitados del Reino, atrasa el despacho de los registros y causa otros perjuicios que son notorios" (AGI, Indiferente general, leg. 2415).

22 Memorial del comercio gaditano a Carlos III, 1-XII-1778.
AGI, Indiferente General, leg. 2415. Las R.O. de 25 de diciembre exigió el pago de los aranceles a las vituallas incluidas en el registro como rancho.

de transacción. Hay que aclarar que estos costes financieros no afectaban a todos los exportadores sino sólo a los cargadores españoles que comerciaban por su cuenta, es decir, los teóricamente protegidos por el "comercio libre". Ni las grandes casas extranjeras establecidas en Cádiz, que utilizaban como testaferros a los cargadores gaditanos, ni algunas grandes empresas privilegiadas españolas, muy en especial los Cinco Gremios de Madrid, tenían necesidad de endeudarse, o al menos de hacerlo en la misma medida que el cargador privado. Por añadidura, también aquí nuestra estimación peca necesariamente por defecto, pues considera que los tipos de interés que regían en plazas con un mercado de capitales relativamente amplio como eran Cádiz y Barcelona eran los mismos que en otras como Santander, La Coruña, Málaga, etc.

Finalmente, en IId resumo la repercusión porcentual sobre el precio de la mercancía de los diferentes componentes de los costes de transacción en los tres supuestos contemplados. El resultado muestra que, lejos de reducirse, los costes marginales de transacción aumentaron como resultado del cambio institucional debido a que la mayor carga fiscal no fué compensada por un descenso proporcional de las restantes partidas.

CUADRO III:
Costes de transacción de una partida de 8.000 cueros al pelo de Buenos Aires, valorada en origen en 205.712,5 rs. vn. y destinada a La Coruña para su posterior reexportación a Europa[23]

Del Río de la Plata a Montevideo		*De Montevideo a La Coruña*		*De La Coruña a Europa*	
embarque en lancha	400	flete hasta La Coruña	54.857,1	gastos embarque	1.983,0
flete a Montevideo	10.000	gastos de desembarco	1.382,9	derechos reexport.	112.941,2
ramo de guerra	40.000	derechos entrada	28.235,3	Consulado	1.800,0
alcabala	9.600	Consulado	1.800,0		
Total (%)	60.000 [29,2]	Total (%)	86.275,3 [41,9]	Total (%)	116.724,2 [56,7]
TOTAL (%)					262.999,5 [127,8]

El cuadro III traslada los cálculos de II a los cueros sin curtir, una de las materias primas industriales cuya importación resultó en teoría mas favorecida por el nuevo sistema al permitir a través de la habilitación de los puertos del Río de la Plata al "comercio libre" la llegada masiva de una mercancía de gran demanda en la industria europea. También aquí la realidad defraudó los paternales deseos de Carlos III. Los cueros que se destinaban al mercado nacional pagaban sólo de derechos fiscales el 38,7% de su precio de compra hasta su entrada en

23 Fuente: AGI, Indiferente general, leg. 2442, "Cuenta figurada del coste, derechos y gastos de 8.000 cueros al pelo de Buenos Aires comprados en aquellos parajes, conducidoa a la Coruña y extraidos a dominio extranjero".

puerto español. Es cierto que el arancel de 1778 había considerado los cueros como una mercancia de libre entrada en España; pero una R.O. de 15 de julio de 1785, que afectó también a otros productos anteriormente declarados "libres", como el azúcar o el papel, estableció sobre los cueros una contribución de 4 maravedis por libra, equivalente, a un 7,3% "ad valorem"[24]. Si el cargador deseaba reexportar los cueros al mercado europeo, la repercusión fiscal sobre el precio en origen alcanzaba se situaba en torno al 94,5% del dinero destinado a la compra de los cueros. En resumen, para un comercio que se financiaba a través de cambios marítimos y otras formas leoninas de contrato, los costes de transacción de importar una mercancía especialmente protegida requerían del desembolso adicional de un volumen de recursos financieros que superaba en un 27,8% la inversión realizada en su compra en origen.

A partir de la información contenida en los cuadros I, II y III es posible ya esbozar algunas conclusiones generales respecto al impacto que a corto plazo pudo tener el sistema de comercio libre sobre los intercambios entre España e Hispanoamérica. En primer lugar, resulta difícil de creer que el *Reglamento* representara una reducción en los niveles de presión fiscal sobre los que funcionaba la Carrera de Indias. Tanto las manufacturas "nacionales" como las "extranjeras" y los productos agrarios de consumo masivo debieron contribuir más como resultado de la aplicación de los nuevos impuestos "ad valorem" a la salida de España y a la entrada en Indias, de la modificación al alza de las valoraciones arancelarias que tendieron a situarse muy por encima de los precios corrientes en 1778, y del mantenimiento y aún aumento de las contribuciones y arbitrios locales vigentes tanto en los puertos habilitados espanoles como en los americanos. Es cierto que algunas manufacturas compatibles con la producción doméstica en el marco de la "industria popular" se vieron favorecidas con ventajas fiscales; o que el "comercio libre" reservó la demanda de transporte a los buques de fábrica española - aunque esta reserva distara mucho de ser efecti-

---

24 AGS, Dirección General de Rentas, 2a^{r}, leg. 433.

va[25]; pero resulta difícil encontrar en esta protección sectorial indicio alguno de una voluntad modernizadora, destinada a favorecer el desarrollo de una industria y un comercio más competitivos; los únicos intereses que primaron sobre los de la Hacienda mientras José de Galvez, el reformador por antonomasia se mantuvo al frente de la Secretaría de Indias, fueron la defensa del orden social establecido y los intereses de la marina y del ejército.

La segunda reflexión hace referencia a la evolución de los costes de transacción. Su eventual reducción hubiera constituido la mejor prueba de los efectos modernizadores del cambio institucional introducido en la Carrera de Indias por el "comercio libre". Pero los cuadros II y III indican que, salvo el descenso de los fletes ligado no tanto a un aumento de la eficiencia del nuevo marco legislativo como a un desplazamiento de la presión fiscal de la actividad naviera al comercio, no hubo mejora entre el período del monopolio gaditano y la nueva etapa que se abre en 1778. Si a ello agregamos el incremento de la presión fiscal y de la incertidumbre generada por el cambio en las reglas de juego del comercio colonial que aumentó la probabilidad de cometer errores en el cálculo de las previsiones de coste / beneficio por parte de los agentes económicos, no resulta difícil concluir que el contenido de la reforma esterilizó los posibles estímulos que que pudiera haber generado una liberalización efectiva del tráfico con América[26].

Esta valoración del cambio institucional es necesariamente provisional y se basa únicamente en un análisis de sus efectos a corto plazo. Para confirmarla, o modificarla, es preciso considerar otras variables que permitan descubrir, por ejemplo, posibles cambios en la orientación de la política reformista dirigidos a corregir efectos no deseados de la

---

25 Esperamos al respecto un próximo y esclarecedor trabajo de Marina Alfonso sobre la marina gaditana del "comercio libre".

26 Sobre el papel inhibidor de los costes de transacción, aún en el marco de un cambio institucional que permita una mejora en los costes de producción, D. C. NORTH, Transactions Costs in History, pp. 558 - 559.

nueva legislación o valorar la respuesta de los usuarios a través de su participación en el "comercio libre".

Por si acaso el *Reglamento y los Aranceles para el comercio libre* ofrecían alguna duda respecto a los objetivos de la reforma, la normativa complementaria posterior acentuó el sentido depredatorio de la política comercial española. A grandes rasgos, las modificaciones introducidas hasta 1787 en el marco institucional del "comercio libre", fueron escasas y siempre en la misma dirección. De forma coyuntural, la guerra contra Inglaterra sirvió de excusa para establecer nuevos derechos y aumentar los ya vigentes. Una R.O. de marzo de 1780 - no derogada hasta febrero de 1784 - dobló la percepción en concepto de almojarifazgo de América, mientras que otra de diciembre de 1781 "para sostener el armamento en corso de 20 navíos", impuso un 3% adicional de entrada en España y un 4% a la salida de Indias[27].

Otras innovaciones más duraderas se introdujeron a través de un casi imperceptible goteo de las órdenes de rentas que resolvían consultas planteadas por las administraciones fiscales de los diferentes puertos habilitados en su diaria aplicación del *Reglamento*. En su mayoría, las dudas surgían como resultado de su aplicación casuística bajo circunstancias no contempladas por la norma, o en aquellas otras en que su redacción confusa podía admitir más de una interpretación. Con pocas excepciones, la Dirección General, apoyó a través de sus dictámenes resoluciones favorables a la Real Hacienda. Así sucedió, - entre los numerosos conflictos que enfrentaron al comercio de Barcelona y a la aduana de la ciudad -, con la R.O. de 16 de abril de 1779 que exigía el cobro del derecho de puertas y equivalente de bolla sobre el azúcar procedente de América, y un 3% de las indianas fabricadas con algodón maltés[28], o, más tarde, con otra de marzo de noviembre de 1781 que imponía el derecho de lezda sobre algunos productos catalanes de exportación libres según el *Reglamento*, como los sombreros,

27 AGI Indiferente General, leg. 1831; MATILLA TASCÓN, Catálogo de la Colección de ordenes generales de rentas, n. 3197, p. 293.

28 MATILLA TASCÓN, Catalogo, p. 265, y n. 3169, p. 294.

el papel o los curtidos[29]. Otras disposiciones de aplicación general a todos los puertos habilitados se dirigieron a reducir el margen de exenciones y desgravaciones a que por costumbre tenía derecho el comerciante según las Leyes de Indias. Así, dos RROO limitaron en 1784 y 1785 los beneficios fiscales concedidos al cargador de materias primas y frutos coloniales afectado por una avería de mar[30]; otra de 1786 redujo el margen exento de la caja de soldadas a 400 ps. fs.[31] y una de febrero de 1787, incluyó al rancho de la tripulación entre la base imponible de los registros de los buques del comercio libre[32].

Los nuevos impuestos sobre mercancías libres de gravamen según los aranceles de 1778 fueron aún mas significativos por el volumen de ingresos adicionales que pudieron reportar al erario. Dos RROO de 15 y 16 de julio de 1785 crearon nuevas contribuciones para el azúcar, cueros y papel[33]. Otra datada un año antes se insertaba más en el ámbito de la política de fomento de la "industria" popular, al imponer sobre las medias de algodón, encajes e indianas fabricadas en Cataluña el 3% con independencia de que fueran o no "indubitablemente" manufacturadas en el reino[34].

Estas disposiciones tuvieron un complemento adecuado en una abundante normativa represora del fraude y el contrabando. La convicción de la Corona de que era preciso endurecer las medidas preventivas y punitivas en defensa del comercio legal indica una extrema desconfi-

---

29 MATILLA TASCÓN, Catálogo, n. 2856, n. 265.

30 La R.O. de 30-X-1784, limitó a un 3% la rebaja por avería deel cacao (MATILLA, Catálogo, n. 3467 p. 294. Otra de 16 de julio de 1785 fijó el límite mínimo para solicitar la desgravación por avería en el 50% de la carga,(AGS, D.G.R., 2ʳ, leg. 433).

31 R.O. de 24 de noviembre (AGI, Indiferente General, leg. 2213).

32 AGI, Indiferente general, leg. 2435.

33 MATILLA, Catálogo, n. 3542, p. 330, y AGS DGR, leg. 433. Los 34 marav. por libra sobre los cueros se percibía a su reexportación.

34 RO. de 12 de febrero de 1784, (AGS, DGR, 2ʳ leg. 1017).

anza hacia sus propias promesas liberalizadoras y hacia la previsible reacción negativa de sus súbditos.

Los resultados del "Comercio Libre". La evolucion del trafico entre 1778 y 1796

Corresponde a J. Fisher el mérito de haber reconstruido a partir de la documentación del archivo de Indias la serie más completa, larga y fiable del "comercio libre" entre España y América, cuyas cifras agregadas recogemos en el cuadro IV[35]. Según sus conclusiones, el comercio libre promovió una "expansión masiva" en el valor de las exportaciones españolas a América[36]; que se multiplicaron en "valores constantes" por cuatro durante el período 1782 - 1796, respecto a la base de 1778. En gran medida, esta expansión sería protagonizada por las remesas de géneros nacionales que aumentaron su participación en la carga total del 38% al 52%. El crecimiento de las importaciones pone de manifiesto un éxito aún mas resonante de la política imperial de Carlos III[37] al multiplicarse nada menos que por 11[38], lo que pare-

---

35 Entre otros, Imperial "Free Trade" and the Hispanic Economy, 1778 - 1796, en: *Journal of Latin American Studies* 13 (1981), pp. 21 - 56; "The Imperial response to "Free Trade": Spanish Imports from Spanish America, 1778 - 1796, en: *Journal of Latin American Studies* 17 (1985), pp. 35 - 78; Commercial Relations between Spain snd Spanish America in the Era of Free Trade 1778 - 1796, Liverpool 1985; El impacto del comercio libre en América durante el último cuarto del siglo XVIII, en: El Comercio Libre entre España y America Latina, pp. 29-38; The Effects of Comercio Libre on the Economies of New Granada and Peru: A Comparison, en: FISHER / KUETHE / MCFARLANE (edits.), Reform and Insurrection in Bourbon New Granada and Peru, Baton Rouge 1990, pp. 147 - 163. En su último trabajo, Relaciones económicas entre España y América hasta la Independencia, Madrid 1992, p. 246, FISHER completa su serie hasta 1810.

36 FISHER, Commercial Relations, pp. 46 y 88.

37 J. FISHER, Spanish Imports from Spanish America, p. 62.

ce indicar una mejora en las relaciones de intercambio entre España y sus colonias tras la puesta en práctica del "comercio libre".

CUADRO IV:
La expansión del "comercio libre" según J. R. Fisher
(millon. rs. vn.)

año	export. nacional	export. extranjera	export. total	import América
1778	28,2	46,3	74,5	74,6
1782	57,1	55,5	112,7	110,8
1783	71,5	65,3	136,8	171,5
1784	196,7	238,9	435,6	550,9
1785	213,0	244,7	457,7	1.149,8
1786	170,4	168,9	339,3	810,8
1787	116,8	141,9	258,7	609,1
1788	153,5	151,7	305,2	947,8
1789	175,3	151,2	305,2	993,0
1790	149,3	142,9	292,2	941,7
1791	184,8	185,5	370,3	1.203,8
1792	226,6	214,9	441,5	933,8
1793	164,2	143,1	307,3	888,6
1794	113,7	72,1	185,8	1.061,6
1795	165,7	116,4	282,1	905,4
1796	143,6	108,3	251,8	1.149,2

Los resultados espectaculares ofrecidos por las cifras de Fisher pueden convencer al lector mas receloso del éxito de la reforma del comercio colonial y, por ello, han resultado perfectamente asimilables en los esquemas interpretativos que hablan de una modernización económica durante el reinado de Carlos III. Sin embargo el mismo

---

38 FISHER, Commercial Relations, p. 61.

cuadro IV, parece desmentir algunas de las conclusiones de Fisher. Las exportaciones, en especial, no parecen mostrar un crecimiento sostenido sino que alcanzan sus máximos hacia 1785, durante la fiebre exportadora que siguió a la paz de Versalles, para caer luego de forma rápida y recuperarse en 1791 - 1792 pero en niveles inferiores a los de 1785. Si en lugar de utilizar el engañoso procedimiento de los números-índice medimos su evolución a través de tasas de crecimiento acumulativo, resulta que las exportaciones crecieron entre 1778 y 1785 en torno a un 25,5% anual, para caer durante los dos años siguientes a razón de un 16,6% anual. Después de la crisis de 1787 no hubo crecimiento real; entre este año y 1796, el último de normalidad antes del estallido de las guerras contra Inglaterra de fines de siglo, permanecieron prácticamente estancadas en torno a una tasa negativa del 0,3% anual.

En trabajos ya publicados hace algunos años[39] hice mención de alguno de los inconvenientes que plantea el uso de las series sobre el "comercio libre" elaboradas por Fisher. Mi crítica destacaba dos aspectos concretos que cuestionaban los resultados obtenidos. En primer lugar la elección discutible de 1778 como año base para medir la evolución posterior del comercio libre, no tanto por ser un punto de referencia "anormal" donde la actividad de los exportadores está condicionada por los rumores de un inminente guerra contra Gran Bretaña[40], como por la distorsión que provoca la introducción, por los Aranceles de 1778, de nuevos criterios en el cálculo de la base imponible de las mercancías y en la determinación de su procedencia nacional o extranjera. De este modo, la serie resultante aumenta

---

39 El modelo catalán dentro del sistema de libre comercio, en: El comercio libre entre España y América, pp. 53 - 70; y: Libre comercio. Mito y realidad, en: T. MARTÍNEZ VARA (edit.), Mercado y desarrollo económico.

40 Esta inseguridad afectó especialmente al período en que comienza a operar el "comercio libre". Según muestra Spooner, las primas de seguros en el mercado de Amsterdam se doblaron en las rutas que tenían por destino Cádiz, Malaga, Alicante o Barcelona, entre octubre y noviembre de 1778 (Risks at Sea, pp. 257 - 286).

automáticamente el valor de las exportaciones y las importaciones, en la medida en que lo hacen las valoraciones arancelarias e incrementa la participación de las exportaciones "nacionales" con la inclusión de mercancías que no merecían en las aduanas tal calificativo hasta octubre de 1778. El reciente trabajo de A. M. Bernal sobre la financiación de la Carrera de Indias muestra con claridad el efecto distorsionador que sobre las magnitudes reales del tráfico puede tener el uso de las valoraciones arancelarias.

CUADRO V:
Comercio y crédito en la Carrera de Indias (1778 - 1788)[41]
(mill. rs. vn.)

año	cambios marítimos	exportaciones Cádiz	exportaciones España
1778	76,1	50,2	74,5
1779	72,9	--	--
1780	39,6	--	--
1781	5,1	--	--
1782	50,8	97,9	112,7
1783	75,6	107,3	136,8
1784	95,1	362,1	435,6
1785	186,1	358,2	457,7
1786	113,4	256,1	339,3
1787	36,8	196,1	258,7
1788	45,8	220,7	305,2
media (79-88)	72,5[95,0]	228,3[454,8]	292,3[392,3]

Desde que en 1760 se reafirmara la obligación de inscribir las escrituras de riesgo de mar en la contaduría del Consulado de Cádiz, la información que proporciona el registro de los cambios marítimos es

41 A. M. Bernal, Riesgos y cambios en la carrera de Indias (1760 - 1788), en: Actas del Congreso Internacional sobre Carlos III, pp. 89 - 313. Los datos de Fisher proceden de la misma fuente que el Cuadro V.

tanto o mas fiable que la contenida en las fuentes fiscales de los archivos de Indias y Simancas, y, en opinión de Bernal, quien ha llevado a cabo su estudio exahustivo[42], garantiza una mejor cobertura del tráfico con América que las series convencionales utilizadas por García Baquero y Fisher. Desde mi punto de vista, además de las virtudes ya señaladas por el profesor Bernal, la contratación de cambios marítimos tiene dos ventajas adicionales para el investigador del comercio colonial. En primer lugar, ofrece una evolución a precios de mercado de los intercambios con América aún en el supuesto de que sólo una parte del comercio de exportación se financiara a través de este procedimiento[43]-; en segundo lugar, la serie no está afectada por cambios en las valoraciones arancelarias puesto que el criterio que rige el acuerdo contractual gira en torno al valor concedido a la porción de mercancías que constituye la garantía real del préstamo cambiario. El Cuadro V recoge el monto anual de la financiación en cambios marítimos para el período 1778 - 1788 y la compara con las series de Fisher de exportaciones totales y a través sólo del puerto de Cádiz.

El resultado es el esperado. Según los datos de Bernal no existe crecimiento entre 1778 y la media del período 1779 - 1788; según Fisher las exportaciones casi se cuadruplican para el conjunto de los puertos habilitados, mientras que se multiplican por 4,5 en el de Cádiz. Igualmente significativo resulta el hecho de que hasta la puesta en práctica de los Aranceles de 1778, la coincidencia entre el valor de los cambios contratados en Cádiz y el volumen de las exportaciones según su valor oficial es casi idéntico - 76,1 millones de reales frente a 74,5 - para

---

42 A. GARCIA BAQUERO ha trabajado sobre la misma fuente para estudiar la financiación de las flotas de 1765 y 1768. (Un modelo de financiación del tráfico con Indias: El riesgo marítimo en las flotas de 1765 y 1768, en: *Archivo Hispalense* 219 [1989], pp. 219 - 245).

43 Las cifras que García Baquero ofrece para las flotas de 1765 y 1768 indican que la abrumadora mayoría de los cambios se concertaron con la garantía de las mercancías embarcadas - el 85,3 y el 86,7% respectivamente - (Un modelo de financiación del tráfico con Indias, pp. 234 - 235).

alejarse bruscamente a partir de 1782, con los primeros cálculos oficiales sobre el nuevo arancel. La serie completa ofrecida por Bernal queda recogida en el gráfico - I - y sitúa con claridad la culminación de la etapa expansiva del tráfico ultramarino en torno a 1774 - 1776, justo en el momento de la preparación de las últimas flotas a Nueva España.

Nuestras dudas sobre la magnitud del crecimiento constatado por Fisher se acrecientan en el análisis de las importaciones procedentes de Indias. En este caso, el motivo de desacuerdo no es tanto el procedimiento utilizado en el cálculo de las cifras sinó el "olvido" de los 550 millones de rs. de vn. transportados por la flota de Antonio de Ulloa a la hora de calcular el valor de los retornos llegados a España en 1778. Esta flota "fantasma"[44] transportó a Cádiz una carga que el propio virrey de Nueva España había valorado en 27,5 millones de ps. fs. con lo que las llegadas a la metrópoli procedentes de América se situarían en torno a los 624,6 millones de rs. vn., en lugar de los exiguos 74,6 estimados por Fisher. De este modo, unas importaciones que se habían multiplicado por 11 de media en 1782 - 1796 respecto a su base, sólo crecieron según sus propias cifras, en un 32,6%, porcentaje que no contabiliza el impacto del cambio en las valoraciones arancelarias sobre las estimaciones oficiales, mas limitado en el caso de las importaciones por la presencia mayoritaria de metales preciosos[45].

---

44 El de retorno de la flota de Ulloa tampoco es recogida por GARCÍA BAQUERO en en su estudio monográfico sobre el comercio colonial durante la etapa del monopolio gaditano. GARCIA BAQUERO conoce de su existencia Cádiz y el Atlántico, I pp. 280 - 281 pero no incluye su carga en el apéndice estadístico (Cadiz y el Atlántico, II cuadro n. 40, p. 252, y cuadro n. 43, p 265.). Si lo hace, en cambio, MORINEAU (Incroyables gazettes, p. 415).

45 Michel MORINEAU utiliza en sus *Incroyables Gazettes* una serie alternativa de los retornos del comercio libre construida a partir de la información aparecida en la *Gazeta de Madrid* y el *Correo Mercantil* que presenta notables diferencias con respecto a la de FISHER:

Existe una alternativa hasta ahora no ensayada para tratar de medir cómo afectó en el largo plazo el comercio libre la evolución de los in-

Retornos de Indias en metales preciosos (Morineau), y retornos totales (Fisher)
(en millones de rs. vn.)

año	retornos en metales preciosos (Morineau)	retornos metales (Fisher)	retornos totales (Fisher)
1778	647,2	?	74,6
1779	71,3	--	--
1780	230,0	--	--
1781	180,1*	--	--
1782	n.p.	4,2	100,8
1783	294,7	51,8	171,5
1784	843,8	480,9	550,9
1785	794,9	758,81	149,8
1786	653,8	460,9	810,8
1787	514,5	258,3	609,1
1788	488,0	463,1	947,8
1789	398,5	364,3	993,0
1790	386,4	411,0	941,7
1791	549,0	570,4	1.203,8
1792	476,6	408,9	933,8
1793	435,1	410,9	888,6
1794	434,9	659,6	1.061,6
1795	526,4	502,3	905,4
1796	603,5	596,4	1.149,2

* estimación mínima.

Estas cifras (Incroyables gazettes, pp. 430 - 435) plantean asimismo algunos problemas. Pese a no recoger hasta fecha muy avanzada - 1792 - las remesas en metales llegadas al puerto de Barcelona, y aún de forma incompleta, logran superar hasta el año 1789 sin excepción la información proporcionada por las hojas de registro de los buques. Con el desmantelamiento del aparato de propaganda organizado desde el Ministerio de Indias por Gálvez en defensa de los logros de su política reformista, las cifras "oficiales" tienden a reflejar mas fielmente la realidad de los niveles del tráfico y a situarse por detrás del recuento de la información del Archivo de Indias. La manipulación de la información no era nada nuevo ni en Gálvez, ni en la *Gazeta*. Ortíz de Landazuri ya había descubierto años atrás la habilidad del entonces visitador de Nueva España para jugar con los números, y su protector el marqués de Grimaldi era un experto en el uso de la *Gazeta* ¿Qué mejor prueba de lo que decimos el intento de ocultar al público la terrible crisis de 1787 con unos resultados que doblan a las reales?

tercambios entre España y América que consiste en comparar las magnitudes del tráfico antes y después de 1778. Si descartamos por excesivamente groseros indicadores como el del número de navíos, o su capacidad de carga, sólo las estimaciones sobre el valor de las mercancías pueden ofrecer nuevas vías de aproximación a la evolución del comercio con las Indias. Pero dos problemas dificultan la construcción de una serie homogénea sobre los valores del comercio colonial durante el siglo XVIII. El primero es cómo unir series calculadas sobre diferentes criterios de valoración arancelaria; el segundo afecta únicamente a las mercancías exportadas en calidad de géneros de palmeo, cuyo adeudo fiscal se realizaba en función de su volumen en palmos cúbicos y no del valor de las mercancías. La solución adoptada para confeccionar las series representadas en los gráficos II a XIII es la de trasladar hacia atrás los valores fijados por el Arancel del "comercio libre" y aplicarlos sobre las cantidades ofrecidas por García Baquero[46]. La estimación de las mercancías sujetas a palmeo se ha realizado a partir de los cálculos efectuados en 1765 por el Contador de Indias Ortíz de Landázuri sobre el valor de una tonelada de mercancías de palmeo que hemos reproducido en el cuadro I. Pese a que la serie de las exportaciones se resiente de la laguna de un cuarto de siglo que existe en las cifras del comercio colonial durante la etapa del monopolio gaditano elaboradas por García Baquero[47], indica que las exportaciones crecieron entre la primera mitad y el último cuarto del siglo XVIII en torno a un 4,9% anual, desde una media anual de 34,5 millones en el período 1720 hasta 300,2 en 1782 - 1796. Sin embargo, no sabemos a ciencia cierta que parte de este crecimiento puede atribuirse propiamente al "comercio libre". La cuan-

---

46 García Baquero, *Cádiz y el Atlántico*, II pp. 180 - 275; Fisher, Commercial Relations between Spain and Spanish America in the Era of Free Trade, pp. 92 - 151.

47 Cádiz y el Atlántico, II pp. 180 - 219. La serie de exportaciones se interrumpe en 1751, justo cuando el comercio con América iniciaba su etapa de mayor dinamismo, y para el siguiente cuarto de siglo sólo incluye la carga de las flotas a Nueva España.

tificación del tráfico en "toneladas mercantes" también ofrecida por Garcia Baquero, parece indicar que el crecimiento de las exportaciones se aceleró en la etapa final del monopolio gaditano[48].

La información sobre las importaciones es mucho más completa y permite llegar a mayores precisiones tanto respecto a su evolución general como a la particular de sus principales componentes. El gráfico - VI - recoge la suma de todas las importaciones de cuenta de particulares y del sector publico en valores arancelarios de 1778, y apunta la importancia de las dos décadas anteriores a la generalización del comercio libre como el período de mayor dinamismo en el comercio con América. Esta impresión se acentúa a medida que desagregamos las cifras. Los gráficos VII y VIII representan por separado las importaciones realizadas por el comercio y aquéllas que corrieron a cargo de la Real Hacienda. Las primeras incluyen los retornos de las exportaciones, ya sea en metales o reinvertido en la compra de materias primas y productos agrarios tropicales, más los ingresos de los navieros por flete de ida y vuelta y los salarios retenidos durante meses de navegación a la marinería. El peso de este componente dentro de los retornos en plata es difícil de precisar año por año pero osciló durante toda la etapa del comercio libre en torno al 25% y al 30% de las remesas de particulares[49]. Por lo que respecta

---

48 GARCIA BAQUERO, Cádiz y el Atlántico, II cuadro 20, pp. 126 - 128. La existencia de una correlación muy baja entre las variables "tonelaje mercante" y valor de las exportaciones para el período 1720 - 1751 - r2= 0,15 - desaconseja el construir una serie de valores a partir de la información disponible sobre el tonelaje.

49 La transferencia por servicios más fácilmente identificable es la de los salarios de la marineria, consignada bajo la partida de "caja de soldadas" en los registros de retorno y que reunía los salarios retenidos a la tripulación desde su partida de España hasta su retorno a puerto español. Las contratas deä tripulación establecían como cláusula fija que el pago de las retribuciones por un viaje redondo a las Indias se realizase una vez el barco estuviera ya de retorno para evitar las deserciones entre la marinería. Las sumas debidas se registraron regularmente en la "caja de soldadas" mientras ésta fué exenta del pago de los derechos de entrada en España; pero cuando dejó de serlo, perdió

al sector público, el grueso de los retornos corresponde al excedente neto obtenido de la administración colonial, mas algunas materias primas industriales cuyo comercio estaba estancado. Por último, en los gráficos - IX a XIII - hemos representado por separado la evolución de las importaciones de los productos más relevantes del comercio americano - plata, azúcar, cacao, tabaco y añil.

CUADRO VIa:
Importaciones de América (1717 - 1796)
(millones rs. vn. de media anual)

	privadas	%	estatales	%	total
[1717-1738]	155,3	(86,7)	23,8	(13,3)	179,1
[1747-1778]	365,0	(87,7)	51,1	(12,3)	416,1
[1782-1796]	518,9	(72,1)	200,6	(27,9)	719,5

CUADRO VIb:
Importaciones de metales preciosos
(millones rs. vn. de media anual)

	privadas	%	estatales	%	total
[1717-1738]	137,7	(85,7)	22,9	(14,3)	160,6
[1747-1778]	267,3	(91,5)	24,7	(8,5)	292,0
[1782-1796]	310,0	(75,4)	101,2	(24,6)	411,2

La consideración desagregada de los retornos permite discernir con claridad quienes fueron los beneficiarios de la reforma. Respecto a la plata, el cuadro VII indica que las remesas consignadas a particulares

toda relevancia el incluirlas o no. Hacia 1784, cuando la "caja" aún significaba un beneficio fiscal representaba el 7,2% de las remesas de metales consignadas a particulares, según los dastos de FISHER (Commercial Relations, p. 67.)

crecieron con especial rapidez entre 1747 y 1778, a razón de una tasa anual del 1,7%, para reducir su crecimiento en la etapa del comercio libre a menos de la mitad - 0,8% -, tras alcanzar sus máximos máximos seculares entre 1765 y 1778, con cifras sólo superadas luego excepcionalmente en 1785. La serie que recoge el saldo neto de la administración colonial remitido a España muestra un comportamiento totalmente distinto. Entre el primer y el segundo tercio del siglo XVIII, las remesas de metales de cuenta del sector público sólo crecieron en torno a un 0,2% anual, para saltar despues de 1778 a una tasa del 8,2%. En términos relativos ello representó que la Real Hacienda pasó a controlar directamente la remisión de la cuarta parte de los caudales enviados desde America durante la etapa del comercio libre. Estos resultados en poco se modifican si contabilizamos el valor arancelario de los frutos y materias primas coloniales. Las consignadas al sector privado crecieron en torno a un 2,2% anual, para reducir su ritmo de expansión a un 2% durante el "comercio libre; las importadas directamente por la Real Hacienda en cambio pasaron de aumentar a razón de un 0,7% en las décadas centrales de siglo, a un espectacular 10,9% anual, en buena medida gracias al rendimiento del estanco del tabaco. Aún los defensores de la bondad intrínseca del "comercio libre" podrían argumentar que, pese a todo, las importaciones de frutos coloniales crecieron a un ritmo casi similar al del período anterior. Pero tanto si consideramos la evolución agregada de las importaciones de frutos como alguno de sus componentes más significativos - azúcar, cacao, o añil - hay que concluir que la continuidad de este crecimiento poco o nada tiene que ver con la política económica de Carlos III. Salvo la euforia pasajera de 1785, las importaciones de frutos sólo alcanzaron altas tasas de crecimiento a partir de 1789 - 1791 como resultado de los cambios registrados en el mercado mundial de productos tropicales tras la revolución de Haití que eliminó a una de las economías de plantación más eficientes[50]. Una parte de la demanda europea de coloniales tradicionalmente cubierta por las re-

---

50 D. WATTS, The West Indies. Patterns of Development, Culture and Environmental Change since 1492, Cambridge 1987, p. 253 y 299 - 300.

exportaciones francesas se desvió coyunturalmente hacia los frutos importados por el comercio español, que pudo aprovecharla durante poco mas a un lustro gracias a que la nueva política colonial auspiciada por Floridablanca tras la muerte de Gálvez, se preocupó por desmantelar parte de las trabas fiscales y burocráticas que habían determinado el fracaso del sistema de "comercio libre"[51]. En el caso de aquellos productos que como la grana - gráfico XIII - dependían exclusivamente de la oferta española, el estímulo derivado del cambio en la estructura de la oferta no existió, y las importaciones durante el "comercio libre" nunca alcanzaron los niveles de la última etapa del comercio de flotas.

Finalmente, un comentario respecto a la evolución de los términos intercambio. Según Fisher, éstos evolucionaron favorablemente a España al crecer más rápidamente las importaciones que las exportaciones[52]. Pero si abandonamos la movediza base de 1778 para estimar a largo plazo la evolución del tráfico la conclusión a que se llega es totalmente distinta. Mientras las exportaciones crecieron en torno a un 4,9 anual entre el segundo y el último cuarto del siglo XVIII, los retornos en plata y frutos consignados a particulares sólo lo hicieron a razón de un 2,8% anual. O en otras palabras, el comercio español para importar lo mismo de las colonias debió exportar cada vez más.

---

51 Sobre la incidencia de la coyuntura revolucionaria en el mercado español de coloniales, vid. mi investigación financiada por una Beca V Centenario del Banco de España, Comercio colonial y crecimiento económico (1776 - 1808). Una interpretación a partir de los precios, Barcelona 1989 (policopiada).

52 Commercial Relations, pp. 60 - 61.

GRAFICO I:
Cambios marítimos, Cadiz (1760 - 1788)

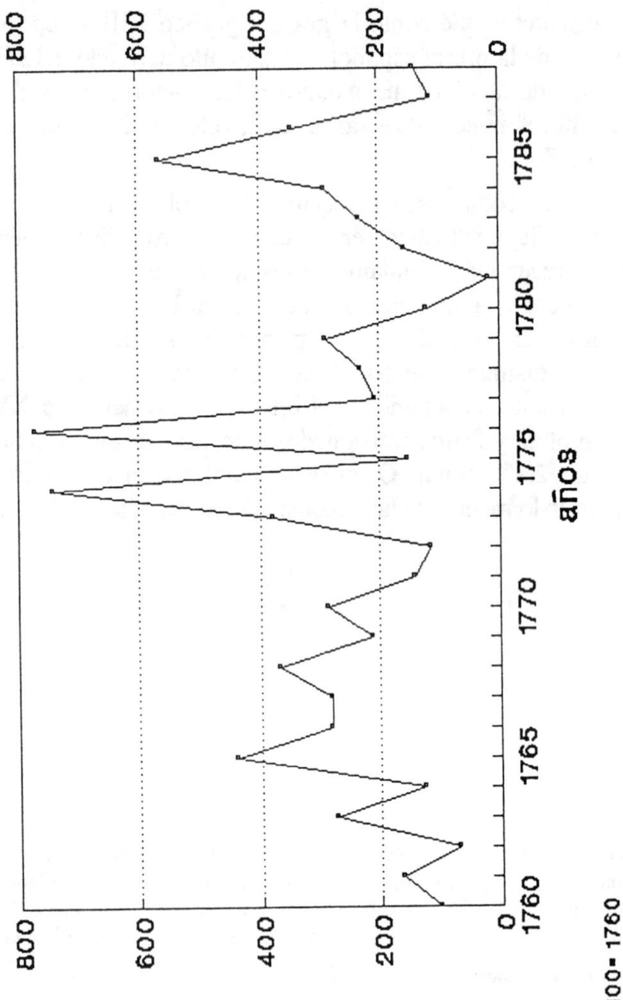

GRAFICO II:
Exportaciones a Indias, 1720 - 1796

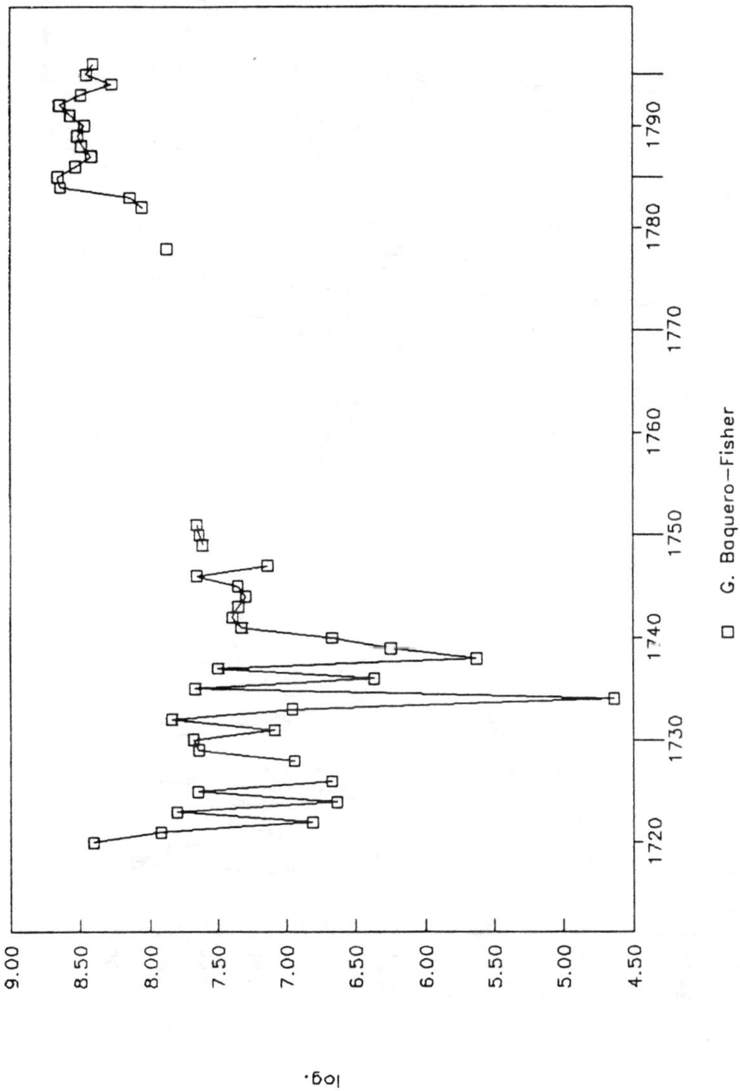

GRAFICO III:
Exportaciones en "tn. mercantes"

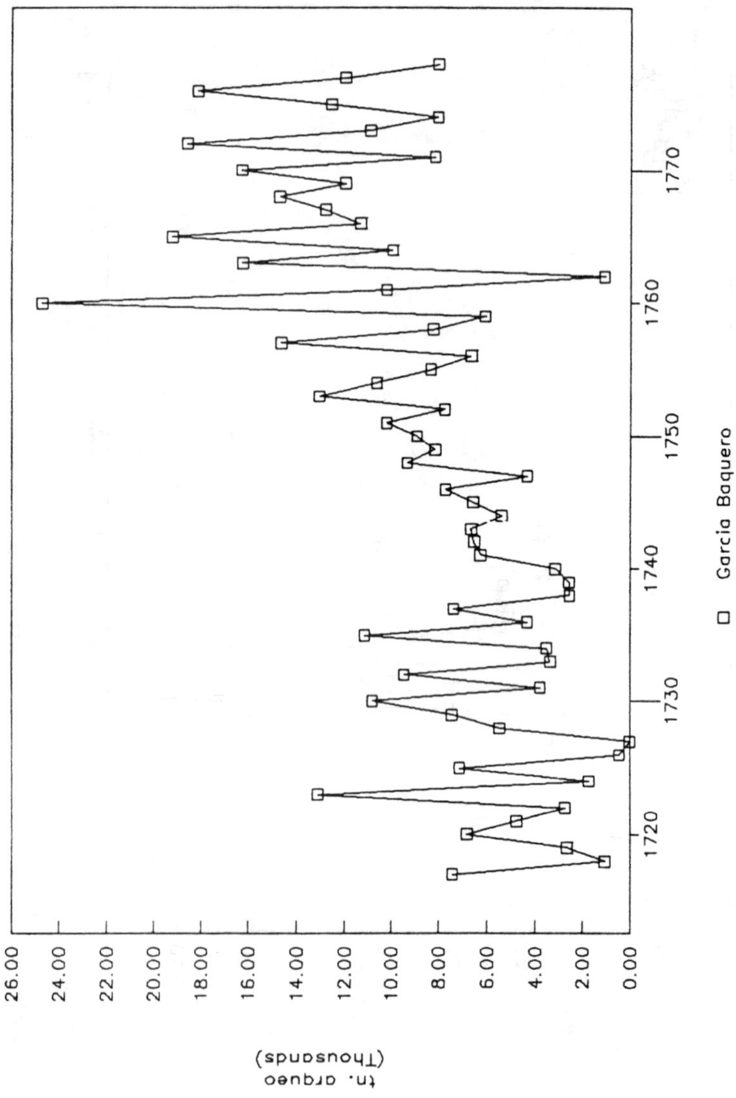

GRAFICO IV:
Importaciones de Indias, 1717 - 1796

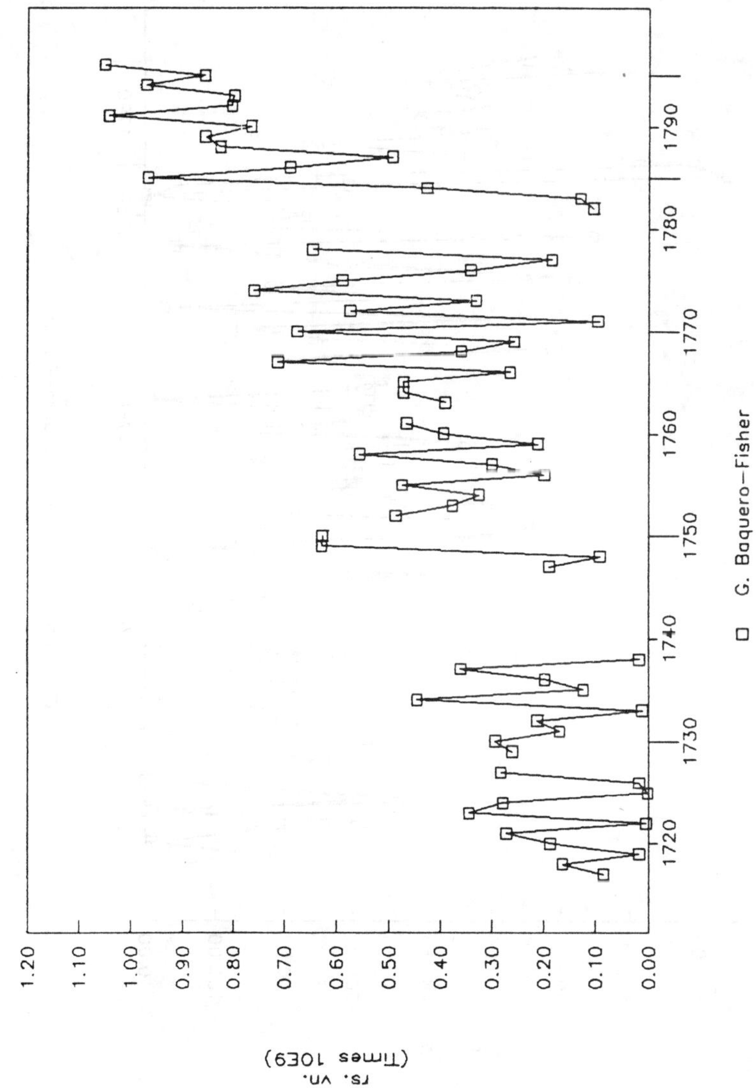

GRAFICO V:
Retornos en metales preciosos

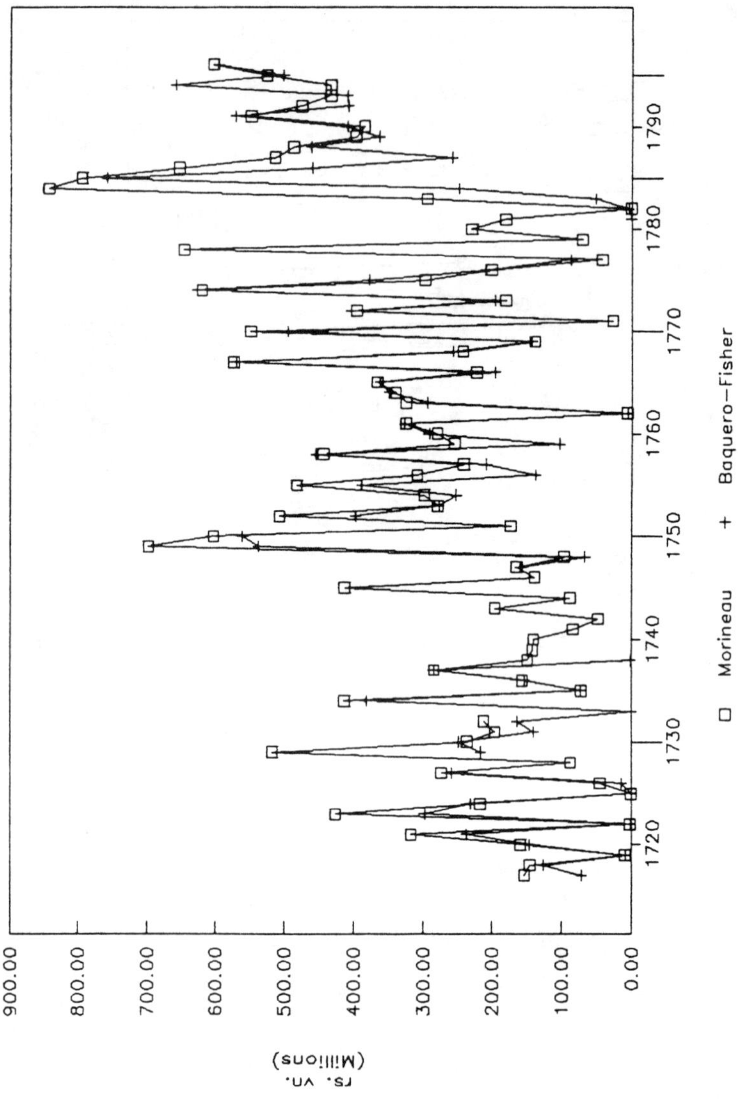

GRAFICO VI:
Importaciones privadas y publicas

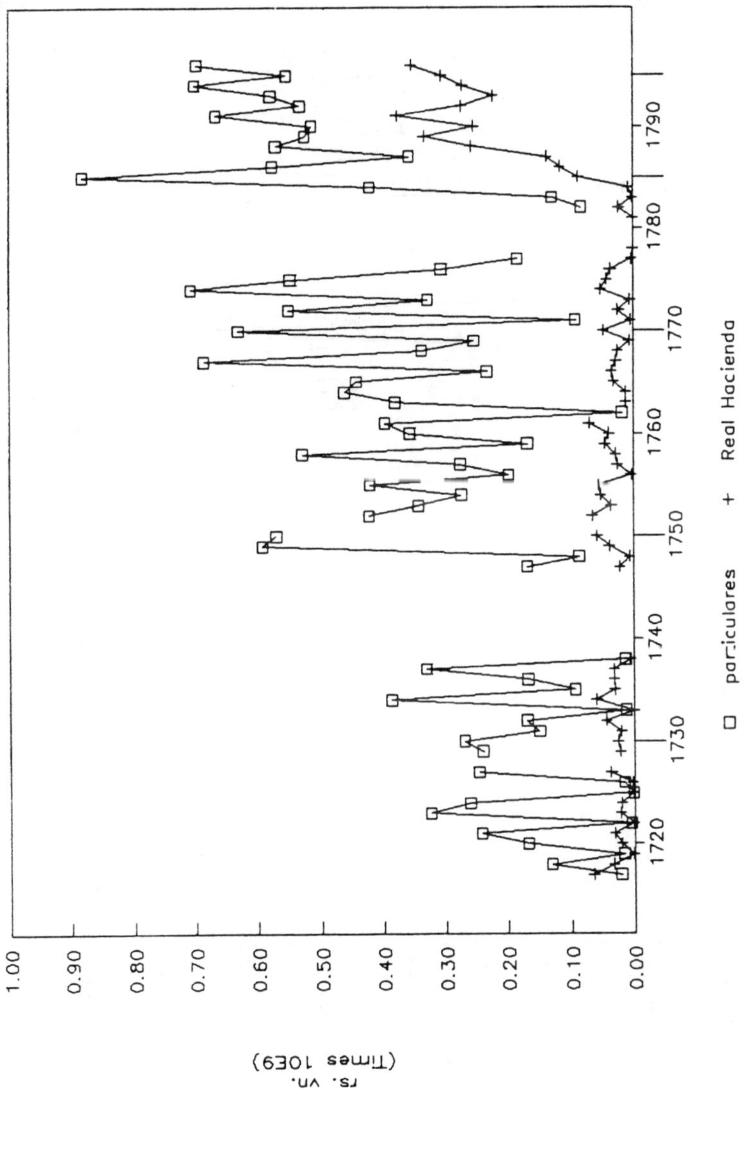

GRAFICO VII:
Metales preciosos de particulares

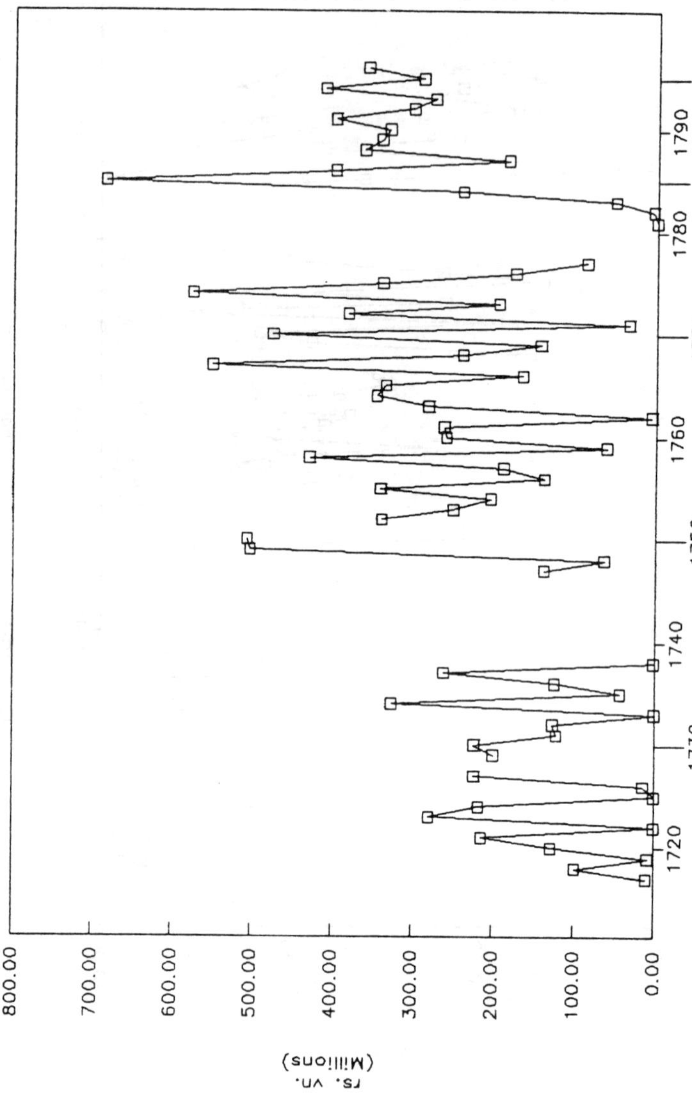

GRAFICO VIII:
Metales preciosos Real Hacienda

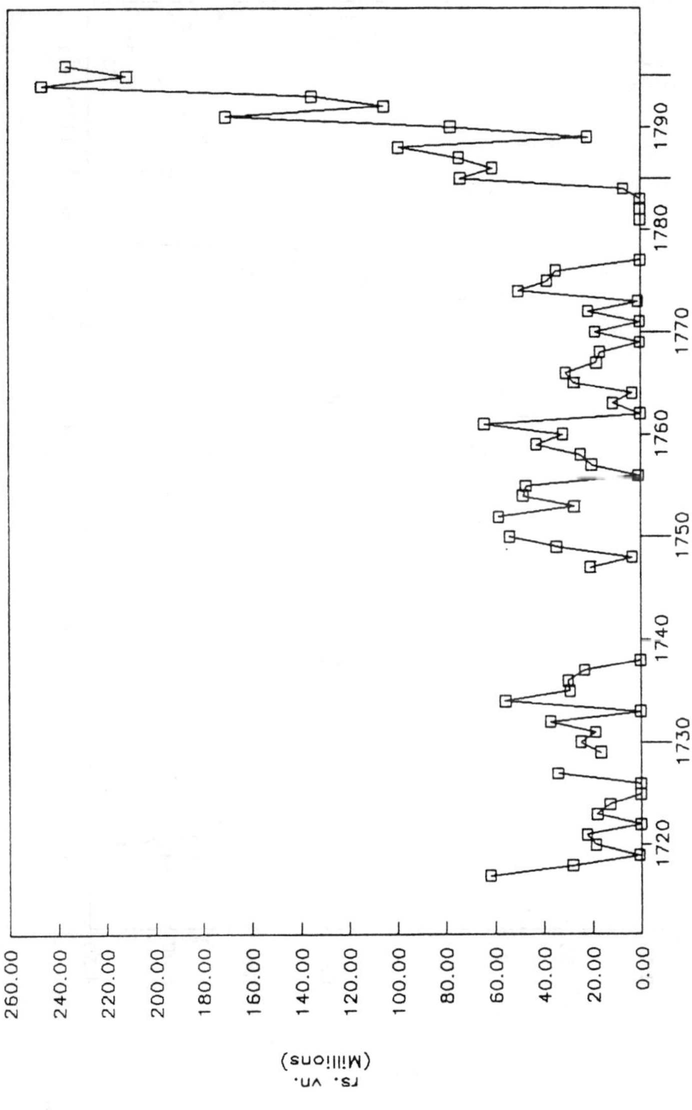

GRAFICO IX:
Importaciones de azúcar

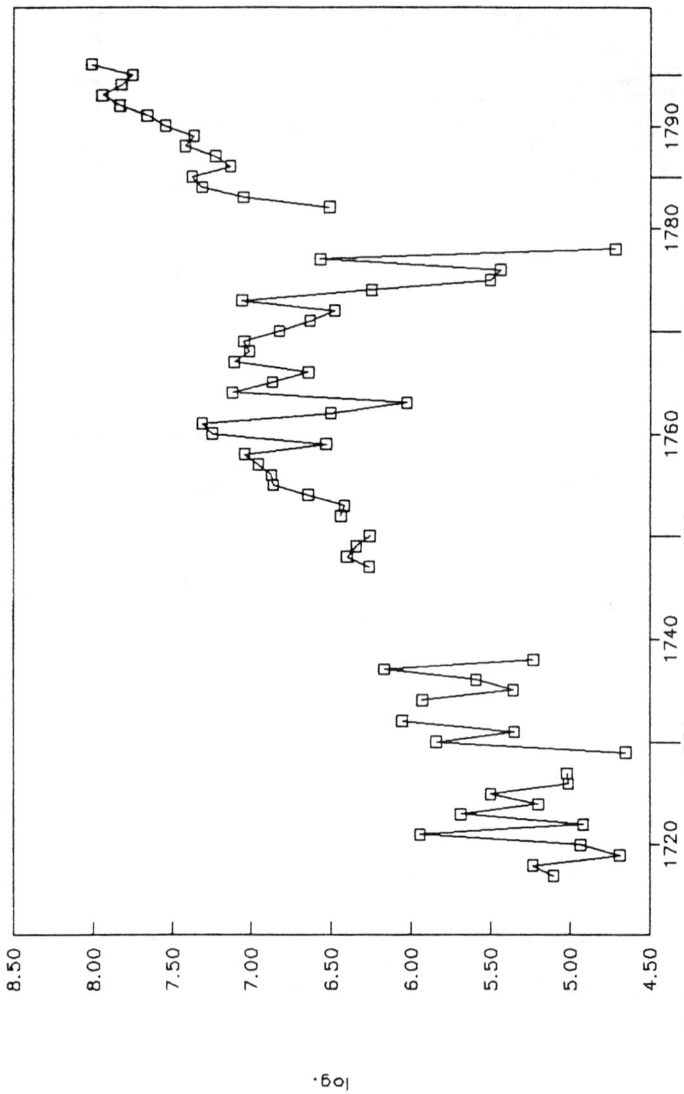

GRAFICO X:
Importaciones de cacao

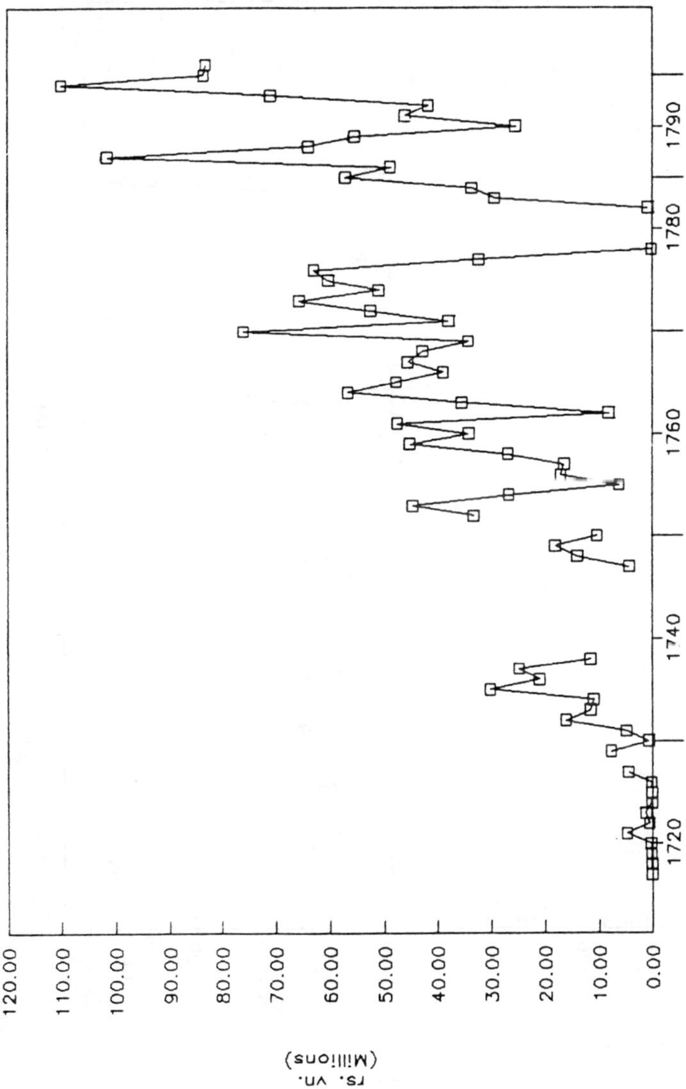

GRAFICO XI:
Importaciones de tabaco

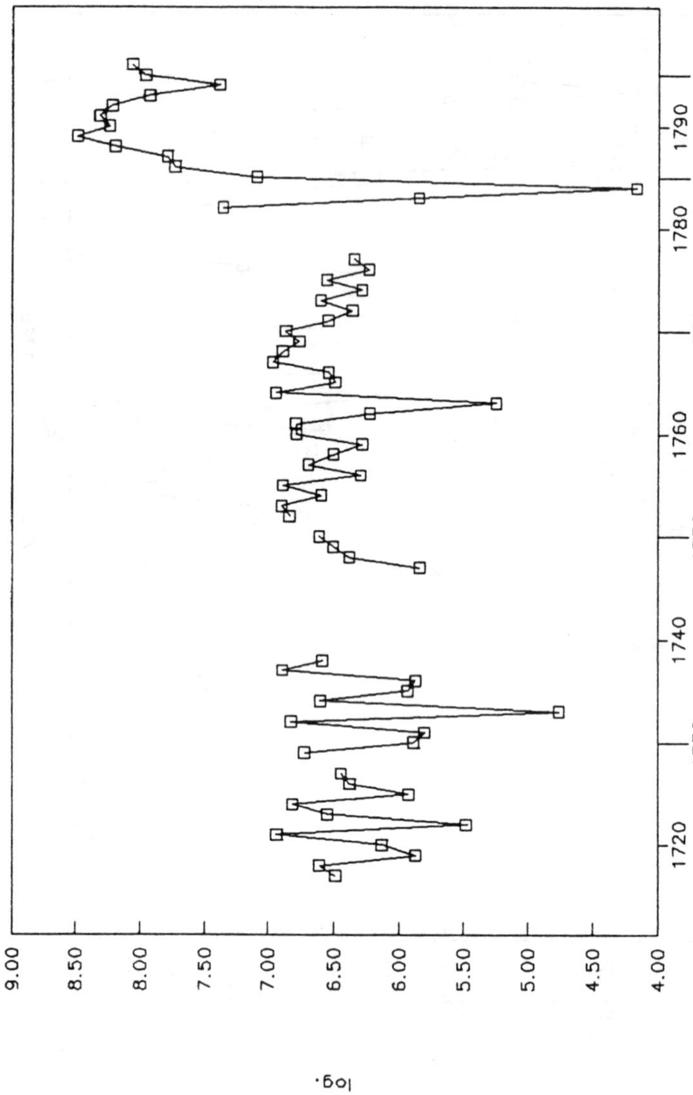

GRAFICO XII:
Importaciones de añil

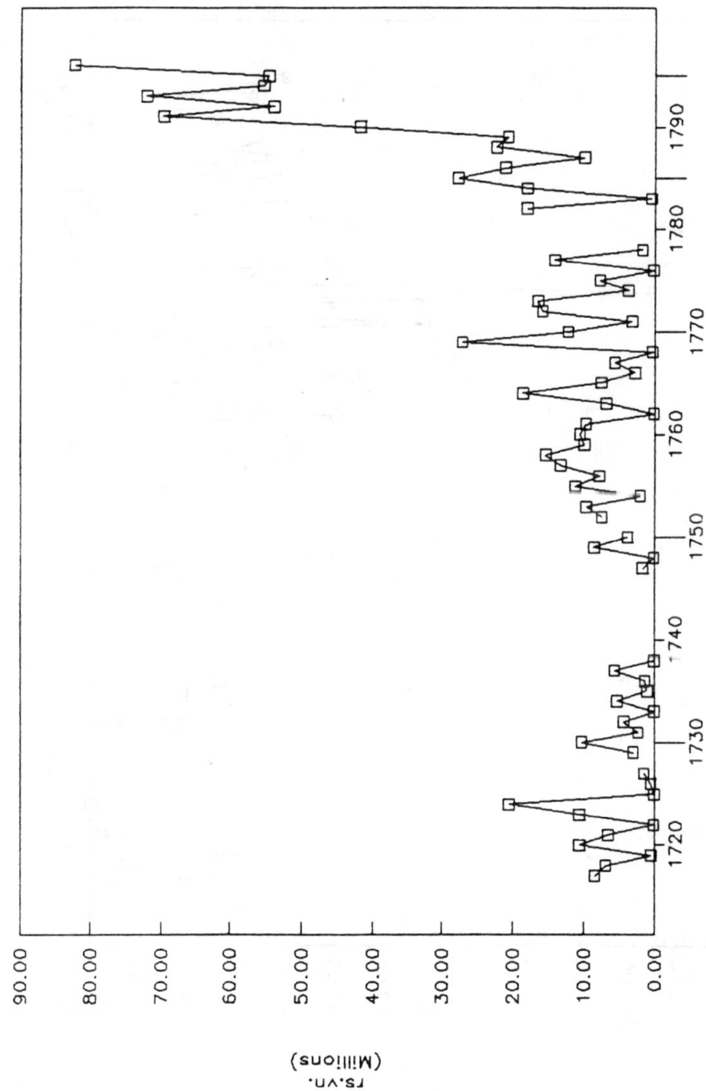

GRAFICO XIII:
Importaciones de grana

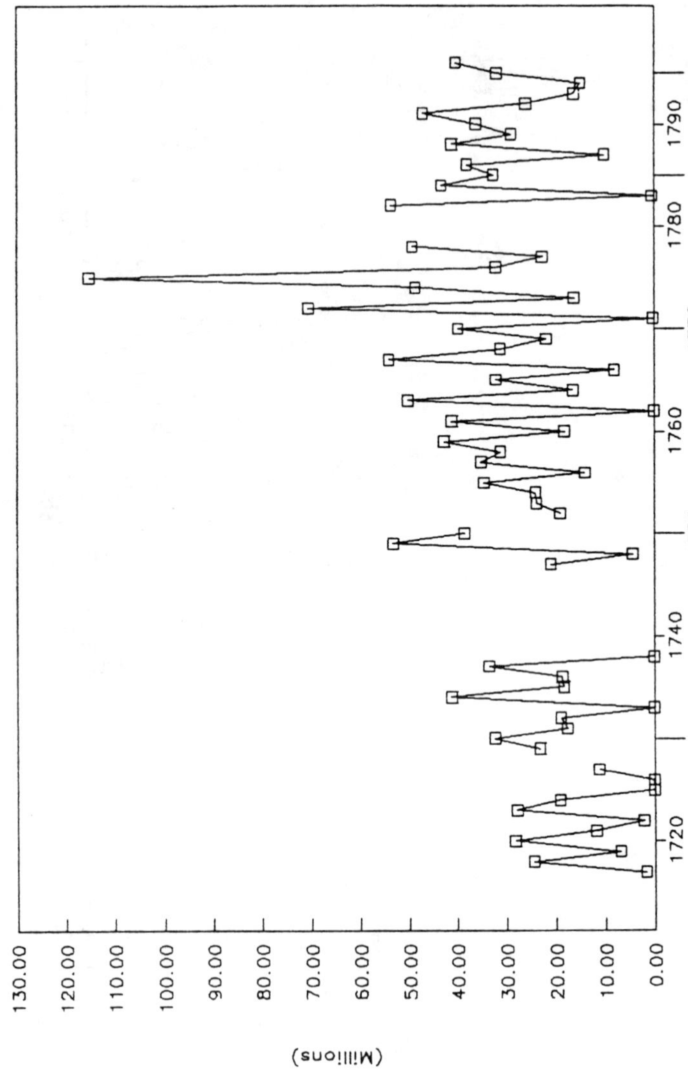

Some Effects on Asian Economies of the European Maritime Discoveries

By ANTHONY REID

> The vessels of the Frank appeared at sea [in Aden in 1502] en route for India, Hormuz and those parts. They took about seven vessels, killing those on board and taking some prisoner. This was their first action, may God curse them[1].

> Then came a Frankish ship from Goa [in 1509], and it came to trade in Melaka [Malacca]. The Franks saw that the city of Melaka was magnificent, and its port was exceedingly crowded. The people crowded round to see what the Franks looked like, and they were all surprised at their appearance. The Melaka people said, "These are white Bengalis!" Dozens of Melaka people surrounded each Frank; some twisted his beard, some knocked his head, some took off his hat, and some grasped his hand. The captain of the ship then presented himself to the Bendahara [Chief Minister] Sri Maharaja. The Bendahara adopted him as his son, and gave him honorific cloths [as for ambassadors]. The ship's captain presented Bendahara Sri Maharaja with a golden chain studded with jewels. He himself put it around the neck of the Bendahara. At that everybody was angry at the Frankish captain, but they were stopped by the Bendahara, who said, "Don't get

---

1 Arab chronicle of Hadhramaut, translated in K. N. CHAUDHURI, Trade and Civilization in the Indian Ocean, Cambridge 1985, p. 65.

> carried away, for these are people who know nothing of manners"[2].

In words like these Asians recorded their first reactions to the arrival of European ships - anger and outrage where the Portuguese began with pillage and violence; bewildered tolerance further east where the initial Portuguese approach was more cautious. These reactions in various combinations would continue to dominate Asian responses over the next two centuries. At best the Europeans were welcomed as another group of outsiders bringing opportunities for trade and military assistance against local rivals. At worst their aggressiveness drove Asian states into a defensive hostility. Remarkably absent from Asian records of the sixteenth or seventeenth century are suggestions that the newcomers had brought new ideas or technologies worthy of emulation.

Nevertheless the effects of European naval expansion were, as we know, profound. In the short run these effects were largely negative and disruptive, which accounts for much of the difficulty Asians had in perceiving anything positive in European civilization. In the longer term the story was much more mixed, and various factors have to be disentangled.

New crops

The major staples of interest to Asians - rice above all, wheat in temperate climes, fish, pork (in the east), mutton (in west and south Asia), cane sugar, cotton and tea - were widely dispersed before the arrival of European trading ships. Undoubtedly European bulk trade did

2 My translation from the Malay chronicle of Melaka, Sejarah Melayu, ed W. SHELLABEAR, 10th edition, Singapore 1961, p. 248. For a full English translation of a different text of the chronicle see C. C. BROWN (ed.), Sejarah Melayu or 'Malay Annals', in: *Journal of the Malayan Branch of the Royal Asiatic Society* 25, parts 2 & 3 (1952).

something to further stimulate their internationalization. For example Chinese tea and Arab coffee became more popular elsewhere in Asia in the course of the seventeenth century as a result of Dutch trade. There were no specifically European crops popularized by the European discoveries.

American crops were a different thing. The potato which had such an impact on Europe was of virtually no interest in Asia, but tobacco, maize, chili, and papaya were taken up remarkably quickly. All four appear to have been brought directly by the Spanish across the Pacific as early as the sixteenth century. It is difficult to imagine South or Southeast Asian food without the chili, and it must have been taken up with enthusiasm. Already in 1596 the first Dutch expedition noted that the Governor of Banten, in Java, used it instead of pepper, "though it is not widespread"[3]. Similarly papaya spread not only as a food source but as a central part of Southeast Asian pharmocopea, valued for its antiseptic properties.

More important in terms of basic diet was maize. It appears to have arrived as early as 1540 both in Yunnan (presumably by an overland route from Europe) and in the Moluccas (eastern Indonesia), where it may have been brought by one of the early Spanish expeditions. Those who could grow rice scorned to eat this inferior cereal, but in dryer hill areas inappropriate for rice it made possible a significant increase in the reliability of harvests, and hence of population.

Tobacco was taken up in Southeast Asia even more enthusiastically than in Europe. It was introduced to Manila by the Spanish within a few years of their conquering that port in 1571, and by the end of the century it was being grown far beyond the limits of Spanish control in the Archipelago. Indonesian rulers in Java and Sumatra were smoking it in long pipes of Dutch style in the first years of the seventeenth century, but the populace preferred a kind of cheroot made by bun-

3 Willem LODEWYCKSZ, "D'eerste Boeck" (1598), in: De eerste schipvaart der Nederlanders naar Oost-Indië onder Cornelis de Houtman 1595 - 1597, ed. G. P. ROUFFAER / J. W. IJZERMAN, Vol. I, The Hague 1915, p. 146.

dling together shredded home-grown tobacco and wrapping it in a stiffer leaf of palm or maize. By the second half of the seventeenth century men and women in many parts of China, in South India, Thailand, the Philippines and Indonesia were reportedly addicted to the new stimulant[4].

Trade organization

I have argued elsewhere[5] that the fifteenth century was more important than the sixteenth in stimulating maritime trade in the Indian Ocean and the South China Sea. The increasing demand for tropical spices from China following the Cheng Ho voyages, and from Europe and the Mediterranean as a result of a century of relative prosperity, gave rise to a regulated system of trade in the fifteenth century based on a number of major stapling ports where trade was effectively open to all comers.

From April to August the monsoon winds blow dependably northwards towards the Asian land mass; from December to March they blow equally dependably southward, from the land masses into the Indian Ocean and the South China Sea. It was this predictability which determined the pattern of Asian maritime trade. Shipowners sought to minimise the risky period at sea by making long journeys at times of good following winds, and to return within the year on the opposite monsoon. For this reason ships were not well equipped for manoeuvring and tacking close to the wind.

---

4 Fernand BRAUDEL, The Structures of Everyday Life, New York 1979, pp.262 - 264; Anthony REID, Southeast Asia in the Age of Commerce, Vol. I, New Haven 1988, pp. 44 - 45; Thomas HÖLLMAN, Tabak in Südostasien: Ein ethnographisch-historischer Überblick, Berlin 1988, pp. 30 - 45.

5 Anthony REID, An 'Age of Commerce' in Southeast Asian History, in: *Modern Asian Studies* 24/I (1990), pp. 5 - 7.

Chinese (and Japanese and Ryukyuan) ships sailing south to the Nanyang always used the northern monsoon in January or February, and returned to China when the wind was from the south in June, July or August. South Indian ships found the southwest monsoon of the Indian Ocean between April and August the most dependable way to sail eastward. They could return with the same monsoon after a short stay, but most stayed to trade "below the winds" until at least December, avoiding the cyclone-prone change of monsoons in October and returning with the northeast monsoon. Gujarati vessels had the longest and most difficult voyage to Southeast Asia. The southwest monsoon was the best for sailing to Sumatra or Malaya, but they had either to leave home in March before these winds closed the Indian ports, or wait until August or September when they opened again. Gujaratis were usually away for at least a year, making sure that they were in a Southeast Asian market for the arrival of the Chinese ships in January or February.

This seasonality of voyaging ensured that entrepots arose in Southeast Asia where traders could await the change of monsoon or the arrival of trading partners. Although individual traders, with their goods, might be away for several years, changing ship for each of the different sectors between Cairo and Canton, Asian ships no longer made such long voyages in the fifteenth century. Their owners were eager to see them back in the home port on the following monsoon. During the months traders were in an entrepot they populated whole quarters of the city, enlivened its markets and took part in its ritual occasions.

The major entrepots in tropical Asia were necessarily located at the intersections of these monsoonal trading sectors, in the Red Sea and Persian Gulf, southwest India, the Straits of Melaka, and the north coast of Java. In the fifteenth century Jidda and Aden in the Red Sea area, Hormuz at the mouth of the Persian Gulf, Surat and Calicut in India, Pasai in northern Sumatra, Melaka on the Straits and Gresik in Java became the key entrepots, and the relative security they brought to the maritime routes reduced the need for difficult caravan routes. The Portuguese conquest of Melaka in 1511, and their subsequent attempts to control passage of the Straits drove trade to alternative caravan routes across the Peninsula and down the west coast of Sumatra to the Sunda Straits. This shift gave birth to new entrepots and stimulated old ones at Aceh, Tenasserim, Ayutthaya, Patani, Pahang, Johor and Banten. Manila, Makassar, Brunei, Cambodia, Champa, and the seventeenth century Vietnamese port of Faifo (Hoi-An) were too far east for Indian ships, but became major entrepots for trade between Chinese, Japanese, Southeast Asian and European shippers. After a very pluralistic century and a half, it was Dutch Batavia which began by about 1650 to assume as dominant a role in the inter-Asian trade as Melaka's had been in 1500.

If the location of these ports was determined largely by the needs of foreign traders, they quickly developed their own parallel home-based shipping. The trade voyages of the Malay epic hero Hang Tuah from Melaka to South India and South China were not invention; the Portuguese also noted that such longer voyages were equipped each year in Melaka - "Melaka sends junks out, and others come in"[6]. Tribute missions to China provided a natural training-ground for Southeast Asian seamen on the run to Canton. No doubt there were always some locally domiciled Chinese involved in these missions, since a knowledge of the language and procedures of China was essential. Some envoys were simply sent on returning Chinese ships, but the commercial advantages of these voyages persuaded most states to purchase their own ships to send to Canton with local trade goods and a mixed crew. That growing numbers of non-Chinese did reach not only Canton but Peking is attested by Chinese attention to Southeast Asian languages in the official translation office (*Ssu-i-kuan*) at the capital, where a special Thai section was created in 1579.

The seasonal flow of ships across each sector of the Asian trade routes therefore included ships based at both ends of the sector. Of Melaka it was estimated that of the 100 ocean-going junks in port at

---

6 The Suma Oriental of Tomé Pires [1515], ed. A. CORTESÃO, London 1944, p. 285.

the peak season, at least 30 belonged to the ruler and merchants of that city, the others being based in India, China, Pegu, Java and elsewhere[7]. That all major ports were active players in the international trade, however, does not mean that all major nations or ethnicities were. Hindus of non-commercial castes, and ethnic Thais, Burmans, Cambodians, Vietnamese and Balinese are seldom if ever mentioned as traders in other ports than their own. Even though Ayutthaya was a major power in the Gulf of Thailand it had no sea-going ships of its own until the reign of Prasat Thong (1610 - 1628). A royal fleet of trading vessels was subsequently built up, but it was predominately manned by Chinese, Muslims and Europeans.

The Asians who were identified as maritime merchants and shippers were concentrated in a small number of specialized ethnic, religious or caste categories. In the Indian Ocean these were primarily Muslims who might be Arab (especially from Cairo, the Hejaz and Hadhramaut), Persian, Gujarati, Bengali, Mappila (of Kerala) or Chulia (Tamil); Jains; and Hindu commercial castes collectively known as *Vaniya* (Anglified as *Banya*) in the north and *Chettiar* (predominately Telugu-speaking) in the south. In the South China Sea diplomatic letters were written in standard Chinese but the shipboard language was the rough Hokkien of the Chinese homeports in the Fujian coast. In Southeast Asia seagoing merchants were known by ethnic markers such as Malay, Minangkabau, Aceh, Java, Cham, Luzon (Muslim Tagalogs of the Manila area), Banda, Makassar, Pegu (Mons of lower Burma) and Chinese. Labels changed, but the reality of a strong trading group continued. Chams and Luzons faded from the international commercial scene in the 16th century, no doubt assimilating under the label "Malay", which was essentially that of the commercial diaspora of Malay-speaking Muslims dispersed by the Portuguese conquest of Melaka in 1511. The Mon merchants of Pegu, the Bandanese, and the

---

7 Ruy DE ARAUJO, Letter from Melaka, 1510, in: Documentacão para a história das missões do padroado português do Oriente: Insulindia, ed A. B. DE SÁ, Vol. I, Lisbon 1954, p. 22.

Javanese of the northern coastal ports similarly disappear soon after the destruction of their home bases (in 1599, 1621 and 1621 - 1624 respectively). Acehnese and Makassare-se were frequently mentioned in the seventeenth century, but thereafter were presumably reclassified as Malays or Bugis (seldom mentioned as traders before 1670). The necessity of being "foreign" in any given port-city will be discussed below. Here it is important to understand the role of the Southeast Asian trading city as a pluralistic meeting-point of peoples from all over maritime Asia.

The Dutch described the mix of merchants that greeted them in Banten in 1596 as follows:

> The Persians, who are called Khorasans in Java, are those who usually earn their living in [precious] stones and medicines ... The Arabs and Pegus are the ones who mostly conduct their trade by sea, carrying and bringing merchandise from one city to another, and buying up much Chinese merchandise, which they exchange against other wares from the surrounding islands, and also pepper, against the time when the Chinese return to buy. The Malays and Klings [South Indians] are merchants who invest money at interest and in voyages and bottomry. The Gujaratis, since they are poor, are usually used as sailors, and are those who take money in bottomry, on which they often make one, two and three times profit[8].

If the long-distance trade from China, India and the Moluccan spiceries brought these multitudes together, it in turn evoked an even busier local trade in supplying the port-cities with foodstuffs, building materials, and local trade items. The great majority of shipping movements were by small local craft bringing rice, vegetables, dried fish, livestock, palm-wine, sugar and salt to feed the urban areas and cash-cropping centres, moving local metalware, ceramics and cloth from producers to consumers, collecting export items and redistributing imports.

---

8 LODEWYCKSZ, 1598, pp. 120 - 121.

The long-distance trade which carried spices all the way from the Moluccas in eastern Indonesia to Venice provides one means of measuring the effectiveness of this Asian trade system. In the 1490s shipments reached a temporary peak. About 570 tonnes of pepper were arriving each year in Venice alone, along with about 75 tonnes of cloves, 26 tonnes of nutmeg and 12 tonnes of mace. In payment for these and other Asian luxuries, Magalhães-Godinho has calculated that Europe was sending to the east the equivalent of about 17 tonnes of silver a year.

The effect of the Portuguese arrival in the Indian Ocean, combined with some other negative factors such as Venice's conflict with Turkey in 1499 and with Egypt in 1505 - 1508, was to depress these figures dramatically. Even including the cargoes brought to Lisbon by the Portuguese ships, largely as a result of plunder, the amounts of pepper reaching Europe did not rise in the first decade of the sixteenth century while the amounts of clove and nutmeg fell to less than a quarter. The drop in European treasure sent east in exchange for spices was spectacular - to the equivalent of only three tonnes of silver[9]. This is not difficult to understand in terms of the attacks launched by the early Portuguese fleets on Muslim shipping in the Arabian Sea and on the coast of India. The Portuguese carried modest amounts of specie to the east with them, and almost no trade goods of interest in Asia. Most of their early return cargoes were obtained by seizing "Moorish" ships they regarded as the enemy, but the disruptive effects of such seizures and naval battles on the Asian shipping networks was far greater than the prizes themselves brought back to Lisbon.

In the longer term the Portuguese impact on Asian trading was probably minor in terms of volume, but considerable in terms of routes and the way trade was organized. By about 1530 the old levels of spice and pepper shipments to Europe and the Middle East had probably been regained, and in the second half of the century they were two to

---

9 V. MAGALHÃES-GODINHO, L'économie de l'empire portugais au XVe et XVIe siècles, Paris 1969, pp. 316, 334. REID, An 'Age of Commerce', pp. 7 - 8.

four times what they had been in the 1490s. On the one hand the Portuguese succeeded by the 1520s in regularly shipping substantial amounts to Lisbon; on the other the Muslim routes gradually reestablished themselves and found ways to combat, evade or buy off the Portuguese. Europe certainly increased its share of the long-distance trade in spices in the sixteenth century, but this was a trend which had begun in the fifteenth century in the capable hands of the Islamic and Venetian traders.

New naval tactics and trade routes

The chief novelty introduced by the Portuguese in the Indian Ocean was the effective use of shipboard artillery, and the determination to use it in pursuit of commercial objectives. The Chinese had of course invented gunpowder and artillery, and even used them on such naval expeditions as those of the Mongols against Japan and Java (in the late 13th century), and of Cheng Ho throughout Asian waters in the early 15th. But China did not feel the need to pursue a consistent naval policy, and tended to lose interest in shipboard artillery at the point around 1500 when the European "military revolution" was rendering it really effective for the first time[10]. Seaborne raiding was also well known from earlier periods in Asian history, but in the late fifteenth century a much more sophisticated system of trade had developed which had greatly increased the safety of unarmed or lightly armed merchant shipping. It was based on a network of entrepots which were strong enough to protect themselves and their trade by suppressing piracy in their immediate environment, but peripheral to the serious power struggles of the Asian mainland. Port-states such as Hormuz, Calicut, Melaka and Gresik lived by trade and needed to

---

10 Geoffrey PARKER, The Military Revolution: Military Innovation and the Rise of the West, 1500 - 1800, Cambridge 1988, pp. 82 - 90.

create conditions where Muslims, Hindus, Chinese, Christians and Jews could all compete in relative safety and tolerance.

These factors help explain the extraordinary success of Afonso de Albuquerque in capturing Goa in 1510 as a permanent Portuguese base in the Indian Ocean, and then seizing two of the key links in the Muslim trade network - Melaka in 1511 and Hormuz in 1515. Albuquerque narrowly failed in his attempts to take Aden and Calicut, which would have completed the chain. The Red Sea remained a Muslim lake and the major source of eventual Turkish counterattacks into the Indian Ocean.

These successes required Asian and especially Muslim traders to change their routes and their tactics. The west coast of India, the Persian Gulf and the Straits of Melaka became dangerous areas for Muslim shipping, and new routes were developed which avoided them. Muslim ships learned to use the west coast of Sumatra and the Sunda Straits to avoid the narrow passage off Melaka, while Aceh at the northwest tip of Sumatra became the major Muslim entrepot for shipping Southeast Asian spices and pepper to the westward. By the 1550s a direct route had developed which carried Southeast Asian produce from Aceh to the Red Sea by way of the Maldives, avoiding the centres of Portuguese strength. This route was carrying at least as much as the Portuguese were in the 1560s[11]. By putting the Indonesian islands in direct contact with the Arab world and the Ottoman empire, albeit for little more than a half-century, it stimulated a more militant and orthodox spirit of Islam in Southeast Asia.

The Portuguese onslaught fundamentally altered, therefore, the fifteenth century pattern of trade by sectors between staple entrepots which were not themselves major powers. The *Carreira da India*

---

11 Fernand BRAUDEL, The Mediterranean and the Mediterranean World in the Age of Philip II, New York 1976, Vol. I, pp. 545 - 554; Charles BOXER, A Note on Portuguese Reactions to the Revival of the Red Sea Spice Trade and the Rise of Atjeh, 1540 - 1600, in: *Journal of Southeast Asian History* 10/III (1969), pp. 415 - 428.

pioneered shipments in a single bottom from Asia to Europe, or looked at another way, reintroduced to Asian trade the long-distance shipping which Arabs and Chinese had previously at times conducted. It stimulated a similar development by its rivals in the shipping from Sumatra to the Red Sea.

The introduction of naval warfare also forced Muslim trade to find more secure bases not vulnerable to Portuguese (and later Dutch and English) raids. The Mogul port of Surat, Turkish-protected ports at Aden and Jidda, the Persian port of Gombroon and Golconda's port of Masulipatam in south India became dominant by 1600. In Southeast Asia Melaka and the autonomous port-states of the north Java coast were replaced by stronger powers - Ayutthaya (Siam), Pegu (lower Burma), Aceh (Sumatra), Banten and Mataram in Java. The promising development of autonomous city-states where a mercantile ethic had an opportunity to develop did not continue.

Even these strong states did not succeed in keeping abreast of European naval armament, so that the Portuguese retained the military edge at sea. They did, however, discourage further Portuguese conquests of major strategic importance. After the Spanish occupation of Manila in 1571 the union of Portuguese and Spanish crowns in 1580 and the much increased flow of American silver through both Spanish and Portuguese routes to the east, the Iberians had greater strength at their disposal. Grandiose plans were developed for conquests of Aceh, Cambodia, and even China, but none of these had any permanent influence (except a destabilizing one in Cambodia). Philip de Brito had more success in salvaging from the Burmese destruction of the Pegu capital in 1599 a little kingdom for himself at the port of Syriam. This lasted for fourteen years before de Brito was defeated and impaled by a Burmese army. His long-term influence, like that of much other European intervention, was to help undermine the capacity of coastal port-states to hold their own against Asian continental powers little interested in commerce.

Military technology

The introduction of naval warfare to Asian waters had other effects. The Portuguese built larger ships in the course of the sixteenth century as they became more confident of a safe voyage home. The great freight-carrying *náo* of the *carreira da India* were about 400 tonnes burden at the beginning of the century and nearer 1000 tonnes at its end[12]. Asian ships grew smaller. Manguin[13] has drawn attention to the size and distinctiveness of the Southeast Asian "junk" which flourished at the arrival of the Portuguese, claiming that they averaged around four to five hundred tonnes. Even if these were in reality the top of the range, their counterparts at the end of the century were less than half as big. Dutch accounts make clear that only the biggest Javanese junks, those taking rice from Java to cities in Sumatra and the Malayan Peninsula, still exceeded 200 tonnes in 1600. Ships had become smaller but more numerous, so that one Dutch traveller reckoned "a thousand or more" vessels of 20 to 200 tonnes in the Surabaya area alone[14]. Not having seen the largest rice-carrying junks, Lodewycksz reported that "The East Indian islands are very rich in ships, but all little vessels, so that the largest junk I have seen would not carry more than forty tonnes"[15]. By the middle of the seventeenth century Southeast Asian craft were no longer referred to as junks at all. Even though Europeans had learned the word "junk" from Malay and Javanese, from this point they applied it only to Chinese vessels of two to eight hundred tonnes. Gujarati vessels based in the secure home port of Surat also remained in the 600-tonne range, but they gradually

---

12 C. R. BOXER, The Portuguese Seaborne Empire, 1415 - 1825, Harmondsworth 1973, pp. 209 - 211.

13 Pierre-Yves MANGUIN, The Southeast Asian Ship: An Historical Approach, in: *Journal of Southeast Asian Studies* 11/II (1980), p. 268.

14 'Verhaal van eenige oorlogen in Indie' (1622), reprinted in: *Kroniek van het Historisch Genootschap te Utrecht* 27 (1871), p. 532.

15 LODEWYCKSZ (1598), pp. 132 - 133.

lost the contest for the lucrative Southeast Asian trade during the seventeenth century, and concentrated on the Red Sea.

The disappearance of the large but unwieldy Southeast Asian junk is not difficult to understand when Portuguese accounts are read of the havoc the Europeans wrought among them. The very large ships maximized the profit on peaceful trading voyages, but they were not designed with either the speed to flee or the manoeuvrability and fire-power to fight against European vessels. Even before he reached Melaka in 1511, Albuquerque had seized several richly-laden junks and confiscated their cargo. Thirty-five of the largest Javanese junks, each of about 500 tonnes, were reportedly employed transporting troops to attack Melaka in 1513, but virtually all were burned or sunk in a naval battle with the Portuguese[16]. After the defeat of Patih Yunus' fleet, Tomé Pires claimed:

> they do not have any junks, because most of the Javanese junks came from Pegu, where the Javanese - and other people who bought in Melaka - used to send for them to be made; ... And because ... the Governor of India burned and defeated all the enemy junks, they were all left without any[17].

This was an exaggeration, and both Javanese and the Mons of Pegu continued to build large vessels. The risks of sending valuable cargoes in the unwieldy junks was becoming too great, however. Their vulnerability was proved again in relation to much improved Dutch fire-power in the early seventeenth century. Thereafter the biggest Southeast Asian vessels came to be war galleys, and it was only Europeans who felt secure enough (and, increasingly, who had the necessary capital) to equip very large freight-carrying ships.

If the seventeenth century saw the demise of the Southeast Asian junk, there were also positive responses to the European maritime challenge. The probability that Makassar, Moluccan and Filipino terms for the great outrigger galleys which dominated their warfare - *galle'*, *kora-*

16 Lettera de Giovanni da Empoli, ed. A. BAUSANI, Rome 1970, pp. 148 - 149.

17 Tomé Pires [1515], p. 195.

kora and *caracoa* (the two latter ultimately from Arabic *kurkur*) - derived from Portuguese or Spanish suggests that major changes were introduced in response to foreign example. This is confirmed by the Thai and Makassar chronicles, which assert for Ayutthaya and South Sulawesi respectively that the first war galleys were built at the beginning of the seventeenth century[18]. This must have meant only an extension of older techniques, to cope with shipboard cannon and larger numbers of warriors. In their replication of the *naga* (dragon) form, in their speed, and in their craftsmanship, these vessels always astonished Europeans.

It must be said that Asian trade suffered more immediately and profoundly from European techniques of naval warfare in the Indonesian and Philippine Archipelagoes than it did in the continental kingdoms - especially China, the Mogul Empire and Safavid Persia. For India Ashin Das Gupta has gone so far as to claim that "the golden period for Indian maritime trade" occurred in the late seventeenth century, as a result of increased European demand for Indian textiles and the greater cost-effectiveness of Indian than of European shipping, though it collapsed quickly after 1700[19].

European military technology was not limited to the sea. The part played by firearms introduced by the Portuguese in 1543 in the unification of Japan by Nobunaga and Hideyoshi has been well documented. While no other Asian state was as successful in keeping Europeans out (after 1639), most experienced the same rapid escalation in the number and effectiveness of firearms. Europeans were not the only source of arms - they were also transmitted through Turkey, both by land (as the rising Mogul power testified) and by sea. In

---

18 Jeremias VAN VLIET, The Short History of the Kings of Siam [1640], trans. Leonard ANDAYA, Bangkok 1975, p. 89; Sejarah Kerajaan Tallo' (Suatu Transkripsi Lontara'), ed. Abd. RAHIM and Ridwan BORAHIMA, Ujung Pandang 1975, p. 17.

19 A. DASGUPTA, Indian Merchants and the Trade in the Indian Ocean, in: The Cambridge Economic History of India, Vol. I, Cambridge 1982, p. 432.

Southeast Asia, as in Japan, however, it was the arrival of European ships which marked a sudden leap in the effectiveness of firearms, and which challenged local powers to acquire or replicate them. Rulers who commanded important ports were best-placed to acquire and replicate such arms, and the consequence was that they tended to subordinate their rivals and build unusually strong and centralized states.

Perhaps the most striking case was Burma, unified in the period 1531 - 1581 by two successive rulers who took energetic advantage of the new firearms as well as Portuguese and Muslim mercenary artillerymen[20]. According to Cesar Frederici, who visited in the 1560s,

> the Burmese king's arquebusses are most excellent, and always in his wars he has eighty thousand arquebusses, and the number of them increases daily ... by continual exercise they become most excellent shot; also he has great ordinance made of very good metal[21].

To a lesser degree this pattern was replicated throughout Southeast Asia, with sometimes Turks but more often Portuguese as the technological intermediaries. Arakan, Ayutthaya (Siam), and the southern Vietnamese state known to Europeans as Cochin-China, were all able to extend and centralize their power on the Southeast Asian mainland through this means. In the Archipelago Aceh (Sumatra), Banten and Mataram (Java), and Makassar (Sulawesi) all accumulated large armouries in the late sixteenth and early seventeenth centuries, with European and Turkish help.

The Portuguese and their successors stimulated the trend towards fewer, stronger states in two ways - by conveying the new military

---

20 Victor LIEBERMAN, Europeans, Trade, and the Unification of Burma, c. 1540 - 1620, in: *Oriens Extremus* 27/II (1980), pp. 203 - 226.

21 The voyage of Master Cesar Frederick into the east India, and beyond the Indies, Anno 1563, in: Richard HAKLUYT (ed.), The Principal Voyages, Traffiques & Discoveries of the English Nation, London 1907, III p. 248.

technology and by presenting a challenge to maritime states not strong enough to defend themselves.

A monetary revolution

As noted above, silver and gold from Europe and northern Africa was already flowing to Asia in large and increasing quantities in the fifteenth century, and the initial effect of the Portuguese penetration of the Indian Ocean was to reduce this sharply. The recovery of the Levantine trade, still largely paid for in gold, and greater Portuguese access to silver supplies, caused a rapid climb in the export of precious metal in the second half of the century. In particular the enormous increase in output of silver from Spanish America after 1570 proved irresistibly attractive as a means to fund the *carreira da India*. The union of the Spanish and Portuguese crowns in 1580 removed another barrier, and in the 1580s there are two independent estimates that the Portuguese were shipping to Goa each year about 42 tonnes of silver (a million cruzados). In total Magalhães-Godinho estimates that Europe was sending 72 tonnes of silver equivalent to the east at the end of the sixteenth century, through both Portuguese and Levantine routes[22].

The addition of shipments direct from Mexico on the Manila galleon from about 1580, and of Dutch and English shipments from 1600, accentuated this vast influx of American silver into Asia. Still more dramatic than the flow of American silver was the sudden expansion of production and export from the Japanese silver mines. This may probably be considered an indirect effect of the European maritime discoveries, in that the Japanese appear to have heard about the new mercury extraction process in Mexico from a Portuguese visitor. Statistics on the dimensions of Japanese silver exports are frustrat-

---

22 MAGALHÃES-GODINHO (1969), pp. 329 - 330, 335.

ingly fragmentary, but there no longer seems much doubt that they overshadowed the flow of American silver into Asia, peaking at the same period but more dramatically. Table 1 summarizes the flow of silver to Asia through European official channels (less than a half of the total European flow), and a rough estimate of Japanese exports.

TABLE 1:
Supplies of Silver and Gold in Eastern Asia[23]
(Decennial annual averages in metric tonnes of silver equivalent)

Period	Portugese	VOC	English	Manila galleon	Japanese exports
1581-1590	8.6	--	--	4.00	30
1591-1600	?	--	--	2.67	40
1601-1610	5.9	5.7	1.3	12.00	80
1611-1620	4.7	10.9	4.7	19.40	110
1621-1630	4.4	12.7	7.7	23.10	130
1631-1640		8.7	5.5	18.40	130
1641-1650		9.5	?	10.10	70
1651-1660		8.6	?	9.00	50
1661-1670		11.8	9.9	8.00	40

Most of the silver disbursed in Asia from Japan and the Manila galleon was eventually absorbed by China, where it helped fuel the commercialization and urban expansion of the late Ming. It has been calculated that the internal Chinese production of silver, at its peak in the early fifteenth century when the Ming had taken control of Asia's most productive silver mines in northern Burma and northern Vietnam, was not above 30 tonnes a year. This dropped steadily thereafter to barely four tonnes p.a. in the decade 1511-20. The influx of American and Japanese silver was of a different order, delivering unprecedented amounts of silver into the Chinese market in the period 1590-1630.

23 Sources in: REID, An 'Age of Commerce', p. 20.

This was fortunate for the Ming regime, which had abandoned the inflation-prone paper currency about 1450 in favour of a silver standard (by weight). The burden of tax was progressively shifted from payment in kind to payment in silver between then and 1620. China became dependent, in fact, on a steady inflow of foreign silver[24].

India had since Ancient times been the major destination of the European silver sent eastward in payment for spices. That pattern continued during the silver boom of the late sixteenth and early seventeenth century. Even though the Portuguese, Dutch, and English were all buying most of their spices and pepper in Southeast Asia during this period, the lion's share of their silver was spent, either by them or their Southeast Asian trading partners, to buy the Indian cotton cloth which was the principal item of Southeast Asian import. A consistent silver coinage of 178 grains troy, the rupee (Hindi: *rupaya*), was first minted under the Mughal Sultan Sher Shah in 1542, but became firmly established throughout India under Akbar (1555 - 1605). It has been calculated that the supply of silver rupees in circulation in India expanded threefold between 1591 and 1639[25]. At the end of his reign Akbar had stockpiled 70 to 100 million rupees, that is more than 800 tonnes of silver[26]. In 1595 there were fourteen imperial mints producing these rupees, while the number expanded with the empire and its money supply to forty mints in 1700[27]. A high degree of commercialization and financial sophistication was achieved in Mughal India of the early seventeenth century.

---

24 Brian MOLOUGHNY and Xia WEIZHANG, Silver and the Fall of the Ming: A reassessment, in: *Papers in Far Eastern History* 40 (1989), pp. 54 - 57. See also W. S. ATWELL, Some Observations on the Seventeenth Century General Crisis in China and Japan, in: JOURNAL OF ASIAN STUDIES 45/II (1986), pp. 223 - 244.

25 Irfan HABIB, The Monetary System and Prices, in: The Cambridge Economic History of India, Vol. I, Cambridge 1982, pp. 363 - 365.

26 John F. RICHARDS, The Seventeenth Century Crisis in South Asia, in: *Modern Asian Studies* 24/IV (1990), p. 627.

27 HABIB (1982), p. 361.

Southeast Asia has been much less studied, but the effect of the silver influx is likely to have been the most profound there. Because China was difficult of access, particularly for Japanese (regarded as "pirates" by the Ming), Japanese and American silver reached it through entrepots in Southeast Asia - especially Hoi-An (southern Vietnam), Manila, Patani (Malayan peninsula) and Ayutthaya. Much Portuguese, Dutch and English silver was also expended in the spice and pepper markets of the Indonesian Archipelago. Although there are no available means of measuring the quantity of silver which remained in Southeast Asia, the threefold increase noted for India in the period 1590 - 1630 must at least have been replicated there. Spanish silver rials became the effective international currency of Southeast Asia during the first half of the seventeenth century[28]. There is little doubt that this influx reached its peak in the 1620s, and that it served in Southeast Asia, as elsewhere, to shift the tax base towards money, to encourage urban growth, to stimulate demand for trade goods and to increase the commercialization of society.

The numerous Southeast Asian states rising on the back of trade revenues might have been expected to seize the opportunity of adopting and enforcing their own silver currencies as a means to control their internal economies, as India did. Although Banten and some other Indonesian states experimented with silver minting, the only serious attempts at a silver coinage in Southeast Asia were in the Buddhist countries. The first true silver coins known to have been issued by rulers "below the winds" were minted in Arakan and Cam-

---

28 The English, French, and especially the dominant Dutch of course attempted to have their own silver coins accepted, but the rial was always preferred. The Dutch Company had to resort to its equivalent of the rial, the Rijksdaalder, for trade in the east. As the Company established a monopoly position in many areas in the late seventeenth century it gradually succeeded in establishing the guilder, which was known in the Malay World as a rupiah because it was almost identical in value to the Indian rupee.

bodia, both around 1600[29]. The Thais, however, had an older tradition of silver weights of standard size.

This was the so-called "bullet" coin, in effect a lump of standard weight with two small stamps of varied design on it. At least by 1600 the weight and shape of this Siamese silver tikal (Thai *baht)* had become standardised. Throughout the seventeenth century it consistently weighed about 14.6 grams, representing one quarter of a tael (Malay, *tahil*), and maintained its international value at about three-fifths of a rial, or thirty English pence[30]. Its kidney shape was obtained by casting it into an elliptical mould, then cutting the flat side so that it could be bent in at both ends. It was then stamped on each side with an animal, shell, lotus or wheel device[31].

Despite the silver resources in its north, Burma had no currency in the sixteenth century except weights of the cumbrous lead-alloy known as *gansa*. By the early decades of the seventeenth century, however, Burma had effectively adopted the Thai system of silver by tikal weight, with brokers authorized to see to its consistency. Tikal was the word used by foreigners for the weight of silver in both countries, but the indigenous words were *baht* and *kyat*, terms still used for the units of currency in Thailand and Burma respectively. In Burma it was one hundredth of a *viss*, equivalent to about 24 grams.

This type of coinage did not exclude other currencies such as the all-powerful rial, but it was an effective response to the silver revolution. It may seem perverse that the Muslim states of the Indonesian Archipelago instead persisted with a system of gold coins which were increasingly irrelevant to the market. Gold was undoubtedly more abundant in the Archipelago than in the rest of Asia, and was cheaper in relation to silver than in India, China or Japan. Before 1620 the ratio

---

29 Reginald LE MAY, The Coinage of Siam, Bangkok 1932, pp.4, 7.

30 R. S. WICKS, A Survey of Native Southeast Asian Coinage, circa 450 - 1850: Documentation and Typology, Cornell University Ph.D. Dissertation 1983, pp. 169 - 170.

31 LE MAY, 1932, pp. 63 - 65.

was about 1:7 in Southeast Asia and 1:10 in India; by the second half of the century it had risen to 1:12 in Southeast Asia and 1:15 in India[32]. Sumatra and the Philippines continued to export gold throughout the century. Moreover the traditional reverence for gold as a symbol of power and prestige made it seem the only possible material to bear the king's name. It was gold with which the Buddhists of the Mainland adorned and honoured their statues; it was gold which kings sought to accumulate as an expression of their power, and it was gold with which the ordinary man adorned his wife and saved against a time of difficulty.

Most importantly, Southeast Asia was more politically fragmented than India or China, and the equation between international and domestic markets was very different. No local coin could compete with the Spanish rial as an international currency. It quickly became the currency and unit of account for the international transactions which dominated the business of the large city markets. The demand of Chinese and Indian traders for Japanese and American silver to take back to their own countries would have imposed a great strain on any indigenous mint. The rulers who issued coins were only engaging in what proved to be a losing battle to maintain an internal realm where they had economic sovereignty distinct from the international market by which they lived.

One way or another silver had become irresistible as the effective international currency of Asia by about 1630, whether in rials as in most of the island world, in weight as in China, Vietnam, Siam and Burma, or in Mughal rupees. The triumph of silver undoubtedly furthered the integration of maritime Asia into a world economy. A fundamental problem (at least for Southeast Asia, southern India and to some extent China) was that foreigners controlled the supply of money

32 Calendar of State Papers, Colonial Series 1625 - 1629, p. 371; Letters Received from the East India Company from its Servants in the East, London 1896 - 1901, III p. 156; Simon DE LA LOUBÈRE, A New Historical Relation of the Kingdom of Siam [1691], Kuala Lumpur 1969, p. 72; HABIB (1982), p. 367.

and through it had direct access to the growers of cash crops. Blussé has called foreign coin a "trojan horse" for Southeast Asian states[33]. It was a key weapon in the struggles of the seventeenth century for economic control of the region.

The marked decline in the availability of Japanese and American silver after 1635 was a major factor in the crisis which affected China and much of Southeast Asia and India in the middle of the seventeenth century. I have argued elsewhere that Southeast Asia and China may only now be shaking off the effects of that crisis on their relative standing in the world[34].

Some more speculative thoughts

In the really long term, the discovery and establishment of the European global sea-trading routes had more negative than positive consequences in Asia, and particularly for the development of a merchant class in maritime Asia. The counter factual case is of course absurd. To imagine the Cape route between Europe and Asia not having been established we would have to extend the African coast southward until it joined Antarctica. Nevertheless to make that leap of imagination for a moment may shed some light on the Asian dilemma.

The great expansion in European trade and prosperity would still have taken place in the long sixteenth century, and would have stimulated ever greater activity along the trade routes between Europe and Asia. American silver would have further fuelled this trade, sending ever greater quantities of specie eastward to pay for Asian spices and

33 Leonard BLUSSÉ, Strange Company: Chinese settlers, mestizo women and the Dutch in VOC Batavia, Dordrecht 1986, pp. 35 - 48.

34 Anthony REID, The Seventeenth Century Crisis in Southeast Asia, in: *Modern Asian Studies* 24/IV (1990), pp. 646 - 649, 656. But see RICHARDS (1990) for a more sceptical reading of the Indian evidence.

precious cloths. The expansion of trade would have continued to strengthen the Asian trading communities, and the port-states where they concentrated, against the continental empires. Europeans would no doubt have travelled eastward in the sixteenth century as they did in the fifteenth, but as guests rather than intruders, much as they continued to be on most of the Asian land mass, and in China and Japan, until the nineteenth century. The military technology and scientific ideas of Europe would have seeped gently and imperfectly eastward through various cultural filters, much as they did in China through the Jesuits and in Japan through the Dutch at Deshima, respectively.

Instead the Europeans came to Asia armed to the teeth, with little to offer by way of trade except minerals, especially gold and silver, and military supremacy by sea. The temptation to use this military supremacy to establish commercial monopolies was irresistible. The Portuguese caused much initial disruption, but after the first few decades it became clear that their only effective monopolies were of Sri Langkan cinnamon, and after 1570 of the direct China-Japan trade. There was some technology transfer through the Portuguese casados and missionaries, not only in China and the Mughal court, but in Makassar, Burma, Sri Langka and the Malay World.

The Dutch world-trading system was far more effective. By the middle of the seventeenth century the VOC had taken over the cinnamon monopoly from the Portuguese in Sri Langka, and established its own monopoly over nutmeg (in 1621) and cloves (complete by 1656). The long-distance trade in these items no longer enriched Asians at all. The VOC shared an effective monopoly with the English Company in the carriage of pepper westward (to northern India, the Middle East and Europe), though not to China and Japan. The "closure" of Japan in 1635 gave the VOC a near-monopoly on the supply of Japanese minerals to Asia - first silver and later copper. The caravan routes through the Levant were eclipsed, as was the direct route between Sumatra and the Red Sea. In consequence northern Indians and Arabs virtually ceased sailing to Southeast Asia, and vice-versa. Asian maritime trade of course continued to flourish, but it shifted to a kind of guerrilla strategy against the heavily capitalized Dutch - small vessels, low overheads, local trading routes, partnerships with private Europeans[35].

The commercial centres of the most intense interaction with foreign ideas were the great ports, which were also the most vulnerable to European pressure. Those port-states which had lived by trade were either conquered by the Portuguese and Dutch or were reduced to insignificance by the diversion of the long-distance trade into VOC hands[36].

A number of larger states appear deliberately to have turned their back on the international market after the period of frenzied involvement with it turned sour. The Japanese case is the most striking. The period 1570 - 1630 was exceptional in Japan's pre-modern history for its intense involvement with world trade. Ten large "red-seal" ships each year were licensed for trading with Southeast Asia over the period 1604 - 1635, exporting silver and metalware in exchange for Chinese silks and porcelain, Southeast Asian pepper, spices, deerskins and sugar[37]. Hayami has labelled this "the great transformation" which brought about the unification and commercialization of the Japanese economy, and the dawn of its modernity[38]. Yet in 1635 all

---

35 An admirable recent demonstration of this trend in south India is S. ARASARATNAM, Merchants, Companies and Commerce on the Coromandel Coast, 1650 - 1740, Delhi 1986, esp. chapter 6.

36 For greater detail see Anthony REID, The Seventeenth Century Crisis, pp. 639 - 657; idem, The System of Trade and Shipping in Maritime South and Southeast Asia, and the Effects of the Development of the Cape Route to Europe, in: The European Discovery of the World and its Economic Effects on Pre-industrial Society, 1500 - 1800, ed. Hans POHL, Stuttgart 1990, pp. 91 - 96.

37 R. L. INNES, The Door Ajar: Japan's Foreign Trade in the Seventeenth Century, Ph.D. Dissertation at the University of Michigan 1980, pp. 51 - 66.

38 HAYAMI Akira, A Great Transformation: Social and Economic Change in Sixteenth and Seventeenth Century Japan, in: *Bonner Zeitschrift für Japanologie* 8 (1986), pp. 3 - 13.

Japanese were prohibited to travel abroad under pain of death. The power of Buddhism having already been broken, Christianity was suppressed and all Japanese obliged to undergo an annual scrutiny of religious beliefs. Foreigners were banned from the Shogunate, save only for Dutch and Chinese access to the tiny island of Deshima off Nagasaki.

Japanists tend to see this as the Tokugawa shogunate's determination to assert a monopoly over the foreign trade as well as the loyalty of Japanese. Seen in a broader Asian context, however, it seems clear that the balance between the costs and benefits to the Asian state of openness to trade tipped towards the former during the second quarter of the seventeenth century, if not before. Burma in the period 1599 - 1635 and Java in the period 1600 - 1624 underwent a similar process, with the capital moving as far as possible away from the coast and the trading ports destroyed, abandoned or strictly controlled. Siam in the 1680s also took a major step towards isolation by making it impossible or unprofitable for Muslim and European merchants to continue their intense involvement.

This was the essence of the "seventeenth century crisis" for Asia. Many of its principal states remained strong or became stronger, including Tokugawa Japan, Ch'ing China, Safavid Persia and Mughal India. But the monopoly policies pursued with increasing determination by the VOC and others made foreign trade appear threatening to the state, and dependence on it to be downright dangerous. There was a symbiosis, sometimes explicit (like the VOC's alliance with Mataram in Java), more often implicit, between the European trading companies and the great continental powers, with the losers being just such interstitial islands of urbanism and commerce which played a crucial role in Europe's own transformation.

The islands of Southeast Asia (and Sri Lanka) had given themselves particularly to cash-cropping for the world market, and were therefore most affected by the monopoly policy of the VOC, as well as the fall in prices in the second half of the century. There are numerous cases of states cutting down their pepper and clove trees, intensifying their rice-cultivation, and reverting to a relatively self-sufficient policy. The corollary of this trend was an inability to buy imported Indian cloths, which the VOC itself complained of in the latter decades of the seventeenth century[39].

The effects in the intellectual area of the way Asia encountered Europe are much harder to assess, though ultimately especially important. It is striking how hard it is to find positive views of Europeans in Asian records of the seventeenth and eighteenth centuries. They appear to have been perceived primarily as a threat to be held at bay, and almost never (the closest to an exception is Japan) as a source of useful new ideas. As a Chinese memorialist put it: "the kingdoms of Siam, of Tongking and the others pay us tribute every year, and have no evil intentions. It is only the Europeans who are to be feared, as they are the most evil and intractable of men"[40].

The Dutch were particularly feared in the seventeenth century, so that even those states with which they traded more or less peacefully, like Siam, Burma, China and Mughal India, appear to have learned less from them than several states learned from the Portuguese. As one of their most experienced soldier-diplomats in Asia pointed out, "There is nobody who wishes us well in all the Indies, yea we are deadly hated by all nations"[41].

Ironically it was only at the end of the nineteenth century, when the European powers were at the arrogant height of their colonial power, that Asians began seriously to examine what they had to offer in sci-

---

39 REID, An 'Age of Commerce', pp. 23 - 24.

40 Letter of P. DE MAILLA, S. J., Peking, 5 June 1717, in: Lettres édifiantes et curieuses, écrites des missions etrangères, Paris 1781, 19, p. 11.

41 Rijklof VAN GOENS, 1655, cited in: C. R. BOXER, The Dutch Seaborne Empire 1600 - 1800, London 1965, p. 84. See also William DAMPIER, Voyages and Discoveries [1699], London 1931, p. 83; FU Lo-Shu, A Documentary Chronicle of Sino-Western Relations (1644 - 1820), Tucson 1966, p. 60.

entific and intellectual terms. It is impossible to say whether this would have happened earlier had they not arrived in gunboats in the sixteenth and seventeenth centuries.

The Foundations of European Industralization: From the Perspective of the World*

By PATRICK KARL O'BRIEN

1. Exogeneous and Endogeneous Impulses Behind the Development of Western Europe 1492 - 1789

Historical sociologists have been courageous enough to write history in the tradition of the Enlightment. Their narratives and analyses span centuries of time and range across continents in order to generalize about social and economic change in audacious and entirely stimulating ways. For example, their hypotheses occupy the high ground of current endeavours to provide historically based answers to Adam Smith's famous question about the causes of the wealth and the poverty of nations.

That question interested Marx, preoccupied Weber and returned to the academic agenda as the global problem of development after the second world war. Since then the literature of the social sciences,

---

* The title is adapted from F. BRAUDEL, Civilization and Capitalism, 15th -18th Century. (Vol. 3) The Perspective of the World, London 1988. An earlier version of this argument appeared in H. POHL (ed.), The European Discovery of the World and its Economic Effect on the Industrial Society 1500 - 1800. Papers of the Tenth International Economic History Congress, Stuttgart 1990.

concerned largely with immediate preconditions for modernization and higher levels of productivity has swamped a more limited body of investigations into the historical antecedents of inequality among the nations.

Nevertheless the perceptions which have emerged from the history of underdevelopment are that differentials in living standards and technological sophistication between the peoples of north western Europe on the one hand and the rest of the populated world on the other first appeared during the mercantile era - an era which succeeeded the Voyages of Discovery at the end of the 15th century and notionally ended with the industrial revolution in the second half of the 18th century. At that juncture the gaps in per capita incomes across countries or continents cannot be measured with confidence but they certainly widened as Europe urbanized and industrialized over the following century and they became really pronounced when population growth accelerated throughout most of the Third World during this century[1].

Modern debates between historians, historical sociologists and a smaller number of economists, who have turned their thoughts to la longue durée, are focussed on the relative strength of the exogeneous and endogeneous forces behind the pace and type of economic growth experienced by Western Europe for some three centuries after 1492[2].

According to what is now designated as "World Systems Analysis" this period witnessed the consolidation of a "European world economy based upon the capitalist mode of production"[3]. The evolution of that global economy over two long cycles, the first of expansion from 1450 to 1600 and the second of stagnation from 1600 to 1750 created

---

1 P. BAIROCH and M. LEVY-LEBOYER (eds.) Disparities in Economic Development since the Industrial Revolution, London 1981.

2 A. G. FRANK, World Accumulation 1492 - 1789, London 1978; S. AMIN, Accumulation on a World Scale, 2 Vols., New York 1974; idem, Unequal Development, New York 1976.

3 I. WALLERSTEIN, The Modern World System, Vol. 1, New York 1974.

conditions for development and underdevelopment in the nineteenth and twentieth centuries[4].

As this "school" perceives it, the rapid advance of Western Europe and the retardation of Asia, Africa, Latin America and Eastern Europe originated in the mercantile era when Europeans (the core) turned the terms and conditions for trade in their favour and exploited the periphery. Through superior military technology and forms of organization Western Europeans either plundered and colonized the territory and resources of other continents or reduced the weaker economies of Eastern Europe (the semi-periphery) to conditions of dependency. They actively created of encouraged forms of labour control such as slavery or peonage at the periphery (or serfdom and sharescropping at the semi-periphery) which maintained prices of producing exports sold on Western European markets close to the level of subsistence wage costs[5]. Institutions, property rights and modes of conducting trade emerged to control the marketing of minerals and primary produce of the periphery and semi-periphery; and to set highly unequal terms under which surplusses from these parts of the world economy exchanged for the manufactured goods, temperate farm produce and commercial sevices imported from the core[6].

Over time, the politically imposed institutions of a mercantilist economic order created patterns of specialization and sustained terms of trade which at one and the same time propelled the economies of Western Europe along paths of economic growth leading to industrialization and higher standards of living and demoted the economies of the periphery (and semi-periphery) towards primary production, monoculture and lower levels of per capita income.

---

4 W. H. Gold FRANK (ed.), The World System of Capitalism, Beverley Hills 1979.

5 I. WALLERSTEIN, The Capitalist World Economy, Cambridge 1979.

6 A. EMMANUEL, Unequal Exchange. A study of the Imperialism of Trade, London 1972.

Obviously the conclusions of World Systems Analysis carry ideological overtones. Furthermore, the approach appeals to sociologists anxious to escape from the more or less crass simplifications and anti historical concepts embedded in modernization theories and structural functionalism[7]. Historians have also welcomed attempts to pose and answer big questions. They need to be reminded of a global context, of an exogeneous dimension, for historical research too often myopically focussed upon the development of countries, regions, towns and even villages which were (even in the sixteenth century) in some way and in some degree part of an international economy.

Nevertheless most of the economic history of Western Europe has been written as if the sources of agrarian improvement, technological progress, capital formation, the accumulation of skills, population growth and internal migration, institutional change and the diffusion of factor and commodity markets which occurred between 1492 and 1789 can be explained almost without reference to shorter or longer cycles of expansion and contraction in the international economy as a whole[8].

There is no doubt that seaborne trade expanded more rapidly in the wake of the Voyages of Discovery. Some Western European ports and their hinterlands became more involved with a wider economy and linked directly or indirectly to long distance trade. Some kind of embryo international division of labour did appear during the mercantile era. There is no need to deny that gains from participation in international trade were unequally distributed between core and periphery as well as between the different states, regions and cities of Western Europe. Military power strongly influenced the shares of world trade seized and defended by each participant national economy as well as

---

7 T. Skocpol (ed.), Vision and Method in Historical Sociology, Cambridge 1984.

8 Even the modern bibliography demonstrates that the nation state remains as the focus for analysis. External relations are usually covered but the international economy as a whole is never considered as an interconnected system.

the terms and conditions of that trade[9]. Observed patterns of specialization cannot be explained in Ricardian terms as the manifestation of the long run evolution of comparative advantages based upon factor endowments located within national frontiers and to differing responses to changes in relative prices. That kind of response occurs within a liberal economic order with more or less free markets for trade in commodities and services and the absence of political impediments to movements of capital and labour across frontiers. Such an order did not really emerge until after 1846[10].

Even if we accept in general terms their depiction of the mercantile economic order, the bulk of modern historical research nevertheless severely qualifies the significance attached by World Systems Analysts to exogeneous or global forces for the economic development of Western Europe over the mercantile era. Whatever may eventually emerge as satisfactory explanations for the retardation at the periphery or semi-periphery of the world economy, the case has not been established that the creation of preconditions for the early industrialisation of Western Europe occurred because that favoured region of the global system dominated international commerce for three centuries after 1492. Obviously most of the interconnexions between trade and economic growth have been explained piecemeal by economic historians but their macro perception is that as long as commerce with the periphery and semi-periphery remained as a tiny (albeit a growing proportion) of total economic activity, commerce cannot be represented as *the* engine of growth which eventually transformed the agrarian societies of early modern Europe into industrial economies.

For the most part economic historians explain that transformation in relation to forces which are seen as relatively detached or even unconnected from commerce between Western Europe and its expanding

---

9 C. TILLY, Coercion, Capital and European States, Oxford 1990.

10 P. K. O'BRIEN / G. PIGMAN, Free Trade, British Hegemony and the International Economic order in the nineteenth Century. in: *Review of International Studies* 18 (1992).

trades with the periphery and semi-periphery. Their stress is upon forces endogeneous to the region including agricultural improvements, technical change, population growth and internal migration, the accumulation of skills, institutional changes including the growth of centralized states, above all to the diffusion of markets and the growth of trade within Western Europe itself. How these several elements in the growth process were connected to an evolving world economy has not been thoroughly investigated, but at present the consensus must be that such connexions were weak, tenuous and in no way necessary or sufficient for the industrialization of Western Europe.

To engage seriously with this issue concerned with the relative significance of endogeneous and exogeneous forces, time, place and mechanisms must be brought into historical analysis and there seem to be two entrées into that engagement. We can either move directly from knowledge available in secondary sources about commerce between Western Europe, the Americas, Asia, Africa and Eastern Europe, to enquire into when and where it influenced the pace and pattern of that region's industrialization. Alternatively we can investigate the growth of major European industries and ascertain when, how and to what degree their development from 1500 to 1800 can be linked to world trade. The first path is far easier to travel because the route from foreign trade to the European economy is not only well trodden but can be marked here and there with some statistical signposts[11]. Moving outwards from the history of particular industries towards global trade is far more difficult because a big picture of European industrialization from 1500 to 1800 is impossible to paint. Histories of several industries are available but the rate and pattern of industrialization, across Western Europe as a whole, eludes not only measurement but clear conception[12]. Industrial regions and towns

11 The data is well tabulated by P. KRIEDTE, Peasants, Landlords and Merchant Capitalists: Europe and the World Economy, Leamington Spa 1983.

12 PARKER's essay remains the best synthesis: W. N. PARKER, Europe, America and the Wider World, Vol. 1, Cambridge 1984.

have been located on maps and described, but "proto-industry" remained dispersed and organized on a scale too small to leave sufficient records for historians to analyse anything other than a fraction of Europe's manufacturing activity for the early modern era[13]. Textiles, mining, basic metallurgy, and shipbuilding have all been studied but printed references to most of the manufactures, artifacts and commodities that would find a place in any modern census of industrial production do not exist[14]. This means that the macro context for an analysis of the interconnexions between the world economic system and industrialization will remain at best impressionistic. Furthermore, the overall significance of that connexion for the progress of industry could be easily exaggerated by focussing upon just a small sample of manufacturing activity.

This survey concentrates upon recent historical writings on the trades between Western Europe, Asia, Africa, America and the European periphery, and attempts to work back to European industrialization. Along this easier but less illuminating route two features of the chronological development and concentration of new trans-oceanic trades need to be emphasized. First, their volume and value particularly with the Americas (but also around the Cape with Asia) did not reach a level that impinged on the European economy until well into the second half of the sixteenth century[15]. For some five decades after the

---

13 N. J. Pounds, An Historical Geography of Europe 1500 - 1840, Cambridge 1979; H. Kellenbenz, The Organization of Industrial Production, in: E. E. Rich / C. Wilson (eds.), The Cambridge Economic History of Europe, Vol. 5, Cambridge 1977; P. Kreidte et al., Industrialization before Industrialization, Cambridge 1981.

14 H. A. Miskimin, The Economy of Later Renaissance Europe, 1460 - 1600, Cambridge 1977; J. de Vries, The Economy of Europe in an Age of Crisis 1600 - 1750, Cambridge 1976; D. Sella, European Industries 1500 - 1700, in: C. Cipolla (ed.), Fontana Economic History of Europe, Vol. 2, Glasgow 1974.

15 K. Glamann, European Trade 1500 - 1750, in: C. Cipolla (ed.), Fontana Economic History of Europe, Vol.2; J. H. Parry, Transport and Trade Routes,

Voyages of Discovery, (while the Portuguese and the Spanish invested in the consolidation of conditions for seaborne commerce with the Americas and Asia) Europe's export exceeded imports from more continents by a large if diminishing margin. Returns on the threshold investment required to establish regular commercial relations took decades to mature[16]. Tangible manifestations of gains from the Discoveries eventually emerged in the form of imports of bullion (principally silver) from South America, fish, fish oil, furs and wax from North America, and drugs, silks and spices (especially pepper) from Asia. The overall scale of these imports remained small before the middle of the sixteenth century. Meanwhile the growth of the European economy (which had been underway since the second half of the fifteenth century) continued to respond to such endogeneous forces: as population growth, urbanization, intra-regional trade within the continent, and a modicum of organizational and technical progress in agriculture and industry.

Thus the short-run impact of the integration of new regions into trans-oceanic trade can be depicted in terms of a "drain" upon European resources and capital. How long that drain persisted will be difficult to determine because inter-continental balances of trade are impossible to reconstruct. Some historians impressed with the loot and the fortunes of adventurers continue to write as if the Discoveries and the *consolidation* of a world economy represented instantaneous windfalls. Benefits were surely not obvious before "net" inflows of imports began to arrive in quantity at European ports during the second half of the sixteenth century. I will concentrate in this essay on those imported commodities as the tangible manifestation of gains from commerce

in: E. E. RICH / C. WILSON (eds.), Cambridge Economic History of Europe, Vol.4, Cambridge 1967.

16 B. W. DIFFIE / G. D. WINIUS, Foundations of the Portuguese Empire 1415 - 1580, Minneapolis 1977 and C. VERLINDEN, The Beginnings of Modern Colonization, Ithaca 1970; D. W. MEINIG, The Shaping of America, New Haven 1986.

with Asia, Africa and the Americas and propose to explore their connexions to Europe's development and industrialization[17].

Secondly, for most of the sixteenth century the gains from trade, and plunder, accrued in very large measure to Portugal and Spain, whose rulers, aristocrats and merchants had committed and risked more capital to open up seaborne commerce with Asia, Africa and the Americas than any other European people[18]. For sound fiscal reasons, Iberian monarchs sought to reserve the new trades for themselves and their own subjects, by using force to exclude or to regulate "aliens". But despite high and mounting levels of military expenditure to protect their investments neither of these Iberian Governments (nor the mobilization of armed power by private investors) could prevent the benefits from the oceanic trade from being more widely diffused around Europe, especially to Italian, Dutch, French and English "interlopers".

Spillovers occurred not simply because bellicose European rivals refused to recognize territorial claims, but because the industries and agricultures of Spain and Portugal could not supply more than a proportion (and apparently a diminishing proportion) of the commodities and services required to sustain the new trades. Demand for textiles, weapons, processed food, tools, construction materials, slaves, shipping and mercantile services spilled over into imports purchased throughout Western Europe for re-export to the Americas, Africa and Asia. Profits which accrued to Spaniards and Portuguese from the expansion of Iberian trade also diffused as purchases across national

---

17 This illuminating approach was adopted by D. LANDES, The Great Drain and Industrialization, in: E. MALINVAUD (ed.), Economic Growth and Resources, London 1979.

18 G. V. SCAMMEL, The World Encompassed: The First European Empires c. 1600 - 1650, London 1981; V. MAGALHAES-GODHINO, L'économie de l'empire portuguais au XVe et XVIe siècles, Paris 1969; K. R. ANDREWS, The Spanish Carribean: Trade and Plunder 1530 - 1630, New Haven 1978 and R. DAVIS, The Rise of the Atlantic Economies, London 1973.

borders[19]. Right from the start the Spanish government allowed Genoese and other foreign merchants to organize commerce with the New World[20]. At the same time the endeavours of the Portuguese to maximize profits from marketing spices, silks, drugs and pepper were not only checked by the survival of competition from overland routes to the Mediterranean but shared with Dutch, French, Italian and English merchants, who also distributed these Asian luxuries around Europe. Thus Portugal and Spain failed to "concentrate" the gains from trade within their national boundaries. Politically they lacked the power to exclude interlopers from other nations. Iberian agriculture, industry and commerce could not for long respond elastically enough to confine trade within the Portuguese and Spanish economies[21]. In the short run the stimulus afforded to several industries: woollens, at Valladolid and Segovia, Valencian silks, metals from Bilbao, shipbuilding in the Basque country, and to processed foodstuffs such as wine and olive oil, was important. But growth was not sustained. Export demand led neither to technical transformation nor to the reorganization of production[22]. Meanwhile the "leakage" from expenditures into the European economy implied that the early industrial growth which followed from the initial consolidation of a global economy would be extensive and dispersed across several industrial regions of the continent. Commercial and industrial profits, internal and external economies of scale, became more visible and more concentrated after 1650, when first Holland and eventually England captured

---

19 J. H. ELIOT, The Decline of Spain, in: *Past and Present* 20 (1961); J. V. VIVES, An Economic History of Spain, Princeton 1969 and A. H. DE OLIVEIRA MARQUES, A History of Portugal, New York 1972.

20 On Genoa see F. BRAUDEL, Civilization and Capitalism, Vol. 3.

21 C. CIPOLLA, Before the Industrial Revolution, London 1976; and I. WALLERSTEIN, The Modern World System, Vol. 1.

22 D. SELLA, European Industries 1500 - 1700, in: C. CIPOLLA (ed.), Fontana Economic History of Europe, Vol. 2; P. KRIEDTE, Peasants Landlords, and Merchant Capitalists.

"disproportionate" shares of European commerce with the Americas, Africa and Asia[23].

2. Silver, Inflation and the International Monetary System

For three centuries after the Voyages of Discovery the return cargo which captivated the European imagination (and which in value terms probably exceeded all other imports from the Americas and Asia by a considerable margin) consisted of silver and gold. Statistics which seek to estimate the value of American precious metals imported into Europe and sent on to Asia are well known[24]. Debates about the economic and political significance of these flows began almost with the arrival of the earliest shipments into Seville and have continued right up to the present day[25]. As usual it seems easier to outline the problems involved than to hazard guesses at answers. First, the relevant orders of magnitude can only be approximate because the quantities of silver and gold imported or smuggled into Europe on private account are not known and the available data omit the very large quantities of American bullion transhipped directly from Acapulco to Manila - shipments which nevertheless, and through trade with Asia eventually impinged on the development of European economies[26]. In

---

23 I. WALLERSTEIN, The Modern World System, Vol. 2, New York 1980.

24 References to the data are to be found in D. O. FLYNN, The Microeconomics of Silver and East West Trade in the Early Modern Period, in: W. FISCHER / R M. MCINNIS / J. SCHNEIDER (eds.), The Emergence of a World Economy 1500 - 1914, Stuttgart 1986.

25 P. VILAR, A History of Gold and Money 1450 - 1920, London 1976 and D. O'FLYNN, A New Perspective on the Spanish Price Revolutions, in: *Explorations in Economic History* 15 (1978).

26 A. ATTMAN, The Bullion Flow Between Europe and the East, Gothenburg 1981 and O. PRAKASH, Precious Metal Flows and World Economic Integration

view of the unsettled debate about the magnitude of imported flows, it may be sensible to return to Soetbeer's estimates for global production of gold and silver first published in 1879[27].

His figures show the overwhelming importance of American production from the 1540s to say the 1720s. Supply was not steady year by year and peak production achieved in the early seventeenth century was probably not surpassed until the mid-eighteenth century. Neverthless, American mines surely provided the world economy with most of the *extra* bullion required for monetary and also for industrial purposes for something like 160 years[28]. As for the latter use, production of artifacts from gold and silver may have formed a sizeable component of industrial output in the sixteenth and seventeenth centuries. But their functions as money (as specie reserves, and as an asset for the settlement of imbalances in foreign trade) was surely far more significant than the production of jewels, paintings, church furnishings, household ornaments, table utensils, decorated textiles, furniture and weapons[29].

Minted into coin and utilized as liquid and acceptable collateral for instruments of credit and paper circulation, silver and gold constituted the base for the expansion of Europe's money supply. After two decades of inconclusive debate between Keynesians and Monetarists on the role of money in macro models of growth and stability, historians have become more cautious in making suggestions about the significance of New World silver and gold for European development over a statisti-

---

in the Seventeenth Century, in: W. FISCHER et al., The Emergence of a World Economy.

27 A. SOETBEER, Edelmetall-Produktion und Werthverhältnis zwischen Gold und Silber, Gotha 1879.

28 F. BRAUDEL and F. SPOONER, Prices in Europe from 1450 to 1750, in E. E. RICH / C. WILSON (eds.), Cambridge Economic History of Europe, Vol. 4.

29 Nine of fourteen papers submitted for Theme A.3 of the Ninth Congress of International Economic History Association and published in W. FISCHER et al., The Emergence of a World Economy, deal with bullion as money and reserve assets.

cal dark age from 1530 to 1800[30]. Alas they cannot even accurately guess at America's contribution to the *growth* of Europe's money supplies because the size of its initial stock is unknown and other components (including the substitution of a penumbra of paper instruments for specie; as well as the scale of European, African and Japanese production of precious metals) cannot be estimated[31]. Perhaps it is *still* safe to accept the established view that the transhipment of gold and silver from the Americas to Europe and to Asia relieved a potential monetary bottleneck to the spread of trade and specialization both within Europe and also for intercontinental trade[32]. But we cannot be certain. Long before treasure fleets arrived at Seville and Cadiz, European merchants, bankers and rulers had responded to monetary restraints on transactions by substituting bills of exchange, letters of credit and banknotes for specie. Throughout the middle ages Princes refused to recognize constraints on state expenditures and "economized" on scarce specie by transforming gold and silver coins into fiat money through the technique of debasement[33]. While there can be no doubt that American metals added greatly to the stock of money available for national and international transactions for almost three centuries after 1492, they were by no means the only element underpinning the diffusion of monetized transactions within and beyond Western Europe. Moreover, it seems highly unlikely that Europe's capitalists and rulers would have permitted their policies,

---

30 But see D. FISHER, The Price Revolution, in: *Journal of Economic History* 4/XLIX (1989).

31 F. BRAUDEL / F. SPOONER, Prices in Europe, and J. SCHNEIDER / O. SCHWARZER, International Rates of Exchange: Structures and Trends of Payments Mechanism in Europe, 17th to 19th Century, in: W. FISCHER et al., The Emergence of a World Economy; F. BRAUDEL, Civilization and Capitalism, Vol. 1.

32 J. DAY, The Great Bullion Famine of the Fifteenth Century, in: *Past and Present* 79 (1978).

33 H. A. MISKIMIN, The Economy of Later Renaissance Europe, is excellent on this topic.

drive and enterprise to be shackled by avoidable constraints on the growth of the money supply. Perhaps American specie is best depicted as a lubricant, not as a propellant; as oil but not petroleum for the engine of European growth.

The ramifications of observed connexions between bullion imports and the formation of capital in Europe may also have been explored almost as far as they can be taken on the basis of available evidence. For example, we know that super normal profits accrued to owners of mines in the Americas especially in the earlier decades of their exploitation. Over time profitability declined as rising unit costs of mining silver and gold set in at one location after another, and as the purchasing power of ever increasing supplies of silver and gold on European markets diminished[34]. Furthermore profits were divided between monarchs and private investors. No estimates exist for their respective shares but in Spain royal taxation in one form or another increased steadily from a low point of 20% at the beginning of the sixteenth century. As their military expenditures mounted Spanish and Portuguese monarchs not only appropriated a rising share of the profits from the exploitation of American minerals but throughout Europe, Kings taxed away a substantial proportion of the increment to national incomes imputable to the expansion of internal and external trade[35].

Thus historians suppose that a "large share" of the windfall offered to Europe in the form of American silver and gold was dissipated on warfare over the mercantile era[36]. Before 1815 the value of resources

---

34 O'FLYNN, The Micro Economics of Silver, in: W. Fischer et al., The Emergence of a World Economy.

35 VILAR, A History of Gold and Money; DIFFIE / WINIUS, The Foundations of the Portuguese Empire; H. KLEIN / J. A. BARBIER, Recent Trends in the Study of Spanish American Colonial Public Finance, in: *Latin American Research Review* 23 (1988).

36 P. KENNEDY, The Rise and Fall of the Great Powers: Economic Change and Military Conflict from 1500 to 2000, New York 1987; M. MANN, States, War and Capitalism, Oxford 1988.

used for military purposes usually ran at a multiple of expenditures on all forms of gross national capital formation; but what exactly might this signify?[37] First there seems no reason to suppose that the escalating costs of warfare during the military revolution of the sixteenth and seventeenth centuries failed to absorb a rising percentage of national incomes and thereby "crowded out" potentially more productive forms of investment. Secondly historians are only just beginning to analyse complex interrelationships between military expenditures, the rise of the state and economic growth[38]. For example are we now prepared to discuss the long term economic benefits from "American" mineral resources allocated to check the expansion of the Ottoman Empire? How far did the diffusion of markets depend upon properly funded states, capable of protecting commerce within and beyond national borders?[39] Whatever is eventually concluded about the fiscal appropriation and expenditures of Spanish, Portuguese and other European monarchs, it is worth emphasizing that the bulk of the profits from the discovery of American gold and silver accrued in the first instance to private capitalists. Even the transactions of monarchs were serviced by merchants, bankers, contractors and other businessmen who took a not inconsiderable slice of the treasure in the form of monopoly profits[40]. If in retrospect the potential for productive investment provided by this huge windfall seems somehow to have been unrealized, even dissipated, (both within and beyond the Iberian peninsular), then it may not be enough to concentrate criticism upon those profligate, warlike and "ostensibly unprofitable" expenditures by Habsburg and other European monarchs!

---

37 P. K. O'BRIEN, The Political Economy of British Taxation 1660 - 1815, in: *Economic History Review* XLI (1988); idem, Taxation and the Rise of the State 1485 - 1815, in: *Historical Research* (Forthcoming).

38 M. MANN, Sources of Social Power: A History of Power from the Beginning to A. D. 1750, Cambridge 1986.

39 C. TILLY (ed.), The Formation of National States in Western Europe, Princeton 1985.

40 VILAR, A History of Gold and Money.

Correlations between inflows of American specie and movements of the general level of prices continues to fascinate scholars[41]. But debates about the importance to attribute to monetary or real factors in initiating and sustaining: the inflation of the long sixteenth century, deflation in the seventeenth century and the renewed upswing in prices across Europe from around 1750 through to the end of the Napoleonic wars remains inconclusive[42]. Increasing supplies of silver could hardly be expected to maintain a constant level of purchasing power through time and variations in the rates of change of national price levels in general, or groups of prices in particular, do not correlate well with supplies of new world silver coming onto European markets. Given the paucity of relevant statistics such correlations are probably not worth pursuing. In any case even the theoretical connexions between the rather modest inflations and deflations of these centuries and economic growth remain uncertain. Wages did in general lag behind prices but that lag was more pronounced for agriculture than for industry and urban services. If industrial profits constituted a primary source for capital accumulation then the faster rise in primary product prices operated to reduce industrial investment. If urban wage earners formed an important segment of the market for manufactured goods the erosion of their incomes by higher food prices reduced demand for industrial output. If landowners and farmers simply consumed windfall profits contingent upon inflation the overall rate of investment would not be pushed upwards[43]. Optimal conditions for industrial advance normally occurred when agriculture delivered a rising volume

---

41 FISHER, The Price Revolution.

42 P. VILAR, Problems of the Formation of Capital, in: D. LANDES (ed.), The Rise of Capitalism, New York 1966 and P. KRIEDTE, Peasants, Landlords and Merchant Capitalists, for a recent survey.

43 On this topic see the debate between C. G. REED / H. A. MISKIMIN, Price Movements, Balance of Payments, Bullion Flows and Unemployment in the Fourteenth and Fifteenth Centuries, in: *Journal of European Economic History* 8 (1979) and J. DE VRIES, The Economy of Europe.

of food and raw materials to towns at stable or declining prices[44]. During the price revolutions of the long sixteenth and the eighteenth centuries the terms of trade turned against industry. To put the point moderately: it is not at all clear how or whether long swings in the purchasing power of bullion promoted or retarded industrialisation[45].

Its role (if not its significance) as lubricant for internaitonal trade may be less difficult to expound. Within Europe, American silver and gold moved across frontiers towards places and goals where its purchasing power was highest. A modern economist might present the process as one where differential rates of inflation stimulated flows of commodities and services from economies of higher towards economies of lower prices. Thus the former (Spain and Portugal) ran deficits on their transactions with other states which they funded with American bullion, and the latter (Holland, France and England) ran surpluses (of commodity exports less imports) for which they accepted payment in the form of silver and gold. Historical research has been adept at tracking both trade and (the contingent balancing item) bullion flows across national frontiers within Europe and also from Europe to Asia[46]. Although the details are complex and its commodity composition changed over time, the geographical patterns and basis for trade remained constant enough to allow for a simplified depiction of the role of bullion in world trade as it evolved for some three centuries after 1492. For example, American treasure provided Western European economies with the means to settle their adverse balances of

---

44 I try to deal with the ramifications of this debate in P. K. O'BRIEN, Agriculture and the Home Market for English Industry 1660 - 1820, in: *English Historical Review* 100 (1985).

45 For recent attempts to make inferences see J. S. GOLDSTEIN, Long Cycles, Prosperity and War in the Modern Age, New Haven 1988, and R. W. JASTRAM, The Golden Constant, New York 1977.

46 See the papers and references by O'FLYNN, CHAUDHURI, PRAKASH, GAASTRA and ATTMAN in W. FISCHER et al., The Emergence of a World Economy, and H. KELLENBENZ (ed.), Precious Metals in the Age of Expansion. Papers of the XIVth International Congress of the Historical Sciences, Stuttgart 1981.

trade with Asia and the Baltic. In this way it facilitated higher levels of international specialization. Without silver and gold gains from trade over the mercantile era would surely have been smaller.

Something like a third of Western Europe's strategically important imports from the Baltic (particularly grain, but also bar-iron, hemp, timber, potash, flax, fur and tallow) may have been paid for with bullion. That proportion diminished over time largely because Dutch, French and English merchants organized the transhipment of ever increasing supplies of American groceries (tobacco, rice, sugar and coffee) and Asian luxuries (tea, spices and textiles) for sale on Prussian, Scandinavian, Russian and Polish markets[47]. Precious metals, textiles and tropical groceries from the Americas (and from Asia) thereby reinforced and pushed forward patterns of specialization within the European economy which had existed for centuries before the Discoveries[48]. We could speculate about how far this process might have gone without the additional supplies of bullion, spices, tobacco, sugar, calicoes and coffee. How easily could the economies of North Western and Mediterranean Europe have found substitutes for imports from the Baltic region, which were not impossible (but certainly more expensive) to procure elsewhere in Europe? Would development have been seriously restrained by changes in the terms of trade between Europe's major economic regions?

Similar speculations (which are basically concerned with necessary or sufficient conditions for progress towards the Industrial Revolution) are required if historians are ever to pronounce on the significance of the entire range of American, African and Asian foodstuffs imported into Europe. Pepper, sugar, tobacco, tea, coffee, spices improved the European diet, and these "luxuries" may well have stimulated greater

---

47 See the papers by ATTMAN and JOHANSEN in W. FISCHER et al. (eds.), The Emergence of a World Economy.

48 K. GLAMMAN, The Changing Patterns of Trade, in: E. E. RICH / C. WILSON (eds.), The Cambridge Economic History of Europe, Vol. 4.

efforts from the work force in order to eat tastier food[49] Claims that pepper, sugar and Asian textiles pioneered in the development of cultural attitudes and institutions conducive to the diffusion of mass markets are also currently under debate[50].

For centuries before Vasco da Gama charted the sea route to India, bullion had provided Europeans with an indispensable commodity for the conduct of commerce with the Orient[51]. European demand for pepper and other spices, for jewels, silks, calicoes, dyestuffs, and tea, was price elastic and responded to the decline in transport and transaction costs when trade between Europe and Asia moved gradually away from the overland route through Venice and the Mediterranean, towards the Cape route and into the new entrepôts of Antwerp, Amsterdam and of London[52]. European manufactures, foodstuffs and raw materials could not in general command prices on Asian markets which made the terms of trade profitable enough to support a large scale expansion of commerce between the two continents. Fortunately silver, gold and copper continued to be highly profitable commodities to ship to Asia where their command over local tradeable goods rose during the price inflations in Europe during the sixteenth and eighteenth centuries[53]. Until late in the eighteenth century the bulk of the spices, foodstuffs and textiles procured in Asia and shipped to Europe, Africa and America continued to be purchased with silver and other

---

49 Mercantilist thinkers thought so - L. GOMES, Foreign Trade and the National Economy: Mercantilist and Classical Perspectives, London 1987.

50 R. A. AUSTEN / W. SMITH, Private Tooth Decay as Public Economic Virtue, in: *Social Science History* 14 (1990).

51 K. N. CHAUDHURI, Trade and Civilization in the Indian Ocean, Cambridge 1985.

52 The shift was gradual - C. H. H. WAKE, The changing pattern of Europe's pepper and spice imports, in: *Journal of European Economic History* 8 (1979).

53 K. N. CHAUDHURI, The Trading World of Asia and the East India Company 1660 - 1760, Cambridge 1978, and K. GLAMMAN, Dutch Asiatic Trade 1620 - 1740, Hague 1958.

precious metals. That dependance diminished through time as Portuguese, Dutch and English merchants and shippers forcibly inserted themselves, first as carriers in intra-Asian trade and then as territorial rulers (providing highly priced Governmental services) in Ceylon, Java and Bengal[54]. By the second half of the eighteenth century when English textiles and metal goods became more acceptable on Asian markets, the terms of trade improved and the share of bullion represented within exports to Asia fell away sharply[55].

3. Tropical Groceries, Industrial Inputs and Cotton Textiles

After bullion, tropical groceries represented the most visible and material gain from trade with the Americas and Asia. Down to the time of the French Revolution, European investment in the equipment, manpower and organization required to cultivate, transport, refine and distribute sugar, tobacco, rice and coffee must have constituted a multiple of European capital committed to all other productive enterprises in the New World and Asia. In the absence of a known and expanding demand for tropical groceries, the contribution of the Americas to European welfare might have been pretty much confined to silver and gold, to fish, and to a less valuable range of industrial raw materials (indigo, timber, furs, wax, fish oil and cotton fibres). Until the end of the eighteenth century all the other resourcs of that

---

54 N. STEENSGAARD, The Asian Trade Revolution of the Seventeenth Century, Chicago 1974, and H. FURBER, Rival Empires of Trade in the Orient, Minneapolis 1976.

55 H. HOSSAIN, The Company of Weavers in Bengal, Delhi 1988 and O. PRAKASH, The Dutch East India Company and the Economy of Bengal 1630 - 1720, Princeton 1985.

vast continent remained in the realm of unknown and unrealized potential[56].

Meanwhile capital and enterprise moved overwhelmingly into the production of foodstuffs for which consumer markets had been pioneered long before 1492[57]. European investment and entrepreneurship in the New World catered for demand that was both highly income and price elastic[58]. Furthermore, the trades in tropical groceries enjoyed externalities in the form of strong state support because they generated taxes and served as a nursery for seamen and ships transferable when required to serve the military ends of Kings and Princes[59].

Slave plantations (as the most effective mode of exploiting under utilized land for the cultivation of cane sugar) had demonstrated their profitability on Mediterranean and Atlantic islands centuries before Europe's inhumane institutions were transplanted to the New World[60]. Their diffusion can be tracked and correlated either with time series related to tons of sugar and tobacco and other produce imported into European ports of with the import of African slaves into the Americas. On the latter index imports of slaves ran at around 5,000 a year in the last quarter of the sixteenth century, at 10,000 a year in the second quarter of the seventeenth century, doubling again to reach 20,000 per annum by the third quarter of the seventeenth century, and rising to a peak of 75,000 slaves a year in the 1780s. Some 5.8 million slaves entered the Americas in the eighteenth century, compared with

---

56 K. G. Davies, The North Atlantic World in the Seventeenth Century, Minneapolis 1974.

57 F. Braudel, Civilization and Capitalism, Vol. 1; C. Cipolla, Before the Industrial Revolution.

58 R. B. Sheridan, Sugar and Slavery, Baltimore 1973; J. de Vries, The Economy of Europe in an Age of Crisis. S. Mintz, Sweetness and Power: the Place of Sugar in Modern History, New York 1985 regards sugar as a drug.

59 I. Wallerstein, The Modern World System, Vols. 1 and 2.

60 B. L. Solow, Capitalism and Slavery in the Exceedingly Long Run, in: *Journal of Interdisciplinary History* 17 (1987); C. Verlinden, The Beginnings of Modern Colonization.

1.3 million over the previous century[61]. They and their descendants provided the indispensable supply of labour required for the expansion of commerce between Europe and the Americas before the Industrial Revolution. Almost the whole of the *increment* to *non-bullion trade* between Western Europe and the New World from 1600 to 1800 depended directly and indirectly on the exchange of tropical foodstuffs, tobacco and industrial raw materials, cultivated basically with slave labour and exchanged for manufactured goods and commercial services produced by Europeans. The rise of an "Atlantic economy" based on commodities other than bullion could only have proceeded at the rate and on the scale witnessed for two centuries before the French Revolution with the assistance of African slaves. Counterfactual speculation based on the voluntary emigration of free white labour to the New World and a pronounced shift in the net barter terms of trade against Europe only serve to emphasize the significance of the connexion between slavery and the growth of trade between the two continents[62].

Nevertheless the importance of cash crops cultivated on plantations and farms located on tropical soils in the Americas was almost certainly of more importance for the development of Brazil, Venezuela, Cuba, other Carribean islands and the Southern United States than it was for the industrialization of Western Europe. In other words the long term significance of slavery resides more in the development of the New World than in the economic history of Europe.

After all, these groceries were luxuries. Their calorific and energy content did little to transform per capita food intake among

61 P. D. CURTIN, The Atlantic Slave Trade, Madison 1969; P. KRIEDTE, Peasants, Landlords and Merchant Capitalists.

62 B. L. SOLOW / S. L. ENGERMAN (eds.), British Capitalism and Carribean Slavery, Cambridge 1987); B. L. SOLOW, Carribean Slavery and British Growth: The Eric Williams Hypothesis, in: *Journal of Development Economics* 17 (1985).

Europeans[63]. Only in so far as sugar, coffee and rice (and we should add Chinese and Indian tea and Oriental spices) substituted for food and drink processed from grain did they do anything more than complement European food production. Foodstuffs imported from the New World (and Asian spices and tea) did not serve to release much labour and capital for employment in industry and urban services. Along with American silver they procured some grain from the Baltic which helped to feed Dutch and Southern European towns[64]. Eventually (but not until rather late in the eighteenth century) did the transplating of American potatoes and maize add a larger but still somewhat marginal supplement to Europe's food supplies[65]. Industrial capacity to process and refine tropical groceries developed in and around European ports, but the value added by these "new industries" probably represented (less than 1%?) of Europe's total industrial output.

Imported industrial raw materials (cochineal, indigo, logwood, furs, fish oils, wax, cotton fibres) and such finished goods as Chinese silks and Indian calicoes, carry more obvious links with the coming of the Industrial Revolution. Textiles procured in Asia with silver and gold transhipped from the Americas extended and pioneered a mass market for a light weight cloth which eventually matured into the first fully mechanized factory industry in England[66]. Transoceanic trade provided the matrix within which the cotton industry first emerged in Europe during the second half of the seventeenth century. These fifty years witnessed a "challenge and response" to Asian textiles carried into Dutch, English, French and Danish ports by European multina-

63 AUSTEN and SMITH, Private Tooth Decay as Economic Virtue.

64 JOHANSEN, How to Pay for Baltic Imports, in W. FISCHER et al., The Emergence of a World Economy.

65 This topic is surveyed by G. B. MASEFIELD, Crops and Livestock, in: E. E. RICH / C. WILSON (eds.), The Cambridge Economic History of Europe, Vol. 4.

66 K. N. CHAUDHURI, The Trading World of Asia and the East India Company.

tional corporations trading with the Indies[67]. To the east their ships carried bullion. Return cargoes (dominated for more than a century by pepper and spices) shifted increasingly over the seventeenth century towards cotton cloth, attractively finished and competitive with European woollens, linens and silks[68]. From about 1660 onwards, Asian textiles began to penetrate European, African and American markets at a rate that prompted one European government after another to ban their import entirely, or to frame regulations designed to encourage import substitution. In retrospect the English Parliament's delayed response to the threat posed by Asian textiles, to long established woollen and linen industries seems (by political accident) to have created the right legislative framework for the development of a native cotton industry. English law first allowed Asian textiles to pioneer the home market, then it moved to protect and stimulate the rapid expansion of dyeing and printing textiles within the kingdom. Finally in 1721 Parliament excluded Asian textiles in finished and unfinished form from the home market altogether. English spinners and weavers moved more rapidly, than their counterparts on the continent, initially into mixtures of linen and cotton fibres (fustians) and, from the 1750's onwards, enthusiastically into cotton textiles[69]. The young industry found accessible and expanding markets not only at home but also in Africa and in the plantation economies of the Americas. On the coast of Africa fustians and cottons exchanged for slaves who were transported to the Carribean, to the Southern States and to South America to produce more sugar, tobacco and raw cotton for transhipment in European ships for sale on European markets.

---

67 K. GLAMMAN, Dutch Asiatic Trade.

68 O. PRAKASH, The Dutch East India Company; H. HOSSAIN, The Company Weavers of Bengal.

69 This argument is fully developed in P. K. O'BRIEN et al., Political Components of the Industrial Revolution: Parliament and the Cotton, Textile Industry 1660 - 1774, in: *Economic History Review* 3 (1991).

Cotton represents the prime (perhaps the only?) example of a major European industry adopted, nurtured and brought to successful maturity in the context of oceanic trade. Indian calicoes, especially printed calicoes, pioneered European markets. European spinners obtained their raw material initially from the Levant but increasingly from the Americas (first the Carribean islands and then the United States). Textile printers in Holland, France and England imitated Indian patterns and designs. Merchants exchanged cotton cloth for slaves from Africa. Millions of black men, women and children (transported to the sugar, tobacco, coffee and cotton plantations of the New World) were clothed by their American masters in cheap cotton cloth. At the margin expanding demand for cotton textiles from African and American consumers also formed part of the pressure which prompted the rapidly growing fustian industry in Lancashire to seek mechanical solutions in order to increase supplies of yarn and cloth[70]. Cotton, the paradigm case of the first fully mechanized factory industry, surely exercised "demonstration effects" upon other industries, particularly in the textile sector. But as late as 1841 the cotton industry still accounted for only 7% of Britain's gross national product. After decades of research into the origins of industrialization few economic historians (even of the First Industrial Nation) could allow their analysis to be dominated by cotton. That industry was, however, undeniably important and Britain's appropriation of such a large share of the gains from trans-Atlantic and Asian commerce from 1688 to 1815 helps to explain why the Lancashire cotton industry achieved such extraordinary dominance on world markets over the nineteenth century.

Nevertheless, the development of no other manufacturing industry in England or Holland or elsewhere in Western Europe can be linked as closely to transcontinental trade. Processed and refined raw sugar, tobacco, coffee and tea have already been mentioned. Shipbuilding

---

70 J. E. INIKORI, Slavery and the Devclpmcnt of Industrial Capitalism in England, in: *Journal of Interdisciplinary History* 17; idem, Slavery and the Revolution in Cotton Textile Production in England, in: *Social Science History* 14 (1990).

and its ancillary trades come to mind. But only a small proportion of the European fleet were employed in commerce with Africa, the Indies and the Americas[71]. Technological improvements to ships, to their navigation and to the organization of transportation by water preceded the Voyages of Discovery. They cannot be connected in any clearcut way with long distance commerce or with trades in tropical produce[72]. Several other industries (including linens, woollens, silks, metallurgical goods, armaments, books and paper) sold modest, but unknown fractions, of their output to consumers in Asia and the Americas[73].

Although they do not have data to substantiate the point most historians might well suggest that an overwhelming percentage of industrial commodities and artifacts manufactured in Western Europe continued to be sold within the region. Given the share of European exports delivered to the Americas, Africa and Asia (amounting to just 24% as late as the 1790s) arithmetically it would be difficult to argue that the opening up of these new markets at the periphery of the world economy had contributed significantly to the long run expansion of demand for industrial output since 1500[74]. Let us play with stylized numbers to make this point. English industry grew at just over 1% a year from 1700 to 1800[75]. Assume that Western European (including English) industry grew at half that rate for three centuries after 1500. By 1800 the increment to total output would then be three and a half

---

71 P. Kriedte, Peasants, Landlords and Merchant Capitalists.

72 C. Cipolla, Guns, Sails and Empires, New York 1965. But J. H. Parry, Europe and a Wider World 1415 - 1715, London 1966 is inclined to suggest connexions.

73 D. Sella, European Industries 1500 - 1700, in: C. Cipolla (ed.), Fontana Economic History of Europe, Vol. 2; H. Kellenbenz, The Organization of Industrial Production, in: E. E. Rich / C. Wilson (eds.), Cambridge Economic History of Europe, Vol. 5.

74 P. Bairoch, Geographical Structure and Trade Balance of European Foreign Trade from 1800 - 1970, in: *Journal of European Economic History* 3 (1974).

75 N. F. R. Crafts, British Economic Growth during the Industrial Revolution, Oxford 1985.

times its base line level. Even *if* the ratio of exports to industrial output was as high as fifty percent; and an, improbably large, two fifths of those exports found their way outside Europe, only a quarter of the increment to total industrial output could represent exports to Asia, Africa and the Americas.

Most industrial producers did not engage in international let alone intercontinental trade and those that did continued to sell entirely modest proportions of their outputs to markets in other continents or to the semi-periphery of Eastern Europe. In the standard modern economic histories, covering the three centuries after 1500, the oscillations and long run developments of manufacturing activity refer only tangentially to long distance trade[76]. On the demand side industrial expansion is usually depicted as a response to population growth, urbanization, to shifts in the terms of trade between industry and agriculture and to intra regional exchanges within Western Europe[77]. On the supply side, familiar analyses of technological changes, the diffusion of industry into the countryside to exploit cheap supplies of labour and changes in locational advantages from town to town and from country to country pay only limited attention to long distance trade[78]. If the impact of the world economy on industry is approached through industrial history then it is difficult to find more than a few examples where global markets for final outputs and inputs came into the story. And only a single conspicuous case (the development of cotton textiles) emerges as impossible to imagine without its connexions to Asia and the Americas.

---

76 H. A. MISKIMIN, The Economy of Later Renaissance Europe; J. DE VRIES, The Economy of Europe in an Age of Crisis; D. SELLA, European Industries, 1500 - 1700, in: C. CIPOLLA (ed.), Fontana Economic History of Europe, Vol. 2.

77 J. DE VRIES, European Urbanization, London 1984; E. E. RICH / C. WILSON (eds.), Cambridge Economic History of Europe, Vol. 5.

78 P. KRIEDTE et al., Industrialization Before Industrialization.

4. Europe's Gains From Trade

Between 1492 and 1789 international, inter regional and local trade expanded in the wake of the Voyages of Discovery. Neo-classical economists might assume that the intercontinental (and contingent intra-continental) trade of the mercantile era promoted a division of labour which increased world output by reinforcing tendencies to specialization along lines of comparative advantage[79]. Unless they are prepared to believe that payments for slaves on the coast approximated to the capitalized values of black workers' outputs over their lifetimes, then the incorporation of Africa into the world economy led to nothing but underdevelopment on that such continent[80]. In so far as Europeans used political weapons to force production and exports from Africa, America and the European periphery in sub-optimal directions then the expansion of trade cannot really be represented as a response to price signals, prompting the allocation of global resources to ever more productive uses. As their merchants gradually exploited the economic potential inherent in the Discoveries, imperial regulations and military power, together with market forces, operated to push Western European economies towards specialization based upon manufacturing and commercial services[81].

To reap the gains from these exchanges Europeans invested heavily in shipping, ports, processing and refining facilities at entrepôts, in African slaves, military power and commercial institutions. Their investments cumulated and matured for decades before they yielded returns in the tangible form of imported supplies of bullion, tropical groceries, industrial raw materials, cotton textiles and silks. Externalities or spinoffs which flowed from major imports from the

---

79 N. ROSENBERG / L. E. BIRDZELL, How the West Grew Rich, Trowbridge 1986.

80 A. G. FRANK, World Accumulation 1492 - 1789.

81 The great merit of Wallerstein's research has been to integrate political with economic factors behind the growth of a global economy - I. WALLERSTEIN, The Modern World System, Vols. 1, 2 and 3.

development and consolidation of the World economy have been outlined above. In conclusion I will try to guess what the magnitude of Western Europe's gains from the trade might look like *if* it could be brought into some kind of cost-benefit matrix.

Obviously relevant statistics will never be available, but a conceptual framework even without the data may be heuristic to pursue. First the increment to the value of global trade "imputable" to the consolidation of a "European" world economy would have to be demarcated and measured. Next the profits contained in that increment and earned by merchants, traders, shippers, bankers and investors who organized and funded trade with the periphery and semi-periphery would have to be calculated. Current historical literature leaves a very firm impression that these rewards accrued overwhelmingly to Western Europeans who organized and invested in inter (and intra) continental commerce. Arab, African, Indian, Chinese, native American and other European merchants (who also participated in and profited from these trades) are implicitely perceived to have earned normal returns and rather small shares of the overall gains from trade. When and where Europeans exercised "monopsony" power or military strength to procure tradeable commodities from America, Africa or Asia, their share of commercial profits would be augmented still further. Through time, one way or another, first Portuguese, Spanish and Italian merchants and then in the seventeenth and eighteenth centuries their Dutch, French and English successors appropriated "most" of the profits imputable to the expansion of intercontinental commerce after 1492. American settlers derived handsome rewards and their slaves' sustenance by bringing surplus land and minerals into production for Western European markets, as did the landowners and serfs of Eastern Europe. Asians gained from the deployment of underemployed skilled labour. Western Europeans obtained their returns basically by handling and financing trade. Mercantile entrepreneurs made fortunes by organizing the sales of pepper, spices, sugar, tea, coffee, calicoes and silks on European markets. Famous entrepôts (Lisbon, Seville, Antwerp, Amsterdam, London) as well as smaller port cities (Livorno,

Cadiz, Genoa, Bordeaux, Nantes, Bristol, Liverpool, Glasgow) owed their development and prosperity to the enterprise of their merchants, whose ships and cargoes traversed seas and oceans to and from Asia, Africa and the Americas.

The splendour of the whole enterprise fascinated the late Fernand Braudel. He suggested that by the eighteenth century, "It was from all over the world ... that Europe was now drawing a substantial part of her strength and substance. And it was this extra share which enabled Europeans to reach superhuman heights in tackling the tasks encountered on the path to progress. Without this constant assistance, would Europe's industrial revolution - the key to her destiny - have been possible by the end of the eighteenth century?"[82]

Braudel delighted in big questions but the connexions from the world economy to the industrial revolution are not nearly strong enough to seriously weaken the present "Eurocentric consensus" that its mainsprings are to be found within and not beyond the continent. Apart from cotton textiles, imports from other parts of the globe (even bullion) do not emerge as significant enough to generate "large" economic effects. In the end their ramifications are important to analyse but limited.

Europeans probably garnered a "disproportionate" share of the gains from trade, but what did they amount to and how were they deployed? In the 1780's roughly a quarter of Europe's commodity exports were delivered to North and Latin America, the Carribean, Asia and Africa. Is it not reasonable to guess that this percentage might represent imports as well as exports, services as well as commodities? If Bairoch's orders of magnitude are plausible, intercontinental exports plus imports accounted for 2% of Europe's G.N.P in the 1780s[83]. Why not double it to take intra European trade into an equation of "total commerce imputable to the consolidation and expansion of a global eco-

---

82 F. BRAUDEL, Civilization and Capitalism, Vol. 2.

83 P. BAIROCH, Commerce extérieur et développement économique de l'Europe au XIXe siècle, Paris - The Hague 1976.

nomy"? Let's continue with this upper-bound numbers game by positing that half of the value of all trade on income account of Europe's balance of payments with other continents hypothetically accrued as "profits" to European merchants, shippers, financiers and investors involved with the new trades attributable to the Discoveries. This entirely illustrative exercise in stylized numbers tells us that at most 2% of Europe's G.N.P. at the end of the eighteenth century took the form of profits (normal and supernormal, it does not matter) derived from commerce with the Americas, Asia and Africa. Even *if* as much as half of this income was reinvested in the maintenance of and net additions *to* the stock of capital, (an extraordinarily high percentage) the returns from organizing this commerce was sufficient to have funded no more than a fifth of gross domestic capital formation undertaken in Europe as late as the 1780s. For some three centuries after 1492 the small (but rapidly growing) ratio of intercontinental commerce to total European output implies that it could not generate more than a comparable proportion of the funds required to support urbanization and industrialization. Thus it is the streams of rents, interest profits and taxes generated by all other forms of enterprise within the region which must have generated an overwhelming share of the reinvestable surpluses embodied in capital formation between 1492 and the French Revolution.

Local incentives to invest and endogeneously generated funds are behind the long term accumulation of capital which carried European industry forward to a level from where it could take advantage of an ever increasing number of innovations which came on stream after 1750. But because so many of the innovations which raised productivity in European industry, in agriculture and transportation had first demonstrated their viability in Britain, historians who wish to make larger claims for the economic significance of the global economy may wish to rest their case on a traditional model of European industrialization which assumes that "the First Industrial Revolution was, with lags diffused onto the mainland of Europe"[84].

5. British Industrialization and Its Diffusion

The force of the connexions between foreign trade and economic growth was surely far stronger for Britain than for other European economies, with the exception of Holland, and the economic evolution of that Republic raises difficult questions of necessary and sufficient conditions for and industrial revolution[85]. After 1585 first the Dutch and then the English involvement in commerce with the Americas, Africa and Asia surpassed that of other European economies (including France) by a considerable margin[86]. For two centuries by means of military prowess and mercantile entrepreneurship these two nations appropriated a "lion's share" of the gains from oceanic trade[87]. Why Holland "failed" to mature into the First Industrial Nation will not be discussed here, and I will concentrate on the potential significance of world commerce for industrialization in Britain.

By the late seventeenth century the English stood poised, economically, politically and militarily, to garner the largest proportion of gains from further expansion of trade with the Americas, Africa and

---

84 W. DARITY, The Numbers Game and Profitability of the British Trade in Slaves, in: *Journal of Economic History* 45 (1985); idem, British Industry and the West India Plantations, 1988; R. FINDLAY, The Triangular Trade and the Atlantic Economy of the Eighteenth Century (Working paper no. 124), Lisboa 1989.

85 P. K. O'BRIEN et al., Political components of the Industrial Revolution.

86 J. ISRAEL, Dutch Primacy in World Trade 1585 - 1740, Oxford 1989; M. AYMARD (ed.), Dutch Capitalism and World Capitalism, Cambridge 1982; J. RILEY, The Dutch Economy after 1650: Decline or Growth, in: *Journal of European Economic History* 13 (1984).

87 I. WALLERSTEIN, The Modern World System, Vols. 2 and 3.

Asia. English enterprise and capital had established viable colonies and plantations along the Atlantic seabord and on Carribean islands[88]. English merchants, backed by a increasingly aggressive and well funded state, had moved into a leading position in servicing inter-continental trades, including the infamous traffic in slaves[89]. English exports, dominated by finished manufactures (particularly woollen cloth), had for centuries found their markets on the continent. That traditional specialization and long established place on European markets began to change at the Restoration. And the eighteenth century witnessed a radical diversification of comparative advantages - away from dependance on woollen into cotton cloth and into metallurgy and shipbuilding, as well as a move towards markets in the Americas and Asia. Between 1700 and 1800 export volumes multiplied by a factor of 4.6. Almost three quarters of the estimated *increment* to the sales of British made goods sold overseas between 1697 and 1802 went to America, Asia and Africa[90]. Cliometricians have suggested, however, that alternative markets could have been found at home or in Europe to support a similar and sustained rate of expansion[91]. English mercantilists might well have been amazed at this counterfacutal suggestion and historians will wish to concentrate on the observed role of exports[92]. In that context numbers help but cannot validate a case one way or the other. For example the ratio of domestic exports to gross national product just about doubled between 1688 and 1802, and two long "cycles" of growth occurred when 33% (1697 - 1760) and 20%

---

88 I. K. STEELE, The English Atlantic 1675 - 1740, Oxford 1986; K. R. ANDREWS, Trade, Plunder and Settlement, Cambridge 1984.

89 P. CROWHURST, The Defence of British Trade, Folkestone 1977; J. BREWER, The Sinews of Power, London 1989.

90 F. CROUZET, Towards an Export Economy, British Exports During the Industrial Revolution, in: *Explorations in Entrepreneurial History* 17 (1980).

91 R. P. THOMAS / D. MCCLOSKEY, Overseas Trade and Empire 1700-1860, in: R. FLOUD / D. MCCLOSKEY (eds.), The Economic History of Britain Since 1700, Cambridge 1981.

92 L. GOMES, Foreign Trade and the National Economy.

(1783 - 1802) of the increment to total output were sold beyond the borders of the Hanoverian kingdom. As usual for countries of any size, most of the national product was consumed or invested at home. But expressing the value of output produced within any sector of an economy as a percentage of national income seems almost calculated to create an impression of insignificance. Industry not agriculture or services represented the leading sector for economic progress over the eighteenth century, and English exports were dominated by manufactures. Perhaps their role is more illuminatingly measured in relation to two upswings in industrial output. Between 1700 - 1760 the increment to exports expressed as a ratio of the increment to gross industrial output amounts to 56%; between 1760 - 1780 that ratio fell to a negligible 2% but jumped back up to 38% from 1780 - 1801[93]. Most of the increment to industrial output 1700-1800 was not traded across oceans or frontiers. Nevertheless, these taxonomic exercises in quantification help to reinforce contemporary perceptions that the growth of industry continued to depend, "in large measure", on the sale of manufactures beyond the borders of the kingdom.

These ratios do not, however, encapsulate feedbacks, multiplier effects and spin offs which also pushed the British economy forward to the status of First Industrial Nation. Although externalities are well described in the secondary literature, their significance cannot be estimated. Examples of such externalities encompass the savings and skills of merchants acquired in overseas trade which found their way into industrial enterprises. Perhaps, more frequently, merchants became bankers and lent their support and funds indirectly to manufacturing or to the creation of transportation and other forms of social overhead capital upon which industrial expansion in their regions depended. Lobbies from the mercantile community exerted what was, by European standards, rather strong influence on the strategic fiscal and economic policies pursued by "patrician" governments in London[94].

---

93 N. F. R. CRAFTS, British Economic Growth During the Industrial Revolution.

94 J. BREWER, The Sinews of Power.

Merchants' horizons were distant, their knowledge international, and their ambitions global in scope. They demonstrated and diffused advanced industrial techniques and commercial practices to other sectors of the economy. They created and widened markets for British manufactured goods both at home and abroad.

Exports of British textiles and metalwares "fedback" to raise demand for wool, flax, iron and coal. They also augmented demand for the services of internal transport, ships, insurance companies, and other financial intermediaries. Export revenues gave rise to increasing possibilities for importing foodstuffs and raw materials (coffee, tea, sugar, spices, tobacco, wine, spirits, silk, timber, cotton fibres, dyestuffs, and natural oils) which could not be produced in Britain except at prohibitive costs. Tropical groceries (referred to by Malthus and Mill as incentive goods) stimulated the work and investment required to buy such highly desirable and energy-giving foodstuffs. Imported raw materials created the base for processing foodstuffs and tobacco and for the manufacture of cotton cloth and silks. Imports also provided the British state with elastic sources of taxation allocated in large part to expand and defend the Empire[95]. Export industries (such as cotton, woolens, iron, and shipbuilding) ranked among the more advanced sectors of manufacturing and demonstrated what might be accomplished by the rest of the economy[96]. Firms engaged in foreign trade could achieve internal economies of scale; and what was possibly more important, larger export industries, such as Lancashire cottons, Yorkshire woollens, and Birmingham metalwares, generated external economies connected with conglomeration and specialization within regions[97].

---

95 P. K. O'BRIEN, The Political Economy of British Taxation.

96 J. M. PRICE, What do Merchants Do? Reflexions on British Overseas Trade 1660 - 1790, in: *Journal of Economic History* XLIX (1989).

97 P. HUDSON, Regions and Industries: A Perspective on the Industrial Revolution, Cambridge 1989.

Finally, contemporary claims for "benign" effects which flowed through changes in money supplies and lower interest rates emanating from a favourable balance of payments are now appreciated. Commentaries on foreign commerce throughout the long eighteenth century continued to be preoccupied with specie flows[98]. Nowadays the preoccupations of mercantilist writers with monetary reserves are less often dismissed (pace Adam Smith) as a simple-minded confusion of gold and silver with real wealth. Mercantilists certainly failed to appreciate David Hume's analysis of the nature and theoretical ramifications of specie flows across frontiers. Their concerns, entirely explicable, were not, however, with the invisible and not exactly verifiable, properties of a self-equilibrating international monetary system, but rather with the immediate and possibly serious deflationary impact on the British economy flowing from an adverse balance of trade. What they perceived and wrote about were the associations between trade balances, money supplies, output, and employment[99]. They did not expect automatic adjustment mechanisms to work any more effectively and quickly than they do today. Meanwhile, and for the circumstances they lived through, English mercantilists recommended policies designed to obtain export surpluses and inflows of monetary reserves to support an expanding economy and an aggressive polity on its way to hegemony at sea[100].

Alas, neither quantification nor more historical scholarship will settle debates about the significance of world trade for the first Industrial Revolution because the increase of world trade and global income cannot be taken as purely *exogeneous* variables behind the long run growth of British exports. For example, and since such a large pro-

---

98 T. HUTCHINSON, Before Adam Smith: The Emergence of Political Economy 1662 - 1776, Oxford 1988.

99 R. BLITZ, Mercantilist Policies and the Pattern of World Trade 1500 - 1750, in: *Journal of Economic History* XXVII (1967).

100 C. WILSON, Treasure and Trade Balances: The Mercantilist Problem, in: *Economic History Review* II (1949).

portion of the increment to sales overseas from 1688 to 1802 was absorbed by colonial or neo-colonial markets (such as the United States and India), there is a sense in which the expansion of exports depended upon sustained investment by the British Government in military power and imperial rule[101]. Furthermore, it is difficult to assess the degree to which the "growth" of trade between the metropolis and its Empire between 1688 and 1802 can be attributed to economic forces at work within Britain which were then communicated overseas and which elicited a positive response and generated higher levels of external trade. How far was the efficiency of exports as an engine of growth powered by investment and productivity advances within the home economy itself?[102] Finally, counterfactual modes of argument have arisen to taunt historians. Cliometricians observe that the importance of foreign trade can be measured as: the potential thereby created for extra income and consumption, but assert that because "domestic demand or supply could within limits replace foreign demand or supply the actual division of British output between exports and domestic use is an interesting fact but not one obviously significant for British economic growth"[103].

For present purposes it may not be necessary to resolve arguments about the exogeneous or endogeneous nature of export growth in order to reinstate the historical significance of oceanic trade. Discoveries occurred at the end of the fifteenth century, and from 1660 to 1802 the British state invested massively in the naval power required to exploit the potential gains from further expansion of trade with Asia, Africa, and above all with the Americas. Obviously the prior existence of a thriving Atlantic economy and well established waterborne trades

---

101 D. BAUGH, Great Britain's Blue Water Policy 1689 - 1815, in: *International History Review* X (1988).

102 P. DEANE / W. A. COLE, British Economic Growth 1688 - 1959, Cambridge 1962.

103 THOMAS / MCCLOSKEY, Overseas Trade and Empire, in: R. FLOUD / D. MCCLOSKEY (eds.), The Economic History of Britain since 1700.

within the Orient created preconditions for export growth over the eighteenth century. Beyond that it seems extremely difficult to specify the exogeneous or endogeneous forces that initiated upswings in exports over particular cycles of long term development. Even when such forces are located it is the sequence of interactions over time that emerge to carry export industries upward onto higher plateaux of production[104]. Finally the limits within which domestic demand or supply could conceivably replace foreign demand or supply were rather tightly constrained and obviously significant for British economic growth[105]. Contemporary observers were not impressed either with English agriculture's capacity for sustained productivity growth or with the prospective buoyancy of domestic demand[106].

Potentially "all things", as economists are prone to point out, "are substitutes", but the domestic costs of producing alternatives for the foodstuffs and raw materials (imported from the Americas) as well as for such "strategic" goods as pitch, tar, flax, hemp, timber (purchased from the Baltic) could have been expensive. Such trades were not based upon marginal differences in internal transformation ratios between Britain and its American and Baltic suppliers.

In general it seems that rather substantial adjustments in consumption and production would seem to have been required for a British economy hypothetically cut off from oceanic trade and compelled to transform its abundant resources (labour and cheap fuels) into substitutes for food, raw materials and military goods procured with exports of manufactures. Furthermore, mercantilists believed that sales abroad

---

104 T. HATTON et al., Eighteenth Century British Trade: Homespun or Empire Made?, in: *Explorations in Economic History* 20 (1983); W. A. COLE, Eighteenth Century Economic Growth Reconsidered, in: *Explorations in Economic History* 10 (1973).

105 P. K. O'BRIEN / S. L. ENGERMAN, Exports and the Growth of the British Economy from the Glorious Revolution to the Peace of Amiens, in: B. SOLOW / S. L. ENGERMAN (eds.), Slavery and the Rise of the Atlantic System, Cambridge 1991.

106 L. GOMES, Foreign Trade and the National Economy.

provided an addition to employment not readily available elsewhere in the economy. In so far as they were correct (and the British economy operated below full employment levels) then any readjustment could have been even more difficult and costly to achieve[107].

Attempts to apply counterfactual logic and the Ricardian theory of comparative advantage to denigrate the role of foreign trade in the first Industrial Revolution are no longer convincing. The significance of trade was neither as expendable as cliometricians suggest nor as overwhelming as Wallerstein, Braudel and the World Systems school implicitly assume[108]. Meanwhile the locus of significance cannot be found (as Marx, Keynes, Gunder Frank and other economists expect) in the flows of returns (normal and supernormal) appropriated by British merchants, shippers, bankers and investors from servicing commerce with Asia, Africa and the Americas[109]. For 1784-1786 this particular flow of profits amounted to £5.7 million. Assuming that businessmen engaged in international commerce were exceptionally frugal men and invested 30% of their profits in gross national capital formation (running at that time at £10.3 million a year) implies that, at its height in the 1780s, oceanic commerce generated a flow of profits sufficient to have funded *not more* than 16.5% of gross investment expenditures at home and overseas[110].

But is this ratio big or small? Perhaps those profits were sufficient to raise net investment rates in Britain above those achieved by the French and other rival economies? Nevertheless at least 83.5% of the funds required to maintain and add to the kingdom's capital stock emanated from sources other than commerce with the New World,

---

107 The ramifications of this argument and relevant evidence are in P. K. O'BRIEN / S. L. ENGERMAN, Exports and the Growth of the British Economy.

108 I. WALLERSTEIN, The Modern World System, Vols. 2 and 3; F. BRAUDEL, Civilization and Capitalism, Vols. 2 and 3.

109 A. G. FRANK, World Accumulation 1492 - 1789.

110 P. K. O'BRIEN, European Economic Development: the Contribution of the Periphery, in: *Economic History Review* 35 (1982).

Asia and Africa. Again, if the focus is shifted to consider the savings required to fund investment in the industrial sector alone, then these same "mercantile profits" may have been *sufficient* to have funded almost all gross fixed investment expenditures in mining, quarrying and manufacturing industry undertaken in the 1780s[111]. By that decade oceanic trade could potentially provide enough savings from profits to fund the entire cost of fixed capital formation in the industrial sector[112]. Nevertheless industrial revolutions are not made by capital formation, let alone by investment confined to the industrial sector. Industry constituted an inseparable part of an integrated economy and some part of its growth is imputable to productivity changes and to endogeneous sources of innovation[113].

For the British Industrial Revolution the significance of foreign commerce should not be denied, denigrated nor exaggerated. It was obviously important. Nevertheless, only historians who continue to depict the industrialisation of Western Europe as the diffusion of best practice British technology and organization onto the mainland could logically accord foreign trade (and the Discoveries) the same significance for other European economies[114]. For the history of European (and even British) industrialization the "perspective of the world" for Europe emerges as less significant than the "perspective of Europe" for the world[115].

---

111 W. Darity, British Industry and the West India Plantations; R. Findlay, The Triangular Trade and the Atlantic Economy.

112 C. F. Feinstein / S. Pollard (eds.), Studies in Capital Formation in the United Kingdom 1750 - 1820, Oxford 1988.

113 N. F. R. Crafts, British Economic Growth During the Industrial Revolution, and see the special issue of *Explorations in Economic History* 24 (1987) where estimates and sources of productivity growth 1700 - 1830 are debated.

114 S. Pollard, Peaceful Conquest: The Industrialization of Europe 1760 - 1970, Oxford 1981.

115 F. Braudel, Capitalism and Civilisation 15th - 18th Century: The Perspective of the World.

Research Results and New Conceptual Starting-Points

By JÜRGEN SCHNEIDER*

Between 1594 and 1602, about a hundred years after the discovery of America, the Florentine merchant Francesco Carletti made a journey around the world. In his description of his voyage Carletti summed up the great discoveries as follows:

> "The two kingdoms of Castille and Portugal have shown us the way around the world. In doing so the Portuguese journeyed eastwards, thus reaching China and Japan, while the Spaniards travelled westwards and reached the Phillipines, which lie about a thousand miles from the island of Macao in China, where the Portuguese hold away. Together the Spanish and the Portuguese have encircled the world and one cannot possibly overestimate the importance of this achievement of the two nations. It is indeed quite amazing that nowadays anyone, aided by the language of these two nations and by their ships, may enjoy the wonderful experience of circumnavigating the entire globe, by way either of the East or the West Indies, in less than four years!"[1]

Out of these discoveries the great trade routes developed. With the "Carrera de Indias" Spain created a convoy system with military

---

* Translation by Peter ORAM.

1 F. CARLETTI, Reise um die Welt 1594. Erlebnisse eines florentiner Kaufmanns, Tübingen - Basel ²1978, pp. 133s.

protection across the Atlantic, which had as its point of departure Seville - or rather, that city's Atlantic ports of Cadiz and San Lucar de Barrameda - and which from 1564 on had as its points of destination Vera Cruz ("flota de Nueva España") and, on the Columbian mainland, Cartagena ("galeones de Tierra Firme"). The convoy system was slow and costly, yet offered the advantage of mutual protection. By means of the galleons which travelled once a year between Acapulco on the west coast of Mexico and Manila, Spain gained access to commodities from the Coast of Coromandel, Bengal and China. To Manila was exported above all silver and some cochineal.

As early as 1500 Portugal established the "Carreira da India", a convoy system that linked Lisbon with the Portuguese centre of Goa in India. Further lines linked Goa with Melaka, Macao and Nagasaki. The sugar routes an the other hand linked Lisbon with Brazil.

It was the task of the internatianal seminar of the UIMP Valencia to analyse of the "*Consequences of the Discovery of America for the Different Economies and for the Development of Economic Thought*".

MICHEL MORINEAU makes three simple observations: "The first one is about the discovery itself, the second is about the contacts that rise from it and the third is on the value of America's discovery". The observations contain more questions than answers, yet these questions and reflections are thought-provoking. However, Morineau makes the following decisive point: "We must change conception, re-establish the real framework, and accept to follow a humble and prosaic path. ... This means measuring the part of the discovery of America into the development of Europe"[2].

ANTONIO-MIGUEL BERNAL draws attention to the fact that for trade with the New World no innovative commercial techniques were required, for it was possible to finance such commercial ventures by

---

2 M. MORINEAU, Five Centuries After that Day since ..., *in this volume*, pp. 31 and 33.

utilizing the system of maritime credit[3] that had been developed over the past centuries in the Mediterranean, "Desde el principio, la Carrera de Indias fue en cierto modo un oligopolio donde un número reducido de armadores, maestres, mercaderes y financieros controlaban lo sustancial de la negociación e impusieron las maneras y ritmo de las operaciones"[4]. The small group of merchants was from the outset made up of international members. The various types of company had two prime objcetives: to mobilise money and to minimize risk. Of particular interest is the description of how prices were fixed at the fairs of Portobelo/Nombre de Dios and Veracruz for goods which were being brought by the fleet from Spain. At these fairs European commodities stood face to face with silver from Mexico and Peru. By means of a process of mutual adjustment (tâtonnement), offer of goods and demand backed by buying-power were brought into agreement with one another. Bernal warns with justification against citing gross profits. Competition prevented profits from becoming too high. Trade with the New World was now a calculated risk.

RENATE PIEPER investigates the effects of American bullion on European monetary system. "The previous data suggest that at least 50% of the metals coined in Europe after the Reforms at Potosí until the mid-seventeenth century proceeded from Upper Peru" - and: "From the mid-sixteenth century until the discovery of Brazilian gold, overseas bullion determined the european composition of coins and

---

3 Cf. L. GOLDSCHMIDT, Handbuch des Handelsrechts. Teil A: Universalgeschichte des Handelsrechts. Das Grundproblem - Das Altertum. Das Mittelalter, Stuttgart 1891, pp. 362ff.

4 A.-M. BERNAL, Crédito, Financición y Beneficio en el comercio colonial español a través de los cambios y préstamos marítimos (ss. XVI - XVII), *in this volume*, p. 49.

coinage. ... The peso fuerte or real de a ocho ... was a very well known means of payment all over Europe"[5].

For the native inhabitants that Columbus encountered on his discoveries, money was primarily of ornamental value. Since Columbus before long only sought gold from the natives, this soon became for the latter the measure of value for all gifts that they received from the Spaniards. ORESTE POPESCU shows with the help of source material the genesis of a market economy. The price revolution first took place in the precious metal production sites in America, above all in Potosí. In 1569 Bodin stated what was already a "general truth" in Peru. "Value is not something intrinsical and real in things"[6] (Oñate). They gained their knowledge from empirical experience as observers of the economic procedures at the fairs and markets of their own regions. Thus they arrived at the subjective theory of value and anticipated Alfred Marshall. From the expansion of the works of the six principal West Indian scholastics Popescu sums up: "It results that the principal contribution of Spanish American scholastics is rooted in the development of the subjective theory of value, the prices theory system, the market morphology, the integration of the monetary theory with the general prices theory and with this, the ample development of the quantity theory of money and the theory of the parity of the purchasing power of money"[7]. There are points of contact here with "ransom of Cajamarca" (1533) and the discovery of the silver mines of Potosí (1545).

MARJORIE GRICE-HUTCHINSON investigates, in which monetary theory in Spain was effected by the Discoveries. In the 16th century prices rose first in Seville, then in in New Castile and later in Old

---

5 R. PIEPER, American Silver Production and Western European Monetary Supply in the Sixteenth and Seventeenth Century, *in this volume*, p. 94 and 97.

6 O. POPESCU, Latin America Contributions to the Development of the Quantity Theory of Money, *in this volume*, p. 141.

7 Ibid., p. 145.

Castile, Valencia, and the rest of Spain. This could not pass unnoticed in the Spanish Universities. Grice-Hutchinson analyses the writings of three of the pioneer members of the School of Salamanca. In Francisco de Vitoria we find a new realism and a new readiness to take the facts of contemporary business practise into account[8]. Domingo de Soto analyses the fairs in Medina del Campo, Medina del Rioseco and Villalon. These were no longer goods fairs but purely exchange fairs, "clearing centres, mainly places for setting accounts"[9]. Decisive for the rate of exchange is scarcity or abundance of money, i.e. supply and demand. Martin de Azpilcueta explained the various rates of exchange by the differing buying power that money has in different places. the "value" of money is determined by its purchasing power. The doctors of Salamanca "formulated a theory of foreign exchange based on the diversity in the purchasing-power of money in the different countries concerned", and "price should correspond to the 'estimation' or demand for a good that was 'common' to the market as a whole, and not to the claims made by sellers about their costs"[10].

FRANCISCO GÓMEZ CAMACHO points out that the economic writings of the Scholastic were governed by Probability and that this philosophy was forsaken for Scientific Determination in the 18th century. In order to find correct solutions to problems the Spanish Scholastic philosophers added to the innovative dimension of moral reflection the analytical dimension. By means of analysis and by taking into account all the factors that influence price-formation, the Spanish doctors arrive at "the truth of the fact" (Melchior de Soria). The price was the result of a process of trial and error, in order to arrive at (by "tâtonnement", as Walras says) a balance. Currency deteriorations were considered a swindle and were immoral. "The Spanish doctors rejeted the notion of the authorities' being able to

8 M. GRICE-HUTCHINSON, Contributions of the School of Salamanca to Monetary Theory, *in this volume*, pp. 186ss.

9 Ibid., pp. 190s.

10 Ibid., p. 176.

legitimately manipulate the value of the standard unit for their convenience"[11].

PETER BERNHOLZ remembers that Copernicus (1473 - 1543) was the first to invent the Quantity Theory of Money. He formalizes the ideas of Martín de Azpilcueta Navarro. Confronting the results with the theories of the Spanish doctors, put forward by Oreste Popescu and Marjorie Grice-Hutchinson, several puzzles arise[12]. Using a simple model to clarify the relationships he concludes that "the exchange rate would ... be driven up until it reached the upper silver point ... Until then only the domestic (Spanish) price level would increase. Afterwards silver would be exported ... It follows that the price increase in Spain should precede that abroad (in France and Flanders) and the exchange rate should remain above its parity as long as silver is mined"[13] in Spanish America (Peru, Mexico). In a last step Bernholz examines the historical facts, i.e. price data (Hamilton, Van der Wee, Posthumus, Vazquez de Prada). The historical data confirm the theorems of the Spanish doctors up to 1567/68. After that time more detailed empirical work on transport, insurance costs and the length of time lags in silver arbitrage is necessary to determine the location of the lower silver points for different places[14].

In pre-industrial times population and food production moved in close step. JOAQUIM DA COSTA LEITE investigates how the Portuguese population in the country's main regions (Northern Coast, Alentejo and Portuguese Mainland) grew between 1527 and 1801. A decisive factor for the growth of the population was agricultural procuctivity. "Maize introduced from America via Spain seems to have spread vigorously during the first half of the seventeenth century, increasing

11 F. GÓMEZ CAMACHO, Economic Thought in Spain in the 17th Century, *in this volume*, p. 231.

12 P. BERNHOLZ, The Discovery of the New World and the Development of the Purchasing Power Parity Theory, *in this volume*, p. 243.

13 Ibid., S. 246f.

14 Ibid., S. 250.

productivity per hectare and sustaining a remarkable demographic growth"[15]. The significance of the Methuen Treaty of 1703 has been grossly exaggerated. Only the export regions (coastal areas) bought imported goods. The inland regions were protected from foreign competition. In the view of Adam Smith Portugal and Spain were declining as Western European States. This view is being revised. Agricultural productivity - daily bread - was more important for Portugal than Brazilian gold.

JÜRGEN SCHNEIDER shows by using the example of the coffee, how the culture of the coffee tree spread from Arabia to Ceylon and Java, to the Carribean and South America. Decisive for the quick diffusion of the production of coffee was the increasing consumption in Western Europe.

RUTH M. VORNEFELD discusses the consequences of the Bourbon Reforms in the second half of the 18th and the first two decades of the 19th century by reference to the travel reports of European experts. Here the transfer of mining technology has the central place. "The project to introduce modern mining technology in Spanish America by 'importing' skilled personnel and engineers failed completely"[16].

PEDRO PÉREZ HERRERO takes the traditional interpretation of the 18th century in Latin America as a fundament of his research. The success of the Bourbon Reforms got a scientific facade by Alexander von Humboldt. Behind the official statistical figures is hidden a reality quite different from the traditionally accepted one. By reproducing the financial structures of New Spain he came to the result that in the first period from 1750 -1780 there was a equilibrium between net income and total expenditure. In the second period (1781 - 1795) had the net income and perpetual expenses a clear tendency to decrease, while the expenditure for temporals and particulars grew. In the final period

15 J. DA COSTA LEITE, The American Factor in Portuguese Economic and Demographic Growth, *in this volume*, p. 276.

16 R. VORNEFELD, The Transfer of European Know-How and Its Effects on Economic Development in Colonial Hispanic America, *in this volume*, p. 322.

(1796 - 1816) grew the net income almost vertically, at the same time as did total expenditure. The analysis von Pérez Herrero shows, that the beneficiaries of the Bourbon Reforms were the New Spanish Elite and not the Bourbons.

The "Comercio libre" of 1778 has been seen in prior research as on the whole positive, and as a prerequisite for new groth. JOSEP M. DELGADO RIBAS reinterpretates the impact of the reform of the Comercio libre on the Spanish colonial trade. "La consideración desagregada de los retornos permite discernir con claridad quienes fueron los beneficiarios de la reforma ... Entre el primer y el segundo tercio del siglo XVIII, las remesas de metales de cuenta del sector público sólo crecieron en torno a un 0,2% anual, para saltar despues de 1778 a una tasa del 8,2%. En términos relativos ello representó que la Real Hacienda pasó a controlar directamente la remisión de la cuarta parte de los caudales enviados desde America durante la etapa del comercio libre"[17]. If one places the "Comercio libre" in the chronological framework of 1717 - 1796, the results of J. R. Fisher's research cannot be upheld. The terms of trade deterioted for Spain: "El comercio español para importar lo mismo de las colonias debió exportar cada vez más"[18].

The discovery of the New World also had its effects on Asia. Tobacco, maize, chili and papaya were taken up remarkably quickly and appear to have been brought direct by Spanish across the Pacific. ANTHONY REID draws on Magalhâes-Godinho, who estimated that in the 1490's Europe was paying some 17 tons of silver a year for goods from Asia, but already 72 tons by the end of the 16th century. "The chief novelty introduced by the Portuguese in the Indian Ocean was

---

17 J. de DELGADO RIBAS, El Impacto de la Reforma del "Comercio Libre" sobre el Comercio Colonial Español, *in this volume*, p. 419s.

18 Ibid., p. 421. Cf. J. SCHNEIDER, Terms of Trade between France and Latin America, 1826 - 1856, Causes of Increasing Economic Disparities?, in: P. BAIROCH / M. LÉVY-LEBOYER (Eds.), Disparities in Economic Development since the Industrial Revolution, London - Basingstroke 1981, pp. 110 - 119.

the effective use of shipboard artillery, and the determination to use it in pursuit of commercial objectives"[19]. By the end of the 16th century the Dutch and the English were increasingly displacing the Portuguese. The VOC and the EIC were innovative enterprises and more than a match for the Portuguese. The Portuguese paid for spices in the production regions with textiles obtained from Asia, while the Dutch and the English brought silver, which was preferred to the textiles. In the first half of the 17th century Spanish silver-reales became the international currency of S.E. Asia[20]. "The triumph of silver undoutedly furthered the integration of maritime Asia into a world economy"[21].

PATRICK KARL O'BRIEN carries out what Morineau had asked: he analyses the contribution of the non-European world to the Industrial Revolution, i.e. the Industrial Revolution is the framework, the yardstick for the assessment of the impact of overseas trade. He comes to the conclusion that "precious metals, textiles and tropical groceries from the Americas and from Asia reinforced and pushed forward patterns of specialzation within the European economy which had existed for centuries before the Discoveries ... International exports plus imports accounted for 2% of Europe's G.N.P. in the 1780s"[22]. In his research work into the potential significance of world commerce for industrialization in Britain O'Brien draws on the latest research. His contribution can be seen as a synopsis of the international seminar of Valencia.

---

19 A. REID, Some Effects on Asian Economies of the European Maritime Discoveries, *in this volume*, p. 444.

20 Cf. Währungen der Welt IV: Asiatische und australische Devisenkurse im 19. Jahrhundert, ed. by J. SCHNEIDER / O. SCHWARZER / F. ZELLFELDER / M. A. DENZEL, Stuttgart 1992.

21 REID, Some Effects, *in this volume*, p. 456.

22 P. K. O'BRIEN, The Foundations of European Industrializations: From the Perspective of the World, *in this volume*, pp. 480 and 492.

"Mass poverty and hunger crises determined to a large extent the history of pre-industrial Europe. Only with the industrialisation of the 19th century was hunger gradually overcome"[23]. For European history, agricultural productivity was of much greater significance than overseas trade. Trade with America and Asia increased the standard of living, but it did not deliver the daily bread to the population at large.

Adam Smith answered the question of what is important for mankind as follows: "After food, clothing and lodging are the two great wants of mankind"[24]. The trade with America and Asia contributed little to the satisfaction of these elementary needs. It is, therefore, with justification that O'Brien concludes that "For the history of European (and even British) industrialization 'the perspective of the world' for Europe emerges as less significant than the 'perspective of Europe' for the world"[25].

---

23 W. ABEL, Massenarmut und Hungerkrisen im vorindustriellen Europa, Hamburg - Berlin 1974.

24 A. SMITH, The Wealth of Nations. In two volumes: volume one. Introduction y E. R. A. SELIGMAN, London 1960, Book I, chap. XI, p.147.

25 O'BRIEN, Foundations of European Industrializations, *in this volume*, p. 502.

Beiträge zur Wirtschaftsgeschichte

Herausgegeben von Hermann Kellenbenz und Jürgen Schneider

Band 1	**Rainer Gömmel** Wachstum und Konjunktur der Nürnberger Wirtschaft (1815-1914) 1978, X, 242 S., Leinen, ISBN 3-12-912610-4
Band 2	**Precious Metals in the Age of Expansion.** Papers of the XIVth International Congress of the Historical Sciences. 1981, 330 S., Leinen, ISBN 3-12-912670-8
Band 3	**Georg Eibert** Unternehmenspolitik Nürnberger Maschinenbauer (1835-1914) 1979, 421 S., Leinen, ISBN 3-12-912680-5
Band 4 bis Band 8	**Wirtschaftskräfte und Wirtschaftswege. Festschrift für Hermann Kellenbenz** Herausgegeben von Jürgen Schneider in Verbindung mit dem Vorstand der Gesellschaft für Sozial- und Wirtschaftsgeschichte Karl Erich Born, Alfred Hoffmann, Hans Mauersberg, Hans Pohl und Wolfgang Zorn.
Band 4	I.: Mittelmeer und Kontinent 1978, 744 S., Leinen, ISBN 3-12-912620-1
Band 5	II.: Wirtschaftskräfte in der europäischen Expansion 1978, 740 S., Leinen, ISBN 3-12-912630-9
Band 6	III.: Auf dem Weg zur Industrialisierung 1978, 692 S., Leinen, ISBN 3-12-912640-6
Band 7	IV.: Übersee und allgemeine Wirtschaftsgeschichte 1978, 746 S., Leinen, ISBN 3-12-912650-3
Band 8	V.: 1981, 863 S., ISBN 3-12-912660-0
Band 9	**Internationaler Ochsenhandel der frühen Neuzeit 1350-1750** Akten des 7th International Economic History Congress Edinburgh 1978. Eingeleitet und im Auftrag der Economic History Association hrsg. von E. Westermann. 1979, 299 S., Leinen, ISBN 3-12-912690-2
Band 10	**Jürgen Schneider** Frankreich und die Unabhängigkeit Spanisch-Amerikas. Zum französischen Handel mit den entstehenden Nationalstaaten (1810-1850). I. Teilband: Darstellung; II. Teilband: Statistischer Anhang 1981, zus. 1362 S., Leinen, ISBN 3-12-912710-0

Band 11 **Helmut Vogt**
Die Überseebeziehungen von Felten & Guilleaume (1874-1914)
1979, 308 S., Leinen, ISBN 3-12-912700-3

Band 12 **Norbert H. Schneeloch**
Aktionäre der Westindischen Compagnie von 1674. Die Verschmelzung der alten Kapitalgebergruppen zu einer neuen Aktiengesellschaft.
1982, 354 S., Leinen, ISBN 3-12-912720-8

Band 13 **Wachstumsschwankungen.**
Wirtschaftliche und soziale Auswirkungen (Spätmittelalter - 20. Jahrhundert)
8. Arbeitstagung der Gesellschaft für Sozial- und Wirtschaftsgeschichte. Referate und Diskussionsbeiträge hrsg. von H. Kellenbenz.
1981, 340 S., Leinen, ISBN 3-12-912730-5

Band 14 **Evelyn Lacina**
Emigration 1933-1945. Sozialhistorische Darstellung der deutschsprachigen Emigration und einiger ihrer Asylländer aufgrund ausgewählter zeitgenössischer Selbstzeugnisse.
1982, 693 S., Leinen, ISBN 3-608-91117-0

Band 15 **Michael Braun**
Die luxemburgische Sozialversicherung bis zum Zweiten Weltkrieg. Entwicklung, Probleme und Bedeutung.
1982, 666 S., Leinen, ISBN 3-608-91118-9

Band 16 **Gerhart Jacob-Wendler**
Deutsche Elektroindustrie in Lateinamerika. Siemens und AEG (1890-1914).
1982, 376 S., Leinen, ISBN 3-608-91119-7

Band 17 **Thomas R. Kabisch**
Deutsches Kapital in den USA. Von der Reichsgründung bis zur Sequestrierung (1917) und Freigabe.
1982, 413 S., Leinen, ISBN 3-608-91120-0

Band 18 **Peter Höfer**
Deutsch-französische Handelsbeziehungen im 18. Jahrhundert. Die Firma Breton frères in Nantes (1763-1766).
1982, 337 S., Leinen, ISBN 3-608-91121-9

Beiträge zur Wirtschafts- und Sozialgeschichte

Herausgegeben von
Hermann Kellenbenz, Eberhard Schmitt und Jürgen Schneider

Band 19 **Hans Gotthard Ehlert**
Die wirtschaftliche Zentralbehörde des Deutschen Reiches 1914-1919.
Das Problem der "Gemeinwirtschaft" in Krieg und Frieden.
1982, 597 S., Leinen, ISBN 3-515-03938-4

Band 20 **Hermann Kellenbenz (Hrsg.)**
Wirtschaftsentwicklung und Umweltbeeinflussung (14.-20.Jh.).
Berichte der 9. Arbeitstagung der Gesellschaft für Sozial- und Wirtschaftsgeschichte (30.3.-1.4.1981)
1982, 298 S., Leinen, ISBN 3-515-03946-5

Band 21 **Friedrich August Lühdorf**
Acht Monate in Japan nach Abschluß des Vertrages von Kanagawa. Eingeleitet und neu herausgegeben von Jürgen Schneider
1983, 263 S., brosch., ISBN 3-515-03950-3

Band 22 **Rolf Walter**
Venezuela und Deutschland (1815-1870)
1983, 406 S., Leinen, ISBN 3-515-03937-6

Band 23 **Aristide Fenster**
Adel und Ökonomie im vorindustriellen Rußland. Die unternehmerische Betätigung der Gutsbesitzer in der großgewerblichen Wirtschaft im 17. und 18. Jahrhundert.
1983, 343 S., Leinen, ISBN 3-515-93947-3

Band 24 **Michael Rauck**
Karl Freiherr Drais von Sauerbronn. Erfinder und Unternehmer (1785-1851)
1983, 804 S., brosch., ISBN 3-515-03939-2

Band 25 **Peter Kopf**
David Hume. Philosoph und Wirtschaftstheoretiker (1711-1776)
1983, 342 S., brosch., ISBN 3-515-03948-1

Band 26 **Hans-Günther Mertens**
Wirtschaftliche und soziale Strukturen zentralmexikanischer Weizenhaciendas aus dem Tal von Atlixco, 1890-1912
1983, 382 S., brosch., ISBN 3-515-03960-0

Band 27 **Wolfgang Penkwitt**
Preußen und Brasilien. Zum Aufbau des preußischen Konsularwesens im unabhängigen Kaiserreich (1822-1850)
1983, 559 S., Leinen, ISBN 3-515-04087-0

Band 28 **Marianne Gechter**
Kirche und Klerus in der stadtkölnischen Wirtschaft im Spätmittelalter.
1983, 462 S., brosch., ISBN 3-515-04475-2

Band 29 **Rainer Klump**
Wirtschaftsgeschichte der Bundesrepublik Deutschland.
1985, 129 S.,brosch. ISBN 3-515-04475-2

Band 30 **Rainer Gömmel**
Vorindustrielle Bauwirtschaft in der Reichsstadt Nürnberg und ihrem Umland (16.-18.Jh.).
1985, XII u. 300 S., brosch. ISBN 3-515-04481-7

Band 31 **Renate Pieper**
Die Preisrevolution in Spanien (1500-1640). Neuere Forschungsergebnisse.
1985, 170 S., brosch., ISBN 3-515-04570-8

Band 32 **Hans Hesselmann**
Das Wirtschaftsbürgertum in Bayern 1890-1914. Ein Beitrag zur Analyse der Wechselbeziehungen zwischen Wirtschaft und Politik am Beispiel des Wirtschaftsbürgertums im Bayern der Prinzregentenzeit.
1986, 419 S., 21 Stammtaf. und Schaubilder als Beilage, brosch.,
ISBN 3-515-04565-1

Band 33 **Wolfram Fischer / R. Marvin McInnis / Jürgen Schneider (eds.)**
The Emergence of a World Economy 1500-1914. Papers of the IX. International Congress of Economic History. Edited on behalf of the International Economic History Association.
1986, 749 S., in 2 Teilbänden, brosch., ISBN 3-515-04748-4

Band 34 **Knut Borchardt**
Zur Geschichte des Bayerischen Staatsministeriums für Wirtschaft und Verkehr.
1987, 58 S., brosch., ISBN 3-515-04953-3

Band 35 **Wolfgang Protzner (Hrsg.)**
Vom Hungerwinter zum kulinarischen Schlaraffenland. Aspekte einer Kulturgeschichte des Essens in der Bundesrepublik Deutschland.
1987, 188 S., brosch., ISBN 3-515-04954-1

Band 36	**Karl Heinrich Kaufhold / Jürgen Schneider (Hrsg.)** Geschichtswissenschaft und elektronische Datenverarbeitung 1988, 347 S., brosch., ISBN 3-515-05286-0
Band 37	**Vom Heimatvertriebenen zum Neubürger.** Sozialgeschichte der Flüchtlinge in einer agrarischen Region Mittelfrankens 1945-1955. Verfaßt von Paul Erker. Herausgegeben vom Landkreis und der Stadt Ansbach. 1988, 233 S., brosch., ISBN 3-515-05287-9
Band 38	**Thomas Michel** Die Juden in Gaukönigshofen/ Unterfranken (1550-1942) 1988, 712 S., brosch., ISBN 3-515-05318-2
Band 39	**Vierzig Jahre Deutsche Mark.** Die politische und ökonomische Bedeutung der westdeutschen Währungsreform von 1948. Herausgegeben von Rainer Klump. 1989, 91 S., brosch., ISBN 3-515-05455-3
Band 40	**Oskar Schwarzer** Die räumliche Ordnung der Wirtschaft in Deutschland um 1910. Ein historisch-systematischer Ansatz zu einer Theorie wirtschaftlicher Entwicklung und strukturellen Wandels. 1990, 267 S., brosch., ISBN 3-515-05687-4
Band 41	**Johann Georg Sichler** Die Bamberger Bauverwaltung (1441-1481) 1990, 632 S., brosch., ISBN 3-515-05688-2

Beiträge zur Wirtschafts- und Sozialgeschichte

Herausgegeben von Rainer Gömmel und Jürgen Schneider

Band 49 **Jürgen Schneider, O. Schwarzer, F. Zellfelder und M. Denzel (Hrsg.)**
Währungen der Welt VI:
Geld und Währungen in Europa im 18. Jahrhundert
1992, 322 S., brosch., ISBN 3-515-06072-3

Band 50 **Jürgen Schneider, O. Schwarzer, F. Zellfelder und M. Denzel (Hrsg.)**
Währungen der Welt VII:
Lateinamerikanische und afrikanische Devisenkurse im 19. und 20. Jahrhundert
1993, ca. 400 S., brosch.

Band 51 **José Casas Pardo (ed.)**
Economic Effects of the European Expansion 1492 - 1824
1992, 512 S., brosch., ISBN 3-515-06240-8

Band 52 **Leonhard Lutz**
Wirtschaft und Gesellschaft Nürnbergs unter Otto Freiherr von Stromer
(1. Bürgermeister 1867 - 1891)
1992, 343 S., brosch. ISBN 3-515-06241-6

Band 53 **Edgar Feichtner**
Die Bauernbefreiung in Niederbayern: Die Änderung der ländlichen Wirtschafts- und Sozialstruktur in Bayern durch die Reformierung der Agrarverfassung in der ersten Hälfte des 19. Jahrhunderts
1993, 267 S., brosch. ISBN 3-515-06280-7

Stand: Januar 1993
In Kommission bei
Franz Steiner Verlag Stuttgart